POVERTY AND UNDERDEVELOPMENT

Poverty and Underdevelopment

Attar Chand

GIAN PUBLISHING HOUSE
DELHI

GIAN PUBLISHING HOUSE
29/6 Shakti Nagar, Delhi-110007

ISBN 81-212-0104-7

PRINTED IN INDIA

Published by Gian Publishing House, Delhi (India) and
Printed by Godwall Printers, Delhi.

Dedicated to

Rajiv Gandhi
Prime Minister of India
for his New 20-Point Programme
to eradicate poverty from the Indian soil

ATTAR CHAND

FOREWORD

Mass poverty continues to be a serious problem of the developing countries of Africa, Asia and Latin America. This is primarily because the developing world is still in the grip of the same forces which made one part of the world rich and the other poor, which concentrated the ability to exploit and manipulate all resources in one section of the international community and deprive the other of the same.

"The wretched, humiliated, despised, insulted and oppressed of the human race", wrote American novelist Richard Wright, who attended the Bandung Conference (1955), "left their calling cards on the table of history, announcing their arrival on the international scene". Arrive they did. But with all the past burdens of inequity and injustice on their head and their vision blocked by old reflexes and models, they remained powerless to take a new turn and chalk out a new path towards economic emancipation, both externally and internally. What was earlier taken by erstwhile colonial masters and their collaborators through political and military domination began to be taken through trade and exchange-rate manipulation. And within the city community, old elites, who were beneficiaries of the colonial rule, were replaced by new elites who kept the same system going, the only difference being that the latter were more powerful and articulate than the old ones.

Process of urbanization in the Third World continues to be controlled by external forces and mode of production in which both the urban and rural poor continue to subsidize the local elites and the erstwhile colonial rulers by way of cheap goods, services and labour. In essential ingredients, the plot of the drama remains the same, though the actors now wear different masks, speak different languages, and act in a more subtle and refined way.

The State in the developing countries—in most cases unwittingly perhaps—is strengthening the powers of the elite both in the rural and the urban areas. The trickled-down effects of economic growth have not materialized, and millions are now living and working in what is called the informal sector, a twilight zone between the formal industrial and rural sectors, without any hope of ever getting absorbed in the formal industrial sector.

It is well to recognize that in developing countries any programme that seeks to ensure a minimum level of living to all sections of the population will require redistribution of income and consumption as well as change in the composition of national product. If necessary redistribution of income and consumption is of large dimensions, as is invariably the case when poverty and unemployment exist on a massive scale, conventional policies are seldom sufficient. To achieve the desired objective, more radical measures have to be adopted. Whether they are feasible or not depend heavily on the balance of political forces in the country concerned. What are regarded as organizational obstacles to redistribute measures are often a reflection of specific social and political constraints. Unless there is sufficient political commitment to the surmounting of these constraints, efforts to combat poverty are destined to fail.

For a drive against mass poverty, it is essential that Governments of the developing countries should start with a clear idea of what, in their own social context, they would regard as the components of a minimum level of living consistent with human dignity. They should identify those sections of the population whose consumption standards do not meet this minimum. Formulating development programmes and policies in terms of average per capita income or consumption, or of the rate of which these averages might be increased, is not adequate for focusing attention on the points at which attacks on acute poverty are most needed. While in most developing countries much remains to be done to furnish a precise measurement of mass poverty—and, as emphasized in the following section, action is urgently needed for this purpose—sufficient information does exist to enable Governments to mount an attack. Once the dimensions of poverty are quantified, however, roughly it should be possible to determine how far the problem can be tackled during a defined period by general measures for accelerating economic growth, and how far such measures need to be supplemented by specific measures to increase the income and consumption of those below the poverty line. In this respect, employment programmes need to be regarded as a means both for accelerating economic growth and for redistributing income and consumption.

In our own country, poverty eradication continues to be the main aim of the present Government headed by Shri Rajiv Gandhi. All current Plan programmes, especially programmes relating to rural development, rural employment tribal advancement, social forestry etc. are manifestation of this aim. The New 20-Point Programme has been designed to give maximum benefit to the poorer sections of the people.

I am impressed by the author's awareness of the urgency of the problem of eradication of mass poverty in global perspective. I realize, that unless radical institutional and social reforms are initiated, the problem would acquire catastrophic proportions within the next decade or two. I hope, the solutions suggested by the author will help to alleviate the sufferings of millions of poor people all over the developing world.

Raj Bhawan.
Jammu.

JAGMOHAN
Governor,
Jammu & Kashmir

ACKNOWLEDGEMENT

I am indebted to a sizable army of fellow scholars who, through their writings, their teaching, or their conversation, have enriched my understanding of the nature of global economic problems, socialism, democracy and the foundations of national and international cooperation. A book such as this is obviously dependent on the contributions of any other men, for no one analyst can possibly explore at first hand all of the ramifications of a field as broad as this aspect of global economic and social issues. I have tried to give to my fellow writers proper credit through appropriate entries in the book, but many have, no doubt been neglected, including some, I am sure, whose influence, though significant, was not consciously recognized as such even at the time.

Many friends at the Universities and Institutions assisted in this venture through discussion of these topics and through some strenuous arguments about them. Their critical views were of great importance in the development of my own ideas. Academicians—Professor V.P. Dutt, Dr. K.R. Sharma, Dr. Dharampal, Dr. Harjinder Singh, Dr. M.K. Saini, M.K. Dhar (Hindustan Times), Lalit Bhasin (Advocate, Supreme Court of India), Dr. J.S. Yadava (Indian Institute of Mass Communication), Vinay Raj (Managing Director, Usha Rectifier Corporation, India Ltd.), Nandraj Jog (Secretary-General, PHDCCI), V.D. Chopra (Patriot) K.S. Ramachandran (Financial Express) S.N. Yadav (FICCI) and Jagmohan (Governor, Jammu and Kashmir) read sections of the manuscript. Their comments and suggestions are especially appreciated.

ATTAR CHAND

ABBREVIATIONS USED

Eberstadt, Nick ed. *Fertility decline in the Less Developed Countries.* New York, Praeger, 1981. p. 370=FDLDC

Effective anti-poverty strategies. Bangkok, Economic Commission for Asia and the Far East, 1973. p. 332=EAPS

George, V. and Roger Lowson. *Poverty and inequality in Common Market Countries.* London, 1980. p. 253=PICMC

Hamilton, E.E. ed. *Industrialization in developing and peripheral* regions. London, Croom Helm, 1986. p. 363=IDPR

Johnston, R.J. and P.J. Taylor. *World in crisis ? Geographical* perspectives. London, Basil Blackwell, 1986. p. 308=WIC

Misra, R.P. and Nguyen Tri Dung. eds. *Third World peasantry : A Continuing saga of deprivation.* 2 vols. New Delhi, Sterling, 1986. p. 262, 346=TWP

Parish, William L. ed. *Chinese rural development : the Great* transformation. London, M.E. Sharpe, 1985. p. 278=CRD

Saini, Mahander Kumar, ed. *Global giants : The other side.* Delhi, Indian Institute of Research on Transnational Corporations, 1986 p. 222 =GGTOS

Townsend, Peter. ed. *Concept of Poverty.* London, Heinemann, 1970 p. 260=COP.

January=Jan.
February=Feb.

Autumn—Aut.
Summer—Sum.

March=Mar.
April=Apr.
May=May.
June=Jun.
July=Jul.
August=Aug.
September=Sep.
October=Oct.
November=Nov.
December=Dec.

Spring—Spr.
Winter—Win.

CONTENTS

INTRODUCTION

GLOBAL POVERTY AND UNDERDEVELOPMENT

POVERTY is a worldwide legacy, though the countries of Asia, Africa and Latin America are more amply endowed with it—nevertheless, from the ghettos of the United States of America, the favlas of Brazil, to the tin-and-mud shacks of South-East Asia and India, the cry is the same. . . 'why, why should this be. . . ?' The answer, no doubt, can to an extent be gauged by running to books of ancient and contemporary history, examining the nature of the people, the climate, the endowments of natural resources, the exploitative capital available or not available, the techniques of agriculture and agricultural improvement plans adopted, and the colonial legacies. But, often, the real answer can only be grasped by examining the political system and elite strata, the instruments—legalistic, constitutional, or otherwise that are tortured, strained and twisted to suit the needs of a privileged section who simultaneously mouths the phrases of socialism and egalitarianism, while their people starve. There is an unending debate and uncertainty about what styles of development to adopt—should the target be to provide all citizens with the basic necessities and shelter, or to hold these in temporary abeyance till the 'furnitures of an industrialized society' are obtained ? (after all, India is a tropical country, and the elements are not to hostile to a camp in the countryside, and improved and minimal dietary patterns can wait till the State has achieved its task of Gross National Product escalation through 'rapid' industrialization). There is seen the necessity of State regulation of private enterprises, and at the achievement same time there is the reluctance to accept the rigors inherently necessary for the achievement of a true socialist order, there is the dabbling in the mechanics of free enterprise, and simultaneously a fear that this is not the system for us ; we want the advantages of every system, but seldom have the will or spirit to meet the preconditions. So long as we are in a muddle about what path of developmental style to adopt, we will fail economically and socially to make use of our capacity to develop. The resources are not lacking nor presently, the technical skills. What we lack is the political will. There is no use pointing to the poverty and the colonical legacy. Since these causes are not static. Poverty need not necessarily be a debit factor. It is only a result, and not a cause. It is in meeting the cause that the instruments of planning and the kind come into focus.

Poverty, now-a-days is viewed both in absolute and relative sense. In the absolute sense, it is referred as a condition of acute physical wants—starvation, malnutrition, disease, want of clothing, want of shelter and almost total lack of medical care. Relative poverty, unlike the absolute poverty is more a matter of subjective definition than of objective conditions. In such a situation a person may have everything that a normal human being requires—nourishment, clothing, shelter, entertainment—yet he may have the uncomfortable feeling that he is poor in comparison to the person next door.

Absolute poverty is a growing phenomenon in both developing and industrialised countries. There is a wider concern at the worsening spiritual and material conditions of the weakest and most vulnerable elements of the community : children, youth, women, the aged and the disabled.

Absolute poverty, is understood as a condition of falling below the minimum standards of subsistence appropriate to each society.

The African countries which were the last to throw off the colonial yoke have found themselves in a particularly great plight. Of the 31 countries which the UN lists as the least developed, 20 are in Africa, and approximately 80 per cent of the continent's population lives in what is in fact poverty. Unemployment stands at 70,000,000. The African population will double by the year 2000, topping 800,000,000, while self-reliance in food will be up to only 60 per cent. It has become customary to associate the debt syndrome with such of its victims as Brazil, Mexico, Argentina and Venezuela, whose aggregate debts have reached, by early 1984, $ 300,000,000,000. But a no less acute situation in this respect has shaped in Africa, with Nigeria's debts, for example amounting to $ 23,000,000,000, while its debt servicing payments have gone up from 4 per cent of the total cost of exports in 1980 to 30 per cent in 1986. In per capita terms the debts of many African countries are on the whole higher than those of Asian and Latin American countries.

All these trials have fallen to the lot of the developing countries of Africa when they are faced with particularly acute problems of development options and strengthening their national sovereignty. Definitely, the West has considered the moment "propitious" for filling the sails of this continent with North-Atlantic wind and for attempting to have many African states make a U-turn in their independent policies.

Sixty million people in China have an annual income lower than the Government poverty line of 150 Yuan annually plus 200 kgs of grain.

The World Bank report estimate shows, for two standards of energy requirements, the share and number of people with energy deficient diet in various regions (Table 1), are the people who face chronic food insecurity. If the energy standard adopted is merely enough calories to prevent stunted growth and serious health risks, an estimated 340 million people or 16 per cent of the people in these developing countries (excluded China) had energy deficient diets. If the standard is raised to enough calories sufficient for an active working life, some 730 million people or 34 per cent of the people lived with dietary deficits. Around 80 per cent of these people were in low income countries.

The above illustrations and magnitudes of the hungry in the world and in specific regions and nations had led some governments to devote substantial resources to increasing food production. Preoccupation with food production is misguided, however, when the concern should be the reasons for the inability of these people to get even a modest share of the world's abundant food supply.

Data show that the growth in global grain production has more than kept pace with the growth in population (Table 2). But for the regions of Eastern Europe, the Middle East and Sub-Saharan Africa, the grain output increased faster then population during the 1970s for developing countries as a group.

Table 1

PREVALENCE OF ENERGY-DEFICIENT DIETS IN EIGHTY SEVEN DEVELOPING COUNTRIES, 1980

Country group or region	Not enough calories for an active working life		Not enough calories to prevent stunted growth & serious health risks	
	Share in population (%)	Population (million)	Share in population (%)	population (million)
Developing Countries ...	34	730	16	340
Low income ...	51	590	23	270
Middle income ...	14	140	7	70
Sub-Saharan Africa ...	44	150	25	90
East Asia Pacific ...	14	40	7	20
South Asia ...	50	470	21	200
Middle East & North Africa ...	10	20	4	10
Latin America & the Caribbean ...	13	50	6	20

Table 2

GRAIN PRODUCTION & POPULATION GROWTH BY COUNTRY GROUP, 1970-82

Country group or region	Average annual percentage change		
	Cereal Production	Population	Cereal Production per capita
World ..	2.3	1.8	0.5
Industrial market economies	2.3	0.7	1.6
East European non-market economies ..	0.6	0.8	−0.2
Developing countries ..	3.0	2.1	0.9

East Africa	.. 0.8	3.0	—2.2
West Africa	.. 1.9	2.7	—0.8
East Asia & Pacific	.. 3.5	1.7	1.8
South Asia	.. 2.7	2.4	0.3
Middle East & North Africa	.. 1.7	2.9	—1.2
Latin America & The Caribbean	.. 3.2	2.4	0.8

In most countries, the gross domestic product (GDP) grew much slower in the early 1980s than in the 1960s and 1970s (Table 3). Annual GDP growth in the middle income developing countries fell from almost 6 per cent in 1973-80 to about 1 per cent in 1982. Similarly the growth of GDP in developed countries dropped from 2.8 per cent a year during the middle and late 1970s to 1 per cent in 1981. Simultaneously purchases by the developed countries of wheat and coarse grains from world markets stagnated and in some cases fell. For the removal of food insecurity it is imperative to eradicate poverty, or what amounts to the same thing promote policies to boost the purchasing power of the masses. In this sense, poverty and hunger are the obverse and reverse side of a coin.

Table 3

GROSS DOMESTIC PRODUCT 1980 AND GROWTH RATE 1965-84 BY COUNTRY GROUP

Country Group	1980 GDP ($ per capita)	Average annual percentage change in G.D.P.					
		1965-73	1973-80	1981	1982	1983	1984
Developing countries	670	6.6	5.5	3.0	1.9	2.0	4.1
Low-income countries	260	5.5	4.9	4.0	5.0	7.2	6.6
Middle income oil importers	1690	7.0	5.6	2.0	0.8	0.7	3.3
Middle income oil exporters	1270	7.1	5.8	4.6	0.9	—1.0	2.7
High income oil exporters	10650	9.2	7.7	0.1	—1.7	—7.0	0.6
Industrial market economies	10420	4.7	2.8	1.4	—0.3	2.3	4.8

Hunger is acurious thing. At first it is with you all the time, waking and sleeping and in your dreams, and your belly cries out insistently, and there is a gnawing and a pain as if your very vitals were being devoured, and you must stop it at any cost, and you buy a moment's respite even while you know and fear the sequel. Then the pain is no longer sharp but dull, and this too is with you always, so that you think of food many times a day and each time a terrible sickness assails you, and because you know this you try to avoid the thought, but you cannot, it is with you. Then that too is gone, all pain, all desire, only a great emptiness is left, like the sky, like a well in drought, and it is now that the strength drains from your limbs, and you try to rise and find you cannot, or to swallow water and your threat is powerless, and both the swallow and the effort of retaining the liquid tax you to the uttermost.[1]

Poverty in Indian society is an old disease, but the demand for its amelioration has gathered momentum with the increasing awareness of what poverty means. And awareness is the product of political processes. Nothing brings this out more than the manner in which land reforms have been carried out. If land reforms initiated immediately after Independence still remain incomplete and, if despite repeated exhortations by Nehru and Indira Gandhi during their years in office, redistribution of surplus land remains an unfulfilled expectation one reason is the absence of assertion by public opinion on these issues. Land reforms have been carried out only to the extent that there was a demand for it—which also explains the differences in the land reform laws of different States.

The reason is, as repeatedly pointed out by India's Planning Commission, the absence of an organisation of the beneficiaries which could ensure that ceiling laws were not violated or circumvented. For the successful implementation of the revised 20-Point Programme also the beneficiaries need to be educated about their rights and organised to attain these rights. Incidentally, by running the campaign and taking the lead in organising the poor, the ruling Congress Party will also revitalise itself, forge again its links with the poor and attract activists from their ranks instead of affluent adventures out for pastures new.

Many welfare programmes remain unimplemented for lack of awareness among those for whom they are meant. Eradication of poverty is the declared purpose of the programme, but amelioration of poverty is not merely a question of economic uplift. It is a political issue, related to the level of the political awareness of the people.

India's economic progress and development has not transformed the state of the unemployed. 26 million are registered at the country's employment exchanges. And there is a view that the actual figure is a shocking four times the number. Moreover, the situation deteriorates each year as lakhs of fresh graduates join the labour force in the search for elusive jobs. The result is frustration, anger and despair. Economic planners from the early days of the republic may have perceived joblessness as a serious social and economic problem. But none of the many schemes and programmes listed in the nation's six previous plans have brought the crisis to heel. Rajiv Gandhi's government has now mounted a sustained assault against joblessness in the Seventh Plan. New avenues of employment are to be created both in the urban and rural areas through a multi-pronged developmental campaign.

The World Bank in its 1981 World Development Report placed India among the 10 poorest nations in the world. The rankings base on per capita Gross National Product (GNP) put Bhutan as the poorest country with a GNP of 80 dollars for each of its, 1.3 millions citizens. Bangladesh was second poorest with a per capital GNP of 90 dollars.

It was followed by Chad with 110 dollars Ethiopia, Nepal and Mali with 140 dollars. Then came Burma and Afghanistan.[2]

India remains the eleventh poorest country in the world with a per capita GNP of 260 dollars.

Given all the hazards of such cross country comparisons, the world development report 1986 ranks India not only below China but also Pakistan and even Sri Lanka.

This is not all. Not only is the country's per capita income one of the lowest, but it is growing at a meagre annual rate of 1.6 per cent compared to China (4.5 per cent) Sri Lanka (2.9 per cent) and Pakistan (2.5 per cent.) as the following figures would show.[3]

1.	Kuwait	13,000	Dollars.
2.	Switzerland	9,870	,,
3.	Sweden	9,500	,,
4.	Saudi Arabia	9,210	,,
5.	West Germany	8,400	,,
6.	U.S.A.	7,800	,,
7.	Australia	6,830	,,
8.	Japan	6,010	,,
9.	U.K.	4,360	,,
10.	U.S.S.R.	3,990	,,
11.	Romania	2,630	,,
12.	Venezuela	2,590	,,

13.	South Africa	1,450	,,
14.	Mexico	1,180	,,
15.	Algeria	1,100	,,
16.	Turkey	1,070	,,
17.	South Korea	880	,,
18.	Jordan	870	,,
19.	Nigeria	500	,,
20.	Phillipines	460	,,
21.	China	390	,,
22.	Egypt	380	,,
23.	Indonesia	310	,,
24.	Pakistan	200	,,
25.	India	140	,,
26.	Afghanistan	130	,,
27.	Ethiopia	100	,,

Although massive efforts are being made since the introduction of the slogan (Garibi Hatao) India could gain only one place from no. 11. At this rate, it would take years to remove poverty and attain higher position better than China and Pakistan.

The abolition of poverty and eradication of unemployment is crucial in a country like India, where roughly 40 per cent (even more) live below the poverty line. Though the early five year plans drew up schemes to push people beyond this plimsoll mark, the strategies were faulty. The organised sector which provided comparatively fewer employment opportunities were fattened by excessive credit, while the unorganised component, which accounted for the bulk of employment, got virtually no capital at all.

The socio-economic profile of rural Bangladesh depicts an agrarian economy in bondage, wherein the poor have become institutionalized into a culture of poverty. This poverty is not merely a legacy from the past, but has also been maintained through fiscal and administrative policies of post-colonial governments. The government machinery was built up under the British rule and stlll retains much of its colonial ancestry. Administration is in the hands of a highly centralized bureaucracy that has little ability to collect direct taxes. The major direct agricultural tax is on land. But rates are low and have been increased only once during the past ten years. The general price level has risen sharply since independence in 1971, so that land taxes constitute a very small share of the agricultural product. Increasing the rate of land taxes poses obvious administrative and political problems, as no government desires to make itself unpopular with the overwhelmingly large majority of the population.

Bangladesh has about as much cropland per inhabitant as Britain and West Germany and twice as much as South Korea and Taiwan. Also the quality of the country's soil is second to none and the climate permits the cultivation of up to three crops per year in most parts of the country. A World Bank report even concluded that the current rice production could be quardrupled by the end of the century with already known techniques.

"What then," One might ask, "is the cause of hunger in Bangladesh?" The answar is: a composite of the semi-feudal agrarian structure, slow paced development and inequitable distribution of the small gains of development. Hunger is the child of poverty and poverty is aggravated by an economic system autocratically geared to maintaining the political, social and economic preponderance of privileged groups. Bangladesh, is just like a big ship divided into three classes : the rich, the not-so-rich and the poor. And when a ship begins to founder, third class passengers do not share a common fate with first class passengers. The well-to-do rarely if ever share the fate of the poor. More commonly they determine it.

In the United States of America, the poverty rate for black Americans decreased in 1985 as black incomes rose but was still three times the poverty rate for whites, poverty rate for black fell to 31 per cent from 33.8 per cent in 1984. The rate for the general population was 14.0 per cent, about the same as in 1984 but up one point the 1980 level when President Reagan was first elected to the White House. The number of blacks in the US below the poverty level fell to six per cent to 8.9 million in 1985.

The black poverty rate far exceeded the rate for whites of 11.4 per cent, which was unchanged from the previous year.

The rate for all Americans of 14.0 per cent 33.1 million were poor in 1985 compared with 33.7 million the year before.

In 1980, the povery rate was 13.0 per cent.

The poverty level was determined by the government and based of that a typical family needs for food. The poverty level for a family of four during 1986 was an income of $ 10,989.

A significant segment on the American middle class is likely to slip into the ranks of the impoverished if current economic trends continue. There is an urgent need for changes in the welfare system so that it will provide a decent living standard and also a ladder out on poverty.

According to the *International Labour Organisation* (ILO) one half of the labour force in the world today is unable to provide even the basic necessities for their families. Mass unemployment continues to grow and this is, in fact, deliberately created by the policies of capitalist employers and governments.

With one-third of industrial capacity lying idle and up to one-fifth of skilled labour redundant, the tremendous destruction of productive resources has reached an unprecedented level.

In the capitalist world, under the cover of the crisis antiworker laws, limiting trade union rights and collective bargaining and requiring further sacrifices of the workers, more benefits for the employers and more subsidies for private companies are being forced upon the working class.

The anti-trade union offensive is imposed more and more obviously as part of monopoly capital's strategy in seeking a way out of the capitalist crisis, to the detriment of the workers and people.

With the pretext of the crisis, the capitalist economists claim that what is needed is to give greater incentives to the private monopolies and hand over them the vital sectors of the economy, such as transport, telecommunications, hospitals and health care, energy and other profitable parts of the public sector.

This offensive looks exclusively for immediate maximum profit, at the expense of the real needs of the majority of workers and countries, while forcing the workers to give up the achievements of their struggles for wage standardisation and social security. Scrapping jobs and closing factories are ways of pressurising for "concession bargaining", i.e. wage cuts and worsening working conditions.

These arguments for "economic liberation" are used in the capitalist countries to ensure a further division of income in favour of the capitalists, with an ever smaller part given to wages and social benefits.

The policies of "deregulation", "privatisation", and other measures to enhance further the arbitrary powers of capitalist employers, aggravate the crisis. In fact, they constitute a reward to the very forces responsible for the crisis.

Under such circumstances, obviously, workers and their trade unions overwhelmingly refuse to accept the responsibility for or to bear the burden of the current disastrous situation. This discontentment and dis-approval is manifested in the unprecedented upsurge of working class militant struggles in all possible forms, with the participation of millions of workers all over the capitalist world.

Six million un mployed and thousands of school—and university—leavers now on the job-market since the summer vacations ended : that's the gloomy end-of-year picture for Western Europe's industrialised nations as they struggle to recover from the worldwide recession.

"The Common Market Nine" are almost all treating the latest reports on unemployment with top priority efforts to cope on a short term basis but no one has yet worked out how to face up to the problem in the long run.

A recent Council of Europe seminar on Youth Unemployment heard that in the last 20 years the number of unemployed youngsters rose 900 per cent in France, 600 per cent in West Germany, 500 per cent in Britain, Belgium and the Netherlands and 200 per cent in Italy. Overall statistics showed that 30 and 40 per cent of all unemployed were young peopled under 25.

Two factors have made the youth unemployment picture worse : the fact that too many youngsters have emerged from school and university with the wrong skills and the fact that western Europe has for year steadily cut back on its physical labour needs by computerisation and mechanisation.

Thus arts, letters or legal degrees are out and wider-ranging general technical skills are in. Faced with the worst youth unemployment figures since 1960, governments are concentrating on trying to channel youngsters into sectors where new skills can be made use of.

Britain, where for example about a third of all the 1.6 million out-of-work or under 25, is offering to subsidise companies which offer teenagers six-months crach-courses—but the government admits there is no guarantee of an eventual permanent job linked to the scheme. Italy is paying out over £200 million in subsidies to firms offering jobs to youngsters.

In West Germany the trade unions have themselves recognised the dangers and have pressed the government for action on creating more jobs by public investment. The West German unions also are campaigning for a cut in working-hours, earlier retirement and longer job-training or schooling, keeping youngsters off the labour market until much later.

A recent report for the European Community, however, expressed strong reservations about these Malthus-based ideas for coping with population-growth and related job-opportunity decline. "These measures are prompted by a quick generalisation. They are costly and, while being irreversible, involve in the long-run a cutback in production potential. In some cases they can even prove unproductive,'' the Community experts warned.

They want to see efforts made to create more jobs but, rather than doing so but cutting a person's work-hours or work-life, the EEC experts advise creating more flexibility in job training to marry working skills to industrial and social needs.

In this context, some experts have particularly stressed to inadequacies of the present labour exchanges system pointing out that these exchanges have proved inefficient in their somewhat "cupid-like" efforts to introduce job-hunters to the right employers and vice-versa.

Priority should be given by the government to improving these national and even European-wide services. And especially a Community perspective to formulate a community policy should be adopted, most experts say.

It has been suggested that government should try further to control the ebb-and-flow of the labour markets by channelling in funds from the welfare sector to force an adjustment on a regional or professional basis. However, some critics, accusing governments of failure in their attempts to achieve similar directive control over general economic policy are doubtful how far this guidance can be achieved.

By contrast, let me turn now to two developing regions of the world that have been making impressive progress against poverty : East Asia, including China, and the Mediterranean.

Not so long ago, these regions were characterised by widespread, miserable poverty. But now the bulk of their people have enough to eat, substantial improvements have been made infant mortality and life expectancy, and virtually all children go to school. Poverty is still pervasive only in remote areas, like the two Yemens, or in countries scarred by way, like those of Indochina.

The People's Republic of China is a special case. It is much poorer than the rest of East Asia but China has eliminated the worst aspects of poverty. Notwithstanding much progress, the government still considers about one-fifth of China's population to be unacceptably poor.

Redistribution of wealth has helped to reduce poverty in several countries – including China, of course, but also including a country as capitalistic as the Republic of Korea. And most of developing countries of East Asia and the Mediterranean have also made special efforts to help the poor on an ongoing basis—through the expansion of public education, for example. But it is no coincidence that these regions have also been characterised by economic success generally. Rapid and sustained economic growth has been basic to the reduction of poverty in East Asia and the Mediterranean.

Most of the developing countries in East Asia and the Mediterranean have maintained special efforts to reduce poverty throughout the recent recession. And now that their economies are growing again, we can expect them to make further progress in reducing poverty.

The world can also take encouragement from the development saga of South Asia. Only 20 years ago, the prospects for South Asia looked as dismal as the prospects for Africa seem right now. Yet South Asia has made some progress against poverty.

Poverty eradication continues to be the main aim of the present government of Rajiv Gandhi. All Plan programmes, especially programmes relating to rural development, rural employment, educated unemployment, family welfare, social forestry etc., have a thrust on this.

But the level of poverty continues to be about 49 per cent. And all people living below the poverty line cannot obviously be lifted in a small or limited period.

In fact, because of paucity of financial resources desired result would not be achieved. According to official estimates, during the Seventh Plan period, that is by the end of 1990, only 52 million people may cross the poverty line. This is in sharp contrast to 75,000,000 people lifted above the line during the Sixth Plan Period. However, the thrust in the new 20-Point Programme is to give maximum benefit to the poorer sections of the people, particularly in rural areas, and thus help them to lift themselves above the poverty line.

In an article Lakshmipat Singhania (1910-76) India's noted industrialist wrote in the *Hindustan Standard* (Calcutta) of 13 May 1970, he regretted the industrial decline of West Bengal over the three preceding decades, and observed: "Industrialisation is not the creation of anybody. It is the will of the people. Entrepreneurship is their job. No single agency can push up entrepreneurship."

In this context, the conversation between Lakshmipat Singhania and Jyoti Basu, then deputy chief minister of West Bengal, on 25 September 1969, is interesting. The industrialist had gone to Basu's Hindustan Park residence to seek his assistance in setting an industrial dispute in the Aluminium Corporation of India. The discussion proceeded as follows :

Jyoti Basu, "We would like people like you to take charge of industries and industrial development in West Bengal if you give up your profit motive."

Lakshmipat Singhania : "If profit was the motive, I think I have enough for me and for my family for seven generations to live more comfortably than at present. Why are you, a brilliant barrister from London, living in such a poor and miserable condition? The reason is that you love what you do, irrespective of profit or loss. The same is the situation with me. I want to build more and more industries to remove poverty and increase India's wealth."

In the 1960s, India and its neighbours were forced to import massive amounts of food, especially in years of bad weather. There was every reason to be concerned that population would continue to increase faster than food production. We had visions of endemic famine and violence in South Asia. But most of South Asia has achieved food security through the "green revolution". Economic growth has more than kept pace with population growth, and India and Pakistan have managed to establish large industrial sectors.

Pakistan is the only country in the region that actually reduced the number of its citizens in poverty during the 1970s. India reduced the proportion of its population in poverty, but, because of population growth, the number of poor people increased, Sri Lanka has long scored relatively high on indicators of social welfare, but at the other extreme is Bangladesh—where more than three-quarters of the population remains trapped in absolute poverty.

South Asia still includes at least half of the world's poorest people. Yet the heroic efforts of the last 20 years have averted what could have been a nightmare, and parts of South Asia have demonstrated economic promise.

Average per capita income in Latin America is higher than in the developing countries of East Asia. Yet the incidence of absolute poverty in Latin America remains disproportionately high. There is little absolute poverty in countries like Argentina or Costa Rica. But poverty is still a serious problem in most of Latin America, and the region includes countries like Bolivia end Haiti where the extent of poverty is not much different from Sub-Seharan Africa.

Latin America was dealt a bloody blow by the international debt crisis. In Mexico, for example, real wages fell 25 per cent between 1981 and 1983. In Chile, urban unemployment reached 30 per cent. The nations with the biggest debts have now all adopted economic adjustment programmes and arranged to reschedule their debts, but some of the smaller countries seem to be floundering.

Poverty has become more severe and widespread throughout Latin America and the Caribbean, and the prospects are grim in those countries that can't settle on reasonable programmes of adjustment.

So then, the historical record shows that progress against poverty is possible. But progress is probably more difficult as we enter the 21st century than it has been for decades.

The problem of poverty cannot be solved by a country alone ; it needs the cooperation of all countries in the world, it needs a worldwide attack, and the responsibility of a world community. I believe that a solution under these conditions would be possible, but this is still utopia. Nobody can be so naive as to believe that one of the Western countries could succeed in increasing their help for the people of the Third World when at the same time the standard of living of western people has to be lowered. In that case, no western government would survive the next election. Therefore, in a realistic view, what we can do as a nation and what is an important as the direct help, is to try to increase the knowledge of our countrymen and their understanding of the problems of our sisterly developing states, and creating by this the basis for more help. I would be glad if we could contribute to eradicate at least some of the inhuman facts existing today, for example, that in one part of the world people die of hunger and that in the other part food is destroyed to stabilize a certain price level.

In many countries in the Asian-African-Latin American regions the situation regarding mass poverty, especially in recent years, has deteriorated. The continued rural-to-urban migration of people, who are in search of work opportunities in the cities which they envisioned to be better than the prevailing condition in the villages, has further aggravated the problem by spreading slums and shanty towns and exacerbating the misery of poverty. Unemployment, including that of youth and the educated has increasingly assumed serious proportions in many of these countries. These are apparently true even in those countries that achieved relatively high rates of growth of production.

While large segments of the population in these countries have inadequate work opportunities, are grindingly poor, suffer from malnutrition and disease and live in miserable housing conditions, a very small segment of the same population enjoys great affluence. The contrast between the rich and the poor within these countries, is becoming more pronounced while the growing disparities generate urges and pressures that cannot be contained indefinitely. It is therefore imperative that we give particular attention to policies and programmes that would sustain or accelerate the growth-process in developing countries and, simultaneously, begin making major inroads into the problems of mass poverty and unemployment.

These problems are basically a reflection of the Under-development of the poor countries and the structural imbalances associated with it. The rapid growth of population——resulting from the substantial reduction in death rates after World War Second that have not been accompanied by significant drop in the birth rates——has contributed to the rapid increase in manpower that has been coming to the labour market in the 1960's. And their ranks will continue to swell, at least, at the same rapid rate.

The economic growth process in these countries in the past four decades has not been conducive and effective in absorbing these new entrants into the labour force, let alone those in the rural areas that would like to benefit from a higher income through better employment opportunities. One factor contributing to this is the pattern of production which has tended to favour those industries that require more capital intensive techniques. This is caused generally by the factor bias of capital goods imported from developed countries, that generally have relative shortage of labour, and also the types of products that reflect the pattern of income distribution in the society. For example, the assembling and eventually production, of luxurious consumption goods, at high cost, has been permitted or even induced. Another factor is the inability of the growth process to sustain itself, because of the problems usually associated with the process of what has been called the import substitution industrialization. On the other hand, the lopsided pattern of income and wealth distribution has not been effectively redressed because of the ineffectiveness of public policies that is in turn caused by institutional and/or political factors.

From the experience of the past four decades, it is clear that sub-stantial changes have to be made in governmental approach to planning of the strategy to overcome these problems. Programmes aimed at reducing mass poverty and unemployment should be conceived as essential components of the overall process of economic and social development. Problems of distribution of income and wealth, of which mass poverty is an explicit reflections, *have* to be brought into the new framework of planning. In combating poverty, the Governments should find means of representing the interests of all major sections of their societies, particularly the economically and socially most disadvantaged and politically weekest segments, and the relevant stages of their planning process. They should also strive persistently to establish the appropriate machinery and procedures for consultation on matters relating to distribution of income and wealth.

For a direct drive against mass poverty, it is essential that governments of the developing countries should start with a clear idea of what, in their own social context, are regarded as the components of a minimum level of living consistent with human dignity. They should identify those sections of the population whose standards of consumption do not meet this minimum. While in most developing countries much remains to be done to furnish a precise measurement of mass poverty, the dimension of poverty should be established, however, roughly. This would enable the Governments to determine how far the problem can be tackled during a defined period by general measures for accelerating economic growth, and to what extent such measures need to be supplemented by specific measures to increase the income and consumption of those below the poverty line. In this respect, employment promotion programmes should be regarded as a means both for accelerating economic growth as well as for redressing the imbalance in the distribution of income and consumption.

The extent of under-utilized labour in the developing countries indicates the scope for accelerating economic growth through its more productive use. Developments in science and technology should be orientated towards opening up potentialities for economic growth through production techniques that could absorb the idle labour at rising levels of productivity. The aim here should be to link up the mobilization of idle labour as far as possible with measures for increasing production and, particularly, for raising the rate of capital accumulation. Through appropriate political, economic, social and technological measures, it should be possible to strengthen the complementarities in the development process. Sometimes, however, choices of the margin between promotion of economic growth and the alleviation of mass poverty and unemployment may be necessary. For example, for certain products, capital-intensive techniques of production are the more efficient over a very wide range of factor costs. In this case, the developing countries have no alternative but to adopt them. But for other products, there is usually a wider choice of processes and techniques.

The measures to increase income and consumption of the poor have to be complemented by a change in the pattern of output towards producing more labour-intensive items of mass consumption, such as food, cloth and cheap clothes, shoes and simple domestic utensils. Furthermore, measures that could result in greater efficiency of both more labour-intensive and smaller scales of production would reinforce those measures designed to reduce income disparities. Adequate provisions have to be made for improving the state of health, sanitation, education and training, housing, public transportation and other social services. On the other hand, many countries may find it desirable to impose heavy indirect taxation on consumption of luxury items to a level that it becomes more sensible to import them rather than produce them at home.

I have tried to give a brief outline of a strategy which, in my opinion, could significantly contribute to the attainment of the main development objectives in the longer run. Adjustments resulting from such actions are not, however, likely to meet the urgent need of alleviating mass poverty and unemployment, particularly in the short and medium terms. Some of these adjustments require a good deal of time to have their full impact felt. It is therefore necessary for Governments to supplement these measures with policies and programmes that can provide more immediate results and still be an integral part of the overall development design. Construction activity and land improvement—building, levelling, draining, ditching, fencing and the same sort of activities-are peculiarly well suited to this role, since efficient labour-intensive methods can be used in such tasks. Many of these projects, both in the rural and urban areas, have high benefits in relations to costs, and therefore, in terms of social returns, could repay their investment rather rapidly. Other constructions, particularly in low-cost housing, could constitute an important part of the more equitable patterns of consumption that a poverty reduction programmes seeks. Labour-intensive construction therefore has the potential for meeting the problems of utilizing idle and low-productivity manpower to productive tasks on a large scale ; while, at the same time, converting it into a resource.

The idea of employing masses of people in construction and land improvement activities is, of course, not new. But in the past experience of many countries this approach has been disappointing. The technical implementation of schemes has often been hasty and inadequate, and also projects, once constructed, have often been poorly maintained. The approach has suffered from organizational weaknesses, especially with respect to the achievement of effective local control and participation in decentralized schemes. Notwithstanding this experience, Governments should still give consideration to this approach, but in a substantially transformed way. First, the approach needs to be adopted boldly as an integral part of the national development effort. Secondly, Governments would need new instruments for effectively implementing these programmes. It would also entail more decentralization of project choice, management and financing. This implies the strengthening of local planning and technical competence, and also the use of match-grant techniques for inducing adequate efficiency, probity and coherence in the programmes. Construction programmes also offer an opportunity for deliberately building up selected rural growth centres and, in general, activiating an explicit regional plan strategy. Such centres could themselves generate a variety of continuing productive employment and permit a greater interchange between rural and urban activities which would reduce the problems of seasonal unemployment in agriculture, and urbanization.

Finally, the advanced countries should, in turn, recognize the importance of the programmes aimed at alleviating mass poverty in the developing countries, and adapt their contribution to the efforts of those countries through trade and assistance programmes that we formulated with these objectives in mind.

I have tried to express my thoughts on the many aspects of the serious problem of mass poverty. I hope they will be useful in stimulating further thoughts in any attempt to formulate policies, programmes and projects within the context of planning economic and social development.

Rural public-works programmes stimulate higher land prices, raise the productivity of capitalist farms and promote stratification among peasants. True, some countries of the region have tried to minimise the gains of landowners from land conservation and improvement. In part, they have attempted to raise the level and progressiveness of taxes on land property, but, perhaps with the exception of the Scheme of Guaranteed Employment in the Indian state of Maharashtra, this has failed to produce any positive results.

So the solution of the unemployment issue is inseparable from profound social transformations, above all in the realm of property. This will also greatly affect the outcome of income redistribution measures. Quite a potential for increasing the number of new jobs and improving the life of the poor is contained in rural transformations aimed at more equitable distribution of land and water resources, as well as at improving the conditions small tenants and farmlands. In other words, a radical solution of the unemployment problem calls for changes that go beyond partial reform. Only a serious remodelling of the economic and social structures, which slow down economic development and social progress, can put an end to dire poverty, hunger and unemployment.

Transnational monopoly capital, which shaped up in the post-war decades and gained unprecedented strength by the early 1980s, is now monopolising whole lines of production in individual countries and the world capitalist economy as a whole. By the early 1980s, the TNCs accounted for about one-third of industrial production, more than half of all foreign trade and nearly 80 per cent of patents and licences for latest machinery and technology in the capitalist countries. The TNCs figure even more prominently in the economies of developing countries. By sharply increasing their activities in the young developing states of Asia, Africa and Latin America, the TNCs have established-control over 40 per cent of industrial production and almost 60 per cent of foreign trade turnover in those countries.

The US-based TNCs, which have turned into veritable empires in the past decades, hold a major place in the transnational structure of modern imperialism. The ideologists of monopoly capital in the West continue advocating the proposition concerning an "important contribution" by the TNCs to economically developing countries. Facts, however, testify to the contrary. The super-monopolies' interest lies not in laying the foundation for the economy, but only in plundering those countries, in pumping enormous profits from them through the exploitation of local manpower and raw material resources. The developing countries have to part annually with about 200,000 million dollars flowing to the headquarters of the TNCs based in the United States and other Western countries. In the past ten years, the profits squeezed out of the developing countries by US corporations alone exceeded their investments in the economies of those States four-fold.

Besides the machinations to which the TNCs resort within the framework of intra-corporation trade, they transfer a considerable portion of profits from the developing countries in the form of royalties. According to available data, during 1980-84 alone, the annual transfer of funds from India to holding companies in this form grew six times over, reaching 350 million dollars a year.

The TNCs transfer considerable funds from the developing countries under the agreements on technical cooperation concluded by them with local companies. The agreements made by the Japanese TNCs, Honda and Yamaha, with Indian companies late in 1985 envisage the one-time payment of 500,000 dollars to each of the two monopolies plus the annual payment of certain sums in the form of royalties.

Neo-colonialism, with the TNCs as the most typical representatives of it, has "inherited" the exploitation of raw material resources in a number of former colonies. And here, in this strategically important sector of the economy, the rapacious nature of the big corporations has manifested itself in full measure.

The transnationals' activities in the raw materials sector of the economies of developing countries amount, in fact, to an arrogation by them of a right to exploit the developing countries' natural resources, up to their complete depletion. Cashing in on their monopoly of latest achievements of scientific and technological progress, the TNCs are trying to make up for the loss of direct control of mining industry in the developing countries, extending their positions in the sphere of processing raw materials.

There and many other facts are a proof of the need to activate the struggle against the transnationals' growing expansion in newly free States and for strengthening their economic independence. This struggle is not successful in those countries which are following a consistant course for limiting the TNCs' activity, for developing the major sectors of the economy, strengthening their progressive form—the public sector.

A number of characteristic features of underdevelopment may be identified, at the obvious risk of over-simplification and generalisation. In the economic sphere there is above all progressive dislocation and distortion of the economy involving restriction of autonomy. Capitalist structures are imposed on already existing economic and social formations. These imposed structures, not being indigenous, widen the divergence between the domestic and export-oriented economies. Thus, as production processes in certain sectors are progressively oriented to the economic needs of the metropolitan countries, there is greater divergence between domestic resources and domestic needs and demand. Production for the satisfaction of domestic needs suffers as a result of a dominant export orientation and characteristically domestic manufacturing is severely limited with heavy reliance on imported manufactures. The nature of economic relations between the metropolitan countries and the underdeveloped countries is such that the surpluses are transferred to the former, leaving the latter relatively impoverished and chronically dependent. Put simply then, the essential point is the distortion of underdeveloped economies, they may grow but that growth is primarily geared to the economic interests of the metropolitan powers. The lack of fit between economic activity and the achievement of real development is, to a large extent, the result of this external orientation and the lack of internal dynamics and coherence.

The importance of the process of underdevelopment cannot be overemphasised; the penetration of the cash economy which now dominates the societies of the Third World not only influences profoundly the contemporary patterns of social formation, dut dramatically restricts the range of future options. The majority of Third World populations are in the rural areas. Of these, very few are now untouched by the money economy although large proportions remain primarily within the subsistence economies. In a number of countries the interactions between the 'modern' and the pre-existing subsistence economy and its related social systems is of major significance. A number of those who have argued for alternative development paths stress the values of pre-existing systems and the possibilities of expressing those values in national development strategies which reject the domination of the inter-national capitalist economy and its attendant social forms.

The debate on the nature of development has continued for many years and will go on for many more. A recent major event was the public acknowledgement of its importance to the West contained in the Brandt Report (*The Independent Commission on International Development Issues 1980*) This, despite its rhetoric, essentially argues a case related to the self-interest of the industrial nations and in its discussion of development demonstrates a lack of conviction in its attempt to separate development from growth:

> Development never will be, and never can be, defined to universal satisfaction. It refers, broadly speaking, to desirable social and economic progress, and people will always have different view about what is desirable. Certainly development must mean improvement in living conditions for which economic growth and industrialisation are essential. But if there is no attention to the quality of growth and to social change one cannot speak of development.
>
> It is now widely recognised that development involves a profound transformation of the entire economic and social structure. This embraces changes in production and demand as well as improvements in income distribution and employment. (*The Independent Commission on International Development Issues*, (*1980*; *p. 48*).

A number of underdeveloped societies have attempted to break the chains of underdevelopment and adopt strategies for genuine development. In this context the socialist countries of the Third World, notably India, Cuba, China and Vietnam, have served as inspiration; but because of profound differences of historical experience, political organisation and levels of ideological development cannot serve as models. Among the non-socialist Third World countries which have had profound influence on their contemporaries, however, both Tanzania and Mozambique have demonstrated, despite massive problems and only partly-achieved goals, that alternative strategies are possible. The Tanzanian leader Julius Nyerere has consistently engaged the fundamental questions of the nature of development. His emphasis on the real purpose of development and the possibilities of a self-reliant development which serves the mass of people has given his writing a unique place in a popular literature which is still dominated by the pronouncements of international agencies which are fundamentally wedded to international capitalist growth.

There is much politics in poverty. Economists of the advanced countries have been advising the developing states to adopt the models of growth which had succeded in their own lands. They refuse to believe that there can be any other ways of getting rich, or less poor, except those suggested by Adam Smith, some 200 years ago. The West says that what is good for the rich must be good for the poor.[4]

Climate is said to be another reason for poverty. The tropics all over the world are poor. There is a recognisable tendency of a decline in income as one moves from north to south for the hot climate reduces the capacity to work hard.

The colonial legacy is also to blame for the colonial masters enforced backwardness for reasons of commercial interests. They destroyed the self-confidence of the people they governed and created a habit of dependence. The miseries of Asia, Africa and Latin America can largely be explained in these terms.

Even after independence these countries had to overcome many psychological, physical and religious divisions. These took many wars and long sufferings to settle. Many conflicts remain. The glaring example is Africa which was divided by the conquering nations at the Berlin conference, 100 years ago, ignoring ethnic homogeneity, geographical area and the topographical contours.

The same is true of India and Pakistan. Gulf conflict between Iraq and Iran, Vietnam and Cambodia. Name any crisis or dispute in the world, and you will find a former colonial power behind it. Colonialism has been the one single most notorious source of poverty in the developing countries. Population comes next in order. However, the population boom has many linkages, like illiteracy, lack of medicare and religious taboos.

"I know that what poverty means to people. I have been unemployed. I have stood in an employment office, waiting for an assignment and a placement. I have shined shoes as a boy. I have worked on a highway crew from daylight until dark for a dollar a day (Rupees seven per day in those days)" wrote the U.S. President Lyndon B Johnson in his book *My Hope for America*, p. 39.

He added "I know the meaning of poverty. It means waiting in a surplus food line rather supermarket check out. It means going without running water rather than worrying about whether you can afford a colour television it means despairing of finding work rather than wondering when you can take your vacation. It means coming home each night empty handed to look at the expectant faces of your little children who lack the things they need. Poverty not only strikes at the needs of the body : it attacks the spirit and undermines human dignity."

No other President thus had suffered the pangs of poverty as Lyndon Johnson which is why he writes with his own bitter experience. It is true he became a teacher afterwards but he never forgot the days when he had worked as a labourer or done work as a shoe shine boy.

Although Harry Trueman could not be bracketed with Johnson, he too could not go beyond matriculation because he could not afford further education. Thus the man who had ordered to drop the first Atom-bomb on Hiroshima had also suffered partly of course the experience of wanting something and then being deprived of it. There are a few cases more of top men who had suffered poverty.

In India there is no better example than that of late Lal Bahadur Shastri, formely Prime Minister. Like hundreds of million of his countrymen, Shastri had suffered object poverty most of his life. His school teacher father died when Shastri was a year and half old. To get an education Shastri sometimes swam the broad Ganga river, books on his head because he lacked the ferry fare. Thus Shastri who was born poor, will be more useful to the poor Indians because he can understand their sufferings.

To those who are eagerly awaiting the entry into 21st Century, the golden era of technology, it might come as a shock, that when India enters 21st century it will take amongst its population 309 million poor below the poverty line. Of this 220 million will be in the rural areas and 89 million in the urban. For India as a whole the absolute number of persons in poverty would increase by 20.7 per cent. However, the increase in poor specific to rural and urban areas would be 10.5 and 56.3 per cent respectively.

This is not a picture to be proud about. Inspite of all the efforts of a welfare state government to eradicate poverty a per centage of 20.7 below poverty line poor going into the 21st century to a great extent is due to the selfish attitude of the society.

In all countries there is a grave lack of information about the conditions in which millions of poor people live. A two-fold conceptual problem also arise, which sooner or later social scientists will have to resolve. On the one hand, the subsistence concept, invented and worked out in England by Charles Booth and Seebohm Rowntree in the late nineteenth century, was coming under fire as providing a basis for defining poverty. In societies which were changing fast it seemed reasonable to suppose that human needs were changing too. The subsistence concept seemed too static, somehow locked up in the distant youth of the grand-parental generation.[5]

On the other hand, the dire needs of the nations had also come to the forefront of public awareness and the paradox of poverty in America, judged by one standard, and poverty in the developing countries, judged by other standards, had somehow to be explained. Despite the frustrating lack of information an intellectual framework, consistent cross-nationally as well as through time, had to be created into which new information could be fed.

This book aims to enlist literature on poverty and underdevelopment since earliest times to 1987.

The book is devoted to themes of poverty and underdevelopment in their over all perspectives. The conditions of the poor can best be understood as a special feature of social stratification. In studying the life-styles of the poor we should pay particular attention not only to ways in which behaviour deviates from middle-class norms but to norms and aspirations which are resistant to change. We should try to create experimental situations to find how people respond to new opportunities. However formalized teaching, instruction and information is of great importance in ameliorating poverty. Poverty among the aged in rural areas is at least as extensive and in some ways more severe than among the aged in urban areas. There is need to draw attention of the governments to the uneasy and complex relationship between the labour market and social security in the causation of poverty.

Although several of the authors listed in this book are well-known for their writing on social policy, this is not a theme deeply pursued in a single volume. The authors including myself are agreed in believing that the most constructive contribution to the development of policy will occur as a result of a more penetrating analysis of the nature of the problem of poverty—and that will be possible only with a radical change and improvement in methods of investigation.

July 1987
Delhi

ATTAR CHAND

REFERENCES

1. Kamala Markandaya. Nectar in a Sieve. *Congress Varnika International* (New Delhi) September, 1985.
2. S.L. Parashar. Poverty. *Madhya Pradesh Chronicle* (Bhopal) 3 Sep 1986.
3. See *Newsweek*, 28 May, 1979.
4. See S.P. Singh. Sources of Poverty. *Hindustan Times* (New Delhi), 5 Dec 1985 9, New Delhi.
5. Seebohm Rowntree did in fact develop a more generous human needs standard, but the subsistence standard was extremely influential both in shaping views about the nature and extent of poverty in different countries and in supplying a basis for the payment of social insurance or public assistance. For criticisms see, *Poverty: Ten Years After Beveridge*, Planning No. 344, 1952 : Townsend, P., "*Measuring Poverty*", British Journal of Sociology, June, 1954 ; Townsend, P., "*The Meaning of Poverty*", British Journal of Sociology, September, 1962.

SOURCES OF POVERTY

IN LINE with this book's concern about poverty, my focus of attention is "absolute poverty." By absolute poverty I mean that people are too poor to obtain a 'calorie-adequate diet." I use World Health Organisation (WHO) guidelines regarding the number of calorie—deficient do not have much energy to spend—to earn a living or do anything else. When families fall substantially below this standard, children are more vulnerable to disease; they are more likely to die in the first years of life, or, if they live, to be stunted physically and mentally.

Some people imagine that poverty in developing countries is a hopeless situation, that progress is impossible. This image of the world is demonstrably false.

The situation is most bleak in sub-Saharn Africa. In nearly all the nations of Africa, one-half to three-fourths of the population subsists in absolute poverty. Statistics about the number of people in absolute poverty can only be very approximate. But the poverty is no less deadly because we cannot measure it precisely :

In Gambia, for example, over half of all rural children die by age five.

In Guinea-Bissau, almost the entire population suffers from malaria and diarrohea. Sixty per cent of the people in Guinea-Bissau suffer from respiratory infections.

Even in Nigeria, with one of the highest per capita income levels of sub-Saharan Africa, over a third of urban families and over half of rural families are unable to obtain a calorie-adequate diet.

For Sub-Saharn Africa as a whole, life expectancy at birth is 49 years, compared to 75 years in the world's industrial countries. There is still only one nurse for every 3,000 Africans, one doctor for every 21,000 Africans ; in the United States, they have one nurse for every 140 people, one doctor for every 520 citizens. Of the school-age children in Africa, one in five is not enrolled in school.

As low as these indicators of health and education in Africa are, they were even lower two or three decades ago. The number of doctors and nurses in proportion to population has doubled since 1960. The proportion of children in school has also doubled since 1960.

But in the early seventies, average income began falling in the poorest countries of Africa. Food production fell behind population growth. Today, even if all the food available in Africa, including imports were divided equally, it would not be enough to meet minimum per capita calorie requirements.

Population growth in Africa is higher than anywhere else in the world—and it's accelerating. The efficiency of investment in Africa is lower than anywhere else in the world—and it is declining.

Economic malaise has contributed to mounting political instability. Violence within and between nations has increased, and, mainly as a result, one in 200 Africans today is a refugee.

The global recession has accelerated the process of economic decay in Africa. Some African governments are not able to provide basic services like road maintenance anymore or, for that matter even pay their own employees regularly.

By contrast, let me turn now to two developing regions of the world that have been making impressive progress against poverty, East Asia, including China, and the Mediterranean.

Not so long ago, these regions were characterised by widespread, miserable poverty. But now the bulk of their people have enough to eat, substantial improvements have been made in infant mortality and life expectancy, and virtually all children go to school. Poverty is still pervasive only in remote areas, like the two Yemens, or in countries scarred by war, like those of Indochina.

The People's Republic of China is a special case. It is much poorer than the rest of East Asia, but China has eliminated the worst aspects of poverty. Notwithstanding much progress, the government still considers about one-fifth of China's population to be unacceptably poor.

Redistribution of wealth has helped to reduce poverty in several countries—including China, of course, but also including a country as capitalistic as the Republic of Korea. And most of developing countries of East Asia and the Mediterranean have also made special efforts to help the poor on an ongoing basis—through the expansion of public education, for example. But it is no coincidence that these regions 'have also been characterised by economic success generally'. Rapid and sustained economic growth has been basic to the reduction of poverty in East Asia and the Mediterranean.

Most of the developing countries in East Asia and the Mediterranean have maintained special efforts to reduce poverty throughout the recent recession. And now that their economies are growing again, we can expect them to make further progress in reducing poverty.

The world can also take encouragement from the development saga of South Asia. Only 20 years ago, the prospects for South Asia looked as dismal as the prospects for Africa seem right now. Yet South Asia has made some progress against poverty.

In the 1960s, India and its neighbours were forced to import massive amounts of food, especially in years of bad weather. There was every reasons to be concerned that population would continue to increase faster than food production. We had visions of endemic famine and violence in South Asia. But most of South Asia has achieved food security through the "green revolution." Economic growth has more than kept pace with population growth, and India and Pakistan have managed to establish large industrial sectors.

Pakistan is the only country in the region that actually reduced the number of its citizens in poverty during the 1970s. India reduced the proportion of its population in poverty, but, because of population growth, the number of poor people increased. Sri Lanka has long scored relatively high on indicators of social welfare, but at the other extreme is Bangladesh—where more than three-quarters of the population remains trapped in absolute poverty.

South Asia still, includes at least half of the world's poorest people. Yet the heroic efforts of the last 20 years have averted what could have been a nightmare, and parts of South Asia have demonstrated economic promise.

Average per capita income in Latin America is higher than in the developing countries of East Asia. Yet the incidence of absolute poverty in Latin America remains disproportionately high. There is little absolute poverty in countries like Argentina or Costa Rica. But poverty is still a serious problem in a most of Latin America, and the region includes like Bolivia and Haiti where the exent of poverty is not much different from Sub-Saharan Africa.

Latin America was dealt a body blow by the international debt crisis. In Maxico, for example, real wages fell 25 per cent between 1981 and 1986. In Chile, urban unemployment reached 30 per cent. The nations with the biggest debts have now all adopted economic adjust--ment programmes and arranged to reschedule their debts, but some of the smaller countries seem to be floundering.

Poverty, has become more severe and widespread throughout Latin America and the Caribbean, and the prospects are grim in those countries that can't settle on reasonable programmes of adjustment.

So then, the historical record shows that progress against poverty is possible. But progress is probably more difficult as we enter the 21st century, then it has been for decades.

1. Abel-Smith, B. and P. Townsend. *Poor and the poorest.* London, Bell, 1965.

2. Adler-Karlsson, G. Eliminating absolute poverty : An approach to the problem. In *Reducing global inquities.* Ed. by W.H. Wriggins and Gunnar Adler-Karlsson. New York, 1978 ; 121-80.

There have been recent attempts to construct new methods of comparing real purchasing power between rich and poor nations. The results to date indicate that the situation in poorer societies may be somewhat better in terms of actual levels of well-being than earlier estimates have indicated. Fourth, the mutual support of the extended family is a much more important factor in poorer nations than in the wealthier societies. Finally, it should be stated as a general rule that where we have good statistics there is no absolute poverty ; where absolute poverty is common, we have no good statistics.

It should be observed, however, that even if aggregate figures of income levels are not very meaningful, the problem of low levels of income decidedly is. What is common to all who live under conditions of absolute poverty is the lack of income with which to buy essentials. They have no money with which to buy food, no money that can be taxed to finance schools or safe water and sewage systems, and no money to provide basic medical care or secure housing. Yet to get a meaningful picture of the dimensions of poverty and to design an attack on it, one must look at its manifestations : malnutrition, inadequate and unsanitary housing and water, and chronic illness and poor health care. Education and employment must also be considered in any measurement of absolute poverty because of their importance in providing the means to overcome these problems.

These six aspects of absolute poverty are discussed in this essay. However, they are not the only ones that ideally should be treated. That one does not live by bread alone is an old truth, and absolute poverty also has a non-material dimension. In the United Nations Declaration of Human Rights, the material problems are listed after the political and spiritual ones. The right to travel within one's nation, to travel freely out of it and return to it are proclaimed as basic human rights, but we know that these rights are seriously infringed upon in many places. Similarly constricted in many nations are the rights to follow one's conscience, to express one's thinking freely, to worship in whichever religion one chooses, and to participate in free assemblies, all rights that Articles 18, 19 and 20 in the UN Declaration have granted and that most nations, communist as well as Western, have recognized by signing the Declaration.

To ignore these non-material aspects of the human condition in an assessment of global poverty is a serious limitation, particularly since certain governments have demonstrated a willingness to sacrifice political and spiritual freedom in their attempts to eradicate material deprivation. The ommission of a discussion of this trade-off is not made in an attempt to hide the problem. It is simply a recognition that the issue is too complex to treat in the context of this essay.

As a first step—which is all this essay aims to take—to putting eradication of absolute poverty at the center of focus of development efforts, it is necessary to get a sense of the material dimensions of the problem. We need to determine indicators that allow us to evaluate the satisfaction of basic needs and to establish policy targets for the specific social groups whose situations are most critical. As concern with the persistence of poverty has increased in recent years, various international agencies and groups have begun to attempt to do just that. The information that follows on the dimensions of the poverty problem represents a synthesis of this ongoing effort.

Roughly 460 million people lack sufficient quantities of food to meet their minimal nutritional needs. This is the conclusion of the Food and Agriculture Organization (FAO) report prepared in 1974 for the World Population Conference and used at the World Food Conference. As the report adds, the true figure may be very much higher since the criteria used to determine global dimensions of malnourishment were based on conservatively low criteria of sufficiency. The measure "insufficient protein/energy supply" was defined as being below a limit of 1,900 to 2,000 calories per day.

"In all countries employment enters into a basic-needs strategy as a means and as an end. Employment yields an output. It provides an income to the employed. And it gives a person the recognition of being engaged in something worth his while." The first part of this statement—that employment is an important means by which to provide for basic needs—can hardly be challenged. The second part of the statement—which embraces employment in an end in itself—is more questionable. It can be seriously questioned how many of those employed today really consider the work they do meaningful or worthwhile.

No doubt, however, in the world as it is today, unemployment and underemployment are major causes of absolute poverty. In most nations the social security and unemployment benefits are non-existent or so small that those who do not have a job and therefore an income easily fall into the category of the absolute poor. Thus the creation of productive employment should be recognized as a goal at least as important as the growth of GNP in any development strategy.

It is of interest to know the dimensions of the unemployment/underemployment problem. In addition to the 17 million potential workers who were unemployed in the developed capitalist economies in 1975, there was a total of nearly 300 million unemployed or under-employed people in so-called developing countries. As indicated in table 8, about 5 per cent of this labour force is openly unemployed and 36 per cent is underemployed. Of the total unemployed and under-employed about 80 per cent are rural.

While developed-country unemployment figures are susceptible to fairly rapid increase or decrease according to the general "health" of the economies in the West, unemployment and underemployment in the developing world appears to be on a steadily upward trend caused by rapid population increases together with structural rigidities and economic policies that fail to provide employment—generating incentives.

Related to this is the effect of the "Green Revolution" on the poorest stata of the rural population. Extensive irrigation is required to achieve the high productivity these modern agricultural techniques promise. It is now generally recognized that the more well-to-do farmers have benefited disproportionately from the introduction of these techniques, and in many cases the irrigation employed may have taken place at the expense of the natural water-flows used by the poorer farmers. The Green Revolution, thus, not only may have created higher productivity and accelerated growth for the farmers able to benefit from it, but it may at the same time have reduced the physical water resources available to the poor.

Economic growth and the catch-up mentality may also intensify the maldistribution of health facilities in the developing countries discussed earlier. This operates both on the demand and the supply side. The purchasing power of the middle and upper classes, as well as their political influence, is able to direct the limited medical resources and health funds available to their own service and away from the needs of the poor. On the supply side, doctors tend to be drawn to the most lucrative regions and practices. Monetary, career, and status motives all combine to intensify the process, and as the disparity between the poor and the well-to-do widens, the problem becomes ever more severe. Furthermore, it operates not only domestically, but is also apparent in the stream of physicians included in the international brain drain. According to a study by the UN Conference on Trade and Development (UNCTAD), between 1961 and 1970 over 14,500 doctors from the underdeveloped countries went to the United States alone.

3. Agarwal, K.G. *Poverty, deprivation and intelligence.* New Delhi, Deep and Deep, 1986. p. 370.

4. Aiyyar, Swaminathan S. Decline of poverty—I & II. *Indian Express* (New Delhi) 15 April 1985; 6; 16 Apr. 1985 ; 6.

5. Alleviating poverty. *Indian Express*, 17 Jan. 1985 ; 6.

Poverty is massive, pervasive and growing in most poor countries of the South. But it is by no means a hopeless task. Many individual countries have shown how to fight their way out of poverty into prosperity. The South as a whole needs to imbibe lessons from these success stories, and the North needs to help finance a replication of these success in other countries. This was the message of Mr. Tom Clausen, President of the World Bank, in a recent lecture at the Martin Luther King Centre in the US. He made the important point that political problems can play a big role in exacerbating poverty. Sub-Saharan Africa presents the bleakest landscape, with half to three-quarters of the population failing to get adequate calories. It is also a place in which one person in 200 is a refugee from some of persecution. Tribal violence, insurgency, and wars have wreaked havoc. What Mr. Clausen failed to say was that the absence of democracy has also contributed to a lack of concern about the condition of the poor. Too many countries of the South have dictatorships which are interested in catering to the ruling power elite rather than the masses. Democracy is no guarantee that poverty will disappear—India and Sri Lanka remain poor. But it does mean that considerable effort will be put into poverty alleviation, and that this will always be a live political issue.

Both growth and redistribution are important for tackling poverty. Latin America has a relatively high GNP but the incidence of poverty is disproportionately high because of a highly-skewed income distribution. There are other countries (Tanzania, Mozambique) which have redistributed assets but failed to grow fast, and poverty is very widespread in these cases too. South Korea and China are outstanding examples of redistribution plus growth though in different ways. The Mao era was best known for redistribution and under Deng agricultural growth has taken off, thanks to the new incentive system which has raised peasant incomes by up to 50 per cent. India is no longer dependent on food aid, with agricultural growing keeping ahead of population growth. The opposite has been happening in Sub-Saharan Africa, which has much to learn from Asia about the green revolution. However, it must be added that even in South Asia the absolute number of those below the poverty line has risen in every country against Pakistan (which has managed to export a big chunk of its poor to the Gulf).

The poorest countries of the South need large injections of finance to get over the hump. But they also need proper policies and priorities. Education and family planning are vital in Africa, where fertility rates are extraordinarily high. Agricultural prices must be remunerative and Governments must ensure the availability of inputs as well as channels for marketing output. Exchange rates should be fixed so as to encourage local production, not cheap imports for the elite. It is not necessary to ask World Bank experts what is needed. One simply has to ask those who have already succeeded in the South.

6. Anderson, Ch. H. *Political economy of social class.* New York, Prentice-Hall, 1974.

7. Anti-poverty programmes : Major short fall in target achievement *Financial express*, 17 Mar. 1986, 7.

8. Arrighi, S. Amin et. al *Dynamics of global crisis.* New York, Monthly Review, 1982.

9. *Assistance to the needy in less-developed areas.* New York, United Nations, 1956.

10. Bailly, F.G. ed. *Gifts and poison*, Oxford, Blackwell, 1971.

11. Bajpai, Rajendra Kumari. National policy on upliftment of weaker sections. *Secular Democracy* Jan.-Feb. 1986 ; 51-52.

12. Balogh, T. Cause and solution of poverty. In *Economic development* Bombay, Vora, 1966 ; 18-32.

The magnitude of the possible effect of a successful mobilization of idle manpower has been consistently underestimated. This failure of appreciation has been mainly due to the assumptions about the shape which development programmes ought to take. It has been implicitly assumed that development would, in the main, have to take the form of industrial growth absorbing the unemployed or underemployed of the rural areas, of a removal of surplus labour from land. Elaborate calculations have been made, therefore, to determine how much "true" under-employment existed. This was defined as that part of the labour force, the removal of which would not affect output. As primitive agriculture is highly seasonal in character, this severely limits the availability of labour. In the context in which some of these calculations were made (e.g., Prof. Rosenstein-Rodan, for Southern Italy) these assumptions were legitimate. Nor can there be any doubt that the process reducing the absolute numbers on the land and not merely their proportion in total employment is an essential part of the effort at increasing national income. What is not justified is to assume that this is to be the main or sole means of rural improvement. Two considerations have been, I think, consistently neglected in shaping these programmes.

The first is that the demand for labour in modernized agriculture based on irrigation increases very rapidly, while even after the removal of the "true underemployed" the seasonal character of the traditional methods of agriculture would leave unemployment which can be estimated between one-third and one-half of the ramaining labour force. Thus productivity in agriculture would still remain so low and so inflexible as to render any development planning difficult, if not hopeless, because of the potential inflationary threat if a programme of expansion is superimposed on this type of economic system.

The second consideration was that agriculture presented at one and the same time not merely an investment opportunity with exceedingly high marginal productivity, which was not utilized only because of the structural and institutional impediments to development, but one which could use manpower for intensive methods of construction. Thus there was here a chance for the seasonal utilization of unemployed rural labour the only reserve and at the same time the greatest curse of underemployed areas. Thus fuller employment could be attained without incurring the extra cost of transportation and the necessary urban rehousing investment which is so terrible an obstacle to national economic planning in dams, irrigation canals, drainage and roads would increase permanent employment opportunities and productivity.

Success in establishing conditions needed for economic progress thus requires a substantial change in the rural social framework. This means the carrying out of a fundamental land reform scheme, which reduces the maximum holding to a certain level at which the inputs, and especially monetary inputs, have to be increased in order to increase income sufficiently to maintain accustomed living standards.

The structure of agricultural costs must become monetized, because without a monetization of the inputs it is difficult to expect the normal profit mechanism to work. Monetary input in a great many areas of Latin America does not reach 30 per cent of the total selling values. Labour is not, in the main, paid in mo ey but in kind. Thus price does not refulate production because in the extreme case of share-cropping, the receipts of the landlord represent a surplus.

Even the use of the pricing system to deflect people from one crop to another under these conditions is extraordinarily difficult. The traditional adherence to certain cropping patterns will be very much higher because there is only a positive incentive non-rural programme will have to be concentrated on basic industries producing intermediate products and capital goods, which, because of technical considerations, are likely to be capital-intensive in the sense of providing relatively few employment opportunities.

Rural reorganization, if linked with public works programmes, might be accepted with less resistance, as it might help with the initial stages by assuring due compensation for old rights. Their being channelled through cooperatives (together with the marginal increase in income) might weaken the stranglehold of tribal or feudal relations which have in the past widely prevented even in India the effectiveness of community development schemes. A new source of income of placed into the hands of "outsiders" might as in the Gezira and in some regions in Egypt provide that loosening of the impediments to rural reform and progress wihch is essential if a new deal is to be introduced.

The rich peasant will stay out and is probably right to do so. They can adopt improved techniques and carry out improvements in their own way. The incentive of self-interest might well offset the draw-back in that having scattered holdings he will not be able to carry out large scale improvement works or to have technical assistance channelled to him, though he ought to be given access to communal improvement on the basis of due payments.

13. Banerji, B.K. Alleviation of poverty : Dimensions of the problem. *Economic Times*, 14 Dec. 1985;5.

14. Barling, S.S. *Poverty, power progress.* Delhi, Panchsheel Publishers, 1983. p. 255.

15. Baster, N. Development indicators : An introduction. *Journal of Development Studies* 8 (3) 1972 ; 1-20.

16. Bauer, P.T. Vicious circle of poverty and the widening gap-myth and reality. *Swarajya* Annual Number (Madras) 1970, 167-70.

17. Beck hold, George. *Persistent poverty.* New York, 1971.

18. Bhagwati, P.N. Strategy for removal of poverty. *Yojana* (New Delhi) 16 Dec. 1984 ; 4-5.

19. Bhatia, B.M. Poverty and growth strategy. *Indian Express,* 14 Sep. 1985 ; 6.

20. Blaikie, Piers. M. Natural resource use in developing countries In *WIC*, 107-26.

21. Blaney, Harry. C. *Global Challenges* : A world at risk. New York, 1979.

22. Blau, Peter M. Structural effects. *American Sociological Review* 25, 1960 ; 178-93.

23. Bourke-White, Margaret, *Halfway to freedom.* New York, 1949.

24. Bowles, Chester. Priority for human dignity. *International Development Review* 7 (3) Sep. 1965.

25. Cole, J.W. and E.R. Wolf *Hidden frontier*, New York, Academic Press, New York, 1974.

26. Cua, Mardino R. Cooperation-an effective tool for anti-poverty programme. In *EAPS*, 150-52.

Our involvement in the cooperatives has been premised on the assumption that the best way to help people whom we have by convention labelled the poor, is to enable them to see the necessity of helping themselves *via* an organization. For, without an organization which they themselves operate in a democratic framework, the attempt to help the poor will never be adequate to meet their needs, but at the same time it will rob them of the spirit of challenge of what others might call initiative. For, poverty is not merely the absence of material needs ; far more brutalizing is the so-called poverty of the spirit, a sense of deprivation. We are not positive whether the poverty of the spirit only comes when material needs are not present or whether the opposite is true. But whatever pattern holds true in any case, both meanings are evident among today's poor whatever they are.

Since organizing the poor to help themselves is the most efficacious way, we are left also here with some alternatives—the trade unions, the organization of farmers into cooperative groups and the organization of urban worker's through cooperatives of many form.

The cooperative idea and its techniques are Western in origin. Our experience in cooperatives is recent. In 1908, some of our legislators were discussing cooperatives, which they did not understand at all, because it was only in 1915 that they passed a law for the cooperatives. 571 agricultural credit cooperative associations were organized under the inspiration of this law On 9th December 1927, a companion legislation was also enacted by our Congress. This second law paved the way for the organization of marketing cooperatives. By 1939, 160 cooperative marketing associations (the forrunners of our present FACOMAs) together with 571 agricultural credit cooperatives, were listed in our statistical records. In 1938, a Protestant minister brought to the country the idea of credit cooperatives. This showed some degree of success, but the war in 1941 decimated all the cooperatives that were to be found in the country except those that eventually became dorment because most members did not understand what they were building. From 1908 to 1957, the history of cooperatives in the Philippines was a history of failures. A new law was passed by our Congress on June 11, 1957 which attracted the interest of the private groups, and efforts to build a cooperative system was renewed with vigor.

We are private groups supported through funding, coming from cooperatives themselves, and whenever support is insufficient to carry on higher programmes some private funding institutions like the Friedrich-Ebert-Stiftung, a major partner of SPECC particularly in the field of cooperative education and training, can also help. We have always been conscious that help from outside can be both a help or a punishment. And help from outside does not only come form private funding institutions but also from the government and form international funding agencies which are too numerous to be listed.

There is one aspect of cooperatives in our country that you might find interesting and which might explain why it has been most difficult to make them succeed. A cooperative is built solely on the idea that people helping themselves can help one another particularly, in providing themselves can help one another particularly, in providing themselves with their economic needs—whether it be providing themselves with credit at competitive interest rates, or consumers items without having to pay for additional mark-ups, or getting the best price for their product by eliminating too many middlemen. And so the cooperative marketing enterprise could lead to the most juicy economic activity processing their own product and getting the finished goods go to the member consumers *via* their "coops". But a project based on a self-reliance is most difficult to introduce in a land which has had a long experience of colonialism. People long under colonialism develop the value of being "right conscious". While cooperatives considered to be "miniature-democracies-in-action" are designed to make people "obligation conscious". As long as this idea is not understood by the members, cooperatives will only become attractive to those who believe that cooperatives would provide them material advantages without necessarily the obligation to give for the communal interest of all the others.

Seeing this as a real problem, we have rationalized our approach. The indigenous system we have developed is to provide our prospective members with graded lessons before they can be enrolled as members of any cooperative. Since we have found out that our people have fallen easy victims to moneylenders charging interest from 100% to 1.000% annually, we begin with a credit "coop". Graded lessons are given requiring the formal attendance of prospective members. Only upon the completion of the required lessons which vary taking into consideration the situation where they are placed, can one become enrolled in a "coop". The general thrust of the lessons which we call (pre-membership educational programme) is to provide them with some cooperative ideals, gradually impressing upon them the need to become obligation-conscious before any economic success can follow. We have discovered to our surprise that people have become interested in studying concepts of economics, community needs, history and government.

27. Dandenar, V.M. On measurement of poverty. *Economic and Political Weekly* 16 (30) 25 Jul. 1981.

28. Dasgupta, K.K. Problems of poverty. *Link* 19 Apr. 19-22.

29. Davis. K and W.E. Moore. Some principles of stratification : A critical analysis. *American Sociological Review* 18 (4) Aug. 1953.

30. De, Nitish. Poverty programmes. *Economic Times* (New Delhi) 1&2 Nov. 1985, 5.

31. De Rosen, Leon. Needed a global strategy of development. *Development, Southern Africa* 1, Apr. 1974, 40-42.

32. Defining poverty. *Financial Express* (New Delhi) 11 Oct. 1984,5.

33. Dey, Tarun. Way to banish poverty. *Tribune* (Chandigarh) 16 Jul 1985 ; 4.

Every year the World Bank brings out a voluminous compendium called "Development Report" which gives a picture of the changing economic world. But the report itself is not as interesting as the statistical appendix at the end which lists data for over a hundred countries.

The United Nations also does this kind of thing but the World Bank information seems to be more authentic, though not perhaps more accurate. For there is a catch in all such international statistics, particularly when they are used to making international comparisons. These are made after converting national currency figures into U.S. dollars at official exchange rates though these rates do not accurately measure the relative purchasing power of currencies.

"The World Development Report (1985)", released last week, also makes similar comparisons. You will find India bunched up along with countries like Kampuchea, Bhutan, Laos and Burundi near the bottom rung of the ladder.

What have Rwanda, Somalia, Tanzania and Vietnam in common with India ? Very little, apart from the fact that their gross national product (GNP) ranges between 250 and 280 U.S. dollars per head ; so they are conveniently grouped together under one head "low income".

The entire industrial sector of Tanzania or Rwanda can be accommodated under the roof of a single private sector factory in India. But to the World Bank statisticians, India is just another Somalia or Tanzania, even though we are one of the top industrial nations of the world.

Going by the World Bank's figures, a business executive in Japan (which has a per capita income of 10,120 U.S. dollars) should be about 40 times better off than his counterpart in Bombay or Delhi. But we all know he isn't. An Assistant Bank Manager in Tokyo may drive a better restaurants but that's about all. He is likely to live in a much smaller house, have less money in the bank and take fewer holidays.

34. Donovan, J.C. *Politics of poverty.* New York, Pegasus, 1967.

35. Douglas, M. Relative poverty. In *Traditions of social policy.* Ed. by A.H. Halsey. Blackwell, 1976.

36. Dutta, Indrani. Problem of poverty. *Deccan Chronicle* 27 Jul. 1986; 6.

37. Epstein, T.S. and D. Jackson ed. *Paradox of poverty.* New Delhi, Macmillan, 1975.

38. Erb, Guy F. ed. V. Kallab eds. *Beyond dependency.* Washington, Overseas Development Council, 1975.

39. Feinstein, O. ed. *Two worlds of change.* New York, Doubleday Anchor Books, 1964.

40. Forsythe, David. *Present role of the Red Cross in protection* Geneva, The Red Cross, 1975.

41. Friedman, R.D. *Poverty : Definition and Perspective.* Washington, American Enterprise Institute for Public Policy Research, 1965.

42. Frobel, Folker *et al.* Global crisis and developing countries. In *Development as social transformation.* London, 1985; 111-24.

43. Galbraith, John Kenneth. *Affluent society* Boston, 1960.

44. Galbraith, John Kenneth, *Nature of mass poverty*. Cambridge, Harvard University Press, 1979.

45. Gallet, P. *Freedom to starve*. Baltimore, Penguin, 1972.

46. Glazer, J.C. Why are the poor still with us. *Public Interest* 1, 1965.

47. Green, C. *Negative taxes and the poverty problem*. Brookings Institution, 1963.

48. Green, Stephen. *International disaster relief: Toward a responsive system*. New York, Mcgraw-Hill, 1977, p. 101.

49. Guin, Catherine, Introduction : Poverty and inequities-strategies for change. In *Reducing global inequities*. Ed. by. W.H. Wriggs and Gunnar Adler--Karlsson. New York, 1978 ; 1-20.

Recently, the developing countries have begun to explore the potential for increased cooperation and interaction among themselves—not as an alternative to relations with the North but as an additional feature of their development strategies. While initial interest in this activity may have stemmed from a desire to enhance the developing states' bargaining power in negotiations with the North, such "collective self-reliance" can have significance for developing countries that seek to meet the needs of the poor. A poverty strategy requires increased production of basic consumption goods and an expansion of basic consumption goods and an expansion of employment opportunities. This can be the basis for mutually beneficial trade. In simple mass-consumption goods, often produced by labour-intensive, capital-saving processes, the developing countries have a comparative advantage and could expand trade among themselves.

Other potential benefits of collective self-reliance exist as well. The exigencies of hunger and rural poverty and underdevelopment put a high premium on innovative rural development programs and new small-scale technologies. Cooperative efforts to design and implement such programs and to develop the technologies could lead to a saving of scarce human and financial resources in the Third World. In addition to creating new markets for simple producer and consumer goods and stimulating research and development in appropriate technologies, joint ventures among developing countries might be able to mobilize new sources of capital within the developing world and generate new earnings. Joint ventures in the processing and manufacture in the Third World of raw materials that are currently exported have already been undertaken, and joint endeavours in transportation, marketing, and consultancy to facilitate this production and trade are likely to follow. Assuming that these efforts are countries in international economic affairs, they should be viewed in the North not as tactics of confrontation but as efforts at improved international economic relations.

However, such actions, important as they may become, do not substitute for needed world economic reform that could accelerate development and help create the conditions under which basic needs can be met. Expanded access for developing countries to the markets of the North is important to the task of meeting basic needs. Many development analysts have already made the point that a substantial growth in markets for LDC labour-intensive manufactured goods could contribute significantly to an expansion of urban employment opportunities in developing countries and thus to an increase in effective demand for basic goods and services. In addition, concessions to poor countries in agricultural trade could make a significant impact on the living conditions of the rural poor.

International support for the stabilization of commodity—export prices could both help to smooth out fluctuations in foreign-exchange earnings in developing economies and help governments plan for the development of rural sectors. Since over three-fourths of the low and poor in developing countries live in rural areas, the development of the agriculture sector, rural infrastructure, and rural industries could create an economic impetus that would reach many of the abject poor (even though, it might be added, the direct effects of establization might initially benefit large farmers and exporting firms). These and other international economic reforms that afford the LDCs a larger share of the world's wealth can provide means to reduce poverty and inequality, provided that these countries choose to orient policies and priorities toward that end.

However, both reform of the international economic system and domestic reforms are likely to be painfully slow processes. If, therefore, the international community is to realize its obligation to help all people escape from abject poverty within a reasonable period of time, expanded international aid policies, targeted more directly toward meeting basic needs will be needed through the next several decades. In making significant amounts of resources available for support of basic needs, programs in the South, the rich countries of the North will undoubtedly demand some assurance that the resources reach those most in need. Yet, given the sensitivity of developing states to political dominance or interference, some way will have to be found to direct aid resources to the appropriate recipients without being unduly intrusive.

Various proposals have been made to obtain international funds from "non-appropriated" sources—e.g., a tax on deep seabed mining or an international tax on personal income—that are not dependent on annual government approval. A next step seemingly should be to devise a means of allocating such funds to those developing countries that apply for them for support of domestically designed basic needs programs.

Implementing some such international needs program would obviously not meet the bulk of the claims that the developing countries are making for a more equitable sharing of the world's resources and increased international status. Indeed, not all of those claims rest solely on the issue of basic human needs. Other issues - which have more to do with the principle of sovereign equality and the expectations that flow from it—will continue through the decade of the 1980s to involve more and less developed states in negotiations over rules, mutual obligations, and the "Just distribution of benefits" among states. For both political and economic reasons, the issues of inequities in relations among states and inequities within societies have become inexorably linked. The South cannot easily continue to demand a "fairer share" in international dealings nor can it expect smooth growth and development without paying heed to the need for a more equitable domestic distribution of the benefits of development. Nor can the North hope to make a significant contribution to eradicating poverty without accepting the need for changes in the international economic order that will themselves facilitate the task of meeting basic needs.

50. Haq, M. *Poverty curtain.* New York, Columbia University Press, 1976.

51. Harrington, Michael. *Vast majority : A journey to the world's poor.* New York, Simon and Schuster, 1977.

52. Hayter, Teresa. *Creation of world Poverty.* London, Pluto Press, 1981.

53. Hildebrand, C. *Poverty, income maintenance and negative income tax*, Cornell, 1967.

54. Holman, R. Poverty ; Consensus and alternatives. *British Journal of Social Work* 3(4) Win 1973.

55. Horowitz, David. *Abolition of Poverty*. New York, Praeger, 1969, p. 178.

56. Horowitz, David. Poverty. *In Abolition of Poverty*. New York, Praeger, 1969, 20-48.

57. How many poor ? *Pioneer* (Lucknow) 4 Mar. 1986, 4.

58. How to fight poverty ? *Telegraph* (Calcutta) 3 Mar. 1986 ; 6.

State governments and institutions like banks have a big role to play in anti-poverty programmes and therefore the problems of implementation have to be addressed by all three. Generations of indebtedness and deprivation perhaps inevitably lead to the first time loan being consumed instead of the necessary asset bring created. Thus good money will have to be sunk after bad for sometimes three years in a row before the loans start being repaid. What has to be ensured by both the Union and state governments is public sanction against non-repayment of bank loans. This is best achieved by keeping ambitious political leaders away from the identification of borrowers and leaving the job to panchayat level operatives who both know and are known to their respective village communities. The administering of the loans should be entrusted to the regional rural banks and their sponsoring nationalised banks. There is now considerable expertise in them to manage rural employment programmes and what is needed is romoval of political interference and motivation for the bank staff and officers from the top management. Also, an attack on poverty, without a simultaneous attack on disease and malnutrition is meaningless. The state governments, which run primary education and look after public health have their roles clearly demarcated. The higher central allocations should now provide a new impetus for greater action.

59. Huang—Thio, S. M. Equal protection and rational classification, *Public law* 1963 ; 412-40.

60. Humphrey Hubert H. Discussions of poverty. In *War on poverty*, New York, 1964 ; 17-30.

61. Humphrey, Hubert H. Disaster insurance. In *War on poverty*. New York, 1964 ; 107-20.

62. Humphrey, Hubert H. *War on poverty*. New York, Mcgraw-Hill 1964. p. 206.

63. Hurry, Jamieson B. *Poverty and its vicious circles*. London, Churchill, 1917. p. 180.

64. Increasing poverty with growth. *Nagpur Times*, 23 Mar. 1984 ; 4.

65. Inder Mohan. How not to help the poor. *Hindustan Times* 29 Oct. 1984 ; 9.

66. Ingram, Derek. Poverty bomb may explode in 1987. *Pioneer* 17 Jul. 1984 ; 4.

Chicago burned. Parliament in Westminister set up a passable imitation of an apartheid state in Britain. In South Africa uprising and sabotage combined with a campaign of non-violence led to the non-delivery of every essential even of water, and broke white supremacy.

Disruption by a racial minority created disruption in a computerised society that no one knew how to cope with. Checkout counters in super-markets went haywire. Poor house-wives found themselves charged £ 300 for their weekend groceries and millionaires wives were told they had no credit. Wall Street crashed.

This is small part of a world scenario that William Clark, former Vice-President of the World Bank, sets down in a new book called *Cataclysm* (Sidgwick and Jackson), published on the day the World Bank produced its own annual *World Development Report*.

Clark has written his dramatic book as a warning to the world that the earth can be destroyed not only by the atom bomb but by what he calls the poverty bomb. It is a response to the fact that the industrialised world has chosen to ignore the Brandt Report and all it stands for.

If everyone goes on ignoring the dangerous situation that is building up between the rich and poor of the world then there can be an economic holocaust just as there can be a nuclear one.

Clark is well qualified to write such a book. At the World Bank for many years he was at the centre of international economic politics and personally witnessed world leaders grappling—or rather failing to grapple—with the great economic issues.

He is also a journalist, having been Foreign Editor of the *London Observer* for ten years, and then Press Secretary to Prime Minister Anthony Edeh.

In that job at 10, Downing Street London, he saw at first hand how a major international crisis developed – the Suez affair which led to the French, British and Israeli military confrontation with President Nasser of Egypt. He resigned the day the Suez invasion ended.

Cataclysm suggests that in William Clark's view little time is left before the poverty bomb explodes. It is the debt situation, already currently grave, which starts the chain of events he describes. Clark set his book only three years ahead—in 1987.

He draws a horrifying picture in which the economic slide produces confrontation between the industrialised powers, notably the US and Britain, and the Third World and leads quickly to black-white racial confrontation.

An international organisation known as the *Black Hand*, based in Nigeria, quickly shows how the computerised world as it is developing today is totally at the mercy of the poorer, and therefore usually black section of communities, and that the poor have it in their hands to cripple the rich world.

67. Jha, Sanjeev. Poverty: Global perspective *Economic Times*, 26 Jun. 1986.

68. Johnston, R.J. and Peter J. World in crisis ? In *WIC*; 1-11.

69. Joshi, P.C. Crossing the barriers of poverty. *Mainstream* (New Delhi) 26 Nov. 1983 ; 9-10; 29.

"I remain committed to planned development and the removal of poverty has to be the main plank of national planning". In these few words Indira Gandhi, reaffirmed her faith in the continuing relevance of economic planning to India and in the fundamental objectives and imperatives of Indian planning.

The occasion of this major policy speech, inadequately covered by the national press, was the inauguration of the Silver Jubilee celebrations of the Institute of Economic Growth (Delhi) on November 16, 1983. Indira Gandhi called upon economists and sociologists to provide intellectual support for the national war against poverty "which is the most degrading experience of human existence and an intensely moral question". She candidly stated that "growth by itself does not end poverty ; it is the manner in which we plan to grow that matters". She could have added that in India today growth induced poverty has also become backwardness.

Indira Gandhi stressed how the national commitment to planning as a method of attacking poverty was irreversible as had deep historical roots in the struggle for freedom. She recalled the rich intellectual and moral legacy of Dadabhai Naoroji, R.C. Dutt, Gokhale and of Gandhi and Nehru on the basic approach to development and specially in regard to their interpretation of development as alleviation of mass poverty. One can recall how Jawaharlal Nehru defined planning "as a process whereby we stop those cummulative forces at work which make the poor poorer and start a new series of cummulative forces to enable the poor to cross the barriers of poverty". Indira Gandhi is fully justified in her assessment that without planning India would not have achieved the transition from the colonial to an independent economy. Nor would India have been put on the path of breaking away from the colonial mould of mass poverty.

We must not forget that poverty under colonial rule represented, to use a phrase from K.S. Shelvankar's *The Problem of India* (1940), "an extremity of destitution", produced and perpetuated by the retrograde colonial structure and buttressed by the colonial state power. The peculiar character of this poverty was that the destitution-stricken masses had no hope of any improvement in their condition within this structure. The problem of the labouring poor under colonialism was not that they were at the bottom of the economic ladder; but that they were on no ladder at all. This colonial mould was broken by the intervention of the national-state which had behind it the powerful support of the national movement, including the toiling masses. The structural changes and the developmental processes initiated by the new nation-state as part of the planning process made the first major attack on the colonial order and opened a new era of hope for the poor. If all these hopes have not fructified, it is at least partly due to the pernicious and stubborn survivals of colonialism in large parts of the country. Three and a half decades of independence have not proved adequate to eliminate the distortions and arrested growth of almost two centuries of colonial rule.

Let us not forget that the battle against mass poverty faces the toughest impediments in the most poverty-stricken States of India's Eastern region which were exposed to the so-called "civilising influence", of colonial rule for the longest period. The socio-economic and cultural distortions created by the British had struck deep roots in these States. The war against poverty in such areas of concentrated poverty requires not less but more and better planning suited to specific conditions of these States. Let us also not forget that the national perspective on the Indian economic problem had its origins in the Eastern region. It had as its major premise from Rammohun Roy to Jawaharlal Nehru the elimination of the conditions of mass immiserisation created by the colonial rule.

One must take serious note of Indira Gandhi's reference to the independence struggle which shaped the anti-poverty approach of the national leaders. The perception expectations and urges of the Indian people and their sensitiveness to socio-economic inequality have been shaped by these historical processes. To ignore them is to have serious gaps in one's approach to India's economic problems and their solutions.

70. Kahn, H. *et al.* eds. *Next 2000 years*. New York, Willian Morrow, 1976.

71. Kakwani, Nanak. On a class of poverty measures. *Econometrics* 4(2) 1977. 48, 1980.

72. Khusro, A.M. Poverty of poverty analysis. *Economic Times*, 1 Oct. 1984; 5.

73. Kohr, Leohold. Low cost poverty. In *Development without aid*. Llandybie, 1973; 57-60.

74. Kossmann-Putto, J&E. Witte. *Historical research in the low countries, 1981-83: A critical survey*. Leiden, E.J. Brill, 1986. p. 120.

75. Kripalani, J.B. *Pomp and poverty*. Delhi, Navchetan Press, 1957. p. 46.

76. Kulkarni, Shanad, *Poverty: An interdisciplinary approach*. Somaiya, 1982. p. 296. Bombay.

77. Kundu, Amitabh. Measurement of poverty—some conceptual issues. *Anvesak* 11 (1-2) 1981.

78. Laslett, P. *World we have lost*. London, Methuen, 1965.

79. Lee, R.B. and I. Devore. *Man the hunter*. Chicago, Aldine, 1968.

80. Lerner, D. *Passing of traditional society*, Glencoe, Free Press, 1958.

81. Lewis. H. *Culture, class and poverty*. Washington, cross-Tell, Feb. 1967.

82. Lenis, Oscar. Culture of poverty. In *on understanding poverty*. Ed. by D.P. Moynihan. .New York, Basic Books, 1968.

83. Lipton, Michel. *Why poor people stay poor.* Cambridge, 1977.

84. Lister, R. Take-up: The same old story. *Poverty* (34) Sum 1976.

85. Marsden, Keith: Global development strategies and the poor. *International Labour Review* 117, Nov. Dec. 1978; 675-96.

86. McCarthy, Kathleen D. Short and simple annals of the poor: Foundation funding for the humanities, 1900-1983. *Proceedings of the American Philosophical Society.* 129 (1) Mar. 1985; 3-8.

87. McGreevey, W.P. ed. *Third-World poverty: New strategies for measuring development progress.* Lexington Books 1980.

88. Mc Hale, John and Magda C. *Basic human needs: A framework for action.* Transaction Books, 1978.

89. Mead, N. *New lives for old.* New York, Morrow, 1956.

90. Meier, Gerald M. Emerging from poverty : *The economics that really matters.* New York, Oxford University Press, 1984.

Since the mid-forties the international community has been concerned with the problems of mitigating the pains of poverty and raising the totally inadequate living standard of more than 2 billion peoples of over 100 developing countries of Africa, Asia and Latin America. In spite of the efforts of these developing countries and international agencies these problems have remained persistent. It is now, imperative to review the development record of the last forty years to know what has gone wrong with the development policies adopted by the poor countries; what policy changes were adopted as a result of the interplay of development experience of the poor countries and the thinking of the development economists; and what are the appropriate policies that should now be adopted to make these countries 'emerge from the depths of poverty'.

The book is an excellent attempt to answer these questions by explaining the development economics in simple and non-technical language. With unusual clarity and range, the author—a Professor of International Economics at Stanford University (USA)—has offered a retrospective appraisal of the development record of the last forty years giving a prescriptive analysis of the urgent policy measures to be pursued by the developing countries for accelerating their development processes. The author's retrospective analysis of what has happened in the developing countries and how scholars and statesmen have analysed these happening, is a story, which is both exciting and disappointing.

Divided in three parts, the first part of the book audits the record of the development efforts of poor countries since World War II and provides a critical assessment of people's expectations, governments on both economic and political fronts.

91. Mesarovic, M. and E. Pestel. *Mankind at the turning point.* London, Hutchinson, 1975.

92. Miller, S.M. and Pamela Roby. Poverty : Changing social stratification. In *COP* ; 124-45.

Poverty can be viewed in many contexts. Generally neglected has been the context of social stratification. The limited results of poverty programs based upon subsistence standards are now forcing a realization that not pauperism but inequality is the main issue within high-income industrial societies. When we begin to discuss poverty in terms of relative deprivation and inequalities, we are posing question about the over-all social stratification of a nation : What are considered 'acceptable' gaps between the poor and other groups ? What are the relevant dimensions for viewing differences among groups within the society today ?

This chapter's first objective is to recast approaches to poverty in terms of stratification. A thorough poverty analysis questions the level of living of the non-poor as well as the poor. As the late Polish sociologist Stanislaw Ossowski Wrote in his brilliant analysis of social stratification, '. . . a class (is) a member of a certain system of relations. This means that the definition of any class must take into account the relation of this group to other groups in this system. Not just the poor but the entire society is at issue. As yet, poverty programs have not been adequately seen as efforts to engineer changes in the stratification profiles of the United States.

A stratificational analysis requires not only viewing the poor as those who are lagging behind relative to others in society, but extending the concept of poverty beyond the narrow limits of income. When poverty is viewed within the stratificational frame-work, we see that Max Weber and Richard Titmuss have already made major contribution to its analysis. One of Weber's outstanding contributions to social science was to untwine three components of stratification : class, status, and power. The Marxian analysis centered on the economic (or class) dimensions of stratification, but Weber believed that the prestige (social honour) and political dimensions of stratification were sometimes independently important. These other dimensions could change without change in the economic they could remain stable despite changes in the economic dimension of stratification. With his widely ranging erudition, Weber illustrated his thesis by showing that, for example, a high status group, such as the Prussian Junkers, could retain considerable political power despite its reduced economic importance. Conversely, rising economic group, like the bourgeoisie, could have a long struggle to obtain prestige equivalent to their economic position. Weber sought not to overturn Marx's analysis but to go beyond it, to broaden its perspectives.

In this century, Titmuss has further refined our tools of analysis by conceiving of income as the command over resources over time. He argues that wage-connected benefits (e.g. pensions) and fiscal benefits (e.g. tax deductions for children which benefit the better-off more than the low-income tax payer) as well as welfare (transfer) benefits must be included in any discussion of the command over resources.

Recently we have suggested that governments in any society with significant inequalities should at least provide for rising minimum levels not only of incomes, assets, and basic services, but also of self-respect and opportunities for social mobility and participation in many forms of decision making. To gain a better understanding of the objectives of various poverty programs and the relationships between these goals, we can look at efforts to reduce poverty in terms of (i) what aspect of poverty is the program aimed at, e.g. the economic, political, educational and social mobility, or status dimensions of stratification ; and (ii) who is the program aimed at, e.g. is the program aimed at improving the social conditions of those who are poor (e.g. jobs, income, housing, health, self-respect) or at moving some of those who are poor out of poverty.

93. Mehta, M.K. Poverty eradication : A far cry. *Daily* (Bombay) 9 Jun. 1984 ; 13.

94. Moynihan, Daniel P. ed. *On understanding poverty : Perspectives form the social sciences.* New York, Basic Book, 1968.

95. Mr. Saouma (Edward) on poverty. *Economic Times* 16 Oct. 1985 ; 5.

On the occasion of the Food and Agricultural Organisation's (FAO) fortieth anniversary, its Director-General Edward Saouma, has stated, perhaps more in sorrow than in anger, that "hunger persists and its victims increase each year in absolute if not proportionate terms." In this context, in an analysis of the rural-urban gap in developing countries, Mr. Saouma states : "Millions upon millions of the third world's rural youth saw little incentive for staying on the land and joined the swelling urban masses seeking a more promising life style". There has not been an overwhelming migration from the rural to the urban areas in India but even small rise in the proportion of the urban to the total population that has been captured by the 1981 census should be a cause for concern. Hopefully, the various anti-poverty programmes and the successive run of good harvests experienced in recent years may have staved the migration. Mr. Saouma's criticism in this context takes the shape of an indictment of development policies fostered by the developed countries : "Food aid on a bilateral government—to government basis (was) a means to providing cheap food to urban consumers. With a ready-made palliative applied to the problem of provisioning politically volatile urban populations, it was much easier to accord agriculture a lower priority".

All this is true for the developing countries as a group, as it was for India, say, upto the mid-sixties. What Mr. Saouma has to say next is also relevant to the Indian situation : "When financing could be found for the development of food and agricultural production, it was often more convenient to channel it to highly visible projects in the modren sector, such as major irrigation works, rather than to devise ways of reaching small holders practising rainfed agriculture". Valid though these criticisms are in respect of the political regimes of the developing countries, the question is whether the limited elitist strategy alone was responsible for the unbalanced pattern of growth achieved in the post-colonial era. Mr. Saouma notes in passing that an "abundance of low-cost labour has not proven to be of significant advantage in efforts to promote industrial growth". For this unsatisfactory situation, he points to the "political strength that labour organisations in developed countries have been able to exercise in protecting domestic jobs". True enough, but can one take up such proximate causes without going into the impact of the dark era of colonialism, when for a century or so industry was not allowed to grow (as in India) and take away population from the land, when land in the colonies had to accommodate increasing numbers ? Backlog is at bottom responsible for low-cost labour (and for low labour productivity in agriculture) and for the current inability of industry to absorb the vast numbers of low-cost labour. For rapid and adequate industrialisation, the scale of resource flows from the multilateral institutions should have been much larger than it has been. There is no question that development strategies have been distorted both by the international framework and the regimes in power in the developing countries. The fact of inadequate resource flows cannot, however, be wished away nor can the fact of the undue cost that is demanded for even the limited resources transferred to the developing world. It is no consolation in this context, to point to the other half that the "industrial growth of Europe and North America, after all, was achieved not in one generation but many" the very half that for generations was stultified by those who bought time for their generations. If "rediscovering a sense of urgency" be the objective of

FAO, as highlighted by its Director-General, surely the objective calls for significantly mitigating the impact of unequal development among nations in a time frame that does not extend beyond a generation or two.

96. Myrdal, Gunnar. *Challenge of world poverty.* Middlesex, Pelican Press, 1970.

97. Myrdal, Gunnar. World poverty problem. In *Against the stream.* New York, Pantheon Books, 1972.

98. Naidu, K. Munirathna. Regional development and a new strategy. *Economic Studies* 22 (1) 1981 ; 3-80.

99. Nambiar, Shri Shankaran. Poverty--An area of study. *Indian Labour Journal* (12) Dec. 1984 ; 1831-35.

100. Nehru, B.K. Removal of poverty I-II. *Economic Times* 9 & 10 Jan. 1986 ; 5.

101. Orr, D.W. and M.S. Soroos. *Global predicament.* University of North Carolina Press, 1979.

102. Orshansky, Mollie. and J.S. Bretz. Born to be poor. *Social Security Bulletin* 39(1) Jan. 1976.

103. Orshansky, Mollie. Counting the poor : Another look at the poverty probill. *Social Security Bulletin.* Jan. 1965 ; 3-29.

104. Orshansky, Mollie. Recounting the poor. A five year review. *Social Security Bulletin.* Apr. 1966 ; 2-19.

105. Orshansky, Mollie. Who's who among the poor : A demographic view of poverty. *Social Security Bulletin.* Jul. 1965 ; 3-33.

106. Panshar, S.L. What is poverty. *Madhya Pradesh Chronicle* (Bhopal) 16 Apr. 1983 ; 4.

107. Politics of poverty. *Financial Express* 20 Sep. 1984 ; 5.

108. Poor advise the rich. *International Herald Tribune,* 16 Aug. 1986 ; 6.

109. Poverty and waste. *Statesman* 6 Mar. 1986 ; 6.

110. Poverty calculations. *Times of India* 9 Dec. 1983 ; 8.

111. Poverty line. *Statesman* New Delhi 3 Nov. 1985 ; 6.

112. Poverty ratio. *Patriot* 14 Mar. 1985 ; 4.

113. Poverty theme. *Economic Times* 6 Oct. 1980 ; 5.

114. Poverty trap. *Financial Express*. 5 Feb. 1985 ; 5.

115. Prais, S.R and H.S. Hauthakker. *Analysis of family budget*. Cambridge, 1955.

116. Ramadas, P. Problems of peace and poverty. *Akashvani* (New Delhi) 11 Jul. 1982 ; 1-2.

War and peace are the two age-old antipodes of human existence. War destroys the works of man and kills man himself. Peace means life. Human history spanning many centuries has seen a great many wars, armed conflicts and clashes. It has been estimated that 15,000 wars, big and small, have revaged the surface of our planet. Peace has seemed little more than a brief break, a halt in between murderous conflicts while war has seemed all but a natural condition of men.

Wars are not fatally inevitable. Time was when men did not know war. Wars are not the natural concomitant of the progress of mankind. They are the result of the combination of social and historical circumstances. Wars are begun with the emergence of antagonistic, class-divided forms of human society. It occurs from a set of deliberate actions by the leaders of certain exploiting classes to achieve definite goals. The victims of those action were the popular masses, ordinary men and women to whom war had always been abhorrent.

The post-war experience of relations between opposing systems—socialism and capitalism—has disclosed to man a new stage in his historical development the universal human importance of principles of peaceful co-existence. It is based on Appointments, the idea of preserving human life and the culture of peoples.

Under the present conditions of the unprecedented and ever-growing scientific and technical might of states, any approach that ignores the necessity for the idea of peaceful co-existence is fraught with consequences of mass mutual extermination of mankind. This truth is now obvious to all.

For many centuries men are never tired of condemning and cursing war. The peoples have had visions of lasting pace, but almost every page in the history of mankind is marred by the history of mankind is marred by the sinister reflection of the flames of wars, big and small. Neither the lessons of history, nor man's natural aversion to killing have ever prevented new blood-baths, because the forces of war, who stood to gain from war were too great. In our epoch this state of affairs has changed fundamentally. Today, the struggle against war has a reliable basis in the strength of the forces of peace and the forces of democracy and in the freedom and independence of nations.

117. Ramaswamy, A. and N.V. R. Ram. *Poverty : Is it understood* ? Inter-Asia Publications, 1985.

118. Rao, T.N. Dimensions of poverty. *Hindustan Times* 27 Mar. 1985 ; 9.

119. Rein, Martin. Problems in the definition and measurement of poverty. In *COP* ; 46-63.

The problems of how to define and measure poverty cannot proceed until we clarify the conception of poverty we wish to employ. Three broad concepts of poverty can be identified. Poverty may be regarded as subsistence, inequality or externality. Subsistence is concerned with the minimum of provision needed to maintain health and working capacity. Its terms of reference are the capacity to survive and to maintain physical efficiency. Inequality is converned with the relative position of income groups to each other. Poverty cannot be understood by isolating the poor and treating them as a special group. Society is seen as a series of stratified income layers and poverty is concerned with how the bottom layers fare relative to the rest of society. Hence, the concept of poverty must be seen in the context of society as a whole. The study of the poor then depends on an understanding of the level of living of the rich, since it is these conditions relative to each other that are critical in the conception of inequality. To understand the poor we must then study the affluent. Externality is concerned with the social consequences of poverty for the rest of society rather than in terms of the needs of the poor. The poverty-line should serve 'as an index of the disutility to the community of the persistence of poverty'.

People must not be allowed to become so poor that they offend or are hurtful to society. It is not so much the misery and plight of the poor but the discomfort and cost to the community which is crucial to this view of poverty. We have a problem for those who are not poor. Poverty then consists of social problems correlated with low income. Hence only when income-conditioned problems are randomized can poverty be eliminated. To improve the level of living of the poor without reducing disutility to the rest of community, is insufficient.

Each of these concepts presents numerous problems of definition and measurement. Should we define poverty only in terms of economic insufficiency, economic inequality and economic dis-economy, or should the definition be broadened to embrace non-economic variables such as prestige, power and social services ? For example, Titmuss has insisted that 'we cannot . . . delineate the new frontiers of poverty unless we take account of the changing agents and characteristics of inequality ! . . Although the concept of poverty Titmuss holds is that of inequality, he is posing the broader question that poverty is more than the lack of income.

When a more encompassing view of poverty is : ccepted which extends beyond the distribution of income, two critical issues emerge—where to establish the cut-off points which separate the poor from the non-poor and which non-economic conditions should be taken into account.

Paradoxically, we measure poverty in subsistence terms, but the programmes and policies we have evolved to reduce poverty in America are based on a broader conception of the dimensions of well-being for which no systematic statistical information is available. These include the lack of accepted minimum or inequalities in the distribution of power, education and legal justice. These dimensions of the level of living are not included in the goods and services which make up a minimum personal market basket, on which the measurement of poverty is based, because these items cannot be purchased by the individual with low income in the market. However, little organized effort has been directed at conceptualizing and measuring a conception of poverty which is more closely related to the programmes we have developed, or at developing a programme to reduce poverty (cash transfers) which is more closely tied to the concept of poverty we employ—the lack of minimum income for subsistence.

However, a small body of literature is being developed which does attempt to spell out the wider dimensions of poverty. Townsend, influenced by Titmuss, defines poverty as inequities in the distribution of five resources, including income, capital assets, occupational fringe benefits, current public services and current private services. A national study of poverty in England based on an empirical.

120. Robbins, C. and J. Ansari. *Profits of doom*. London, War on Want, 1976.

121. Rodgers, Gerry B. *Poverty ten years on.* Geneva, ILO ; 1983.
122. Rout, Sarat. Battle against poverty. *Patriot* (New Delhi) 1 Apr. 1986 ; 9.

When Mahatma Gandhi visited Orissa in 1921, he was shocked to see the poverty prevailing at that time. He called Orissa the epitone of India's poverty and started his famous *padayatra* (a long walk by feets) there. He deputed a number of his devoted followers like Thakkar Baha, Iswarlal Vyas and many other noted social workers to remain in Orissa and work among the people. Orissa has always been considered one of the poorest States in India. According to recent estimates of the Planning Commission, 67 per cent of the people lived below the poverty line in 1977-78. By 1983-84 happily the extent of poverty has been reduced to some extent and the number of people now living below the poverty line constitutes 45 per cent of Orissa's total population.

But, what is the reason behind the poverty in the State. Thirty-seven per cent of Orissa's total population constitutes scheduled caste and scheduled tribes. They are the most deprived section of the community. Besides this, nearly 30 per cent of the house-holds own less than one hectare of land, 28 per cent total work force are of the agricultural labours are practically landless. During British rule, Orissa suffered most. The State was politically fragmented and the economic development was totally neglected. The State suffered from successive spells of famine and ravages of flood. It is only after independence that concerted efforts were made to improve the rural economy.

Though rural development programmes were being implemented in the State since the First Five Year Plan, no specific attempt was made to attack poverty directly. Since 1980 an integrated approach has been made and feasible schemes were drawn up for different groups of people belonging to the weaker section. The most important measure taken in this regard was the implementation of the Integrated Rural Development Programme. Under this programme, 500 beneficiaries were selected in each block and were provided with assistance. Since many of the beneficiaries were totally landless, emphasis was given one development of rural crafts, village industries and small business. The District Industries Centres and DRDA projects jointly conducted training programmes to impart necessary skills. Animal husbandry, dairy farming, sheep rearing, poultry, pisciculture etc. were also encouraged.

The Government of Orissa felt that the pattern of IRDP was not beneficial to the poorest among the poor. Therefore, the State Government introduced a scheme of its own known as Economic Rehabilitation of the Rural Poor (ERRP). Under ERRP scheme, the selected beneficiaries are allotted land, if available, and given all facilities for cultivation. They are also given training and provided tools, equipments, credit etc. Under the ERRP scheme, the beneficiary gets a subsidy at 50 per cent and the tribal beneficiary gets 75 per cent subsidy. The basic objective of this programme is to attack poverty at its root. In all villages, 10 of the poorest families were selected by a People's Committee and assistance was provided to them. A recent evaluation made of the programme has shown that gradually this scheme has been able to make an impact.

123. Rowntree, S. *Poverty and progress : A second social survey of York*, London, Longmans, 1941.

124. Rowntree, S. and G. Lavers. *Poverty in the welfare State*. London, Longmans, 1951.

125. Russett, B.M. *et. al. World handbook of political and social indicators*. London, Yale University Press, 1964.

126. Rutter, M. and N. Madge. *Cycles of deprivation*. Heinemann, 1976.

127. Sagar, Vidya. Poverty analysis. *Economic Times*, 25 Oct. 1985 ; 5.

128. Sambasiva Rao, K. Attack on poverty. *National Herald*, (New Delhi) 17 Dec. 1985 ; 5.

129. Schachter, Oscar. *Sharing the world's resources*. Columbia University Press, 1977.

130. Sen, A.K. Issues in the measurement of poverty. *Scandinavian Journal of Economics* 81(2) 1979 ; 285-307.

131. Sen, A.K. Poverty : An ordinal approach to measurement. *Econometrica* 44 (2) Mar. 1976 ; 219-31.

132. Shankar, Kripa. Obstacles to poverty removal. *Mainstream* 23 Apr. 1983 ; 15-16.

133. Sharma, O.P. Parameters of poverty. *Indian Express* 17 Oct. 1984 ; 6.

134. Sheehan, M. *Meaning of poverty*. Dublin, Council for Social welfare, 1974.

135. Sinfield, A. Comparative view of poverty research. *Social Studies*. 4(1) Apr. 1975.

136. Sinfield, A. Poverty rediscovered. In *Planning for change*. Ed. by J.B. Culling worth. London, Allen & Unwin, 1973.

137. Singh, S.P. Poverty line. *Hindustan Times* 4 Apr. 1985 ; 9.

138. Singh, S.P. Sources of poverty. *Hindustan Times* 5 Dec. 1985 ; 9.

139. Sopher, D.E. Measure of disparity. *Professional Geographer* 26 (4) 1974.

140. Subramaniam, C. Anatomy of poverty I & II. *Financial Express* 9 & 10 Oct. 1984 ; 5.

141. Sukhatma, P.K. On measurement of poverty. *Economic and Political Weekly* 16(32) 8 Aug. 1981.

142. Thapa, Nomesk. Sins and sinners. *Economic Weekly* 7 Oct. 1961.

143. Tinbergen, J. Concept of unbalanced growth. In *Economic development*. Bombay, Vora, 1966 ; 14-7.

In recent years a phrase has been launched into the arena of "growthmen" meant as a challenge to the concept of balanced growth as an aim for development policies. It is this author's contention that the phrase is rather unfortunate. In this note it will be analysed a bit further than has so far been done.

"Balanced" is another word for "equilibrated", or "in equilibrium". The word equilibrium, in its simplest meaning, indicates one situation on a demand curve, namely; the point of interaction with the supply curve. Alternatively, it can be seen as one point on a supply curve, namely; the point of intersection with the demand curve. Again as an alternative, an equilibrium point may be a point in a more complicated structure. But always, equilibrium represents one among a large number of conceivable situations; there are many more (infinitely more) disequilibrium points than equilibrium points. While the requirement that something be in equilibrium represents a well-defined choice, the inverse requirement that something be unbalanced does not define it at all; it leaves us with an infinity of points, with the suggestion, that any of them be desirable, if only not the equilibrium point. The phrase "unbalanced" therefore is indeterminate and in a very general philosophical sense cannot be the alternative to "balanced". In fact, what the proponents of "unbalanced growth" means is something balanced in another way. Hence the phrase unbalanced is unfortunate.

As is well known, the proponents of unbalanced growth point out that development policy, apart from direct government investment in some fields, should create inducements to the private sector—and, presumably, the lower public authorities—to complement the activities in the sector of central government. This main point is well taken and applies to any regime, including communist regimes. Nowhere can everything be done by a central government alone. As soon as the activities needed for the development of an economy have to be distributed over various agents, those undertaken by the central government alone will show lacunae (to be filled up by the other agents) and may hence be called "unbalanced". But, as already pointed out, they should not barbitrarily unbalanced. They should be unbalanced in a very specific way, such as just to create the necessary inducements. The idea—or at least the portion of it which is acceptable—does not imply that what should be unbalanced (in this particular way) is the economy's growth. Hence, if "unbalanced", not "unbalanced growth". Growth should be balanced anyway; whatever imbalance is needed is imbalance in the central government's action. The combination of the words "unbalanced" and "growth" does not make sense, therefore, either.

The policy advocated consists of a number of elements. To begin with, decisions must be taken about which activities should be left to the private sector and to lower public authorities. Next, the institutions and their instruments shall be indicated which are supposed to create the desired inducements to the private sector and the lower public authorities.

144. Townsend, Peter ed. *Concept of poverty*, London, Heinemann, 1970. p. 260.

145. Townsend, Peter. Measuring poverty. *British Journal of Sociology*, Jun. 1954.

146. Townsend, Peter. Meaning of poverty. *British Journal of Sociology*, Sep. 1962.

147. Townsend, Peter. Measures and explanations of poverty in high income and low income countries. In *COP*; 1-45.

The structural developments I have described have the effect of introducing a more hierarchical, or similarly hierarchical form of social stratification, with the consequence of increasing, or at least perpetuating, poverty. There is the rural poverty of large sections of the population who live on the margins of dietary sufficiency and some of who struggle for survival. The arrival of nationhood, the extension of systems of communication and the growth of urban areas contributes to the deepening of their poverty. But what are conditions like? There are great difficulties in establishing the true resources and in particular the nutritive content of the diet of many peoples in the agricultural regions. The Food and Agriculture Organization has made recommendations that the average daily calorie intake for a man should be around 3,000. Most experts consider that fewer than 2,500 represents under-nourishment, under 2,000 acute shortage and around 1,500 famine. But while the food supply in Bolivia, Chile, Peru and Ecuador does not reach 2,000 calories a day, Josue de Castro, for example, argues that this is in fact supplemented to a greater extent than is usually assumed by home production and 'natural' foodstuffs which are peculiar to particular areas. In the period immediately before the harvest, when stocks of food are low, the intake drops in some areas of Africa below 1,000 calories a day. Where the diet appears to be on the borderline of sufficiency, as among the

Senoufo, special account may have to be taken of the quite frequent festival days. The average daily ration here was found to rise as a result from 2,586 calories a head to 2,750. In one fertile district on the lower Senegal river a careful year's investigation by one team from the Organization for Research into Food and Nutrition in Africa showed an average daily intake per person of 2,175 calories. These are the kind of problems that arise in attempting any exact measurement of malnutrition in these areas. Moreover, care has to be taken not to assume that the prevalence of deficiency diseases such as kwashiorkor, beriberi, scurvy, pellagra, glaucoma and anaemia are due solely to a shortage of food. While is primarily protein deficiency, may become common because it is scarcity of meat as such. Beriberi would not be so prevalent if highly miled rice was not so popular. And the slender margins of nutritional sufficiency of some people in these areas can be lost in a drought, by the repressive act of an overlord, by the introduction of less nutritious commercial foodstuffs and by the influx of refugees.

The poverty of the people in these agricultural regions is a resigned or compliant poverty, or at least, so it has seemed in the past. With limited social horizons and reference points, it is not surprising that they find it difficult even to conceive of vastly improved standards of living. But the establishment of nation, states and the ideology of nationalism are changing all this, and introducing a second form of poverty. There is the miserable poverty of those in the cities and towns whose share of national resources, whose conditions of life and whose opportunities are for below either average real, or average computed, resources. In addition to the shortage of simple foodstuffs the insanitary squalor of shanty town conditions is imposed upon them. Knowledge of the gross disparities between elites, regular wage-earners and agricultural workers in standards of living and career opportunities is gradually percolating through to the rural areas. Men and families are attracted temporarily or permanently to the towns. The new wage-earners are jealous of their pay and their security. The movement into the urban centres is bigger than growth to capacity to provide employment and population increase makes the problem worse. As a consequence there are large groups of destitute families and individuals living in shanty towns, many of whom hope they are on their way up the income and social scales, others of whom, after continued disappointments, still find compensations in urban life. When the Moroccan Trade Union was formed in 1955 more than half its 600,000 members were unable to pay their dues because they were either under-employed or unemployed altogether. There is the extreme situation described by Ahmed Mezerna.... the bands of men, women and children and aged, almost totally naked, whom misery and death have pushed towards the cities and who, each morning, search the garnage pails, disputing with dogs and cats for remnants of food, the rags and the empty tin cans.

In Lima, Peru, hordes of poor wait for the city scavengers to unload the next lorry-loads of refuse. This kind of poverty is a direct and inevitable consequence of the overall social structure—a creation of relative wage-earning prosperity, which is concentrated in the cities, of subsistence farming in the rural regions, of 'pedestal' elites and of nationalist ideology.

The thesis of this chapter has been that systems of international social stratification and social stratification interact to produce poverty. We started with a puzzle: does it make sense to say there are considerable numbers of people in poverty in the United States when they can buy far more than the masses of the population in, say, Asia, Africa or Latin America? I have tried to show that it is in attempting to give a systematic and comprehensive answer to this 1950 and mid-1960s. Unemployment grew and more persons of working age were excluded from the wage-system. The pay structure seems to have become slightly more unequal Employment benefits in kind and occupational pension and sick pay schemes expanded rapidly, but did not include millions of manual workers within their scope. Interest and dividend income grew rapidly in the late 1950s, but again, for only a restricted section of the population. Some parts of social security income, especially family allowances, did not keep pace with wage and salary increases during that period. Finally there was a disproportionate increase in dependency. Thus there was a shift in structure of the adult population towards the older age-groups; a revival of the birth-rate together with an increase in the number of families with four or more children, and small increases in the numbers of chronic sick, disabled and handicapped among the middle and older age-groups. All these groups tended to have relatively low incomes. There are, of course, many other factors in the explanation—including external ones, for the internationalization of industry, politics and the professions is doing much to widen the distribution of rewards within any particular society and national sentiment about 'great' powers, sporting prowess and the brain drain helps to maintain pay differentials by increasing the incomes of elites at the expense of the poor.

This approach to theory does, of course, have direct implications for action. Theories which place responsibility for poverty with the individual or with 'the culture of poverty' are rejected. The concept of the culture and poverty concentrates attention upon the familial and local setting of behaviour and largely ignores the external and unseen social forces which condition the distribution of different types of resources to the community, family and individual. The elimination of poverty requires not the reform, education or rehabilitation of the individual or even, bearing in mind a major strategy of the American war on poverty, the creation of more opportunities of upward mobility for the individual. It requires reconstruction of the national and regional systems by which resources are distributed, or, alternatively the introduction of additional systems which are universalistic and egalitarian. Systems which are confined either to the rich (like the ownership of land or of stocks and shares) or to the poor (like public assistance and free school meals) tend towards privilege on the one hand, and disprivilege on the other. They separate society into more rigidly defined strata.

Given this analysis of poverty there can be no single remedy. Poverty can be reduced by introducing and strengthening systems of social security (particularly family allowances, allowances for fatherless families and pensions for the old and disabled); by extending (through legislation) employer benefits in kind to all employees; by developing free community welfare services for all; but also by restricting the privileges of the prosperous sections of society—partly by restricting excessively high salaries amomg elites and by maintaining a strong system of progressive taxation, but also difusing wealth by the elimination of substantial private ownership. These policies have positive value in breaking down rigid attitudes about human superiority and inferiority, which is required if the dominant wage-system is to become more egalitarian. The restraints placed on elites by, for example, the Tanzanian Arusha Declaration, suggest one strategy. Poverty is not just lack of resources required to live a normal life. It is lack of resources in fact used, and felt to be rightly used, by the rich.

148. Townsend, Peter. Measures of income and expenditure as criteria of poverty. In *COP* ; 100-12.

The poor tend to be under-represented in income and expenditure surveys. They have difficulties in keeping records Their educational level may be low, their homes and their days may be crowded with children, or they may be old or sick.

There is the further problem of deciding whether 'current' or 'normal' income or expenditure is the best criterion of their living standards. A man who is unemployed may have a low income but his expenditure may still nearly reflect the wage he was receiving, say, five weeks previously. His weekly wage may have been spread out over the first two or three weeks of unemployment. He may have received an income tax rebate and payments from a trade union, and he may have relied on various forms of temporary 'credit' or loans. Yet he is also using up the financial and psychological 'reserves' which most other people in society retain, and in certain important senses is much worse off. It is now customary in the Ministry of Labour surveys not to treat income in unemployment or sickness as 'normal' unless it has been received for at least 13 weeks. In a survey of poverty it is necessary to distinguish between temporary and long-term poverty, but it seems important not to assume that high income can be averaged with low income over certain periods for purposes of calculation unless families not only have the powers (whether formal or informal) to redistribute fluctuating income in this way but also reasonable fore-knowledge that income is in fact going to fluctuate.

This paper is destructive rather than constructive. It produces evidence to show that in household income and expenditure surveys a big discrepancy between total income and total expenditure is found for (i) all income groups except, sometimes, the highest groups, and (ii) a high proportion of individual households. The discrepancies are sufficiently serious to justify a review of the general technical direction of such surveys but also the special problems that are involved in carrying out future surveys of poverty. In particular we need to reconsider the nature and size of the financial resources that are to be measured.

Until further pilot research is undertaken the conclusions that can be reached must be highly provisional. First, it seems desirable to concentrate on improving income information rather than expenditure information. There is reluctance among some sections of the public to provide this information, but for most households it is a less complex matter to obtain, though new techniques must be developed if it is to be reliable. If an accurate representation of levels of living is to be reached, expenditure information cannot be confined to limited periods of the recent past. For some items the time period must be fairly extensive. This means that accuracy is almost as difficult, if not as difficult, to ensure for expenditure as for income.

Second, the wisest possible definition of income must be used. 'No concept of income can be really equitable that stops short of the comprehensive definition which embraces all receipts which increase an individual's command over the use of society's scarce resources—in other words, his 'net accretion of economic power between two points of time". For low-income households special efforts will have to be made to trade fluctuations in income during the previous year (carefully noting the changes in sources and size of income during sickness, unemployment and so on).

Third, supporting measures of other resources such as assets, private gifts and income in kind from the social services, will need to be worked out.

At this stage research on small groups of households is likely to be of greater value than large-scale surveys. In particular, studies with follow-up interviews which seek to 'explain' discrepancies between expenditure and income.

149. Townsend, Peter. Poverty as relative deprivation. In *Poverty, inequality and class structure*. Ed. by D. Wedderburn. Cambridge University Press, 1974.

150. Vanaik, Achin. Poverty leads to disasters. *Times of India* (New Delhi) 13 Sep. 1984 ; 8.

151. Watts, M. On the poverty of theory. In *Interpretations of Calamity*. Ed. by K. Hewitt. London, 1983 ; 231-62.

152. Wedge, P. and H. Prosser. *Born to fail*. London, Arrow Books, 1973.

153. World Bank. *Assault on world poverty*. Baltimore, Johns Hopkins Press, 1975.

154. Young, M. *ed. Poverty report*, 1975. London, Temple Smith, 1975.

Agriculture

155. Agricultural development in the People's Democratic Republic of Yemen. *Contemporary* (New Delhi), Jul. 1978 ; 43-44 ; 49.

The national economy of the People's Democratic Republic of Yemen (PDRY) depends substantially on agriculture. As much as two thirds of the population earn their livings from agricultural production and related activities.

Before independence land ownership system was semi-feudal. Only a small proportion of the potentially cultivable area was brought under cultivation. Most cultivated land belonged to a few sultans, emirs, shaikhs and other large landowners. The overwhelming mass of the common people were poor peasants and agricultural labourers who were always at the mercy of the big land-owners, money-lenders and speculators. In these circumstances, the Politburo of the National Front of Democratic Yemen considered it of prime importance to bring in legislation on agrarian reform. The first Agrarian Reform Law was announced on the 22nd June, 1969 as a fundamental step towards removing the obstacles on the path of progress in agriculture. A second Agrarian Reform Law was promulgated on the 5th November, 1971, with a view to finding effective solutions to the whole question of landownership. The following are the main features of the law :—

1. Confiscation of land belonging to the *sultans, shaikhs* and officials of the ancient regime and various other properties.
2. Maximum land holdings to be limited to 20 feddans per individual and 40 feddans per family.
3. Establishment of a public corporation (The Directorate of Agricultural Cooperation and Land Reform).
4. The foundation of agricultural cooperatives on the confiscated land-membership to be obligatory for all those who have obtained such land through land reform.
5. An obligation on the part of the state to create collective farms and demonstration farms to stimulate collective activity amongst the peasantry.
6. Abolition of all exploitative mortgages on land taken out more than five years ago.

This law enabled the revolutionary occupation to confiscate 1,24,139 feddans of land and distribute them among 25,778 poor peasants.

The political committee of the Ministry of Agriculture and Agrarian Reform was set up on the 25th March, 1971, which took up immediate transformation of the patterns of land-ownership by concentrating on two main principles.

The first principle was that cooperatives were to be based on common ownership of means of production, the pursuit of agricultural productivity, the provisions of goods and services at the lowest cost, better human relations, and the inculcation of cooperatives, members with a spirit of initiative. Cooperative activity has different areas of production and consumption such as :—

1. Cooperatives producing agricultural services, which supply services such as fertilisers, fuel, spare parts and seasonal loans.
2. Irrigation Cooperatives undertaking irrigation services through digging wells, installing pumps, constructing canals and building dams.
3. Fishery Cooperatives dealing with all aspects of fishing industry, etc. etc.

Cooperative activity of the countryside of Democratic Yemen is of two kinds. In the first, irrigation is undertaken in common and marketing takes place without any merging of land holdings. The second is based on the merging of land holdings, on common ownership of the instruments of production and on cooperative work.

156. Agricultural records vaunted. *International Herald Tribune* Jun. 1978.

"Last year our farmers broke all the records," announced the huge, double-page advertisements that appeared recently in the Venezuelan press. "In more than 20 products, the 1977 harvests were the highest volume in our entire history. The new agricultural Venezuela is moving ahead."

These costly advertisements, paid for by the government and displayed prominently all over the country, also carried a photograph of President Carlos Andres Perez and a list of the impressive 1977 crop results in grains, vegetables, fruits, poultry and pork.

Despite nagging problems in boosting output of beef and other products, last year's excellent crop results are of particular significance to the government. The Perez administration has placed heavy emphasis on agriculture ever since taking office in March 1974, and has pledged to reform the country's agricultural system. Since that year, the government has spent an unparalleled sum of money. 19.7 billion bolivars ($54.6 billion), on agriculture in an attempt to make the country self-sufficient in several widely used foods, as well as to breathe new life into neglected rural areas and convince businessmen to invest in agricultural projects. This figure does not include other expenditures made for public works, subsidies, tax relief and other incentives offered by the Perez administration.

The numerous official initiatives in agriculture include extending billions of bolivars in low-interest credits for large and small farms and ranches, and to other agribusiness enterprises; wiping out over 1.6 billion bolivars in agricultural debt ; setting minimum, guaranteed prices for producers, and building a wide range of public works directed at aiding farmers, such as rural roads and highways, silos, irrigation systems and flood control projects.

The government has also declared earnings on agriculture and agri-business activities tax free; offered incentives on imported agricultural hardware ; and sold seeds, fertilizers and breeding cattle at subsidized prices often on credit.

157. Agriculture. *International Herald Tribune* Oct. 1978.

158. Agriculture : Development efforts paying off. *International Herald Tribune* 10 Mar. 1983; 12, 14.

159. Agriculture and the Village. *Economic Times* 23 Aug. 1980 ; 8.

160. Alauddin, M. and Mustafa K. Mujeri. Growth and Change in the crop sector of Bangladesh : A disaggregated analysis. *Journal of Contemporary Asia* 16 (1) 1986; 55-74.

161. Alavi, H. Peasant classes and primordial loyalties. *Journal of Peasants Studies* 1 (1) 1973; 23-62.

162. Bhaduri, Amit. Study in agricultural backwardness under semi-feudalism. *Economic Journal* 83 (329) 1973.

163. Bhambhri, C.P. Peasant mobilization in China and India. In *TWP* Vol. 2; 204-17.

164. Bonilla, F. Rio's Favelas. In *Peasants and cities.* Ed. by W. Mangin. Houghton, Miffin, 1970.

165. Brazil's agrarian problem. *Patriot* 21 Jul. 1986 ; 7.

The pattern seen in Peru is repeated almost every where. Brazil is more stable than Peru or Colombia but at the same time it faces even more complex and daunting problems. In 1964, it was the increasing social tensions in the rural areas, with Jutliao and his peasant leagues, an active and radialised elergy mobilising the peasantry in support of agrarian reforms and the Latifundistas recruiting gun elingers to resist the reforms that provided the background to the military coup.

The agrarian reforms remain on the statute book but the military rule has weakened the peasant organisations and the landowners are not, hesitating to murder persists who have become the principal spokesmen of the peasants. Most congressmen, state governors and military officers come from the class of landowners and are related to them and, thus, are not sympathetic to peasant aspirations.

They are not in favour of reforms and are willing to turn a blind eye to the activities of security companies which resort to strong-arm methods to defend the property rights of the landlords. The Government of President Sarney was sufficiently alarmed by the increased violence in the rural areas to send federal and local policemen to get hold of unclinched arms in an 'operation clean up'.

It is not that there is an immediate threat to the Government, the possibility of the Government collapsing because of the inability to handle the agrarian crisis appears, at the moment, to be rather limited. What is significant about the crisis is that it enables one to have a better understanding of why the continuous military interventions have been successful. It is only because the rich and affluent have looked upon the military to protect their interests against the just demands of the oppressed.

Even when the proposed reforms are timid the opponents are able to win considerable support by claiming that they are communist inspired. It is not surprising that Minister for Land Reform Nelson Ribeiro resigned in May and, to replace him. Sarney brought in Dante de Olievera, a former guerilla with solid left-wing credentials.

The appointment is hardly likely to please anyone, indeed, it is likely to be seen by the right and its allies in the military as a provocation. It is more likely than not to aggravate violence in the countryside. In Latin America, only the moderates can carry out reforms and they have not the slightest interest in any reforms which will lead to a shift in favour of the dispossessed classes. Those who favour basic social reforms can be accused of supporting communism and even the church is not immune from the accusation. In May, the Minister of Justice was accusing priests of creating difficulties for agrarian reforms and the Governor of Sarney's home state Miranha, Luis Roche was attacking subversive priests.

166. Brown, Lester R. Agricultural revolution in Asia. *Foreign Affairs* Jul. 1968.

167. Brown, Lester R. *Man, land and food : Looking ahead at world food needs*. Washington, Economic Research Service, U.S. Deptt. of Agriculture, Nov. 1963.

168. Cernea, Michael. Modernization and development potential of traditional gross-roots peasant organizations. In *TWP* Vol. 2; 242-58.

169. Chayanov, A. *Theory of peasant economy*. Illinois, 1968.

170. Coulborn, R. ed. *Feudalism in history*. Princeton, 1956.

171. Critchley, J. *Feudalism*. Winchester, George Allen & Unwin, 1978.

172. Dalton, George. Modern transformation of European peasantries. *TWP* Vol. 2; 25-50.

173. Desai, A. R. ed. *Peasant struggles in India.* Bombay, Oxford Univ. Press, 1979.

174. Dhanagare, D. N. *Peasant movement in India, 1920-59.* New Delhi, Oxford Univ. Press, 1983.

175. Feder, Ernest. New World Bank programme for the self-liquidation of the Third World peasantry. *Journal of Peasant Studies.* 2, 1975 ; 343-45.

176. Gaud, William S. Green revolution. *International Development Review* Jun. 1968.

177. Guggenheim, Scott. Poverty, peasants, patrons and proletarization in Piat, Philippines. In *TWP* ; 90-109.

178. Gupta, Amit Kumar. *Agrarian structure and peasant revolt in India.* New Delhi, Deep & Deep, 1986. p. 250.

179. Hiroshima, S. *Structure of disparity in developing agriculture.* Tokyo, Institute of Developing Economies, 1978.

180. Hobsbawm, E. J. *et. al.* eds. *Peasants in history : Essays in honour of Daniel Thorner,* New Delhi, Oxford Univ. Press, 1980.

181. Huizer, Gerrit. Peasant movements reacting to pauperization : the dialectics of liberation. In *TWP* ; 13-59.

182. Hunter, G. *et al. eds. Policy and practice in rural development.* London, Croom Helm, 1976.

183. Islam, Nuru. ed. *Agricultural policy in developing countries.* New York, Macmillan, 1974.

184. Jones, E. L. and S. J. Woolf eds. *Agrarian change and economic development.* New York, Methuen, 1969.

185. Joshi, P. C. Perspectives of agrarian reconstruction : India in the Asian context. In *TWP* ; 60-89.

186. Krishnaji, N. *Notes on agrarian structure and family formation.* Trivandrum, Centre for Development Studies, 1979.

187. Lela, Uma J. and J. W. Mellor. Jobs, poverty and the "Green Revolution". International Affairs (London) Jan. 1972 ; 20-32.

188. Lewis, W. Arthur. *Tropical development 1880-1913.* Evanston, Northwestern Univ. Press, 1970.

189. Lopreato, J. *Peasants no more.* Chandler, San Francisco, 1967.

190. *Low incomes in agriculture*. Paris, OECD, 1964.

191. Mintz, S. Note on the definition of peasantries. *Journal of Peasant Studies* 1(1) 1974 ; 91-107.

192. Mortimer, Rex. *Stubborn survivors, dissenting essays on peasants and Third World development*. Monash University, 1984. p. 180.

193. Nyong, P. A. Who the friends of the peasants are and how they pose the question of the peasantry. *Review of African Political Economy* 22, 1981 ; 17-26.

194. Paige, J. *Agrarian revolution*. New York, Free Press, 1975.

195. Pausewang, Siegfried. New international economic order for the peasant in the third World. *TWP* Vol. 2 ; 8-24.

196. Perry, Hayden. Farmers reap a bitter harvest. *International Viewpoint* 25 Mar. 1985 ; 21-22.

197. Popkins, S. *Rational peasant*. Berkeley, 1979.

198. Prasad, Pradhan H. Poverty and agricultural development. *Economic and Political Weekly* (Bombay) 20(50) 14 Dec. 1985 ; 2221-25.

199. Rao, V. K. R. V. *Growth with justice in Asian agriculture*. Geneva, 1974.

200. Scott, James. *Moral economy of the peasant*. New Haven, 1976.

201. Sen, Sunil. *Agrarian struggle in Bengal*, 1946-47. New Delhi, PPH, 1972.

202. Seth, A. N. Agrarian reform and integrated rural development for small farmers. In *EAPS* ; 91-105.

The concept of a small farmer in terms of extent of land may perhaps be more readily understood among the farmers themselves and administratively it may be more convenient also than the concepts of income or employment. The level could be expressed in terms of the average availability of land (i.e. the average size of holding in the area), allowance being made for the class of land (irrigated or unirrigated, upland or lowland etc.), and its productivity. One possible approach would thus be to define 'small farmer' as one who works in agriculture by his own or his family labour ; if he cultivates land on his own, whether as owner, tenant or share-cropper, the extent of land operated is less than the average size of holding of a comparative class, quality or tenure of land in the area ; but in either case he does not hire other workers except during peak season. We have dwelt at length on the definition of a small farmer with a view to evolving some rough and ready yardstick for determining the magnitude of the problem. Refinements could of course be made for any country or area in the light of the objectives in view and the nature of data available.

In any democratic welfare State, which has adopted planned development as its policy instrument, a major objective of socio-economic development would be to extend its benefits to the weaker sections of the community through their participation in the development processes, and thus to reduce glaring disparities within the community. And the small farmers comprise most of the "poor" of Asia. To study the magnitude of the problem of small farmers is therefore essential to any democratic planning.

To illustrate, let us take the example of India for which reasonably reliable data are readily available to us. In their study on *Poverty in India*, Dandekar and Rath had estimated-based on data collected in the National Sample Survey (seventeenth round), 1961-62 that nearly 36 per cent of the rural households either did not cultivate any land or cultivated less than 0.5 acres (0.2 ha) each : about 58 per cent, less than 2.5 acres (1 ha) each ; and over 80 per cent, less than 5 acres (2 ha) each They concluded that "inspite of these rather old and fragmentary data, it is clear that the rural poor consist predominantly of agricultural labour households and small landholders with cultivated holdings of less than 5 acres (2 ha) each, and particularly those with less than 2.5 acres (1 ha). The two groups would also include village artisans progressively thrown out of the traditional employment. The urban poor, they observe, are only an overflow of the rural poor into the urban areas. Fundamentally they belong to the same class as the rural poor.

The rural poverty at the lowest level is largely accounted for by the agricultural labour households. About their working conditions Dandekar and Rath observe that about 60 per cent of the labour households had no land and hence they depended almost entirely on the personal labour of their members. The remaining 40 per cent cultivated small pieces of land ; nevertheless their main dependence was on wage-employment in agriculture or outside agriculture. Nearly three-fourths of the labour-households worked as casual labourers, that is, they worked if and when work was available. Otherwise they were unemployed. The remaining one-fourth were attached labourers, that is, they worked for a single employer under some kind of a contract extending to at least a period of one year. The nature of this contract varied from a proper agreement of an annual farm servant to the feudal tie of a bonded labourer.

About the magnitude of the problem of tenancy or of share-croppers, the situation varies a great deal in different parts of the country. Generally it is still wide-spread in high density areas of West Bengal and Bihar in North-eastern India, and in Andhra Pradesh and Tamil Nadu in Southern India ; though it has been eased considerably in Uttar Pradesh (North India), Maharashtra and Gujarat (Western India) and Kerala (Southern India) through successive measures of reforms. However, we could not get hold of any recent data in the regard.

203. Slicher, Van Bath, B.H. *Agrarian history of Western Europe. A.D. 500-1850.* London, Edward Arnold, 1963.

204. Smith, Thomas C. *Agrarian origins of modern Japan.* Staford, 1959.

205. *State of food and agriculture, 1966.* Rome, FAO, 1966. (DOC. CL/47/2).

206. Stigler, G. Cost of subsistence. *Journal of Farm Economics* 27, 1945.

207. Sundarayya, P. *Telengana people's struggle and its lessons.* Calcutta, Desray Chadha, 1972.

208. Thorner, David. Peasantry, In *International Encyclopaeaia of Social Sciences, vol. 11*, 1968. New York, Macmillan, 1968 ; 503-10.

209. Triu, N. Ngoc. Problems, achievements and prospects of Vietnamese' agriculture. *Vietnam Courier* (2) 1986 ; 9-13.

210. Venezuela embarks on agricultural development. *Baghdad Observer*, 7 Jul. 1978 ; 4.

Farmers are not benefiting from Venezuela's massive oil revenue. Agriculture and cattle breeding were economic mainstays before the discovery and exploitation of oil. But by 1974, when oil income increased fourfold and domestic consumed demand started soaring, 80 per cent of the food consumed in this country of 13 million people was imported, mainly from the United States.

By 1976, ports were congested with ships waiting to unload food and industrial products and the government of President Carlos Andres Perez authorised an airlift to speed up imports of essential food items.

Past governments relied on oil to keep domestic consumer prices frozen, doing virtually nothing to develop other sectors of the national economy.

Now the government is using oil revenue to undertake vast economic diversification programmes. One of them is for agriculture and the effects started to show last year.

Millions of dollars have been spent on rural infrastructure projects such as secondary roads, and the government has raised gradually its financing to one billion dollars budgeted for this year.

Private banks have been required to set aside 20 per cent of their lending resources for agricultural loans, and by the end of last year these had reached two billion dollars.

In the past, loans to farmers were regarded as being too risky.

As a result of the programme, the food shortage which developed in 1976 and the first half of 1977 was overcome.

Agricultural output grew 11 per cent last year and the overall sown area increased 14 per cent. By last September, some emergency imports such as cattle-on-the-hoof were suspended, and food imports this year were expected to slow down.

211. Wadekin, K.E. Income distribution in Soviet agriculture. *Soviet Studies*, 1975.

212. Warner, C.K. ed. *Agrarian conditions in modern European history*. New York, Macmillan, 1966.

213. Wolf, Eric. *Peasants*. New Jersey, Prentice-Hall, 1966.

214. Wolf, Eric. *Peasant wars of the twentieth century*. New York, Harper and Row, 1969.

Backward Classes

215. Bose, Nirmal Kumar. Who are the backward classes. *Man in India* 34, 1954; 89-98. See also *Culture and Society in India*. Bombay, Asia, 1967.

216. Rodman, H. Lower class value stretch. *Social Forces* 420, Dec. 1963; 205-15.

Black Money

217. Agarwal, S.K. Black money in politics. *Newstime* (Hyderabad) 14 Sep. 1984 ; 9.

218. Gupta, Sanjeev. How big is India's black economy. *Indian Express* 18 Nov. 1981; 6.

219. Mallick, Asmi Raza. Black economy: Myths and realities. *Patriot* 18 Jul. 1986; 4.

The dimensions of 'black economy' in India has been increasing at an alarming rate over the years, and, at the same time, various models of estimation of 'black wealth' are being devised. But for a common man what is more important is the policy framework which can contain the havoc created by the parallel economy in his economic status and purchasing power.

'Black' money is simply unaccounted money, tax-evaded concealed income and undisclosed wealth.

This money is illegally accumulated and is usually spent on conspicious consumption and incorrupt practices to further generate income and wealth. Many and ingenious are the ways and means employed by industrialists, export houses, the film industry, businessman and above all the corporate sectors to hoodwink the taxman in the ongoing game of hide and seek.

The Wanchoo Committee appointed by the Union Government in 1970 to investigate the problem, was of the view that tax evasion and black money have reached such a stage in our country which can only be a menace to our economy and a challenge to the fulfilment of the avowed objectives of distributive justice and setting up of an egalitarian society. The effects of 'black economy' can only be disastrous.

The 'parallel' economy in India is the reflection of the prevailing economic and social policies being pursued by the ruling classes. Their ways are in indirect conflict with our declared objective of achieving a just society. The system of 'black economy' plays a negative role with the planning mechanism, and does the greatest damage to the national fabric as a whole.

The latest report on 'black' economy has been prepared by the National Institute of Public Finance under the leadership of Prof. Raja J. Chellaiah. The authors of the report have come to the same old reasons advanced by most other previous committees. The present structure of high rates of taxation and the range and complexity of control of the economic activities in India, according to authors, are awesome and lead to the creation of tax-evaded income.

No doubt, high tax rates make tax evasion more attractive and profitable. But we cannot come to a hasty conclusion that decrease in the rate of taxation will necessarily lead to a halt in the generation of 'black' income and wealth. In India, taxation is not only concerned with instability of income and employment, but with a number of problems connected with economic growth on one hand and removal of poverty and inequality on the other. We have the additional problem of chronic unemployment and regional disparities.

220. Sandesara, J.C. Black income. *Economic Times* 18-19 Dec. 1981; 5.

221. Sarber, S.C. Black money in USA—*Mainstream* (New Delhi) 8 Dec. 1984. *Commerce* (Bombay) 10 Nov. 1984.

222. Sundaram, K. and V. Pandit. On black money. In *Readings in Indian public finance*. Ed. by. D.N. Dvivedi. Delhi, 1981; 142-56.

223. Trivedi, Y.P. No steps to curb black money. *Industrial Times* 3 Mar. 1986, 10.

Bonded Labour

224. Bonded labour (in India). *Deccan Chronicle* (Secundrabad, Andhra Pradesh) 27 Aug. 1986; 6.

Every few months the Centre (New Delhi) finds it necessary to urge the State Governments to speed up rehabilitation of released bonded labourers. And most States promptly release impressive statistics about the work done by them. But the fact is that the progress of identification, release and rehabilitation of bonded labourers is disturbingly slowpaced. Periodically those championing the cause of bonded labour agitate for effective implementation of the Bonded labour (Abolition) Act. Right now there is an agitation, at the mandal offices of Ibrahimpatnam and Yacharam in Andhra Pradesh, for the implementation of the Act. A bonded woman labourer, participating in the agitation, has said that her children have been working for a landlord for a monthly wage of Rs. 50. Her recent complaint to the officer concerned resulted, according to her, in a reply to the effect that her children were not working for the landlord any longer and that, therefore, the children could not be treated as bonded labourers. There seems to be an understanding among the landlords on how to frustrate official attempts at protecting the interests of bonded labourers. These unfortunate people are steeped in ignorance and poverty. Their employers are often cunning and brutally exploitative. They have the power to delay the implementation of the Act. This law directs the officials concerned to identify and release bonded labourers. The released workers are entitled to relief and rehabilitation. Child bonded workers are to be admitted to social welfare hostels. Many leaders of bonded labour have alleged that there is a nexus between landlords exploiting their workers and the officials concerned with the implementation of the Act. The class structure in villages being what it is, landlords are in a position to obstruct social and economic reforms.

225. Bonded labourers in M.P. *Madhya Pradesh Chronicle* (Bhopal) 6 Jun. 1986; 5.

226. Das, S.K. Bonded labour unchained. In *Changing image of India.* New Delhi, 1977; 48-51.

227. Dogra, Bharat. Hard Choice. *Hindustan Times* 31 Aug. 1986; 9.

228. Fernandes, Vivian. Bonded for life. *Hindustan Times* 31 Jul. 1986; 17-22.

229. Freed from bonds of slavery. *Times of India* 15 May 1986; 17.

230. Mahoney, Robert. Millions of Indians still live in bonded labor. *International Herald Tribune* 20 Aug. 1986; 11.

231. Of inhuman bondage. *Tribune* 27 Apr. 1986; 4.

"In giving freedom to the slave", Abraham Lincoln said, "we assure freedom to the free—honourable alike in what we give and what we preserve." Necessary words, even resonant. But neither word nor action can alter history or altogether heal its wounds. That is the moral to be drawn from what has recently been happening in India to the "liberated" bonded labourers. When Mrs. Indira Gandhi included in her 20-point programme (widely believed assomething designed to cushion the blow of the Emergency) abolition of bonded labour, it did not mean much to most people. Curiously, even today it does not, notwithstanding Mr. Rajiv Gandhi's periodical expressions of concern over the continuance of this system of slavery. That may well be because bonded labourers have no voice. If they had, certain recent incidents would not have taken place. For instance, a woman released from the stone queries of Rajasthan has "died of starvation and disease" shortly thereafter in Guna district of Madhya Pradesh, according to the *Bandhua Mukti Morcha*. "She died of hunger because we had had nothing to eat for several days after we were brought from Rajasthan," according to her husband, Kishan Lal, one of the 633 bonded labourers released from the stone queries of Kota last November. Kishan Lal approached several district officials, including the Sub-Divisional Officer of Mungaoli, repeatedly seeking food and medical aid for his ailing wife, "but they did not help us and my wife died of hunger," he told reporters at Bhopal.

232. Prasad, Pradhan H.S. Poverty and bondage. *Economic and Political Weekly*, Special Number 11 (31-33) Aug. 1976.

Capitalism

233. Ackerman, Frank and Andrew Zimbalist. Capitalism and inequality in the United States. In *Capitalist system.* Ed. by Reich Edwards and Weisskopf. Prentice-Hall, 1978.

234. Aglietta, M. World capitalism in the eighties. *New Left Review* 13, 1982; 25-36.

235. Bazelon, David T. Facts and fiction of U.S. capitalism. *Reporter* 21, 17 Sep. 1959 ; 43-48.

236. Desai, A.R. World hunger: How capitalism starves 100 million people *Economic and Political Weekly* 12 Apr. 1986 ; 619.

Hunger project is an international institution started in 1977. It is spread over 152 nations, with a membership of about 3 million. Its object is to spread awareness about the grave situation of starvation and hunger on a global scale, particularly in the context of mankind having developed enough productive power to produce ample food to feed the entire population of the world, if only a proper system of distribution could be worked out. Hunger Project has been carrying on a systematic campaign to draw attention to the grim dilemma which humanity is facing in the form of millions of people living in a perpetual state of starvation in the midst of ample availability of food. It has recently published a Report urging people to stri ve to end starvation and dealth arising out of non-access to food.

The Report presents some startling facts generally kept hidden by the rulers of advanced capitalist countries as well as Third World countries pursuing the capitalist path. The document highlights the following facts about the spectre of starvation and hunger that haunts humanity:

—More than one thousand million people in the world suffer from acute hunger today.

—Every year more than 15 million people die of hunger; 24 persons die of starvation and hunger every minute; every 24 hours 35,000 people die of hunger.

—Out of 24 persons who die of hunger every minute, 18 are children below the age of five years.

—More people have died of starvation during just the last two years than died in the first and second World wars together.

—More people die of starvation every two days than died in the bombing of Hiroshima.

—In 1976 a terrible earthquake in China took a toll of 2 lakh lives. More people die of starvation in the world every seven days.

Out of the 1,000 million persons living in starvation, the overwhelming majority belong to Third World countries pursuing the capitalist path of development in Latin America, Africa and Asia. Of this starving population, 50 per cent of nearly 500 million people live in the five countries of India, Bangladesh, Nigeria, Pakistan and Indonesia. It is estimated that if starvation were eliminated from India alone, the extent of starvation in the world would be reduced by one-third. It is significant that the crusader for a computers-led entry of India into a twenty-first century of prosperity, by relying on the profit-chasing classes as the agents of growth, is shrewdly silent about how these millions of the Indian people, constituting one-third of world's hungry, are to be freed from starvation.

237. Halliday, Jon. Capitalism and socialism in East Asia. *New Left Review* 124, Nov-Dec. 1980; 3-24.

238. Halliday, Jon. *Political history of capitalism.* New York, Pantheon Books, 1975.

239. Heilbroner, Robert L. *Limits of American capitalism.* New York, Harper Torchbooks, 1966. p. 144.

240. Jazani, Bizhan. *Capitalism and revolution in Iran.* London, Zed Press, 1980.

241. Lenin, V.I. *Development of capitalism in Russia,* Moscow, Foreign Languages Publishing House, 1956.

242. Marshall, Byron. *Capitalism and nationalism in pre-war Japan.* Stanford, 1967.

243. Marshall, T.H. Value problems of welfare capitalism. *Journal of Social Policy* 1 (1)Jan. 1972.

244. Miller, Raymond W. *Can capitalism complete*? New York, Ronald Press Co., 1959. p. 263.

245. Reitsma, H.J.A. Development geography, dependency relations and the capitalist scapegoat. *Professional Geographer* 34, 1982; 125-30.

246. Rodinson, Maxime. *Islam and capitalism.* Suffolk, 1974.

247. Shonfield, A. *Modern capitalism.* Oxford, 1969.

248. Westerguard, J. and H. Reisler. *Class in a capitalist society.* Heinemann, 1975.

249. Williams, Eric. *Capitalism and slavery.* New York, 1966 (1944).

Caste System

250. Charan Singh. Poverty, caste bane of poll system. *Newstime* (Hyderabad) 12 Mar. 1985; 7.

250a. Pandey, Rajendra. *Caste system in India : Myth and reality.* New Delhi, Deep & Deep, 1986. p. 250.

Child Labour & Development

251. Aries, Phillipe. *Centuries of childhood,* New York, Vintage Books, 1962.

252. Baig, Tara Ali. Dilemma of child workers. *Sunday Mail* 27 Jul. 1986; 6.

253. Blood, R. *Developmental and traditional child rearing philosophies and their family situational consequences.* Chapel Hill, 1952.

254. Boonpala, Pamudda, Child labour in Nepal. *Amrita Bazar Patrika* (Calcutta) 18 Aug. 1986; 7.

255. Child labour (India). *Economic Times* 21 Aug. 1986; 5.

The much-bruited child labour Bill is unlikely to abolish such labour if one goes by the government's approach to the problem. The annual report of the ministry of labour (1983-84) has accepted child labour as a "harsh reality", the total elimination of which would be neither feasible nor possible in the present stage of economic development. The report has underlined the need for improving their working conditions and providing facilities for education and health care. The picture of this sector is dismal. Of the 310 million children in the country (between five and fifteen) about 110 million are employed. From the army of children working inordinately long hours for a pittance in the match factories of Sivakasi to the thousands of little boys and girls working in Calcutta 16 to 18 hours a day for just two meals, child labour is the story of exploitation. It is even more gruesome in the bonded labour sector. The government sought to put some teeth into the employment of children Act by an amendment last year. But there is no change in the present nefarious practices of factory owners partly because the collusion between supervising officials and exploiting could not be broken and partly because the monitoring agency is weak. If the new Bill takes care of these two deficiencies, a beginning could be made in improving the working condition of child labour. A state enquiry committe has suggested the establishment of child labour boards for implementing both the labour and welfare provisions of the proposed new legislation which should regulate working hours and guarantee minimum wages. Child labour institutes should be opened to provide basic education and health care to child labour. Mobile schools (at construction sites) and hostels should be run by these institutes. What is equally urgent is a 10-year plan to phase out child labour. But a ban on the employment of children in hazardous occupations cannot brook any delay.

256. Child labour bill. *Deccan Chronicle* 24 Jul. 1986; 6.

257. Fernandes, Walter and Neera Burra. Child labour: A law that will not protect. *Indian Express* 18 Aug. 1986; 6.

258. Gubhaju, Bhakta. B. Health problems in Nepal: With special reference to infant and child health. *Asian Profile* 14(2) Apr. 1986; 165-74.

259. Hollnsteiner, M.R. Hope is whatever we find: The future of poor urban children in developing countries. *UNICEF News* 97 (3) 1978; 20-26.

260. Huber, J. and G. Spitze. *Sex stratification: Children, housework and jobs*. New York, Academic Press, 1983.

261. Innocent children in bondage. *Hindustan Times* 20 Jul. 1986; 9.

262. Jeliffe, D.B. Emergency feeding of young children. *Journal of Pediat* 75, 1969.

263. Lewis, H. *Child rearing among low income families*. Washington, Centre for Metropolitan Studies, 1961.

264. Lindert, Peter H. Child costs and economic development. In *Population and economic change in developing countries*. Ed. by R.A. Easterlin. Chicago, 1980.

265. Mardsen, Dennis. Fatherless families on national assistance. In *COP* ; 205-19.

266. McClements, L.D. Equivalence scales for children. *Journal of Public Economics* 8 (2) Oct. 1977.

267. Mueller, Eva. Economic value of children in peasant agriculture. In *Population and development*. Ed. R.G. Ridker, Baltimore, 1976.

268. Nag, Moni. Economic value and costs of children in relations to human fertility. In FDLDC ; 274-94.

269. Puffer, R.R. and C.V. Serrano. *Patterns of morality in Childhood.* Washington, 1973.

270. Raina, Jay. Children face brunt of poverty. *Hindustan Times* 24 Oct. 1984; 3.

271. Ray, N.K. Child labour : Not by legislation alone. *Patriot* (New Delhi) 3 Sep. 1986 ; 4.

272. Repetto, Robert. Economic value of children : Some methodological questions. In *Population and development*. Ed. by Ronald Ridker, Baltimore, 1976.

273. Richman, Harold A. and M.W. Stagner. Children in an aging society. *Daedalous*. Win 1986 ; 171-90.

274. Saha, Maitreyee. Child labour : Legislation no solution. *Mainstream* 16 Aug. 1986 ; 39.

Fifty thousand children work in the match and fireworks factory in Shivakasi in Tamil Nadu ; an equal number of them are working in the glass factories in Ferozabad ; 95,000 children are providing their labour to the carpet weaving industry in Mirzapur Badohi—Varanasi and Jaipur—the number totals to a 44 million working in no less than 18 small-scale industries and in the agricultural sector. If we were shocked to read about the condition of children working in factories in the novels of Charles Dickens, the tales of child labourers in India in the 20th century are no less horrifying.

The Government, however, with its "ultimate objective to eradicate child labour" has sought to propose a comprehensive bill legalising child labour or, as its recent position paper states : " "legally permitting child labour in many areas (other than factories mines and other hazardous occupations) where it is banned at present . . . in some processes of the carpet weaving industry, match making industry, child may be permitted". Giving reasons as to why it is necessary, it states that "under the present legal framework, no protection is available to the children who are working in the banned sectors of employment and, whose conditions are most unsatisfactory". The law, if enforced will "clearly define the areas where employment of children is to be banned and where it is to be permitted with adequate protection and welfare measures".

275. Schidlovsky, J. India may lead world in child labour. *Sun* (Baltimore) 24 Jun. 1982.

276. Schorr, A.L. *Poor kids.* New York, Basic Books, 1966.

277. Shagari, Shehu. Role of Children in Nation-building. In *Challenge of Change*. Lagos, 1980 ; 13-16.

278. Somen, Suman and G. Narayana Reddy. How programmes on child development can effectively be planned. *Kurukshetra* (New Delhi) Mar. 1986 ; 25-28.

279. Srinivasan, G. New hope in child labour welfare project. *Patriot* 26 Jul. 1986 ; 4.

280. Srinivasan, G. Useless child labour laws. *Amrita Bazar Patrika* 25 Jul. 1986 : 6.

281. Subramaniam, Chitra. Child labour rights move raises controversy *Baghdad Observer* 16 Jul. 1986 ; 6.

282. Those who live off society's waste (in India). *Statesman* (New Delhi) 29 Aug. 1986 ; 3.

283. Toer, P.A. *Child of all nations.* Penguin Books, 1984; p. 285.

284. Vlassoff, M. Labour demand and economic utility of children. A case study in rural India. *Population Studies* Nov. 1979.

285. Ware, Helen. Economic strategy and the number of children. In *Persistence of high fertility.* Ed. by Caewell.

286. Wishy, Bernard. *Child and the republic.* Univ. of Pennsylvania Press, 1968.

Civil Wars

287. Brownile, Ian. Humanitarian intervention. In *Law and Civil war in modern World.* Ed. by J.N. Moore. Baltimore, John Hopkins Press, 1874.

288. Davis, Morris. *Civil wars and the politics of international relief.* New York; Praeger, 1975.

289. Moore, John Norton ed. *Law and the civil war in the modern world.* Baltimore, John Hopkins Press, 1974.

290. Never again a civil war. *International Herald Tribune* 22 Jul. 1981 ; 4.

Colonialism

291. Horvath, R.V. Definition of colonialism. *Current Anthropology* 13(1) 1972 ; 45-57.

292. Ranger, T.O. *Colonialism in Africa, 1870-1960*. Cambridge, 1969.

293. Volsky, Dimtry. Back to colonialism. *New Times* (Moscow) (36) Sep. 1984; 18-19.

294. Wolf, R.D. *Economics of colonialism, Britain and Kenya, 1870-1930*. London, 1974.

Community Development

295. Alldred, N. Some contradictions in community development. *Community Development Journal* 11 (2) 1976 ; 134-40.

Cultural Dimension

296. Gans, Herbert J. Poverty and culture : Some basic questions about methods of studying life-style of the poor. In *COP* ; 146-64.

The methods to be used by any study are determined by the purposes of that study, and this chapter addresses itself to what I consider the basic question about method : why, for what purposes, study the life-styles or the culture of poor people ? By the purposes of a study, I mean more than its formal subject or its hypotheses, but also its intellectual aims, and especially its political aims and policy implications.

All studies have political aims and implications, whether these are consciously formulated or not, for as Louis Wirth once wrote, 'every assertion of a "fact" about the social world touches the interests of some individual or group. The study of culture as we know it derives largely from nineteenth—and twentieth-century ethnologists who wanted to describe pre-industrial cultures, sometimes to preserve them (at least in books), sometimes to show their own industrialized countries the virtues of pre-industrial ways of life. Today, anthropologists more often study reactions to modernization, although with a similar political agenda ; they now argue that the values of pre-industrial cultures ought to be taken into account in the processes of urbanization and industrialization. Many anthropologists are still seeking to preserve at least parts of these older cultures in order to build humane and vital elements into a sometimes inhumane and bureaucratic process of modernization.

The study of poverty has followed a somewhat different political path. The early studies of the ways of the poor were simple and moralistic, in the nineteenth century cataloguing their moral lapses ; in the twentieth century, their pathologies. Some of the first students of American poverty understood that immorality and pathology resulted from economic deprivation, but many explained the life-styles of the poor by what one would today call culture, particularly the non-Puritan cultures of the Eastern and Southern European immigrants. Indeed, these observe, mostly people of high status who were struggling to maintain their culture and political power in a rapidly urbanizing society, proposed that proverty could be abolished by ending the European immigration—thus excluding the masses of potential American citizens who were threatening the dominance of the Protestant middle and upper classes. By the twentieth century, American social scientists no longer held to such a simple view ; even so, the studies of the Chicago school of Sociology are, at one level, detailed statistical descriptions of lower class pathology and deviance. The causes of the pathology and deviance were ascribed largely to the peculiar social and economic environment of the city, and some of the researchers seemed to imply that the solution to these ills lay in a non-urban society. But most were debating sociological and theoretical issues, and paid little attention to the political implications.

Current sociological research among the working and lower class has developed in reaction to this tradition. Religion of researchers has exposed the myth of total social disorganization and pathology among the poor. For example, Whyte emphasized the complexity of the working class social organization ; Young and Willmott, and others, showed the persistence of kinship and traditional kinship forms ; Walter Miller stressed that what the middle class called pathology was a viable and independent culture ; Oscar Lewis demonstrated how much vitality and joy existed alongside the deprivation and pathology ; and Hylan Lewise called attention to the diversity, pragmatism and strength he found among low income people.

297. Peet, Richard. Destruction of regional cultures. In *WIC* ; 150-72.

298. Rainwater, L. *Problem of lower class culture.* Washington University, Sept. 1966 (Mimeographed).

299. Riessman, F. *Culturally deprived child.* New York, Evanston and London, 1962.

300. Rosenmayr, Leopold. Cultural poverty and working class youth. In *COP* ; 165-83.

By cultural poverty we understand the total or partial lack of productivity of and/or receptiveness to symbols, norms and values in societies and their subsets, and in small groups and interpersonal relations.

We consider the constellations and systems of symbols as the 'core of culture' and the poverty in respect to symbolic culture as the central problem of cultural poverty. By symbols we understand the wide range of formalized means of information, learning, influence, and expression in the sciences, arts, literature, fact-representation and in legal, moral and religious codes. To an important degree norms and values depend on symbols for their formulation and transmission. On the other hand, values and norms - individual and socially stabilized ones—are reflected in symbolic representation and information ; aside from this general relationship, symbolic culture, its products or the processes of its reception may be classified according to intellectual and/or scientific, aesthetic, technological, economic criteria i.e. values or value systems.

It is the underlying yet unproved and still unspecified hypothesis of this chapter that the overcoming of poverty in symbolic culture is of great importance in the processes of the amelioration of physical, economic and social poverty. This hypothesis has several implications :

(a) Learning processes (formal schooling, occupational training etc.) are part of and depend on socialization processes in symbolic culture – although, of course, formal training in school systems inversely enhances at least certain aspects of the access to symbolic culture.

(b) If symbolic culture is produced or assimilated consciously it effects the perception of physical, economic and social poverty. (The 'interaction' of poverty variables and the 'intensifier phenomenon' need further research in order to arrive at system- and cycle-models of poverty on the one hand and of amelioration on the other).

(c) Amelioration of physical, economic and social poverty is based on certain elements of symbolic culture. The latter are a necessary condition for amelioration. Socio-economic welfare, however, is not a sufficient condition for the further development of symbolic culture. (A study in the logical relations of poverty elements is needed, and formal process analyses for amelioration may be fruitful from a methodological and theoretical point of view).

Our study is meant to furnish material for implication (a) and (c), and should bridge the gap between classical poverty studies on the one hand and educational sociology on the other. It emphasizes the necessity for more rigid research on processes of social development in youth, in depressed areas, etc., on the basis of a strict control of variables and duration. On the other hand, it attempts to generalize theoretically over different types of development.

Here we describe briefly different models of socialization, related to different types of social mediation of 'symbolic culture'.

For this purpose, we defined as 'cultural activities' of our respondents their (Mainly receptive) participation in symbols. The study is based on measuring and analyzing several areas of such activities. For each of these areas—reading, movie-going, music, theatre-going, etc.—we investigated some factors with which these differences are associated. We also studied the interrelationships between the different activities. We particularly attempted to ascertain the respondents' position on the dimension of 'cultural level' in terms of their attitudinal preference for, or factual participation in, sets of symbols of different quality represented by the various works of literature, theatre, music, and art.

Our research was designed as a comparison between boys who start work at the age of 15 and those who receive a full secondary education. We therefore drew random samples among adolescent males of 800 apprentices and 897 high school students of equal age—15 and 17 years old. The samples covered the same geographical areas ; the city of Vienna and the province of Lower Austria. High school finishes with a diploma (Matura)—the entry requirement for Austrian universities—and therefore lies at the top end of the whole range of training and occupational possibilities open to male adolescents between the ages of 14 and 18 in Austria. Conversely apprenticeship lies nearly at the bottom end of that range. Apprentices constitute the largest group among boys aged 14 to 18. They work four days a week in a workshop or factory, receiving on-the-job training lasting for about three years, which is supplemented by attending a trade school ('Berufsschule') for one day per week.

As was to be expected from research in other countries, apprentices and high school students differ in their education and social origin. As a matter of fact, there were so few high school students from working-class homes—only 7 per cent—that we had to define the three social classes used for main analyses throughout this study somewhat differently from Anglo-American practice. Classifying by parental occupation gave the following result.

The geographical spread of our samples permits regional comparisons by the size of the community in which the respondents live (city of Vienna, towns with more than 20,000 inhabitants, small towns and villages), and the distribution of the cases along the rural-to-urban dimension.

Our data were collected in 1959, 1960 and 1961 by written questionaires that were filled in by the boys in their classrooms at school , under the immediate supervision of our research staff, with no teachers being present. More recent studies on female youth with similar methods confirm the results.

301. Schwartz, A.J. Further look at culture of poverty : Ten Caracas barriors. *Sociology and Social Research* Jul. 1975.

302. Valentine, C.A. *Culture and poverty.* Chicago, 1968.

Debt Problem

303. Bernstein, Blanche. *Pattern of consumer debt, 1935-36.* New York, 1940.

304. Biggest debtor. *International Herald Tribune* 1 Aug. 1986 ; 4.

305. Bolin, William H. and Jorge Del Canto, LDC debt : Beyond crisis management. *Foreign Affairs* 61 (5) Sum 1983 ; 1099-1112.

306. Castro (Fidel) speaks out Latin American debt problem. *International Viewpoint* 10 Feb. 1986 ; 17.

307. Chhabra, Hari Sharan. Africa's mounting debt burden. *Times of India* 21 Jan. 1984 ; 8.

Since the beginning of the oil crisis, a number of African countries have been sinking deeper, some more than others, under the mounting weight of their external debt. With rising prices for the oil they import and generally lower prices for the commodities they export, the non-oil countries of Africa were left with no option but to borrow from any source they could. At least 30 out of 50 countries of Africa import food. This further multiplies the economic woes of the continent.

Today on average, the debt-service ration in Africa is 10 per cent as compared to 0. 75 per cent on IDA soft loans. While there are countries where debt-service is less than this figure, there is also the Ivory Coast which has the disturbing ration of 35 per cent. Zaire at, one time a cooper-rich country, is the most notoriously indebted country. Here the debt-service ration has risen to 45 per cent—the country is literally sold out or at the least mortgaged.

Oil-rich Nigeria is cash hungry these days and since it has the potential to pay back the loans, private banks have come to its rescue. Nigeria, a class by itself in Africa, is practically the only country in Africa in which private banks have full faith. Since Nigeria needed ready cash in 1982 and 1983, it kept signing on the dotted line. The result was that the debt-service ratio which stood at 2 per cent in 1980 rose to 7 per cent in 1983.

The Nigerian federal ministry of finance has released statistics which show Nigeria's foreign debt outstanding at Naira's foreign debt outstanding Naira 10 billion, of the end of March 1983, which is roughly equal to $ 14 at billion. The March 1983 figure, which is frightening, does not include the country's backlog of trade debts. They are said by international banks to total about $5 billion. The difference probably represents trade payments for which documents are still being processed.

Nigeria may be able to fend for itself when the demand for oil rises, but the future of other African countries, including financially sound (till recently) countries like Kenya and Madagascar, seems rather bleak. Their prospects of increasing foreign exchange earnings are not bright because the prices of most commodities are not increasing. And with worldwide interest rates expected to rise, a number of African contries will have to pay out more to service their debts.

Project financing in Africa by the World Bank is receiving generous attention, but will decrease because equity from African countries is on the decrease. A World Bank official claimed recently that Kenya can get million of dollars, but since it cannot make its own countribution, many projects have ground to a halt. There are many such cases in Africa.

The African Development Bank lends money to African countries only and offers some hope that it will help many a project. The recent doubling of its capital base $ 6 billion by opening membership of the bank to non-African countries is a happy sign. India has recently become a member of the African Development Bank by making a small contribution. By doing so Indian companies can get orders through tenders for projects financed by the African Development Bank.

308. Cline, W.R. *International debt systemic risk and policy response.* Cambridge, 1984.

309. Cody, Edward. In Mexico, repayment squeeze into the hinterland. *International Herald Tribune* 5 Sep. 1986 ; 7.

310. Creeping debt crisis. *Statesman* 20 Sep. 1984; 6.

In this season for reminding the world's economic managers of the mess in which they have landed the global monetary and trading systems, the international institutions have come forward with their customary assessments of the outlook ahead. There is very little in their reports to cheer us, unless we share the view that the economic recovery in the industrial countries, especially the USA, will trickle down in time to the needy debt-ridden developing nations. For obvious reasons, it is difficult to subscribe to this optimistic view and these reasons have been highlighted in the timely analysis of the Commonwealth expert group which calls for a collective and adequate international response to the worsening debt crisis. The warning that the world's financial system is now involved in dangerously unstable arrangements is neither premature nor exaggerated. The IMF's report for the year echoes it, although in more circumspect language, while pointing out that between January 1983 and April this year there was a rescheduling of 94 billion dollars of bank debt of 17 developing member countries, which was made possible by an "unprecedented degree of cooperation among banks, debtors and national and international agencies". Indeed, they all have a vital stake in the future stability of the monetary and financial systems since most debtors would like to avoid defaults which will damage their creditworthiness while creditors realize that they have more to lose than gain by any precipitate action to force repayments.

Even conceding that this mutuality of interests will continue to be a major factor in promoting orderly arrangements in respect of existing debts, there remains the problem of the developing countries' ability to cope with the burden of even these rephased debt repayments while also exporting enough to meet their current essential import requirements for consumption and development. It is a truism that larger exports will not be possible without dismantling protectionist barriers in the major industrial markets and the two reports reiterate this point—but there are few signs of a relaxation of the known imediments to free flow of trade. The IMF finds some consolation in the apparent willingness of the industrial countries to agree to requests for special measures to open up trade on a case by case basis. Whether such guarded responses are sufficient to solve the problem is a matter on which the Fund prefers to be non-committal.

311. Debt-cum-growth. *Economic Times* 27 Jul. 1984; 6.

What of the future ? The immediate future is worrisome. The debt servicing obligations of 12 countries (including India) are estimated to spurt from $ 74 billion in 1983 to $ 107.5 billion in 1987 and to $ 122.8 billion in 1990. The rapid rise in debt service during the coming three years by close to 50 per cent stems from recent reschedulings. In the immediate future, the commercial banks will have to vary the terms of the loans and interest rates to make debt servicing manageable. The banking objective will be to increase net lendings to developing countries as a group by 6 per cent a year so that their share in the portfolio of the banks comes down to 20 per cent by 1990. But this is contingent upon a real export growth of 6.35 per cent a year over 1983. What is being visualised is an annual trade surplus of $ 5 billion during 1984 to 1987 against the deficit of $ 19 billion recorded during 1980 to 1883. This is a staggering task. The problem is not only the unpredictability of the policies of the rich countries but the structural limitations many developing countries face. Capacity constraints have developed in countries like India, Korea, Brazil and Yugoslavia in the production of tradeables. Furthermore, traditional, labour intensive and low technology, capital intensive and low technology, capital intensive products like textiles and steel are either already subject to OECD quotas or are likely to be barred by new restrictions. Restrictive features will continue during the decade even if the economic growth rate of the rich countries rises significantly given this prospects, high or rising interest rates will put even the credit worthy developing nations of today in serious difficulty. The kind of burdens that conventional wisdom enforces on the developing countries—but not on the rich countries—involve consumption restraints that are not politically feasible. The key issuing restoring confidence in the international banking and financial system then is the promotion of high growth rates in the developing countries. For this IMF prescriptions are not as only inadequate but counterproductive.

312. Day of action against the debt. *International Viewpoint* 28 Oct. 1985; 26.

313. Debt and development *Economic Times*. 26 Aug. 1986 ; 5.

314. Debt main obstacle to Africa's growth. *Economic Times* 5 Jul. 1984; 7.

315. Debtor meets debtor. *International Herald Tribune* 11 Sep. 1986; 4.

316. Delamaide, D. *Debt Shock* London, 1984.

317. Devilliers Claude way out of the debt crisis. *International viewpoint* 10 Feb. 1986; 9-16.

318. Dornbusch, Rudiger. Debt solution : link relief to long-term trade concessions. *International Herald Tribune* 29 Aug. 1986; 4.

319. Easing on debts. *Financial Express* 11 Aug. 1986; 5.

320. Fagen, Melvin M. Nine proposals for coping with third world debt. International Herald Tribune 18 Aug. 1986 ; 4.

321. Graham, Bradley. Faces of latin debt : In Buenos Aires, rapid deterioration as investment dries up. *International Herald Tribune* 5 Sep. 1986; 7.

322. Hansen, Peter M. Nine steps for debtors. *International Herald Tribune* 29 Aug. 1986 ; 4.

323. Harris, Laurence. South Africa's external debt crisis. *Mainstream* 16 Aug. 1986; 11-21. *Third World Quarterly* 8 (3) Jul. 1986.

In London on 20 February 1986, an extraordinary meeting of bankers approved, in principle, terms for rescheduling outstanding debts owed by South Africa to foreign bankers. Since the end of the 1970s the world has seen many countries enter into such negotiations on outstanding debts and agree 'rescheduling' terms with their banker, but this meeting fully deserved the special attention it received, for South Africa's debt crisis in unique.

Its outstanding special feature is the dominant role played by political developments ; the impasse of apartheid, the fragmentation of the forces that traditionally bolstered it, and the prominence of the anti-apartheid forces. Most countries' debt negotiations involve some political element and are shaped by the interplay of domestic and international political forces. In some cases these have been very promiment. The rescheduling of Argentina's debt after the Malvinas/Falklands war and of Poland's after the announcement of martial law have been the most notable precedents. The negotiations over Brazil's, Peru's, Mexico's and other countries' external debts in the first half of the 1980s have also been strongly influenced by political developments in those countries. Nevertheless, the exceptional significance held by political developments makes South Africa's debt crisis a special case.[1]

Since the problem became acute in the summer of 1985, the politics of black township revolts, black trade union unrest, African National

Congress (ANC) actions, President Botha's contradictory stance on reform and anti-apartheid sentiment in the US and Europe determined its course. In October 1985 the Sunday Times reported Businessmen and bankers inside and outside South Africa are united in believing that the crisis and its resolution are political not economic'[2] and they appeared largely correct, at least regarding its immediate causes. In 1985 the debt crisis emerged not because of an immediate shortage of export earnings with which to service the debt, as with many other economies, but because of foreign creditor's reactions to the State of Emergency declared in July 1985.

A second special feature of the crisis was the nature of the debt itself. When Third World countries have been forced to reschedule their liabilities, the debts at the core of the problem have commonly been 'sovereign debt' the direct or indirect liabilities of the state, and most have been medium-term loans that, as a result of economic circumstances, the state has found it difficult to service. By contrast, South Africa's problems centred on the renegotiation of credit to private enterprises and a high proportion of this credit was short-term credit arranged through foreign banks lending to South African banks. The significance of this type of debt over recent years had, in turn, arisen largely as a result of political pressures against more 'regular' credit facilities.

The third unusual feature of South Africa's debt crisis has been the appointment of an 'intermediary' to produce a solution (at least a temporary one) instead of the usual negotiating machinery. This, too, was prompted by the political sensitivity of the issue, although some bankers now feel that it may become a model for other countries with debt problems.

Although South Africa's debt problems are unique in these ways, there are, too, several elements that are common to many countries' experience. Although (Following austerity measures in 1984) the current account of the balance of payments has been in surplus, the economy has suffered a severe recession like that which has compounded the difficulties of other debtor nations. Although the international banks have been subject to pressure from their share-holders and depositors against supporting apartheid, they have largely been as much influenced by normal considerations of banking prudence. And although their central banks are sensitive to political and diplomatic problems, their concerns in the debt negotiations have been to prevent disruption to the international banking system.

324. Hattori, Masaya Debt problem : An institutional solution. *Economic Eye* (Tokyo) Jun. 1986; 8-12.

325. International Debt: Reading the Crunch. *Economic and Political Weekly* 15 Feb. 1986; 270.

Peru has ploughed a lonely furrow for over six months now since President Garcia announced that Peru would limit the servicing of its external debt, official plus private, to 10 per cent of its annual export earnings. His Latin American counterparts saw the logic of what Garcia was driving at but stopped short of supporting his line of action on external debt. It almost looked as if Peru had been isolated and it was generally believed in US financial circles that one day, sooner than later, Garcia would be made to eat his words.

Then, when oil prices started slipping and even before the fateful OPEC decision to confront the non-OPEC exporters of oil with a choice between either coming to a production-sharing arrangement with OPEC or facing sharp declines in oil prices; Nigeria announced that it would limit its debt servicing payments to 30 per cent of its export earnings. The ceiling put on its debt services by Nigeria was a delayed but clear vindication of the message from Peru, namely, if sovereign countries in debt have to meet their debt servicing obligations they must first be able to have adequate export earnings. The creditor countries could not on the one hand pursue increasingly protectionist policies and feel thrilled about the decline in commodity prices and at the same time expect their loans to be services as before.

But even Nigeria is a relatively small debtor by Latin American standards. Its outstanding external debt is less than a third of Mexico's Mexico's oil exports earnings 70-75 per cent of its total export earnings as against Nigeria's almost 90 per cent but almost half of Mexico's oil export earnings, even in 1984 (not too bad a year, all things considered) were needed for debt servicing as against 15-16 per cent for Nigeria.

These numbers are important to bear in mind in assessing the present situation. Nigeria has already served notice that it would allow more than 30 per cent of its export earnings to be used up in debt servicing. When and where will Mexico draw the line ?

It can certainly be argued that unlike Peru with less than $ 14 billion external debt and Nigeria with obligations about twice as large, creditor countries, certainly the US, cannot allow Mexico, the second largest third world debtor after Brazil, owing close to $ 100 billion abroad, to be so cornered as to be forced to resort to the Peru-Nigeria course of action. That will create a serious crisis for the Western banking system.

But look at what is happening right now. in December 1985 Mexico asked for $ 4 billion in new loans in 1986 in order to repay its interest dues on time. Thanks to the way oil prices are falling, with the price reaching almost $ 15-16 a barrel, and given the assumption that Mexico will still export 1.5 million barrels a day, Mexico would need an additional $ 5 billion to keep its head above water. The underlying assumption is that loan restructuring will result in postponing repayments due on principal. The creditor banks were earlier quibbling over $ 4 billion in new loans. What now when Mexico will need $ 9 billion in new loans in one year ? Meanwhile, Mexico is reaching a situation where practically all of its oil export earnings will be absorbed by just interest charges.

Isn't it time for the international community to consider seriously a collective step to link debt servicing to export earnings ? As for the implications of that step for international banking, let that also be provided for.

326. Khanna, K.C. New Debt bomb in making. *Times of India* 2 Oct. 1984; 8.

Judging by the outcome of the last weeks meetings of the world Bank and IMF in Washington, the economic future of the Third World is not grim; it is horrendous. "Neo-colonialism" was a term coined by Kwame Nkruman to vivity the crass exploitation of the less developed countries (LDCs) of Africa, Asia and Latin America but it soon fell into disfavour partly because the Soviet bloc made cynical use of it during the Cold war of the 'fifties and the early sixties' but mainly due to the fact, in that period of no-war—no-peace with the East, the West's economic relations with the LDCs were marked by a degree of enlightened self-interest, if not idealism. Ironically, the surge of western economic power since the mid-sixties has progressively dimmed that spark. Today the US seems to be going through a phase of intense paranoia. While some European nations on occasion make weak gutural sounds in protest before going along, others do so with the aplomb of proud courtiers.

327. Konstantinor, Yuri. Debt Crisis : is there a way out ? *Moscow News* (33) 17 Aug. 1986; 5.

328. Mc Queen, Charles A. *Bolinian public debt* Washington, 1924.

329. Merritt, Giles. Debt crisis: out of sight but still burning. *International Herald Tribune* 21 Jul. 1986; 4.

330. Murhij, Jassim M. Debt and world responsibility. *Baghdad observer* 5 Oct. 1984; 5.

The debt crisis has, no doubt, tremendously affected the Third World and its development. It has further aggravated an already deteriorated economic situation. What makes it more difficult is the intransigent Western and American attitudes towards this problem. Despite the fact that Third World countries are earnestly seeking a way out of this crisis, we find on the other extreme, strong opposition on the part of the creditors to any drastic solution or compromise.

Many proposals, however, have been presented to the creditors but were only met with total rejection.

According to analysts the current economic crisis may ease over the next few years but Latin American's need for external resources will not.

In fact, Latin America is facing its worst economic and financial crisis since the depression of the 1930s. Reliable figures show that the hard-pressed countries are struggling with a general reduction in economic activity, including a 3 to 4 per cent decline in production and an extraordinary increase in unemployment and the consequent waste of economic potentials.

Domestic inflation as well worsened during 1982-83, with prices in the region rising by some 85 per cent, the highest rate in the last three decades. The balance of payments deficit reached a record 39 billion dollars in 1981 and 36 billion dollars in 1982.

This state of affair has been largely attributed to foreign debt. In many Latin American countries, the growing costs of interest on amortization or foreign debt absorb a high proportion of their external payments. Capacity, virtually eliminating the possibility for development. This situation has compelled some states to adopt severe domestic adjustment measures, and special external resources have been mobilized to deal with emergency situations.

Towards the end of 1983, the total external debt of Latin American countries rose to around 336 billion dollars, compared with 75.4 billion dollars in 1975, according to Inter-American Development Bank Report.

The report also say that the accumulative amount of that debt is equivalent to 56 per cent of the gross domestic product, or 325 per cent of the region's exports of goods and services last year, compared with 26 and 166 per cent, respectively in 1975.

Some 86 per cent of Latin America's foreign debt is concentrated in the larger and most developed countries : Brazil, 27 per cent of the total;

Mexico, 26 per cent ; Argentina, 12 per cent ; Venezuela, 10 per cent ; Chile, 5 per cent ; and Colombia and Peru each with 3 per cent.

However, Latin American countries have repeatedly sought a collective approach to the problem to free the region from the heaviest economic yoke it has ever known. During a Latin American parliamentary meeting in Costa Rica recently, Latin American leaders were urged to work together soon to hammer out a joint agreement to tackle the crisis.

Argentine President Raul Alfonsin, meanwhile has warned that "failure to act on the problem of the region's debt will have serious political consequences."

But the US stand remains unchanged. US and Latin American representatives have recently ended a two day conference on the foreign debt crisis. Sharp differences remained but they agreed to continue talks in the Organisation of American States (OAS).

The annual meeting of the (OAS)--Inter-American Economic and Social Council produced what Latin American delegates considered token debt relief in the form of a US agreement to urge relaxed lending policies by US funded development agencies such as the World Bank.

But the US has rejected as "politically unrealistic" the demands raised by economy ministers for ceilings on interest rates and debt services payments by all of the region's countries.

Argentine economy Minister Bernardo Grinspun told reporters : "This conference (OAS) 23-nation conference achieved nothing to ease out debt burden, but I would say it contributed to changing the state of public opinion."

Argentina has played a key role in setting up a system of consultations among Latin American debtors in a conference three months ago at Cartagena, Colombia, Argentina has also called for parallel negotiations on debt issues with the United States in the OAS, starting with the OAS General Assembly in Brazil. The Assembly is to meet in November after the US presidential elections.

Only Colombia and Brazil, which have adopted a go-it-alone policy in talks with the banks, dissented from the idea of seeking more US concessions through the OAS.

The search for a solution, however, has never ceased. Towards the middle of September, 40 government ministers, bankers, academics and civil servants assembled in Vienna for an international forum.

They proposed eight major steps to serve as guidelines for solving the Third World's debt problems.

The gathering, organised by the United Nations Development Programme and North-South Roundtable issued the package which suggested a cut in United States interest rates and phased reduction of the American budget deficit as crucial steps to reduce debt in developing countries.

It also proposed long-term debt rescheduling, capping of interest rates, writing off debts of the poorest nations, formation of a new world debt refinancing body, new multilateral trade talks, revision of Third World development strategies and steps to boost the flow of funds into the developing countries.

These measures were meant as guidelines to break North-South deadlock over treating national debts case-by-case with strings of economic adjustment attached to loans.

Pakistani planning and development minister Mahbub UL Haq stressed that "the debt problem is not behind us. Its more serious repercussions are ahead of us. The cost of earlier solutions has been extremely high in social terms, loss of needed investments, unemployment and decline in living standards of society's poorest people."

The meeting studied debt along with its implications for trade and the development of human resources.

They are welcomed recent reports of a rescheduling arrangement between Mexico and the commercial banks, with eased financial and extended repayment periods. But they recommended "creditors should encourage further adjustments in bank lending terms".

The final statement also called for a "measure of debt forgiveness" for the poorest countries, mostly in Africa, saying that in the least developed countries "a strong case existed for cancellation of all official debts."

No doubt, the problem is not entirely of the debtor countries and both internal and external factors have contributed to its exacerbation. Therefore, there should be a spirit of international shared responsibility to tackle it, otherwise its consequences will be grave. Chief agents in the world economy must participate actively and jointly in the efforts to arrive at a solution ; the governments of the creditor and debtor countries; the international banks ; representatives of industry and trade and the multilateral financing agencies. These are all faced with the common challenge of reestablishing the conditions necessary for economic growth and expansion of world trade, and a stable equilibrium in international monetary and financial relations.

331. Murhij, Jassim M. In search of genuine solution to debt crisis. *Baghdad Observer* 3 Sept. 1984 ; 4.

Five Latin American presidents and senior officials from four other countries assembled recently in Quito for the swearing-in of Ecuadorean President Leon Febres Cordero. They seized the opportunity and met US Vice-President George Bush over a variety of subjects covering, among other things, debt, drug-smuggling and Central America's wars.

According to the Colombian President, Belisario Betancur, the Latin American leaders have sought "fresh moves to ease their crippling debts,"—the second such meeting since last June when 11 of the region's indebted nations met in Cartagena, Colombia.

The Cartagena group is due to meet again in Buenos Aires, Argentina, next month to review responses from creditors to its proposals and prepare a joint position ahead of the joint annual meetings of the International Monetary Fund (IMF) and the World Bank on September 26.

Argentine President Raul Alfonsin, however, has warned that failure to act on the problem of the region's 350-billion-dollar debt "will have serious political consequences". He also repeated his call for negotiations between debtors and creditors on the issue.

So far, the United States has rejected joint negotiations. Instead, US officials have recently been calling on Latin America to open up to foreign capital "as a means of helping solve its debt problem".

In Cartagena, however, Betancur proposed easing restrictions on foreign investment "to stimulate a greater flow of capital to the region".

332. Nakarmi, Laxmi. Prospects of growth ease debt burden. *International Herald Tribune* 25 Sep. 1986 ; 5, 7.

333. Nelson, Doniel, Debt crisis may cause a Third World change of direction. *Pioneer* 13 Mar. 1984 ; 6.

Most of the attention has been focussed on the potential threat to the banks—the damage which would be caused to the international banking system if developing countries defaulted on their loans.

This misplaced emphasis is hampering the discussion of proposals aimed at achieving a major restructuring of debt and at finding ways of enabling Third World countries to speed up their development.

As Calusen observed, the real problem is for the borrowers not the lenders : the financial system has "weathered the storm quite well" but "for heavily indebted countries, the dilemma is acute".

Now that so many countries have burned their fingers by large-scale borrowing, perhaps the concept of development through foreign funds will be replaced by greater stress on mobilisation of domestic resources. Self-reliance may yet come into fashion.

334. New Ways for old debts. *International Herald Tribune* 5 Sep. 1986 ; 6.

335. Ongpin, Jaime V and Solita Monsod. Debt : Is repudiation an answer. *Asiaweek* 20 Jul. 1986 ; 78.

336. Onis, Jnan de. Third World and its creditors deadlocked. *International Herald Tribune* 22 Sep. 1986 ; 1, 6.

337. Out of the debt trap. *International Viewpoint* 9 Dec. 1985 ; 28.

338. Pai Panandiker, D. H. Burden of debt. *Hindustan Times* 22 Jul. 1986 ; 9.

339. Panigrahi, Chintamani Facing up to foreign debt (in India). *Link* 15 Aug. 1986 ; 51-52.

340. Payer, Cheryl. *Debt trap : the IMF and the Third World.* Harmondrworth, Penguin Books, 1974.

341. Raghavan, C. Sharp increase in debt—servicing. *Patriot* 6 Apr. 1984 ; 4.

The comparable increase is much greater for the LDCs—from 8.6 per cent to 22.8 per cent—while for countries with a per capita annual income of 600 dollars or less, the increase was from 9.5 per cent to 28.4 per cent. ODA debt as a percentage of the GNP has risen rapidly for countries with a per capita annual income of 900 dollars or less. For LDCs it went up from 18 per cent of GNP to 28 per cent during that period.

Projections of debt service payments based on the World Bank's debtor-reporting system and on commitments (disbursed and undisbursed) at the end of 1981, show that for the 95 countries the annual debt service payments will average around 4.8 billion dollars for the period 1985-87.

This would be a 40 per cent increase over the average level of 3.5 billion dollars attained in the period 1979-82.

About 60 per cent of debt service payments in each of the projected years would represent the liabilities of countries with per capita income of 600 dollars or less, including major ODA recipients. The combined share of LDCs in the total debt service is expected to average 13 per cent annually.

The distribution of the projected ODA debt and debt service, the Secretariat note says, is "highly skewed" among donors from the 24 Western industrialised nations of the OECD. Japan and the United States would together account for about two-third of both the total ODA debt and debt service in 1985-87.

"These broad orders of magnitude indicate the potential scope for measures which can be applied to deal with the debt-servicing problems of the developing countries during that period," the Secretariat concludes.

342. Rajwade, A. V. Debt bomb. *Economic Times* 24 Feb. 1986 ; 8.

The Baker Plan presented by (and named after) the U. S. treasury secretary at the last annual fund bank meeting as a comprehensive proposal for a solution to the problems of 15 of the world's major debtors, does not seem to be getting off the ground. It may be recalled that the plan envisaged :

The debtors to adopt market-oriented adjustment policies to promote growth, lower inflation, and reduce external imbalance.

The multilateral agencies, particularly the World Bank, to increase their gross annual lending to the 15 countries from 56 bn. to 59 bn. for the next three years.

The commercial banks to increase their exposure by 250 bn. over the three years.

The debtors are not too enamoured of the market-oriented adjustment policies, despite the emphasis on growth. Economic growth is of-course essential if political convulsions—and an international banking crisis are to be avoided. The reason is simple. If an additional percentage of GNP is to be exported to reduce the external imbalance, there would result a fall in the living standards, and political crisis, unless the GNP growth rate is plus. Political strains could force governments to repudiate debt, leading to a major banking crisis. To avoid it, economic growth in debtor countries is a must. Indeed, this emphasis on economic growth is a welcome shift from the earlier, IMH prescribed, approach.

The World Bank initially made some welcome noises regarding the Baker Plan. But it does not seem to know what concrete steps to take next. One reason for this is perhaps the fact that the incumbent president of the bank ends his term in June and is hardly in a position to provide major leadership initiatives.

343. Ramachandran, K. S. External indebtedness in Asia and Pacific region. *Financial Express* 11 Aug. 1986 ; 5.

344. Ramachandran, K. S. International debt problem. *Financial Express* 4 Oct. 1983 ; 6.

345. Rowen, Hobart. Banks fold as the debt ratio soars. *International Herald Tribune* 12 Aug. 1986 ; 4.

346. Saini, Mahander Kumar. *Debt Crisis : The future—the situation in the Third World.* Delhi, Indian Institute of Research on Transnational Corporation, 1986 p. 112.

The economic revival in a number of industrialized countries, first and foremost the United States, which began after the severe crisis of 1980-82, noticeably slowed down in 1985. Thus, according to UNCTAD estimates, the aggregate increase of the gross domestic product in the OECD member-states did not exceed 2.5 per cent. According to GATT estimates, there was also a noticeable slowing down in the growth rate of world trade in 1985, and this will have a detrimental effect on the developing nations. On the whole, the short-lived economic revival of 1982-84 spread very unevenly and practically by-passed completely most of the developing world. This showed once again the complete groundlessness of the US claim to the tole of the moving force behind the development of the Third World. This claim was time and again voiced both by U.S. President Reagan and members of his administration.

Indeed, in the seventies and eighties, especially in 1980-83, in the conditions of a deep economic crisis in the west, there was a sharp deterioration (first and foremost, as a result of an unprecedented growth of interest rates) in the terms of servicing the foreign debt of the developing countries which had reached an astronomical figure, while the debt problem, itself had for many of these countries, especially in Latin America, turned into the core of their economic policy. There was a sharp drop in the real prices of the main export commodities of the developing countries ; serious difficulties shaped out in the sale of manufactured goods on western markets. Thus, the drop in price of the raw materials exported by the developing nations in 1982-84 had, as against 1981, a cumulative negative effect totalling 38 billion dollars, while the increase of the interest rates in 1980-82 more than doubled the foreign debt service payments.

In many developing countries the hard currency losses, resulting from the drop in raw materials prices and an increase in the interest rates, reached 10 per cent of their GDP; while in some countries, for example in Jamaica and Sri Lanka, the respective figure was some 33 per cent.

In 1984 the net influx of fresh financial resources to the developing countries had, in actual fact, stopped. It might seem paradoxical, but many countries and even entire regions (for example, Latin America) became net exporters of capital. Thus, the net outflow of resources from Latin America in 1982-84 comprised 77 billion dollars, while the aggregate outflow of resources in interest payments and profits on capital investments reached 134.7 billion dollars in 1981-84. At the same time due to the necessity of servicing a vast foreign debt many of the developing countries were forced to step up their exports and artificially reduce their imports to the utmost. As a result, in 1983 the trade surplus of the developing countries comprised 22 billion dollars, while in 1954 it soared to nearly 50 billion dollars.

Under the influence of unfavourable trends in their relations with the western states and the heavy burden of unresolved domestic problems the social and economic situation of the overwhelming majority of developing nations to remain extremely unfavourable. One billion people in these countries live in poverty, 500 million are unemployed, a considerable part of the population is deprived of normal housing conditions, access to education, medical aid, etc.

In the first half of the eighties the obstructionist policy of the western powers, first and foremost the United States practically brought to a standstill the process of international negotiations aimed at achieving a restructuring of international economic relations both within the UN frame-work, and on a wider scale within the frame-work of the North-South dialogue.

So we see that for the developing countries the mid-eighties have become a period of gloomy reflections about the prospects of their further economic development, the possibilities of improving their positions in world trade, and achieving, even to a limited extent, the aims and tasks of the restructuring of international economic relations. Therefore, as the date of the holding of the eighth non-aligned conference approaches, a critical analysis of the state of affairs and the prospects of relations with the west as a whole, as well as of separate aspects of their foreign economic ties, becomes an increasingly vital task for the non-aligned countries and other developing nations, And the elaboration on this basis of proposals to overcome the existing difficulties acquires similar importance.

347. Saini, Mahander Kumar. *Debt trap or death trap.* Delhi, Indian Institute of Research on Transnational Corporations 1986. p. 68.

According to the data published by the United Nations Economic Commission for Latin America, in 1982 and 1983 the Latin American countries transferred abroad in real terms 50 billion dollars in the form of interest payments and other sums connected with servicing their foreign debt. The main sources of those payments were export earnings and official gold and foreign currency reserves. In 1984 the countries of the region covered 38.5 billion dollars in interest payments and 12.9 billion dollars in servicing the foreign debt itself. Those payments amounted to 40 per cent of their export revenues. It should be noted that major international commercial banks sharply curtailed the granting of new credits to the developing countries. While in 1981 the net inflow of capital to the said countries amounted to 16 billion dollars, in 1982 there started a reverse process—an outflow of foreign exchange reserves to the banks of industrialized Western countries, first of all to those of the United States, amounting to 7 billion dollars. In 1983 the sum reached 21 billion dollars accompanied by a reduction in direct investments into the economy of the Third World form 14 billion dollars in 1982 to 10 billion dollars in 1983. A net outflow of capital in 1982-84 amounted to 75 billion dollars.

The above-mentioned data, though far from giving a complete picture of the problems being faced by the developing world, poses a serious question. How, under current conditions these countries can settle the problem of servicing their external indebtedness. In order to overcome the consequences of the gravest monetary and socio-economic crisis of the last 40 years it is necessary for the developing countries to undertake joint, well co-ordinated measures. For the industrialised countries it is necessary to realise that it is in their interest to remove the causes of that crisis and (this is true especially as regards the United States) to accept responsibility for the resulting situation.

Suggestions to reconstruct the current international economic order are dealing primarily with technical aspects of the matter. However, this is quite insufficient for its really good solution. Favourable general economic conditions, as well as correction of political outlook (which occasionally prevents from casting an objective look at the actual state of affairs) and right and responsible decisions, are also needed. Leaders of the industrialized countries have to display certain political courage and awareness of the fact that in case of catastrophe, of a complete breakdown of the machinery that regulates world economic processes, including functioning of the monetary and financial system, their countries will suffer greater losses, whereas the Third World will lose only its debts.

348. Sweezy, Paul M. Two faces of Third World debt. *Mainstream* 18 Feb. 1984; 27-28, 34.

The tremors that shook the financial world during 1982 and most of 1983 have for the time being subsided. But the ensuing calm is an uneasy one : clearly, the crisis has merely been postponed to another day.

The sense of panic among the financiers and governments of the leading capitalist nations is not the product of idle rumours or vague fears. It has been obvious for some time that the vast expansion of Third World debt would sooner or later create serious problems for the international bankers. But the outsize profits to be made in the Third World have been too tempting to be resisted by even the most prudent of bankers. The chickens began to come home to roost in 1982. In that year, 22 countries were forced to negotiate debt rescheduling because they could not meet their contractual payments. And it is evident that the fat was indeed in the fire when the three largest Third World debtors—Mexico, Brazil, and Argentina—let it be known that they did not have the foreign exchange to pay interest and amortization due on their loans.

A default by one or a combination of these countries, as will be shown below, could lead to the bankruptcy of some of the biggest US banks. Default was avoided because of prompt and energetic rescue measures taken by the US government, by central bankers, and by the Bank for International Settlements, the IMF, and the World Bank. One thing, however, needs to be clearly understood about these heroic efforts in the heartland of finance : it was the banks that were rescued, not Mexico, Brazil, Argentina, and the other potential defaulters. As a matter of fact, an essential feature of the whole rescue operation consisted of pushing the affected Third World countries further down the road of debt enslavement, with a consequent imposition of severe economic contraction and a decline in the already miserable living standards of the masses. Neither was the financial system of the imperialist countries strengthened: a crucial aspect of the rescue operation was a continued increase in Third World debt and with it enhanced vulnerability of the international banks. On the other hand, the bankers have done well for themselves, at least for the time being. Not only was their skin saved, but they have managed to use the crisis to squeeze even more profits out of the Third World.

349. Varma, Kewal. Walking into debt trap. *Mainstream* 22 Feb. 1986 ; 11-14.

The Government finances are in extremely bad shape. According to latest estimates, this year's budgetary deficit would be between Rs. 6,000 crore and Rs. 7,000 crore. It remains to be seen how much statistical jugglery will be employed to show a lower deficit. This is despite the fact that there has been an artificial boom in revenues as a result of the unusually large number of raids.

Polite hints have come to the Finance Ministry from the right quarters that enough in enough – the raids should start petering out now. Even otherwise it is not possible for the tax administration to keep on the raids at this level for too long. In other words, tax revenues will not look up too much next year. The only windfall V.P. Singh can expect is the Rs. 500 crore as a result of court cases.

The exercises in the Finance Ministry indicated that at the existing level of taxation and prices of public sector and departmental undertaking products and services, the budgetary deficit next year could cross the Rs. 10,000 crore mark. V.P. Singh has made it a Rajput prestige issue that he will not raise the level of income taxes. He is under pressure to reduce the general level of excise duties also. The only tax area from where he can raise revenues is customs. In view of the yawning trade gap, there is a greater case for raising customs duties. The increase is also painless as it does not attract public attention as income tax and excise duties do.

The Finance Minister knows the secret of why the huge budgetary deficit of this year has not produced run-away inflation. The inflationary impact of this large budgetary deficit was moderated by massive imports, as a result of which the foreign exchange reserves were eroded to the tune of Rs. 450 crore in the first 40 weeks of the current financial year as against an accretion of Rs. 1,200 crore last year. In other words, there has been a negative turnround of Rs. 1,650 crore in foreign exchange reserves. Consequently, the expansion of money supply was moderate. It expanded only by 13.9 per cent in the first 40 weeks of the current financial year, as against 16.2 per cent in the corresponding period of the previous year. This naturally kept the lid on deficit-induced inflationary pressures in the economy.

The Finance Minister tries to explore a soft option this year too. Recently he sent an SOS to the World Bank which can be summed up in these words: "Debt servicing crosses prudent limits. Liberalisation (effected at Bank-Fund's behest) in danger. Rush concessional aid. Most urgent." Pat came the reply from the Bank: "IDA governors express inability to increase aid. Advise foreign commercial borrowings. Don't abandon liberalisation, sending copy of our report".

350. Vasudevan, Mullath. Third World's debts. More helpful role for World Bank. *Statesman* (New Delhi) 29 Aug. 1986; 6.

351. Yanzhoung, Guan. and Tong Leli. Latin America. New efforts to solve debt crisis. *Beijing Review* 24 Sep. 1984; 15.

352. Zhongwen, You and Zhen Bingxi. Third World debt. *Beijing Review* 14 Nov. 13-16, 25.

Defence

353. Brara, J. S. Poverty Vs. armament. *Searchlight* 21 Nov. 1982 ; 4.

354. Cervantes, Nestor. Arms race, *Searchlight* (Patna) 24 Dec. 1980 ; 4

Deserts and Wasteland

355. Chitwadgi, S. S. Desertification Control. *Madhya Pradesh Chronicle* 3 Jun. 1984.

Desertification is the diminution or destruction of the biological potential of the land, and can lead ultimately to desert-like conditions. It is an aspect of the widespread deterioration of ecosystems, and has diminished or destroyed the biological potential, i.e. plant and animal production, for multiple use purposes at a time when increased productivity is needed to support growing populations in quest of development.

Let us protect our soils ! Soil is a non-renewable resource ; once it is gone, the loss is permanent. Nature takes from 100 to 400 years, or more to generate 10 millimeters of top soil and 3,000 to 12,000 years would be needed to generate soil to a depth of 30 cm.

Grave through the loss of top soil may be, it is quiet crisis, one that is not widely perceived. Unlike earthquakes Volcanic eruptions, or other natural disasters, this manmade disaster is unfolding, gradually. It is not always widely recognised because the intensification of cropping patterns and the plowing of marginal lands that leads to excessive erosion over the long run can lead to production gains in the short run can lead to production gains in the short run, thus creating the illusion of progress.

Although soil erosion is a physical process it has numerous economic consequences, affecting productivity growth income distribution food sufficiency and long terms external debt. Ultimately it affects people.

When soils are depleted and crops are poorly nourished, people are often under nourished as well.

World environment day 5 June 1984 is focused on desertification control. Desertification means people : people help cause it, suffer because of it and can help stop it.

Despite missed opportunities by the international community to contain the march of the deserts by the year 2000, UNEP's. Executive Director MOSTAFA TOLBA says, there is still hope, given political will, to do so even though the deal may have shifted further down the time scale. Desertification is not just simply a problem of planting TREES. It is social, it is economical and technical, it is about population and other aspects.

In India desertification control is attempted by the Governments. Despite are on the march despite control efforts. The environmental degradation day by day is constantly observed by those who have an eye to see it. Now desertification control measures in Indian condition include, mainly saving the soil is a crucial life support system, since the bulk of all food production depends on it. Soil erosion is a natural and continuous process, but in undisturbed ecosystems but in undisturbed ecosystems, with a protective cover of plants.

356. Ghose, Arabinda. Derchping Wasteland, a compulsion. *Yojana* (New Delhi) 1 May, 1986 ; 21-23.

357. Glantz, M. H. *Desertification.* Boulder, Westview Press, 1977.

358. Ishwar Prakash. Combating desertification. *Financial Express* (New Delhi) 3 Jun. 1984 ; 6.

The desertification processes in the India subcontinent are extremely varied. In the Thar desert, the diminution of the biological productivity of the land is more in areas receiving about 400 mm of rain in a year than in the drier areas, and it is mostly due to escalation of the human and livestock populations, whereas the processes are active in Sri Lanka even in zones of rainfall of 635 to 1,900mm. Bangladesh has posed an entirely new aspect of desertification resulting from a drop in riverine flow in the dry season in a high-rainfall area. In Nepal, the human population increase has led to felling of forests at such a rate as to cause severe problems of soil erosion.

With a variety of factors causing desertification in different rainfall zories and terrains, it is but natural that efforts to combat it should be location-specific, with the broad objective of increasing productivity and restoring the biological potential of the land. Whereas in the Thar desert, serious research and development works to combat desertification have been going on for 35 years, they are still at a take-off stage in other countries. The close association of actions for combating desertification with land-use patterns in arid lands is based on a fragile balance, which can be easily upset. It is essential, therefore, that plans of development should be based on (i) maintaining optimal, sustainable productivity, (ii) the application of ecologically and socio-culturally sound technologies that will not upset the ecological balance, and (iii) the development of innovative modalities for administration and extension services.

It is necessary in this context that the implementation of the strategies to combat desertification should involve the participation of the desert-dwellers, in particular the farmers. This is because the agricultural practices adopted in low rainfall arid areas are injurious to the land and aggravate sand movement. As a consequence, emphasis has to be laid on high-yielding forage grasses and legumes, improved grasslands and livestock production.

It is essential to assess problems and their magnitude on ecological principles, keeping in view critical indicators of desertification. Since vast geographic expanses are involved, remote-sensing techniques are needed quickly to delineate vulnerable areas, sand-pilling and salinity encroachments, and to monitor biotle disturbances. Based on interpretation of Land sat imageries (Bands 4 and 5, supplied by the Indian Space Research Organisation ISRO) and ground truth data, the central Arid Zone Research Institute (CAZRI), Jodhpur, has prepared maps of the Rajasthan deserts on 1 : 2.5 million and 1 : 2 million scales. These are supported by a new concept of composite mapping—major land resources unit (MLRU)—which has been developed at CAZRI. This unit enables composite mapping of areas having similar resource potential and management needs. In other words, besides the recurring pattern of soil, landform and vegetation, MLRUs also indicate the pattern of human activities and the resource potential of an area for development planning. The human factors are determined by socio-economic surveys. Integrated natural resource surveys in the Rajasthan desert, parts of Haryana, Gujarat and Andhra Pradesh are being extensively used by various developmental agencies for natural resources and land use management.

359. Sarkar, R.P. Climatic variations, drought and desertification *Yojana* 1 May 1986; 30-31.

WEATHER DOES NOT RECOGNIZE manmade boundaries. Weather phenomena travel from one country to another. Atmospheric changes in one part of the world influence the weather and climate in another. Further, meteorological events greatly influence the economy and development of individual nations. The importance of meteorology in daily life and long term planning is, therefore self-evident. A special theme is chosen by the World Meteorological Organisation (WMO) every year to focus attention on one particular activity. This year's theme is "Climate Variations, Drought and Desertification".

The WMO could not have chosen a more apt theme because in recent memory severe climatic events have disrupted life rather frequently in many countries. The Sahelian drought of 1968-73 in North Africa attracted considerable public attention. The drought recurred recently with increased intensity and spread to Ethiopia, Somalia and the neighbouring countries of that region. This prolonged drought has demonstrated the realities of climatic variability and its significance for the human societies, particularly those of the developing world.

Until recently, any variations in climate and their associated impacts were assumed to be natural events beyond the control of man. There is now an increasing awareness that human activities themselves can also affect the climate on a large scale. Many examples can be quoted. However, suffice it to say that human intervention has caused important changes in large areas of the Earth's surface and in the composition of the atmosphere. The effects of these changes will, in time, work their way through to the complex system that determines the global climate. It is likely that the consequences will become noticeable in the next few decades.

The study of climate, climatic variations and drought have received much attention in the 'United Nations' and in other specialized agencies. At the United Nations Conference on the Human Environment in 1972, it was emphasized that the world was facing an international problem of an unprecedented nature, the solution of which could be achieved only by the closest collaboration among nations.

360. Slow action against first desertification. *Newstime* 9 Jul. 1984 ; 12.

The Chinese drylands have a long history of land use matched by a record of desertification. It is reported that of the 170,000 square kms. severely desertified there, only 50,000 sq. kms. have been desertified in this century.

Wind is seen as the most important cause. In the arid lands of Western China, desertification is seen in the encroachment of dunes, sand drifting, deflation of topsoils on the edges of irrigations, and the salinisation and sand-burial of low river beds. Also to blame are overgrazing and fuelwood gathering, mis-management of water supplied, the consequent abandonment of once-irrigated lands and population growth.

In the rainfed croplands of Australia, accelerated wind erosion of light soils is the most wide spread problem. The soils are made vulnerable by repeated tillage and left bare in dryfarming systems. Moderate desertification in the rangelands is caused by overgrazing. Shrubs of little pastoral use have invaded some areas.

An assessment made by Executive Director Dr. Mostafa Tolba of the UN Environment Programme (UMEP) on desertification points to "continuing and locally accelerating desertification in South Asia (notably in the upland rangeland) in several irrigated areas and in Nepal". High and increasing population pressure and no alternative resources in the drylands threaten a serious desertification hazard. Desertification of irrigated lands is typified by Pakistan where shallow water tables now affect half of irrigated areas and salinisation about one-third. In Bangladesh, conflicting upstream requirements have reduced winter flows in the Ganges.

This has allowed an inland advance of saline water. Accelerated water erosion and deterioration of soil fertility are common in areas of clearing agriculture, notably in the dry zone of Sri Lanka and in the Deccan.

In Middle Asia and Khazakistan in the Soviet Union, there have been major successes in reclaiming formerly saline steppes and degraded irrigated lands. Desertification there continues to be brought under control. Some hazards remain from current construction and mining projects and recovery of rangelands will be slower although productivity has increased.

Dowry

361. Bhatnagar, Rakesh. Who will monitor the new anti-dowry act ? *Patriot* 22 Oct. 1985; 4.

The amended Dowry Prohibition Act came into force from 2 October 1985. It has given sharper teeth to the original act of 1964, but still may not be sharp enough to eliminate the malady.

Although the amendment has been made in good faith and for the betterment, of those harassed, certain lacunae prevailing in the 1964 law have been left unattended by the formulators which may, ultimately, prove that the amended Act is hardly an improvement upon original one.

The procedure laid down for computing or listing "dowry" is so cumbersome and unsuited to the Indian way of life that if followed in toto it may make solemnisation of marriages more of an account's job in which one party exchanges inventory with the other.

Under the law, any property or other valuable security given or agreed to be given in connection with a marriage to the bride or the bridegroom, or any other person, will be dowry. It will not be necessary to show that the same was given as "consideration" for the marriage. Any person directly or indirectly demanding dowry defined as property given in connection with (not consideration of) marriage, from the parents or other relatives or guardians of the bride or bridegroom will invite imprisonment for a term up to two years and a fine of upto Rs. 10,000. Similarly, any person giving or taking dowry or abetting the giving or taking of dowry will be subject to the same punishment as one demanding dowry, directly or indirectly, and a fine up to Rs. 10,000 or the value of dowry whichever is higher.

362. Dogra, Bharat. How they devalued dowries. *Hindustan Times* 20 May, 1984.

363. Dowry act not sufficient. *Nagpur Times* (Nagpur, Maharashtra) 25 Feb. 1986; 4.

364. Gurucharan. Path-breakers. *Hindustan Times* 20 May; 1984.

365. Harihar Rao, V. Multipronged attack on dowry. *Newstime* 10 Nov. 1985; 7.

The dominant intention of the Dowry Prohibition Act is to do away with the pernicious practice of dowry which has spread its tentacles deep into the vitals of society. There are several systems of personal law in the country like Hindu, Muslim, Christian and Parsi, including the matriarchal system in Kerala. It is indeed a pity that the dowry system has spread like an infection to other religions and is also taking roots among Muslims and Christians. Among Muslims besides the Mehr and other formalities incorporated in their Nikahnamas, the dowry is being shown as a composite part of dahez articles. Ingenious no doubt, but it indicates the vulnerability of the people to fall a prey to the obnoxious institution of the dowry.

The word 'dowry' has been defined under Section 2. The basic ingredient to constitute dowry is that the property or 'valuable security' should have been given by one party to the other, in a marriage, or by the parents of either party to a marriage or to any person as consideration for the marriage of the spouses at or before or after the marriage. It can therefore be seen that when property or valuable security is given as consideration for the marriage, then only it falls within the purview of the definition of dowry.

It is significant to observe that the word 'Stridhana' is not used in the Act. Prior to codification of Hindu Law the woman was entitled to hold the property with restricted rights. Her rights were enlarged after enacting the Hindu Succession Act of 1956. The Supreme Court has recently held in Pratibha Rani's case that 'Stridhana' is an absolute property of the woman, and her husband or in-laws in whose custody it is kept would be deemed to be the trustees and are bound to return the same if and when demanded by her. Consequently when the property is not returned by her husband or in-laws they would be held guilty of breach of trust under Section 406 of Indian Penal Code.

Mr. Justice Varada Rajan, who, gave the dissenting judgment in Pratibha Rani's case (AIR 1985 SC Page 628), was of the view that in the absence of any specific agreement for entrustment of the property by the wife to her husband or in-laws, the appropriate remedy would be to file a civil suit, which affords the scope for the parties to the marriage to come together. Without such an agreement a complaint invoking Section 406 of Indian Penal Code would have a disastrous effect and consequences on the peace and harmony which ought to prevail in matrimonial homes.

366. Sharma Mithlesh. Brides are not for burning. *Nagpur Times* 2 Mar. 1986 ; 6-7, 27.

According to the Hindu scriptures, dowry or 'dahej' is a necessary adjunct to the marriage sacrament as 'var-dakshina' (gift to the bridegroom) for the act of 'Kanyadaan' (giving away of daughter in marriage). This 'var-dakshina' which was a token amount willingly given earlier has now become painful extortion, blatant blackmail and worse. Besides hefty cash, dowry assumes diverse forms like T. V. or video set, expensive jewellery, household utensils etc. Even an ordinary 'dulha' can expect a bicycle, a transistor-radio, or a wrist-watch, a golden chain and of course, the wedding-bedding. Modernisation and urbanisation have resulted in the insatiable demand for consumer goods.

The rationale of dowry was and is the simple fact that a daughter's claim to ancestral property, family wealth and assets is next to nothing while the son alone inherits it. This is tantamount to deliberate discrimination or deprivation for the poor girl who should be compensated for suitably at the time of marriage by generous dowry. Dowry, unfortunately, is no longer a voluntary gift from an affectionate father to a daughter but a diabolical tool of torture and harassment for the bride who is constantly pestered and bullied to bring in dowry in cash or kind after marriage over and above and the substantial gifts at the time of marriage. In order to ensure happy married life for their daughters, most of the parents to oblige and even run into debts to satisfy the 'sasural-wallahs'. But the litany of demands increases day by day.

The way out for the greedy in-laws is simple arithmetic. Burn the bride and marry another. So much more dowry, they argue. Murders everywhere conceive the plot and plan the strategy meticulously enough to escape conviction without any fuss or publicity. Indian ingenuity has devised a fool-proof method of doing away with the young bride-stove accident. Forget the anomaly of an antiquarted kereosene stove in a house boasting of gas-burners or replacement of sensible cotton sari with the combustible nylon Sari. A contrived spark or a deft push is enough. Engulfed in fire, this distraught daugther-in-law may cry for help, scream agonisingly but she knows for sure who are the perpetrators of this dastardly crime.

Even the dying declaration is recorded mostly under duress or out of cultural conditioning in this grisly drama. And should she point an accusing finger at her mother-in-law, husband's brother etc. (who are invariably involved in this sordid affair), legal loopholes see to it that nobody is convicted in the end. In fact, burning by fire is a perfected technique to dispence with an inconvenient bride without the least little incriminating clue or evidence left after the 'accident'. The rich harvest of 'bride-burning' is more widespread in Delhi, Punjab, Haryana, Uttar Pradesh and Bihar where the 'consumer culture' and 'keeping up with Joneses' syndrome seem to have deep roots.

367. Tackling dowry deaths (in India) *Hindustan Times* 29 Aug. 1986 ; 9.

Economic Growth

368. Albin, Peter S. *Progress without poverty, socially responsible economic growth.* New York, Basic Books, 1978.

369. Alexandersson, G. and B. I. Klevebring. *World resources.* Berlin, Walter de Grynterm, 1978.

370. Angana, J. J. *Strategy of economic development.* Poona, Gokhale Institute, 1971. p. 15.

371. Anseleoponlos, Angelos T. *For a new policy of international development.* New York, Praeger, 1977.

372. Bairocs, Paul. *Economic development of the Third World since 1900.* Berkeley, 1975.

373. Bairoch, Paul and Levy-Lebouer, M. *eds. Disparities in economic development since the industrial revolution.* New York, 1981.

374. Banks, J. A. *Prosperity and parenthood.* Atlantic Highlands : Humanities, Mar. 1979.

375. Baller, P. T. and B. S. Yamey. *Economics of undeveloped countries.* Cambridge, 1957.

376. Beenstock, M. *World economy in transition*, London, 1983.

377. Bluestone, Barry. Tripartite economy : Labour markets and the working poor. *Poverty and Human Resources* Jul--Aug. 1970.

378. Brown, Lester R. *Global economic prospect : New Sources of economic stress.* Washington, 1978.

379. Calleo, David P. Europe has economic levsons for America. *International Herald Tribune* 11 Aug. 1986 ; 4.

380. Carr-saunders, A. M. *Condition of economic progress.* London, Macmillan, 1940.

381. Coloman, David. and F. Nixson. *Economics of change in less developed countries.* New York, Willy, 1978.

382. Fishlow. A *et. al. Rich and poor nations in the world economy.* New York, McGraw-Hill. 1978.

383. Frankel, S. Herbert. *Economic impact on underdeveloped Societies.* Oxford, 1953.

384. Galbraith, John Kenneth. Positive approach to economic aid. *Foreign Affairs* 39 (3) Apr. 1961.

385. Giananis, Nicholas V. *Economic development thought and problems.* North Qwinay, Mass : Christopher Publicity House, 1978.

386. Gill, Richard T. *Economic development : Past and present.* Prentice-Hall, 1973.

387. Ginsberg, N. *Atlas of economic development.* Chicago, 1961.

388. Go for the growth. *Far Eastern Economic Review*; 24 Jul. 1986 ; 54-55.

389. Gregor, A. James. Economic reform in the People's Republic of China. *Asian Profile* Mar. 1986 ; 1-15.

390. Heller, Walter. *New dimensions of political economy.* Cambridge, 1966.

391. Higgins, Benjamin. *Economic development.* New York, W. W. Norton, 1959.

392. High inflation and hungry masses, *Pioneer* (Lucknow, Uttar Pradesh) 15 May 1986 ; 6.

"Oh, for the good old days when a rupee was a rupee and not just 10 paise or less ! This is how the oldsters moan nostalgically about the days which are no more and will never recur in future. Mind-boggling inflation is now a world-wide phenomenon. No currency in the world, whether it is rupee, dollar, pound or any other coin that is legal tender in the country concerned, has escaped the sharp bite of inflation, during the last four decades. But inflation perhaps was not so galloping as it has been in the last decade. According to statistics prepared by the International Labour Organisation (ILO), Israeli food prices have increased by a mind-boggling 94,491 per cent over 10 years from 1974 to 1984. Israel, of course, stands in a class by itself. But a comparison of the 1974 and 1984 annual averages, writes a Geneva based correspondent, after scanning the ILO report, confirms whether by comparatively modest or astronomically amount, prices in general and food prices in particular, have gone spiralling up sky-high.

In India we may feel ourselves particularly severely hit by the inflation-ridden decade, but according to the ILO survey India experienced food prices rises of 76.7 per cent, a remarkably low figure compared with the soaring increase in other countries, notably in Latin America. Even Yugoslavian food budgets went up by 1177 per cent, although most of the other East European countries with their controlled prices recorded very low changes in food costs over the ten years. The freer market economics of the West reeled with increase of 452 per cent in Greece and 207 per cent in the United kingdom.

However, the West Germans, the Swiss, and the Japanese suffered far less with 44;53 and 66 per cent respectively. Singapore was the most mildly affected with an increase of only 37 per cent, while all the other Asian countries, with a few exceptions saw inflationary food price sweeping up beyond 100 per cent. The same pattern, records the surveyor, was found for prices in general across the world during this economically turbulent decade. Switzerland reported the lowest inflation rate of 43 per cent, following by Singapore fractionally higher 43.3 per cent.

Where India is concerned inflaticn has hit us most as millions are literally starving amidst plenty due to higher food prices. It is on record that the per capita net availability of cereals and pulses has gone down from 480 grammes in 1965 to 463 grammes in 1985. And we talk of glut in our food production. So much so that the Government of India have reportedly decided to permit the export of wheat even at a loss.

The Indian press has rightly pointed out that when on the basis of the estimate of the Government itself, nearly 40 per cent of the population of the country live below the poverty line, which means that they cannot afford two square meals a day—the considerations which had prompted the government to decide on exporting wheat are difficult to understand much less of appreciate. There is a great difference between the so-called availability of food-stuff and its actual consumption.

"Commerce", the prestigious periodical has voiced the general opinion by going on record with the candid statement : "It should be the duty of every democratic government to devise measures to enable the hungry people to get a share of the available supplies rather than to deny this possibility by exporting the supplies abroad to subsidise the consumption by foreigner". It is an accepted maxim that charity begins at home. The benefits of the much-trunpeted 'green revolution' should first reach the hungry masses before the produce is shipped for consumption abroad to earn foreign exchange.

393. Hopkins, A.G. *Economic history of West Africa*. London, 1973.

394. Horonitz, David. Capital. In *Abolition of poverty*. New York, Praeger, 1969 ; 72-109.

395. Jalan, Bimal. *Essays in development policy*. New Delhi, Macmillan, 1975.

396. Jumper, Sidney R. *et.al. Economic growth and disparities : A world view.* Prentice-Hall, 1980.

397. Kahn, H. *World economic development. : 1979 and beyond.* Boulder, Westview Press, 1979.

398. Kamarck, Andrew M. *Tropics and economic development : A Provocative inquiry into the poverty of nations. India,* Johns Hopkins Univ. Press, 1976. p. 113.

Rain is a preoccupation for most people throughout the Tropics. A remark by Washington Post reporter Jim Hoagland on Africa applies to most of the Tropics : "More than 85 per cent of Africa's 300 million people eke out their livings as peasant farmers, and a failure of the rains to come can be a devastating economic disaster. If the question, 'How do Africans live ?' means how do most of them spend the majority of their time, the answer probably is "Thinking about rain". Life tends to be organized around it, in the way that consumer goods are the centerpiece of Western societies". In 1973 the world became aware of the tragic drought in the six west African countries bordering the Sahara—Chad, Mali, Mauritania, Nigeria, Senegal, and Upper Volta—following a decade of low and badly distributed rainfall and three years of severe drought. Fragmentary information indicated half of Senegal's groundnut crop was lost, 30 to 40 per cent of the cattle in the region died, and around one-third of the 30 million population was affected by severe malnutrition and hunger.

Continuous heat and the absence of frost mean that life and re-production go on throughout the year. The great executioner of nature, winter, is absent. No winter temperatures constrain continuous plant growth or the continuous reproduction and growth of all other kinds of life ; weeds, insects, birds, parasitic fungi, spider mites, eelworms, microbes and all kinds of viruses, pests, and parasites on man, his animals, and his crops. Life over most of the Tropics therefore takes on an infinite multiplicity of forms, but fierce competition results and only a relatively few individuals in every generation of any species survive in any one place. The conditions are ideal for rapid evolutionary change to adapt to any new opportunities.' (It is not at all surprising that evidence now indicates that even man first evolved in Africa).

These central biological parameters of the Tropics have considerable economic implications. Because of the multiplicity of species and the rapid evolutionary potential of the Tropics, there is a high probability that any new plant or animal introduced into an area by man will soon be attacked by some rapidly multiplying enemy. A crop successfully established always runs the considerable risk of attracting some new pest that has suddenly appeared. For example: "coffee rust which climinated the arabica coffee industry in Ceylon (Sri Lanka); ......blister blight of tea before control measures were found in Ceylon, South India and Indonesia; (sudden death) in the Zanzibar cloves; 'swollen shoot' in West Africa cocoa; 'wither-tip' of Dominican limes; and Panama disease of 'Gross Michel' bananas". The Philippines became self-sufficient in rice in 1967 but had to import rice again in 1971 becuase of a major outbreak of disease among the new rice varieties.

The Tropics are littered with the ruins of development projects that refused to recognize these special problems. A British Colonial Development Corporation million-dollar chicken-raising scheme in. The Gambia was completely wrecked by a disease that killed off chickens by the hundreds of thousands. A similar cause wrecked the Overseas Food Corporation's pig-raising scheme in Queensland. The Richard Toll rice-growing scheme in Senegal has not yet learned to cope with the hundreds of thousands of weaverbirds (Quelea) that descend on the paddies each year when the rice is ripe. The Ford Motor Company tried for twenty years, beginning in 1927, to establish rubber plantations in the Amazon Basin of Brazil. Because of health problems that occurred in spite of massive help from the U S. government during World War II, as well as tree blight and infertile soil, Ford finally gave up, losing practically the whole of its investment of $ 15 million. The Gezira Scheme in Sudan started with splendid crops but after a few year "the virgin land...... appeared to be worthless, filthy with weed and foul with disease". Only the fact that the Gezira company recognized the critical importance of research in the Tropics kept the whole scheme from collapsing in disaster. The tropical Northern Territory of Australia can show numerous examples of failures. In the 1950s, a California consortium invested in a rice project at Humpty Doo and produced small crops with large costs. A Texas company invested in a sorghum growing project at Tipperary Station, which never produced a profitable crop.

399. Khan, M.H. and J.A. Zerby. Socio-economic positions of India, Pakistan and Bangladesh in the Third World. *South East Asian Economic Review* 3(1) 1982; 85-100.

400. Kilborn, Peter T. U.S. economic downturn throws Reagan's record into doubt. *International Herald Tribune* 28 Jul. 1986; 1-2.

401. Kindleberger, Charles P. and Bruce Herrick. *Economic Development* New York, McGraw-Hill, 1977.

402. Kirby, E. Stuart. Raw material base. *In Economic Development in East Asia.* London, 1967 ; 98-115.

403. Kumar, B. *Planning poverty and economic development.* New Delhi, Deep and Deep 1985. p. 271.

404. Kumarappa, J.C. *Public finance and our poverty.* Ahmedabad, 1948 p. 110.

405. Kuzenets, Simon. *Economic development and cultural change.* New York, 1960.

406. Kuzenets, Simon *et.al eds. Economic growth Brazil, India, Japan.* Duke Univ. Press, 1955.

407. Leibenstein, Harvey. *Economic backwardness and economic growth.* New York, 1957.

408. Leontief, Wassily *et al. Future of the world economy.* New York, Oxford Univ. Press, 1977.

409. Lew, Roland. Economic reform against the workers. *International Viewpoint*, 11 Nov. 1985, 15-20.

410. Little, I.M.D. and J.M. Chifford. *International aid.* London, 1965.

411. Louis, M. Victor. Plan, the budget and poverty. *Economic Studies* 22 (9) 1982 ; 413-16.

412. Mandel, Ernest. World economic situation in 1985. *International Viewpoint* 22 Apr. 1985, 22-25.

413. Margirier, G. Eighties : A second phase of crisis ? *Capital and Class* 21, 1983, 61-86.

414. Mathur, Gautam, *Planning for steady growth.* New Delhi, 1966.

415. Meier, Gerald M. *Emerging from poverty : the economics that really matters.* New York, 1984. p. 268.

416. Myint, H. *Economics of the developing countries.* London, Hutchinson, 1964.

417. Paul, Swaraj. Indian economy is neither truly--public, nor truly private. *Sunday Observer* (Bombay) 27 Jul. 1986.

418. Peadu, K.K. Cooperation for economic development. *Inter economics* Feb. 1973 ; 38-41.

419. People's Democratic Republic of Yemen builds new socio-economic structures. *Contemporary* (New Delhi) Nov. 1978 ; 24-25.

When the oppressed peoples of Yemen rose in revolt on the 14th October, 1963, it was in a way a continuation of the Revolt of 26th September, 1962 in the northern part of the homeland. The objective was to liberate the national economy from the grip of foreign monopolies, wipe out the feudal and primitive production relations, and thus release the retarded productive forces of the masses to build a new life, free from socio-economic exploitation and poverty.

It took years of armed struggle to establish republican forms of government in the north and the south driving out the British from the latter and the feudal imamate and its foreign supporters from the former.

In the south, the new government of the People's Democratic Republic of Yemen (PDRY) found itself burdened with an underdeveloped economy, and primitive agricultural land.

With very little land left for the rest of the population there was tremendous pressure on it. The situation was aggravated by fragmentation which meant unproductive utilisation of land.

There was practically no industy, except an oil refinery at Little Aden. Even local handicrafts and fisheries had been destroyed.

Yemen had been converted into a market for British goods. Even the essentials of life—cloth, household utensils, wheat and maize, milk, cooking oil, and certain vegetables—had to be imported.

Even after the achievement of freedom it was not possible for PDRY to take any significant step forwards a fundamental reconstruction of the socio-economic structure. It was only the corrective movement of 22nd June 1969, led by the Left of the National Front supported by other Left parties that the first steps for the Socio-Economic transformation could be initiated. Moreover that process was accelerated by the unification of the Political Organisation National Front, People's Democratic Union and the People's Vanguard Party. The unification was based on the acceptance of the ideology of scientific socialism and a programme of national democratic development, avoiding the path of capitalism.

To bring about far-reaching socio-economic changes necessary to raise the country from the morass of stagnation, the new government first seized the key sectors of the economy. Through the nationalisation of banks, shipping, petroleum distribution, insurance and trade, the economy was liberated from the domination of foreign monopoly capital.

In 1970, the Agrarian Reform Law ended feudal hegemony. The large-estates were broken up and land redistributed to the mass of the peasantry. These measures were accompanied by agricultural and agro-industrial cooperatives and the setting up of state farms.

After these two basic measures had been taken towards a radical transformation of existing socio-economic relations, a three-year plan was launched in 1970. The perspective was that of a multi-structured economy, with social ownership of the means of production represented by the state and the cooperative sectors. Apart from these two sectors, which were to emerge as the dominant feature of the economy, mixed projects were also encouraged.

420. Poverty and growth. *Economic Times* 3 Jul. 1984 ; 5.

421. Poverty and growth. *Economic Times* 10 Dec. 1984 ; 5.

422. Prest, A.R. *Public finance in underdeveloped countries.* London, Weidenfeld and Nicolson, 1962.

423. Preston, Julia. In Micanagna, economic crisis is extreme. *International Herald Tribune* 26-27 Jul. 1986 ; 1-2.

424. Real de Azna, Carlos. Small nation and the constructive style of development. *Cefal Review*, Second Semester, 1977; 153-75.

425. Rosenthal, Gerald. Identifying the poor. *Economic measures of* In *understanding poverty*. Ed. by D.P. Moynihan. New York, Basic Books, 1963.

426. Rostow, W.W. *Stages of economic growth : A non-communist manifesto* Cambridge, 1962.

427. Schumpeter, Joseph A. *History of economic analysis.* Oxford, 1954.

428. Shafei, Mohamed Z. *Three lecturers on economic development.* Beirut Arab University, 1970.

429. Shanin, T. Nature and logic of the peasant economy. *Journal of Peasant Studies*, 1973.

430. Sheth, D.L. Problem of reservations: Economic backwardness or social injustice? *Radical Humanist* (New Delhi) Apr. 1986, 9-14.

431. Singhania, H.S. *Today and tomorrow: Perspectives for Indian economy* New Delhi, 1980. p. 218.

432. Spiegelglas. S. and O.J. Welsheds. *Economic development challenge and promise*, Prentice-Hall, 1970.

433. Stein, Leslie, *Economics relatives in poor countries*. London, 1972.

434. Storper, M.J. and A.J. Scott. eds. *Production, work and territory*. London, Allen & Union, 1985.

435. Streeten, Paul. *Development perspectives*, New York, 1987.

436. Taylor J. *From modernization to modes of production*. London, Macmillan, 1979.

437. Thrift, Nigel, Geography of international economic disorder. Fn *WIC* 12-67.

438. Todaro, Michael P. *Economic development in the third world* London, Confmans, 1977.

439. Walker, John 1. Africa's economic reforms need fuel. *International Herald Tribune*. 24 Jul., 1986 ; 4.

440. Watts, Nita *ed. Economics of the world*. New York, Oxford University Press, 1978.

441. Williams, G. *ed. Nigeria : Economy and society* London, 1976.

Economic Planning

442. Agarwala, Virendra. Planning for ending poverty. *Economic Times* 27 Dec. 1979; 5.

443. Gans, Herbert J. *People and plans*. New York, Basic Books, 1968.

444. Ghosh, A. and P. Majumdar. Planning for poor I & II *Statesman*. 6 Feb., 1985; 6; 7 Feb. 1985; 6.

445. Jha, Radhanamdan. Planning to eliminate poverty. *Indian Nation* (Patna, Bihar) 29 Sep. 1986: 4.

446. Masion, Edward S. *Economic planning in underdeveloped areas : government and business*. New York, Fordham Univ. Press, 1958.

447. Matthews, Allan F. Resources and norms in development planning *International Development Review*, 9 (2) Jun. 1967.

448. Mehmet, Ozay. *Economic Planning and social justice in developing countries*. London, Crown Helm, 1978.

449. Narayan Rao, J.S. Poverty and planning : Monumental failure *Newstime* 6 Dec. 1984: 9.

450. Plan and poverty. *Tribune* 24 Oct. 1985; 4.

451. Poverty and planning *Sentinel* (Assam) 30 May, 1984; 4.

452. Prashad, Kamta. *Planning for poverty alleviation*. New Delhi, Agricole, 1986; p. 240.

The need to alleviate poverty has become a matter of urgent concern for all of us. The book brings out that, while we have achieved break-through in certain areas, the magnitude of the problem calls for greater effort on our part although several measures have already been taken. "Why? And what improvements are possible?" are the most important questions before us today. The significance of the book lies in the fact that it is mostly concerned with these very questions. The book attempts to provide a review of the strategies and policies followed until the Sixth Five Year Plan for alleviation of poverty and suggests new policy measures that should be considered for the alleviation of poverty.

This book deals, in a comprehensive manner, with the various aspects of the poverty alleviation programmes and tries to provide a systematic approach to the problem of poverty. The author has made a number of suggestions covering both economic and administrative aspects at both macro and micro levels. He has also spelt out the various implications of the strategy advocated by him and suggests operational details.

453. Rangnekar, D.K. Nehruism and the second plan. *Economic Weekly* 16, Jul. 1964.

454. Sethi, J.D. Prices, poverty and the plan. *Indian Express* 11 Nov. 1983; 6.

455. Todaro, Michael P. *Development Planning* : *Models and methods.* London, Oxford University Press, 1971.

456. Wasterston, Albert. *Development Planning Lessons of Experience.* Johns Hopkins Univesity Press, 1979.

Education

457. Abrams, Mark. Rewards of education. *New Society* 4(93) 9 Jul. 1964.

458. Abdul Noor, S.M. Investment on human resources : Education, a strategy for eliminating mass poverty. In *EAPS* 183-98.

The war of liberation brought in its trails, a number of formidable difficulties in the field of education. The uncoordinated educational development of the past left its legacy. The task of correcting the prevailing chaos was onerous. The endeavour to mobilize the full potentials of t he economy and to ensure sustained economic growth, with greater social justice and self-reliance presented an existing challenge. The task aimed not only at a shift from the past to which the country had been used to, but also to provide measures for the future to which the country would be marching ahead. An appreciation of the directions sought, and the rate of progress considered desirable, was imperative to discern the trend of change.

The first step of the course was an understanding of the right strategy. What should we define as our basic strategy for education ?

(a) Development of Education as a deliberate and reasoned str ategy fitted into properly times stages, to accelerate economic development as a whole; and thereby assist the climination of the mass poverty?

(b) Development of Education as a catalyst, as a builder of the proper social framework of a new society, the creator of a national unity?

(c) Development of Education as a pre-investment essential to the fulfilment of political goals?

Within the framework of the choice for a broadened strategy remains the necessity of resolving some basic policy issues. They may be stated as follows :

(a) How to identify the society which we are aiming at and the technology through which we can attain that ;

(b) for what values, ethical or moral, in such a society the youth of today would prepare themselves or will be prepared ;

(c) whether the repaid change in science, in technologies, in techniques of production, in social organizations and in human adjustments will provide a new set of valued and a complex mechanism for creating such attitudes ;

(d) whether the new schools should be "autonomous schools" i.e., schools deeply imbibed with the spirit of social environment; and finally.

(e) how to strengthen the base of an educational system within the shortest possible time.

It is of course obvious that the questions raised in previous paragraphs cannot be answered within a few months. In the meantime, in order to plan, we have to proceed with certain fundamental assumptions. We have identified some which we may narrate as follows:

First, the existing traditional system of education, despite its incoherence and alarming inefficiency, has been able to provide manpower to run the administration, the management, the political and economic system with considerable success. The system is equipped to generate enterpreneurship, ability and political acumen among the masses. It is this process of learning that has steered us to our goal of freedom and is aiming at our economic emancipation. It still contains a certain amount of merit and consideration.

The system is at present partially incapable of providing the trained manpower, due to extremely rapid economic and technological transformation of the society and inadequate upliftment of the educational process. Education has remained as an exogeneous element of the economic system. It may therefore be justifiable to amend the system and not to discard a heritage, only because it is at present, not meeting the total need. May be what it warrants is a modification and an overhaul, but not a disposal over the window.

Second, even if we draw a profile of a complete break-through for our educational system which is theoretically and academically possible, yet we would not be able to provide the necessary technical capability and facilities within the country to undertake and implement the break-through.

Third, incidental learning (non-formal education) which has been an assest and corrolary of our educational pattern from the historic ages have not been given due emphasis in the past. It would be our endeavour to reconstruct the missing profile of incidential learning, and place it as a viable alternative to the formal system. For this purpose, the resource and time-period of FFYP would be devoted for wide scale research and development.

459. Amin, Samir. Education, ideology and technology. In *Imperialism and unequal development*. Succex, Harvester Press, 1977 ; 153-68.

In capitalist society the economic factor is, for the first time, obfuscated by generalized commodity exchange. The division of labour becomes so complex that the producers no longer have a direct relationship to one another, and distribution no longer appears as directly related to production. This obfuscation explains the emergence of social laws as we understand them. In the natural sciences, a "law" refers to forces which impose themselves objectively as autonomous forces independent of the observer. The notion of social laws distinct from moral laws was inconceivable before the rise of the capitalist system. It is with the emergence of social laws that appear to be autonomous with respect to society that capitalist society could develop a new science of society, distinct from ethics and religion.

The principal aspect of this social science is the economic aspect. These social laws, which impose themselves as autonomous forces, are primarily economic laws--the laws of market exchange. The prices of goods, the prices of labour, the destination of goods appear to result from the market confrontation between supply and demand - with respect to commodities, labour power, capital goods, investments.

In capitalist society, therefore, ideology has an economistic rather than religious character. This is paralleled by a demystification of politics which becomes detached from ethics and religion and increasingly appears as a branch of social science. This point is essential for an understanding of the changes that occurred in the area of education.

At the same time—and this is a second basic aspect of the question--there is a spectacular development of the productive forces resulting from the division of labour within occupations combined with the utilisation of increasingly effective means of production.

In considering education and training in nineteenth-century capitalist society, we can find several characteristics. First, the education of the elites is still largely traditional, based on the humanities, and certainly less religious ; it increasingly incorporates "scientific knowledge" but retains its basic philosophical, linguistic, and literary orientation. Training in reasoning is provided by the gradual extension of instruction in mathematics as a foundation of formal logic.

Second, the training of skilled workers (and, to a less degree, of more advanced technicians and engineers) is at first quite restricted and frequently considered inferior to the humanist education of the elites, i.e., of the new bourgeoisie, including its political members and leading ideological and intellectual representatives. Much of this training, especially that of skilled workers, is acquired through practical work experience and permits social mobility toward more advanced levels, notably that of engineering.

Third, the gradual spread of basic education. This is a general education in citizenship combined with elementary scientific and technical knowledge in preparation for eventual skilled work.

To understand these three characteristics we must relate them to the specific characteristics of capitalism—the obfuscation of social relations ; the emergence of objective, especially economic, laws ; the predominantly economistic character of ideology ; and the development of the productive forces in keeping with the division of labour within occupations (i.e., the growing separation of policy-making tasks and unskilled performance tasks).

The schooling provided for the people under the guise of generalized primary education is essentially a training for citizenship. This civic training becomes gradually detached from religion (although it may retain some elements of religious origin or character) because politics has been demystified ; and with the emergence of economic and social laws which impose themselves on society as natural, autonomous forces, the religious element shifts from the political to the economic domain.

The education of the elites, therefore, involves primarily the acquisition of an ideological body of closely interrelated opinions, ideas, and information concerning the social order and the objective character of the laws of society. This education is paralleled, with respect to the organization work, by a division between skilled work and the unskilled work of the mass of producers. The growing division of labor underlies not only the problems of education but, more generally, the problems of civilization, social perspectives, and the ultimate purpose of economic development. This situation has given rise to many of the contradictions that underlie the chaos of the modern world.

The first contradiction is the increasing degradation of work in the industrial world, i.e. downgrading of the work skills of a growing number of workers. Labour and Monopoly Capital, an American study by Harry Braverman, gives a powerful description of the degradation of work in the United States. At the beginning of the twentieth century, the percentage of unskilled workers barely exceeded a third of the active population : in 1970, this figure had risen to 70 per cent, and it now includes not only the great majority of workers in the secondary sector, but also a growing majority of workers in the tertiary sector. This massive degradation of work skills of the majority of producers is paralleled by the increasing specialization of a minority.

This first contradiction gives rise to another. At the very moment when under the impact of affluence and democratic pressures, the educational system tends to become generalized on the secondary level— that is, at the very moment when the citizens of these countries are acquiring an increasingly lengthy formal education—it is becoming increasingly difficult for a majority of these citizens to find work. For a growing majority of the population, education is becoming dysfunctional, a kind of superfluous luxury.

This second contradiction derives from the specialization of skilled work. Skilled lobour used to be distributed almost evenly over the entire work force in keeping with a social division of labour among occupations but not, by and large, within occupations. During the nineteenth century, the utilization of increasingly modern and effective techniques designed to increase over all labour productivity gradually created a closer connection between science, the source of knowledge, and technology, the application of knowledge in a particular area of production.

During much of the nineteenth century, the dominant branch of scientific knowledge was mechanics, the foundation of applied technology. Owing to a less pronounced division of labour, this afforded a measure of social mobility through the acquisition of relatively accessible knowledge. This period saw the widespread diffusion of popular technical and scientific works on mechanics that were read and studied by large number of workers. The training of skilled workers was not yet highly specialized, except for certain occupations such as medicine and other professions which were in any case restricted to bourgeois practitioners.

Today the situation is quite different. The branches of technology have undergone considerable diversification and the scientific foundations of technology are therefore much less unified around mechanics. Today, electronics, mechanics, biology, and other branches are equally important scientific sources of technology. The training of skilled labour is becoming increasingly specialized and involves many more workers than the small number of engineers trained in the nineteenth century. This training nevertheless involves but a small minority of workers. The training of highly skilled workers is the condition for the degradation of work for the majority of workers.

The third contradiction bears on what may be called the crisis of the humanities. This crisis is closely related to the changes that have occurred in the ownership and control of capital—the gradual disappearance from the bourgeoisie of the individual or family entrepreneurs of the nineteenth century, and the emergence of a class which tends to exercise collective control over much more highly centralized capital. The centralization of capital, an expression of the growing contradiction between the social character of production and the exclusive control of this production through formal ownership of the means of production, is reflected in the fact that exclusive family ownership of the enterprise has been supplanted by social forms of ownership, by the corporations which control capital. The bourgeoisie of the nineteenth century is increasingly being replaced by what Galbraith, among others, has ambiguously termed the "technostructures".

This change calls attention to another aspect of social reproduction—the reproduction of the bourgeoisie itself as a social group composed of individual and families. In the nineteenth century, the bourgeoisie reproduced itself through the bourgeois family, through marriage and family inheritance. Owing to the centralization of capital and the transfer of formal control over capital to the corporations, family inheritance is no longer of major importance. Since, on the other hand, the mass of producers are able to acquire an elementary and secondary, and in certain cases even a college education, the training of the "elite" is increasingly based on a socio-political process of internal selection. This selection is disguised as recognition of individual "qualities" or practical on-the-job experience (whether valid or not), but it conflicts with the democratic pretensce of social mobility. This provokes a crisis in the humanities-oriented system of education (which is bound to disappear since the bourgeoisie is no longer reproduced primarily through the family), and transforms the character of the training and education of the ruling class.

The training and education of the ruling class are now based on science and technology viewed as ideologies, ruling-class education is no longer designed primarily to produce scientists and technicians ; its principal objective is to inculcate the notion that science and technology are autonomous forces external to society. This is one of the aspects of the crisis of the universities with respect to the teaching of the social, political, and economic sciences ; at the same time, the premise that technology must replace ideology is giving rise to a new philosophical orientation.

This, then, is the context of the contradictions of the modern world in the area of education. How do these contradictions relate to the underdeveloped countries ? These countries are integrated into the world capitalist system—economically (decisive role of external relations in the transformation and development of these countries) and socially (borrowed models of consumption, culture, and technology, and transmission of the dominant ideologies). As a result, all these contradictions are present in the periphery of the system although they are here scaled down and, for this very reason even more violent.

In the underdeveloped countries the traditional economic system has been gradually destroyed by its integration into the world capitalist system. The handicrafts have almost disappeared due to the competition of manufactured goods, and the system of agricultural production has deteriorated due to external pressures which have forced it to adjust to the requirements of the world market. We can see extreme exampled of this in African societies in which food production involving sophisticated accumulated technical skills was gradually supplanted by the production of export goods fabricated in centers run by technical researchers and consultants who have no relations to the producers, and whose output is "transferred"—forced upon the producers through managerial systems, cooperatives, and supervisory companies which disposes the peasants of their ancestral skills. Owing to the penetration of capitalist ideology into the underdeveloped countries, the destruction of the traditional system of on-the-job training is paralleled by the deterioration and gradual disappearance of the elitist systems of education, especially those based on traditional philosophy and religion : this is happening, for instance, to Koranic education in all the Moslem countries.

Moreover, this destruction leaves nothing in its wake. Whereas in the center of the capitalist system traditional education was gradually replaced with a new kind of schooling, which I have criticized in the preceding pages, in the underdeveloped countries the destruction of traditional education has in numerous instances resulted in total illiteracy and in the loss of the traditional technical skills accumulated through practical work experience in agriculture and the crafts.

This process of destruction can be observed in various domains.

First, in the most important domain—economic life. It is the study of this domain that led to the gradual discovery that underdevelopment results from development in the center, expansion of the center, the center's domination of the periphery—destruction of handicrafts, dominant role of agriculture—and, at the same time from a belated and inadequate industrialization based on technological and consumption models borrowed from the advanced world, which therefore cannot provide work for the majority of the producers it "marginalizes".

The effects of this process of destruction can also be observed in the domain of language. There is good reason to believe that the languages of the Third World as they are actually used are gradually deteriorating as a result of the degradation of work. I am thinking of African languages which, in keeping with the prevalence of skilled handicrafts, incorporated a corresponding technical vocabulary and an underlying conceptual system that presupposed an implicit body of theoretical knowledge.

In the underdeveloped countries, the contradictions of the system thus assume a violent and almost caricatured form. We are witnessing not only the dispossession of work in the industrial world, but also the degradation and dispossession of a mode of work which is not even being replaced with industrial labour. In other words, there is a growing number of unemployed who are unskilled in the full sense of the term—they are neither artisans nor peasants, having no longer those skills, and they are not even degraded industrial workers. Since the models of industrialization are borrowed from the developed countries, we are also witnessing the specialization of skilled work, but this specialization is such that the capacity for mastering these work skills is practically non-existent. This difficulty is dealt with by the massive purchase and use of imported skilled workers and expensive technology. But when complex machinery is imported, the difficulty is not to operate it, but to get to know its "secrets", i.e., to be able to reproduce it, and eventually to adapt it to ends different from those for which it was designed. And finally, we are witnessing a transfer of nineteenth century elitist educational models which are here perfectly absurd, since they are not even rooted in local tradition, as they were in Europe.

What is the purpose of literacy or mass education campaigns in such a society? Stated bluntly, they are dysfunctional, they are out of place, not required in terms of the social reproduction of the dominated peripheral system, and consequently, serve a purpose only when pursued in conjunction with an upgrading of work.

What do we mean by the upgrading of work? In this respect, as in others, the underdeveloped countries cannot retrace the path followed by the developed countries. Each must transcend the capitalist system from the outset and develop technology that will enable it not only to solve its own particular economic problem, that of underdevelopment, but also to open up new perspectives for world civilization. This is an extremely complex and difficult problem which will take a long time to solve. It is, moreover, not excluded that the currently developed world will also participate in the creation of this new world civilization by challenging the forms of social and work organization which are now characterized by massive degradation.

460. Anderson, C.A. and M.J. Bowman. *Education and economic development.* Chicago, Aldine Press, 1965.

461. Anderson, J. *Struggle for the school.* London, Wyman, 1970.

462. Berry, S. Albert. *Education, income productivity and Urban Poverty.* World Bank 1980, Washington.

463. Blang, Mark. *Introduction to the economics of education.* Penguin, 1972.

464. Bowen, W.G. Assessing the economic contribution of education. *In High Education* (Robbins Report) London, HMSO, 1963.

465. Bowles, Samuel, Schooling and inequality from generation to generation. *Journal of Political Economy* May-Jun. 1972.

466. Carter, M.P. *Home, School and Work.* London, Pergamon, 1963.

467. Court, D. and D.P. Ghai. *Education society and development.* Nairobi, Oxford University Press, 1974.

468. Cullen, K. *School and family* Dublin, 1969.

469. Education and Subversion. *New Quest* (39) May-Jun. 1983; 167-70.

470. Floud, J. Social class factors in educational achievement. *In Ability and educational opportunity.* Ed. by A.H. Halsey. So Swedish Ministry of Education, 1961.

471. Foster, P. and J.R. Sheffield. *World Year book of education, 1974.* London, Evans Bros., 1975.

472. Humphrey, Hubert H. People for jobs: the urgent crisis in education. *In War on Poverty.* New York, 1964, 121-42.

473. *Investment in education*. Dublin, stationery office, 1965.

474. Jolly, R. *ed. Education in Africa*. Nairobi, East African Publishing House, 1968.

475. Joshi, Navin Chandra. Mass literacy in Indian democracy. *Patriot* (New Delhi) 3 Sep. 1986; 4.

476. King, T. *ed. Education and income*. Washington, 1980.

477. Miyashita, H. *et al.* Effect of population growth on the quantity of education children receive. *Review of Economics and Statistics*. 64, May 1982.

478. Moody, Harry R. Education in an aging society. *Daedalus* Win 1986, 191-210.

479. Most illiterate. *Amrita Bazar Patrika* (Calcutta) 10 Sep. 1986; 6.

480. Psacharoponlos, G. *Returns to education*. San Francisco, 1973.

481. Ramachandran, G. Illiteracy and poverty. *Gandhi Marg* (New Delhi) Jan. 1976; 38-45.

482. Ray, Kamlesh. Education and employment *Mainstream* (New Delhi) Annual, 1970; 27-31.

483. Schultz. T.W. *Economic value of education*. New York, Columbia Univ. Press, 1963.

484. Sexton, P. *Education and income*. New York, 1961.

485. Sheshinsky, E. Relation between a social welfare education and the Gini Index of income inequality. *Journal of Economic Theory* 4, 1972.

486. Smolenstey, E. Investment in the education of the Poor: A pessimistic report. *American Economic Review Supplement* 55, May 1966.

487. Tupe, S.D. Role of educational institutions in poverty eradication. *Kurukshetra* (New Delhi) Jun. 1986; 10-11, 19.

Election System

488. Chanan Singh. Poverty; caste bane of poll system. *Newstime* 12 Mar. 1985; 7.

Employment

489. Dinesh, C. Handicrafts: Employment for Weaker sections. *Financial Express*, 27 May 1986 ; 5.

Removal of poverty and improving the quality of life of urban and rural poors appears to be a major challenge for the developing countries of Asia, Africa and latin America.

The development plans of an increasing number of developing countries indicate that their development strategies tend to favour employment generation and a more equitable income distribution expansion of rural industrialisation and the improvement of rural incomes, and the local production of consumer goods in accordance with the needs, lastes and purchasing power of low-income groups. With respect to the manufacturing sector, these strategies favour small-scale production and the use of technologies suitable to local resource endowment.

In other worlds, it is recognised that industrialisation strategies which emphasize the establishment of medium-scale and large-scale industries and the use of imported technologies, capital, and skills may not achieve the socio-economic objectives of these countries. Obviously it is not suggested that medium-scale and large-scale industries should not be promoted at all. These industries have certainly an important role to play in any industrial development strategy. It is only suggested that the very small production units (e.g. cottage industries and handicrafts) may also need to be promoted if balance economic and social development is to be achieved.

Expansion of this sector should have very important effects, including the following; substantial employment generation, rural industrialisation, iptimal use of local human and material resources, considerable multiplier effects on the economy (through backward and forward linkages) etc. Despite these contributions, most developing countries have generally focused their efforts exclusively on the promotion of medium-scale to large-scale enterprises based on imported technologies and skills (e.g. turnkey factories) and promoting goods which cannot generally be afforded by a large majority of the population. While the establishment of some of these enterprises may be justified, many others have proved to be "white elephants" which heavily depend on governmental subsidies or unwarranted protection (e.g. prohibitive tariffs). Why then this emphasis on the promotion of medium-scale and large-scale industries, and the neglect of cottage industries and handicrafts? A number of answers may be provided.

Firstly, many developing countries seem to have adopted the strategy successfully used by Western Countries during the industrial revolution in the hope that a similar strategy would yield similar results. It is now recognised that given the substantially different circumstances of developing countries (as compared to those of the Western countries during the industrial revolution), heavy industrialisation may not always yield the expected socio-economic benefits.

Secondly, the establishment of medium-scale and large-scale industries has often been the result of the activities of foreign investors who were not interested in the establishment of small-scale enterprises. As these investors brought in the necessary capital and skills, governments did not object to the establishment of medium-scale and large-scale industries.

Thirdly, the majority of developing countries are not equipped to provide assistance to the very small enterprise sector. This sector includes a large number of geographically dispersed production units which may not be easily reached. Thus, any kind of assistance, whether it consists of the provision of credit, training or supporting services would require an extensive staff to assess the needs of these production units and provide the necessary assistance. Unfortunately, few countries have recognised the need to establish the right type of institutions to assist the very small enterprise.

Furthermore, it is often mistakenly of thought that given the smallness of the production units constituting the above sector, no assistance or special measures are required. There may be other reasons for the neglect of the very small production sector; however, the above three reasons are probably the most prevalent ones.

Any effort to structure policy and design projects in favour of very small enterprises should take into account the very large number and location of the production units within the sector. In some developing countries, the number of small units have been recorded in tens of thousands. In most developing countries the bulk of traditional small enterprises has been found to be located in rural areas.

Given the vast number of very small enterprises in both rural and urban areas, it is clear that the sector provides substantial employment opportunities for the benefit of the rural and urban poor. In addition, the sector palys an important role in mitigating the trend of labour migration from rural to urban areas, and the increasing social unrest and congestion in most urban centres of developing countries. However, it needs mentioning that the large numbers of the widely dispersed small units constitute a major problem whenever governments undertake to design programmers that could effectively reach the target group at reasonable costs.

Kerala, endowed with its breath-taking natural beauty, has to her credit a variety of handicrafts products which add glamour to the rich cultural heritage of the State. The highly intelligent and gifted craftsmen of the State, with their age old contacts with different civilizations at home and abroad, have adopted special type of designs which have good demand in the markets at home and abroad.

Famine & Drought

490. Bernstein, T.P. Stalinism, Chinese peasants and famine : Grain procurements during the Great Leap Forward. *Theory and Society 13 (2)* May 1984; 339-78.

491. Blix, G. *et. al. eds. Famine*. Uppsala, Sweden, Almquist & Wikselle, 1971.

492. Brass, Paul R. Political uses of crisis: The Bihar famine of 1966-67. *Journal of Asian Studies*. 45 (2) Feb. 1986; 245-68.

493. Famine continues unabated. *Congress Varnika International* (New Delhi). Sep. 1985 : 6-7.

The images of Africa's dead and dying no longer flicker across our TV screen nightly, nor are we confronted with pictures of the continent's agony in the morning papers. The world community, once alerted to the nightmare of starvation in Ethiopia and other countries, responded with a generosity that many say has never before been seen, and the first world conference ever to focus on a whole continent—in Geneva in March—resulted in the assurance that most of the food needed in Africa for 1985 would be forthcoming.

So the public in the donor countries can be forgiven for believing that the critical situation, while not exactly a thing of the past, has at least been brought under control.

The reality, unfortunately, is much grimmer. While the death rates in relief camps and easily accessible drought-stricken communities have dropped, in many cases sharply, tens of thousands continue to die every month of hunger and hunger-related illnesses in the most critically affected African countries. In fact, said FAO Director General Edouard

Saouma recently to a conference specially convened by his organisation to discuss the African crisis, the famine could see the extinction of many nomadic communities.

"The harsh reality is that the famine shows no sign, so far, of abating," he told the conference. "A head count of its mounting victims is simply not possible. Too many who cannot make it to feeding camps lie in unmarked graves."

Mr. Bradford Morse, who described the African drought as the greatest human disaster in history when appointed to head the new OEOA late last year, is hopeful that the emergency will be contained in long run. But he acknowledges that thousands are dying every day across the continent.

"We said at the beginning of the year that 30,000,000 Africans are threatened by starvation and that continues pretty much to be the case today. Unless the world community maintains its commitment and its current pitch we could quickly revert to the kinds of scenes we saw late last year."

His comments are echoed, sometimes too sharply for comfort, by a wide variety of field assessments. David MacDonald, Canada's Emergency Coordinator for African relief operations, warned in a report to Foreign Minister Joe Clark that the famine in Africa may not have reached its peak yet. "Urgency is even more the central issue," he wrote. "Sudan is now at the point at which Ethiopia was (in December... And they are both) just the tip of the iceberg."

In Ethiopia, RRC commissioner Dawit Wolde Giorgis told a recent meeting of U.N. government and NGO officials that despite more and more people being reached by food aid, the number in need was continuing to rise, with over 8 million now incapable of meeting their own needs.

Frank Carlin, Catholic Relief Services Representative in Ethiopia, reports worsening malnutrition even amongst the non-drought groups as they accommodate relatives on already-reduced incomes (all working Ethiopians contribute one twelfth of their salaries to the national releif effort). Addis Ababa, he notes, whose population has swelled with drought victims, is not a beneficiary of food aid.

"I'd say at least 1,000 people are still dying everyday in Ethiopia," he says.

The situation in Chad is equally precarious, according to Bertram Collins, UNICEF's Regional Director for West Africa, "Chad has a famine demographic profile almost identical to Ethiopia's." he reported in New York. "The only difference between the two is that Chad's infrastructure for distributing food is infinitely less developed."

In Sudan, P.A. Stanissis, OEOA's Special Representative there, says that the situation continues to deteriorate rapidly, and at least five million—perhaps even more—now need food aid. Sudan's situation is complicated by the continuing arrivals of refugees from Chad and Ethiopia, currently estimated at over a million. A major problem, according to Mr. Stanissis is the shortage of fuel to move the trucking fleet.

Field people cite one or more of the following causes as giving rise to the feared deterioration.

The logistical difficulties—shortage of trucks, spare parts, fuel, inadequate road infrastructure, inaccessibility of certain regions—of moving food and other emergency supplies off the ships and docks to the areas in need.

494. Franke, R.W. and B.H. Chasin, *Seeds of famine*. Montclair, N.J., Allanheld, Osmun, 1980.

495. Green, E. R. R. Great famine. *In course of Irish history*. Ed. by ; T. W. Moody and F. X. Martin. Cork, Meroier Press, 1967.

496. Hewitt, K. *Ed. Interpretations of calamity*. London, Allen & Unwin, 1983.

497. Jaisingh, Hari. Drought management, *Indian Express* 2 May 1986 ; 8.

Those who play politics and thrive on people's ignorance and misery generally become insensitive to sufferings that go with poverty, deprivation and natural calamities. While the initiative shown by Prime Minister Rajiv Gandhi to acquire first-hand knowledge of the country's drought-affected areas is to welcome, the experience shows that such VVIP trips at best produce cosmetic changes. They have not helped to take our collective blinkers off so that problems are tackled squarely.

What needs to be realised is that the drought situation in parts of the country requires far more serious efforts than have been visible so far. Rains do fail occasionally in drought-prone areas of Gujarat, Madhya Pradesh, Rajasthan, Maharashtra, Karnataka. But more than nature's wrath, it is man's recklessness—both at the official and non-official levels—that make matters worse.

Providing relief is one thing. The spending of millions of rupees on relief works year after year has not brought cheer to those who suffer quietly. Doles don't solve problems. They only cushion one's suffering.

True, the country today can painlessly absorb disaster shocks of drought and floods. Gone are the dark days of mass starvation and deaths seen during the 1942 Bengal famine. Still, we seem to be creating conditions for a prolonged drought by conveniently overlooking ground realities.

Though the administrative machinery has the infrastructure to meet the challenges thrown up by a natural disaster, the basic thinking and approach remain either distorted or lopsided. A colonial hangover blurs the vision and cripples the efficacy of the system that suits the corrupt and the inefficient. The rest is all politics played in league with corrupt middlemen and power brokers. The result is the pathetic helplessness of the common man as echoed by 70-year-old Jadha Amdhar Patil of the drought-hit village Jamoulka in the Nashik belt : "I gave everything—my savings and gold—to the call of the nation. Now, no one is coming to our rescue as we struggle for the very survival. Politicians make promises but never fulfil them. My dreams have gone sour."

The whole scenario of man-made-cum-natural calamities has to be viewed afresh. There is need to evolve both long-term and short-term disaster management perspectives in the absence of which precious resources would continue to be plundered by vested interests.

A disaster of any magnitude does cause a set-back to development efforts. As it is, not even 60 per cent of the money earmarked for development projects actually gets spent on them. Parasites and middlemen constantly nibble at development funds at all levels. Even the Prime Minister's own constituency is not spared. The plight of ordinary constituencies without their VVIP godfathers can be imagined.

Relief operations throw up their own rackets. As Dr. V. M. Dandekar, Director of the Gokhale Institute of Economics and Politics, told Anand Agashe, our staff correspondent at Pune, "The situation cannot be improved if the present system of carrying out the works (he was referring to the employment guarantee scheme operating in the drought-affected areas of Maharashtra) through government departments is persisted with. The problem is further compounded as a large number of MLAs and MPs have been getting the kickbacks from the corrupt officials."

Tne picture is frightening ; mini-Ethiopias and mini-Brazils could be in the making in parts of the country. Brazil suffered the worst drought in its living memory in 1983-84. The disaster was mainly due to the massive before-station in the past quarter century. A senseless plunder of forest wealth brought ruin to Ethiopia.

What is true of Brazil or Africa is also true of India. Nearly one-third of Maharashtra is in the grip of yet another dry spell. Drought has gripped 30 per cent of Madhya Pradesh. The Saurashtra region of Gujarat too faces an unprecedented crisis of drinking water. The situation is equally gloomy in parts of Rajasthan, Karnataka and Andhra Pradesh.

498. Ladurie, E. L. Famine Amenorrhea (17th Centuries). In *Biology of man in history*. Ed. by Robert Forster and Orest Ranum. Baltimore, Johns Hopkins University Press, 1976.

499. Makwane, Francis. Bombs have not killed us, but famine has, *Newstime* 28 Oct. 1984 ; 12.

Some 60,000 refugees from the Mozambican province of Tete, now living in Zimbabwe, face an uncertain future in their homeland as security problems and transport difficulties frustrate the massive international relief operation launched in May.

The refugees fled famine at the beginning of the year, as anti-government guerillas of the Mozambique National Resistance (MNR) cut the province's supply lines, isolating it economically.

A refugee spokesman at Marymount Mission Zimbabwe, said : "More than anything we want to return to our lands, but we are afraid there will be no food to eat and no seeds to plant. The hunger is worse than any war we have experienced. Bombs and bullets haven't killed us, but famine has."

These people's enemies are neither the MNR guerillas nor government troops, but hunger and drought. Mozambique has suffered war virtually uninterupped for 20 years. Tete in particular has a history of poverty, drought, slavery and war.

In the Sixties it became the western front of Frelimo, the Liberation front fighting Portugeuese colonial rule and now the single party in power. While parts of the province became liberated zones, other suffered massacres at the hands of Portuguese commandos, as in the village of Wiriamu.

Tete became a training ground for ZANU guerillas fighting the Smith regime in what was then Rhodesia. The population endured Rhodesian bombing raids.

Throughout, the tenacious Nyungwe peasants in the valleys south of the Zambezi have clung to their lands, surviving on subsistence agriculture, supplemented by a healthy barter trade in goats. The region suffers cyclical droughts. Roughly two years out of every five are dry, and rarely does a grain harvest last the year.

Only now has a combination of drought and war forced people from their lands. The MNR's bloody campaign against Frelimo has paralysed the province's transport network, blocking the movement of food and trade in goats and cattle.

The mass exodus brought the situation to the world's attention. Administrative changeovers, appalling communications and a reluctance to admit the scale of the problem posed by the MNR, kept national government in the capital, Maputo, 1000 kms. to the sought, ignorant of the growing disaster.

In Zimbabwe plans to repatriate the migrants were recently reversed, as international funding was secured to build five new refugee centres in remote northern lands. The Zimbabwe Social Services Ministry aims to cater for 45,000 people for up to one year.

The new camps are being completed just as many refugees are returning to Tete in the hope of good rains next season, having lived nine months in makeshift shelters, dependent for food on the goodwill of local people and the efforts of voluntary organisations.

500. Masefield, G. B. *Famine : Its prevention and relief.* London, Oxford Univ. Press, 1963.

501. May, Brian. *Third World Calamity.* London, 1981.

502. Mayer, A. C. *Indians in Fiji.* London, Oxford Univ. Press, 1963.

503. Mayer, A. C. *Peasants in the Pacific : A study of Fiji Indian rural society.* London, Rontledge, 1961.

504. Mayer, A. C. History of Fiji. *Popular Science Monthly*, 1915.

505. Mayer, Jean. Coping with *famine Foreign Affairs* 53 (1) Oct. 1974.

506. Meillassouse, C. Development or exploitation : Is the Sahel famine good business ? *Review of African Political Economy* 1, 1974 ; 27-33.

507. Midha, Tania *et al.* Drought in India : Scorched earth *Telegraph* (Calcutta) 4 May 1986 ; 4-11.

508. Orissa : Drought and poverty : A report from Kalahandi *Economic and Political Weekly* 2 Nov. 1985 ; 1857-61.

509. Scott, E. *Ed. Before the drought.* Boston, Allen & Unwin, 1984.

510. Sen, A. *Poverty and famine.* Oxford, 1981.

511. Shiveshwarkar, Shyamala. Famine report. *Hindustan Times,* 15 Jun. 1986.

512. Summer rains, drought in Asia kill hundreds and derastate crops. *International Herald Tribune* 7th Aug. 1986 ; 6.

513. Venkatachary, R. Recurring drought : Need for permanent plan. *Deccan Herald* (Bangalore) 25 Oct. 1984 : 6.

In the current uncertain socio-political climate of ours the Orwellian perception of 1984 seems to have relevance since one is compelled to wonder whether the poignant human problem, drought, is a bane or a boon.

There can be little doubt that drought is an economically debilitating occurrence which turns crop lands into dusty bowls, dries up wells and canals, compels the victims to migrate to cities, deprives cattle of their fodder and diverts huge development resources to relies work.

Drought also provides some opportunity to score political points and denigrate those in power.

The controversies raised in the wake of drought do not strictly pertain to the measures to be adopted to prevent the tragic event or present permanent solutions to mitigate the sufferings of the victims.

Generally, they serve to confuse the issues. But then the steps taken generally by those in power to tackle drought are like a firefighting job i.e., allowing a grim situation to develop and frantically seeking ways and means to meet the challenge. Such rearguard actions, in fact, make a mockery of the claims of the State and Central Governments that the numerous programmes put in operation in the country are tuned to eliminate conditions leading to the occurrence of droughts.

The long-range remedial steps should naturally centre programmes for expanding irrigation potential, particularly minor irrigation, extensive use of ground water, mass bunding, introduction of drought resistance, short duration crops, contingent crops production plan, massive infrastructure development in the traditionally drought-hit areas, creation of fodder bank for cattle and foodgrain buffer stock in rural areas.

Apart from all these measures, the development of dry agriculture technology, post-harvest technology, and dairying is also necessary. One of the most important measures that commends itself in a perspective plan is the crop insurance scheme. The scheme, introduced in 1979, covers all the risks operating during the crop season and provides indemnity to all the insure farmers if the average yield of the area falls short of a guaranteed yield. The scheme was adopted by three States—Gujarat, Tamil Nadu and West Bengal during 1979 and 1980. Later 12 States, including Karnataka, also adopted the scheme. It is not clear how successfully and extensively the scheme has been implemented and to what extent the farmers have derived benefit during periods of drought. If the traditionally drought-prone States were to scientifically plan and adopt both short term and long term drought filthing programmers, there will be no need for them to carry the bagging bowl to the Centre seeking funds and succour.

Feudalism

514. Polanyi. K. Primitive feudalism and the feudalism of decaly. In *Economic development and social change* Ed. by G. Dalton. New York, 1971.

Food and Hunger

515. *Ad Hoc Consultation on world food scarcity.* Washington, World Bank, 1975.

516. Allen, G.R. *Impact of food aid on donor and other food-exporting countries.* Rome, FAO, 1965. p. 52.

517. Banerjee, Subrata. Food policy (of the World Bank). *New Age* (New Age) 22 Jun. 1986 ; 15.

An important aspect of the report on India presented by the World Bank to the Aid India Consortium is the re-commendation to reduce the growth rate target for food production in the seventh plan. This is to be done by reducing the farm profitability margin.

Our self-sufficiency in food is really marginal. We are pound of a surplus, when millions lack the purchasing power to buy food. If 700 million people had the purchasing power to buy 500 gm. of foodgrains per day, our immediate requirements would have been for nearly 160 million tonnes, taking into account the need for seeds and wastage.

Secondly, the World Bank wants us to export wheat. This is at a time when foodgrain prices have been falling on the international market. The objective is very clear. If we reduce the growth rate of our foodgrains production and export wheat we shall soon find ourselves with our begging bowls again.

This will be a wonderful opportunity for the transnational agro-business of the USA and some of the advanced capitalist countries of Europe to sell foodgrains to us and make profits.

This is not all. The World Bank is also against increasing the production of coarse grains and pulses which feed the poor. After all, our green revolution has primarily benefitted wheat and to a lesser extent rice. This is another reason why we have still miles to go to reach food self-sufficiency.

518. Bondestam, L. *Political economy of food : Proceedings of an international seminar.* Tampere, Peace Research Institute, 1976.

519. Bradley, P.N. Food production and distribution and huger. In *WIC*; 89-106.

520. Brown, Lester. R. *By bread alone.* New York, Prayer, 1974.

521. Chakravarty, S. and P.N. Rosenstein-Rodan. *Linking of food aid with other aid.* Rome, FAO, 1965. p. 39.

522. *Climate change, food production and interstate conflict.* New York, the Rockfeller Foundation, 1976.

523. Dandekar, V.M. and N. Rath. Imperative of hunger. *Financial Express* 3 Nov. 1982 ; 7.

524. Dandekar, V.M. *Uses of food surplus for economic development* Poona, Gokhale Institute of Politics and Economics, 1956.

525. De Castro, Josue. *Geopolitics of hunger.* New York, Monthly Review, 1977.

526. De Hevesy, Paul. *World Wheat planning and economic planning in general.* London, 1940.

527. Dessan, Jan. *Role of multilateral food aid programs.* Rome, FAO, 1965. p. 38.

528. *Development through food : A strategy for surplus Utilization.* Rome, FAO, 1962.

529. Drogat, N. *Challenge of hunger.* London, Burns and Oats, 1962.

530. Dumont, R. and N. Cohen *Growth of hunger : A new politics of agriculture.* London, Marion Bayara, 1981.

531. Eberstadt, Nick, Myths of the food crisis. *New York Review of Books* 19 Feb. 1976.

532. Ezekiel, Hannan, Food requirements. In *Second India Studies Overview.* New Delhi, Macmillan, 1978 ; 92-108.

533. Fitz genald, D.A. *Operational and administrative problems of food aid.* Rome, FAO, 1965. p. 63.

534. Food policy sell out. *Economic Weekly* 21 Nov. 1964.

535. *Food situation in India* : New Delhi, Ministry of Food and Agriculture, 1954.

536. *Fourth world food survey*, Rome, FAO, 1978.

537. Freeman, Oriville L. *World without hunger.* New York, Prayer, 1968.

538. George, S. *Feeding the few : Corporate control of food* : Washington, Institute for Policy Studies, 1979.

539. George, S. *How the other half dies : The real seasons for world hunger*, Penguin, 1976.

540. Gramling, Linda. Progress in food processing. *China Business Review* 13 (2) Mar.-Apr. 1986 ; 33-38.

541. Harris, N. *Of bread and guns : the world in economic crisis.* Penguin, 1983.

542. Hightower, P. *Eat your heart out : Food profiteering in America.* New York, Crown, 1975.

543. Hopkins, R. F. and D.J. Puchala. *Global Political economy of food.* Madison, Univ. of Winconsin Press, 1978.

544. Hunger amidst World plenty. *Patriot* 19 May 1982 ; 10.

545. Ignorance of hunger. *International Herald Tribune.* 26 May 1986 ; 4.

546. Increasing food security for poor. *Industrial Times* (Bombay) 31 Mar. 1986 ; 45.

The world has plenty of food, but some 700 million people in developing countries do not eat sufficiently well today to lead an active working life, and nearly half of them are acutely undernourished ; they barely subsist on a minimum survival diet.

The basic cause of hunger or food insecurity which affects almost a third of the population in the Third World, excluding China, according to a new World Bank report : Poverty and Hunger : Issues and Options for Food Security in Developing Countries, is poverty or lack of purchasing power. Hunger persists, even in countries that have reached self-sufficiency in food. Food insecurity cannot be eliminate without alleviating the poverty of countries and people. This is the central conclusion of the Report.

Economic growth will ultimately provide poor household with enough income to acquire enough food, and such growth should be a primary goal of economic policy. But growth will increase their purchasing power only slowly and may not reach everyone. In the long run, poverty alleviation linked with economic growth is the best way to reduce malnutrition and chronic food insecurity. But in the short run, specific programmes designed for the poor and malnourished, in cost-effective ways, are also needed.

A.W. Clausen, President of the World Bank, says in the Report : "The World Bank stands ready to help countries address their food security problem. It is also prepared to contribute resources. The alleviation of poverty and hunger are, after all, the primary purposes of economic development."

547. Joshi, Navin Chandra. Hunger persists amidst plenty, *Hindustan Times* 9 Apr. 1986 ; 19.

548. Kakudo, Kenichi. Stability and self-sufficiency : Japanese policy on food and agriculture. *Speaking of Japan.* Apr. 1986 ; 22-25.

549. Kirby, E. Stuart. *Food shortage. In Economic development in East Asia.* London, 1967 ; 42-60.

550. Kopi, Ocei. World food shortage can oyesters fill the gap ? *Baghdad Observer* 6 May 1986 ; 4.

551. Lappe, F.M. and J. Collins. *Food first.* London, Abacus, 1980.

552. Marching to 21st on empty stomachs. *New Age* (New Delhi) 3 Aug. 1986 ; 16.

In one year between 1984 and 1985, the number of registered unemployed in India has increased by three million – from 23.5 million to 26.3 million, a rise of 11.6 per cent. Vacancies are not being filled up and other avenues of employment are getting more and more restricted.

Prices are shotting up, making life of common people more miserable than ever before. Between June 1985 and June 1986 wholesale prices of essential commodities have gone up by 4 per cent.

All-India consumer price index number rose in March 1986 with 1970-71=100. Retail prices are rising steadily and sharply.

Government appears to be bent upon demolishing the public sector which has been serving the nations and the national economy. 'Gadgets' is the key word for everything. We seem to be marching towards the 21st century on futuristic planning virtually on empty stomachs.

No wonder, Rajiv Gandhi flared up when asked by CPI, Member of Parliament Indrajit Gupta to explain how the government had taken the same line as the Birlas and Bharat Rams to link interim relief to productivity as far as the Delhi textile workers were concerned.

He resorted to bluster and calumny against trade union leaders because he could not have honestly answered the most point.

553. Masefield, G.B. *Food and nutrition procedures in times of disaster.* Rome, FAO, 1967.

554. Mayer, Jean and Johanna Dwyer. *eds. Food and nutrition policy in a changing world.* New York, 1979.

555. Mckenzie, J.C. Poverty : Food and nutrition indices. In *COP*: 64-85.

One of the most difficult problems to deal with is one which a community does not believe exists. Such a statement in many ways summarizes the major difficulties concerning any evaluation of nutritional deficiencies in the affluent society. In developing countries there is no debate as to whether or not people are malnourished. This can be obviously and fairly simply demonstrated just by looking at the population and the conditions in which they have to live. In consequence the debate becomes one on the extent of the problem and the best ways of dealing with it. But in the so-called affluent world many are not prepared even to consider whether or not any problem of malnutrition still exists and certainly there is no longer very obvious visual evidence of chronic deficiencies to remind them. In this area, therefore, the major issue becomes one of isolating the key nutrition indices and of indicating in real terms the nature and extent of the problem, if indeed a problem exists. As such this chapter will be concerned primarily with isolating the indices, indicating limitations and pointing out the problems surrounding such measurements. They will be considered in the context of a study to assess whether or not there are any indications of malnutrition in the United Kingdom.

The economic and social history of the twentieth century paints a picture of substantial improvement for the community as a whole. Poverty and hardship for large sections of the population in the 1920s and 1930s was replaced in the 1950s and 1960s by full employment and the attractions of a 'boom' economy. I shall review the extent to which the nutritional status of the United Kingdom population has shown a similar improvement over the period. Such an investigation requires the collection and assessment of several types of evidence and I will examine each in turn. Inf rmation is required on the food consumption and nutrient intake of the population. Details of clinical examinations are needed to indicate the extent to which health has been affected by differing diets. The results of biochemical tests may be used to indicate the level of nutrient reserves within the body. The study of vital statistics and anthropometric data will demonstrate the impact of dietary variations. Too often in the past attempts have been made to investigate the nutritional status of a community using only one of these methods and unjustified deductions based on these findings have been published. Only after an examination of all these areas and their inter-relationship can an adequate assessment of nutritional status be made.

Evidence on the dietary intake of the population of the United Kingdom has rested mainly with the National Food Survey. This is a continuous sampling enquiry into the domestic food purchases of private households in Great Britain. A sample is selected by means of a three-stage stratified random sampling scheme. In 1964 the effective response rate was only 52 per cent. The housewife is asked to keep a record of the description, quantity and cost of food which enters the household during one week. Items such as soft drinks, icecream, alcohol and other items likely to be purchased by the other members of the family are not included.

556. Miller, D.S. and P. Mumford. *Getting the must out of food.* London, 1966.

557. O' Neill, Onora. *Faces of hunger : An essay on poverty, justice and development*. London, Allen & Unwin, 1986 ; p. 178.

558. Osam, P. *Accelerating food grain production in low-income food-deficit countries : progress, potentials and paradoxes*. Hanevil, East-West Center. May 1978.

559. Penn, J.B. *Food and agriculture policy challenge of the 1980's*. Washington, USDA, Jan. 1980.

560. Rai Chowdhari, Satyabrata. Twilight areas cry for food. *Tribune* 18 Apr. 1986 ; 4.

With the population growing by 3.2 per cent a year, the per capita food production falling sharply, the foreign debt rising to around $ 170 billion, the economies stagnating and civil conflicts persisting, Africa's 500 million people can look to the future only with apprehension.

"The harsh truth is that Africa today faces a crisis of unprecedented proportions," Mr. Robert S. McNamara, former World Bank President, said in a recent lecture in Washington.

The commission on World Hunger set up in 1978 by President Carter once declared that there should be a ban on "the use of starvation as a method of warfare". Yet, President Carter's first reaction to the Soviet presence in Afghanistan was to order an embargo on grain supplied to the Soviet Union.

A prominent Latin American journalist reported that the military rules of Argentina refused to join the embargo as a "lever to coax Washington into helping them suppress publication by the Inter-American Human Rights Commission of a list of tortures and assassinations". These are only two instances out of many to highlight the political dimensions of food.

561. Ramachandran, K.S. Food outlook for Asia. *Financial Express*. 28 Jul. 1986 ; 5.

The FAO forecast of world production of cereals in 1986 is 1.835 billion tonnes, a slight decline from the record of 1.844 billion tonnes in 1985. This is given in its Food Outlook, June 1986, While production of rice and wheat is expected to rise to 520 and 480 million tonnes, respectively, that of coarse grains is likely to fall by 4 per cent to 835 million tonnes. The forecast assumes normal weather for the remainder of the season.

On the basis of a large harvest and a high level of carryover stocks FAO projects a total supply of 2.066 billion tonnes, an increase of 3 per cent over last year's level. World trade in wheat and coarse grains might remain at the 1985 level of even fall slightly, with the major importing countries producing more.

Since the crop outlook in major exporting countries is favourable, exports might be well in excess of import demand, leading to depressed prices in international grain markets.

The estimate of closing stocks in December 1985, is now put at 390 million tonnes. This is considered a record, both in absolute terms and as proportion of expected consumption during the current year. While there has been some increase in stocks of major exporting countries, those held by developing countries are said to have fallen from 131 million tonnes at end 1984 to 127 million tonnes. Much of the decline occurred in China following a smaller cereal harvest in 1985.

The preliminary forecast of production of rice in the Asian regions for 1986 is 443 million tonnes, 4 per cent above the level of 1985. According to FAO, the planting of the early 1986 crops has, more or less, been completed and the harvesting of some of the crops has begun.

In China, heavy rainfall and above normal temperature have benefited the early and intermediate crops. With renewed official stress on raising overall cereal production, the paddy crop this year is likely to be significantly larger than last year's. An official survey of planted area indicates a big rise in plantings of paddy. This is in sharp contrast to 1985 when production fell due to a shift from paddy to cash crops and use of land by agriculturists for purposes other than farming.

In Vietnam, though the main crop now being sown is expected to be larger, any increase in production in 1986 over the previous year is considered unlikely. In Indonesia, a bumper harvest of the main crop is expected. FAO has made a similar assessment in respect of Malaysia. In Sri Lanka, however, the main crop has been seriously affected by the damage caused by floods.

562. Reultinger, Shlomo. Food Security and poverty in LDC's *Industrial Times* 18 Aug. 1986 ; 47-50.

The world has ample food. Global food production has grown at an even faster rate than the unprecedented population growth of the past 40 years. Prices of cereals on world markets have been even falling. Yet many poor countries—and hundreds of millions of poor people—do not share in this abundance. They suffer from lack of "food security", mainly caused by a lack of purchasing power.

Food security, though interpreted in many ways, is defined here as access by all people at all times to enough food for an active, healthy life. Its essential elements are the availability of food and the ability to acquire it. Conversely, food insecurity is the lack of access to sufficient food and can be either Chronic or transitory. Chronic food insecurity is a continuously inadequate diet resulting from the lack of resources to produce or acquire food. Transitory food insecurity, on the other hand, is a temporary decline in a household's access to enough food. It results from instability in food production and prices, or in household incomes. The worst form of transitory food insecurity is famine.

The costs of inadequate diets to individual families and to nations as a whole can be enormous. Inadequate diets increase people's vulnerability to diseases and parasites, reduce strength, curtail the benefits of schooling and training programmes, and result in a general lack of vigour, alertness, and vitality of the affected groups. Low productivity, due to inadequate "human capital," depresses output and hence income, making it more difficult for families and nations to extricate themselves from the cycle of poverty.

The level of food security to be achieved must be determined by individual countries. Their choice will be influenced by many, often conflicting factors. For example, cost-effective food security interventions can accelerate the rate of human capital formation required for economic growth. But attempting to reach the entire malnourished population too rapidly may entail such large costs and losses in resources efficiency that it will impair food security in the future.

563. Richards, P. People's Science : *Ecology and food production in West Africa*, London, Methnen, 1985.

564. Schneidar, Keith. Global demand for U. S. food falls Sharply. *International Herald Tribune* 21 Apr. 1986 ; 3.

565. Scott, John, *Hunger* : *Must we starve* ? New York Time, 1966.

566. Shanker, Vineeta. Dangers of global food politics. *Patriot* 29 Jul. 1986 ; 4.

Far more important than efficiency is the question of food security. Having accepted the framework of free trade, the Report makes a sweeping assumption that relations between nations are determined by economics alone, that politics has no róle to play. It, therefore, argues for food security in term of raising agricultural and not food production. In accordance with the law of comparative advantage, agricultural export production could be exchanged for food. In its scheme of things, food imports appear to be without political costs. Which is why it quotes approvingly a study by the International Food Policy Research Institute which has suggested that India could have achieved its stabilisation objectives at a third of the actual costs by increasing its reliance on international trade. A liberal import policy would have reduced the costs of carrying buffer stocks, it suggests.

On purely technical grounds, there is no doubt that India incurs high monetary costs in carrying large buffer stocks. But the question is whether it can rely on world trade without having to compromise her independence. We have a precedence of food aid under PL 480 which had to be given up because it involved unacceptable infringement of our sovereignty. The fact the surplus producers of foodgrains can and do impose economic sanctions against importing countries is no secret.

Can India afford to leave itself vulnerable to such pressures, given her external environment? Surely, this question of depleting buffer stocks through exports, as it is being argued in some quarters, and depending on crisis purchase of foodgrains, cannot be measured only in terms of dollars.

It would be naive to believe that the World Bank is not aware of the political compulsions for food self-sufficiency and food security. It, however, prefers to overlook them in its message for trade liberalisation. If taken seriously, surely this message could have dangerous implications for developing countries' sovereignty, integrity and independent development.

567. Singh, S. P. Requiem for the dying. *Congress Varnika International* (New Delhi) Sep. 1985 ; 80.

Demand for food is no revolutionary dalliance with Marxism, nor a challenge to the authority of the nations which produce enough foodgrains to feed the world on their own. The unsettled social and political conditions in Africa and Asia and their belligerence in World forums do not reflect their love for leftist ideology or capitalist infatuation but their impartience with their present miserable living conditions.

The recent FAO warning that about five lakh children will be dying per day in the hunger-belt, stretching from the Sahara to Saigon (now Ho Chin Minh City), even if the present rate of the 2 per cent growth of grain output continues, sounds quite catastrophic. But, this is no news. African has been the stamping ground of all colonial powers where slaves were traded, their women stripped and sold by the weight of their flesh. They were exported abroad to grow cotton. We all know it.

However, no country alone is to be blamed for African miseries. All imperial powers of the world will have to explain their conduct on the day of reckoning, if ever it comes. Now, Ethiopia is very much in the news because more people seem to be dying there than anywhere else in the world.

The fact of the situation is that the entire African continent owes its miseries to the conclave held in Berlin, 100 years ago, when diplomats of the West divided the continent into spheres of influence. And, thus, ushering an era of colonial rule whose effects are still seen across the starving countries.

It was at the Berlin conference that Africa was carved up by diplomats, with each of them fighting for his share in the plunder and loot. It was virtually a scramble for Africa in 1878 when great powers gathered at Berlin, then the capital of Prussia, to discuss the affairs of Turkey. While diplomats at the conclave made Romania, Serbia, and Bulgaria independent of the Turkish Sultan, Africa was permanently made slave.

And, after nibbling at the edges, the Europeans began to rush into the interior. Armed with superior weapons, the Bible and make shift treaties, imperial agents had laid claim to more than 25 million sq. km. of territory, inhabitated by more than 100 million black Africans. It was a chaotic process that plunged the European powers into war. Bismarck, who disliked disorder and wanted a piece of the spoils for Germany, decided to lay down some norms. His competitors, the French and the British, agreed to the idea of systematic exploitation of Africa.

Fourteen nations attended the Berlin conference which lasted for three months and Africa was divided amongst them. The only people which did not attend the conference were the African who surrendered their land and liberty in Berlin, without a shot being fired, or a man being killed. After the conference was over, Europeans came and assumed the command of the areas allotted to them according to the Bismarck compromise formula.

Africa of a century ago, consisted of several hundreds of independent states, large and small, weak and powerful. The diplomats at the conference condensed these states into 40 pieces of territories, without concern for homogeneity ethnic or racial, and a new Africa was created. It was not a clean job. Ethnic groups were cleaved into fragments—the Ovambo split in half by the boundary dividing Portuguese Angola from German South-West Africa, now Namibia. The Ibos and Yorubas of West Africa were combined with Muslim tribes of the north into a country that became the British-rules Nigeria, where rivalries set off the Biafran war, that is still continuing unabated. The Germans were given title to what became Tanganyika, not that they claimed it but the British wanted to placate Bismarck.

568. Sinha, G. N. *Introduction to food economics.* Allahabad, Kitab Mahal, 1956. p. 169.

569. Sinha, R. P. *Food in India.* Oxford, 1961.

570. Smil, Vaclay. Food in China. *Current History* Sep. 1978 ; 69-72, 82.

571. Sop, Li Gun. Dynamic efforts to solve food problem. *Korea Today* Apr. 1986 ; 43-44.

The non-aligned and developing countries are beding great efforts to develop agriculture.

They have backward agriculture left over by prolonged colonial rule, and because of the abnormal weather which has lasted in recent years, they are facing hardships in their endeavour for the solution of the food and agricultural problems.

Their serious shortage of food is shown by the data and reports prepared by the United Nations Conference on Trade and Development, the Food and Agriculture Organization and other UN specialized agencies. More than a billion people are starving throughout the world. Of them, six hundred millions are undernourished. This disaster takes place mainly in the developing countries, particularly in African countries.

Africa is inhabited by 514 million people or 11 per cent of the world's population, but produces only 3.5 per cent of the world's food output. This continent's average annual per capita consumption of food is 120 kg. This is less than a third of the world's average.

Taking advantage of this situation, imperialists try to meddle in the domestic affairs of the developing countries and dominate them by wiedling the "food weapon".

Developing agriculture to solve the food problem is the most important and urgent task confronting the non-aligned and developing countries, at present.

Today the non-aligned and developing countries give top priority to agriculture and the solution of the food problem and are exerting energetic efforts to develop agriculture.

572. Specially subsidised grains for poor. *Economic Times* (New Delhi) 25 Apr. 1986 ; 4.

Conceding that the recent hike in prices of certain essential commodities has affected people below the poverty line, minister of state for planning A. K. Panja told the Rajya Sabha today that food grains at "Specially subsidised rates" are being provided to them.

In a written reply, he stated that people living in tribal areas, pregnant women, young children and nursing mothers and those involved in various rural works programmes would get relief as a result of the supply of some essential commodities at specially subsidised rates.

The poverty line used in the Seventh Plan is the per capital monthly expenditure level of Rs. 107 in rural areas and Rs. 122 in urban areas at 1984-85 prices. This corresponds to the calorie requirements of 2400 per capital per day in rural areas and 2100 per capital per day in urban areas, the minister stated.

This poverty line would be updated for subsequent years by using the Central Statistical Organisation private consumption deflator (as a proxy for rise in the price of the consumption basket).

The estimates of poverty are based on the National Sample Survey (NSS) data on household consumption expenditure. The estimates for 1983-84 are based on the 38th Round of the National Sample Survey.

The next Survey will be undertaken only in 1988 or 1989 and, therefore, it is not possible at this stage to indicate the change in the number of persons living state to indicate below the poverty line.

The public distribution system is a permanent feature of the strategy to protect all consumers including poor families from hike in prices of essential commodities. Apart from this, the government has proposed various measures for the improvement of level of living of those below the poverty through distribution of foodgrains at concessional prices. These include programme for distribution of foodgrains, particularly, rice and wheat to the people in the Integrated Tribal Development Projects, expansion of the coverage of Rural Landless Employment Guarantee Programme and National Rural Employment Programme and for the nutrition.

572a. Srinivasa-Rajhavan, T.C.A. Question of hunger. *Indian Express* (New Delhi) 17 Apr. 1986 ; 6.

573. Tang, A. and B. Stone. *Food production in the People's Republic of China.* Washington, 1980.

574. Thavaraj. Foodgrains : The case for rationing. *Economic Weekly* 3 Oct. 1964.

575. Toynbee, Arnold. *Population and food supply.* Rome, FAO, 1959. (McDougall Memorial Lecture).

576. Trans-Atlantic food war. *International Herald Tribune* 10 April 1986 ; 6.

577. Varma, Kewal. Food and world Bank politics. *Mainstream* 28 Jun. 1986 ; 4-6.

The World Bank has launched a concerted attack on India's policy of food self-sufficiency. In its latest 1986 report, India : Economic Situation and Development Propects, the Bank has raised following major objections to India's agricultural strategy :

First, the foodgrain economy appears to be in considerable disequilibrium as evidenced by high grain stocks (23 million tons) and the seemingly limited options for disposing of surplus supplied.

Second, the 3.7 per cent growth target of the Seventh Plan may underestimate the difficulties of disposing of current surplus stocks through exports (markets are seak and India is a relatively high-cost producer) and through expansion of "Food for Work" programme at home (there are significant organisational impediments). The Bank has recommended "a somewhat lower target growth rate for foodgrains production."

Third, "the proposal to initiate procurement operations for oilseeds, pulses and other major crops which remain unprotected is worrisome." Providing stable and favourable returns for a range of crops through public procurement could saddle the country with a rigid pricing and production structure in which comparative advantage, whether for individual farmers or the economy as a whole, disappears from view.

The India Report was preceded by a World Bank policy study poverty and Hunger. This study became the basis of a seminar of policy-markers and opinion-makers held recently in the Capital. Some of the observations of the Study are :

—So far the progress in diminishing food insecurity has been disappointing partly because of the widely-held misconception that food shortages are the root of problem.

—Food self-sufficiency or a rapid increase in food production will not necessarily increase food security in a country, although these goals may be desirable for other reasons.

—There is no necessary link between national food self-sufficiency and food security. In fact, where a country cannot produce food efficiently, self-sufficiency can reduce a country's purchasing power and therefore its food security.

—There are two well-known difficulties in pursuing the objective of economic growth. First, economic growth takes time. Second, given the current distribution of assets and opportunities, even with economic growth a large number of poor people will increase their purchasing power only slowly and some will remain poor.

—In the shorter run, redistributing purchasing power and food itself among those who are undernourished can help, and the Government can do much to improve the food security of its people if programmes for redistribution are carefully designed and selected on the basis of cost-effectiveness.

—In most countries, the surest, and probably the cheapest, way to stabilise domestic food prices is through international trade.

—Some governments also keep excessive buffer stocks. Large stocks are seldom cost-effective because of high storage losses, low capacity utilisation of storage facilities and high interest charges tied up in inventories. Countries with access to foreign exchange will usually find it cheaper to stabilise prices by varying their exports and imports rather than by using buffer stocks even if world market prices are unstable.

There is an orchestrated attempt among influential indigenous sections to project this line. This year's theme paper of the National Council of Applied Economic Research titled, Focus on Some Major Imbalances in the Indian Economy for instance, attributed the reduction in the poverty rate in recent years entirely to anti-poverty programmes. The paper argued that the rate of growth in agriculture achieved in the Sixth Plan "cannot be bettered except marginally". Within this overall rate of growth of agriculture, the paper advocated a shift from food crops to non-food crops. It says "Large stocks of foodgrains with the Government over the last two years in a row alongwith the steep rise in the prices of oilseeds and pulses as well as imports of edible oils and sugar in the same period, suggest strongly that the output-mix of agriculture is not in consonance with the composition of demand".

This year's (1986) Budget was also cast under the shadow of this Philosophy. Thus, while the outlay in the Central Plan for agricultural developmental programmes was frozen, it was increased by 65 per cent for anti-poverty programmes.

Simultaneously, some influential economists in the Government have started lobbying that the food problem has now been solved and the Government should start dismantling the procurement system which has become a huge financial drain on the exchequer. This point of view was put forward at a meeting of senior economists in the Government held sometime back. This was followed by personal lobbying by economic advisers in the Prime Minister's Secretariat. Their argument is that having helped the farmers achieve a breakthrough in food production the Government can now leave them to cope with market forces on their own.

578. Venugopal, K.R. Foodgrains for the poor. *Indian Express.* 11 Nov. 1986 ; 6.

579. *World hunger-causes and remedies.* Washington, Institute for Policy Studies, 1974.

580. Yud Kin, J. and J.C. Mekenzie. *Changing food habits.* London, Machibbon and Kee, 1964.

Forestry

581. Greening helps. Gansu beat poverty. *China Daily* 10 Mar. 1986 ; 4.

Global Survey

AFGHANISTAN

582. *Afghan progress in the Fourth year of the plan.* Kabul, 1959. p. 88.

583. Goldren, Lee O. Afghanistan in 1985. *Asian Survey* Feb. 1986 ; 235-45.

584. Rupert, James. As village help fades, Afghan rebels stress mobility. *International Herald Tribune* 22 Jul. 1986 ; 4.

585. *Second Five Year Plan.* Kabul, Ministry of Planning, 1963, p. 98.

586. Tytler, William Kerr. *Afghanistan : A study of political developments in Central and Southern Asia,* London, Oxford Univ. Press, 1953.

AFRICA

587. Africa hard hit by economic crisis. *Secular Democracy* Jul. 1986 ; 25.

588. Africa may one day feed us all. *Congress Varnika International* (New Delhi) Sep. 1985 ; 42-43.

Twenty years ago, many Asian countries were also in crisis. They faced acute food shortages, even famine. Yet without much increase in acreage, wheat production in India increased nearly fourfold in 20 years, Indonesia increased rice production two and half times, from 10 million tonnes in 1970 to over 25 million in 1984. China's growth rate in food production has similarly been remarkable in recent years.

Despite continuing population increase in Asia, growth in food production is keeping ahead of population. In Africa, though it is repeatedly stressed that there is insufficient food, and population is outstripping increased yields. Why ?

Michael Pickstock asked if it was because Africa's main food crops, such as maize, millet, sorghum, cassava and yam had missed out on the research effort. In his reply, Dr. Swaminathan addressed this and other issues.

By no means, spectacular advances have been made in the developed countries with important African crops such as maize, sorghum and millet. Agricultural revolution in the United States started with hybrid maize. In its wake, it also revolutionized the production of other crops.

A farmer who has learned the value of good crop management, such as fertilizer application, water management and pest control in hybrid maize begins to apply these to other crops as well.

The wheat revolution was the trigger in the Punjab, for example, where we now see also a rice revolution and a potato revolution.

Once you have a catalyst for change in agriculture, the movement can be very rapid-unless, of course, the market is poor or prices unremunerative.

The improvement of sorghum and millet yield potential in the US is 25 years old. Seven to eight tons per hectare, in many cases, 10 tons for hybrid sorghum in the case of the so called master farmers.

The terrible irony is that wherever these crops are feed crops, they are improving, but in those places where they are food crops, they are stagnating.

589. Arkhurst, F.S. *ed. Africa in the seventies and eighties : Issues in development.* New York, Prayer, 1970.

590. Arnold, G. *Aid in Africa.* London, 1979.

591. Arnold, Guy. African development : New directions for the 1980's. *Africa Report* 26, May-Jun. 1981 ; 58-61.

592. Bachrach, P. and M.S. Baratz. *Power and poverty.* Oxford, 1970.

593. Barnes, Leonard. *African renaissance.* London, 1969.

594. Batten, T.R. Problems of *African development.* London, 1954.

595. Bretton, Henrz L. *Power and politics in Africa.* London, 1973.

596. Browne, G. Orde. *African Labourer.* London, Oxford Univ. Press, 1933.

597. Buell, R.L. *Native problem in Africa. 2 Vols.* Univ. of Cambridge, 1976.

598. Caldwell, J.C. *Africa rural-urban migration.* Canberra, Australian National University Press, 1969.

599. Carpenter, F.W. *Report of the committee on African Wages.* Nairobi, Govt. Printer, 1954.

600. Cleave, J. *African farmers : Labour use in the development of small-holder agriculture.* New York, Prayer, 1974.

601. Clifford, W. *Primer of social casework in Africa.* Nairobi, Oxford Univ. Press, 1966.

602. Coleman, J.S. Sub-Saharan Africa. In *Politics of the developing areas* by G.A. Almond and J.S. Coleman. Princeton, 1960 ; 271-75.

603. Davies, I. *African Trade Unions.* Harmondswarth, Pengwin Books, 1966.

604. Davis, J. Merle. *Modern industry and the African.* London, Macmillan, 1933.

605. Dirham, B. and C. Hines. *Agribusiness in Africa.* London, Earth Resources Research, 1983.

606. Dunn, John. *ed. West African States: Failure and promise* Cambridge, 1978 p. 259.

607. Faul, Michelle. Africa ; After drought the locusts. *Indian Express* 11 Aug. 1986 ; 6.

608. Gaudin, Bernand. Development projects in rural Africa : Two dynamics in conflict. *Development* (3-4) 1981 ; 39-45.

609. Generous World response to challenge in Africa. *Congress Varnika International.* (New Delhi) Sep. 1985 ; 28-29.

610. Ghai, Dharam and Samir Radwan. *Agrarian policies and rural poverty in Africa.* Geneva, ILO, 1983.

611. Gutkind, P. and I. Wallerstein *eds. Political economy of Contemporary Africa.* London, Sage, 1976.

612. Gutto, S.O.B. Law, rangelands, peasantry and social change. *Review of African Political Economy* 20, 1981 ; 41-56.

613. Harden, Blaine. Growing up hungry in Africa : the food can nourish, but there is never enough. *International Herald Tribune* 14 Jul. 1986 ; 1,6.

614. Heister, H. Social Welfare and African Development, *Applied Social Studies* 2, 1970, 81-89.

615. Hughes, C.C. and J.M. Hunter. Disease and development in Africa. *Social Science and Medicine* 3, 1970.

616. Hughes, John. *New face of Africa : South of the Sahara.* New York, Hugmans, 1961. p. 296.

617. Manghezi, A. *Class, elite and community in African development.* Uppsala, 1976.

618. Matheson, Alastair. Stowaways' bid to escape poverty. *Tribune* (Chandigarh) 12 Jan. 1984 ; 5.

Hundreds of jobless Africans are stowing away on ocean-going ships in the hope of finding work in Europe, West Asia and the USA.

Until recently, frontier controls in Africa were lax, enabling the people of poor countries to migrate to wealthier ones where jobs were easier to find. Recession has stopped that easy-going attitude.

Nigeria's recent mass deportation of nearly two million aliens was the dramatic culmination of a trend which has seen more and more African States blocking the way to foreign workers while they have mass unemployment at home.

As a result, the courts of the Kenyan seaport town of Mombassa are experiencing a rush of cases involving stowaways found in the harbour of Kilindini, hiding in ships' hold and engine rooms.

Many of these stowaways are from Tanzania, taking advantage of slack security precautions in the ports of Dar-es-Salaam. Zanzibar and Tanga to smuggle themselves on board ships bound for Europe or Gulf ports.

Recently two bedraggled youths, half-naked and smeared in oil, appeared before one Mombasa magistrate to be sentenced as stowaways.

Another three Tanzanian youth were not so lucky. They had succeeded in evading discovery while in port. But crawled out of their hiding places as the vessel began heading out to the sea from Mombasa to begin a voyage across the Indian Ocean.

The captain of the ship, which had a Far East registration, ordered them to be thrown overboard into the shark-infested waters. Two made it back to the shore. The third was drowned.

There are similar stories from most African port these days as desperation forces men and women to seek devious ways to better their lot. Young women seem to be far more fortunate, and usually find a friendly sailor or two to take pity on them and conceal them until the next port.

Those who evade discovery still have the final hurdle to pass at their eventual destination.

Those without proper papers can find themselves declared "stateless" with no country willing to take responsibility for them. Two men who stowed away on a Dutch ship in an Algerian port were refused entry in quick succession in Britain, Ireland and Portugal.

Then, when they resigned themselves to staying at home back in Algeria, they were turned away from Algiers by the authorities who claimed they had no documents to prove they were Algerian nationals.

One African country whose citizens took to the seas decades ago is Somalia, communities of Somalis, descendants the early migrants, are found today in such places as cardiff, Liverpool and other European ports, especially in Italy where ties with that country's colonial past still ensure a Somali better treatment than might be expected elsewhere.

Those African States with strong ties with the Arab world are able to offer their skilled jobless a better way out as emigrant workers in Saudi Arabia and other parts of the Gulf, where there is still employment to be had on construction projects.

The brain drain—as well as the muscle drain—in now so great that countries like Sudan are seriously questioning the wisdom of the contract labour system, in spite of financial advantages it gives to the individual and the State in the shape of foreign currency earnings.

Most Africans find conditions in the Muslim Gulf too austere compared to the convivial social (and night) life of their native countries.

619. Monod, T. *ed. Pastoralism in Tropical Africa.* London, Oxford Univ. Press, 1975.

620. Ominde, S.H. and C.N. Ejiogn *eds. Population growth and economic development in Africa.* London, 1972.

621. Panikkar, K.M. *Afro-Asian States and their problems.* London, Allen & Unwin, 1959.

622. Plan for Africa. *Indian Express* (New Delhi) 6 Jun. 1986 : 6.

The special UN General Assembly session which adopted a five-year $ 128-billion plan for Africa's development was the first ever of its kind to focus on the economic situation in a particular continent. The historical significance this lent to the occasion, however, was somewhat diminished by the fact that no firm financial commitment is available for the 1986-90 plan which commences this year itself. While the African countries are pledged to provide $ 82 billion under a plan adopted last year by the Organisation of African Unity (OAU), the international community, which is expected to provide the remaining $ 46 billion, has not gone beyond committing itself, through the final document, to "making every effort to provide sufficient resources to support and supplement the African development efforts". Particularly unfortunate has been the attitude of rich nations. Their representatives who addressed the session were not only unwilling to make any specific financial pledges but, with the exception of Canada, Denmark and the Netherlands, even to grant any major concession in respect of debt repayment by the African countries.

Their response is not entirely surprising. The role the United States and Britain have recently played in frustrating UN efforts to end apartheid in South Africa through economic sanctions is well known. What these other rich countries overlook is the fact that peace and prosperity are indivisible and the world cannot be at peace when a whole continent like Africa south of the Sahara is racked by poverty and conflict. One hopeful sign is the growing awareness by the people of their responsibility towards fellow humans, which has produced two outstanding gestures—the "Race Against Time" this year and "Live Aid" last year. But that is obviously not enough and one awaits the day when the pressure of public opinion will change Government policies. Meanwhile, Third World countries have to make a serious effort. As the resolution stated, economic and technical co-operation among themselves could be a key element in Africa's economic recovery. The problem of ecological degradation leading to declining agricultural productivity, the rapid growth in population and distress migration caused by famine and civil strife have combined to aggravate a difficult situation. The General Assembly resolution should signal a global effort to mount a Marshall Plan-type of development effort for the reconstruction of Africa.

623. Post, Ken. *New States of West Africa*. Harmondsworth ; 1968.

624. Power, Jonathan. Africa : Can voluntarism fill the gaps ? *International Herald Tribune* 30 May 1986 ; 6.

625. Power, Jonathan. Listen to Africa's heart beat before rushing into advise. *International Herald Tribune* 16-17 Aug. 1986 ; 5.

626. Rodney, Walter. African Slavery......*Journal of African History* 2(3) 1966.

627. Rodney Walter, *How Europe under-developed Africa.* Dar-es-Salaam, Tanzania Publishing House, 1972.

628. Sandbrook, R. *Politics of basic needs : Urban aspects of assaulting poverty in Africa.* London, Heinemann, 1982. p. 256.

629. Shaw, Timothy M. *ed. Alternative futures for Africa.* Boulder, Westiview, 1982.

630. South of Sahara, the riches and poverty. *New Wave* (New Delhi) 26 Oct. 1986 ; 8-9.

631. Sule, Surekha, Poverty : In Asia and Africa. *Economic Times* (New Delhi) 26 Jun. 1986.

632. Todaro, Michael P. Income expectation, rural-urban migration and employment in Africa. *International Labour Review* 104 (5) 1971 ; 387-414.

633. Taber, Jane. Aid programme that made millions hungry. *Pioneer* 3 Jun. 1984.

As the drought continues its relentless charge through Africa's Sahel region leaving mass starvation in its wake, development officials are begining to realise there is more to the drought than simply the weather.

Officials of the aid agencies UNICEF and Oxiam recently looked behind the weather and found that problem of food distribution allocation of financial resources, concentration on exporting crops rather than domestic production, and government shortsightedness were the main factors in making a fairly serious situation even worse.

As Alan Grainger of Oxford University wrote a couple of years ago : "Drought triggers a crises, but does not cause it".

The eight countries of the Sahel-Niger, Chad, Upper Volta, Mauritania, Senegal. The Gambia, Cape Varde and Mali—should be used to and prepared for drought by now. They have not seen rain for the past two years. And ten years ago the area suffered one of the most severe droughts in memory.

From 1968 to 1973 the rains failed leaving an estimated 50,000 to 150,000 people dead. Donor countries contributed $ 7.45 billion in aid to the region for a five-year period from 1975 to 1980.

But the Sahel countries, with the exception of Niger, do not seem to have learned from the drought experience. In fact this year the Food and Agriculture Organisation appealed for a million tonnes of food aid, the largest amount ever requested for the region.

634. Tianxi, Wu and Li Zhengdong. Africa stresses solving grain problem. *Beijing Review* 6 Jun. 1983 ; 14-16.

635. United Nations Declaration on the critical economic situation in Africa. *Congress Varnika International* (New Delhi) Sep. 1985 ; 2.

1. We the States Members of the United Nations express our deep concern at the profound economic and social crisis that Africa is experiencing. Over the last few years the situation has assumed alarming proportions, seriously jeopardizing not only the development process but, more ominously, the very survival of millions of people.

2. We are alarmed by the spectre of widespread famine hanging over many African countries. Over 150 million people are facing hunger and malnutrition. Prolonged unprecedented drought, accelerating desertification and other natural disasters have compound as already serious situation, dislocating normal life all over the continent. Alarming shortages of food and water supplies and the depletion on livestock have led to the displacement of million of people within and across borders.

3. Africa, despite its enormous potential remains the least developed of all continents, lagging far behind by every economic indicator.

4. Furthermore, the international economic environment continues to affect developing countries adversely, and, particularly, it had a devastating impact on the already fragile African economies.

5. We are aware that African countries recognize they have the primary responsibility for their development and for addressing the present crisis. They have therefore undertaken and continue to undertake painful adjustment measures at very high social and political costs.

6. We agree that in confronting the challenge of development, policies and measures, such as those outlined in the Lagos Plan national

of Aetion for the Implementation of the Monrovia Strategy for the Economic Development of Africa and the Special Memorandum on Africa's Economic and Social Crisis adopted by the ECA Conference of Ministers, provide a framework for national and sub-regional action and international support.

7. We recognize that, in view of the high priority attached by African Countries to food and agriculture, the first urgent task is the early attainment of national and collective self-reliance in food production.

8. Africa is experiencing a very serious debt problem, repayment and servicing of which is taking a very high percentage of already reduced export earnings. The problem is further exacerbated by factors such as deteriorating terms of trade, decline in concessional flows in real terms and increased use of short term commercial credit. Without an increase in net capital inflows and urgent debt relief measures, prospects for recovery and development in Africa will be undermined.

9. Bilateral and multilateral creditors should take concerted measures to ease the debt burden of African countries. For official and officially-guaranted debt, total or partial conversion of official development assistance (ODA) debts into grants, longer maturities and grace periods, lower or concessional interest rates and extended multi-year rescheduling are among the measures to be dealt with urgently within the framework of close consultation with each of the debtor countries concerned, as well as any other measures to be agreed upon.

10. We recognize that African countries, in view of their heavy dependence on concessional financial flows and their limited access to alternative sources of external finance, require a substantial and sustained increase in the volume of these flows through bilateral donors and multilateral channels for development finance and technical co-operations.

11. The heavy dependence of African countries on the export of a few primary commodities renders them particularly vulnerable to the sharp price fluctuations that result in drastic shortfalls in export earnings. Urgent action is therefore needed to stabilize commodity prices on longterm trends and to improve and increase the use of compensatory financing arrangements for export earnings shortfalls, such as the Compensatory Financing Facility of the International Monetary Fund.

12. We urge all organs, organizations and bodies of the United

Nations system to give greater attention to Africa and to continue to mobilize resources to assisting African countries in dealing with the current crisis and its longer-term ramifications.

636. Wallerstein, F. Dependence in an interdependent World. *African Studies Review* 17 (9) 1974; 1-26.

637. Yucheng, On Africa : Poorest countries, largest debts. *Beijing Review* 20 Aug. 1984; 10.

638. Zheng, Yan. Africa efforts to fight serious drought. *Beijing Review* 5 Nov. 1984; 15.

AFRICA, EAST

639. Brett, E.A. *Colonialism and underdevelopment in East Africa.* London, Heinemann, 1973.

640. Hill, Althea. Fertility of the Asian Community of East Africa. *Population Studies* 29 Nov. 1975; 355-72.

ALGERIA

641. Algeria. *Beghdad Observer* 25 Apr. 1975; 3,7.

642. Chopra, V.D. Algeria. *Patriot* 15 Jul. 1972; 4.

643. Gillespie, J. *Algeria, rebellion and revolution.* London, Berlin, 1960.

644. Kaul, Z.L. Algerian Socialism. *New Wave* (New Delhi) 20 Jun. 1976; 8-9.

The disabled population is at the end of the labour queue in all lands and at all times including that of India. In the circumstances competitive employment is a distant unattainable goal. Most ever mentally and physically handicapped, therefore, need special arrangements for preparing them for entry into labour market. Advanced countries have solved the problem by establishing a network of sheltered workshops They are truly the last resort for giving employment to physically handicapped with serious loss of functions. They focus on unskilled, labour-intensive work after proper training such as packaging, bench assembly, collecting, mail sorting, stuffing, mechanical assembly, wood working, metal-working, inspection, custodial work, manufacturing jobs, reclamation, salvage operation etc. India has not yet experimented in this field. Sheltered workshops are indeed indispensable and will go a long way in ameliorating the difficulties of handicapped for these are the final major component of the rehabilitation system and provide employment for those who have few options in the competitive labour market. Sheltered workshops are thus not only the employers of last resort but also a source of service for those most in need-welfare for workfare in its true sense. The magnitude of services rendered by sheltered workshops will be obvious by the fact that they employed nearly 1 million separate clients during the last decade in U.S.A. While the manpower and veteran's programme together reached about 500,000 handicapped in the same duration.

The government must, however, be cautious from the very beginning to see that the employment programme designed for the disabled may not become employment programme for the able-bodied workers. It is suggested that the ratio of the staff in sheltered workshops must be 50:50 between disabled and ablebodied workers, and that, they must work on the principle of industry and commercial establishments. The products and services created by these workshops be subsidised by Government of India to make them competitive and be sold on the pattern of Khadi Gramodyog. These workshops must also provide non-vocational services to the clients like developing skills of independent living—such as personal hygiene, speech therapy, homemaker training, training in mobility, adult education, psychotherapy, transportation, housing and homebound employment. Such services by sheltered workshops will go a long way in inculcating a sense of workfare and will wean them away from public relief and charity. The private sector employers can do a wonderful job by providing suitable placements to the physically handicapped in their industrial and business establishments.

The corner-stone of Algeria's economy is oil and natural gas. The recent hike in the oil prices has brought the country an economic boom. This industry is completely in government hands as are foreign trade and transport. There is very little foreign investment. Agriculture has been reorganized on co-operative and collective basis. The first three year plan (1967-70) was formulated in 1966. It was followed by the first four year plan in 1970. The current four year plan covers the period between 1974 and 1977. The plan envisages an investment of 110 billion Algerian Dinars (Rs. 22000 crores) compared to DA 30 billion (Rs. 6000 crores) in the 1970-73 plan.

The first two plans did not fully achieve the targets. The Algerians are frank enough to admit that the first plan objectives were achieved to the extent of only 65 per cent, and of the second plan only 75 per cent. When I asked the Director of Planning for the reasons for the failure to achieve the targets, he replied. "Perhaps, we Algerians want to achieve too high targets in a short time."

The main thrust of the current plan is on the manufacturing sector and on articles of domestic consumption. For instance, the emphasis is on production of tractors and motor-cycles, and not on cars or luxury goods. The National Motor Vehicle Company (SONA-COME) created in 1967 near Constintine, has set up a modern factory with West Germany collaboration; this has an annual capacity of 9500 engines and 4000 tractors. In the next few years, production will be doubled by introducing a second shift. In order to prevent concentration of industries in one area, the government has disposed other industries in different areas.

One of the problems facing the planners in Algeria is regional development. Four fifths of the country is covered by desert and is therefore, very sparsely populated. Settlements are only around the oases. There is a natural tendency among the people of the desert to migrate to the fertile area, just like in Egypt, where on an average 6000 people come daily to Cairo, in search of livelihood. To stop this migration, the planners have made determined efforts to set up agriculture based industries in the desert area, to dissuade the people from migrating to the cities.

Algeria is not self-sufficient in food production. Irrigation facilities are meagre, and vast areas of land are used for cultivation of grapes from which wine is made. But export of wine has declined, because France which has mounting stocks of its own wine refused to buy Algerian wine. The Algerian government has, therefore, decided to reduce the area under grape cultivation and instead grow cereals. At present the government buys food-grains mostly from Canada against cash payment.

Because of its vast developmental programmes, the country is experiencing inflation. But that is natural in any developing economy. Large loans have been taken from the World Bank and other European countries. But Algeria's economic future is bright. It is estimated that Algeria has a total of 300 billion cubic meters of natural gas, which is 11 per cent of the world's known reserves. At present the bulk of the natural gas is being bought by the USA. There are plans to build two underwater pipelines across the Mediterranean sea to transport gas to Europe. One pipeline will carry gas to Italy; the work on the Sicily side has been completed. The other pipe line will take the gas to Spain. By 1980-82, between 30 and 50 billion cubic metres of gas will be exported to USA, Italy, France and other European countries every year.

Algerians welcome foreign investment, but without any political strings. They say it will only be a commercial deal. The Soviet Union has built a steel plant near Oran. The Chinese have set up a procelean factory. Italy and West Germany have also collaborated in a number of industries. Our own Tatas are about to sign a contract worth Rs. 2 crore for setting up an electric sub-station.

The volume of trade between Algeria and India has been small. Last year it was worth only Rs. 20 lakhs: Various reasons are cited for this low figure. One is that Algerians are used to French specifications, and secondly, the Suez Canal's closure was a factor inhibiting the flow of goods. But now things are gradually changing. With the signing of the trade agreement between the two governments, trade is bound to grow this year. Already an order for 700 tons of tea has been placed with India. Non-traditional items like engineering goods, chiefly diesel pumps are also in demand. Indian manufacturers are surveying the field. When the President's press advisor, Dr. Amimour referred to exchange of goods between India and Algeria, I asked him, "What will we get in return for our tea?" Prompt came the reply, "Algeria, Wine." I said, "We are a prohibitionist country. We don't want wine." He laughed, and said that perhaps we could take other products.

645. Knapp, Wilfrid. Boumedienne's Algeria. *Statesman* 21 Nov. 1974; 6.

646. Ould-Rouis, Bachir, Algeria. *National Herald* (New Delhi) 1 Nov 1968; 5.

647. Zinin, Y. and V. Shelepin. Algeria Looks ahead, *New Times* (Moscow) 27 Jul. 1974; 20-21.

ANTIGUA

648. World Bank. *Antigua and Barbuda : Economic Report*. Washington, 1985. p. 90.

ARGENTINA

649. Ferrer, Aldo. *Argentine economy*. Berkeley, 1967.

650. Potash, R. *Army and politics in Argentina, 1928-1945*. Stanford, 1969.

651. Robles, Juan, Austral Plan austerity, unemployment and a wage freeze. *International viewpoint* 9 Dec. 1985; 25-26.

652. Rowe, James L. Treating Argentina's old ailment. *International Herald Tribune* 18 Jul. 1986; 11.

ASIA

653. Alvarez, F.C. *New horizons for the third world.* Washington, Public Affairs Press, 1976.

654. Angeleponlors, Angelos T. *Third world and the rich countries : prospects for the year 2000.* New York, Prayer, 1972.

655. Asean in the shadow of poverty and military control. *Far Eastern Economic Review* 3 Apr. 1986; 51-60.

656. *Asian development in the 1980s: Growth, employment and working conditions*, Geneva, ILO, 1980.

657. Brecher, Michael. *New States of Asia.* New York, Oxford Univ. Press 1963.

658. Brundtland, Gro Hartem. Helping the poor nations in ways that last. *International Herald Tribune* 23 Sep. 1986; 4.

659. Clausen, A.W. Poverty in the third world. *Financial Express* 4 Feb. 1985; 5.

660. Dasgupta, Jyotirindra. Development and poverty reduction in South Asia. *Journal of Asian Studies.* 42 (1) Nov. 1982 ; 105-118.

661. East, W. Gordon and O. H. K. Spate *eds. Changing map of Asia.* London, Methuen, 1953.

662. Etienne, Gilbert. *Rural development in Asia,* London, Sage, 1986. p. 270.

663. Frank, Andre Gunder. *Crisis in the Third World.* New York, 1981.

664. Garzonzi, Eva. *Economic growth and development : The less developed countries.* New York, Vintage Press, 1972.

665. Ginsburg, N. S. *Asia in modern world.* New York, 1963.

666. Gupta, Pranay. This is the week for a new development agenda. *International Herald Tribune.* 29 Sep. 1986 ; 4.

667. Haq, Mahbubul. *Poverty curtain. Choices of the third world.* Columbia University Press, 1976.

668. Harrison Paul. Inside the third world. *Development and Cooperation* (2) Mar.-Apr. 1980 ; 20-23.

669. Harrison, Paul. *Third world tomorrow*, Brighton, Penguin, 1980.

670. Hermassi, Elbaki. *Third world reassessed.* Berkeley, 1980.

671. Host-Mudsen, Poul. How much capital flight from developing countries. *Finance and Development 2* (*1*) Mar. 1967.

672. Islam, Rizwanul, *ed. Strategies for alleviating poverty in rural Asia.* Bangkok, ARTEP, 1985. p. 327.

673. Khan, A. R. and Eddy. Lee *eds. Poverty in rural Asia.* Bangkok, ILO, ARTEP, 1984.

674. Lack of credit deepens rural poverty in Asia. *Newstime* 27 Jul. 1985 ; 12.

675. Lagos. G. *International stratification and underdeveloped Countries*, Chapel Hill, 1963.

676. Leys, C. *Politics and change in developing countries.* Cambridge, 1969.

677. Lin, Ching-Yuan. *Developing countries in a turbulent world : Patterns of adjustment since the oil crisis.* New York, Prayer, 1981.

678. Mountjoy, A. B. *Third world : Problems and perspectives.* London, Macmillan, 1978.

679. Myrdal, Gunnar. *Asian drama : An inquiry into the poverty of nations.* New York, 1968.

680. Nyun, U. Economic cooperation in Asia. *In Economic development.* Bombay, para, 1966 ; 94-100.

681. Preecha, Suchin. Rural poverty in Asia. *Pioneer* 23 Jul. 1985 ; 6.

Rural poverty remains widespread in the Asia-Pacific region because credit is virtually denied to million of small farmers and landless labourers who need it most.

The lack of credit also helps explain the slow progress of rural development in the region, according to the UN Economic and Social Commission for Asia and the Pacific (ESCAP). A study discovered that production loans at reasonable or legal rates of interest are inaccessible to the small farmers and landless workers.

The absence of such credit also underscores as the "loan sharks" dominate the financial picture in the villages, although usury is outlawed in all countries of the region.

Dominance of loan sharks as a source of credit needed by the small farmers and village entrepreneurs keeps them chained to poverty and also slow down if not snag efforts at rural development, said ESCAP. Of the estimated 2.6 billion population of the region 76 per cent live in the rural areas "amidst widespread poverty".

"Many millions are in desperate need of credit with which they can farm viably or be self-employed in agricultural processing, trade and servicing of farm equipment and other occupations," ESCAP observed.

It also noted that while Asia-Pacific governments are starting to give attention to the credit needs of their rural poor, the volume has failed to loosen the grip of the loan sharks in the villages.

ESCAP said scarce government resources are part of the reason behind inadequate production loans for the rural poor. But there are other causes as well like blast of most lending institutions in favour of big farmers.

While governments have started recognising the counter-productive effects of such a bias on part of the banks, ESCAP pointed out that measures adopted to correct it have not been successful. This is because big farmers are often economic and political powers in their respective localities and that some have influence which extends to the national leadership.

Thus, the big farmer blas of most lending institutions in the region in helping widen the "gap between the well-off and the poor in the rural communities," ESCAP warned.

Another aspect of the credit problem for the rural poor found by ESCAP "is how to reconcile the need to provide adequate credit at reasonable interests to small farmers with the high cost of administering a large number of small loans."

ESCAP also reported that if subsidy strategy adopted by some governments to solve the credit problem of the rural poor often does not work or seldom live up to expectations. In most cases, benefits go to the big farmers because the poor farmers are effectively shut off from production loans.

There have been instances when subsidised credit did reach the small farmers. But one of the consequences was a high rates of default on part of the borrowers due to defective implementation.

What is needed is a fresh approach to the problem, said ESCAP, citing Bangladesh as an example through its Grameen Bank (GB) system.

682. Robertson, R. and A. Tndor. Third World and international stratification : theoretical considerations and research findings. *Sociology* Jan. 1968.

683. Rothstein, Robert, L. *Weak in the world of the strong : the developing countries in the international system.* Columbia University Press, 1977.

684. Sachs, Ignaey. *Discovery of the third world.* Cambridge, 1976.

685. Singh, Mahinder Santokh. Industrial dynamics of newly industrializing countries in East and Southeast Asia : A real path towards a new international economic order. In *IDPR* ; 283-310.

686. Steadman, John M. Myths of Asia. *American Scholar* Spr. 1961.

687. Sule, Surekha. Poverty : In Asia and Africa. *Economic Times* 26 Jun. 1986.

The incidence of poverty in Asia and African countries has been assuming serious proportions during the past couple of years. The poor are getting poorer, even in developing countries with fairly high growth rates. Some Asian countries like Philippines, Thailand, Indonesia, Malaysia have seen their economics growing rapidly over the past two decades, and yet continue to grapple with problems of skewed income distribution and mass poverty.

In many developing countries, the income of the poorer groups have suffered an erosion for three main reasons. First, it is due to the slow pace of labour absorption from agriculture into other sectors. Second, those in the lowest quintile of the income distribution have limited access to both human and physical capital. And third, a large proportion of the rural population has limited access to available land.

It is in Africa—especially in Sub-Saharan countries—that the poverty has been aggravated by the dangerous ill effects of natural disaster, such as in Ethiopia in the aftermath of the famine havoc. A developed nation on the other hand, could better cope with crises of this sort. This implies that these African countries are more vulnerable due to their poverty and the impact of such calamities is to accentuate their poverty. This is the vicious circle.

The per capital incomes in 29 Sub-Saharan countries are among the lowest and as a result of then, farm failures, their current per capita output would be lower than that in 1960 and their current per capita income would be 20 to 30 per cent lower than in 1970, because the overall growth rates have been dismal (Table 1).

Though food production in famine-stricken Africa has recovered dramatically in the current year, the chronic problem remains and some 18 million people will suffer from hunger, malnutrition and disease this year.

Some 21 African countries having 200 million or 40 per cent of the continent's population were identified by Food and Agricultural Organisation (FAO) as facing severe food shortage in 1985. Lives of over 30 to 35 million people in these countries were severely threatened and more than 10 million people have left homes in search of food. Africa was estimated to need 7 million tonnes of food imports during 1985-86 at a cost of emergency of US $ 1.5 billion.

But the fact is different. Though 7 million tonnes of food aid for 21 African countries may be a gross underestimate, the gap between the food required and food grown by them is 12 million tonnes. Again, of the 7 million tonnes of requirement, estimated 5.5 million tonnes of food were promised of which only 3.9 million tonnes were delivered. This means only 3.9 million tonnes out of the 12 million tonnes of food requirement became available i.e. only one-third of the food deficit could be met.

Apart from the far too inadequate food supplies, the food aid was late in reaching the recipient, that is after the pressing need is over. In fact, food aid harms rather than helps when it is delivered behind schedule and at times disturb the recipient country's food plans. Last year, the donated food grains had no room for storage because by the time they arrived, the good rains brought bumper harvest and the warehouses were full to the brim. Under such circumstances, the food rots and is wasted or at time even gets consumed causing more harm.

The hungry rarely get food when they need it, and when it comes, it amounts to oversupply affecting adversely the prices paid to the domestic farmers. Another problem pertains to the transport of grain to the affected areas which are in the interior, with the result, the food rots at the port.

688. Third world warms against poverty. *Patriot* 28 Sep. 1984 ; 4.

689. Ul Haq, Mahbub. *Poverty curtain : Choices for the Third World.* New York, Columbia University Press, 1976.

690. Wint, Guy. *British in Asia.* London, Faber and Faber, 1947.

ASIA SOUTH

691. Raychaudhuri, Tapan. Historical roots of mass poverty in South Asia *Economic and political weekly* 20 (18) 4 May 1985 ; 801-6.

The contemporary phenomenon of underdevelopment is not a continuation of the traditional economic order of pre-modern times. The patterns of economic organisation and levels of economic performance in the traditional societies of Asia, before they were enmeshed into the international economy created by first the merchant and later the industrial capitalism of western Europe, were significantly different from their contemporary counterparts.

In the case of India, the pre-colonial economy in its normal functioning did not generate large groups of half-starving people. The author traces the roots of mass poverty in India, as we know it today, to the new institutional framework of agriculture introduced after 1813 which deprived small holders, both tenants and proprietors, of nearly all their surplus, if it did not actually reduce them to landlessness.

Not only the new institutional arrangements, but even the positive developments in agriculture augmented the traditional disparities of India's agrarian society. Thus development of a market for cash crops implied a change in the ratio of non-food crops to food crops until, with increases in population, the output of foodgrains per head of population declined quite sharply. And where irrigation provided the means of increasing productivity, those in control of large holdings tried and increased their holdings, often at the cost of the poorer agriculturists.

The all-too-familiar phenomenon of today's mass poverty was

thus already an established fact of life by the time population began to increase at a steady pace. Thereafter, given the pyramidal structure of rural society, there was a concentration of the increasing numbers in the lower rungs, until the very poor accounted for a half or more of the rural population.

The approach and method adopted in this essay are very much those of what is now described as 'old economic history'. This implies an emphasis on the qualitative rather than the quantitative, on arguments historical rather than economic in their essence. Of course, any such distinction is, beyond a point, artificial. The reason for this preference goes beyond deficiencies in one's training which are considerable. Where quantitative data are not available—on such crucial matters as national income and population—the attempt to squeeze the blood of aggregated series from the stone of fragmentary evidence is more courageous than prudent. Secondly, this paper is an attempt to present in a few pages the main ideas in what, hopefully, will emerge some day as a medium-sized volume. Some of the statements are hence in the nature of shorthand : the very considerably differences over space and time are 'de-emphasised' and the focus is on the uniformities rather than the variations without, one hopes, distorting the essential historical reality. Finally, the imprecision which marks most of the statements which follow is not accidental. It represents what, to my understanding, is the closest approximation to our present level of knowledge and possible perception.

ASIA, SOUTHEAST

692. Mehmet, Ozay *ed. Poverty and social change in Southeast Asia*, Ottawa, University of Ottawa Press, 1979. p. 288.

ASIA, WEST

693. Asad, T. *Kababish Arabs*. London, C. Hurst, 1970.

694. Arab World faces heavy debt burden. *China Daily* 6 Jul. 1986 ; 4.

695. Yanchun, Shi. Arab countries strive for grain self-sufficiency, *Beijing Review* 25 Jul. 1983 ; 12-13.

AUSTRALIA

696. Barnard, M. F. *Australian Outline*. Sydney, 1943.

697. Borrie, W. D. *Immigration : Australia's problems and prospects*. Sydney, 1949.

698. Brigden, J. B. *Escape to prosperity*. Melbourne, 1930.

699. Bunning, W. *et. al. Housing problem in Australia*. Sydney, 1947.

700. Camenon, R. J. Immigration and labour *Australian Quarterly* Mar. 1950.

701. Carr-Saunders, A. M. *National income of Australia. London*, Angue and Robertson, 1938.

702. Clark, C. and J. G. Crawford. *National Income of Australia*, Sydney, 1958.

703. Copland, D. B. *Australian economy*. Sydney, 1947.

704. Eggleston, F. W. *et. al. Australian standards of living*, Melbourne, 1939.

705. Fighting war and poverty in 1985. *International Viewpoint* 25 Feb. 1985 ; 24-25.

706. Fisher, H. G. B. Crisis and readjustment in Australia. *Journal of Political Economy* 42, Dec. 1934.

707. Fitzhardinge, I. F. Immigration policy. *Australian Quarterly* Jun. 1949.

708. Fitzpatrick, B. C. *Australian people 1788-1945*. Melbourne, 1946.

709. Fitzpatrick, B. C. *British Imperialism and Australia, 1783-1823*. London, 1939.

710. Giblin, L. F. Australia in the shadows. *Australian Quarterly* Dec. 1933.

711. Grattan, G. H. *ed. Australia*. Berkeley, 1947.

712. Greenwood, Gordon *ed. Australia*. London, Angus and Robertson, 1955. p. 445.

713. Harris, H. L. *Australia's national interests and national policy*. Melbourne, 1938.

714. Holt, H. E. *et. al. Australia and the migrant*. Sydney, 1953.

715. Holt, H. E. *Australian production at the crossroads*. Sydney, 1952.

716. Ingleton, G. C. *ed. True patriots all*. Sydney, 1952.

717. Langmore, John and David Peetz *eds. Wealth, poverty and survival : Australia in the world.* Sydney, Allen & Unwin, 1983. p. 225.

718. Laseron, C. F. *Face of Australia.* Sydney, 1953.

719. Lyons, J. A. National plan and after. *Australian Quarterly* Sep. 1931.

720. MacLaurin, W. R. *Economic planning in Australia, 1929-36.* London, 1937.

721. *Peopling of Australia.* Melbourne. University Press, 1933.

722. Portus, G. V. *Australia.* Sydney, 1933.

723. Stevens, B. S. B. Imperial economic development. *International Affairs* (U. K.) Nov. 1936.

724. Tennant, K. *Australia : Her Story.* London, 1953.

725. Wadham, S. M. *Land and the nations.* Melbourne, 1943.

726. Walker, E. R. *Australia in the world depression.* London, 1933.

727. Walker, E. R. *Australian economy in war and reconstruction,* New York, 1947.

728. Walker, E. R. *Unemployment policy : With special reference to Australia.* Sydney, 1936.

729. Walsh, Maximilian. Testing time for Australian economy. *Times of India.* 28 Jul. 1986 ; 8.

730. Walsh, Maximilian. Touch tests ahead for a lately unlucky Australia. *International Herald Tribune.* 18 Jul. 1986 ; 4.

731. Wilde, Peter. Economic restructuring and Australia's Changing role in the world economic system. In *IDPR* ; 16-43.

732. Wood, G. L. *ed.* Australia : *Its resources and development.* New York, 1947.

BAHRAIN

733. Fybe, Ann. Expatriates' jobs may be at risk in tight market. *International Herald Tribune.* 18 Jun. 1986 ; 13.

734. Niederaorn, John H. Reconstruction of the prehistory of Bahrain : Landing place of Noah. *In Bahrain and the Gulf. Ed.* by J. B. Nugent and T. H. Thomas. London, Croom Helm, 1985 ; 14-24.

735. Nugent, J.B. and T.H. Thomas, *eds. Bahrain and the Gulf.* London, Crom Helm, 1985. p. 222.

BANGLADESH

736. Ali, S. *et. al. Labour migration from Bangladesh to the Middle East.* Washington, World Bank, 1981.

737. Bangladesh. *In profiles of rural poverty.* Geneva, ILO, 1979 ; 26-28.

738. Bertocci, Peter J. Bangladesh in 1985. Resolute against the storms. *Asian Survey* Feb. 1986 ; 224-34.

739. Cair, Mead T. Economic activities of children in a village in Bangladesh. *Population and Development Review* 3 (3) Sep. 1977.

740. Cair, Mead T. Household life cycle and economic mobility in rural Bangladesh. *Population and Development Review* 4(3) Sep. 1978.

741. Chen, Lincoln C. *ed.* Disaster in *Bangladesh.* New York, Oxford Univ. Press, 1973. p. 290.

742. Chowdhury, A.K.M. Alauddin and L.C. Chen. Interaction of nutrition, infection and mortality during recent food crises in Bangladesh. *Food Research Institute Studies* (Stanford) 16 (2) 1977.

743. Das, Arvind N. Tale of three countries: Some observations on Bangladesh, Pakistan and India. *Human Futures* (New Delhi) 2 (21) 1979 ; 145-56.

744. Huffman, Sandra L. *et. al.* Nutrition and prestpantum amenorrhea in rural Bangladesh. *Population studies* 32 (2) Jul. 1978.

745. Jung, Anees. Poetry, poverty and God. *Times of India Sunday Review* 18 May 1986 ; 5.

746. Latif, Abdul and N. Chowdhury. Land ownership and fertility in two areas of Bangladesh. *Bangladesh Development Studies* 5 (2) Apr. 1977.

747. Peach, J. and F. Januzzi. *Bangladesh : A profile of the countryside.* Washington, 1979.

748. Wahid, Abu N.M. Analysis of seed-fertilizer technology and rural poverty of Bangladesh. *Asian Profile* 13 (5) Oct. 1985 ; 425-32.

BARBADOS

749. Harlow, Vincent. *History of Borbados, 1625-1685.* London, 1926.

BELGIUM

750. Bergham, Jos. Poverty and inequality in Belgium. *PICMC* : 61-91.

As to the task of fighting poverty in general, this continued to be the responsibility of local social assistance committees, whose activities were quite separate from social insurance and were on the whole little affected by the post-war reforms. Under an Act of 1925 a social assistance committee was set up in each commune, mainly to provide financial assistance, to take any measures to prevent destitution and to secure any help for medical care. This was an entirely decentralised system managed at the local level by a committee which, after having set up a 'social investigation', had complete discretionary power to decide whether a person or family was in need and the kind and amount of assistance that should be awarded. It followed that assistance benefits varied from one communue to another, depending on, for example, the financial resources of the local committee or the size and skill of its professional staff.

The individual character of each decision, which in theory was meant to lead to a fair assessment of person and family needs, made it impossible to develop any set of national assistance level. Hence there was no official poverty line in Belgium, nor indeed any national policy on minimum social incomes. Some reference to national minimum benefits was to be found in the social insurance legislation, where it was accepted that certain groups should be provided with higher pensions and allowances than a mere application of insurance principles would have yielded. However, a bewildering disparity was apparent not only among the different social insurance sectors but also within the same sector. These minima were also based on certain contribution and work conditions ; only 'full career' pensioners, for example, could qualify for minimum pensions.

After the burst of reforming activity in the early post-war period Belgian social policy entered a new phase that was to last until the end of the 1960s. This phase saw some important developments in certain sectors of social security, especially in the pension arrangements for employees. Legislation in the 1950s related pension rights more closely to revalued lifetime earnings, and there were a number of ad hoc adjustments to existing pensions to bring them more in line with changes in national prosperity. There was also a gradual extension of the field of application of social insurance, as some new schemes were created for previously excluded groups. For the self-employed an old-age and survivors' pension scheme was introduced on a compulsory basis in 1956, and this was followed by compulsory medical care insurance in 1964. In 1967, these provisions were co-ordinated in the so-called 'social statute of the self-employed', to which sickness pay and disability benefits were added in 1970.

Despite these developments, the basic character of Belgian social insurance and assistance policies was not really changed during this phase. The new pensions for the self-employed provided only very modest benefits, in most cases well below any acceptable subsistence standards, while the initiatives for changes within the general social insurance system still came from the 'social partners' and tended to emphasise the needs of the ordinary employee. Since successive governments preferred to follow the 'social partners' rather than elaborate different policies, there was little opportunity for a critical or fundamental reappraisal of social insurance, nor indeed of social policy as a whole. Another consequence of this state of affairs and of the continued reluctance of central government to interfere with the activities of social assistance committees was that hardly any information was available at the national level about the existence of poverty or its incidence amongst different social groups.

BOLIVIA

751. Arnade, Charles W. *Emergence of the Republic of Bolivia.* University of Florida Press, 1957. p. 269.

752. Bolivia. *International viewpoint* 14 Oct. 1985 ; 3.

753. Bolivia faces another crisis. *Patriot* 20 Sep. 1986 ; 7.

754. Dion, H.G. *Agriculture in the Altiplano of Bolivia.* Washington, 1950.

755. Dugnid, Julian. *Green Hell.* London, 1931.

756. Marsh, Margaret A. *Bankers in Bolivia.* New York, 1928.

757. McBride, G.M. *Agrarian Indian communities of highland Bolivia.* New York, 1921.

758. McQueen, Charles A. *Bolivian public finance.* Washington, 1925.

759. Osborne, Harold. *Bolivia : A land divided.* London, Oxford University Press, 1964. p. 181.

760. Weeks, D. Bolivia's agricultural frontier. *Geographical Review*, 36, 1946.

761. Wright, M.R. *Bolivia.* Philadelphia, 1907.

762. Zhenya, Zhang. Debt crisis rebounds on West. *Beijing Review.* 18 Jun. 1984 ; 16.

BOTSWANA

763. Knappert, J. *Myths and legends in Botswana, Lesotho and Swaziland.* Leien, E.J. Brill, 1986. p. 248.

764. Kraft, Scott, Botswana's survival on the razor's edge. *International Herald Tribune.* 5 Sep. 1986 ; 2.

765. Lipton, Michael. *Botswana : Employment and labour use. 2 Vols.* Gaborone, Ministry of Finance and Development Planning, 1978.

766. Lucas, R. *Migration amongst Botswana (Mimeo).* Boston University, Mar. 1982.

BRAZIL

767. Baer, W. *Industrialisation and economic development in Brazil.* Homewood, Illionois, Richard D. Irwin, 1965.

768. Becker, Bertha K. Brazilian path of agricultural development and plasant social differentiation. The case of the Amazon frontier. In *TWP* ; 294-313.

769. Bello, Jose Maria. *History of modern Brazil, 1889-1964.* Stanford, 1966.

770. Burns, E.B. *Nationalism in Brazil . A historical survey.* New York, Prayer, 1968.

771. Daland, R. *Brazilian Planning.* Chaphel Hill, 1967.

772. De Onis, Juan. Bolivia's slide into debt and despair has slowed under firm policy of Paz. *International Herald Tribune* 5 Aug. 1986 ; 3.

773. Diaz-Alejandro, Carlos F. *Some aspects of the Brazilian experience with foreign aid.* New Haven, Yale University Press, 1969.

774. Dulles. J.W.F. *Unrest in Brazil.* Austin, 1970.

775. Ellis, H. *Applicability of certain theories of economic development to Brazil.* Wisconsin University Press, 1968.

776. Goldenstein, Lea and S.G. Carvalhaes, Industry and the human and ecological tragedy of Cubatao, Sao Paulo, Brazil. In *IDPR*; 266-82.

777. Ianni, Octavio. *Crisis in Brazil*. New York, Columbia University Press, 1970. p. 244.

778. Machado, Joao. What prospects for the transition to bourgeois democratic rule? *International Viewpoint* 11 Mar. 1985 ; 3-8.

779. Merrick, Thomas W. and D.H. Graham. *Population and economic development in Brazil. : 1800 to the present*. Baltimore, Johns Hopkins, 1979.

780. Mitchell, S. *ed. Logic of poverty : the case of the Brazilian North-east*. London, 1981.

781. Sorj, Bernardo. Agroindustry, state and class formation in Brazilian agriculture. In *TWP Vol. 2* 68-91.

782. Wirth, J.D. *Politics of Brazilian development*. Stanford, 1970.

783. World Bank, *Brazil*. Washington, Oct. 1979.

BRUNEI

784. Ranjit Singh, D.S. Brunei in 1985. Domestic factors, political and economic externalities *Asian Survey* Feb. 1986 ; 168-73.

BURKINA FASO

785. Burkina Faso : The Naam's struggle for self reliance. *Congress Varnika International* (New Delhi) Sep. 1985 ; 26-27.

One could be forgiven if one has come to believe in recent months that Africa is a helpless continent, being ravaged by drought and famine and totally dependent on outside aid to keep itself going. The international media has chosen, not unexpectedly, to focus on the international dimension of the relief effort, and may (unwittingly) have promoted the view that Africans themselves are paralyzed by the tragedy. So Oxfam, Catholic Relief Services and Save the Children are deserved household words now, but few even know of the existence, for example, of the Ethiopian Relief and Rehabilitation Commission.

The fact is that the vast proportion of development and relief efforts in Africa are the result of indigenous, collective endeavours.

In Burkina Faso, for example, when someone was ill or too old to wield a hoe, hosts of young people would gather to turn the soil of their fields. Village musicians marked the rhythm with flutes and drums, helping release the energy that was always available for those in distress. In a few short hours the work was done, accomplished not merely by the strong arms of youth, but by the strong arms of youth, but by the strength of a cultural commitment to the collective. It was the strength of the "Naam."

The Naam movement is a particularly inspiring and successful venture, taping the well of a people's past to bring new life to the present and hope for the future. Traditional strengths are being harnessed to tackle contemporary life-threatening problems.

The movement's success is apparent in many ways. Since their inception in 1967, the Naams have increased in number to over 1,500 throughout the country. And in those intervening eighteen years, their members have built countless retention dams, dirt roads and developed water and soil conservation methods. In order to generate money for projects, groups have undertaken market gardening, handicraft work and poultry and small animal tending. And through their social organization they have provided villages with pharmacies for traditional medicine and classes and demonstrations on maternal and child health.

The name itself is both a departure from development terminology and a merging of traditional cooperation with current needs. It was the deliberate strategy of the creator of the Naam movement, Dr. Bernard Ledea Ouedraogo, to give people an idea that was part of their past : He says, "if one says "Naam" to the farmers, they know what that means. But if you say 'farmers' cooperative, they do not really understand. This is why I preferred first of all to speak the language of the villagers to the villagers."

The Naam movement, besides being firmly rooted in the tradition of the people, is also a technique for empowering them to take control of their problems and to make changes in their lives. Dr. Ouedraogo, Doctor of Sociology from the Sorbonne, describes it as a process of making people responsible for their problems. With that responsibility clear, people confront problems and experiment with solutions.

It also has a potential of creating a national consciousness. What begins as a local effort to deal with localized problems can extend itself, achieving not only local unit but a new perception of national identity. "Then one appreciates one's home ground more, one is less tempted to migrate to the Ivory Coast or Ghana. By extension, one day one attains what is terms as national unity and then one can work towards another goal, that is the construction of a new society."

What becomes apparent in the struggle, waged by the African people for a better way of life, is that they are struggling for their way of life, for cultural authonomy and identity. When problems force the dispersion of a people, alienation and despondency follow. In overcrowded cities of Africa, unemployment and its related ills may turn some young people, like those of Burkina Faso who used to collectively till the fields of the ill and old back home, into criminals. Movements like the Naam are providing options, giving people pride and belief in the value of themselves and their way of life and help prevent such waste.

Funding for the movement comes from the Naam's own projects and also from external sources.

The collective strength of Africa lives on, in many different forms around the continent. Often it is largely unknown outside the small struggling communities where the battles against poverty, illiteracy and disease are waged everyday. And now, especially when the crisis in Africa looms so large in the world's view, the small but significant victories go unnoticed.

However, everday they are won, with amazingly meager resources, victories against drought, soil erosion and staggering infant mortality rates. All over the continent, people are helping to build dispensaries, equip nurseries, dig well and renew their forests through co-operative and self-help efforts. Sometimes, as for example when drought strikes year after year and the soil yields little, the people's own efforts cannot meet the special adversity, and there is no alternative to life-saving relief assistance from outside the community or even the nation.

BURMA

786. MacDougall, Hugh C. and Jon A. Wiant. Burma in 1985. *Asian Survey* Feb. 1986 ; 168-73.

787. Mishra, Satish, At the Crossroads. *Link* 15 Jun. 1986 ; 28-29.

788. Tinker, Hugh. *Union of Burma*. London, Oxford Univ. Press, 1959.

CANADA

789. Unemployment crisis in Canada. *Free Press Journal* (Bombay) 5 Sep. 1986 ; 4.

CARIBBEAN REGION

790. Smith, R. T. Culture and social structure of the Caribbean. *Comparative Studies in Society History*, 6 1963.

CHILE

791. Christian, Shirley. Chileans worried about jobs, prices. *International Herald Tribune* 7 Aug. 1986 ; 3.

792. Gil, Jair, Pinochet's regime facing new crisis. *International Viewpoint* 28 Oct. 1985 : 11-17.

793. Halperin, Ernst. Economic difficulties. In *Nationalism and Communism in Chile.* Cambridge, MIT Press, 1965 ; 24-26.

794. Lehman, David. *Ed. Agrarian reform and agrarian reformism : studies of Peress, Chile and India,* London, 1974.

795. Machicado, F. *Distribution of income in Chile and its impact on the patterns of consumption of essential goods.* Madison, Univ. of Winconsin, Land Tenure Center, 1974.

796. Weinraub, Bernard. Chile rejects proposals for reforms. *International Herald Tribune* 19 Aug. 1986 ; 1, 6.

COLOMBIA

797. Berry R. Albert. Open unemployment as a social problem in Urban Colombia : Myth and reality. *Economic Development and Cultural Change.* Jan. 1975.

798. Dix, Robert H. *Colombia.* New Haven, Yale University Press, 1967. p. 452.

799. *Economic position and prospects of Colombia.* Washington, World Bank Vol. 1, May 1978.

800. Galbraith, W. O. *Colombia.* London, 1953.

801. Henao, J. M. and G. Arruba. *History of Colombia.* Chapel Hill, Univ. of North Carolina Press, 1938.

802. Hirschman, Albert O. *Journeys towards progress. New York*, the Twentieth century Fund, 1963.

803. Hobsbawn, E. J. Revolutionary situation in Colombia. *World Today* 19, Jun. 1963 ; 248-58.

804. Holt, P. M. *Colombia today and tomorrow*. New York, Prayer, 1964.

805. Hunter, John M. *Emerging Colombia.* Washington, 1962.

806. Mohan, Rakesh and Nancy Hartline. *Poor of Bogota : who they are, what they do* and *where they live*. Washington, World Bank, 1984. p. 85.

807. Nelson, Richard R. *et. al. Structural change in a developing economy : Colombia's problems and prospects.* Princeton, 1971.

808. Rippy, J. Fred. *Capitalists and Colombia.* New York, Vanguard Press, 1931.

809. Ruiz, H. R. and Alfredo Molano. Agrarian policies and peasant organizations in Colombia. In *TWP* : 328-342.

COMMONWEALTH

810. Arndt. H. W. *et. al. World economic crisis : A Commonwealth perspective.* London, Commonwealth Secretariat, 1980.

COSTA RICA

811. Hainess, M.R. and A.C. Avery. Differential infant and child mortality in Costa Rica ; 1968-73. *Population Studies* 36 (3) Mar. 1982.

CUBA

812. Alvarez Diaz, Jose Ramon. *Road to nowhere : Castro's rise and fall.* Miami, 1965.

813. Baran, Paul. *Reflections on the Cuban revolution.* New York, Monthly Review, 1961.

814. Batista Y. Zaldivar, Fulgencio. *Growth and decline of the Cuban Republic.* New York, Devin-Adair, 1964.

815. Boorstein, Edward. *Economic transformation of Cuba.* New York, Monthly Review Press, 1968.

816. Buell, R. L. *ed. Problems of the new Cuba.* New York, Foreign Policy Association, 1935.

817. Casuso, Teresa. *Cuba and Castro.* New York, Random House, 1961.

818. Chapman, Charles E. *History of the Cuban Republic.* New York, Macmillan, 1927.

819. Cuba revisited after ten years of Castro. *Foreign Affairs* 48, Jan. 1970 ; 312-21.

820. Farnos, Alfonso. *Role of Women and demographic change in Cuba.* Geneva, ILO, 1983.

821. Horowitz, Irving Louis *ed. Cuban communism.* Chicago, Aldine, 1970.

822. Huberman, Leo. *Socialism in Cuba.* New York, 1969.

823. Leontief, Wassily. Notes on a visit to Cuba. *New York Review of Books.* 21 Aug. 1969 ; 15.

824. Leontif, Wassily. Trouble with Cuban socialism. *New York Review of Books.* 7 Jan. 1971 ; 19.

825. Lockwood, Lee. *Castro's Cuba.* New York, Macmillan, 1967.

826. MacGaffey, Wyatt and Clifford R. Barnett. *Cuba. New Haven,* 1962.

827. Mallin, Jay. *Fortress Cuba.* Chicago, Henry Regnery, 1965.

828. Mesa-Lago, Carmelo and Roberto E. Fermandez. *Labour conditions in Communist Cuba.* University of Miani Press, 1965.

829. Nawarro, V. Health services in Cuba. *New England Journal of Medicine* 287 (19) 1972 ; 954-9.

830. Nelson, Lowry. *Cuba : the measure of a revolution.* University of Minnesota Press, 1972. p. 242.

831. Nelson, Lowry. *Rural Cuba.* University of Minneapolis Press, 1950.

832. O'connor, James. On Cuban political economy. *Political Science Quarterly* 69 (2) Jun. 1964 ; 233-47.

833. O'Connor, James. *Origins of Socialism in Cuba.* New York, Cornell University Press, 1970.

834. Rosenfeld, Stephen S. Light is turned on Castro. *International Herald Tribune* 21 Jul. 1986 ; 4.

835. Seers, D. *ed. Cuba : the economic and social revolution.* Chapel Hill, 1964.

836. Smith, R.F. *Background to revolution : the development of modern Cuba.* New York, Knopf, 1960.

837. Suarez, Andress, *Cuba.* Cambridge. MIT Press, 1967.

838. Thomas, Hugh. *Cuba.* New York, Harper and Rowe. 1971.

839. Wylie, Kathryn. *Survey of agriculture in Cuba.* Washington, U.S. Department of Agriculture, 1969.

840. Zeitlin, Maurice. *Revolutionary politics and the Cuban working class.* Princeton, 1967.

841. Zeitlin, Maurice and Robert Scheer *Cuba.* New York, Grove Press, 1963.

DAHOMEY

842. In solidarity with free Africa. *Baghdad Observer* 21 Jun., 1978 ; 4.

DJIBOUTI

843. Hong, Li and Gao Changyun. Economy makes headway. *Beijing Review* 23 Jan. 1984 ; 15.

DOMINICAN REPUBLIC

844. Ansari, Anis U. Islamic activities in Dominican Republic *Radiance* (Delhi) 5-11 Feb. 1984 ; 5.

ECUADOR

845. Belote, Linda. *Prejudice and price : Indian white relations in Saragwro, Ecuador.* Ph. D. Dissertation Ann Arbor, Univ. of Illinois, 1978.

846. Peek, Peter and P. Antolinez. *Labour migration in the Sierra of Ecuador : Causes and Incidence.* Geneva, ILO, 1980.

EGYPT

847. Abdel—Malek, Anouar. *Egypt : Military society.* New York, Random House, 1968.

848. Baligh, Dalia. Egyptians, rich and poor, feel the pinch of reduced

import, Subsidies. *International Herald Tribune* 30 Sept. 1986 ; 12.

849. Caldwell, Pat. Egypt and the Arabic and Islamic words. In *Persistence of high fertility*. Ed. by John C. Caldwell. Canberra, 1977 ; 593-616.

850. Dourian, Kate. Mubarak confirms Cairo wants new debt accord. *International Herald Tribune* 21 Jul. 1986 ; 7.

851. Egypt's urgent need (President Mubarak visits Paris, London and Bonn for aid) *International Herald Tribune* 19-20 Jul. 1986 ; 4.

852. Egyptian economy in thores of crisis. *People's Democracy* (New Delhi) 24 Aug. 1986 ; 9.

Egypt's enormous foreign debt, which is estimated at more than 30,000 million dollars, is being described as an illness neglected for too long and one with little chance of a cure.

The financial river which brings Egypt the dollars which it needs to repay its debts and interest on is fed mainly by four tributaries : earnings from the sale of oil, the use of the Suez Canal, Egyptians working in other countries, and tourism. However, Egypt's oil exports have declined almost by 50 per cent since the beginning of this year as the price of oil began to sharply fall since last December. The tense situation in the region, which was seriously aggravated by the U.S. attack on Libya, has also had a negative effect on traffic through the Suez Canal. Although in absolute terms revenues from the use of the canal have increased due to a rise in passing charges, they have not achieved the desired level. Moreover, demand for labour in the countries of the region has also declined. As regards tourism, earnings from this source have dropped after some countries of West Asia were blamed for several terrorist attacks in Western Europe. As a result, the influx of tourists to these countries, Egypt included, sharply declined.

Thus, the four main sources of currency earnings have not provided the normal or expected profits. The Egyptian economy is still smarting under the effects of the "open door" policy inaugurated by President Sadat. As soon as the doors of the Egyptian economy were flung open, western capital, especially American capital, rushed in.

The "open door" policy led to the rapid polarisation of Egyptian society. Free enterprise quickly created new fortunes and their owners, both Egyptian and foreign, began to vie with one another for contracts. There are more than 100 billionaires in the country and several tens of thousands of people have seven-digit bank accounts.

853. Fridman, Jane. Pressure to *Don Higab* rises. *International Herald Tribune* 11 Jun. 1986 ; 12.

854. Hill, R. *Egypt in the Sudan*. Oxford, 1958.

855. Lengyel, Peter. Egyptian view of dependency and development. *Studies in Comparative International Development*, 1974 ; 121-25.

856. Levy, Victor. *Cropping patterns, mechanisation, child labor and fertility behaviour in rural Egypt*. (Jerusalam, Manrice Falk Institute), 1983. (Mimeographed).

857. Nundy, Julian. Problems grow for a nation without a safety net. *International Herald Tribune* 11 Jun. 1986 ; 11.

858. Starr, Joyce R. Water clock ticking for people of the Nile. *International Herald Tribune* 11 Jun. 1986 ; 14.

859. Tohamy, Olfat. Debt burden grows to an all-time-high as resources decline. *International Herald Tribune* 11 Jun. 1986 ; 11.

860. Tohany, Olfat. Reforms seek to curb excesses. *International Hearld Tribune*. 11 Jun. 1986 ; 12.

EL SALVADOR

861. Peek, Peter and P. Antolinez. Rural-urban migration and the urban labour market : the case of San Salvador. *World Development* Apr. 1977.

ETHIOPIA

862. Abir, M. *Ethiopia: the era of the princes*. London, Longmans, Misael, 1969.

863. Beguele, A. and E Chole. *Profile of the Ethiopian economy*. Addis Ababa, Oxford Univ. Press, 1969.

864. Bondestam, L. *People and capitalism in the Awash Valley, Ethiopia*. Dakar, IDEP, Sep. 1973.

865. Clapham, C. *Haile Selassie government*. London, Longman, 1969.

866. Cohen. John M. *et. al. Revolution and land reform in Ethiopia.* Cornell Univ. Press, 1979.

867. Cooper, Adi *et. al. Class, state and the world economy : A case study of Ethiopia.* Sussex, Sep. 1975. (Paper presented at the conference on New Approaches to Trade).

868. Ethiopia : Brief historical background. *Congress Varnika International* (New Delhi) Sep. 1985 ; 8-16.

Ethiopia is a unique phenomenon in Africa. Ethiopia and Egypt are the only African nations that can trace their history into antiquity, but Egypt became more and more alienated from its ancient culture by successive conquests while Ethiopia, except for a few years of Italian occupation in the 1930s and 1940s, retained its original character through the centuries. Ethiopia's historic continuity is largely the result of a favourable geographic location ; its high plateaus, which, both fertile and temperate, border on heavily travelled seas on the east and elsewhere, can be defended like fortresses from the hostile deserts that surround it. Thus Ethiopia has been able to preserve and perfect a unique culture born of the ancient encounter and the slow fusion of two equally gifted peoples : the Cushites, a white race with dark skin, who were probably indigenous and Semitic tribes that have emigrated from Arabia.

The Egypt of the Pharaohs believed that it had received certain of its divinities from Ethiopia, which it called punt, or the land of God. Later, the Greeks thought of it as the original home of wheat and of the olive tree. The legends are partly true. The most recent discoveries confirm the ancientness of man's presence in Ethiopia ; even the remains of an archaic hominid (the Paraustralopithecus aethipicus) dating back some 15,00,000 years have been found in the Omo Valley. According to Egyptian hieroglyphic texts, an authentic civilization began as early as the 2nd millennium BC. The pharaohs sent fleets there to buy such precious goods as spices, incense and myrrh. Bas-reliefs in Dayr al-Bahri at Thebes, dating from around 1500 BC, depict certain Ethiopians cultivating myrrh and incense. The text commenting on these drawings calls the Ethiopians Habashat, from which later came the name Abyssinia.

869. Gebre-Medhin, M. and B. Vahlquist. Famine in Ethiopia the period 1973-75. *Nutrition Reviews* 35, 1977.

870. Hiwet, A. *Ethiopia : From autocracy to revolution.* London, Merlin Press, 1975.

871. Hoben, A. *Land tenure among the Anshara of Ethiopia.* Univ. of

Chicago Press, 1973.

872. Huffnagel, H. *Agriculture in Ethiopia*. Rome, FAO, 1961.

873. *Land tenure in Ethiopia*. Addis Ababa, Imperial Ethiopian Government (planning board) 1962.

874. Legum, Colin, *Ethiopia—the fall of Haile selaissie's empire*. New York, Africana Publicity, 1975.

875. Noggo, Yohannes. Agrarian reform and class struggle in Ethiopia. In *TWP* ; 176-229.

876. Pankhurst, Richard. *Economic history of Ethiopia, 1800-1935*. Addis Ababa, 1968.

877. Pausewang, Siegfried. *Peasant and local society in Ethiopia*. Norway, 1979 (DERAP working paper A-105, Bergen).

878. Rule, Sheila. Ethiopians find refuge, and squalor, in Somalia. *International Herald Tribune* 30 Jul. 1986 ; 14.

879. Rule, Sheila. In Ethiopia, hints of economic shift are perceived. *International Herald Tribune* 30-31 Aug. 1986 ; 5.

880. Sven, Rubensen, *Survival of Ethiopian Independence*. London Heinemann, 1976.

EUROPE, EAST

881. Gabor, Hunya. Recent East European regional development experience. In *IDPR* ; 85-113.

882. Neuberger, E. and L.D. Tysoon *eds*. *Impact of international economic disturbances on the Soviet Union and Eastern Europe*. Oxford, 1980.

883. Portes. R. Effects of the world economic crisis on the East European economics. *World Economy* 3, 1984.

EUROPE, WEST

884. Barach, Arnold B. *New Europe and its economic future*. New York, Macmillan, 1964.

885. Behrend, H.A., Knowles and J. Davis. *Views on pay increases*,

fringe benefits and low pay. Dublin, Economic and social search Institute Paper, No. 56, 1970.

886. Bohning, W. *EEC and the free movement of labour*. Oxford, 1973.

887. Bourgeois-Pichat, J. Recent demographic change in Western Europe : An assessment. *Population and Development Review* 7, 1981 ; 19-42.

888. Dewhurst, Cophock and Yates *et. al. Europe's needs and resources*. London, Macmillan, 1961.

889. George, V. and Roger Lawson *ed. Poverty and inequality in common market countries*. London, Rontledge and Kegan Paul, 1980 p. 253.

890. Gouldner, Alvin W. *Coming crisis of Western Sociology*. New York, Basic Books, 1970.

891. Kindleberger, Charles. P. *Europe's postwar growth*. Cambridge, 1967.

892. Lawson, Roger and Vic George. Assessment. In *PICMC* ; 233-42.

The persistence of income and other material inequalities over the years is natural to welfare capitalism, if one accepts the theoretical framework suggested in the first chapter. Without substantial inequalities and without the inheritance of wealth, capitalism loses both its driving force and its raison d'etre as an economic system. The persistence of poverty, in terms of a minimum income for survival in an affluent society, is not, however, a necessary precondition to the survival of welfare capitalism. This type of poverty can be abolished within welfare capitalism. The fact that it has not so far been abolished does not mean that it cannot. In terms of direct costs, a social security scheme that ensures that everyone has an income adequate for a minimum standard of living is not likely to be that much more expensive than the existing schemes of most of the countries in our study. It is the fear of indirect costs to welfare capitalism that is more real : the fear that such a scheme will undermine work incentives and that it will act as a spring-board for demands for further improvements in the guaranteed minimum living standards. In other words, abolition of poverty will lead to increased demands for reductions in income and wealth inequalities. Whether these fear—or hopes—are justified is impossible to say from the existing evidence. Much, of course, will depend on the level at which the guaranteed minimum income is set.

In spite of the failure of all our countries to reduce or to eradicate poverty, a slight change of emphasis in social security policies can be detected during the past decade, with more attention being given to the low-paid and disadvantaged workers : the introduction of the family income supplement and child benefit schemes in Britain ; the new 'social minimum' benefits in Belgium and in France ; and the liberalisation of social assistance and important changes in family allowances in Germany. These and other changes may be the beginning of a new awareness that some of the vast sums spent by social security systems should be redirected to ensure that no one lives in poverty.

Whether these uncoordinated measures will develop into a coherent policy for the low-paid will depend on the strength of the political forces demanding such a change. The population groups in poverty are directly related to the working class but they are not seen as such, nor do they form a unified social group wielding substantial political power.

893. Merritt, Giles. Plan to resolve Europe's job crisis. *International Herald Tribune* 30 Sep. 1986 ; 6.

894. *Perception of poverty in Europe.* Brussels, Commission of the European communities, Mar. 1977,

895. Poverty of economics, *Amrita Bazar Patrika* 5 Jan. 1985 ; 7.

896. Riffault, H. and J.R. Rabier. *Perception of poverty in Europe.* Brussels, EEC, 1977.

897. Roberti, P. Income inequality in some Western countries. *International Journal of Social Economics* 5 (1) Jan. 1978.

898. Sinfield, A. *Poverty research in Britain and Europe.* Conference on Poverty Research, London, 1967.

899. Singer, Hans W. and Javed A. Ansari, *Rich and poor countries.* London, Johns Hopkins University, 1977.

900. Sinha, Radha. Global poverty : Vatican's dilemma. *Patriot* 28 Sep. 1984 ; 4.

Reverned Leonardo Boff, a Franciscan from Brazil stands accused by the Church of Rome of deviations from the true Catholic faith. He was summoned to appear before Cardinal Joseph Ratzinger, the Prefect of the Sacred Congregation for the Doctrine of Faith. The Office of the Prefect is the doctrinal watchdog of the Vatican which the Economist recently (September 8, 1984) called 'the present incarnation of the Holy Office or Inquisition'. By a strange coincidence, the Prefect works from the place which once housed the Inquisition.

March of the anger of the Vatican is directed toward the theological writings of Latin American clergymen like Gustavo Gutierrez and Leonardo Boff, which has come to be known as the liberation theology. Gutierrez argues 'hat Christians must take a realistic look at society and the struggles and conflicts within it. To them Christian love must be founded on commitment to more just society and on action to bring about such a change. The liberation theology draws its inspiration largely from the dependency theory and argues that the inequality and misery of the Latin American masses is the direct outcome of the economic and political dominance of the region by the Western capitalist powers and their surrogates within Latin American countries themselves. Therefore, the solution of the problem of poverty and degradation in Latin America—for that matter in any other developing region--lies mainly in the creation of a new economic, social and political order.

Leonidas Prano, a clergyman from Ecuador defines 'liberation' as a liberation from social domination and economic exploitation, from ignorance and from misery and insecurity resulting from hunger, sickness and other sufferings. To many liberation theologians like Boff, churches acceptance of the status quo amounts to collaborating with the state machinery which has invariably become an instrument of oppression and alienation. The church must support and guide revolutionary changes in societies characterised by extremes of wealth and power. These theologians commonly use 'class-struggle' and other Marxist paradigms and even go to the length of branding the Pope, the bishops and priests as the ruling elite and the laity as the underclass. In many cases radical priests have joined guerilla forces in Central America and Columbia. Four priests have continued to hold ministerial appointments in the Nicaraguan government in defiance of the Vatican directives.

The Vatican itself is in a quandary. Latin America, where almost half of the 800 million Catholics live, is well known for the extremes of poverty and wealth, where inequality of income and wealth is much more pronounced than in India. In Peru 20 per cent of households at the lower and of the income distribution receive only 2 per cent of the income while 10 per cent of households at the top end have as much as 43 per cent. The respective share for Brazil is 2 and 51 per cent and in Costa Rica 3 and 40. As many as 85 per cent of rural households in Bolivia and Guatemala are landless or near-landless. For most other countries the proportion ranges between 65 and 80 per cent. The Gini-Coefficient of land distribution in as many as ten Latin American countries is over 0.8 (the nearer the figure to 1.0 the higher is the inequality). In another five it is between 0.7. and 0.8. Only two have a Gini Coefficient of less than 0.7. The number of people below the poverty line in Mexico is officially estimated at 50 per cent. According to a World Bank estimate, 58 per cent of all Brazilian children under 18 years of age are malnourished.

Lack of access to land has forced the Latin American masses to migrate to the already overcrowded urban slums. Mexico City is expected to have as many as 31 million people by the year 2000 and Sao Paulo 26. Other migrant workers flock to plantations where they are engaged on contract for short periods. Such contracts are given only to the adult males. In practice the entire family including children work, but the entitlement to rations and other benefits are limited to the contracted workers. Other facilities such as accommodation, water supply and medical facilities are either inadequate or non-existent. Contractors often operate as money lenders which adds to the vulnerability of the migrant worker. Their migratory nature itself acts as an impediment to the organisation of labour unions but a more important reason is the hostility of the establishment to such unions.

It is in this context of poverty and degradation that the liberation theology was born in the 1960s. The vatican can ignore these realities at its peril. On the other hand, Pope John Paul-II rivals President Reagan in his deep hatred of Marxism and is obviously intolerant of priests using Marxist analysis so much so that in 1983 on the occasion of his visit to Nicaragua, he publicly chastised Ernesto Cardenal Martinez, a Roman catholic priest who serves as the minister of Culture in the Nicaraguan government. But more threatened by liberation theology is the Vatican establishment itself.

The dilemma of the Vatican is clearly reflected in a 36-page document Instructions on Certain Aspects of Liberation Theology issued early in September under the signature of Joseph Ratzinger. The report condemns the "chocking inequality between rich and poor" and categorically states that the Vatican stand against the liberation theology must not be misconstrued as "some kind of approval, even indirect, of those who keep the poor in misery, who profit from misery, who notice it while doing nothing about it or who remain indifferent to it". This in itself is an endorsement of the basic premises of the liberation theology. Any other action would have cost the Vatican its credibility as the champion of the poor. Besides, the liberation theologians can justifiably claim that they draw their inspiration directly from the Second

Vatican Council (the Vatican-II) which gave birth to a new vision of the Church as a 'Pilgrims People of God', a community of the faithful which learns from its historical setting and is prepared to change its values according to the objective social, economic and political realities of the time. The Vatican II also came out in favour of a preferential treatment of the poor. This change in Vatican attitudes inspired the Second General Conference of Latin American Bishops held in Medellin in Columbia in 1968 which categorically blamed the richer capitalist nations for the deprivation of the masses in Latin America. The Third General Conference of Latin America held in Puebla in Mexico in early 1979 further endorsed the political activism of the clergy.

901. Townsend, Peter. Scale and meaning of poverty in contemporary Western society. *Dependency and Poverty, 1963-64*. Brandies Univ., Colloquium series Paper, July, 1965.

902. Treuner, Peter. Experiences and possible contributions of the industrialised countries. In *EAPS* : 39-48.

Mass poverty occurred as a by-product of the process of industrialisation on the main basis of the mercentilistic idea, that labour should be cheap to increase national wealth. There were some other reasons of which the following four are most important. Some reasons are identical to what you are experiencing in the developing countries :

—the increasing demographic growth rates.

—decreasing agricultural protection which meant a deterioration of agricultural income levels.

—productivity progress in the secondary sector.

—and an almost exclusive legal protection of an entrepreneurial capitalism in all the countries that are industrialised countries today.

The type of mass poverty we experienced throughout different periods of the nineteenth century in most of the North-Western European countries disappeared relatively fast, when it became dangerous for the liberalistic system. Think of Marx's political ideas, not of his historical works ; and maybe, I should just cite the riots of miners in France or some riots of weavers in Germany.

I expressly said that poverty disappeared fast *when* it became dangerous, and I did not say *because* it became dangerous. There are many different reasons for the disappearance, of which the following five are the most important, in my view.

The first, and there is a very important difference to what you are experiencing here, is the very slow pace of industrialization compared to what developing countries are facing today. We had slowed down the production of technical progress and we did not arrive at a phenomenon of economic and/or social dualism, which is the characteristics of the Third World countries.

The second historical reason is an inherent aspect of the capitalistic system of the West, the impact of Protestantism and especially of Calvinism which fostered capitalistic behaviour on a very large scale.

On the very broad basis of rich landlords and rich merchants, we produced in a very short time, within ten to thirty years that is, thousands of rational entrepreneurs to make use of the new technologies and of the "Industrial reserve army", a fact which prevented us to come close to the point of crisis which we can observe here. And at the same time, this religiously motivated society continued to use some traditional charity, which cared for the most spectacular cases of poverty, thus again excluding the danger of a crash-down.

The third and certainly a very important reason was the expanding imperialism during the period of industrialisation which extended old and created new markets and new needs, and thus facilitated continuous industrial growth. This continuity of industrial growth is one of the problems of the new industries in the developing countries. We never had a problem of disrupted industrialization. We continued step by step, and at the same time this imperialism gave the industrialized countries access to the Third World's resources, bringing the living standard beyond what it would have been, if they had been restricted to their own physical resources.

The fourth reason, for this process of overcoming of poverty was the fact that we had no democracy in the industrialized countries. We had "good" kings or dictators, and even in some countries where we had parliaments, it was not democracy in the sense that the poor had a possibility to bring forward their needs, and to translate them into political actions. We had dictatorial systems, which eased the way for industrialization as well as for overcoming poverty.

Finally there were some timid anti-poverty policies of the national governments which date back to the early nineteenth century : for instance, legislation on maximum duration of work, and at the same time, the beginning of social security measures.

I would like to stress once more the decisive role of economic liberalism in the Western countries, namely, the protection of the entrepreneurial capitalism by legal and sometimes by military means. We had free international transfers and exchange of products which again fostered this continuous development for industrialization and even when, from the middle of the last century protectionism grew, it did not restrict economic and technical progress as the economies of scale had not yet reached the level, which is actually today characterizing industry in most fields. The fact of being more and more restricted to the national territories did not harm the process of industrialization—it brought forward customs problems and price problems, but it did not stop the continuous process.

The anti-poverty measures undertaken at that period should be pointed out very shortly. The first were the charitable organizations, especially the churches, which cared for the most spectacular cases. Second point, and I think this might be considered during this Workshop, were the cooperative initiatives of the trade unions during the last century beginning about 1850. For the first time, self-aid was practised by the poor themselves, who organized themselves, who cared for the finance or for the physical means to fulfill their purposes in many different forms. To name the most important :

—assistance to unemployed persons ;

—subsidies to local or regional mobility which was paid by the trade unions and not by the State at that time ;

—educational institutions especially for the adult workers, but with a long run impact on the development of our societies, last but not the least, the cooperative markets for food and consumer goods which were practised on a large scale by the trade unions in many European countries.

To sum up this historical retrospective, mass poverty was a short-time phenomenon which disappeared with processing industrialization and growing productivity, and when accumulated capital lead to mass production which itself fostered mass demand and thus assisted the continuous process up to what we call today, *the customer society*—a perversion of what was the aim of industrialization: that we are producing needs to stimulate demands to keep the system running without most people in our countries asking themselves whether the new needs are suggested are the needs in the sense of *values*.

903. Tuohy, William. Poverty spreads across Europe. *International Herald Tribune*. 14 Mar. 1985 ; 9.

904. Willmott, Peter *et. al. Poverty and social policy in Europe—A pilot study in the United Kingdom, Germany and France.* London, Institute of community studies, 1978.

905. Willenz, Eric. Why Europe needs the welfare state. *Foreign Policy* (63) Sum. 1986 ; 88-107.

FEDERAL REPUBLIC OF GERMANY

906. Dahrendorf, R. *Society and democracy in Germany*. London. 1968.

907. Demand : Peace and jobs. *New Times* (Moscow) (19) 19 May 1986 ; 15.

908. Hallett, G. *Socialist economy of West Germany*. London, Macmillan, 1973.

909. Jantz, K. Pension reform in the Federal Republic of Germany, *International Labour Review* 83, 1961.

910. Jaura. Ramesh. Are foreign creating unemployment ? (in West Germany). *Link* 5 Oct. 1986 ; 37.

911. Kreja, J. *Social structure in divided Germany*. London, Crown Helm, 1976.

912. Lawson, Roger. Poverty and inequality in West Germany. In *PICMC* : 195-232.

A closer look at German social security policies suggests some other interesting relationships with the pattern of economic inequalities. As has been implied, the considerable expansion of social security which took place under the Christian Democrats in the 1950s and 1960s was largely financed by increases in the taxation and social insurance contributions of workers and ordinary employees. It was also concerned much less with establishing national minimum standards for all citizens than with 'protecting the capacities and incentives for gainful employment including the different rewards acquired through economic activity". In practice, this has meant generous standards of protection, particularly in retirement and against sickness and disability, for many workers with regular and stable employment: the standards have been much closer to those traditionally enjoyed by public officials and white-collar employees than is the case, for example, in Britain. But because of their work orientation the schemes have had a less benevolent expression for many low-paid workers and those with poor employment records.

Moreover, a number of studies have linked the good protection given to the majority of workers with demanding and stressful working conditions in factories, leading to higher accident rates than in many other countries and to a surprisingly high proportion of workers leaving the labour force before the official retirement age. A survey conducted in North Rhine-Westphalia in the 1960s put the proportion at 42 per cent of all manual workers, but 54 per cent for the unskilled and semi-skilled. Until the 1970s, too, Germany's social security sechemes have given far less support to larger families than has been given in many other countries. And, in keeping with the emphasis on the ordinary worker with normal responsibilities, they have made few concessions to women but particularly women in one-parent families-or, to use the official jargon, incomplete families'. Again, though, this has begun to change during the 1970s.

The distinctive priorities in social security are best illustrated by the major social reform of the post-war period, the reform of old-age and disability pensions enacted by the Christian Democrats in 1957. This raised old-age pensions for an average wage earner with an average employment record to approximately 50 per cent of gross and 60 per cent of net earnings before retirement, levels above those in many other countries. It also pioneered the principle, at least in state superannuation schemes, that pensions should be given a guaranteed share in increasing national prosperity, by linking subsequent pension increases to the general growth of wages and salaries. Unlike state pensions in most other countries, though, the 1957 reform contained no minimum pension noı any formula favouring the low-paid and pensions were very closely related to lifetime work records. Moreover, in line with the traditional rules in German social insurance, there was no supplement in the new scheme for wives, and a widow continued to receive 60 per cent of her husband's pension. In fact, the whole concept underlying the reform was that a person's pension should reflect the value of his work, as expressed by the wage he receives, the only concessions made at the time to social equity were allowances for periods of sickness, unemployment and wartime service. Although these priorities have since been modified by the so-called 'second pension reform' passed by the Social Democratic Liberal coalition in 1972, the pension schemes still provide relatively meagre benefits for the low-paid and irregularly employed. There is now, for example, a minimum pension, but only for workers with at least 25 years' contributions: for a widow of a worker with a normal employment record it amounts to little more than 20 per cent of national average earnings.

913. Lawson, Roger. Housing allowances in Germany. *Roof* 1 (1) 1976.

914. Lawson, Roger and Cindy Stevens. Housing allowances in West Germany and France. *Journal of Social Policy* 3 (3) 1974 ; 230-38.

915. Unemployment rises to 8.6 per cent in West Germany. *International Herald Tribune* 6 Aug. 1986 ; 9.

FIJI

916. Ahmed, Ali. *Plantation to politics ; studies on Fiji Indians.* Suva, USP and the Fiji Times Ltd., 1980.

917. Ahmed, Ali. *Society in transition.* Bombay, states' people Press, 1977.

918. Arthur, W. *What is Fiji ?* London, 1859.

919. Belshaw, C.S. *Under the Ivi tree : Society and economic growth in rural Fiji*, Berkeley, 1964.

920. Bhooshan. *Human settlement policies in Fiji.* Mysore, Institute of Development Studies, 1982. (Mimeo).

921. Blaikie, W.G. *Mission at Fiji : Catholic Presby terian.* 8, 1882.

922. Brewster, A.B. *Hill tribes of Fiji.* London, 1922.

923. Britton, H. *Fiji in 1870.* Melbourne, 1870.

924. Burns, A. *et. al. Report of the Commission of Inquiry into the natural and population trends of the colony of Fiji*: (Legislative Council Paper No. 1, 1960) Suva, 1960.

925. Chesson, F.W. *Past and present of Fiji.* London, Royal Colonial Institute, proceedings 6, 1874-75.

926. Cooper, H.S. *Fiji : Its resources and prospects.* London. 1879.

927. De Ricci, J.H. *Fiji.* London, 1875.

928. *Fiji today.* Sydney, M.A.T.E. 1886.

929. *Fiji's Eighth Development Plan. 1981-85 Vol. 1.* Suva, Central Planning Office, 1980.

930. *Fiji's Sixth Development Plan, 1971-75.* Suva, Central Planning Office, 1970.

931. *Fiji's Seventh Development Plan, 1976-80.* Suva, Central Planning Office, 1975.

932. Forbes, L. *Two years in Fiji.* London, 1875.

933. France, P. *Chapter of the land ; custom and colonization in Fiji.* London, Oxford University Press, 1969.

934. Gillion, K.L. *Fiji's Indian migrants.* Melbourne, Oxford Univ. Press, 1962 .

935. Gordon Cumming, C.F. *At home in Fiji.* London, 1881.

936. Gunasekera, H.M. *Rural development in the South Pacific : the case of Fiji.* University of Ottawa, Seminar Paper on Rural Development, 29-31 Oct. 1981 (Mimeo).

937. Gunasekera, H.M. Fijian peasantry : History and emerging problems. In *TWP* Vol. 2, 218-41.

938. Horne, J. *Fiji : Remarks on the agricultural prospects.* Levuka, 1878.

939. Kingsell, G. S. Fiji Islands as an imperial opportunity. *United Empire.* New series. 11, 1920.

940. Legge, J. D. *Britain in Fiji 1858-1880.* London, Macmillan, 1958. p. 307.

941. Nation, J. *Custom of respect.* Canberra, ANU, 1978.

942. Norton, R. *Race and Politics in Fiji.* Brisbane, Univ. of Queensland, 1977.

943. Ramachandran, K. S. Fiji's development plan : A non-starter ? *Financial Express* 21 Jul. 1986 ; 5.

Fiji's Ninth Development Plan (1986-90) aims at a growth rate of 5 per cent annually in terms of real GDP. It also seeks to reduce the current account balance of payment deficit to just over one per cent of GDP by 1990. But neither of these goals is realistic considering immediate past trends.

GDP fell by 1.7 per cent in real terms in 1985 and the outlook for the current year is not very encouraging in view of the austerity measures taken by the Government by way of adjustment to a sharp decline in unit value of Fiji's exports last year and the year before. As for the balance of payment position, continued depression in global commodity prices virtually rules out any significant improvement.

It is true that the current account deficit had fallen to 3.7 per cent of GDP in 1984 and remained at the same level in 1985 from 9.4 per cent in 1982 and 8 per cent in 1983. But a reduction to nearly one per cent of GDP by end of the decade seems a tall order, despite gains to the economy from a fall in world oil prices and interest rates.

The accompanying tables show how steep the fall in prices of Fiji's major exports has been. Last year, while the terms of trade of developing countries generally weakened by 3.3 per cent, the deterioration was as much as 13.7 per cent in regard to Fiji.

According to a recent assessment of Fiji's economy by the International Monetary Fund (IMF Survey, June 16), Fiji's economy had been hit hard by a sharp decline in commodity prices during 1984-85. World prices of sugar, the country's major export, fell by about 40 per cent in 1984 and a further 25 per cent in 1985.

In the latter half of 1984, the Government put into effect an adjustment programme in anticipation of a deterioration in commodity prices in 1985. Wages were to be freezed, public expenditure slashed and growth in bank credit and money supply severely restricted.

As a consequence of these measures, growth in domestic demand was checked, so were inflationary pressures. An increase in current account balance of payment deficit was also averted. But a price necessarily had to be paid and, as we noted earlier, GDP in real terms came down by 1.7 per cent.

The IMF study deals at length with the Government's wage policy. Since 1977, the annual cost of living adjustments in all sectors of the economy have been based on wage guidelines formulated by the tripartite forum comprising representatives of Government, trade unions and employers' associations. Although, in principle, the forum must consider the country's overall economic situation in formulating guidelines on wages, in practice the previous year's inflation rate is chosen as the appropriate measure for compensation.

According to IMF researchers, during 1977-84 the rate of wage increase allowed under the forum's guidelines averaged 8.4 per cent annually, broadly consistent with the average inflation rate of 8.2 per cent. Besides, each trade union was permitted to negotiate with employers for additional wage increase based on merit or seniority. In case of Government employees, the increase remained fixed at 4 per cent throughout the period.

944. *Report of the working committee set up to review the Agricultural Landlord and Tenant Ordinance.* (Parliamentary) Paper No. 13, 1975).

945. Roth, G.K. *Handbook of the Colony of Fiji.* Suva, 1936.

946. Shand, R.T *ed. Island States of the Pacific and Indian Oceans : Anatomy of development.* Canberra, ANU, 1980.

947. Snatak, B.D. With the aged in Fiji. *Social Welfare* (New Delhi) Mar. 1984 ; 16, 19.

948. *Social indicators for Fiji.* Suva, Bureau of Statistics, 1979.

949. Spate, S.K. *Fijian people : Economic problems and prospects* (Council Paper No. 13, 1959).

950. Stavenuiter, Stan. *Regional disparities in Fiji.* Suva, Central Planning Office, 1982 (Mimeo).

951. Trotter, C. Fiji. *Blackwoods magazine.* 143, 1888.

952. Udal, R. *Colonization of the Fiji Islands.* London, 1871.

953. Word, M. *Role of investment in the development of Fiji.* Cambridge, 1971.

954. Waterhouse, J. *King and people of Fiji.* London, 1866.

955. Watters, R.F. *Koro : Economic development and social change in Fiji.* London, 1969.

FINLAND

956. Jucker-Fleetwood, Erin E. *Economic theory and policy in Finland, 1914-25.* Oxford, Basil Blackwell, 1958. p. 127.

957. Jutikkala, E. Great Finnish famine in 1696-97. *Scandinavian Economic History Review* 3, 1955 ; 48-63.

FRANCE

958. Gabriele, Jean-Paul. Industry in Haute-Marne : A rural backwater in an advanced economy. In *IDPR* ; 44-58.

959. Heller, H. *Conquest of poverty : The calvinist revolt in 16th Century France.* Leiden, E.J. Brill, 1986. p. 300.

960. Lawson, Roger and Cindry Stevens. Housing allowances in West Germany and France. *Journal of Social Policy* 3 (3) 1974 ; 230-38.

961. Parodi, Maurice. France. In *Low income groups and methods of dealing wtih their problems*. Paris, *OECD*, 1969.

962. Sinfield, Adrian. Poverty and inequality in France. In *PICMC* ; 92-123.

In 1976 the Organisation for Economic Co-operation and Development (OECD) published two reports on its member countries, one on income distribution and the other on poverty. These led Le Monde to tell its readers that their county had been awarded a gold medal' for its great and persistent inequality. Not only that, France also had one of the worst rates of poverty among the western industrial countries studied, despite its very high social expenditure.

In the same year the paper gave further emphasis to a number of national studies which broke 'the long and remarkable silence' and 'the groping in the dark' on the distribution of wealth, and provided detailed data on changes in the earnings spread over time. It headlined one article : 'Fortunes-much greater differences than had been thought', and another 'Wages, the same distribution as twenty years ago'.

The picture of a country concerned with poverty and inequality was reinforced by another international study, published for the European Commission in Brussels with considerable publicity in March 1977. The French population as a whole was shown to be very much more aware of poverty, inequality and social injustice in their own country than were the people of Britain. The French believed that poverty persisted on a very much wider scale than did the British ; and they were also much less likely to attribute it to personal failing or inadequacy and tended to place the blame for the much higher level of poverty on the injustice of their society. Indeed, almost half those interviewed in France believed there was poverty in their country compared with just over one-third in Britain; twice as many of these though it due to injustice, and barely a third as many as in Britain considered it due to 'laziness and lack of will power'.

Yet, despite the image that may be starting to emerge of a society that was aware and concerned to help its poor, poverty, deprivation and inequality seem to have received fairly little explicit attention in France in the last twenty years, compared, for example, with the USA, Britain or Sweden. Apart from individual, and recently growing, activity on a number of disparate issues, evidence of concern has been well below that in those other countries if one measures it by government activity in terms of committees, reports or legislation, by independent research initiatives, or by the extent of sustained and informed official or public debate, however confined this public may be.

The major exception to this picture that may account for some public awareness has been trade union concern with inequality linked to low pay. Their claims of pauperisation of the working class, seen as absolute in the 1950s and then more often as relative in subsequent years, may well have helped to shape popular perceptions. Even so, Jane Marceau reports evidence from the early 1970s of 'sheer ignorance on the part of the mass of the people of some of the important inequalities which remained in spite of "social protection".

Nevertheless there have not been the many detailed analyses and discussions of poverty and measures to reduce it that have occurred in the USA and Britain. In these terms there is no poverty debate in France, no major poverty lobby, let alone any official anti-poverty programme. But any account of poverty simply based on the review of published materials and on discussion and correspondence with a small number of people, and undertaken from another country, must be at best regarded with a certain wariness. At worst it may reinforce stereotypes and pre-judgments, if not prejudices : confirm limited conventional wisdom of a foreign land; and mislead those who seek to gain lessons both for policy and the analysis of industrial capitalist societies from the growing number of comparative studies.

After 1945 the major problems of reconstruction, and an inflation which affected France earlier than most western countries, had the effect both of diverting attention from the specific problems of particular groups traditionally vulnerable to poverty and of a exacerbating, or at best maintaining, regional and occupational differences in economic and social well-being. In addition the French social security legislation of 1945 and 1946 was seen as a 'Working-class victory equal to the social reforms of 1936', and spoken of in terms of its social democratic spirit, solidarity end social justice. Combined with the high rate of economic growth after the War, which brought about many evident changes in the society, it helped to create the belief of poverty-free society even though the new social security scheme provided nothing for the unemployed—a reflection perhaps of the fact that France was less affected than many countries by the inter-war depression.

In early 1964, UNCAF (the Union Nationale des Caissesd' Allocations Familiales), one of the major national organisations in France allocating funds which could be said to combat poverty through its.

Despite the 35 per cent increase in June 1968 (38 per cent outside Paris), which directly helped 12 per cent of workers, average wages after that continued to draw away from the minimum level. The introduction of SMIC in 1970 was an attempt to prevent the lowest wages falling behind. The act stated that SMIC guarantees the lowest paid workers that their buying power will be maintained and they will have a share in economic growth'. From the end of 1972, until the middle of 1974 at least, SMIC grew faster than the average [hourly wage, and by 1975 it had caught up to the proportion of the average wage it had been in 1954.

Although, the use of SMIC to indicate the extent of poverty in work has a certain logic, its value for measuring low incomes for all groups is clearly more debatable. How much should it be adjusted to arrive at the net amount for equitable comparison of the income levels of those in and out of work, and for those outside the labour force altogether ? Even for those in work it does not take account of family allowances and other benefits or taxes, social security and other contributions.

There is an additional problem in using SMIC as an indicator of poverty over time similar to the application of supplementary benefit levels in Britain. A more generous increase by a government that raises SMIC by more than prices or average earnings may show an increase of those in poverty outside the areas of employment covered by SMIC.

SMIC is a useful indicator of poverty among workers, provided two factors are taken into account. One is the problems of relating a minimum hourly rate to weekly earnings data, which is partly dealt with by excluding part-time workers ; the difficulty that remains here is that some will have worked more than the basic week of 40 hours and only the overtime will have taken them over the poverty line. The other major difficulty is the construction of a net monthly measure based on a gross weekly wage of 40 hours at SMIC rates minus contributions to Social Security, the complementary schemes for retirement and unemployment insurance. On this basis Nicole Borel suggests a cut-off point for July 1974 at 1500 F net per month for those in full-time work. But this calculation takes no account of any payment of family allowances or other benefits nor of deductions of tax : and there are no comparable data for the analysis of poverty in work by family size at that date.

Borel's first finding was the large scale of the problem indicated by the measure suggested, and even by less generous ones. One-third of wage earners were receiving less than 1500F net, one-fifth less than 1330F, in July 1974. At both levels the clear majority of workers came from the private and semi-public sectors (69 per cent at 1500 F and 76 per cent at 1300 F.) The second main finding was 'the very great inequality in the distribution of low pay'. The risk of being in working equality varied very much among different groups. Nearly nine out of ten domestic workers received less than 1500 F net a month, and over seven out of ten in local government and farming, compared with three out of ten in the main private and semi-public sectors, and less than two out of ten in central government. The difference between local and central government very largely reflects the much greater preponderance of established as opposed to temporary or non-established civil servants in the latter.

Women in full-time work are much more likely to be low-paid than men (44 per cent and 24.5 per cent respectively below 1500 F net). And, of course, women are also more likely to be in low-paying part-time jobs, especially those having to look after young children by themselves. In part women's greater risk of poverty in work reflects their greater concentration in low-paying sectors such as local government, where the proportion low-paid in each sex does not vary greatly. In public employment as a whole women are less likely to experience discrimination, and it is outside this area that the chance of low-pay for women is almost twice as great as for men.

The risk of low pay is much greater in four main industries, in addition to agriculture and domestic work : clothing, personal services such as hairdressing 74 per cent, hotel and catering 60 per cent, and textiles 51 per cent. Although tips may augment pay in some service industries, low earnings are still very prevalent. These are also industries likely to have an above average proportion of foreign workers who are particularly likely to be low-paid.

The risk of low pay is also of course considerably greater for those workers who do not receive the full protection of SMIC : apprentices, workers under 18 years of age, certain disabled workers, and those working within prisons. In addition many part-time workers are found in the low-paying industries, especially women with young children, but they are not included in the calculations above.

Finally, the self-employed are a very much larger proportion of the working population in France than in Britain. In general the data for this group are much more limited, but the available evidence indicates a much greater heterogeneity among them, and a wider dispersion of income. On 1966 data Scardigli considered that a large number of individuals in this group most certainly have very low incomes : small farmers, craftsmen, small shopkeepers. At the same date Klanfer reported that estimates suggested that there were as many on low incomes among the self-employed as in employment.

963. Weber, E. *Peasants into Frenchmen.* Stanford, 1976.

964. Wright, G. *Rural revolution in France : the peasantry in the twentieth century.* Stanford, 1964.

GHANA

965. Austin, Dennis. *Politics in Ghana.* London, 1964.

966. Dusautoy, P. *Community development in Ghana.* London, 1958.

967. Fitch, Bob and Mary Oppenheimer. Economics in the political Kingdom, 1957-61. In *Ghana*, New York, 1966 ; 81-94.

As Charles Bettelheim has pointed out, the "poor" nations of the world are not underdeveloped : they are oppressed. Their problem is not lack of development but morbid development. This is no more terminological quibble. It is the key to understanding the problem of economic backwardness. When a morphological study is made of the two types, it becomes clear that the industrial nation is not simply the enlarged "mature" form of the poor nation or its "logical" outgrowth :

Today's industrialized countries are not economically dependent. The structure of their production does not correspond to that of "underdeveloped" countries in which a few hypertrophed sectors are narrowly tied to a few foreign markets, deeply penetrated by foreign capital. These economics do not develop or stagnate according to the evolution of the world market for this or that mineral or agricultural raw material. They are not forced to support the cost of heavy foreign financial obligations (interest, dividends, royalties paid to foreign capitalists). Their infant industries do not have to face the competition of powerful, already established industries dominated by the same big capital which already dominates their own natural resources. These economies do not depend for their enlarged reproduction on imports of equipment coming from abroad. Even when they were not fully industrialized, they were not deformed and disequalibrated but, on the countrary, integrated and self-centred.

According to Bettelheim, it is incorrect to say that the poor countries have not developed. They have, but their development has been skewed by their relationship with the West. Consequently, the problem of economic growth is not solved by evolution, i.e., by stimulating growth within the old economic structures and by intensifying the existing relationships. Growth can only be attained by the opposite means –by smashing the old structures and severing the old relationships. Only then is it possible to achieve rational, democratic, collective control over economic inputs and outputs—that is, socialist planning.

Ghana's morbid development—the hypertrophy of her foreign dominated export sectors, the rudimentary growth of her internal productive sectors—typifies the dualism characteristic of oppressed nations. We have seen thus far that during the early years of its rule, the CPP made no effort whatsoever to restructure Ghanaian society : the leaders did not see the institutions left behind by the British colonialists as barriers to national economic development. The CPP, at this time, believed that in order to achieve rapid economic growth the institutions of colonialism needed only to be administered by Africans.

At this point one might ask : "If Nkrumah simply maintained all the old colonial institutions, what made the 'free world' attack him so bitterly ? Why did the Soviet Union consistently single him out for special Praise ? How did Ghana become known as a center of African socialism ?" The answer is that there was not one Ghana, but two—a pro-western Ghana from approximately 1957 to 1961, and a pro-socialist Ghana from 1961 to February 1966. The first Ghana operated as an ordinary neo-colony stagnating within the British sphere of influence. It looked to the British pound as its "anchor of safety", kept its external reserves in London instead of Accra, and allowed the British banks to systematically deflate the economy. Post-1961 Ghana attempted to adopt socialist planning techniques, tried to build up the state industrial sector, and finally brought the British banks under some measure of control.

Pre-1961 Ghana had been guided by a development strategy formulated by W. Arthur Lewis. This strategy, which emphasized total dependence on foreign capital to industrialize the country, brought nearly complete disaster. During the "Lewis era," Ghana experienced rapid deterioration of her balance of payments position, loss of huge amounts of external reserves, and failure to attract anywhere near the amount of foreign capital which Lewis counted on to assure Ghana's industrial future.

Then during the depth of Ghana's 1961 balance of payments debacle, Nkrumah introduced the "Seven Year Plan for Work and Happiness." This plan forms a real watershed in post-independence Ghanaian history. The plan declared socialism to be the national objective and sought to achieve self-sustaining industrial growth by 1967. Contrary to the Lewis strategy, the state was to have the major role in economic development.

Historical accuracy is not the only reason for emphasizing the existence of two stages of Ghanaian history and attempting to describe how one stage led to the next. There are also important political reasons. By telescoping Ghanaian history into one horrendous "socialistic-communistic dictatorship," the NATO intellectuals are able to ignore the neo-colonial background from which Ghana tried to escape; they are not required to defend the embarrassing Lewis period. This period provides an obvious case study of how the most "affluent" of the oppressed nations carefully followed the orthodox teachings of a respected NATO intellectual and achieved rapid progress—to the brink of economic disaster.

By treating Ghanaian history as a monolith, it is possible to ignore entirely the reasons why Nkrumah at last tried to take a non-capitalist path. Instead, his increasingly bitter attacks on neo-colonialism can be discussed in psycho-pathological terms: "paranoia," "love-hate relationship," "increasing megalomania," "transference," etc. Finally, if all of Ghana's post-independence history was an experiment in socialism, and if that experiment failed, then it can be argued that socialism is really unworkable in Africa.

The failure of the socialist experiment in Ghana did not lie in the peculiarity of African circumstances, and still less in the psychology of a single man. It failed because the attempt to break with Ghana's colonial past was not made soon enough, and because when it was made, it was not complete enough. In order to understand the failure of the post-1961 socialist experiment, as well as the earlier failure of the Lewis strategy, it is necessary now to analyze more precisely the neo-colonial mode of production in Ghana and the barriers it presented to balanced, integrated economic growth. Three major sectors of the economy will be touched upon: cocoa, mining and manufacturing.

In the attempt to establish a conservative "image", Ghana had opened the way for the balance of payments difficulties of the 1959-61 period and lost the greater share of her reserves without any tangible benefits. After 1961, the policies of the Nkrumah government changed :

they included large government outlays for consumer—and capital-goods factories, Soviet-inspired planning techniques, stringent import controls, and expanded fiscal and monetary powers. All these policies were part of Ghana's natural reaction against the failures of the neo-colonial period.

In any country, the political elite can derive its income only from tapping the economic surplus. But in an oppressed country like Ghana, there is no inherent tendency for self-sustaining economic growth. How, then is the elite to derive its sustenance without starving its subjects ? In the food-farming sector, a subsistence economy prevails ; cash crops like cocoa have been subject to deteriorating terms of trade ; mining is dominated by foreign firms with varying profit margins. Taxing the foreign-owned intermediary sectors—the banks and import-export firms—is as politically hazardous as trying to tax the mines. This leaves only one sector—manufacturing. In order to increase, or even maintain, its standard of living and its political machine, the political elite must increase manufacturing.

But this cannot be accomplished without the complete mobilization of the organized working class, the same working class that the political elite was forced to discipline in the pre-independence days to placate the colonial interests. And in the post-independence period, the political elite and the organized working class confront each other as potential consumers of the economic surplus. To combat the growing dissatisfaction of the working class and the urban lumpen-proletariat—which in Ghana was expressed both by the Ga Shifimo Kpee and the 1961 General Strike—the political elite is forced to turn more and more to mystification as a source of legitimacy. The cult of the leader is born---not from the nationalist hero's desire for flattery, but because, as Fanon points out, "the leader is all the more necessary now that there is no more party." But even this does not solve the economic problem.

Consequently, the political elite must turn more and more to foreign interests : taxes on the mines, the banks, the firms, small as they may be, provide the only solid source of revenue; suppliers' credits, onerous as the terms may be, remain the only hope for increasing the economic surplus as the population expands and the terms of trade decline. Eventually, however, the foreign investor demands his money back.

By the time the coup occurred, the CPP's relation to the masses had passed through three stages, similar to those experienced by political elites in oppressed countries elsewhere. During the first stage, the CPP derived its legitimacy from its ability to strike bargains with the colonial leaders. During the second stage, it derived legitimacy from its past successes in bargaining with the colonialists. During the final stage, the masses and the other competing elites—the army and the civil servants—began to realize that the bargains struck by the political elite were worthless to them. From this point on, it was only a matter of time before a new elite emerged which would resolve the contradiction either in favour of the masses or in favour of neo-colonialism. The effort to coordinate the interests of both had proved impossible.

The era of postwar colonial independence movements is over now. The political elites who mediated their way to power are giving way to new military/bureaucratic elites who function in the name of austerity and efficiency. But it must not be thought that, simply by acting in favour of the old colonial power, the new rules have put an end to the contradictions which faced and defeated the departing political elites.

How can this "circulation of elites" be stopped? What is needed to put an end to the politics of mediation? How can political and economic independence be combined? The specific answers to these questions can only come from Africans, through the experience of their own revolutionary movements. Already, however, in "Portuguese" Guinea, where the Partido Africano da Independenica da Guin'e Cabo Verde (PAIGC) has liberated over half the country, a general outline of the solution appears to be developing. In "Portuguese" Guinea, starting with a movement very similar in class composition to that in Ghana during the early days of the CPP, the PAIGC has been able to develop a revolutionary movement through the process of anti-colonial war.

968. Foster, P. *Education and social change in Ghana.* London, 1965.

969. Jeffries, Richard. *Class, power and ideology in Ghana.* Cambridge, 1978.

970. Gaisie, S.K. Fertility among the Ghanaian tribes. *In population growth and economic development in Africa.* Ed. by S.H. Iminde and E.N. Ejiogn. London, 1972.

971. Hill, Polly. *Migrant Cocoa farmers of Southern Ghana.* Cambridge Univ. Press, 1963.

972. Kraft, Scott. Leftist Ghana embracing capitalism. *International Herald Tribune,* 23-24 Aug. 1986; 1-2.

973. Rathbone, Richard. Ghana. *In West African States.* Cambridge, 1978; 22-35.

974. Schildkrout, E. Fostering children in urban Ghana. *Urban Anthropology*, 2, 1973; 48-73.

GREECE

975. Dokopoulou, E. Foreign manufacturing investment in Greece. In *IDPR*; 188-204.

976. Egli, David. High inflation persists despite other successes. *International Herald Tribune*, Oct. 1978.

977. Hope-Simpson, John. Work of the Greek refugee settlement Commission (Address before R.I.A.A.) *Journal of the Royal Institute for International Affairs*, Nov. 1929.

978. Labrianidis, Lois. Industrial location—Product of multiple factors : the tobacco industry in Greece in *IDPR*; 232-65.

979. Neher, Jacques. Ailing Greek economy puts a squeeze on the E.C. *International Herald Tribune*, 4-5 Oct. 1986; 10.

980. Papadopoulos, Sofronis. Papandreou's austerity sparks a massive upsurge. *International Viewpoint*, 13 Jan. 1986; 3-5.

981. Warnings are given on wage controls to contain inflation. *International Herald Tribune* Oct. 1978.

GUATEMALA

982. Galeano, Eduardo. *Guatemala occupied country*. New York, Modern Reader Paperbacks; 1967, p. 159.

983. Galeano, Eduardo. Unpunished crimes of poverty. In *Guatemala*. New York, Modern Reader Paper-backs, 1967; 93-102.

GUINEA

984. Johnson, K.W. Guinea. In *West African States*. Cambridge, 1978; 36-65.

GUYANA

985. Abrams, Mark and R. Rose. Must labour last ? London, 1960.

986. Chase, Aghton. *133 days towards freedom in Guiana*. Georgetown, 1964.

987. Chase, Ashton. *Trade Unionism in British Guiana*. London, 1962.

988. Farley, Rawle. African peasantry in Guiana. *Social and Economic Studies* 2, 1954; 8-19.

989. Greene, J.E. *Race Vs politics in Guyana*. University of the West Indies, 1974. p. 198.

990. Herskovits, M.J. *Myth of the Negro Past*. New York, Harper Bros., 1941.

991. Jagan, Cheddi. *Anatomy of poverty in British Guyana*. Georgetown, Guyana : PPP, 1954.

992. Jagan, Cheddi. *Forbidden freedom*. London, 1954.

993. Reno, Philip. *Ordeal of British Guiana*. New York, 1964.

994. Simms, Peter. *Trouble in Guyana*. London, 1966.

HAITI

995. Tuchnin, Ruslan. After baby doc. *New Times* (Moscow) (27) 14 Jul. 1986; 20-21.

On June 10, 1986 Haiti was swept by a nationwide strike. This would have been unthinkable only six months ago. Recent weeks have seen a rash of political demonstrations in the capital Port-au-Prince, in Cap Haitien, Gonaives and other cities. There have been angry crowds, barricades, fierce clashes with riot police. All this is taking place in a country whose people groaned under the cruel Duvalier family dictatorship for almost thirty years when not only open protest against the authorities but even meek criticism provided grounds for arrest, forture, murder or "disappearance".

The people of Haiti have just awakened to political life but the ruling elite is already busy behind the scenes attempting to nip it in the bud. While the U.S. Ambassador in Port-au-Prince who on February 7 offered his plane to Baby Doc, the dictator Jean-Claude Duvalier, was ironing out the last details of the tyrant's escape across the Atlantic, the upper echelons of the military were sharing out government posts. Generals and colonels who had been pushed aside by the fontons macoutes (the security police) but who had served the dictator loyally scrambled to take over control of the state.

To politically inexperienced Haitians, soldiers from barracks looked less odious than the rabid tonfons macoutes. So the appearance of the military in government was at first accepted as the lesser evil. And some quarters even welcomed the army.

Few people realized at the time that the reactionary military, who had seized key positions in the country, were entrusted with the mission of keeping the people in a vice to prevent mass movements from overflowing the bounds set by Washington and the local oligarchy.

This was the reason the Reagan Administration dismissed the bankrupt Duvalier Jr. and sent him to the Old World. The Administration's think tank believed that a safety valve had to be opened in the seething Haitian cauldron if a devastating social explosion was to be prevented.

Following the evacuation of Baby Dock, the "big" U.S. press wrote of the need to fill the "political vacuum" in Haiti. This assessment had a grain of truth in it the Duvalier regime had been so ferocious, its enemies had been destroyed on such a scale and with such brutality (50,000 murders) that in the early days after the tyrant's fall the political arena looked like a desert in which the only visible object was the army barracks. It was from the barracks that the generals and colonels who had formed the elite of the dictatorial regime emerged to claim the role of the country's saviours from chaos.

INDIA

996. Agarwal, C.B. *Harijans in rebellion.* Bombay, 1934.

997. Akbar, M.J. Poor and the 21st Century, *Telegraph* (Calcutta) 10 Feb. 1986 ; 6.

998. Alagh, Yoginder K. *et. al.* Agricultural growth and manpower absorption in India. *In Labour absorption in Indian agriculture* by P.K. Bardhan *et. al.* Bangkok, ILO-ARTEP, 1978.

999. Alexander, K.C. Some aspects of peasant organizations in *South India. Rural Development Participation Review* 1 (1) 1979.

1000. Alleviating poverty. *Patriot* 22 Apr. 1986 ; 4.

It is a double abstraction that tends to make misleading such official claims as have been made about the results of some major poverty alleviation schemes for 1985-86. If the profusion of figures cited lend the achievement an amorphous character, the nebulousness of the concepts employed makes it all the more difficult to get a real measure of the asserted rural progress. A telling illustration is the claim that the Integrated Rural Development Programme (IRDP) has helped more than two million rural families cross the poverty line in the last one year. Given the elasticity of the poverty line (quantified, for the moment, roughly at earnings of Rs. 1,800 per head at current prices), that statement says nothing about whether the stress of the programme implementation has been a favour of the poorest of the poor or how enduring is the new status of the beneficiaries. Such questions are hardly impertinent, and they have been raised before in different terms by many an expert study of the impact of the major programmes and the projects being implemented under them.

1001. Amolak Ram. Picture of poverty. *Hindustan Times* 20 Apr. 1986 ; 9.

1002. Anand. V. Eghwar. Poverty and development I & II : *Statesman*, 17 & 18 Dec. 1985 ; 6.

1003. Anandan, P.I. Coronation and the depressed classes. *Hindustan Review* 24, 1911 ; 529-32.

1004. Anti-poverty schemes. *Economic Times* 25 Nov. 1985 ; 5.

1005. Anti-poverty shortfalls. *Times of India* 18 Mar. 1986 ; 8.

1006. Baig, Tara Ali. Poverty as a national asset. *Times of India* 8 Jan. 1986 ; 8.

Civilisation should mean being civilised. Unfortunately, a vast number of people, who pride themselves on being civilised, which the dictionary defines as "having been reclaimed from a savage state," are often more savage than the so-called savages. When it comes to exploitation, we too have been guilty.

Today democracy and hypocrisy have many faces. The two are often combined now in one facade in India where the democratic process of political evolution has been grafted so expertly onto the old social and feudal systems. A headline in the Times of India says "voluntary bodies urged to fight poverty". Why does the prime minister stress that this is a "crucial role" for voluntary agencies to play, when this did not seem to be the case before or in his mother's political programme ? The slogan of "garibi hatao" and the 20-point programme related to all political cadres of the party and administrators in their jurisdictions. Yet the appeal today is to none of these. In point of fact, voluntary organisations were forced to rely for funds upon the government grant system and not at all on their enterprise or ability to build up financial independence of any kind, thanks not long ago to the income tax amendments that shackled their freedom.

1007. Bajaj, Ramkrishna. *Indian Economy : Emerging perspectives*. New Delhi, Allied, 1986. p. 194.

1008. Bawa, T.S. *Nehru's India.* New Delhi, Freeland Publications, 1956.

1009. Bhatia, Prem. Thank God for poverty. *Newstime* (Hyderabad) 4 Oct. 1986 ; 7.

1010. Bhatte, V.M. *India.* In *EAPS* ; 55-57.

Ownership of capital is even more unevenly divided, with high degree of concentration of wealth. While the statistics of the distribution of corporate and non-corporate capital are not used here, they are known to reveal a high concentration in the hands of the few rich. Further conclusions can be drawn from the pattern of income-distribution in India. The top 5 per cent of the households account for about 20 per cent of the total personal income---17 per cent in the rural and 26 per cent in the urban sector. The ability to save---which can form one of the main bases of capital accumulation by the large mass of low or even the middle income groups—is very low. In fact, recently there seems to be increasing capital consumption among the middle and fixed income groups. The poor and low-income groups of the Indian society have meagre hopes of sharing in any significant part of the capital. To some extent, the state-ownership—through the enlargement of the public sector, nationalisation etc. may mitigate the gravity of the picture of unequal distribution of capital as a means of production. However, the "have-nots" are not likely to have the opportunity or the hope of adequate participation in the development of the modern industrial sector, even in the labour intensive and small-scale production. The pattern of income-distribution is likely to become even more unequal if the economic development process according to the present pattern of planning continues—in spite of its proclaimed aim of a "socialist economy". The rise during the last decade in the concentration ratio—particularly in the urban sector---in indicative of this trend.

The picture of mass-poverty arising from the unequal distribution and ownership of land and capital, and the large and growing mass of "have-nots" is further aggravated by the unequal distribution of the opportunities and benefits derived from literacy, education and skills-formation. The size of the resources devoted to man-power development could be partially judged from the public sector outlays on education and social welfare, and from an investigation as to who really derives main benefits from such outlays. Investment in housing and urban development mostly benefits the rich and the upper-middle class, even if we consider the outlays on worker's housing as a significant redeeming feature of the present plans. But such outlays have been meagre. In case of education, what can we hope from the Fourth Plan which provided (in terms of 1960-61 prices) just about Rs. 0.84 per capita ? India may have produced an adequate compliment of engineers (in fact, thousands of them are unemployed or migrate to other countries), but primary education is still not universally and freely available to all the school going age group of children in urban and rural areas. Millions of youth have no prospects in the foreseeable future of participating in the development process and benefiting therefrom. It is not only a question of lack of resources for man-power development. We have to motivate 60 million families and prepare them mentally to do the job they should do. There is widespread idleness and lack of intensive work performance among the labour force. The apathy to work even among the employed and the trends towards labour-strikes compound the problem even more.

Particularly, the rural land-less labour have nothing to offer except their bare hands, for lack of skills-development, even if they can be employed through a massive programme of public works. While they remain unemployed, the society as a whole—in one way or other—has to keep them alive by providing at least the meagre subsistence for their survival.

The complexity of the problem is aggravated by the very enormous size of the population involved, compounded further by the increasing population growth.

In 1969, there were 245 to 250 million Indian citizens who were below the so-called line of bare-minimum of living—judged by any standard—per capita income, nutrition, employment, clothing, housing, etc. In 1974, even under the most optimistic assumptions, there will still be 225 to 235 million people under the same category. Family planning programmes—even if they are comprehensive, effective and sustained—will result in some decline in the rate of population growth only in the 1980's at the earliest. On the other hand, with the present slow and low overall economic growth (with very sharp cut-backs in food supply which may take place in any year of draught, floods and other disasters), with some 250 million people living below the so-called poverty line whose consumption needs are none-the-less compulsive, what amount of savings, resources, aid etc. for development can be mustered ? We are caught in a vicious circle—which can get even more vicious—since the latest Plan predicts that we can not grow fast enough, and we cannot do much by way of redistribution of wealth, land, income, and opportunities for skills formation of education.

1011. Blair, Harry W. Rising Kulaks and backward classes in Bihar ;

Social change in the late 1970s. *Economic and Political Weekly* 15, 12 Jan. 1983 ; 64-74.

1012. Butler, Harold. *Problems and Industry in the East, with special reference to India, French India. Ceylon, Malaya and the Netherlands Indies* Geneva, ILO, 1938.

1013. Chandran, T.N. *Poverty-affected groups in India.* Trivandrum, 1972.

1014. Changes suggested in anti-poverty set-up (by G.V.K. Rao). *Indian Express* 10 Mar. 1986 ; 11.

1015. Chodke, Manju. Poverty and alleviation programmes. *Economic Times* (New Delhi) 26 Jun. 1986 ; III.

1016. Chopra, Pran. Can we afford our poverty. *Economic Times* 20 Sep. 1981 ; 4-5.

1017. Da Costa, E.W. Portrait of Indian poverty. In *challenge of Indian poverty.* Ed. by A.J. Fonseca, New Delhi, Vikas, 1971.

1018. Dandekar, V.M. and N. Rath. *Poverty in India.* Bombay, Indian School of Political Economy, 1971.

1019. Das, Amritananda, Studying poverty in developing nations : with special reference to India. In *EAPS* : 223-35.

The current widespread interest in empirical studies of poverty in developing nations reflects a new awareness of a critical fact, that rapid economic modernisation (even when this results in impressive increases in GNP per capital does not have much positive impact upon problems of mass poverty in developing nations. Even when "growth" is accompanied by apparently strong redistributive measures, the bulk of benefits go to a thin elite stratum, leaving the masses untouched, if not actually worse off.

This now well-documented fact of the tendency of economic modernisation to result in maldevelopment, indicates that efficient programmes for the elimination of poverty must differ quite radically from conventional strategies for rapid economic growth. Once the distinction is accepted, both humanitarian and mass politics considerations virtually force us to give primacy to poverty-elimination (rather than "growth") and the prime target of national planning.

In order to translate this new priority into praxis, however, much more accurate information than we now possess on poverty problems of developing nations will have to be marshalled. This underlines the need for action-oriented empirical studies of poverty—which have, fortunately become widely accepted.

In one sense, poverty studies in India have a long history dating back to pioneer works like Dadabhai Naoroji's 'Poverty and Unbritish Rule in India'. This and later nationalist writings in the same vein did not, however, constitute poverty studies in the strict sense of the term as we have been using it. That is, they did not contain information directly useful for planning anti-poverty strategies.

Further, most of the "nationalists" were convinced that the cure of mass poverty lay in rapid modernisation. Only Gandhiji was perceptive enough to realise that modernisation can lead to maldevelopment and, therefore, to press for unconventional development strategies with a specific anti-poverty content. Gandhi's seminal insights, however, not backed up by empirical research on broad base.

The early post-Independence era was marked by the dominance of the ideology of poverty-elimination through rapid modernisation plus redistributive measures of the conventional type. It took quite some time to realise that this mixture was not having the expected effects. The beginnings of poverty studies (in our strict sense) can therefore be noted only from late second Five Year Plan onwards.

Certain landmarks of this period may be briefly noted.

A. In 1961, the Study Group on the Welfare of the Weaker Sections of the village community—headed by Shri J.P. Narayan—reported that about 40 to 45 per cent of rural households had an income of less than Rs. 500 ($ 67 approx) annually and 80 per cent less than Rs. 1,000 ($ 135 approx) annually.

B. In July 1962, a high-power working group recommended as a 'bare minimum' an expenditure of Rs. 240 ($ 32 approx) per capita annually, at 1960-61 prices. This has become the conventional "poverty line", with appropriate price-level adjustments.

C. In September 1962, the Reserve Bank of India Bulletin contained the classic study by P.D. Ojha and V.V. Bhatt 'Distribution of income in the Indian Economy 1953-54 to 1956-57'. This revealed, inter alia, that 5 per cent of top households obtained

20 per cent of personal income. Further, the study indicated that distribution of income was on the way towards becoming more unequal.

D. In NCAER study entitled "All India Rural Household Survey, Income, Investment and Saving, vol. II (1965)" and the parallel study "Urban Income and Saving" yielded data which showed that—in the early 'sixties—86 per cent of the population had per-capita income all less than rupee one a day. Also about 20 per cent of rural households were seen to own no land and 25 per cent to have land below one acre. Further, 13.6 per cent households (in the bottom group) had per capita annual income of Rs. 108.40 ($ 14.5) on average. The highest income group contained only 2.2 per cent households with per capita annual income of Rs. 935.50 ($ 124.6) on average.

E. Apart from these influential studies, vast amounts of data were being accummulated by the National Sample Survey (NSS) dealing in particular with levels of consumer expenditure, patterns of land ownership etc.—which (when analysed) could—yield similar findings on mass poverty phenomena.

F. A crop of official reports on various aspects of policy were also coming up, and they yielded valuable but fragmentary information on poverty and maldevelopment. Notable in this context is the *Mahalanobis Commission Report* on concentration of economic power which showed the virtual collapse of the redistributives measures on which reliance had been earlier placed.

G. Individual studies, by social scientists of institutional change and social welfare administration revealed considerable evidence of how—at the gross roots level—most of the policy-initiatives meant to benefit the weaker sections were being frustrated or diverted away from their true aims.

H. Finally, the Planning Commission's Studies on the progress of planning--particularly as related to the unemployment/under-employment situation gave conclusive evidence of the failure to control maldevelopment.

These developments have culminated in a number of high quality technical studies of poverty in the recent epoch 1970—mid '73. In the main, they have been statistical in nature with little emphasis on detailed programmatic analysis. Nonetheless, they represent a fundamental advance on the studies in the preceding period both in the precision and in their relevance to formulation of action-programmes.

1020. Das, Suhas Chandra. Fighting poverty (in rural India) *Amrita Bazar Patrika* (Calcutta) 26 Mar. 1986; 6.

Ajit Panja, the Union Minister of State for Planning said—"A direct assault on poverty was being mounted in the Seventh Plan with the object of bringing down the poverty line." Over the past 33 years, the Government has spent many thousands of crores in rural development programmes which were primarily meant to alleviate poverty.

But it is a sad commentary, that even the specially designed poverty alleviation programmes are not reaching the poor. Nor do they have sufficient depth to make an impression on poverty, let alone eliminate it. Despite claims to the contrary alleviation on poverty in India remains an unfinished task. Poverty in India is essentially a rural problem, because it originates in villages and when it cannot be contained there, overflows to cities like flood-water in the form of slum-dwellers. Therefore, in any discussion on poverty, the focus has to be on the rural people.

1021. Datt, Rudder. Basics of economics: the poverty line. *Career and competition Times* (New Delhi) May 1986; 35-36.

1022. Deo, Jai Mangal. Need for a new service cadre. *Indian Nation* (Patna) 8 Apr. 1986; 4.

1023. *Depressed Classes*. Madras, G.A. Natesan, 1913.

1024. Deshmukh, Durgabai *ed. Social Welfare in India*. Delhi, Publications Division, 1955.

1025. Dhar, M.K. Budget for growth and poverty alleviation. *Indian and Foreign Review* 31 Mar. 1986; 6-11,30.

1026. Djurfeldt, Goran and Staffan Lindberg. *Pills against poverty : A study of the introduction of Western medicine in a Tamil Village*. London, Curzan Press, 1975.

1027. Dogra, Bharat. *Poverty, development and poverty, India. 1947-84*. New Delhi, Social Change 1984. pp. 327.

1028. Dubashi, Jay. Poverty; Figures and fiction. *Tribune*. (Chandigarh) 15 Oct. 1985;4.

1029. Evil spirit brooding over India, says Palkhivala. *Statesman.* 14 Mar. 1986;7.

1030. Fenner, F.J. Destruction of income opportunities in rural India. *Technica* 30(2) 1972.

1031. Financing poverty. *Surya India*. Dec. 1984: 64-65.

American aid, as it is today, has caused more problems than it has solved. It claims to be attacking poverty, but in the countries American aid is concentrated, the poor just don't have the power to secure the items they need. And with the Americans continuing to support tyrannical regimes round the world, animosity towards the USA is bound to grow.

Many nations of the world are poor and needy. The United States of America is wealthy. It follows logically that America should increase its foreign economic aid to help the poor of the world. This is natural response of most Americans when they are confronted by the incredible destitution in which most of the world's people are forced to live.

However, American foreign economic aid is not beneficial to the people of world.

American foreign economic aid has actually fallen on evil days. After billions of dollars have been expended around the world, America has fewer friends: indeed American aid has gained this country more enemies than allies. U S. foreign assistance fails to help the poor because it is necessarily based on one fundamental fallacy that aid can reach the powerless even though it is channelled through the powerful. Official foreign assistance necessarily flows through the recipient governments, and often particularly in those countries to which the U.S. gives most of its aid, these governments represent narrow economic interests.

American economic aid to those countries where economic control is concentrated in the hands of a few bolsters the power of those who have successfully raped the country and its people. Instead of helping, American aid hurts the weak and poor majority. Articles designed to help the poor become the property of the rich. Thus the poor majority dislikes America even more than it initially did. Foreign aid does not transform non-democratic nations, where a few have power, into democratic nations. The outcome of American aid is just the opposite, official foreign aid reinforces the power relationships that already exist.

Another reason why the economic aid policy of the United States of

America is unsuccessful is because of the incorrect belief that American aid is necessary for the world and for freedom. Some administration officials seem to think that freedom is not free and that peace can be bought. They feel that there is peace in the Middle East only because of massive amounts of American aid to both Egypt and Israel. They feel that the future of the world will be bright only if American aid continues. However, as will be seen, American aid often halts the fight for freedom in the third world. Of the top ten recipients of U.S. economic assistance, only five are third world countries. These countries—India, Indonesia, Bangladesh, Pakistan, and the Philippines—are not known for their commitment to the poor. Indonesia, Bangladesh, Pakistan and the Philippines have earned international reputations for their neglect of the needs of the poor and for their repression of those working for change. Thus, American aid does not go to those governments which have shown a commitment to the poor but to those who repress their own people.

1032. Gaiha. R. *On measuring the risk of poverty in rural India* (*Mimeo*), Delhi University, Faculty of Management Studies, 1982.

1033. Gaiha, R. and N. Kazmi, *Aspects of poverty in rural India.* (Mimeo) Delhi University, Faculty of Management Studies, 1982.

1034. Gandhi, Rajiv. We cannot, and will not rest until we have wiped out poverty from our land. *Telegraph* (Calcutta) 7 Jan. 1986;6.

1035. Garibi Hatao: Easier said. *Newstime* 24 Dec. 1985;7,

1036. 'Garibi Hatato' mostrum. *Pioneer* 4 Jan. 1986;4.

1037. Ghodke, Manju. Poverty and alleviation programmes. *Economic Times* 26 Jun. 1986.

There has been a considerable debate on the subject of poverty since the deliberation of the report of the study group (set up by the government) which regarded the nationally desirable minimum level of consumer expenditure of Rs. 240 per capita per annum. While the controversy still rages on the estimation and the extent of poverty in India, many suggestions are advanced to surmount it.

The problem was highlighted in the Fourth Plan and some estimates of poverty level were made in the Sixth plan. The Seventh Plan document has placed the all India poverty level at 37.4 per cent in 1983-84. As many as 40.4 per cent of the total population in the rural areas are established to be below the poverty line and the corresponding estimates for the urban areas are 28.2 per cent.

In the rural areas, poverty assumes sinister proportions. With the majority of the population dependent on an uncertain agriculture, they have no steady source of employment or income. This lack of adequate employment and hence low purchasing power, keeps them in the vicious circle of poverty. The recurrent drought and famines have brought this problem into sharper focus, necessitating timely measures to curb this growing tide of poverty.

In order to give relief to these teeming millions the recent budget has raised the allocations for poverty alleviation programmes by a whopping 64.7 per cent, from Rs. 913 crores in 1985-86, to Rs. 1504 crores in 1986-87. Greater emphasis is being laid on programmes which are of direct benefit to the weaker sections of the society, especially the scheduled castes and scheduled tribes. The budget also highlighted some of the anti-poverty programmes which are likely to receive a boost during the current year. The National Rural Employment Programmes (NREP) is expected to generate over 300 million mandays in the current year as against 253 million in 1985-86. Its outlay has been stepped up by almost 93 per cent from Rs. 370 crores in 1985-86 to Rs. 443 crores in 1986-87.

The Rural Landless Employment Guarantee Programme (RLEGP) is estimated to have generated employment of 264 million mandays in 1985-86. In outlay has been increased by 58 per cent from Rs. 400 crores in 1985-86, to Rs. 633 crores during the current year. The Integrated Rural Development Programme (IRDP) is to get an increased allocation from Rs. 283 crores in 1985-86 to Rs. 428 crores in 1986-87, or by 20 51 per cent. In the seventh plan the IRDP is expected to assist nearly million families.

In order to alleviate the lot of the rural poor, comprising the small and marginal farmers, landless labourers, rural artisans etc., the Department of rural development has been implementing various programmers, the important ones being IRDP, NREP and RLEGP. To mitigate the harshness of poverty arising out of adverse agro-climatic conditions, the Drought Prone Area Programme (DPAP) and the Desert Development Programme (DDP) are also being implemented.

The IRDP was launched in 1976-77 in 20 selected districts. From

1980, IRDP was extended to all the blocks in the country. It is meant for the benefit of the rural poor, with family as the basic unit of development. At least 30 per cent of the Families under this programme should be from among for schedule castes and scheduled tribes. During the sixth plan, against a target of 15 million families, 16.5 million families were assisted for improving their economic conditions such that they may rise above the poverty line.

1038. Ghose, Sankar. Strategy for small farmers and Weaker Sections. In *Changing India.* New Delhi, Allied, 1980 ; 55-61.

1039. Gyan Prakash. Reproducing inequality. Spirit cults and labour relations in colonial eastern India. *Modern Asian Studies* 20 (2) Apr. 1986 ; 209-30.

1040. Hanumantha Rao, C.H. Changes in rural poverty in India. *Mainstream* 11 Jan. 1986 ; 9-12, 33-34.

1041. Harriss, John. Working poor and the labour aristocracy in a South Indian city. A descriptive and analytical account. *Modern Asian Studies* 20 (2) Apr. 1986 ; 231-84.

1042. How to remove the scourge of poverty (in India) ? *Patriot* 20 Jul. 1986 ; 2.

There are several ways of removing poverty.

The Naxalites have found one way—recourse to arms and ammunition. Kill the big landlords. Kill the money-lenders, whether they are executed after a people's court trial or not. Snatch the land from the landlords and give it to the landless poors. If necessary, kill the Police.

But the Police has more arms than the people. They know how to use arms. They are better killers than the people.

So it has gone on for the last 30 years that the Naxalite movement has been killing, and being killed. The poverty has remained where it was.

There are other ways—the—20-Point Programme and all that. The bureaucrats can conceive and do. The *Darbar* is held in the open. The Collector Saheb declares a moratorium of debts incurred by the poor peasants on which they have been paying interest for as long as they can remember. Now the Government announces that the peasants have paid enough interest and they will be required to pay no more. The peasants are legally and technically freed from the clutches of the money-lenders.

1043. Hundred Years ago: Poverty in India. *Amrita Bazar Patrika* 7 Jun. 1986;7.

1044. India has overcome famine, not hunger. *Times of India* 5 Dec. 1986;1,6.

1045. Iqbal Narain. India in 1985. *Asian Survey* Feb. 1986; 253-69.

1046. Iyyampillai, S. Profile of poverty in a prosperous village. *Financial Express*, 1 Feb. 1986;5.

1047. Jabbar Alam, M. Stealing from funds for anti-poverty programs. *New Age* 6 Jul. 1986; 16.

1048. Jain, I.C. Assault on poverty: More glitter than gold. *Times of India* 31 Mar. 1986; 8.

1049. Jasbir Singh. Regional disparities in levels of living standard in India : An integrated approach. *Asian Profile*. 14 (2) Apr. 1986; 141-48.

1050. Jensen, F.N. Programmes for the poor in India. *Social Action* 1969.

1051. Karan Singh. Population, poverty and development. In *One Man's World*. Ed. by Kishore Gandhi. New Delhi, Allied, 1986; 65-72.

1052. Kumarappa, J.M. *Our begger problem* : *How to tackle it*. Bombay, Padma 1945. p. 294.

1053. Kurien, C.T. *Rural poverty in Tamil Nadu. In poverty landlessness in rural Asia*. Geneva, ILO, 1977.

1054. Lakdawala, D. *Growth, employment and poverty*. Tripati, All India Labour Economics Conference, 1977. (Presidential address).

1055. Lehman, David *ed. Agrarian reform and agrarian reformism*: *Studies of Peru, Chile and India*, London, 1974.

1056. Madan, B.K. Poverty : causes and cure. *Yojana* (New Delhi) 15 Aug. 1979; 53-58,86.

1057. Manuja, M. Twenty-first century poverty. *Madhya Pradesh Chromide* (Bhopal) 26 Nov. 1985;4.

1058. Medhora, Phiroze R. Poverty in India. *Economic and Political Weekly* 2 Feb. 1971; 543-48.

1059. Mehta, Manhar. What does she know of our poor and their poverty ? *Organiser* (New Delhi) 26 Jun. 1983; 7.

1060. Metha, Vinod. Growing rich-poor gap. *Tribune* 12 Apr. 1979; 4.

1061. Menon, V.P. *Story of the Integration of the Indian States.* New Delhi. Orient Longman, 1961.

1062. Mies, Maria. Shahada movement : A peasant movement in Maharashtra. *Journal of Peasant Studies* 3 (4) 1976; 473-82.

1063. Mishra, Girish. Party sworn to fight poverty. *Daily* (Bombay) 7 Jan. 1986: 8-9.

The public sector has to play a key role in the times to come. The public sector units must generate resources for investment and must improve their productivity and avoid waste. They cannot be subsidised by the people for all time come. Here a positive response is expected from the leftist parties. Till now, they are silent. They must come forward with concrete proposals and must do something real to motivate their trade unions to fulfil their duty in the grand struggle against neo-colonialism and for real economic independence of the country.

Prime Minister Rajiv Gandhi has warned the private sector which has been interested more in cornering concessions and incentives than in innovations and increasing productivity and improving quality. This situation can no longer be tolerated and the private sector has to reduce unit costs of production and increase its competitive power, if it wants to survive.

The Congress is entering the second century of its existence with a vision of grand India where there would be a determined fight for building an equitable society to guarantee a decent standard of living to every Indian. The fight for an independent modern socialist economy is linked up with the fight against neo-colonialism and poverty. The poor have to be reassured that the Congress cares for it.

1064. Misra, B.B. *Indian middle classes : their growth in modern times.* Oxford, 1961. p. 438.

1065. Modi, L.N. Poverty alleviation in 7th Plan. *Facts for you.* (New Delhi). Feb. 1986;5.

The first question is what is the definition of poverty ? So far it was annual income of Rs. 3500 per family, irrespective of number of family members; on 16th December '85 Mr. Chandulal Chandrakar announced in a press conference that this definition has been changed to yearly income of Rs. 6400 and simultaneously the quantum of assistance has also been raised from Rs. 3000 to 6000 per family.

According to Mr. Chandulal Chandrakar this was done because the past experience had shown that most of the beneficiaries of the poverty alleviation programmes had continued to remain below the poverty line. A second dose of assistance would now be given to them to lift them out of this bracket.

Of about four million people expected to be covered under the poverty alleviation programmes this year, about three million would be old beneficiaries.

From the above it is evident that the definition of poverty is so low that in future years people assisted under poverty alleviation programmes would again come down under poverty line. Therefore need is to assist people in such a way that each member of family can have yearly income of Rs. 3600, so that rural people once out of poverty can sustain themselves with their economic activity. Even under revised norms of poverty it means only Rs. 3.5 per day per man, which is paltry.

1066. Mukherjee, Aditya. *Indian capitalist class : Aspect of its economic, political and ideological development in the colonial period, 1930-47.* New Delhi, JNU History Centre, 1982 (Mimeo).

1067. Mukherji, Aruna. Portrait of poverty : Eradication plans need co-ordination. *Daily* (Bombay) 7 Mar. 1986; 10-11.

The recent Congress (I) centenary re-emphasised that its major goal is the elimination of poverty and hunger. Yet, the most distressing fact in India today is that this country accounts for one-third of the hungry peoples of the world and that over 300 million people live below the poverty line—a concept the economists have evolved to describe the abysmally poor who are not getting the minimum of nourishment to sustain the body.

Some years ago, the Planning Commission made in interesting survey which revealed that of the 304.6 million people in India who continued to live below the poverty line which was put at Rs. 65 per capita income per month, the overwhelming majority 252.7 million lived in the rural areas and 51.84 million in the urban areas.

1068. Mukherji, Aruna. Poverty in India : the great betrayal. *Daily* (Bombay) 19 Mar. 1983; 10-11.

How many realise that today after three decades of planning, as many as 304.6 million people in India continues to live in India continues to live in abject poverty—below the poverty line, which is defined as Rs. 65 per capita income per month ? The estimate is based on a survey made by the Planning Commission.

In other words, 45 per cent, or nearly half the population of India does not get sufficient food to eat. The vast majority of these men, women and children—252.7 million live in the rural areas; while the poverty-stricken people living in the urban areas in slums on the pavement or in some nook and cranny is 51.84 million. There cannot be a greater condemnation of the traversity of "economic growth" which has taken place in India than that millions are condemned to a life of misery and utter degradation after about Rs. 15,000 crores have been poured into the planning process.

Those living in such anguish in the rural areas never make the headlines in the daily press. To the economics they are merely numbers and they analyse in their usual abstruse fashion the reasons for the existence of so much poverty in India.

What the Asian Development Bank had to say is as pertinent today as when the observation was made. It was realistic when it observed that Asia's poor millions are not only unable to earn an income sufficient to meet bare necessities, they are typically also deprived of essential public services such as sanitation, potable drinking water, basic health care and elementary education.

1069. Mukherji, M. *National income of India* : *Trends and structure*. Calcutta, Statistical Publishing Society, 1969.

1070. Nair. G. Ravindran. Uruli Kanchan : Hope for the rural poor. *Economic Times*. 20 Dec. 1985;5.

1071. Naoroji, Dadabhai. *Poverty and un-British rule in India*. Delhi, Publications Division, 1962.

1072. Nath, Trilok. Poverty shift. *Patriot* 20 Jul. 1986.

The urbanised areas generally municipalised, appear to be bursting at the seams. Unlike the spill over in the countryside which results in development of smaller hamlets, the scene in the urban areas is that of utter disorganisation and congestion in the existing municipalities. Allied to it is the discipline syndrome which has affected the urbanised areas in particular. These are the vocal as also focal points of various agitations.

In the urban areas squatters rule the roost. Unauthorised use of vacant premises and encroachments are made for starting workshops and business establishments including shops selling grocery and other wares. Roads in all urbanised areas are glorified shopping centres with eating houses interspersed leading to squallor and unhealthiness.

The problem appears to contain urban growth in the existing townships, so as to avoid vagarancy. In the absence of an appropriate number of living tenements or even of jobs which draw a flood of population from the rural areas to the towns vagarancy, begging and criminality develop. Needless to say control can only be exercised by putting down the obvious evil with a firm and strong hand. Vagarancy in the urban areas could be put down by providing homes in which vagarance could be pulled in for work. Similarly no "squating" should be permitted on any account. Commercial activities should be confined to the premises alloted for the purpose.

The requirements in the urbanised areas at present is quite high and the availability is poor. Some of the not fully organised sectors like the subsections of restauranteers, have a very high level of the shortfall. This need be fully examined so as to organise training in these fields as well. This question of a population audit requires to be gone into rigorously in order to make concerted attack on the problem of unemployment and underemployment as well.

The sight of employed personnel wasting a good bit of their working hours in their favourite pastime of "talking and spitting", naturally results in lower productivity in all the fields. The tendency has been to provide a first line corps of supervisors to ensure that work goes on more systematically with less interruptions. But this provision does not appear to have proved worth-while and in fact it has been counter-productive resulting in development of tier after tier of supervisory cadres which further clog the wheel of progress.

The result has also been of creating multifarious grades in all services and avocations which are a detriment to progress. In any case this does not conduce to the bringing in of a socialistic pattern of society to which the country is wedded after independence was achieved. The stratification of society into snob groups and those at the bottom rungs has gone on. The western impact has given a jolt to some extent yet the old style of evaluation of various rungs in society has gone on, making the entire structure weak.

1073. No poverty after 15 years : (Dr.) Manmohan Singh. *Hindustan Times* 15 Dec. 1985; 8.

1074. Ojha, P.D. "Trickle down" theory does not work. *Economic Times* 26 Jun. 1986.

It is not easy to define in precise terms 'poverty'. It can be relative poverty or it can be poverty in the absolute sense. In the latter sense, who can be considered absolute poor ? Perhaps those who are denied certain basic essential necessities of daily life. Here again, it all depends, what is meant by 'basic essential requirements'. There is a concept of 'Basic' or 'minimum need' which, among others, include food, clothes, education, housing, health, etc. In my scheme of things, when I attempted a measurement of the absolute level of poverty. I attached considerable importance to food grains consumption. It occurred to me that for a country like India, uneven distribution of income measured in terms of Gini co-efficient or Lorenz Curve may not provide sufficient guidance to the problems of poverty. As you know, uneven distribution of income has always been present in all societies. Besides, it is extremely difficult to measure 'income'.

I was, therefore, looking for a measurement of poverty not in the relative sense but in the absolute sense. Various studies had indicated that around that time nearly two thirds or more of total private consumption expenditure in South Asia was being devoted to 'food'. In India itself, the consumer expenditure (1963-64) on foodgrains (cereals and pulses) constituted nearly 45 per cent of the total consumption expenditure in rural areas and 26 per cent in the urban areas; on all food items, the percentage were 70 and 60, respectively.

I decided to measure the level of absolute poverty in terms of food items.

A national Sample Survey on Consumer Expenditure (16th round) had given data for the first time in terms of 'quantity' of foodgrains consumed per capita for various expenditure groups in the year 1960-61.

I used these data of cereal consumption in terms of quantities. The difference in terms of quantity between the minimum calorie requirements and the actual consumption, in my view, constituted a level of 'absolute poverty'. That is how I estimated the number of people being 'absolutely' poor in the rural and urban areas.

The concept which I developed in the sixties, in my view, is still relevant, although there may be need to have refinements with better and fuller information available now. In terms of basic need, there are certain Items e.g., requirements for clothes, housing, health care, education, etc., which can be phased and postponed. Admittedly, these are all very essential for a decent standard of living. However, the requirement for food is such, that it cannot be postponed.

The objectives of various studies which came up in late sixties and early seventies—have, in my view, been more or less fulfilled to a considerable extent. The various studies have succeeded in attracting the attention of the Planning Commission and policy makers about the nature and the magnitude of the problem. As a result, several policy initiatives to alleviate poverty have been taken. Therefore, what is needed now is to focus attention on the overall development package, in particular, the programmes and policy directed towards the problems of solving the absolute poverty. I am not saying that research studies to refine the estimates are not to be encouraged. However, having identified the 'poor people'—scheduled castes, scheduled tribes, landless labourers, small and marginal farmers, people in the dry land (i.e. where annual rainfall is 30 inches or below) etc., the need is to focus attention on the implementation of the programmes designed for their benefit.

1075. Over two million families cross poverty line. *Patriot* 21 Apr. 1986.

1076. Palkhivala, N.A. Anti-poverty programmes degenerate into property programmes. *Industrial Times* 3 Mar. 1986; 6-7.

1077. Pandey, G.K. Fighting poverty in rural areas (in India). *Times of India* 20 Aug. 1986; 8.

1078. Parakal, Anthony. Why do millions starve in our country? *Free Press Journal* (Bombay) 2 Apr. 1984.

That in predominantly agricultural country like India majority of its population should live below the poverty line, grow undernourished and die of starvation is a shame.

That in spite of her vast fertile land, river waters and great manpower. India should resort to import of foodgrains every year is also a shame.

That even countries with limited land and manpower produce more foodgrains than what is produced in India and export to other countries is again a shame.

That due to endless inter-State river water disputes millions of acres of cultivable fertile land remain unutilised is yet another shame.

That every year the quantity of wheat and rice devoured by rats from the storage bins and silos of India is enough to feed more than 25 million starving mouths for a whole year is the greatest shame of all.

What has led to this shocking state of affairs is not far to trace. From the time India took to planning in the year 1951, industrial development has been receiving greater attention than agricultural development, though it should have been the other way round, particularly in view of the fact that majority of our population who live in rural areas are used to, and mainly engaged in, agricultural activities. In fact, had they been trained in modern techniques of farming and supplied with necessary machineries and fertilisers, by now our country would have achieved self-sufficiency in food and become one of the biggest exporters in food grains. For our utter negligence and failures, we are paying through our nose, besides making millions of our poor masses suffer for want of food.

The worst part of the dismal story is that even the huge investments and efforts made so far for industrial development have not produced the desired results, such as steady economic growth, generation of employment opportunities and promotion of better standards of living. Some of the factors attributable to the poor performance on the industrial front are chronic labour unrest created by vested political and trade union interests, unnecessary interference by bureaucracy, red-tapism and rampant corruption. While the position is slightly better in the case of industries falling under private sector, it is worse in public sector undertakings. This unhappy situation is likely to slip further from bad to worse since no one seems to be serious about making efforts aimed at undoing the wrongs.

Yet the worst part of the story is that even though the development of agriculture remained neglected, in the name of land reforms and protection and promotion of the interests of farmers, various political parties and trade unions launched certain movements. In actual practice, they did more harm than any good the farmers and the country as a whole. Kerala provides a typical example of the havoc played by dirty politics. Nearly 25 years ago, the government headed by E.M.S. Namboodripad introduced a land reforms bill. Under the bill, land owners were forced to give 10 cents of land to tenants living in their lands, even if the land owner has only 15 cents and a tenant lives within it. This was alright for big land holders, but it was like an arrow to the wound as far as small landholders were concerned, and in Kerala majority of the land owners belong to the latter category. This led to great unrest among the small land owners, Majority of them paid scant attention to the development of land and cultivation. Of course, for Namboodripad it was a success inasmuch as the votes of those benefited from the so-called land reforms bill continued to be guaranteed for his party.

1079. Parikh, J.M. Statistical anomalies in the measurement of Indian poverty. *Econographics* 3(3) Jun. 1970.

1080. Poverty amidst plenty. *Economic Times* (New Delhi) 23 Mar. 1986; 5.

1081. Poverty and politics. *Link* 14 Sep. 1986; 3.

1082. Poverty and principles. *Searchlight* (Patna) 25 Sep. 1986; 4.

1083. Puzzle of national poverty. *Newstime* 29 Jan. 1985; 7.

1084. Ramamurthy, M. *Poverty and supply of wage goods in Tamilnadu* Madras, Sangam Publishers, 1974; p. 111.

1085. Rangnekar, D.K. *Poverty and capital development in India* London Oxford University Press, 1958.

1086. Rath, Nilakantha. Garibi Hatao: Can IRDP do it ? *Economic and Political Weekly* 9 Feb. 1985.

1087. Reddy, J. Ramadas. Structural change and removal of poverty in rural India. *Kurukshetra* (New Delhi) Nov. 1985; 29-30, 33.

1088. *Report on the beggar survey in Madras city.* Madras, Madras School of Social Work, 1956.

1089. Selbourne, David. Naked and the blood. *In through the Indian looking glass.* Bombay, Popular Prakashan, 1982: 140-42.

1090. Sen, Mohit. Poverty in India. *New Age* 17 Jan. 1971; 13.

1091. Sense and nonsense on poverty. *Telegraph* (Calcutta) 25 Apr. 1986;6.

New Delhi's department of rural development obviously believes in Barnum's famous aphorism that says there's a sucker born every minute. Otherwise, why would it want to regurgitate the same tiresome litany about numerical targets achieved during the Sixth Plan under the Intertargets achieved during the Sixth Plan under the Integrated Rural Development Programme (IRDP) in its latest annual report (1985-86), and go on to claim smugly that a further 2.08 million very poor families have been given some kind of assistance last year with the intention of helping them to step across the poverty line? Are not those who drafted the report aware that such figures have long since been thoroughly discredited by a host of field surveys (including some by such august bodies as the Planning Commission and NABARD) and that highly placed government officials are now publicly admitting that a mountain of effort and rhetoric has produced the proverbial molehill? They must know that the only set of figures that means anything—the one that could tell us exactly how many beneficiaries of IRDP can now eat two square meals a day—is the one that still does not exist, and the best guesstimates put the proportion of assisted families that has actually managed to cross the poverty threshold at anything like 20 per cent.

1092. Sommer, A. and W.H. Moslly. East Bengal cyclone of Nov. 1970. *Lancet* 1, 1972, 1029.

1093. Spear, Percival. *India, a modern history.* Univ. of Michigan Press, 1961.

1094. Sundaram, K. and Tendulkar, S.D. Poverty in India. *Indian Express* 14 Mar. 1985;6 & 15 Mar. 1985; 6.

1095. Suri, Kamla. Financial bodies must be sound. *Economic Times* 26 Jun. 1986.

Over the last decade and half, commercial banks have been involved in rural development programmes. They have been, by and large, extending credit for financing agriculture and allied activities within their areas of operation. What is unique about the integrated rural development programme is that there is a concerted approach by the commercial banks and the government agencies to assist the rural poor in their diverse productive endeavours to bring them above the poverty line. For the urban poor, specific programmes will be drawn up as announced by the Finance Minister in his budget speech.

If we look at the achievements of the commercial banks during the sixth Five Year Plan, the target laid down in terms of number of beneficiaries and quantum of loans, stand fulfilled. The number of beneficiaries assisted were 16.56 million as against the target of 15 million. Subsidy amounting to Rs. 1661 crores was made available from the budget and term loans for Rs. 3102 crores were disbursed by commercial banks, regional rural banks and co-operatives, their respective shares being 49 per cent, 33 per cent and 18 per cent respectively.

Certainly what has been achieved is creditable but in any poverty alleviation programme which is so vital for our country, we must consciously look into its deficiencies for learning lessons for the future. I think there can be no two opinions that as a programme, IRDP is well-conceived, particularly because among other things it emphasises the self-employment aspect in the rural sector and nearly 63 per cent of our rural working force is self-employed in agricultural and non-agricultural sectors.

1096. Suri, Kamla and Sahetiya Srichand. 307 million below poverty line : Alleviation of poverty afar any. *Economic Times* 26 Jun. 1986;III.

Numerous studies have been made from time to time by experts including the Planning Commission evaluating the extent and dimensions of poverty in India. Based on different concepts most of these are controversial but are significant on account of the fact that they have raised a number of important issues relevant to policy formulations. The controversy on the definition of poverty arose in early sixties, and came to its peak in late sixties and early seventies when poverty eradication became more or less a political slogan.

In view of the data deficiencies and the lack of National Sample Survey (NSS) reports on an yearly basis, it is extremely difficult to obtain a comprehensive picture of the evolution of poverty in India. The NSS reports which provide basic data on consumption expenditure are undertaken on a quinquennial basic. However, piecing together the various estimates made by experts in the field, some idea can be had of the magnitude of the problem of poverty in India.

An understanding of some of the estimates relating to the incidence of poverty made by experts within and outside the Planning Commission brings one to the conclusion that whatever be the estimates, there is no secular trend showing that we have made a dent on the poverty line.

Going by a very conservative estimates, there were as many as 307 million or 42.6 per cent people living below the poverty line in India in

1983. This figure is somewhat higher than the Planning Commission estimates of 269 million or 37.4 per cent (chart along side). According to Planning Commission estimates, the proportion of people below the poverty line was as high as 51.5 in 1972-73; it fell to 48.3 per cent in 1977-78 and further to 37.4 per cent in 1983.

1097. Tamil Nadu. *In Profiles of rural poverty.* Geneva, ILO, 1979 ; 29-32.

1098. Thakur, S.C. What is wrong with MNP (minimum needs programmc). *Indian Express* 12 May 1986 ; 6.

1099. United Nations. *Poverty and unemployment and development policy.* New York, 1975. p. 235.

1100. Visaria, Pravin. *Poverty and unemployment in India : An analysis of recent evidence.* Washington, World Bank, Jul. 1978.

1101. War against poverty. *Hindustan Times* 24 Sep. 1986 ; 26.

1102. What is poverty all about ? *Economic Times* 26 Jun. 1986.

Poverty as part of business of administration is a new concept. The removal of poverty as said to be the main "thrust" of our government's policies. The government during the Raj was totally lacking in thrust of any kind. Nor did it have any policy except that of supressing our entreprise and industry.

Like some of us today the British also hated poverty. I mention this because poverty has also been remanticised in India, as much indeed as wealth has been worshipped. The very purpose of the Empire was the removal of British poverty. The British appointed economic advisers to the Government of India who did a fairly good job in enriching Britain. It is doubtful if the economic advisers to the government in free India have had the same degree of success. The question whether by acting on their advice the wrong people have been enriched needs to be looked into.

In faimess to the British it must be recognised that some of them took an interest in our cattle and agriculture. Lord Linlithgow, for instance, He paid more attention to cows and bulls than the political problem of India. There is something to be said in favour of cattle and agriculture in the fight for the removal of poverty. At school I came across in my textbooks one of the most picturesque statements ever made by a Briton in India : that our cows were so starved that a white sahib could hang his hat on their ribs. It was made perhaps by Sir Malcolm

Darling. The cow and the peasant starved together. But the British, like pious Hindus, were more concerned about the cow.

At the time we became free it was fashionable to say that political freedom was not enough, that "real" freedom was economic. Gandhiji's idea of swaraj was swaraj for the poor. For the past 39 years the government has accomplished much but the experts have found it difficult to "quantify" what it has done for the poor. One reason for this is that we have no universally accepted yardstick to measure poverty or prosperity. If poverty to be measured according to the calorific value of the food eaten by an individual (in extreme poverty this is zero), the clothes he wears, the size of his dwelling, the area of the land he owns ?

Poverty is admittedly a relative term. I regard myself a comparatively poor man because I don't possess a colour TV set while all my neighbours have imported colour TV sets. And half these neighbours of mine consider themselves poorer than the other half because they don't own cars. The man who eats only one meal a day is surely poorer than the man who eats two meals. But then there are people who don't eat even one meal a day, though for that reason the man who eats one meal cannot be considered better of.

The peasant who has ordered ear-rings for his wife is richer than his neighbour whose wife is totally unadorned. But poverty, like prosperity, could be concealed.

The peasant with the unadorned wife may be using his money "productively" instead of buying his wife jewellery. The question however arises : is not "productivity" a deceptive term ? Is not economics all about the satisfaction of needs, desires ? Is not the man who buys his wife ear-rings happier than the other man who may have more cash ?

The point to note is that there are different kinds of poverty as there are different layers of poverty. I don't know on what basis the so-called poverty line has been drawn. But the more relevant question I wish to ask is whether such a line could be drawn at all. Or should there not be different poverty lines ?

Poverty, according to me, is not a subject for the economist alone. It is a matter of concern for the sociologist, for the educationist and even the anthropologist. The definition of poverty—if—that is possible at all must vary according to cultures, ethnic groups etc.

The problem worries economists today is how far we have been successful in removing poverty from our midst and how far governmental planning has paid dividend. Different authorities have different views on this. They are not agreed even on the number of people living below the arbitrary poverty line.

Critics of the government have always held that the rich have become richer and that the poor have become poorer. According to Dr. Nilkanth Rath, the Integrated Rural Development Programme (IRDP) has been a flop. In his view Rs. 4,000 crores of the Rs. 4,500 crores allocated in the Sixth Plan have gone to waste. Contrasted with this, a study made by Dr. I.Z. Bhatty and others of the National Council of Applied Economics (NCAER) shows that there has been a decline in poverty. Its findings are based on a survey of over 3,000 of the "poorest households".

Though there has been a decline in poverty, some other points out there has been an increase in the absolute number of the poor. The whole attempt of trying to solve the problem of poverty seems to be futile. There is a saying in the South : you climb a finger's breadth up but slide a cubit down. Such has been the case of our economic development. Will we have greater success with the Seventh Plan ?

I myself am inclined to the view that poverty itself has become a vested interest. The affluent have found it convenient to join the struggle of the poor. As for the government what will it do without poverty ? No sensible government works for the rich. The philosophy of the welfare state is based on the belief that the poor will always be with us. Without the poor the politicians will be idle. Like Voltaire's God, the poor too may have to be invented. Ironically it will be the rich who will invent the poor. After all, in every society the rich have a role in creating the poor.

1103. Woodruff, Philip. *Men who ruled India ; the Guardian.* London, Jonathan Cape, 1954.

INDO-CHINA

1104. Robequain, Charles. *Economic development of French Indo-China.* Oxford Univ. Press, 1944.

1105. Weatherbee, Donald E. Indonesia in 1985 ; Chills and thaws *Asian Survey.* Feb. 1986 ; 141-49.

INDONESIA

1106. Abey, Arun *et. al.* Labour absorption in Indonesian agriculture. *Bulletin of Indonesian Economic Studies* 17 (1) Mar. 1981.

1107. Colletta, N.J. Use of Indigenous culture as a medium for development : the Indonesian case. *Prisma* (1) 2 1975 ; 61-66.

1108. Dadao, Wang. Making economic readjustments. *Beijing Review* 27 Jun. 1983 ; 14.

1109. Duffy, Hazel. Prospect of an economic spurt in Indonesia. *National Herald* 22 Nov. 1975 ; 5.

1110. Garnant, R. and P.F. McCawley. *Indonesia : Dualism, growth and poverty.* Canberra, ANU, 1980.

1111. Geertz, Clifford. *Agricultural ivolution the process of ecological change in Indonesia.* Berkeley 1966.

1112. Gerbrandy, P.S. *Indonesia.* London, Hutchinson, 1950.

1113. Higgins, Jean. *Indonesia : the crisis of the millstone.* Princeton, 1963.

1114. Indonesia 1984. *Asian thought and society.* Jul-Nov. 1984 ; 207-14.

From the beginning, the New Order state has added to its power in successfully surmounting serious crises. In 1966, when General Suharto first assumed governing authority over a week, divided and nearly bankrupt state, he confronted clearly visible, unavoidable, interrelated national, political and economic crises.

To cope with a visible, frightening macropolitical crisis posed by widespread socio-political disorder, General Suharto relied initially on loyal elements of a divided bureaucratic apparatus and on relatively independent Muslim political zealots who acted to annhilate or imprison on purge from official posts many hundreds of thousands of Communists, or citizens labelled as Communists or alleged fellow-travellers of Communists. The shocking slaughter of perhaps half a million of alleged uncompromising leftists by uncompromising religious-political rightists served the state's quest for order by visibly demonstrating the urgent danger posed to national survival by the open mobilization of uncontrolled, uncompromising secular or religious, ideological, passions along competing political lines. Since the 1960's, state leaders have kept fresh memory of the terrible slaughters and lessons of the 1960's by continuing to warn the population of a continuing urgent threat to national survival posed by a continuing danger of uncompromising Communist or Muslim political violence. State leaders have exploited fears of the recurrence of religious-political fanaticism to justify their authoritarian political initiatives to build state power. In the 1960's General Suharto's jailing and purging from state jobs of the alleged leftists also served the state's quest for power by intimidating much of the politically active population and discouraging any subsequent political challenge to state authority from the virtually decimated left. The purging of thousands of leftist military and vivilian bureaucrats from government rolls also served the state's quest for power by creating bureaucratic vacancies for staffing by military and civilian functionaries personally loyal to General Suharto. Consequently, by the late 1960's, New Order state leaders already had publicly proclaimed an urgent and popular and legitimating solution to the crisis—the establishment of political and economic order--and had begun toaccumulate the means to accomplish it.

Economically in the late 1960's, General Suharto confronted a visible, practical macro-economic crisis caused by declining production and rampant inflation. Relying on the clear and urgent danger of general economic chaos and a massive dose of Western financial aid to win support for new state policies. General Suharto reduced inflation, curtailed some economically irrational state expenditures and introduced economically rational guidelines in the form of the state's five-year development plans supported by Western aid and experts, to co-ordinate and expand the activities and powers of state officials on behalf of political stability and economic growth. Since the 1960's the state has used the memory of economic chaos most effectively ; its primary *raison d'etre* and justification for power has been the creation of a widely desired and interrelated economic prosperity and political order.

Continuing in the 1970's, President Suharto relied on the people's of a return to political chaos and economic ruin and persisted in his fear economic-political strategy to strengthen the state by visibly creating political stability and economic growth. Politically, he consolidated state power in the 1970's by reorganizing and unifying the military and making it a more coherent and responsive state governing instrument. To counter a return of political warfare and to dilute the intensity of non-state political identities mobilized on uncompromising religious or ideological grounds, he banned religious and ideological parties unacceptable to the government and forced the remaining parties into two, state-created, umbrella coalitions—one composed of Muslim parties

(PPP) ; the other composed of a mix of Nationalist and Christian parties (PDI). State leaders then weakened the ties of the rural masses to the politcal Parties, which they had forced into these two artificial political coalitions, by interfering in the selection of their leaders and candidates for elections, by denying party politicians access to village voters between five-year elections and by depriving them of access to the state patronage resources needed to sustain their cadres. To replace the declining religious-political parties, the state revitalized its own more accommodating, secular political party, Golkar. The state provided state officials to lead Golkar, provided state military and civilian clients to support Golkar and provided state resources to finance Golkar. Consequently, Golkar became the state's secular vehicle for acceptable political communication, patronage, and electoral mobilization and won over 60 per cent of the votes in subsequent elections. Unlike traditional, religious-based political parties, Golkar's secular officials had daily access to village voters by means of an expanding number of state development programmes extended to all villages and cities and Golkar had visible and imposing military support.

To dilute the intensity and rigidity of the religious identification of elements of the masses with political Islam, the state sought to substitute its own ideology of Panchasila, a diffuse and flexible doctrine based on five vague principles emphasizing such civic virtues as tolerance, compromise and accommodation. In the late 1970's, the state introduced ubiquitous education programmes and applied pervasive pressures on all citizens to embrace the state ideology of Panchasila as state leaders, the state party and most secular political organizations publicly endorsed it.

Economically in the 1970's, the state successfully floated its new economic and political policies on a flood of bonanza oil profits, begun in 1973. With the help of Indonesian and Western economists and also with the help of over 20 billion dollars of Western aid since the 1960's, the state's successive Five Year Development Plans generated visible economic growth while Indonesian entrepreneurs of Chinese origin worked with state functionaries and foreign investors to create new industries and jobs. In a climate of expanding economic abundance, the state used its new material wealth to extend its power and to purchase the electoral support of voters in the countryside where the state heavily subsidized fertilizer and pesticide purchases and farm credit and other development programmes leading to increased rural wealth and production. The state also used its new wealth to expand its influence among voters in the cities where it rapidly raised the basic salaries of civil servants and school teachers, heavily subsidized fuel and food purchases and provided cheap financial credits for indigenous businessmen. Powered by such expansive spending and development programmes, the authoritarian state consolidated and expanded its political power and won successive elections by increasing margins.

1115. Indoneisa—the real issue. *Economist* (London) 26 Jul. 1947 ; 157-58.

1116. Indonesian vows to honour debts. *International Herald Tribune* 16 Sep. 1986 ; 13.

1117. Ingleson, John. Life and work in colonial cities : Harbour Workers in Java in the 1910s and 1920s. *Modern Asian Studies,* 17 (3) 1983 ; 455-76.

1118. Islam, I and Habibullah Khan. Income inequality, poverty and socio-economic development in Indonesia. *Asian Profile* Apr. 1985 : 139-52.

1119. Kaho, J. Ideology and social structure in Indonesia. *Comparative Studies in Society and History* 20(1) 1978.

1120. Kian-Wie, Thee. *Plantation, agriculture and export growth : An economic history of East Sumatra, 1863-1942.* Leknas, 1977.

1121. Mubyarto. Economic history of the Javanese farmer. In *TWP Vol. 2.* ; 182-203.

1122. Mustafa, K.G. Indonesian economy at a glance. *Baghdad Observer* 12 Jun. 1984 ; 5.

1123. Pelzer Karl J. *Planter and peasant : Colonial policy and the AGRARIAN struggle in East Sumatra, 1863-1947.* Nijhoff, 1978.

1124. Poffenberger, M. Towards a new understanding of population *Population Studies* 37(1) Mar. 1983.

1125. Ramachandran, K. S. Indonesian economy : Far from take-off stage. *Financial Express* 4 Feb. 1985 ; 5.

1126. Sajogyo. Modernization in rural development in rural Java. In *TWP* ; 110-44.

1127. Sethuraman, S. V. *Jakarta-urban development and employment.* Geneva, ILO, 1976.

1128. White, Ben. Demand for labour and population growth in *Colonial Java. Human Ecology.* Fall 1973.

IRAN

1129. Alak, B. Economic deceleration in Iran. *Baghdad Observer* 6 Nov. 1984 ; 5.

There is no doubt that the recent Iranian abortive offensive against Iraq in Saif Saad sector, will exacerbate the already chaotic economic situation in Iran. Events in the past have shown that following each Iranian attack on Iraq, business and almost every aspect of the economy begins to feel the impact of the Iranian defeat. In moral and financial terms. For instance, business activity, in both the bazaars and other sectors of the Iranian economy, has been greatly reduced mainly because of lack of funds, manpower and desire on the part of the Iranian peoples to engage in any business activity.

A report recently released by opposition, Mujahedein Khalq Organization shows that since Khomeini's coming to power, economic activity and business transactions in the capital Teheran alone have declined by over 75 per cent, and that the Iranian economy is getting worse as time passes.

The Middle East Economic Digest (MEED) in a report on August 13 said that as a result of cuts in the Iranian budget, imposed earlier in 1984 by the Iranian *Majlis* (Parliament), every facet of the economy has been affected. "Nearly all the cuts are in the development budget", MEED reported. The result has been a slowdown in construction and other activities. "Combined with a slow-down in the issue of Letters of Credit (LCS) for the first three to four months of the 1984-85 Iranian year, the cuts have produced economic deceleration", MEED added.

MEED stressed that merchants in Teheran's bazaar complain of a drop in business since early in the year. They have also been complaining about the interference of Khomeini's guards in their business and personal affairs, and about blackmailing and robbery.

Also, on the microeconomic level, the Iranian regime has been levying heavy taxes on the incomes of the Iranian people in an attempt to compensate for declining oil revenues resulting from the indefinite siege which Iraq has been imposing on major Iranian ports, such as Kharg Island, since February 27, 1984.

Although the Iranian regime and its allies, as well as other suspicious circles have been trying to belittle the significance of this effective siege, numerous economic reports confirm that the siege has in fact done great damage to the Iranian economy.

The Iranian Central Bank Governor admitted recently that as a result of the siege, Iran's Oil revenues declined by over 55 per cent. Also, a report by Middle East Economic Survey (MEES) states that if the Iraqi siege to Kharg Island, Iran's major oil export terminal were to be continued, the Iranian budget for 1985 and following years would be drastically cut, and that a complete halt in economic and business activity would result from this siege.

Only a month after Iraq's announcement of its siege to major Iranian ports, the Iranian Majlis announced a 20 per cent reduction in the Iranian budget. MEED (13 August, 1984) said that the Iranian Prime Minister Hossain Mousavi, instructed the Majlis to slash the budget. Central Bank Governor Moshen Nourbakhsh said at the time that 2 billion dollars had to be cut from the imports planned budget alone.

Economic observers and analysis point out that due to Iran's inability to revitalize the various sectors of the economy, which have for long been neglected by the Iranian regime, the Iranian peoples would be forced to pay more income taxes, thus adding to their already heavy tax burden.

1130. Alak, B. Iranian economy and seeds of destruction. *Baghdad Observer* 17 Apr. 1986.

1131. Farvar, M. Taghi. *Iranian agriculture can become self-sufficient.* CENESTA, 1981.

1132. Farvar, M. Taghi and Wasif Ahmed. Peasants in Iran : Nill they survive ? In *TWP* ; 145-75.

1133. Iran : Economic vision lost. *Economic Times* 19 Jul. 1981 ; 5.

1134. Iran fails again to repay yen 1.5 billion debt, *Japan Times Weekly* 20 Sep. 1986 ; 6.

1135. Khosravi, K. *Peasant society in Iran.* Intesharat Payam, 1979.

1136. Lambton, A.K.S. *Landlords and peasants in Persia.* Oxford, 1953.

1137. Lambton. A.K.S. *Persian land reforms, 1962-66.* Oxford, 1969.

1138. Mansour, Ali, Strain on Iran's economy, *Pioneer* 25 Apr. 1986 ; 4.

The Iran-Iraq war (since 1980) is proving a great strain on Iran's economy. Continuing Iraqi air attacks on Kharg Island—the terminal which handles 80 per cent of Iran's Oil exports are posing severe economic problems for Tehran.

End-of-year forecasts by shipping sources in Bahrain of the probable abandonment of Kharg as Iran's main terminal follow the recent budget statement by Prime Minister Hussein Mussavi that "while the Government this year succeeded in minimising the effects of the enemy attacks against our oil exporting facilities, nevertheless the inevitable effects of these attacks compounded by the undesirable state of the world oil market have meant that part of the government revenue projections was not met".

Mussavi was explaining to the *Majlis* (Parliament) that government revenue is more than one-third lower than planned.

Nevertheless, he announced a 12.5 per cent increase in defence spending. Iranian officials now agree that the cost of the war with Iraq estimated for this year at around $ 14 billion is eating up more than half of the national annual budget.

Baghdad's strategy of forcing Iran to the negotiating table by curtailing its oil exports is slowly biting. There have been over 60 Iraqi air-raids against Kharg in the past year, and the terminal has twice been forced to close for repairs, each time for a few days. According to shipping sources, only three of four of the 14 oil loading berths at the terminal are still operational.

Oil revenues have been falling for the last two years. According to a Majlis deputy, Iran's oil revenue for the current year is expected to the around $ 14 billion, barely enough to pay for the country's most essential imports.

No statistics are available for foreign exchange reserves, a figure regarded as a military secret.

Judging by the hard time the Majlis gave the Finance Minister last year, the level of foreign exchange had reached an alarmingly low level probably more than $2 billion.

The rising cost of the war and diminishing revenues have meant belt-tightening for Iranians.

Government employees have not had salary rises for several years,

Their purchasing power had dropped by more than a half since the revolution. Shortages of raw materials and spare parts have forced many factories to run below capacity or to close down. This has meant fewer goods and high unemployment.

The Government has confined development projects to those needing the least foreign exchange or those closest to completion, so there have been fewer contracts for local construction and engineering firms. Many of the films lucky enough, winsmall government contracts found themselves chasing officials in various ministries for payment.

1139. Mottahedeh, Roy. *Mantle of the Prophet* : *Religion and Politics in Iran*. London, Chatto and Windus, 1986. p. 416.

1140. Naji, Fawziya. Khomeini's regime political, economic problems increasing. *Baghdad Observer* 1 Sep. 1984 ; 5.

Iran has been struggling against a great number of economic, social and political problems ranging from the enormous human losses at the battlefront, to the acute power struggle which has become the main feature of Khomeini's regime.

Since the destruction of its Abadan oil refinery in the early days of the war, Iran's oil production has been increasingly declining. This decline has reached its climax with the Iraqi successful siege of Iran's main oil terminal of Kharg Island.

As President Saddam Hussein put it, the main objective of Iraq's siege of Kharg Island was to paralyse Iran's economy in order to force the rulers of Tehran to end their war against Iraq.

In response, Iran has tried to find a way out of the Iraqi siege. The rulers of Tehran, according to Lloyds investigators, hired mini-tankers to export oil in small quantities in order to meet its basic military and economic needs. However, the Iranian balance of trade, is expected to show a deficit of 4 billion dollars in the near future.

Iran has also offered to pay the insurance rates of all ships heading for Kharg Island to load Iran's oil which has been sold at lower prices than the official price agreed upon by the Oil Petroleum Exporting Countries (OPEC).

Furthermore, the Khomeini regime continued selling gold at low prices in international markets. Banking sources in the Swiss city of Zurich have said that bankers have been buying Iranian gold at reduced prices. These offers were meant to encourage world firms to send their tankers to the Iranian ports.

Generally speaking, Iran's suffering from its ailing economy is no longer a secret. The Iranian parliament in a debate last week criticised the government of Prime Minister Hossein Mousavi for his mis-management and failure to bring order to the economy.

Few ministers escaped criticism and five of them were sacked. Two minister, Defence Minister Mohammed Salim and Industry Minister Mostafa Hashemi were dismissed for economic mis-management.

Furthermore, the parliamentary debate produced more up-to-date economic figures and gave the first sign that the government's proposed Five-Year Plan had been rejected.

As regards its social and political situation, Iran has been undergoing unprecedented disturbances which could be well exemplified in defection of soldiers, army splits and Khomeini's regime international isolation.

1141. Nikbeen, Saber. Clergy serves Mammon, but badly. *International Viewpoint* 28 Oct. 1985 ; 17-20.

1142. Pourkarim, H. Islamic Republic of Iran and the politics of agriculture. *Iranian Agricultural Problems* 2, 1980 ; 23-62.

1143. Rahimi, A.R. Post revolution Persian economy. *Radiance* 27 Jul. 1980 ; 3.

1144. Vanaik, Achin, Steady decline in Iran's economy-I & II, *Times of India* 26 & 27 Aug. 1980 ; 8.

1145. Yavari, A.R. *Traditional agriculture in Iran.* Tehran, Book Publication and Translation Agency, 1980.

IRELAND

1146. Cinneide, S.O. *Law for the poor—A study of home assistance in Ireland.* Dublin, Institute of Public Administration, 1970.

1147. Cinneide, S.O. Poverty and inequality in Ireland. In *PICMC* ; 124-60.

Compared with other EEC countries, Ireland has a high dependency ratio and a low GNP per head of population. For these if for no other reasons poverty is likely to be a more serious social problem in Ireland than in these neighbouring countries. However, we know very little about poverty in Ireland. It has been the subject of research and discussion for only a decade : the 'rediscovery of poverty' in Ireland happened around 1971. Even still the most basic information is missing. There are no comprehensive statistics on income distribution in Ireland. It is possible to build up a picture of income distribution using data from a variety of sources. In 1971 it was estimated in this way that at least 20 per cent of the population were poor. In this chapter an attempt is made to update this estimate to 1975. There seems to have been some positive redistribution in the meantime, but the conclusion as to the extent of poverty in Ireland at present (or in 1975 which is the most recent date dealt with here) must remain very tentative. The greatest deficiency in existing incomes data is that there is no information on low wage earners. With regard to the wider aspect of inequality, such Irish data as are available show the expected association between low income (or low social class) and lack of household facilities, and health and education problems.

Poverty, whatever it is, however it is defined, is enmeshed in the particular social structure and economy to which it belongs in a highly complex kind of way : it can hardly be discussed in isolation. At the outset then it is necessary to highlight some distinctive features of the Irish background which affect poverty and the discussion of poverty in Ireland.

First, of all, the structure of the population of Ireland is different from that of other EEC countries because of demographic trends which have made Ireland unique in the past and which are still very much at variance with those elsewhere. The distinctive Irish population trends were a high level of emigration, low marriage rate, high average age at marriage and high fertility. With regard to total population the Irish experience has recently been summarised as follows.

In the second half of the last century, Ireland suffered an enormous population decline, from 65,29,000 in 1841 to 33,22,000 in 1901 : in the first half of this century the fall continued, almost without interruption, but at a slower rate-by 1961 the total population had fallen to its lowest level of 28,18,000. However, after 1961, with the onset of greatly increased industrial and general economic growth (stimulated by the First Programme for Economic Expansion) the Irish population bagan to show consistent increases. The 1966 Census recorded a population of 28,84,000 some 66,000 higher than the 1961 level and the next Census in 1971 yielded a total population of 29,78,000, representing a further increase of 94,000. At this time a further watershed in the Irish demographic scene was reached when, for the first time in well over a century, the tide of emigration was turned. Since 1972 the annual estimates of net migration have indicated small but consistent net inflows.

With regard to marriage rate, age at marriage and fertility rate, the Irish statistics have changed dramatically over the past fifteen years so that they are now nearer European norms ; but vital differences remain. In the past the combined effect of low nuptiality, late marriage and high fertility was a birth-rate which was in line with that in other countries. The fact that now more people are getting married earlier has not been offset by a matching decline in fertility, which means that the birth-rate is significantly higher than that in other EEC countries. The birth-rate for Ireland for 1971 was 22.7 per thousand ; in other countries it ranged from 12.7 in Germany to 17.2 in France and the Netherlands. Despite a dramatic decline in fertility in recent years, because of the composition of the population the birth-rate is expected to remain high in the foreseeable future.

The significance of these features and trends is not clearly seen by reference to the present composition of the Irish population. The Irish population is particularly young (31 per cent under 15 years of age, 55 per cent under 30) and the overall dependency ratio is high, with obvious implications for public expenditure, particularly on social infrastructure. The most recent population projections (Keating, 1977) postulate a decline in the dependency ratio—but not a dramatic one—to 71.2 in 1981 and 68.9—69.1 in 1986. It is worth mentioning too that a very high proportion of the population in Ireland, 48 per cent, live in rural areas and towns of under 1,500 people ; and about a quarter of the work force is engaged in agriculture (including forestry and fishing) ; this latter figure is the highest for the EEC countries.

The pattern of employment is at once a demographic feature and a feature of the economy. But more needs to be said about the Irish economy as compared with that of the other EEC countries. Taking GNP per head as an appropriate measure. Ireland is by far the least wealthy of the nine EEC countries. In addition :

> it can be seen that Ireland's rate of growth of product and of product per capita was rather lower than in most of the other EEC countries. Nevertheless, it is notable that the Irish growth experience was considerably better than that of the UK despite the close trading and other relations between the two countries. However, if Ireland is

to close the income gap with its EEC partners, a far higher growth rate of GNP per capita will be required.

It is against the background of the Irish demographic and economic conditions outlined in this brief conspectus that the discussion from here on must be read.

Any attempt to collect and collate data on 'poverty' in Ireland will reveal that there is very little material from before 1970 or so ; what exists, which is little enough, dates mainly from the period between then and now. It would seem that at the beginning of the 1970s a re-discovery of poverty took place in Ireland. Perhaps it is not surprising that this happened at a time when Ireland was more prosperous than it had ever been in its recent history.

During the nineteenth century, when Ireland was governed from London, poverty in Ireland was the subject of numerous British parliamentary enquiries and reports by philanthropic bodies and individuals. Many of them centred on the proposal to establish a Poor Law system of workhouses, which proposal was implemented in 1838, and on the subsequent operation of the Poor Law. The nadir of the welfare of the population of Ireland, at least in the social and economic sense, is probably marked by the Great Famine of 1847, when a million people died and a million people emigrated within five years. There is ample documentary evidence of the widespread extent of poverty in Ireland, both in the countryside and in the cities in the last century and at the beginning of this century. The teeming slums of Dublin, in which a quarter of the people of that city live, are a recent memory ; an acute sense of shared material deprivation is part of the mental equipment of the large proportion of Irish people who were brought up on small farms until comparatively recent times.

When these images were beginning to fade, new impressions of poverty were being projected by objective observers. The main way this began to happen was in assertions about the inadequacy of income maintenance payments. Even in 1945 the chairman of the National Health Insurance Society, the social insurance agency, reported that '(everyone) realises how inadequate the sickness and disability benefits are, and how necessary it is to increase them'. In 1964 Kaim-Caudle, in what was the first independent examination of social security provisions in Ireland, concluded that 'the present rates of social assistance appear to be inadequate'.

> The 11,2,000 old age pensioners over 70 received in 1963 (£ 1.63) per week without any additional allowance for rent. . . . It requires little imagination to realise that these pensions are quite inadequate by mid-20th century standards. Yet the (£ 1.63) received by an old age pensioner must appear princely to the unemployed with one adult dependant who in a rural area receives (£ 1.73), i.e. (£ 0.87) per adult per week in assistance payments. Such a man, if he were to purchase nothing whatsoever, not pay anything for rent, fuel and electricity could not buy enough food to maintain himself on a prison diet. It is extremely difficult to understand how ten thousands of people can manage to exist on unemployment assistance at all. They have to rely on help from some quarter—neighbours, emigrants' remittances, family, religious orders, food centres or charities.

In 1963 social insurance payments were about 40-50 per cent higher than the corresponding assistance rates ; i.e., and unemployed worker who was properly insured got 40-50 per cent more than an unemployed worker who was not properly insured and whose eligibility for income maintenance depended on a means test. But even those receiving social insurance benefits were badly off.

1148. *Combat poverty—an introduction to the working of the National Committee on Pilot Schemes to Combat poverty.* Dublin, May 1975.

1149. Foley, Gerry. Sixteen years of resistance in Belfast's lower falls. *International Viewpoint.* 24 Mar. 1986 ; 24-25.

1150. Geary, R.C. and J.G. Hughes. *Central aspects of non-agricultural unemployment in Ireland.* Dublin, Economic and Social Research Institute Paper no, 52, 1970.

1151. Irish language and the fight for national liberation, *International Viewpoint* 14 Jul. 1986 ; 22-25.

1152. Kaim-Candle, P. *Social security in Ireland and Western Europe.* Dublin, Economic and Social Research Institute, Paper No. 20, 1964.

1153. Kennedy, K.A. and R. Bruton, *Irish economy,* Brussels, EEC Economic and Financial series, No. 10, 1975.

1154. MacAirt, J. Irish Urban poverty, *Social studies* (Maynooth, Ireland) 1978.

1155. MacGreil, M. *Educational opportunity in Dublin,* Dublic, Catholin communications Institute of Ireland, 1974.

1156. Woodham—Smith, C. *Great hunger : Ireland, 1845-49.* London, 1962.

ISRAEL

1157. Adler, Chain, *et. al. Education of the disadvantaged in Israel : companions, analysis and proposed research*, Jerusalem, 1975.

1158. Alak, B. Can Zionist economic ailments be cured? *Baghdad Observer* 8 Oct. 1984 ; 5.

As new Zionist Prime Minister Shimon Peres took office recently, major crises on all levels of the economy focused international attention on the plight of the Zionist economy. "Israel's" balance of payments deficit is currently $ 5 billion a year and its annual inflation, which stands at 400 per cent now, is forecast to hit the 1000 mark in few months' time.

The new Zionist government recently cut subsidies on fuel and foodstuffs, adding from 18 to 54 per cent to the retail cost of food-stuffs and gasoline. In addition a one-time tax was imposed on cars, boats and aircraft, business inventories and properties. Steps are being taken to close income tax loopholes which have cost the government $ 150 million a year.

On September 26, the Zionist government announced it had out one billion dollars from its budget in the first step of an austerity plan to heal "Israel's" economy.

Peres listed four stages on "the road to recovery" cutting government spending, soaking up the public's extra cash by slashing subsidies and imposing taxes, agreeing with the labour unions to a price and wage freeze and then seeking to renew economic growth. The austerity measures are expected to push inflation up to a 600 to 700 per cent annual rate in the next few months.

According to cabinet sources. Peres told minister at an eight-hour session on September 20 he wanted most of the planned austerity programme enacted by the time he goes to meet President Ronald Reagan on October 8 to seek additional economic aid.

No details were available of what additional economic aid peres would see. But officials in the Zionist treasury have been discussing and asking the U.S. to write off one billion dollars of the Zionist entity's 9.6 billion dollar debt. Peres also was likely to ask that next year's aid package of 2.6 billion dollars be delivered in one lump at the start of the fiscal year, rather than in instalments.

In a speech on September 16, Peres moved quickly on the economic front, ordering a nine per cent devaluation of the shekel, Israel's currency, to stop a panic run on black market dollars. According to press reports, the devaluation caused little reaction in an entity inured to a daily erosion of salaries by inflation and constant adjustments in the exchange rate. The move also had been widely anticipated.

Finance Minister Yitzhak Modai said about a third of the cuts will come at the expense of government subsidies, which means consumers will pay more for gasoline, food, transportation and education. A monthly education tax of 4,000 shekels (about 10 dollars) will be imposed on families with children at school.

1159. Amin, Y.M. Israeli economy—no remedies prescribed. *Baghdad Observer* 30 Sep. 1985;4.

In an attempt to keep pace with hoper-inflation, the Zionist entity (Israel) on September 4 started a new reform of its currency by introducing a new shekel valued at 1,000 existing shekels.

Certainly this move was neither cosmetic nor was it planned at making everday transactions easier. Neither was it technical nor did it aim at easing computer and cashier calculations as alleged by the Israeli Finance Minister Yitzhak Modai. This new economic move must be yet another clear symbol of inflation.

It is the second time Israel had reformed its currency since the annual rate of inflation, which last year hit a record 445 per cent, first leapt into three figures in 1979. The first reform was in 1980 when the shekel, when valued 17 U.S. cents, was introduced, replacing the Israel lira. And as the present shekel's value is 0,067 of a cent, the new currency is worth 67 cents at present exchange rate. However, even the emergency measures covering a wage-and-price freeze introduced last July proved to be unworkable as the Zionist entity pursues a policy of settlement, expansion and aggression.

To prop up its ailing economy, the entity makes use of every single opportunity to press hard on the US for the aid.

Not long ago, the US approved 1.5 billion dollars in emergency aid to the Zionist entity in addition to 2.6 billion dollar grant for the current years.

Not long age, also Yitzhak Modai was in Washington to brief the United States officials, and particularly Secretary of State George Shultz, on Israel's economic austerity programme.

Moder asked Shultz for help in implementing a recently ratified free trade agreement that fifted most import duties between them.

1160. Berger, David *ed. Legacy of Jewish migration 1881 and its impact.* New York, Columbia Univ. Press, 1983 p. 193.

1161. Blowers, A. and G. Thompson *eds. Inequalities conflict and change* Milton Keynes, Open University, 1976.

1162. Bowles, S. and V. Nelson. Inheritance of IQ and the inter-generational reproduction of economic inequality. *Review of Economics and Statistics* 56, 1974.

1163. Datta, Surinder K. Israel: Arms and economy. *Hindustan Times* 21 Aug. 1984; 9.

Israel has come to stay both as a physical entity (even though on usurped lands) as well as in the minds of its admirers and detractors. The State also is a democracy (a sacrosanct term) and today a big exporter of arms and ammunition. Sophisticated war engines like the futuristic Lavi fighter--bomber, said to be the most potent in the western world, complete with state of the art weapons delivery systems and electronic warfare devices, is a product of Israeli-US collaboration. Washington has earmarked nearly $1 billion in developing the Lavi. The armament question is important. One way out perhaps in the long run of Israel's current economic predicament (a 400 per cent annual inflation rate) is to develop the country's high tech. industries which are derived in large part from weapons research. Israel did $ 1.5 billion in foreign business last year. A big ticket item is the Markaya tank.

It would also be worth mentioning that Israel has a military budget much larger than that of its major opponents combined. Israel's major industrial sector is the one engaged in arms production for the Israeli armed forces as well as for export. Israel has about 120 arms factories.

Israel's persistent economic woes, savere after the 1973 war, were a big election issue but for fear of losing votes, both candidates, Feires and Shamir avoided a detailed discussion of the austerity measures that were to go into effect after the election.

The continuing occupation of Lebanon which Israel invaded in June

1982 and were some 24,000 Israeli troops remain is the albatross around Israel's neck. During his election campaign Labour's Peres promised to remove most of the troops from southern Lebanon within 100 days of taking office. The occupation costs $ 1.2 million a day in addition to the human toll.

1164. Israeli economy. *Patriot* 29 Jul. 1984 ; 4.

1165. Kahn, A.E. Agricultural aid and economic development: the case of Israel. *Quarterly Journal of Economics* 76, 1962: 568-91.

1166. Perera, Judith, Economy will pose the crucial challenge to New Israeli Govt. *Pioneer* 27 Aug. 1984 ; 4.

1167. Shipler, David K. Hidden poverty in Israel, *Amrita Bazar Patrika* 19 Apr. 1983 ; 2.

1168. Taha, Salah, Zionist economy—No way out. *Baghdad Observer.* 22 Jul. 1985 ; 5.

Despite the announcement in the occupied territories that the Zionist entity has reached an agreement with representatives of the industrialists and the trade unions on ways to avert a general strike, political observers and commentators believe that the economic crisis in Israel is far from over. The new measures are but cosmetic attempts to avoid the total collapse which the Zionist entity has been heading for.

Since assuming power last year the Zionist coalition government tried a variety of measures to overcome it a economic difficulties and to control inflation now steaming a head at an annual rate of 285 per cent. The failure of all previous measures has forced the Zionist Prime Minister Shimon Peres to impose a severe austerity programme with all the painful and tough decisions expected to be taken to implement it. Among the austerity measures which the Zionist entity announced was the decision to cut the budget by 750 million dollars, raising prices, freezing wages and devaluation of the shekel.

Even Israel's friends described the move as declaring was against itself. The austerity measures or what Peres called a "recovery programme" was introduced against a background of soaring inflation, sharp decline in foreign currency reserve and the reluctance of Israel's friends to give a hand until the Zionists put their house in order.

Indeed, many of these measures were tried before but with no positive result. The only new measures was the decision to suspend the automatic linkage of wages to inflation index and the use of emergency orders to impose this move along with a price freeze.

In order to convince the settlers with his recovery programme the Zionist Prime Minister appealed directly to every Zionist to help overcome the tremendous difficulties which they are expected to face as a result of cutting public expenditure, dismissing thousands of workers and freezing the wages of several thousands of others. But the workers opposed the programme and threatened to take strong action including a general strike claiming that the austerity measures would reduce public and living standards and would put further burdens on them as salaries are expected to be eroded by 30 per cent.

1169. Warshwsky, Michel. Government of national paralysis. *International Viewpoint* 14 Jan. 1985 ; 14.

1170. Weksler, M. Crisis of the Zionist economy. *International Viewpoint* 14 Jan. 1985 ; 15-17.

ITALY

1171. Allen, K. Italy. *In Pensions, inflation and growth* Ed. by T. Wilson. London, Heinemann, 1974.

1172. Boissevain. J. F. Poverty and politics in a sicilian agro-town. *International Archives of Ethnography* 50, 1966.

1173. Conti-Sergio. Dynamic of the industrial system in a backward region : Crisis and industrial innovation in the Italian Mezzogiorno, In *IDPR* ; 149-74.

1174. Coppola, P. Industrialization North of Naples ; Problems of sectorial and spatial connectivity. In *IDPR* ; 175-87.

1175. Corsini, M. *Problems for the provision of adequate social services in Italy*. Rome, COSSIC, May 1974, (Mimeographed).

1176. Davis, J. *Land and family in Pisticci*. London, Athlone, 1973.

1177. Dolci, D. *Poverty in Sicily*. Penguin, 1966.

1178. Groenewagen, P. D. and Joseph Halevi *ed. Italian economics ; past and present*. Sydney Univ. Press, 1984.

1179. Mose, David. Poverty and inequality in Italy. In *PICMC* ; 161-94.

Post-war growth in Italy's urban population has been explosive. This is true not only in the industrial centres of Liguria, Piedmont and Lombardy—where Turin and Milan have absorbed increases, based largely on immigration, of 63 per cent and 36 per cent respectively between 1951 and 1971—but also in the administrative cities of South Italy where immigration has added to a persistently high birth-rate to show growth most notably in Rome (69 per cent). Cagliari (61 per cent), Palermo (58 per cent) and Bari (44 per cent) over the same two decades. Expansion on such a scale would have created social problems even if the public authorities had planned and carried out provision of housing, welfare and urban utilities. In fact, the demand for those services has been met everywhere no more than partially, for the most part privately, and in some cases not at all.

Housing is the most serious failure. The public sector has managed only a steadily falling share of total housing expenditure (14 per cent in 1962, a trivial 3.7 per cent in 1972), so that cheap subsidised houses for the new urban work force are in very short supply. The consequences of abandoning public initiative and in many cities even effective supervision of development, can be seen in almost any urban periphery, where speculation inland and buildings has combined with the continuing demand for housing to produce at best a chaos of high-density and exorbitantly expensive dwellings with poor access to services, and at worst the re-creation of shacks and shanty-towns which provide a temporary, but too often permanent, urban foothold for immigrants. The worst case, Rome, is the best described, with an officially estimated 16,506 families (62,351) people living in shacks in 1968 and a very much larger number in the borgate, the settlements on the outskirts first established to house the population forcibly removed from the city centre in the 1930s and enormously swollen by recent migrants. The (officially tolerated) chaos of Roman housing, and the resulting evasion of minimum housing standards and access to services, can be imagined from the calculation that in 1974 between one-quarter and one-third of the city population (roughly 8,30,000 people) were living in unauthorised dwellings.

1180. Podbielski, G. *Italy : Development and crisis in the post-war economy*. Oxford, 1974

1181. Serge, Anna. Change in a textile industrial area of Northern Italy. In *IDPR* ; 136-48.

1182. Silverman, S. Agricultural organisation, social structure and value in Italy. *American Anthropologist* 70, 1968.

1183. Silverman, S. Patronage and community nation relationships in Central Italy. *Ethnology* 4 (2) 1965.

1184. Sylos Labini, P. Precarions employment in Sicily. *International Labour Review* 89, 1964.

1185. Youth protest repressive legislation in Italy. *International Viewpoint*. 25 Feb. 1985 ; 27.

IVORY COAST

1186. Campbell, Bonnie. Ivory coast. *In West African States*. Cambridge, 1978 ; 66-116.

1187. Harden, Blaine. Prosperity in Ivory Coast is linked to ties with France, but some lament the coast : *International Herald Tribune* 15 Sep. 1986 ; 6.

1188. Joshi. H. *et. al. Abidjan* : *Urban development and employment in the Ivory Coast*. Geneva, I. L.O. 1976.

1189. Zolberg, Aristide R. *One-party Government in the Ivory Coast*. Princeton, 1969.

JAMAICA

1190. Bell. Wendell *ed. Jamaican leaders* : *Political attitudes in a new nation*. Berkeley, 1964.

1191. Jamaica reels under foreign debt. *Statesman* 14 Sep. 1982.

1192. Long, William R. Jamaican leader's popularity sinks, alongwith the economy. *International Herald Tribune* 6-7 Sep. 1986; 3,

1193. Payne, Tony. Economic crisis in Jamaica. *Pioneer* 17 Jun. 1984 ; 6.

For all the wrong reasons the troubled Caribbean island of Jamaica may soon again be attracting the headlines. Over the last few months its economy has slipped deeper and deeper into crisis.

Following the massive devaluation of the Jamaican dollar late last year, the general shortage of foreign exchange and the news that the US bauxite company, Reynolds, was pulling out of the country, it must have seemed to Prime Minister Edward Seage and his Jamaica Labour Party (JLP) government that Jamaica's bag of economic woes was just about full.

But now have come other ominous developments, including a new tax package brought in near the end of the financial year in an attempt to bring about meaningful reduction in the budget deficit. This include increased taxes on cigarettes, education, hotel accommodation, construction, travel and conveyancing.

Further devaluations of the currency followed. Foreign exchange is now auctioned in Jamaica in daily amounts, the rate within which bids can be made being set by the government. This has allowed a creeping devaluation of the local dollar, bringing the official rate down as far as J$ 3.81 to the US dollar.

Even then the black market was trading at about J$ 4.40, with the feeling within the financial community in Kingston that nothing could prevent it reaching the hitherto inconceivable depths of J$ 5. Until the middle of last November one US dollar was J$ 1.781.

Other bad news included a rise in the price of basic food items following the removal of government subsidies, the likelihood of more job losses, if as rumoured, the state-owned National Sugar Company was to be removed from the budget and further credit tightening.

More severe public expenditure cuts are feared to be in the offing as Seaga is forced, step by step, to implement what is in effect an IMF package before he gets Fund's money.

All in all, Jamaica's economic prospects are very gloomy. Seaga has made major mistakes in economic management. On assuming power in 1980 he let the country, especially the better-off, go on a three-year consumer beings.

Exchange controls were deregulated and imports opened up to a degree the economy simply could not afford in the light of its foreign exchange problems. The evidence of this error is all the Volvos and BMWs now to be seen around the more affluent parts of Kingston.

1194. Smith, M. G. *Social stratification in Jamaica.* Los Angeles, 1965.

JAPAN

1195. Ali, S.M. New economic thrust of Japan. *Mail* (Madras) 23 Jan. 1981.

1196. Bedeski, Robert E. Japan in 1985 : the year in review. *Asian Profile* Mar. 1986 ; 43-48.

1197. Bishan, Sunil. Japan's economic Pearl Harbour. *Blitz* 30 Nov. 1985, 12.

1198. Dynes, Michall. Jobs godown in the land of the rising Yen, *Statesman* (New Delhi) 11 Dec. 1986 ; 6.

1199. Frkutake, Tadashi. *Man and society in Japan.* Tokyo, University Press, 1962.

1200. Higuchi, T. Income redistribution and social security : Interpretation of Japanese society. *International Labour Review* 92(3) Sep. 1965.

1201. Ishida, Takeshi. *Japanese Society.* New York, Random House, 1971.

1202. Japan's economy : Is it looking up or down ? *Financial express* 15 Jun. 1983 ; 25.

1203. Mizoguchi, T. and N. Takayama. *Equity and poverty under rapid economic growth : the Japanese experience.* Tokyo, Kinokuniya, 1984 p. 253.

1204. Nakamura, James I. and M., Miyamoto. Social structure and population change : A comparative study of Tokugawa Japan and Ching China, *Economic Development and Cultural Change* 30(2) 1982.

1205. Odaka, Kunio. Middle classes in Japan. *Contemporary Japan* 28(1) Sep. 1964 ; 10-32.

1206. Panikar, Matthew J. Japan's economic strategy. *Economic Times* 12 Jan. 1986 ; 1.

1207. Pharr, Susan J. Japan in 1985 : the Nakasone era peaks. *Asian Survey* Jan. 1986 ; 54-65.

1208. Smite, T.C. *Agrarian origins of modern Japan.* Stanford, 1959.

1209. Taira, K. *Japan.* Paris, OECD, 1965.

1210. Vogel, Ezra F. *Japan's new middle class.* Berkeley, 1963.

KAMPUCHEA

1211. Eiland, Michael. Cambodia in 1985 : From stalemate to ambiguity. *Asian Survey.* Jan. 1986 ; 118-25.

1212. Etcheson, Craig. *Rise and demise of Democratic Kampuchea.* Boulder, Westview Press, 1984 p. 300.

1213. Gearing up for the dry season. *Asiaweek* 15 Nov. 1985.

1214. Ha, Phnong. Kampuchean economy : Stability and rapid development. *Vietnam Courier* (12) 1985 ; 27.

Right after the overthrow of the Polpot regime seven years ago, the Kampuchean people started rebuilding the country. In their advance, the Kampuchean people have had to overcome many difficulties : a society in ruins left by the Polpot regime, an antiquated backward economy and a multi-faceted war of sabotage waged by hostile forces. However, thanks to their staunch revolutionary traditions, their diligent and creative labour, and the devoted assistance from fraternal countries and friends in the world, the Kampuchean people have reinvigorated their country and recorded brilliant achievements in all fields of activity making the situation in the country ever more stable.

The revolutionary administration has issued policies and carried out measures to step by step transform the old economy, and develop a new economy with ever-increasing labour productivity and product quality on the basis of collective ownership. In the countryside, the peasants, now masters of their land, are boosting production, carrying out intensive cultivation, raising productivity and food output. A remarkable achievement has been the elimination of famine. After liberation, the country had to ask for food relief, but now it can produce enough food for home consumption. More than the hundred thousand solidarity-for-production teams have been set up. As a result, agricultural production has been stepped up. The sown areas has expanded and output and productivity have gradually increased. In 1985, the areas under rice total 1.7 million hectares (compared with 770.500 ha. in 1979) yielding 2.1 million tonnes of rice (as against 696, 850 tonnes in 1979). The average yield is 1.23 tonnes per hectare, even 3 tonnes per hectare in some places as against 0.7 tonnes in 1979. Nearly 1,200 recivoirs and dams, and many Irrigation projects have been restored or built anew in various provinces with a view to effectively serving agricultural production. Every year, hundreds of thousands of hectares are planted with beans of different kinds, more than 20,000 ha. with rubber, 2,500 ha. with sugarcane, 9,000 ha. with tobacco and 500 ha. with cotton. Besides, some 60,000 tonnes of fish are netted. Livestock breeding has been boosted : now the country has two million buffaloes and oxen, more than 5.3 million poultry (as against 8,20,000 in 1979) and more than one million pigs (only 50,770 in 1979.)

In industry, in spite of heavy damage, 60 enterprises out of a total of more than 100 have been restored and put back in operation. They have been re-equipped and enlarged and many new ones built. Many small-industry and handicraft enterprises have also been built using home-produced materials to produce consumer goods. Last year, increases in output value have been recorded in many branches of activity : textiles (58 per cent), consumer goods (28 per cent), rubber (2.5 times), compared with the planned targets. Transport and communications have been quickly restored. The shipping agency "KAMSAB" contributes to expanding international cooperation. Trade services handle goods distribution and circulation, thus promoting production and stabilizing the people's living conditions. Foreign-trade relations have been expanded and the volume of goods exchange increased. The financial and banking departments have contributed actively to the restoration and development of the country's economy :

1215. Huyen, Vu. Rebirth of Kampuchea. *Vietnam Courier* (Hanoi) (2) 1986 : 27-28.

Kompong Som is the only seaport in Kampuchea and the second largest city after Phnom Penh. Coverning an area of nearly 1,300 sq. kms. of which two-thirds is forest land and 16,000 hectares arable land, Kompong Som, the province of the same name, not only is rich in sea resources but also plays an important role in the Kampuchean economy. Its forest, sea and agricultural resources help meet both domestic and export demands.

In Kampuchean Som means beautiful and Kompong port. For generations, the Kampucheans have been proud of their Beautiful Seaport City. To reach Kompong Som, some 200 kms. from Phnom Penh, the traveller has to cross the Pich Nin Pass, noted for its poetic scenery, and the air becomes even fresher as he approaches the port. From a high point near the city, he can see a vast stretch of land and sea : green groves of Coconut palms, timber, and coffee plants. He will also see the coming and goings of ocean liners, smaller ships, and fishing boats.

However, the Beautiful Port, as it is called, at one time shared the tragic fate of the whole nation under the blood-thirsty Polpot regime. The 661 ha. forest of 12,000 coconut palms in Riem village which adorned the seacoast and constituted a source of wealth for the city, was devastated. When the sea dyke protecting the coconut palms started crumbling, Polpot soldiers knocked it down altogether. Everybody was forced to leave the coconut groves, even their owners. An old man in Riem village said : "Why should killers of women and children have cared for the coconuts ?"

Recollections by survivors gave me some idea of the destruction wrought by Polpot men : even the movie house, the only one in the city, was pulled down. Hundreds of children were orphaned by the Killings. On January 7th, 1979. Kampuchea was liberated ; the rebirth of Kampong Som and the whole nation began.

1216. Katigbat, Jose. Specialists discuss estimates on food shortages. *Nation* (Bangkok) 26 Sep. 1985.

1217. Quinn-Judge, Paul. Two old enemies fight Cambodia war. *Christian Science Monitor*. 23 Oct. 1985.

1218. Szymusiak, Molyda. *Stones any out : A Cambodian childhood. 1975-80*. New York, 1986. p. 245.

KENYA

1219. Bager, Torben. *Marketing cooperatives and peasants in Kenya*, Uppsala, 1980.

1220. Buch, Hansen M. and H.S. Maranssen. *Contract farming and the peasantry : case studies from Kenya*. Denmark, Rosklde University, Research Paper No. 18, 1981.

1221. Clark, Mari H. Women headed households and poverty. Insights from Kenya. *Journal of Woman in Culture and Society* 10 (2) Win 1984 ; 33-54.

1222. Godfrey, E.M. and G.C.M. Mutizo. Political economy of self-help Kenya's harambee institutes of technology. In *Education, society and development*. Ed. by D. Court and D.P. Ghai. Nairobi ; 1974.

1223. Harden, Blaine. In rural Kenya. *International Herald Tribune* 12-13 Jul. 1986 ; 1.

1224. Hunt Diana, Chaynov's model of peasant household resource allocation and its relevance to Mbere division, Eastern Kenya. *Journal of Development Studies* 15 (1) Oct. 1978.

1225. *Integrated Rural Survey, 1974-75* : Basic report. Nairobi, Government of Kenya, 1977.

1226. Kimalel, S.K. Kenya. *National Herald* (New Delhi) 13 Dec. 1976 ; 5.

1227. Kitching, E. *Class and economic change in Kenya.* New Haven, Yale Univ. Press, 1980.

1228. Knowles, James C. and R. Anker. Analysis of income transfers in a developing country : the case of Kenya. *Journal of Development Economics* 8, 1981 ; 205-26.

1929. Lamb, G. *Peasant, capitalists and agricultural development in Kenya*, Nairobi, 1972.

1230. Legum, Colin. Kenya : It's family planning or famine. *International Herald Tribune*, 29 May 1986 ; 4.

1231. Leys, Colin. Capital accumulation, class formation and dependency. The significance of the Kenyan case. *Socialism Register*, 1978 ; 241-66.

1232. Leys, Colin. Politics in Kenya : the development of peasant society. *British Journal of Political Science* 1, 1971. 307-37.

1233. Ngethe, Njuguna. Kenyan peasantry in national development. An overview. *In TWP Vol. 2* ; 92-125.

1234. Njonjo, A.L. Kenyan peasantry : A re-assessment. *Review of African Political Economy* 20, 1981.

1235. Nyong, P.A. Development of middle peasantry in Nyanza. *Review of African Political Economy*, 1981.

1236. Rosberg, Carl G. and John Mothingham. *Myth of Man. Nationalism in Kenya.* Nairobi, East African Publishing House, 1966.

1237. Smith, L.D. Overview of agricultural development policy. In *Agricultural development in Kenya.* Ed. J. Heyer *et. al.* Nairobi, 1976.

1238. Sorrenson, M.P.K. *Land reform in the Kikuya country.* Nairobi, Oxford Univ. Press, 1967.

1239. Swainson, N. *Development of corporate capitalism in Kenya. London*, Heinemann, 1980.

1240. Swainson, N. Rise of a national bourgeoise in Kenya. *Review of African Political Economy* 8, 1977.

1241. Swynnerton, R. *Plan to intensify the development of African agriculture in Kenya.* Nairobi, Govt. Printer, 1945.

1242. Wolf, R.D. *Economics of colonialism, Britain and Kenya, 1870-1930* London, Yale Univ. Press, 1974.

KOREA

1243. Aseim, B.S. National economy of Socialist Korea. *Young Indian* (New Delhi) 4 Jan. 1973 ; 17-18.

1244. Attar Chand. Korean; Economy. *NIF Weekly* (New Delhi) 23 Sep. 1984.

1245. *Building of an independent national economy in Korea*, Pyongyang, 1977. p. 264.

1246. Cole, D. C. and P.N. Lyman. *Korean development : the interplay of politics and economics.* Cambridge, Harvard Univ. Press, 1971.

1247. Kerns, H. South Korea's strategic loss. *Far Eastern Economic Review* 5 Feb. 1982 ; 82.

1248. Kim, C.I. Engene. South Korea in 1985. *Asian Survey* Jan. 1986 ; 66-77.

1249. Park, Sam Ock. Regional changes in the industrial system of a newly industrializing country : the case of Korea. In *IDPR* ; 311-34.

1250. Precarious industrial structure. *Far Eastern Economic Review* 19 Jul. 1984 ; 43-44.

1251. Ramachandran, K.S. South Korean economy. *Financial Express* 31 Oct. 1983 ; 5.

1252. Scalapino, Robert A. and Chong-sik Lee. *Communism in Korea.* Berkeley, 1972.

1253. Seale, Patrick. Korea's economic, development--Why ? *Baghdad Observer* 31 Dec. 1981 ; 3.

1254. Suh, Dae--Sook. North-Korea in 1985. *Asian Survey* Jan. 1986 ; 78-85.

1255. Verghese, B.G. Korea's economic miracle, *Indian Express* 19 Dec. 1985 ; 6.

1256. Watts, David. Chill winds sweep S. Korean economy. *Statesman* 4 Jan. 1986 ; 9.

1257. Young-Ki, Park. Korea. In *EAPS* ; 84-88.

Since the beginning of the 1960s, Korea has been experiencing a rapid process of Industrialization ; for example, the annual average GNP growth rate throughout the '60s was well over 10 per cent. Recent growth rate shows an increase of 9.8 per cent and 9 per cent for '71 and '72 respectively, and a 10 per cent growth rate is expected in 1973. Per capita income has also rapidly increased from US $ .3 in 1961 to US $ .302 in 1972.

Among all the economic indices representing rapid industrial expansion, the increase in export is not impressive. During each of the last 10 years the annual export averaged in a 40 per cent increase over each preceeding years. A total of US $ 40 million export in 1960 was increased to US $ 2,350 million in 1972 and US $ 3,200 million is expected to be the total amount of export in 1973.

The process of industrialization was accompanied by a massive change in the industry mix of the economy. In 1961, for example, agriculture and fishing accounted for 43 per cent of the GNP but in 1970 they decreased to 26.4 per cent while the mining and manufacturing industries increased from 14.9 per cent to 27.7 per cent. The structure of employment, or the employment pattern, likewise has been altered. In 1963, the labour force engaged in mining and manufacturing industries together represented only 8.7 per cent of the total employment, but in 1972 it increased to 17.4 per cent.

In spite of all these encouraging economic indices representing successful and rapid industrialization, there has been a growing awareness of the fact that social development, or the human side of the development—which is as important as the economic, in determining whether a given economic growth will endure on a long term basis and which is known as the ultimate goal of economic development, has been almost completely neglected.

The following figures may illustrate the setback on the human side of development and help to clarify the profile of poverty in the midst of industrial expansion. In spite of a marked increase in the total number of wage earners during the last decade, the ratio of the national income destined for renumeration of the employed remained practically unchanged, i.e. from 38.2 per cent in 1958 it rose to 38.8 per cent in 1970. The ratio of agricultural income in the national account has been reduced from 31.2 per cent to 26 per cent, while the income from property, such as interest and dividends, enjoyed a remarkable increase from 4.2 per cent to 7.1 per cent and from 0.2 per cent to 1.2 per cent respectively during the same period.

Again, in spite of an annual average increase of over 10 per cent in the nominal wage during the last decade, the labour cost in the manufacturing industry yet remains only 9.6 per cent or 6.3 per cent for direct labour cost alone—out of the total cost in 1971. The comparable figure for Japan in 1969 was 32 per cent.

Among the wage earners registered with the Office of Taxation as of October 1973, well over 6,00,000 workers are recorded as receiving an amount less than 15,000 Won or US $ 38 a month and thus are exempted from paying income tax. Close to one quarter of the total wage earners are still receiving less than 35,000 Won US $ 88 a month, the amount disclosed by Government as the minimum monthly expenditure per urban worker's household.

In other words, during the last decade, no significant systematic approach has been taken by Government or private institutions within their development plans to deal with the problem of integral human development. As a result, quantitative growth has been attained according to the plan; however, it has resulted in accumulating wealth in the hands of a few and has thus expedited polarization between the haves and the have nots and has induced a widespread feeling of relative deprivation among the people.

Anti-poverty measures which could be undertaken by the Government the innumerable. Economic development will, no doubt and especially in the long run, serve as the basis for eradicating poverty. For an immediate redistributive effect, however, the Government could devise taxation schemes in the interests of the poor, programmes to provide cash payments for the obviously poor, provide free and subsidized government services for the less privileged group, and foster a policy to strengthen the bargaining position of workers. Government could even involve itself in redistribution of wealth by means of land reform or nationalization of industries. The government of Korea, it seems to author, has placed the lion's share of its emphasis on economic development and has had little concern for an immediate redistribution effect.

Perhaps those are the factors that made the Third Development

Plan, designed to cover the period 1972 to 1976, place emphasis on social matters or social programmes related to development. Social programmes appearing in the Third Development Plan may be classified into eight fields: Population, Education, Health, Nutrition, Housing and Environment, Income and Social Security, Social Welfare, and Community Development. The objectives are said to be to improve the level of living, to provide a more equitable distribution of income, and to enlarge the opportunity for social participation and mobility for not only certain groups of society but for people as a whole.

KUWAIT

1258. Kuwait's Crown Prince (Sheikh Saad) calls for New International Economic Order. *Contemporary* (New Delhi) 1979 ; 27.

1259. Kuwaiti economy. *NIF Weekly* 7 Oct. 1984 ; 588.

LAOS

1260. Chung, Viet. Economic growth in Laos. *Vietnam Courier* (12) 1985; 24-26.

With the favourable conditions created by the topography, climate and land, Laos has enormous potentials to develop forestry and agriculture (at present, Laos has 4 million ha. of cultivable land and 1.2 million ha. of meadow).

Looking back to the days before liberation, the basis of Lao agriculture was a small, self-sufficient agricultural economy with rudimentary farming technique and low labour productivity. There was practically no material and technical infrastructure.

Between 1952 and 1965, the whole country had only 10 tractors. Until the early 70's, water conservancy had been unknown to many people. In the whole country there were about 180 small canals (from 6 to 14 kms. long each) especially in Vientiane, Luang Prabang, Saravane, and Sayaboury, enough to serve only about 33,000 ha. of field.

The output of food was reduced with every passing year. In 1955, it was 390 kgms. per capita; in 1970, 305 kgms. and in 1975, 275 kgms.

In the past, unable to meet the needs of its people, Laos usually had to import food, particularly rice. It imported about 1,00,0000 tonnes of rice every year, not to mention other agricultural products and foodstuffs.

Forestry and fishery were in a similar state. Handicrafts were neglected.

When the Lao People's Democratic Republic was born, the Party and Government saw clearly the difficulties and worked out an orientation for the nation's economic development. The party advocated developing agriculture and forestry to meet the needs of the people and create the bases for socialist industrialization.

In agriculture, a cooperative movement was vigorously launched, together with the three revolutions in the countryside. Advances were made towards building a new socialist countryside.

Agricultural cooperatives were set up. In 1976, there were nearly 600 cooperatives. At the beginning of 1985, their number stood at 2,546 (accounting for 40 per cent of peasant households). By the end of 1984, five provinces had basically completed cooperativisation : Huoa Phan, Phongsaly, Xieng Khouang, Ou Dom Say and Champassak.

Many formerly nomadic peasant households in mountain areas have adopted a sedentary mode of life.

Hundreds of agricultural cooperatives have applied new methods of cultivation; especially they have used fertilizers and technical and scientific advances in combination with water conservancy to transform one-crop fields into two-crop fields, thus step by step changing the old method of farming.

Besides agricultural cooperatives, Laos also has thousands of mutual aid teams that are the initial organizations leading peasants to collectivization.

The Lao Party and State pay great attention to the building of technical and material bases for agriculture. Many old water conservation works have been restored and upgraded. More than 1,000 canals and dams now irrigate and drain about 1,00,000 ha; 15 big and medium-size irrigation works have been built. Many of them, namely Hoong Seng, Neum Moun, Neum Houang (Vientiane), Vang He, (Champassak), Manaxay (Khammouone) have been commissioned. From 1976 up to now, the irrigated area has increased 3 times (accounting for more than 20 per cent of the area under rice). In 1982, the irrigated area was

1,14,200 ha. of which 15,000 ha. were irrigated by mechanical pumps. In the whole country there are now 2,000 tractors and pumps.

1261. Dommen, Arthur J. Laos in 1985; the Dear of the census *Asian Survey* Jan. 1986; 112-117.

1262. Lao : Mixing Marx and Buddha, *Asiaweek* 7 Sep. 1986; 64-65.

LATIN AMERICAS

1263. Althimir, Oscar. and S. Pinera. *Decomposition analysis of the inequality of earnings in Latin American Countries*, Washington, World Bank, 1977.

1264. Altimir, Oscar. *Extent of Poverty in Latin America*, Washington, World Bank Staff Working Paper No. 522, 1982, p. 111.

1265. Arcienegas, German. *State of Latin America, New York*, 1952.

1266. Braithwaite, S.N. Real income levels in Latin American *Review of Income and Wealth*, 14 (2) 1968.

1267. Frank, A.G. *capitalism and underdevelopment in Latin America*, Penguin, 1969.

1268. Garcia Calderon, Francisco. *Latin America : Its rise and progress*. New York, Scribner's, 1917.

1269. Gong, Chen. Latin America : Joint efforts to solve debt problem, *Beijing Review* 2 Jul. 1984 ; 15.

1270. Harris, Seymour. E. *ed. Economic problems of Latin America*. New York, 1944.

1271. Horowitz, Irving L. *Masses in Latin America*, New York, Oxford Univ. Press, 1970.

1272. James, Preston E. *Latin America*, New York, Odyssey Press, 1959.

1273. Ortega, Emiliano. Peasant agriculture in Latin America: Situation and trends. In *TWP* : 245-93. See also *CEPAL Review* (16) Apr. 1982.

1274. Santana, Roberto. New context, framework and evolution of small peasant exploitation in Central Latin America and Andes countries. *TWP*; 314-27.

LEBANON

1275. Van Der Laan, H.L. *Lebanese traders in Sierra Leone*. The Hague, 1975.

LESOTHO

1276. Knappert, J. *Myths and legends in Botswana, Lesotho and Swaziland.* Leiden, 1986, p. 248.

LIBERIA

1277. Beleky, L.P. Development of Liberia. *Journal of Modern African Studies* 11, 1973; 43-60.

1278. Clapham, Christopher, Liberia, *In West African States*, Cambridge, 1978 ; 117-31.

1279. Clapham, Chistropher, *Liberia and Sierra Leone*. Cambridge, 1976.

1280. Clower, R.L. *et. al. Growth and without development : An economic survey of Liberia.* Evanston, 1966.

1281. Harden, Blaine. Doe (Samuel K.), under pressure, refashions his fiscal image. *International Herald Tribune*, 28 Jul. 1986; 5.

1282. Liebenow, J.G. *Liberia : the evolution of privilege*, Ithaca, 1969.

1283. Lowen Kopf, M. *Politics in Liberia*, Stenford, 1976.

LIBYA

1284. Economic basis of third universal theory, *National Herald* 1 Sep. 1981 ; 9.

MADAGASCAR

1285. Griffin, Michael. Madagascar enters painful period for its economy. *International Herald Tribune* 3 Sep. 1986 ; 4.

1286. Griffin, M. Rice bowl cure is no miracle for Madagascar, *Baghdad Observer* 20 Jul. 1986 ; 6.

1287. Madagascar faces problems as it shifts political gears. *Mainichi Daily News* 4 May 1986 ; 5.

Madagascar's economy is just like its climate : agreeably unhealthy.

The simile is explained by the fact that the economy is in the process of changing from a socialist to a free-market system, and nobody quite knows what will happen.

The decision was helped by the recent move to life virtually all restrictions on the production and marketing of rice, the country's basic food, in a bid to end the chronic shortages which government control had brought.

But after 10 years of socialism under the regime of President Didier Ratsiraka, officials are proving very reluctant to go along with the changes, for the highly bureaucratic system which has evolved has proved very profitable for many of them.

There is therefore a love-hate relationship between the regime and the World Bank and International Monetary Fund, a foreign financial expert explained. On the one hand, the government has so far managed to keep its commitments, on the other, the two international organizations do not understand why there is resistance to what are turning out to be objective improvements.

For there are now definite signs to recovery, following the austerity programme forced on the country three years ago by the World Bank and the IMF.

Finance and Economy Minister Pascal Rakotomovo said after the consultative group meeting last Friday that the austerity plan had reduced inflation from 35 per cent to 10 per cent, and it was now possible to embark on a more expansionary policy.

State finances have been overhauled nationalized companies reorganized, the industrial base is gradually being renovated, agricultural output is up and the trade balance is better.

But exports are still low, and almost 50 per cent of the revenue they bring in go on servicing the 2.5 billion debt. This year's servicing bill will amount to 365 million dollars, Rakotomovo said.

The government's efforts to export as much as possible have been hit by the weather, with drops revaged by two cyclones in three years, the variation in world prices of raw materials, and continuing defects in the system.

Exports of coffee and cloves were maintained at their 1984 level, but those of vanilla (of which Madgascar is the chief exporter), sugar, prawns and meat all fell.

Imports were reduced to some extent, but the government still had to buy in 1,25,000 tonnes of rice last year, while fixed-rice contracts with the Soviet Union meant it could not take advantage of the drop in oil-prices.

The trade deficit was brought down last year to 6.6 billion Malagasy francs (around 10 million dollars).

With immense agricultural and industrial potential, the return to a liberal economy, foreign capital encouraged and protected by a new investment code, a new policy of exploiting the country's resources in international partnership and a flexible exchange rate, Madagascar's economy should theoretically show real advance from 1987.

To mark a complete break with the past, the 10 million Malagasies are now expecting a thorough reshuffle in a government which has not basically changed in 10 years, and is still paying lip service to the ideology it adopted in 1975.

Much depends on whether President Ratsiraka has the political strength to carry things through.

MALAYSIA

1288. Ahmad, Zakaria Haji. Malaysia in 1985. *Asian Survey* Feb. 1986 ; 150-57.

1289. Alatas, S.H. *Second Malaysian Plan, 1971-75 : A critique.* Singapore, ISAS, 1972.

1290. Anand, Sudhir. *Aspects of poverty in Malaysia.* Aulanko, Finland. (Mimeo) 1975.

1291. Anand, Sudhir. *Inequality, and poverty in Malaysia.* London, Oxford University Press, 1983. p. 372.

1292. Anand, Sudhir. *Size distribution of income in Malaysia. Part-I.* Washington, World Bank, 1973.

1293. Anand, Sudhir and S.M. Kanbur. *Inequality and development.* Oxford, St. Catherine's College, 1978.

1294. Ghee, Lim Teck. *Peasants and their agricultural economy in colonial Malaya.* Kuala Lumpur, Oxford University Press, 1977.

1295. Malaysia. In *profiles of rural poverty.* Geneva, ILO, 1979 ; 33-36.

1296. Mahmet, Ozay. *Development in Malaysia : Poverty, wealth and trusteeship.* London, Croom Helm, 1986.

1297. Nawal, Yunus *et. al.* Malaysia. In *EAPS* ; 63-69.

People of Malaysia are mostly from an agricultural community with a less income group. Available data indicates that average incomes of workers in the five sectors of the economy are as outlined below :

Modern Urban Sector	—High
Modern Rural Sector	—Medium
Government Sector	—
Traditional Urban Sector	—Low
Traditional Rural Sector	—

In the above ranking, the high level of income is about one and half to two times that of the medium level of income. About 60 per cent of workers in the country are found in the Traditional Rural Sector and Traditional Urban Sector which provide a low level of income. Slightly less than one-fifth of the workers in the country are found in the Modern Urban Sector which provides a relatively high level of income, and slightly more than one-fifth in the Modern Rural and Government Sector which provide a medium level of income.

The poor include the unemployed, the underemployed and those in low income occupations in agriculture, industry and services. The poor agricultural workers, many of whom are Malayas, are mainly coconut and rubber small-holders, single crop 'padi' farmers, tenants and share-croppers in 'padi' and rubber cultivation and inshore fishermen. Their low incomes are primarily the result of uneconomic size of their holdings, agronomically poor or unsuitable plots of cultivation, traditional methods of farming and lack of access to modern agricultural inputs. The urban population of all races comprises of the unemployed or those engaged in low productivity traditional urban activities such as small artisans, petty traders, hawkers, stall holders, household servants and others pursuing a multitude of activities requiring little or no initial skill or training. In recent years, their number has been swelled by immigrants from the rural areas.

Despite the high and growing levels of per capita income in Malaysia, inequality in the distribution of income among Malaysians remains wide. The information on household incomes, collected in the post-enumeration survey of the 1970 census population, indicates that the mean household income in Peninsular Malaysia was only (M) $269 per month. As stated below about 27 per cent of households in Peninsular Malaysia had income below (M) $100 per month, while a further 31 per cent had incomes between $100 and $200. Over the top, one tenth of all households accounted for nearly 40 per cent of the total income earned in the economy, while the share of the lowest two fifths of the households amounted to only about 12 per cent of total income.

As stated above, there were also considerable differences in the distribution of household income between urban and rural areas. About 90 per cent of households with monthly income below (M) $100 and 76.2 per cent of households with income between $100 and $200 were to be found in the rural areas. Thus 82.6 per cent of the households in Peninsular Malaysia with incomes below $200 were located in rural areas. About 34 per cent of the rural households had incomes below $100 per month, while 9.4 per cent of urban households was less than half the mean income of $435 or urban households. These marked disparities in income among various groups income and between urban and rural areas in Peninsular Malaysia indicate largely the low levels of productivity in much of the agricultural sector and the service sector.

Compounding the problem of income levels and their distribution is the situation with respect to conditions of living. Information indicates that poor nutrition and lack of access to adequate health, housing, education and transportation facilities remain a sizeable problem. The rural households have a lower number of occupants per dwelling, but they experience a serious lack of piped water, electricity and adequate sanitation facilities. Density of occupation per dwelling is higher in the urban areas. The relative congestion of living quarters and the lack of adequate water and sanitation facilities in many urban areas add to the conditions of greater squalor for the urban poor. Educational enrolments also remain a matter of serious concern in the rural areas and in the poorer urban areas.

The prospects for the future are good, the significant improvements in real earnings in small-holder agriculture, as a result of the past and continuing programmes of new land development, increase in size of holdings and agricultural modernisation policies. In the agricultural sector, about 4,10,000 acres of land were provided with drainage and irrigation facilities, of which over 2,10,000 acres were brought under double-cropping during 1971-73.

1298. Ojha, P.D. Configuration of Indian poverty—Inequality and levels of living. In *Challenge of Indian Poverty* Ed. by A.J. Fonseca. New Delhi, Vikas, 1971.

1299. Snodgrass Donald R. *Inequality and economic development in Malaysia*. Oxford, 1980.

1300. Young, Kevin. *et. al. Growth and equity in a multiracial society.* Baltimore, 1980.

MALDIVES

1301. Bell, H.C.P. *Maldives islands*. Colombo, 1940.

1302. Gayoom. Maldives looks to the future. *Far Eastern Economic Review* 5 Oct. 1979; 42-43.

1303. Hussain, Adnan. *Maldives islands today*. Colombo, Information Department, 1967.

1304. Lateef, K. Sarwar. ed. *Maldives : An introductory report*. Washington, World Bank, 1980. p. 172.

1305. Maloney, Clarence. Maldives : New stresses in an old nation. *Asian Survey* Jul. 1976.

1306. Selwyn, Percy. *Small, poor and remote : Islands at a geographical disadvantage.* Brighton, England, 1973.

1307. UNDP. *Report of a mission to the Maldives Islands*. 1966.

MALI

1308. French, Howard. Relief and rain barely avert disaster in Sahel. *International Herald Tribune* 28-29 Jun. 1986 ; 15.

1309. French, Howard. Seeking traces of empire along Mali's great river. *International Herald Tribune* 28-29 Jun. 1986 ; 17.

1310. Mali battles drought. *Congress Varnika International* (New Delhi) Sep. 1985; 24-25.

The choking red dust of the summer Harmattan hangs over Mali like a threatening shroud.

The Niger river is at its lowest level since 1913 and near the village of Farana, just a day's drive north of the capital of Bamako, women are digging in the dry river bed for water. Near Lake Debo cattle in their thousands crisscross the Niger at knee depth to graze the last green tufts of a season still three months from rain, while northern nomads—their herds long gone—struggle southwards to the fringes of towns like Mopti, Timbuktu and Gao.

In the last few months displaced families have swelled the populations of these centres by 10,000, 20,000 and 40,000 respectively and at least 1.2 million people nationwide are said to be on the knife edge of starvation.

Sixteen years of drought and three consecutive crop failures have brought Mali to these desperate straits. The northern harvest of sorghum, millet and rice was 65 to 70 per cent lower than normal last years and the 1985 food deficit stands at 4,81,000 tonnes a—crippling shortfall for a country of 6.5 million people which was self-sufficient until 1960 and lacks the logistical capacity to distribute more than 2,00,000 tonnes of Cereals a year without airlifts and other extraordinary measures.

In purely climatic terms, the country is the third most seriously affected by drought in Africa today after Ethiopia and Niger, but political stability and the government's resolve to meet the emergency head-on have so far prevented the scale of human devastation seen in other Sahelian countries.

President Moussa Traore lodged a formal appeal for 2,33,000 tonnes of food aid with international donors last October. About 1,66,000 tonnes-more than one-third of it from the U.S.—is already on the docks in Abidjan in the neighbouring Ivory Coast. An additional 1,50,000 tonnes is expected to enter the country through private traders, and a 20,000 tonnes government purchase is to be used to buffer price fluctuations. Comments one senior representative of the World Food Programme which is monitoring food aid distribution here : "A little more than 2,00,000 tonnes in food aid has been committed, and while there will be malnutrition, it will not be a catastrophe. It will be a grave situation and there will be starvation, but it will not be like Ethiopia."

MAURITANIA

1311. Schissel, Howard. Mauritania moving to save Oasis towns. *International Herald Tribune* 28-29 Jun. 1986; 15.

1312. Wilkinson, Ray. Mauritania: A nation disappears in tides of sand. *International Herald Tribune* 29 May, 1986; 9.

MEXICO

1313. Grebler, L. *Mexican immigration to the United States : The record and its implications*. Los Angeles, Univ. of California Press, 1966.

1314. Hicks, W.W. Economic development and fertility change in Mexico, 1950-57. *Demography 11*, 1974; 407-21.

1315. Illich, Ivan. Development myth—the Mexican experience. *Gandhi Marg* (New Delhi) Jan. 1986 : 687-91.

1316. Lewis, O. *Children of Sanchez : Autobiography of a Mexican family*. New York, Random House, 1961.

1317. Lewis, Oscar. *Five families : Mexican case studies in the culture of poverty*. New York, Random House, 1959.

1318. Vaughan, Mary Kay. *State, education and social class in Mexico, 1880-1928*. Northern Illinois Univ. Press, 1982. p. 327.

MICRONESIA

1319. Tiny Islands, Big Ambitions. *Asiaweek* 7 Sep. 1986 ; 41-44.

MONGOLIA

1320. Heaton, William R. Mongolia in 1985. *Asian Survey* Jan. 1986 : 86-92.

NEPAL

1321. Islam R. *et. al. Employment and development in Nepal*. Bangkok, ILO, 1982.

1322. Khanal, Y.N. Nepal in 1985 : An uneasy year. *Asian Survey* Feb. 1986 ; 246-52.

1323. Seddon, David. *Peasants and workers in Nepal : The conditions of the lower classes*. Warminister, P. Aris and Phillips, 1978.

1324. Sharma, Jan. Nepalese women hardest hit by unemployment. *Pioneer* 19 Dec. 1985 ; 6.

NEW GUINEA

1325. Strathern, A. *Rope of Moka : Big men and ceremonial exchange in Mount Hagan, New Guinea*. Cambridge, 1971.

NEW ZEALAND

1326. Condliffe, J.B. *New Zealand in the making*. London, 1959.

1327. De Bres, J. *How Tonga aids New Zealand.* Wellington, South Pacific Action Net Work, 1974.

1328. Jackson, Keith. and John Harre. *New Zealand.* London. Thames and Hudson, 1969. p. 224.

1329. Oliver, W.A. *Story of New Zealand.* London, 1963.

1330. Sinclair, K. *History of New Zealand.* London, 1961.

1331. Sutch, W.B. *Quest for security in New Zealand, 1840-1966.* Wellington, 1966.

1332. Wilson, E.W. *Land problems of the New Zealand settlers of the forties*. Dunedin, 1935.

NICARAGUA

1333. Bernard, Jean Claude. Revolution on its sixth anniversary. *International Viewpoint* 14 Oct. 1985 ; 3-7.

1334. Mukherjee, Sadhan. Nicaragua : Seven years of revolution. *New Age* 20 Jul. 1986 ; 12.

1335. Nicaragua poses no threat. *International Herald Tribune* 18 Aug. 1986 ; 4.

NIGERIA

1336. Akerle, A. Facing up to unemployment in Benin city. In *Urbanization and Nigerian economic development*. Ibadan, 1979.

1337. Ayida, A.A. and H.M.A. Onitiri. *Reconstruction and development in Nigeria.* Ibadan, 1971.

1338. Beer, C.E.F. *Politics of peasant groups in Western Nigeria.* Ibadan, 1976.

1339. Bulloch, J. Nigerian anger at leaders' rich living. *Sunday Telegraph* 21 Jun. 1964.

1340. Coldwell, John C. Education as a factor of mortality decline : An examination of Nigerian data. *Population Studies* 33 (3) Nov. 1979.

1341. Coleman, J.S. *Nigeria, background to nationalism.* Los Angeles, 1958.

1342. Collins, P. ed. *Administration for development in Nigeria.* Ibadan, 1979.

1343. *First report of the wages and salaries review commission, 1970.* Lagos, 1970.

1344. Lagemann, J. *Traditional African farming systems in Eastern Nigeria.* Munich, Weltforum Verlag, 1977.

1345. Mabogunje, A. L. Demobilization of the Nigerian peasantry. In *TWP* ; 230·44.

1346. Miller, J.P. Medical relief in the Nigerian civil war. *Lancet* 1, 1970; 1330.

1347. Nigeria spreads family planning message. *China Daily* (Beijing) 23 Apr. 1986 ; 4.

1348. Peace, A. *Social change at Agege.* University of Sussex. 1973. (Ph. D. Thesis).

1349. Raju, R.K. Exforced austerity in Nigeria. *Statesman* (New Delhi) 24 Jul. 1986 ; 6.

1350. Riesman, M. Humanitarian intervention to protect the Ibos. In *Humanitarian intervention and the United Nations.* Ed. by Richard B. Lillich. Univ. Press of Virgina, 1973.

1351. Seers, D. ed. *First things first : Meeting the basic needs of the people of Nigeria,* Addis Ababa, 1980.

1352. Shagari, Shehu. *Challenge of change*. Lagos, 1980. p. 95.

1353. Shagari, Shehu. Economic development is vital to technological advancement. In *Challenge of change*. Lagos, 1980; 28-30.

1354. Williams, Gavin. and Terisa Turnner. Nigeria. In *West African States*, Cambridge, 1978.

1355. Yugui, Qian. Developing its national economy, *Beijing Review* 27 Jun. 1983; 15-16.

OMAN

1356. Birks, J.S. Development or decline of pastoralists : the Bani Qutab of the Sultanate of Oman. *Arabian Studies* 4, 1978 ; 7-19.

1357. *Women and revolution in Oman.* London, International Defence and Aid Fund, 1975.

PACIFIC REGION

1358. De Bres, J. *et al. Migrant labour in the Pacific.* CORSO, Auckland Resource Centre for World Development, 1974.

1359. Lambert, S.M. Medical conditions in South Pacific. *Medical Journal of Australia* 2, 1928 ; 362-78.

1360. Rada, Edward L. and Kan, Wn. *eds. Self-help in Pacific Asian development.* Taipei, Soochow Univ. Press, 1975.

PAKISTAN

1361. Ahmed, A. Democracy and dictatorship in Pakistan. *Journal of Contemporary Asia* 4, 1978, 44-512.

1362. Alauddin, T. Mass poverty in Pakistan. *Pakistan Development Review* 4, 1975 ; 431-50.

1363. Burki, S.J. Eradication of mass poverty : the Pakistan experience in *EAPS*; 236-68.

In Pakistan, as in so many other developing countries, a Family as a "production unit" functions in an environment that is considerably different from the one in which families produced children when the present-day industrial countries were passing through a similar stage of development. Then the family functioned without much outside interference and determined its supply of children to what it perceived to be its demand for them. The very rapid rate of population growth in recent years has brought another factor in the family's decision making framework : the role of the State. While the State does not coerce the individuals to adopt a certain reproductive behaviour, it is in many cases, vigorously trying to influence it. Family planning propaganda and social pressures to reduce the size of the family have definitely changed the environment in which the family now decides about its size. In most cases there is a basic conflict that results from differences in perception between what the family regards to be its optimum size and what the State considers to be the appropriate size of the family.

The most difficult problem is that of distinguishing between the demand for children and their supply, because parents are both the demanders and suppliers simultaneously. Pecuniary and non-pecuniary factors are important on both demand and supply side. On the pecuniary side of demand for a child is the tangible return that would accrue to parents because of the child's anticipated contribution to parents' income. The non-pecuniary benefit is of course the psychic satisfaction of having children. Similarly, on the supply, side there are opportunity costs and psychic costs of the time invested by the parents in begetting and bringing up children. A mother invests a certain amount of time in bearing a child and parents spend a certain amount of tangible resources on rearing him. On the non-pecuniary side are such factors as the pain of child-birth.

Leaving non-pecuniary costs and benefits aside, it is possible to use well established conceptional framework to determine what parents consider to be the right size of their family. A number of factors contribute to this, and some of them are subject to change as a result of State interference. The most important factor that influences parental decision is their anticipation of the cost involved to sustain themselves at a certain level of well being beyond their own economically productive stage. This is an important consideration in the countries where old age pension and welfare are not available. The estimate of requirement for old age in societies without a great occupational mobility is usually based on the level of consumption attained by the parents when they embark on family building. Two more calculations are needed before the parents arrive at the suitable size of the family; first, the expected level of child's earnings when he reaches his economically active life and, second, the probability of his surviving to that point in time. In the former case, in an underdeveloped country, most parents calculate their off-spring's earnings on the basis of their own at the time of family formation. In the second case, the parents' estimate is based on their perception of the rate of infant mortality. These three calculations taken together determine for the parents the size of their family.

1364. Burki, S.J. Food and fertility. *In prologue to development policy and population policy—the Pakistan experienee*. Washington, ICP, 1975.

1365. Burki, S.J. Interest group involvement in West Pakistan's rural works program. *Public Policy*. 19, Winter 1971.

1366. Burki, S.J. *Pakistan under Bhutto, 1971-77.* London, Macmillan, 1980.

1367. Callard, Keith. Political stability of Pakistan. *Pacific Affairs* 29 Mar. 1956.

1368. Chaudhari, G. Whither Pakistan. *New Wave* 20 Jul. 1986 ; 8-9.

1369. Feldman, H. *From crisis to crisis. Pakistan in 1962-69.* London, 1970.

1370. Hashmi, A.H. Slums and slum improvement in Karachi. In *EAPS*; 199-210.

Poverty might be considered as basic to the very existence of the slum phenomenon. In Pakistan, as elsewhere, slum inhabitants comprise those belonging to the lowest income groups. Surveys have revealed the rate of unemployment and under employment to be high. Even in slums populated largely by industrial labour the rate of expenditure is frequently at subsistence level because of remittances to their relatives in other parts of the country.

The other major problems of Karachi's slums are also common to those in many other Asian countries in particular the problems of housing, sanitation, roads and streets, health and education, municipal services and public utilities.

Housing presents the most momentous of these problems. At present the largest proportion of dwellings in the slum are consists of *jhuggies*, followed by kucha, semi-pucca and pucca dwelling. Several factors might be considered to be productive of this situation of unsatisfactory and inadequate housing: the more important among these are lack of necessary means; lack of sufficient incentive to invest in improved housing because of the unauthorized legal status of the slum in question ; lack of motivation to improve one's living conditions; and the supposedly temporary nature of a particular slum specially in the case of a squatter settlement.

The increase in Karachi's slum areas has been occasioned by the bloating and expansion of slums already in existence for decades and the emergence of new slums frequently starting off as squatter settlements and gradually acquiring permanence and definite slum characteristics. In both cases the haphazard nature of growth precluded proper planning so that congestion, absence of proper roads and streets and the existence of narrow, tortious alleys is a conspicuous characteristic of most slum areas in Karachi. In many cases proper planning of the area would necessitate total rebuilding and the dislocation of large numbers.

The provision of municipal services in the slum areas presents another major problem. At the crux of the problem is the inability of the slum residents to pay for services provided or to pay any other taxes levied by the municipality. The rate of tax evasion in the slum areas has been found to be extremely high.

The inability of the inhabitants to pay and the unwillingness of the municipality to improve its services sometimes assumes the nature of a negative circular causation: the slum dwellers refuse to pay for unsatisfactory service, whereas the municipality finds itself unable to improve unless it is paid. The major municipal services relevant to the slum areas are water supply, the provision of hospitals and primary schools, garbage collection and sewerage.

The supply of water in Karachi is an elaborate undertaking since water is conveyed to the city from the river indus, over a distance of some 70 miles. Water shortage has thus been one of the city's constant problems. In the slum areas this problem is particularly acute. With a few exceptions, which can be overlooked for statistical purposes, piped water is not available in any of the slum dwellings. The provision of water from community taps which have been provided by the municipality in most slum areas is limited to certain hours of the day.

The educational, recreational and medical facilities available in the slums of Karachi and other Pakistani cities present the same, inadequacies that are generally characteristic of slums everywhere in Asia. Paucity of educational facilities has particular grave implications for the future in that the young slum generation of today is denied the opportunity to acquire skills and knowledge that will help to enhance earning the capacity in the future and to change the "slum attitudes" that have been found to be so instrumental in perpetuating the slum way of life. Karachi slums are similarly denied the benefits of uplift efforts by social welfare organizations; on paper there are many but in practice most are totally or largely dormant.

Garbage collection and sewerage are the other areas in which the municipality has been either unable or unwilling to cope with the result that environmental sanitation is a shockingly deplorable characteristic of almost all the city's slums.

Most slums are not in total darkness as they are provided with street lights, although few dwellings have domestic electricity.

1371. Khan, Dilawar Ali and Chaudhri Haider Ali. Income impact of the green revolution. *Pakistan, Economic and Social Review.* 11(1) 1973; 67-82.

1372. Khan, Liaquat Ali. *Pakistan : Heart of Asia.* Harvard Univ. Press, 1951.

1373. Khan, M.H. and J.A. Zerby. Socio-economic position of Pakistan in the third world. *Pakistan Development Review* 20(3) 1981; 347-65.

1374. Khandker, R.H. Distribution of income and wealth in Pakistan. *Pakistan Economic and Social Review* 11 (1) 1973; 1-39.

1375. Nabi, Iraz. *Quality of life in Pakistan : studies in social factor.* Lahore, Vangu and Books, 1986.

1376. Naseem, S. M. Mass poverty in Pakistan : Some preliminary findings. *Pakistan, Development Review* 4, 1973 ; 317-60.

1377. Naseem, S. M. Rural poverty and landlessness in Pakistan. *In Poverty and landlessness in rural Asia.* Geneva, ILO, 1977.

1378. Nazeer, Mian M. Urban growth in Pakistan. *Asian Survey* 16, Jun. 1966 ; 310-18.

1379. Papanek, G. *Pakistan's development.* Harvard, 1968.

1380. Qureshi, M. L. Pakistan. In *EAPS* ; 51-54.

Knowledge about the degree and extent of poverty in Pakistan is rather limited. In the first instance there is the problem of the estimation of the 'poverty line', that is, the level of per capita expenditure that fails to satisfy the minimum human needs. This requires detailed investigations into nutritional requirements, housing standards and other necessities in various regions of the country, and these have not yet been carried out. Secondly available information about employment and household incomes and expenditures, which is essential for an estimation of the magnitude of poverty, is rather scanty. However, a recent study sponsored by the Pakistan Institute of Development Economics (PIDE), has attempted to prepare rough estimates of the extent of poverty in Pakistan. The study has used two arbitrary poverty lines, namely annual per capita expenditures of Rs. 250 (US$ 52.5) and Rs. 300 (US$ 63) for the rural areas and Rs. 375 (US$ 78.75) for the urban areas. Higher poverty lines were assumed for urban areas because of the higher cost of living in these areas compared with rural areas.

In the rural areas, assuming a poverty line at an annual per capital expenditure of Rs. 250;27 per cent of the population was below this line in 1969-70. However, if the poverty line is drawn at Rs. 300, about 60 per cent of the population was poor. In the urban areas in 1969-70, 25 per cent of the population was below the poverty line of Rs. 300, and 59 per cent below the poverty line of Rs. 375.

Taking the rural and urban populations together, about one-quarter of the population, namely 16 million, was below the lower poverty line (Rs. 250 for rural and Rs. 300 for urban areas) and about 60 per cent, namely 36 million, was below the higher poverty line (Rs. 300 for rural and Rs. 375 for urban areas) in 1969-70. In other words about one-quarter of the population was living in abject poverty in 1969-70 and another 35 per cent was slightly better off but was not much above the subsistence level.

It will be seen from the above that the estimates of the degree and magnitude of poverty are sensitive to the choice of the poverty line. This is so because a large part of the population is concentrated in the narrow range of per capital consumption of Rs. 250 to Rs. 300 per annum in rural areas and Rs. 300 to Rs. 375 per annum in the urban areas.

The trend overtime shows a substantial reduction in abject poverty since 1963-64. The percentage of rural population below the lower poverty line has declined from 43 per cent in 1963-64 to 27 per cent in 1969-70 and of urban population from 55 per cent to 25 per cent. However, the rural population below the upper poverty line has remained constant at about 60 per cent of the total during the 1963-64 ; 1969-70 period but that of the urban population has declined from 75 per cent to 59 per cent.

The conclusion about some reduction in poverty over time is supported by some indirect evidence also. The benefits of the increase in GNP, particularly the increase due to the green revolution, have spread to some extent to the poorer sections of the population resulting in some improvement in income distribution. A study on the distribution of income in Pakistan shows that incomes have become less concentrated during the period of 1963-64 to 1966-67 and another study on the distribution of income and wealth in Pakistan also shows a declining trend in income inequalities in rural and urban areas during the period 1963-64 to 1969-70.

The data, namely the household, income and expenditure surveys of the Central Statistical Organization (CSO), on which the above studies are based, are subject to serious limitations. So the conclusions arrived at one the basis of such data cannot be regarded as firm. Nevertheless, the broad magnitudes of the problem of poverty as indicated in the PIDE study mentioned above are not likely to be far different from the actual situation.

However, the sections of the population which are poor have to be identified and the causes of poverty have to be analysed. A thorough study of the problems of employment and income distribution is essential for a proper analysis of the causes of poverty. Available information on which such studies could be based is meagre. However, two surveys are being carried out to fill some gaps in information, namely the Housing Economic and Demographic Survey by CSO, and the Benchmark Survey for the Integrated Rural Development Programme jointly by the PIDE and the Ministry of Agriculture, Government of Pakistan. These surveys are expected to provide reliable information on income, employment, housing, land-holdings, irrigation facilities, farm inputs, agricultural production, livestock, and age, sex and education of household members. This information will provide a basis for further studies on the problem of poverty.

1381. Richter, William L. Pakistan in 1985 : Testing time for the new order. *Asian Survey*. Feb. 1986 ; 207-18.

1382. Sayeed, K. B. *Pakistan : the formative phase 1857-1948*. Oxford University Press, 1968.

PAPUA NEW GUINEA

1383. Amarshi, A. *et. al. Development and dependency the political economy of Papua New Guinea*. Melbourne, Oxford University Press, 1979.

1384. Conroy, J. D. *Education, employment and migration in Papua New Guinea*. Canberra, Australian National University 1 ; 1976.

1385. Levine, H. B. and M. W. Levine. *Urbanisation in Papua New Guinea*. London, 1979.

1386. MacPherson, S. *Health and underdevelopment in Papua New*

Guinea. Auckland, New Zealand Association for the Advancement of Science, Jan. 1979.

1387. Nelson, H. *Papua New Guinea Blackunity or blackchaos* ? Penguin Books, 1972.

1388. Premdas, Ralph R. Papua New Guinea in 1985. *Asian Survey* Feb. 1986 ; 196-206.

PARAGUAY

1389. Churilov, E. Twilight of a dictatorship. *New Times* (Moscow) 23 Jun. 1986 ; 27-28.

Grave economic crisis......Factories operating at half capacity at best...... The building industry virtually paralyzed......Up to four-fifths of the incomes from traditional exports—soybeans, cotton, timber and tung oil—going into the payment of interest on a foreign debt that is appalling for a country with a population of four million—15 billion dollars. Such is the state of affairs in the Paraguayan today. No wonder that Latin American and West European countries are increasingly reluctant to grant new loans to the regime, whose corrupt chieftains have no scruples about embezzling public funds.

Paraguay's economic problems are symptomatic not merely of a cyclical crisis, but of the collapse of the "Paraguayan development model" geared to the production of farm products for export. Meat packing plants are now standing idle for want of orders. The benefits of last year's bumper crops of soybeans and cotton have been reduced to nothing by the plummeting of world market prices. Although the volume of exports has grown by 40 per cent, export earnings have gone down by 6 per cent. At the same time, the prices of bread, sugar and meat on the domestic market are climbing steadily, which his working people hard. The national monetary unit, the guarani, was devalued by 75 per cent last-January. As a result, the prices of various commodities have jumped still higher.

The serious economic difficulties have catalyzed nationwide opposition to the dictatorship. Protest action by working people in town and countryside is gaining in scale. They have put forward political as well as economic demands.

The student movement is assuming massive proportions. Discontent is spreading to the middle and even big bourgeosie and part of the military.

1390. Reichert, John. Unpopular austerity proposals in Paraguay. *Baghdad Observer*. 31 May 1986 ; 4.

Falling exports, foreign debt repayments and rising unemployment are forcing Paraguay to consider a tough economic austerity programme that analysts say could take a high political fall.

Paraguay, which has been ruled for 32 years by General Alfredo Stroessner, 73, has enjoyed a reputation as an oasis of economic stability in a region plagued by foreign debt, runaway inflation and economic stagnation.

But in early May, a team of Central Bank official handed Stroessner a package of proposed reforms that would sharply devalue official exchange rates and lead to hikes in public service tariffs.

Stroessner is also facing a budding opposition movement which has staged one of the first challenges to his strong-arm rule. Police broke up with tear gas, water cannons and clubs a series of unprecendented public protests a month ago for more democratic freedoms and better pay.

Economic analyst Pablo Herken Krauer said the government was torn between ignoring economic problems in an effort to ratain a ploblem-free image, and adopting reforms that could be politically costly.

"The problem is one of indecision", a banking source said.

Paraguay enjoyed rapid growth in the late 1970s and early 1980s, benefiting from its participation with Brazil in building the multi-billion dollar Itaipu hydroelectric dam.

But banking sources said the country's economic problems began to emerge over two years ago and have been left unattended. The land-locked nation of 3.5 million people is dividing into a recession after four years of lacklustre economic performance, they said.

The drop in economic activity has been aggravated by a drought that is expected to cut the cotton and soybean crops, the two main exports, by over 30 per cent.

Monsignor Jorge Livieres Banks, who has headed a church call for a national dialogue on the nation's political, economic and social crisis, said the drought had severely affected the large rural population that depends on subsistence farming.

People's Republic of

CHINA

1391. Aziz, S. *Rural Development : Karning from China.* London, Macmillan, 1978.

1392. Baum, Richard. China in 1985 : the greening of revolution. *Asian Survey* Jan. 1986 ; 30-53.

1393. Blecher, Marc. Balance and cleavage in Urban-rural relations. In *CRD*, 219-45.

1394. Butler, Steven B. Price scissors and commune administration in post-Mao China, in *CRD* 95-116.

1395. China. *In Profiles of rural poverty.* Geneva, ILO, 1979 : 37-42.

1396. Circular outlines plans to help poor. *Beijing Review* 5 Nov. 1984 ; 7-8.

1397. Decision on solving urban employment problem. *Beijing Review* 8 Feb. 1982; 21-24.

1398. Developing regional industrial systems in the people's Republic of China. In *IDPR*; 335-52.

1399. Diamond, Norma. Taiton revisited: State policies and social change. In *CRD*; 246-70.

1400. Eberstadt, Nick. *Poverty in China.* New York, 1975.

1401. Eliminating rural poverty in China, *Amrita Bazar Patrika* 24 Jan. 1985 ; 9.

China's strategy of self-reliance in rural development, based on the use of collectives, had reduced inequalities in areas such as education and public health, including sanitation and nutritional levels. But the strategy has not led to an alternative path to higher agricultural production or to the income levels of advanced countries.

This is one of several important findings in a new World Bank study, Rural Development in China, which analyzes China's agricultural performance over the past 30 years. The authors are Dwight H. Berkins, director of the Institute for International Development at Harvard University and Shahid Yusuf, a senior economist at The World Bank.

They note that China's agricultural future does not appear to be "markedly different" from that of other nations, particularly in East Asia, which have achieved substantial economic development. Agricultural research and the increasing use of modern "inputs" will keep production growing, and rising incomes will keep demand for food growing at an even pace with, or a bit faster than, supply.

The authors state that as in these other countries, the gap in China between urban and rural incomes will only be solved by moving people in the countryside into urban employment with higher productivity. This was an option that had been delineratelyeschewed by the Chinese authorities. Mobilizing labour: In implementing, village-level programme, China's "surplus" workers were mobilized at a historically unprecedented level. Going beyond conventional sources of growth analysis, the World Bank study examines the organizational and political means that World enabled the Chinese to mobilize so much labour for developmental purposes.

The authors find that the Chinese leadership see their future and the future of their policies as being intimately tied to the prosperity of the countryside. A logical follow-up to this belief was China's emphasis on preventive medicine and on helath efforts that reached remote regions of the country, and a land reform programme under which the poorest villagers received most of the benefits.

Analyzing the role of agriculture in overall development strategy, the authors emphasize the fact that China's agricultural and industria development strategies have been carried out, to an unusual degree, in isolation from each other. Thus, China still has many of the characteristics of a "dual" economy, despite three decades of rapid industrial growth. While agriculture has benefited from the existence of a modern industrial sector, rural development in China has been a self-contained effort, compared with other rapidly growing economies.

Other findings by the authors are that health improved dramatically mainly as a result of collective effort in sanitation and inoculation campaigns, and that the significant rise in incomes among the poorest quarter of the population was a result of land reform, not gains in production. And farm production increased, but not faster than in many other developing countries that invested in much less effort, the authors say.

In 1979, the government initiated a programme for reform and adjustment. Various types of "production responsibility System" were introduced in the rural areas, giving small groups and households more autonomy in decisions regarding production and investment, as well as linking incomes directly with output.

The authors of the World Bank study state that in order to achieve gains in agricultural productivity the Chinese leadership, for the immediate future, is counting on the incentive effects of the responsibility system and increased production. The main gain of the responsibility system, as evidenced by the record of early 1980s, is a marked improvement in farmer incentives and a resulting rise in farm production. Since the responsibility system could lead to an abandonment of collectivized agriculture and a return to the system of individual family farms, the question arises as to whether China's leaders would allow such an extreme.

The authors conclude that however this question is resolved, it is clear from the experience of three decades that a strategy of self-reliant community development based on collectivized agriculture cannot, by itself, solve China's problem of agricultural production or income distribution, China's arable land is not potentially productive enough to result in high rural incomes through agriculture alone, and collectivization is not able to solve the problems of the poorest regions. Thus, the need to rely on urban industry as a method of eliminating rural poverty and achieving higher productivity.

1402. Gartrell, John. Inequality within rural communities of India. *American Sociological Review* 46, 1981.

1403. Griffin, Keith and Ashwani Saith. *Growth and inequality in rural China*, Geneva, ILO, 1981.

1404. Griffin, Keith and Ashwani Saith. Pattern of income inequality in rural China. *Oxford Economic Papers* 34 (1) Mar. 1982; 175-79.

1405. Has China eliminated poverty? *Economic Times* (New Delhi) 26 Jun. 1986; IV.

In China as many as 112 million or 11 per cent of the total population lived below the poverty line in 1982. The urban and rural break up was 1 per cent and 13 per cent respectively. The minimum annual per capita income according to the Chinese concept for falling below the poverty line, in Yuan 140 ($ 50) for rural areas and Yuan 167 ($ 60) for urban areas at 1985 prices. This compares with the average annual per capita income in China of $ 300 in 1983.

China's problem of poverty is therefore more or less confined to rural areas. Although there is substantial income inequality between the rural and urban sectors, the rural poverty is also not uniformally distributed. There are wide inter-provincial variations in the incidence of poverty e.g. the poverty percentage in Gansu province was as high as 41 per cent as against only 3 per cent in Jiangus and Hubei provinces. There is also a growing concern that the per capita output and income gap between the coastal areas and the interior is likely to widen significantly.

Despite all these differences, it is a fact that China has banished hunger, disease, high birth and infant death rates, general illiteracy and constant fear of destitution and starvation which haunt the very poor in other developing countries. As quoted in a recent world bank country report on China, the Chinese are making all out efforts to improve their levels of living. Many of the poorest in rural area are among the first to introduce the production responsibility system and have benefited from rapid growth in crop production. Poor areas of eastern and southern China have become richer by swithing to crops like cotton rather than sticking to foodgrains which was unsuitable under their existing agroclimatic conditions.

Between 1952, and 1982, China's per capita national income grew at an average annual rate of 4 per cent, while since 1979 the per capita income grew at an enviable 6.8 per cent per annum. In an attempt to improve living standards and eliminate poverty the Chinese government has set targets of quadrupling the gross value of industrial and agricultural output between 1980 and 2000, and increasing per capita income from around \$ 300 to \$ 800 (about 5 per cent per annum). Given their track record, this does not seem an impossible target.

1406. Ishikawa, S. China's food and agriculture. *Food Policy* May 1977.

1407. Lard, Nicholas R. State intervention and peasant opportunities. In *CRD* ; 33-56.

1408. Mallony, W.H. *China : land of famine.* New York, America Geographical Society, 1926.

1409. Maun, Jim. China phasing out right to lifetime job security. *International Herald Tribune* 3 Sep. 1986; 1,6.

1410. Nee, Victor Peasant household individualism. In *CRD*; 164-92.

1411. Peasants climbing out of poverty. *China Daily* 9 Mar. 1984; 3.

1412. Perkins, Duight. Meeting basic needs in the People's Republic of China. *World Development.* 1978.

1413. Qing, Huang. Platform for economic growth, *China Daily* 18 Aug. 1986; 4.

1414. *Report on food problems* Nanking. International Dept. Ministry of Information, 1947; p. 12.

1415. Self-help crusade beats poverty trap. *China Daily* 13 Feb. 1986; 1.

1416. Unger, Jonathan. Remuneration, ideology and personal interests in a Chinese village, 1960-80. In *CRD*; 117-40.

1417. Urban housing shortage (in China). *Beijing Review* 31 Aug. 1981;28.

1418. Watson, Rubie S. *Inequality among brothers : class and kinglup-in South China.* Cambridge, 1985. p. 193.

1419. Whyte, M.K. Social trends in China : The triumph of inequality ? *In Modernizing China.* Ed. by A. Coak Barnett and Ralph N. Clough. London, Westview, 1986; 103-24.

1420. Whyte, M.K. and W.L. Parish. *Urban life in contemporary China.* Chicago Press, 1984.

1421. Wiens, Thomas B. Poverty and progress in the Huang and Huai River Basins. In *CRD*; 57-94.

1422. Xiaong. Zhang. Why be afraid of poor getting rich ? *China Daily* 10 Nov. 1986;4.

1423. Xingping, Kang Teenager fled poverty for prosperous future. *China Daily* 21 Mar. 1985;6.

1424. Yanan bids poverty farewell. *China Daily* 14 Mar. 1986; 6.

1425. Yun, Tian. Assisting the rural poor. *Beijing Review* 19 Sep. 1983; 23-27.

It has always been one of the major goals of the Communist Party-led revolution in China to overcome class polarization and secure common prosperity in the countryside. The land reform of the early post-liberation years and the 1956 movement to establish agricultural producers' co-operatives removed the root causes of class polarization. But they could not possibly eradicate the differences in people's labour ability and income, differences which exist throughout the historical period of socialism.

For more than two decades after the cooperative movement, China has tried to bridge the income gaps between the peasants with large-scale egalitarian collective management and egalitarian methods of distribution. By arbitrarily equalizing the peasants' incomes these methods only crippled the peasants' enthusiasm for work, and held back the growth of agricultural production which even came to a standstill in some places. As a result, the peasants' standard of living did not improve as expected.

After the adjustment of the rural economic policies in 1979, new management methods—chiefly the contracted responsibility system based on the household—have been introduced within the framework of the collective economy of the production teams. While peasants are encouraged to earn as much as they can, no effort is spared in assisting those who have difficulties in rapidly boosting their incomes. This has considerably improved the standard of living in rural areas.

During the period from 1979 to 1982, the value of China's total agricultural output increased at an average annual rate of 7.5 per cent, as against the average annual rise of 3.2 per cent for the 26 years between 1953 and 1978. The peasants' incomes averaged 270 yuan per capita in 1982, which, after deducting incomparable factors, meant a 92.7 per cent increase over what they earned in 1978. The actual increase in the four years from 1979 to 1982 far outstripped that of the 26 previous years. The relatively backward rural areas which made up one-third of the countryside and poor households that embraced one-tenth of the rural population are now diminishing quickly.

Today, most poor families in China's rural areas are those without able-bodied members, funds or technology, and those impoverished through natural or other causes. They need to be helped. The remaining poor include the physically handicapped, childless senior citizens, and members of revolutionary martyrs' families that lack able-bodied members. The government or collective economic organizations issue regular allowances to ensure their decent living.

In the last few years, 3.27 million families across the country have received help in labour, funds and technology, and 1.09 million of them have shaken off poverty. The experience of Laian Country in Anhui Province's Chuzian Prefecture has been a model in assisting the poor. Its methods are being popularized nationwide.

1426. Yun, Tian. Moving a mountain of poverty. *Beijing Review* 24 Aug. 1981; 21-26.

1427. Zweig, David. Narrowing the urban-rural gap. *China Business Review* Mar-Apr. 1986 ; 18-19.

1428. Zweig, David. Peasants, ideology and new incentive systems : Jiangsu Province, 1978-81. In *CRD*; 141-63.

1429. Zweig, David. Prosperity and conflict in post-Mao China. *China Quarterly* (105) Mar. 1986; 1-18.

PERU

1430. Deadline for Peru. *International Herald Tribune* 9-10 Aug. 1986 ; 4.

1431. Einandi, Luigi. *Peruvian military : A summary political analysis.* Santa Monica, the Rand Corporation, 1969.

1432. Jikang, Hu. Debt. problem cries for cooperation. *Beijing Review* 8 Sep. 1986 ; 12-13.

1433. Lehman, David *ed. Agrarian reform and agrarian reformism : studies of Peru, Chile and India.* London, Faber and Faber, 1974.

1434. Military role in Peru. *Patriot* 20 Jul. 1986 ; 7.

1435. Peru. New York, United Nations, 1952.

1436. Plaza, J. Orlando. Peasantry, power and region : An approach to the Peruvian case. In *TWP Vol. 2* ; 51-67.

1437. UP and down in Peru. *International Herald Tribune* 22 Aug. 1986 ; 4.

1438. Year later in Peru. *International Herald Tribune* 6 Aug. 1986 ; 4.

PHILIPPINES

1439. Bautista, Romeo. Employment promotion in a small, open economy : the Philippines. In *EAPS* : 132-49.

From an attitude of general complacency about the employment problem in the past, development economists, other social scientists and even policy makers are increasingly being awakened by the accumulating evidence of heavy unemployment and underemployment existing at present and showing unfavourable trends in most developing countries. A natural accompaniment to the increasing number of unemployed and underemployed is the growing incidence of poverty in the affected households in the midst of an already low income economy. In view of such direct relationship between poverty and labour force under utilization, it hardly needs justification to assume that the generation of productive employment would be an effective measure in the battle against widespread poverty afflicting most developing economies of Asia at this time.

Indeed, poverty, measured in whatever way, lies at the heart of the employment problem, the conventional measures of unemployment and underemployment being only imperfect indicators of the magnitude of the employment challenge facing these countries.

As several reports of ILO-sponsored employment missions to a number of developing countries have demonstrated, various aspects of development policy on employment generations and instances are not lacking in which prevailing policies serve to inhibit the absorption of labour in productive activities. In the present discussion, I would like to use the Philippine experience as a case-study to examine some causes and possible solutions to the employment problem. I shall confine myself to an analysis of the industrialization policies adopted in the post-war period, from which will emerge certain policy guidelines that need to be followed at this time as part of an effective employment-promoting development strategy. The deliberate ommission of the other aspects of development policy bearing on the employment problem, should not be construed as a rejection of their significance. The reason for ignoring them here is simply that other lectures and discussions in this Workshop, as indicated in the agenda, will take up such important topics as agricultural development, poverty redressal programmes, demographic aspects, etc.

In discussing employment promotion policies, it would be useful to distinguish at the outset between long-term and short-term policy measures. Certain policy prescriptions to remedy the employment problem are in the nature of long-run solutions aimed at providing a reasonably sound basis for sustained employment generation in the future.

Where the pattern of economic development has acquired, for

instance, a strong bias against the use of labour in production, policy measures might be devised to effect a change in the economic environment and set the economy on at new development track, hopefully combining a fuller utilization of the labour force and a rapid rate of growth of national output.

On the other hand, there might be political and social pressures to mitigate the severity of the employment problem in the short run, in which case policy measures yielding immediate employment benefits would be appropriate. It is not easy, of course, to indicate precisely the degree of unemployment and underemployment warranting classification as an emergency case. In any event, the point needs to be recognized that any short-term approach to the employment problem should be consistent with and if possible also contribute to the long-term objectives. We shall return to this issue latter on.

It seems generally agreed by now that a rapid growth of output does not necessarily bring about a high rate of employment generation. However, one would also admit that sustained labour absorption can be achieved only in the context of a growing economy. Given the currently low levels of per capita income among most Asian countries, it is obviously desirable that employment creation policies be made compatible with rising national products. These considerations would seem to imply the necessity of a development oriented strategy aimed at exploiting possible complementaries between output growth and employment generation. Although trade-offs between these two policy objectives may not be avoided, especially in the short run, it is frequently the case that the elimination or even a reduction of existing biases in the economy against labour absorption leads to an even better climate for output expansion. The dentification of these factors inhibiting the growth of both employment and output is critical. I would think, to the solution of the employment problem in the long run.

It may be helpful to give a brief statement of the major points that I would want to make following the presentation of certain dimensions of the Philippine employment problem. Although they are discussed in the context of the Philippines, it will perhaps not be far-fetched to claim that other developing economies in Asia are more or less similarly placed.

The first hypothesis I will advance is that Philippine postwar economic policy has generally biased the industrial structure towards import-dependent, regionally concentrated, large-scale industries that require in production relatively more capital than is appropriate, given the country's resource endowments. At the same time the comparative advantage in labour-intensive manufactures for export failed to be exploited due to the neglect of industries not oriented towards the displacement of imported consumer goods in the domestic market. The consequence has been a disappointing rate of labour absorption in the industrial sector despite a fairly respectable growth performance of the economy.

1440. Branigin, William. Aquino : Beset with problems : *International Herald Tribune* 15 Sep. 1986 ; 1-6.

1441. Chanda, Najan. Stability's high cost. *Far Eastern Economic Review* 4 Sep. 1986 ; 52-53.

1442. Ho, Teresa J. Time cost of child rearing in the rural Philippines. *Population and Development Review*. Dec. 1979.

1443. Hollnsteiner, M R. Development research versus poverty research : Two sides of the same coil ? (Philippines) : In *EAPS*; 218-22.

What is the difference between action-oriented research aimed at the development of the Asian masses, and action-oriented research geared towards the elimination of poverty ? At first glance they seem to represent two sides of the same coin, the difference merely lying in which side one chooses to look at. After all, everyone knows that development aims at eliminating poverty and raising levels of living among the masses.

Two decades of development have cast doubt on this one solid assumption. For development deemed successful in terms of economic growth rates seem not to have diminished poverty very much after all. Development moves forward but so does poverty. If the actual association between development and poverty turns out in fact to be a positive rather than a negative one, that is, the greater the development, the greater the poverty, then correspondingly, development research cannot be synonymous with anti-poverty research. If the elimination of poverty is allegedly the aim of development research, but poverty is growing rather than declining despite notable development increments, then the researcher needs to pause and take serious stock of his conceptual frameworks. Development research and poverty research, it seems are not two sides of the same coin after all, but rather represent two different coins altogether.

Let us examine these two types of research and delve deeper into their differences.

Using development as a framework means identifying oneself with a process that is simultaneously an ideology. It embodies a conscious thrust forward towards higher levels of living, a sharing of these levels in more equitable proportions throughout the society, a heightened sense of dignity, efficacy, and self-worth among the once poor, and anything else that fits into that elusive concept called quality of life. If, on the other hand, the researcher chooses poverty as his conceptual framework, then he is focussing on a social system—a way of life that enmeshes members of society into so intricate a pattern that every part of it is related to every other part, and all parts make up an interwoven whole. If poverty flourishes with development, then there must be a functional relationship between the two that bears further investigation.

Since in most developing countries, development has been not only a process but an ideology as well, researchers have been caught up in its bandwagon effect. Hence, the question they usually start out which matches this orientation, namely ; what strategy should be employed to move the masses from point A on the modernization scale to point B ? Further, how can this particular strategy be enhanced for maximum efficiency, measured by quantitative improvements in levels of living and qualitatively higher assessments by the target population of their current states ? The development researcher thus examines agrarian reform programmes, and how new land-systems affect production. Or he looks into agricultural development schemes involving credit, cooperatives, fertilizer-distribution, irrigation systems, marketing patterns, and farmers' understandings and perceptions of how such innovations fit into their daily lives. Still others opt to assess programmes in family planning, urban community development among squatter populations, resettlement schemes and the like. Their queries ultimately ask, 'are these programmes working or not ?' Why or why not ? And, how can we make them work better ?

The poverty researcher by contrast starts out with a much more fundamental question. What is poverty ? So apparently simple an inquiry camouflages a whole series of complex questions. What are the components of poverty ? Do all poverty populations embody these components, or are there different components and mixes depending on the population under study ? How are these components related to one another ? Given the systemic character of poverty, what will be the effects of new inputs ? What kinds of new inputs are necessary to effect outputs geared to the elimination of various kinds of poverty ? Do the people believed to all into the poverty sector, perceive themselves as poor ? Relative to whom ? What are their aspirations for themselves and their families, given their present status ?

Where the development researcher focusses on specific strategies linked to particular situations in a society, the poverty researcher takes a more holistic view, even though he may also select a particular problem for investigation. The former studies people in categories appropriate to his own development strategy interest ; the latter assumes nothing, creates no dominant categories initially but starts simply with people in their own terms.

Thus, the two sets of researchers may take an interest in the same kinds of information, let us say, household income and expenditure patterns. But the development researcher will view the data in the context of, for example, a proposed new savings and small loan scheme to be initiated by a local bank or a newly devised applied nutrition scheme. The poverty researcher, on the other hand, may be more interested in how a pattern relates to the family's status in the community, or the number of children the parents expect to send to school in line with career aspirations, or a host of other linked behaviors.

Then there is the matter of who or what is to be studied. Basically, two classifications apply. The first involves specific ecological or occupational groups. Here one might look into various types of farming and fishing villages, especially those in the chronically depressed typhoon-ridden areas, stagnant towns, and urban slum or squatter enclaves ; occupational groups might include disadvantaged ethnic or hill-tribe minorities, landless rural labourers, and urban scavengers, pier hands, and hawkers. The second subject classification entails a look at systems as such. While in a sense, ecological and occupational groups are already being studied in terms of their relationship to a larger poverty-perpetuating system, there is need to focus separately on systems in themselves. One would thereby understand the connection between the poverty of the groups cited above and the operations of the larger society of which they are a part. A cybernetic approach which, among other things, discovers just how people actually cope with poverty and somehow manage to survive should yield significant insights, for example, by looking a system, one makes them a central concern instead of relegating them merely to the secondary status of a supporting framework.

1444. Hollnsteiner, M.R. Notes on urbanization and poverty in Asian countries with special reference to the Philippines. In *EAPS* ; 213-17.

1445. May, R.J. and F. Nemenzo. ed. *Philippines after Marcos*. London, Groom Helm ; 1985.

1446. Mydans, Seth. Philippine town awaits changes and targets past.

International Herld Tribune 23 May 1986 ; 18.

1447. Parry, Antony. Putting money in the pockets of the poor. *Baghdad Observer* 31 Mar. 1986 ; 4.

1448. People are going hungry. *International Viewpoint* 13 Oct. 1986 ; 10.

1449. Petitjean, Paul. Decisive tests facing the Aquino government. *International Viewpoint* 21 Apr. 1986 ; 3-5

1450. Reyes, P.S. and T.L. Chan. Family income distribution in the Philippines. *Statistical Reporter* 9 (2) 1965.

1451. Seno, Cecilio T. Philippines. In *EAPS* ; 77-83.

The Philippines in 1973 saw a new push. The advent of the New Society envisioned by President Ferdinand E.Marcos ushered in significant changes. This year finally witnessed basic alterations of the old social, political and economic systems.

Over the years, the country had been in a sad state of confusion and disorder. Prior to the New Society, its social, economic and political systems had worked out for its own destruction. The old order was, as the President of the Republic once admitted, literally sitting on a social volcano about to erupt.

It was a candid admission. But that was supported by facts. The situation was acute in Luzon and Mindanao. The rebels, mostly communist-inspired, had lorded over some towns, barrios and mountains of a number of provinces in Central and Eastern Luzon, even including the Bicol Region. And in Mindanao, conflicts between the Muslim and Christian Filipinos created cleavage in the unit of the people as a whole.

In the main, all these conflicts and resistance to the old order stemmed not from ideological or religious differences and sheer outrage, but from poverty. The revels saw clearly the inequitable distribution of wealth. At a time when they were longing for social justice, they saw the rich becoming richer. And in Mindanao, the Muslims cashed in one the mass sentiment of people driven from their own lands.

These mass social discontent and unrest were the children of hunger and want.

1452. Villegas, B.M. Philippines in 1985. *Asian Survey* Feb. 1986 ; 127-40.

POLAND

1453. Boyes, Roger. Jaruzelski's failure to see need for change. *Statesman* 14 Jul. 1986 ; 6.

1454. Wesolowski, W. Some notes on the functional theory of stratification. *Polish Sociological Bulletin* 3-4, 1962.

PORTUGAL

1455. Anderson, Perry. Portugal and the end of ultra-colonialism *New Left Review* 15, May-Jun. 1982 ; 83-102.

PUERTO RICO

1456. Friedrich, Carl J. *Puerto Rico : Middle road to freedom.* New York, Rinehart, 1959. p. 86.

1457. Lenis, Gordon K. Puerto Rico : A case-study of change in an underdeveloped area. *Journal of Politics* 17, 1955 ; 614-31.

1458. Magruder, Calvert. Commonwealth status of Puerto Rico. *University of Pittsburgh Law Review.* 15, 1953.

1459. Steward, Julian H. *et. al. People of Puerto Rico.* New York, 1956.

1460. Wells, Henry. Ideology and leadership in Puerto Rican politics. *American Political Science Review* 49, 1955 ; 22-32.

RWANDA

1461. Ping, Xin. Rwanda developing national economy. *Beijing Review* 16 May 1983 ; 13.

Rwanda, a landlocked African country with a dense population and poor natural resources, has steadily improved its national economy in the past 10 years.

Efforts to develop the mainly agricultural economy began with the country's independence 20 years ago and have grown since 1973 when President Juvenal Habyarimana took office.

The country now has a balanced state budget, a stable currency and a steady increase in foreign exchange reserves. Its GDP (Gross Domestic Product) has grown by an average of 4.8 per cent annually for 10 years.

Cultivated land in Rwanda increased from 7,20,000 ha. in 1973 to 9,80,000 ha. in 1980. Agricultural output rose from 3.12 million tons to 4.24 million tons in the same period. The yearly increase rate for grain in the period of the Second Five-Year Plan (1977-81) was 3.5 per cent and for livestock it was 4 per cent.

The country has 133 industrial plants including 29 agricultural plants including 29 agricultural processing and food factories. The volume of foreign trade increased from 9.5 billion Rwandan francs (92.84) Rwandan francs equal one US dollar in 1974 to 28.5 billion francs in 1979.

National economic growth has boosted living standards as well. The income of the peasantry has increased considerably because the government has raised the purchasing price of agricultural products many times. Meanwhile, the government also raise the pay for urban employees in 1978 and 1980 by 10-25 per cent. Now, the home market is flourishing and commodity prices are stable.

Observers note that Rwanda can maintain a stable economy while the world economy is torn by crisis mainly because its government has pursued domestic and foreign policies that conform with the country's specific conditions.

The country is now facing such problems as a lack of skilled workers and a rapid population growth rate which is larger than the increase rate of grain.

The Rwandan Government is concentrating on surmounting these difficulties during its Third Five-Year Plan (1982-86). In that period the country will make efforts to attain self-sufficiency in grain, reform secondary and higher education, improve public health, housing and recreation and develop relations with other countries.

SCANDANAVIA

1462. Lofgren, O. Historical perspectives on Scandanavian peasantries. *Annual Review of Anthropology* 1980.

SENEGAL

1463. Bashizi, B. Day-care centers in Senegal. *Assignment Children* (47-48) 1979 ; 165-71.

1464. O'Brien, Donal B. Cruise *Mourides of Senegal.* Oxford, 1971.

1465. O'Brien, Donal B. Cruise. *Saints and politicians: Essays in the organisation of a Senegalese peasant society*. Cambridge, 1975.

1466. O'Brien, Donal B. Senegal. In *West African States*. Cambridge, 1978 ; 173-88.

SIERRA LEONE

1467. Allen, Christopher Sierra Leone. In *West African States*. Cambridge, 1978 ; 189-210.

1468. Barrows, W.L. *Grassroots politics in Sierra Leone*. New York, 1976.

1469. Pitt-Reviews, Julian. *People of the Sierra*. Chicago, 1969.

1470. Riddell, J B. *Spatial dynamics of modernization in Sierra Leone*. Evanston, Illinois 1970.

SINGAPORE

1471. Chee, Chan Heng Singapore in 1985. *Asian Survey* Feb. 1986 ; 158-67.

1472. Govindasamy, N. Singapore. In *EAPS* ; 70-76.

Singapore has been a fully independent nation since 1965 and has a population of over two million people. Geographically it is 226 sq. miles in area and has a population density of 9,499 per sq. miles.

The population composition is made up mainly, of 3 major ethnic groups—75 percent Chinese, 15 per cent Malays and 8 per cent Indians.

Singapore has a modern exchange economy based on commerce, trade and industry, the last only spearheaded within the last twelve-thirteen years.

Efforts in formulating a definition of poverty have utilised both quantitative measures (e.g. A specified Income level) as well as more qualitative measures (e.g. 'relative deprivation').

In Singapore, there has not been much of an attempt to define the 'poverty level' nor is there a ready profile of the current poverty situation.

The early social surveys, one conducted in 1953 and the other in 1966 represent efforts to systematically study the socio-economic and especially family-living conditions of households in Singapore.

The 1966 Sample Household Survey conducted by the University of Singapore obtained information relating the number of wage-earners to household size. Although no 'poverty level' was defined, it is possible to hazard a rough estimate of those living at poverty or near poverty levels from these correlations. Taking only these households with none or one wage earner in households of no less than 7 persons, a conservative estimate of 15 per cent of total households living near or at poverty levels is arrived at. This assumes that all house-hold members are dependent on the single wage earner.

The 1953 survey on Urban Incomes and Housing made explicit the derivation of a "physical" measure of poverty. Poverty was seen as a function of the "disposal income" i.e. the net income after deduction of requisite expenses for rent and transport. Where the household Disposal Income Relations fell below 100 per cent, this was described as a 'poverty' or 'poor' household. Below this level, the disposal income for the household was inadequate to provide the given family with goods and services included in the computation for minimum living standards based on prevalent living costs.

Using this measure, the study revealed that 19 per cent of the households included in the survey sample were in the "poverty" category.

Both these reports provide some basis on which some reasonable assumptions can be made regarding the current extent of poverty. Most important are the characteristics of households in which the incidence of poverty is significantly high. It is not possible to discuss all these correlations. The variables selected for the present purposes are those which can give some idea of the trends in terms of the prevalence of poverty through comparability with similar currently available data.

High incidence of poverty was found among the following groups in the 1953 survey :

1. The unemployed—those not working but looking for work
2. Families on Public Assistance

3. Households in poor housing/living conditions.

1473. Singapore bourse rises on economic optimism. *International Herald Tribune* 15 Aug. 1986 ; 11.

SOMALIA

1474. Cholera epidemic claims hundred in Somali Camp. *Congress Varnika International* Sep. 1985 ; 27.

Cholera, a disease that relief workers dread because it quickly gains root in the often overcrowded and unsanitary conditions of emergency shelters swept through a camp for Ethiopian refugees in north-western Somalia in late March killing at least 1,000 people and possibly as many as 1,600. The epidemic broke out on 27 March in a refugee camp at Gannet near Hargeisa, and while most of the deaths were in the camp of 45,000 many of the victims were from surrounding settlements. There was a speedy local and international response, but the debilitated and malnourished condition of the refugees led to a very high mortality rate. Had remedial measures not been undertaken immediately, however, the toll would have been substantially higher.

The international response was led by the Office of the U.N. High Commissioner for Refugees, which dispatched 22 tons of medicines and 12 tons of medical equipment to the scene by a special charter flight from Amsterdam. At the same time the League of Red Cross and Red Crescent Societies (LRCS) sent a medical team with an additional 12 tons of medicines and medical equipment. The efforts, combined with those of the Somali government and its refugee health unit, the Somali Red Crescent, several voluntary organizations and other U.N. agencies such as UNDRO, WHO and UNICEF, brought the cholera under control.

Leon Davico, a spokesman for UNHCR, said that the cholera outbreak had abated, but cautioned that a recurrence was still possible since 200 to 300 new refugees, potential carriers of the disease, arrive in the area every day. The Somali government has established a separate camp for the new arrivals, and all non-affected residents of the Gannet camp were evacuated to a new site nearby. Health centres are being set up and supplementary feeding and sanitation programmes have started in these camps. Measles immunization for new arrivals is underway, and other preventive measures are being instituted for which UNDRO has sent to donors a list of urgent necessities.

Newcomers are medically screened, registered and sheltered at the new centre (Gannet 'B') a few kms. away, pending their transfer to a long-term holding camp. While the worst appears to be over, relief workers remain cautious and continue to monitor the situation closely. The improvement of water and general sanitation facilities in the camps is a priority. Ironically, this goal has been hampered by the arrival of the long awaited rains which have already caused flooding in this drought-stricken region.

Community health workers trained by the government's refugee health unit have intensified a public health information campaign among the refugees. A buffer stock of medical supplies is being established in Mogadishu and Hargeisa to be ready on the spot in Somalia should another cholera outbreak occur.

Measures are also underway to place an emergency epidemic medical supply stock in a central location in Europe, from where it could be dispatched to a point in Africa in a matter of hours if the need arose.

In Ethiopia, meantime, the government has denied that cholera has been verified in any of the death at Koream or Kobo camps. It has characterised the cause of some 40 deaths there as acute diarrhoea.

1475. Jamal, Vali. *Nomada and farmers : Incomes and poverty in rural Somalia.* Addis Ababa, JASPA, 1981.

1476. Rule, Sheila. President's health is key to Somali succession. *International Herald Tribune* 23 Jul. 1986 ; 6.

SOUTH AFRICA

1477. Sharp, John. Report on poverty conference. (Cape Town, Apr. 1984) *Journal of Southern African Studies* 11(1) Oct. 1984 ; 154-58.

1478. South Africa : Economic sanctions. *Update* (Bombay) 3 Sep. 1985; 14.15.

SPAIN

1479. Chislett, William. Joblessness : Bitter pill. *International Herald Tribune* 16 Sep. 1986 ; 8.

1480. De La Serna, Victor. Unemployment, budget deficit cast shadow over economy. *International Herald Tribune* 16 Sep. 1986 ; 9.

1481. Debelius, Harry. Many financial woes : Hope is for stable economy after the transition period. *International Herald Tribune* May 1977.

1442. Meister, Stanley. 50 years later, Spain is still haunted by civil war. *International Herald Tribune* 16 Jul. 1986 ; 1-2.

1483. Vazquez—Barquero, A Transformation of the industrial system in Spain. In *IDPR* ; 114-35.

1484. Wiston, Colin M. *Workers and the right in Spain, 1900-1936.* Princeton, 1985. p. 374.

SRI LANKA

1485. De Dilva, K. M. D. *Sri Lanka ; A Survey.* London, 1977.

1486. Farmer, B. H. *Pioneer, peasent colonization in Ceylon.* London, 1957.

1487. Isenman, Paul. Basic needs : the case of Sri Lanka. *World Development* 8(3) Mar. 1980.

1488. Jayaweera, N. Credit support for high yielding varieties in Sri Lanka. *Marga Quarterly Journal* 2(2) 1973.

1489. Kearney, Robert N. Sri Lanka in 1985. *Asia Survey* Feb. 1986 ; 210-23.

1490. Moore, M. P. and G. Wickramasinghe. *Agriculture and society in the low country.* (Sri Lanka) Colombo, ARTI, 1980.

1491. Oliver, Henry M. *Economic opinion and policy in Sri Lanka.* Durham, Duke Univ. commonwealth studies center, 1957. p. 158.

1492. Peiris, G. H. Agrarian transformation in British Sri Lanka. *Sri Lanka Journal of Agrarian Studies* 2(2) 1981 ; 1-26.

1493. Wickramasekara, P. Development and the peasantry : the Sri Lankan experience. In *TWP Vol 2* ; 141-81.

1494. Wijesekera, N.D. *People of Ceylon.* Colombo, 1949.

SUDAN

1495. Awed, M.H. Evolution of land ownership in the Sudan. *Middle East Jonrnal* 1971 ; 212-28.

1496. Barbour, K.M. *Republic of the Sudan.* London, 1961.

1497. Bearing the refugee burden, *Congress Varnika International* Sep. 1985 ; 23.

1498. Disaster fears grow in Sudan. *Congress Varnika International* (New Delhi) Sep. 1985 ; 21.

Most relief workers grimly acknowledge that a year end toll of at least 100,000 is likely under even the most optimistic scenario. Children, more vulnerable than adults, are already estimated to be dying in unprecedented numbers. Accurate figures are difficult to come by, especially in a developing country as vast and diverse as Sudan (it is larger than all of western Europe). But on the basis of national surveys which show unprecedented malnutrition, experts estimate that at least 20,000 more children are now dying every month than do normally.

"The worst of the famine has spread from Ethiopia into Sudan," says David MacDonald, the Canadian Government's Emergency Coordinator for Africa.

David Willis, of the *The Christian Science Monitor* wrote that the "scale of the famine and drought in Sudan surpasses anything seen in this century." He reported that veillages within 30 miles of the Nile were emptying as normally fertile alluvial land dried out at a quickening pace. Sudan just a few years ago was seen as a potential breadbasket for much of Northeastern Africa.

Jim Henry of the League of Red Cross and Red Crescent Societies is not sanguine about Sudan's prospects over the coming weeks. "Even with full international support, it's not going to be easy," he says. "Over 11,000 tons of food must be brought in by us alone into Northem Darfur very quickly. Unless it gets there, the situation in Darfur will make Ethiopia look good by comparison." "The League has launched an additional appeal of $ 16 million for the balance of the year, making their Sudan operations the largest in Africa. Adding to the urgency is the fear that impending rains will make many of the roads impassable. Relief Agencies are concerntrating therefore on one single priority, getting as much food and other relief items to key distribution points to build bufferstock before the end of July. It is unlikely that stocks sufficient to meet the need can be moved in time.

The international aid effort was intensified in response to the growing crisis in late May with emergency airliftings of food and other survival items to the critically affected Darfur and Kordofan provinces in Western Sudan. The EEC, Western European nations, Saudi Arabia and Libya started mercy flights once the gravity of the situation became apparent.

Winston Prattley, whose appointment as the Secretary General's Special Representative to Sudan reflected the organization's intense concern over the deterioration, says "the airbridge is saving lives but delivering very limited tonnages at very high cost and is not a large scale alternative to overland transportation". He was speaking after flying to the western regions immediately upon arriving in the country. Mr Prattley, who is also UNDP's Resident Coordinator in Sudan, is also investigating the potential of alternative forms of transportation, such as dirigibles (hot air balloons). More urgently, since any significant importation, of needed trucks cannot materialize in time, he is working closely with government officials in coordinating negotiations with truck fleet owners to mobilize their resources on agreed-upon standardized rates which will streamline deliveries. The absence of a comprehensive agreement has contributed to the severity of the crisis.

1499. El-Dawi, T.A. Migration in Western Sudan, *Sudan : Notes and Records*, 56, 1975.

1500. El-Dawi, T.A. Peasantry and national development : the case of Sudan. In *TWP Vol. 2* ; 126-40.

1501. Galal-el-Din, M.A. *Population and development in the Sudan and the Third World.* Khartoum, 1977.

1502. *Growth, employment and equity : A comprehensive strategy for the Sudan.* Geneva, ILO, 1976.

1503. Handerson, K.D.D. *Sudan republic.* London, 1972.

1504. Harden, Blaine. Hunger is a weapon in Sudan's Civil War. *International Herald Tribune*, 20 Aug. 1986 ; 1, 5.

1505. Holt, P.M. *Mahdist state in the Sudan.* Oxford, 1958.

1506. Krotki, K.J. *Twenty-one facts about the Sudanese.* Khartoum, Ministry of Social Affairs, 1958.

1507. Lebon, J.H.G. *Land use in Sudan.* London, 1965.

1508. MacMichael, H.A. *History of the Arabs in the Sudan.* Cambridge, 1922.

1509. Madeley, John. Breadbasket that was not. *Congress Varnika International* (New Delhi) Sep. 1985 ; 20.

1510. Osman, M.S. and H.E. El-Haq. Irrigation practices and development in the Sudan. *Sudan Notes and Records*, 55, 1974 ; 96-110.

1511. Pons, V. ed. *Urbanization and urban life in the Sudan*. Khartoum, Hull, 1980.

1512. Shannon, Don. Threat of famine is reported in Sudan. *International Herald Tribune*, 5 Aug. 1986 ; 6.

1513. Sorbo, G.M. *How to survive development : the story of New Halfa*. Khartoum, 1977.

1514. Sudan : The struggle is on many fronts. *Congress Varnika International* (New Delhi) Sep. 1985 ; 22.

1515. Sudan : Those who suffer. *International Herald Tribune* 21 Aug. 1986 ; 4.

1516. *Sudan Report of Mission on Needs Assessment for Population Assistance*. New York, UN Fund for Population Activities, Report No. 9, Feb. 1979.

1517. Sudan's starvation war. *International Herald Tribune* 25 Sep. 1986 ; 8.

1518. Tothill, J.D. *Agriculture in the Sudan*, 1948.

SWAZILAND

1519. Knappert, J. *Myths and legends in Botswana, Lesotho and Swaziland*. Leiden, 1986, p. 248.

SWEDEN

1520. Gandhi, Arun. Economic woes catch up with Sweden. *Sunday Observer* (Bombay) 25 Mar. 1984.

1521. Joshi, G.S. Sweden today : Enviable economy. *Economic Times* 25 Jan. 1976 ; 7.

1522. Poverty on the rise in Sweden. *Indian Express* 7 Nov. 1985 ; 6.

In Sweden, a country where it was believed poverty had been

abolished, there are clear indications that it has not only crept back, but is speeding.

The number of those who must seek welfare assistance to make both ends meet—an unfailing proof of poverty—has gone up for four years, in a now and last year, six per cent of the population received welfare assistance. It is estimated that another 25,000 persons will join their ranks this year.

This is happening at a time when there has been a clear improvement in the employment situation. Sales of new cars during the first half of this year set new records and retail trade expects 1985 to be its best year in the 80s.

It is not the jobless or the social dropouts, the categories that the welfare assistance is mainly intended for, that are swelling the numbers of recipients. For some years now, "ordinary" persons with jobs have been in growing numbers seeking welfare assistance, as their earnings are not enough to meet their expenses.

However, being well off is a relative concept and from an Indian point of view, few Swedes are well off. It has come to be accepted in this country that no average Swede can afford the luxury of non-working wife.

It is only when both the spouses work full time, besides the woman's household chores, that the Swedes have the means to buy the gadgets, domestic appliances and cars that in international comparisons reflect their high standard of living. In the Stockholm region, single men constitute the largest group of welfare recipients.

1523. Venkatachary, R. Swedish economy : Tasks ahead of Palme. *Economic Times* 8 Oct. 1982 ; 5.

1524. Yukolov, N. Economic solutions of whose expense ? *New Times* (3) Jan. 1985 ; 14-15.

SWITZERLAND

1525. Economy that works. *Pioneer* 1 Sep. 1985 ; 6.

SYRIA

1526. Dodd, stuart Center. *Controlled experiment on rural hygiene in Syria.* American University of Beirut, 1934.

BEIRUT

1527. Kopeluk, M. Syrian economics today. *Palestine and Middle East* (Tel-Aviv) 9 (3) 1937.

TAIWAN

1528. Chang, C.C. Taiwan's international cooperation programme. *Inter-economics* Dec. 1972 ; 384-86.

1529. Howe, Russell Warren. Island in Limbo : Taiwan's growing identity crisis. *Statesman* 29 July 1986 ; 6.

1530. Hsiung, James C. Taiwan in 1985 : Scandals and Setbacks. *Asian Survey* Jan. 1986 ; 93-101.

1531. Kang-Sheng, Liu. Biggest litte economy. *Free China Review* Oct. 1977 ; 13-20.

Taiwan probably has the biggest little economy in the world. The Province ranks only 37th in size among the islands of the world. Two-thirds of Taiwan's 14,000 square miles is mountainous. Population is large for the area. Taiwan has in fact the highest population density in the world. But except for a few states of Western Europe, no country has established such a big economy on such a small geographic and population base. With a population of about 17 million, the Republic of China is competing with South Korea, which has three times the land area and twice as many people, and even with Japan and its more than 100 million people.

For this year, the Gross National Product will be close to US $ 20,000 million and per capita income around US $ 900. These figures indicate that the Taiwan economy of the Republic of China is fast approaching developed status : Up to a quarter of a century ago. Taiwan had a Thriving agriculture and scarcely any industry. In 1952, agriculture supplied 35.7 per cent of the net domestic product and industry less than 18 per cent. These figures have been turned around in only 25 years. By 1981, agriculture is expected to be down to about 10 per cent and industry up to nearly 40 per cent. Industrial growth got under way in the 1950s with small factories making substitutes for imports. Textiles became the first sizable industry and still leads in export volume despite the upward surge of electrical machinery apparatus. Today's trend is toward heavier and more sophisticated industry as iron and steel, shipbuilding, petrochemicals annd advanced electronic products. Even so, Taiwan's economic miracle is still largely attributable to light industrial diversification that provides a wide variety of export goods.

1532. Liu, Paul K.C. Determinants of income inequality over the family development cycle : the case of Taiwan. *Income distribution and the family, population and development Review* supplement 8, 1982.

TANZANIA

1533. Blacker, J.G.C. Fertility trends of the Asian population of Tanganyika. *Population Studies* 13, Jul. 1959 ; 46-60.

1534. Bucke, Andrew Tanzania's crumbling economy. *Tribune* 7 Jan. 1985, 5.

People used to say that the old airport Dares Salaam prepared you for what was to come. The arrivals section was three small rooms. Baggage collection meant picking up your cases from a counter which opened directly on to the apron. You went straight outside to a row of decrepit taxis which would take you town - about a 10 minute ride-for the equivalent of $ 15.

At least this system worked. Now the new $ 50 million airport, built with French aid and just opened, has the internationally expected glass and concrete. Shining convey or belts carry the luggage. The taxis are the same but slightly more expensive.

Yet it stands in stark contrast to the condition of near collapse which afflicts virtually every other part of the country's transport sector.

On a recent trip between Dar and Arusha, Tanzania's two most important towns, our Landrover suffered, in three separate incidents a broken leaf spring, then a smashed exhaust pipe and finally a wrecked shock absorber. This is part of the old Great North Road, coming up from Zambia and leading through to Kenya, yet there are miles of vehicle -wrecking and potentially lethal potholes. On long stretches the surface has gone completely, leaving dirt that may turn to impassable mud in the rains. This is the country's most important road. The state of the feeder roads can be imagined.

1535. Chengbo, Huai. Tanzania ! Lasting solution to refugee, *plight. Beijing Review* 16 Jul. 1984 ; 15.

1536. Doherty, J. *Location of health facilities in Tanzania*. Dar-es-Salaam University, 1973.

1537. Hyden, Goran, *Beyond Ujamma in Tanzania ; Under development and an uncaptured peasantry*. Berkeley, 1980. p. 270.

1538. Kilama, W.L. et. al. Health care delivery in Tanzania. In *Towards Ujamaa : twenty-years of Tenu leadership* Ed. by. G. Rulhnmbika. Dar-es-Salaam, 1974 ; 191-217.

1539. Kimambo, I.N. and A.J. Temu *ed. History of Tanzania*. Nairobi, 1969.

1540. Moffett, J.P. *Tanganyika : A review of resources and their development*. Narwich 1955.

1541. Mwansasu, B.U. and C. Pratt *eds. Towards socialism in Tanazania*. Dar- es-Salaam, Tanzania Publishing House, 1979.

1542. Nyerere, J.K. *Freedom and development*. Dar-es-Salaam, 1973.

1543. *Report of the Territonial Minimum Wages Board, Tanganyika, Dar-es-Salaam,* Govt. Printer, 1962.

1544. Sarda, Shyam. Socialism in Tanzania. *Socialist India* 16 Sep. 1972 ; 23-25.

Tanganyika lies on the coast of Africa just south of the equator. It is surrounded in the south by Mozambique (Portuguese control), Malawi and Zambia, in the West by Zaire (Congo-Kinshasha), Rwanda and Burundi in the North by Uganda and Kenya and in the East by Indian Ocean. It became independent on December 9, 1961 under the leadership of President Julius Kambarage Nyerere. In 1964, Tanganyika and Zanzibar combined to form Tanzania.

To understand Tanzania, one has to understand politico-socio-economic development of Tanzania under both German and British colonial rules and the personality of President Nyerere. Tanzania remained very much undeveloped under the colonial rule and at the time of independence, it was the least socio-economically developed of its other two East African neighbours Kenya and Uganda. Since it was the least expendable, it was given independence first of all in the region. But in all fairness to the man and the political party that led Tanganyika to independence, I must stress the great role played by President Nyerere and Tanganyika African National Union (TANU). Today amongst African political parties, TANU holds a high position, with a good organisation, reaching the village level where most of the people live. Tanzania is a one-party State with TANU as the only political party. President

Nyerere ranks h igh amongst Africa's progressive and enlightened nationalist leaders.

President Nyerere basically is a liberal socialist and not one inclined towards dictatorial socialism. He is pragmatic and has sense of judgement of what his country and people want. Only a month after leading his country to independence, he resigned the office of Prime Minister in January, 1962 to devote his full time to the consolidation of his party's role, to reach his people and given thought to future line of action. This step inculcated in the country a spirit of self sacrifice, put a stop to the mad rush of holding of high political office which is inevitable when transfer of power took place and consolidated the position of the party.

After about six years of independence, TANU gave thought to what it had achieved, where it was going and where it wanted to go. The result was the famous Arusha Declaration, wherein, political party's and through the party Government's, role and duty were defined including those of a leader.

1545. Shivji, I. *Class struggles in Tanzania.* London, 1976.

1546. Tanzania's shift from socialist. *Free Press Journal* 23 May 1985 : 4.

1547. Van Etten, G. *Rural health development in Tanzania,* Assen, Van Gorcum, 1976.

1548. Von Freyhole, *M. Ujamaa village in Tanzania.* London, Heneiman 1979.

1549. Williams, G. Taking the part of peasants: Rural development in Nigeria and Tanzania. In *Political economy of contemporary Africa.* Ed. by P. Gutkind and I. Wallerstem. London, Sage, 1976.

THAILAND

1550. Amyot, Jacques. Studies of the low income groups in relation to development strategies in Thailand. In *EAPS*; 269-306.

Formal social science research is a relatively recent phenomenon in Thailand. One of the first efforts along this line was launched by Cornell University after World War II by its now classical Bang Chan Project in a rural community in the outskirts of Bangkok. This was the beginning of an ever increasing stream of foreign scholars, predominantly anthropoligists, coming to Thailand to conduct community studies, first in the centre and north of the country, then in the north-east. To this day, the south of Thailand remains relatively untouched by research. The product of this effort is a number of village study, monographs which are included in any standard bibliography on Thailand.

The past fifteen years also witnessed the introduction of the social sciences for planning and evaluation purposes of government programmes. The use of economics of course is not a recent innovation but the behavioural sciences are. The National Statistical Office had been conducting field surveys for many years, but gradually other branches of the government began conducting research for their specific purposes adding research and evaluation divisions to their organizations. Most active in this field were the Department of Community Development, the Department of public Welfare, and others. Because of lack of total local trained personnel, these relied mainly on foreign advisers in the beginning. These were provided by foreign aid programmes of national and international organizations who also conducted research in support of their projects. A not inconsiderable amount of research was conducted under US/AID and UN auspices, for example.

Responding to this need for research, Thai universities began strengthening their behavioural science programmes. Thammasat University launched its Institute of Public Administration which eventually achieved separate university status under the name of National Institute of Development Administration (NIDA). It conducted research in the fields of public administration and economic planning. Thammasat also has a thriving Department of Social Welfare, also active in research. Kasetsart University has a good record of research in the field of agricultural economics and other agricultural fields.

1551. Goldstein, S and Alice. Thailand's urban population reconsidered, *Demography* 15, 1878; 239-58.

1552. Goldstein, Sidney. Urbanisation in Thailand, 1947-1967. *Demograph* 8, 1971 205-23.

1553. Ingram, James C. *Economic Change in Thailand since 1850* Stanford, 1955.

1554. Krongkaew, Medhi, Agricultural development, rural poverty and income distribution in Thailand. *Developing Economics* 33(4) Dec. 1985; 325-46.

1555. Panitchpakdi, Prom. Thailand In *EAPS*; 58-62.

Data on income distribution in Thailand, as in most developing countries, is not sufficiently reliable, accurate or detailed to construct a clear and comprehensive picture of the country's income distribution situation. We can only hope to paint a crude picture of income distribution in Thailand from the statistics available. At present, the average income per capita for the nation as a whole is about 4,000 baht present, the average income per capita for the nation as a whole is about 4,000 baht (US$200). There is considerable income disparity among the various regions in Thailand. For instance. GDP per capita for the Central Region is nearly 7,000 baht (US$ 350) while the comparative figure for the Northeast Region is about 1,680 baht (US$84). If we split the national economy into two sectors, namely the agricultural and non-agricultural sectors, GDP per capita in 1970 was 1,300 baht (US$65) for the farm population and 9,100 baht (US$452) for the non-farm population. From this, we can say that the farmers in general are the poorer members of our Society. Of course, these statistics only give rough magnitudes and "averages" can be rather misleading. A recent NFSDB rural manpower survey revealed that among farm households in four different villages in Khon Kaen Province in Northeast Thailand, the average income per head was 1,250 baht (US$63), but the income per head statistics for these farm households ranged from 440 baht to 3,010 baht. This example in not exceptional and the NESDE rural manpower study is full of examples of a similar nature.

Assuming that the main objective is to increase the income of the poorest farmers in order to increase the welfare of the poorest groups, and that the job-opportunities outside agriculture are very limited, let us consider what measures can be taken to help achieve this objective. To increase income, we can in the first place, take measures to directly reduce the farmer's cost of production. Secondly, measures can be taken to increase land and labour productivity, to influence the supply and range of agricultural crops produced and lastly, something can be done to stabilise and to raise the price of agricultural products. In what follows, we shall use these broad strategies as the framework for the discussion of more specific strategies, programmes and projects.

To reduce the direct costs of production, the Government is providing production credit, subsidising the price of some production inputs and in some cases, is distributing agricultural inputs to poor farmers free of charge. With respect to credit facilities, the Thai Government has been providing production credit through the Bank for Agriculture and Agricultural Cooperatives (BAAC) for quite some time now.

1556. Ramachandran, K.S. Emerging economic crisis in Thailand. *Financial Express* 23 Sep. 1986;5.

The abortive coup in Thailand a fortnight back, apparently was provoked by the country's critical economic situation. There are many who believe that after 20 years of rapid expansion with the growth rate averaging about seven per cent annually, it now faces a threat of recession. The men who led the coup themselves claimed that they were seizing power "to correct the seriously deteriorating situation of the economy."

The civilian Government and the military are known to be having serious differences on the management of the economy, and the supreme military commander, Gen. Arthit Kamlang-ek, some time back publicly denounced the Government's decision to devalue the national currency, Baht.

Though the coup attempt was master minded reportedly by three former top military officers and was made when General Arthit was out of the country, it still indicated the military's want of confidence in the civilian Government. especially its economic administration.

Thailand's deficit in the current account balance of payments is large enough to cause concern. In recent years, the country consistently had a big shortfall in external trade, as shown in table I. The country's cumulative commerical borrowing at the end of last year was also considerable ($8-682 billion and it ranked eighth among the top 10 borrowers in the Asian and Pacific region, as per data compiled by OECD and the Bank of International Settlements. This was dealt with in these columns last week.

The Government was compelled to take a number of measures for reducing the external resources gap. Severe restrictions were clamped on foreign borrowings, the currency was devalued by 14.8 per cent, development spending was curtailed, a credit sqeeze was introduced and tax rates hiked.

1557. Sricharatchanya, Paisal. Structural unadjustment. *Far Easten Economic Review*. 2 Feb. 1984; 53-54.

Two years after implementation of the fifth plan (1982-86) and assisted by two Structural-Adjustment Loans (SALs) from the World Bank, Thailand appears to be making headway in correcting chronic imbalances in its economic structure. But, though the government remains committed to continue the overall adjustment programme—a principle feature of the fifth plan---the momentum is slowing because of bureaucratic complications and political and economic setbacks.

The broad objective of the programme is to improve the country's payments position in the medium term in order to sustain longer-term economic development. A condition of the SALs, it involves major policy reforms in five main areas: agriculture, industry, fiscal managment, energy and institutional development.

Fiscal-policy reform has been given a higher profile in view of the economic slowdown during 1981-82, which led to substantial government revenue shortfalls. The reform places heavy emphasis on domestic-revenue mobilisation, with the target of raising revenue as a proportion of gross domestic product to 16 per centby 1986. It also calls for elimination of losses among serveral major state-run corporations (Review, 19 Jan.).

The thrust of industrial restructuring focuses on making local industry which has largely been performing the function of import substitution over the past two decades – more export-oriented. Agricultural reform centres on reclassification of former forest reserves, destroyed by poaching as well as general agricultural marketing and pricing policies. Energy-policy reform not only aims at correcting distorted price structures but also calls for implementation of an energy matter plan combining development of new energy sources, conservation and utilisation.

On top of normal budgetary resources, the Thai Government intends to achieve these reforms with the assistance of about five quick-disbursing SALs over the fifth plan period. The first US$150 million SAL granted by the World Bank in early 1982 was followed exactly one year later by a US$175 million loan in early 1983. However, given the Thais' inability to stick to the timetable for effecting the various changes required, there may be a considerable delay before the third loan is forthcoming.

1558. Thailand: Entering the home stretch. *Asiaweek* 27 Jul. 1986 ; 18-22.

1559. Thailand takes on economic challenge. *Economic Times* 6 Apr. 1978;5.

1560. Thais must revive economy. *China Daily* 18 Aug. 1986;4.

TRINIDAD AND TOBAGO

1561. Bhatia, Krishan. Trinidad and Tobago. *Hindustan Times* 14 Jan. 1973.

1562. Braitwaite. Lloyd, Social stratification in Trinidad. *Social and Economic Studies* 2, 1953; 5-175.

1563. Mackoon, Lindsay. Trinidad to the rescue of Caribbean economies. *Bangkok Post* 26 Jan. 1978.

A formula has been found to help those Caribbean islands currently reeling under the effects of widespread inflation and massive unemployment.

The Caribbean Aid Plan. as it is to be known, was announced by Prime Minister Dr. Erice Williams it will be funded by Trinidad and Tobago, the wealthiest Caribbean state, initial efforts to involve metropolitan powers having so far failed.

A four-man team, including the Governor of the Trinidad and Tobago Central Bank, Victor Bruce, has been named to work out the plan. Other members are Dr Euric Bobb, the bank's deputy governor-designate; Dr. John Spence, Chairman of the Food and Agriculture Corporation; and Cecil Wyke, former trade officer, who will be secretary.

Among other things, the team will be required to operate on guidelines laid down by the Trinidad Government; report to parliament through the auditor-general; operate through the government-owned National Commercial Bank; and consult regularly with the International Monetary Fund (IMF) in respect of help to Caribbean countries provided that IMF agrees to the arrangement.

Caribbean islands are leaning heavily on Trinidad for influsion of loans. The latest appeal, for $60 million, from Guyana, appears to have been turned down. Similar requests have come from Dominica, Jamaica, and Barbadoa.

1564. Williams, Eric. *History of the people of Trinidad and Tobago*. London, Andre Dentsch. 1964.

TURKEY

1565. Dervis, Kemal and S. Robinson. *Source and structure of inequality in Turkey, 1950-73*. Washington, World Bank. 1977.

1566. Gursel, Mustafa R. Outdated agriculture sector is slowly adjusting to a freer market. *International Herald Tribune*. 2 Jun. 1986; 12.

1567. Hopkirk, Peter. Turkey restores law and order: Economy revived. *Statesman* 30 Mar. 1982.

1568. Krause, Axel. Austerity plan draws praise, but future is uncertain. *International Herald Tribune* 3 May 1984; 7-8.

1569. Senatalar, Burhan. Open economy shows growth but inequalities increases as well. *International Herald Tribune* 2 Jun. 1986;11.

1570. Toye, Eremy. Turkey's economic outlook. *Baghdad Observer* 10 Jun. 1978.

UGANDA

1571. Farrant, M. *et. al. Kampala's children.* Kampala, UNICEF, 1972.

1572. Gargan, Edward A. In Uganda, Children made homeless by war find a home in army. *International Herald Tribune* 5 Aug. 1986;6.

1573. Gargan, Edward A. In Uganda, Slaughter has Stopped. Economic mismanagement still threatens recovery. *International Herald Tribune* 15 Aug. 1986; 1-2.

1574. Harden, Blaine. In Uganda, Children who never know peace, *International Herald Tribune* 16 Jul. 1986; 1-6.

1575, Harden, Blaine. Thousands of Ugandans trying to start life over. *International Herald Tribune* 18 Jul. 1986; 1-2.

1576. Mamdani, M. *Politics and class formation in Uganda.* London, Heinemann, 1976.

UNITED KINGDOM

1577. Ascherson, Neal. Gap between rich and poor grows. *Amrita Bazar Patrika* 6 Jun. 1986;6.

Under the surface of London, there are strange tremors. Something is rising to the surface, and when it bursts through it will so I begin to believe—create a new and almost unrecognisable type of urban society. It will shatter out expectations about social progress, and eventually threaten the whole management of the British economy. That something is middle class money.

A few months ago, I wrote about the way that London was ceasing to be a city with a large, organised factory proletariat and reverting towards a capital in which a huge, underemployed plebs or 'people' work to service a wealthy minority. Since then, it has become clear that the coming changes may be far more dramatic and fightening.

This theory starts with something now familiar: the price of private housing in central London. Ever since about 1970, the value of this housing stock—above all old, 'gentrified' and renovated houses has been rising steeply. So far this year alone, the prices of Secondhand houses in the central area has gone up by around 20 per cent, although in other parts of Britain the value of all private housing has scarcely kept pace with inflation or even dropped below it. One colleague lives in a one-bedroom, third-floor flat in the inner London area of Paddington which cost him £ 60,000 some 18 months ago and can now be sold for £ 80,000.

Until now, there has been a habit of regarding these colossal values as 'fairly money'. If you have to pay as much or more to buy another when you sell a flat or house (unless you move to the provinces), then its effect on your bank account, is slight. But this may be about to change—a thought I owe to Michael Elliot of The Economist magazine who is writing a book about it.

For cashing-in time is coming. It's a matter of time and generations. James and Lavinia Yupsley, London-based journalists in their late twenties, are living on a mortgaged house in Islington worth £ 120,000. His father Daniel Yupsley, a successful lawyer, and his wife Vanessa are living in a paid-off house worth the same. Just possibly, old Bill Yupsley, James's grandfather, is living in yet another inflated value house, having decided not to retire to the country after his career as a smart dentist. All this may also be true of Lavinla's family.

Take education, for example. Twenty years ago, the liberal middle class of London sent children through the whole state system. By the late 1970s, there was an embarrassed consensus that comprehensive 'were n't good enough yet', but state primary schools remained acceptable. Today, the same group not only assumes that comprehensive schools are unthinkable, but is beginning to pay for private primary education at new day schools in central London.

With the new wealth, this simply means that a large hereditary caste with its own culture will regain the monopoly of power once enjoyed by the products of the public schools. The period when class barriers seemed to be crumbling and growing permeable will appear as a brief reversal of the normal trend, a 20-year blip in the history of class in England.

The New Class of the capital would tower over the rest of Britain, distorting its whole development. In the end, its power would not be tolerable. Perhaps the provinces would challenge it. Perhaps the Londoners themselves. Cabinet makers, coachmen, lawyers, clerks make the bloodiest revolutions, not orderely factory workers.

There are bad dreams here. Let the new money flood London : for a time, it would be Ben Jonson's "Fleshfly, summer is with thee now;" But then a very hard wind would rise.

1578. Atkinson, A. *Poverty in Britain and the reform of social Security* Cambridge, 1969.

1579. Booth, Chanles, *Life and labour of the London.* Macmillan, 1902.

1580. Booth, Charles and Seebohm Rowntree. *Poverty : Ten years after* London, 1952 (Planning No. 344, 1952.)

1581. Brown, Henny Philips. *Origin of trade Union power.* Oxford, 1983. p. 328.

1982. Coates, B. and E. Rawstron. *Regional variations in Britain.* Balsford, 1971.

1583. Coates, K. and K. Silburn. *Poverty : The forgotten Englishmen.* London, Penguin, 1970.

1584. Collins, E.J. Migrant labour in British agriculture in the 19th century. *Economic History Review* 29 (1) 1076 ; 38-59.

1585. Daniel, W. *Racial discrimination in England.* Penguin, 1968.

1586. *Domestic food consumption and expenditure, 1964.* London, HMSO, 1966.

1587. Eden, F.M. *State of the poor* London, Routledge, 1928.

1538. Fischer, Louis. *This is our world.* London, Jonathan Cape, 1985.

1589. Freeman, C. and M. Jahoda *ed. World futures : The great debate.* Oxford, Martin Robertson, 1979.

1590. George, V. Poverty and inequality in the U.K. In PICMC ; 24-60.

Though the various groups of people in poverty have been discussed separately, there is a common thread joining most of them together :

they belong to the manual, particularly the unskilled, occupational groups. The unskilled workers earn wages that are lower than those of other occupational groups ; they are more likely to have larger families and to suffer from unemployment, sickness and disability ; vice versa, they are less likely to be covered by occupational schemes for sickness, widowhood and retirement: they are less likely to satisfy to the full the insurance contributions entitling them to the various insurance benefits ; and they are, of course, less likely to have any savings or strong financial support from their extend family network. Bearing in mind that these misfortunes are inter-connected, the unskilled are not only more likely to find themselves in poverty but more likely to remain in it. As a 1978 government report on lower incomes put it :

> The effects of disadvantage can be cumulative. There are links between the incidence of low skills, low earnings, sickness disablement and spells of unemployment, and those who have less earnings from work are also likely to have lower incomes when out of work. Poor housing conditions are less clearly associated with lower incomes but those with lower incomes are more likely than others to occupy poor housing.

Incomes and wealth inequalities are almost as great today as they were at the beginning of this century, though the concentration of both has been dispersed from the top 1 per cent to the top 10 per cent of the population. Some of this dispersal is illusory, for it is dispersal from husbands to wives or other members of the family. In spite of the various forms of personal and company taxation, these inequalities have survived and, on present evidence, they will continue in the future. Poverty, too, have survived in spite of the fact that the standard of supplementary benefit level today in relation to average earning is similar to the standard of absolute poverty adopted by Rowntree in 1899. The social security system provides financial help to millions of people in need but it fails to ensure that no one has an income below even the basic supplementary benefit level for two main reasons. First, many, of those who are entitled to supplementary benefit fail to apply for a variety of reasons. Second, many of those in receipt of supplementary benefit receive reduced amounts, again for a variety of reasons. Theoretically, it is quite possible to abolish this form of poverty among the non-employed section of the population through administrative changes. In practice, however, it may not be possible, partly because of cost and partly because some of the existing rulings that are responsible for some of the poverty reflect core social values relating to work and the family. Poverty among the working population is much more difficult to abolish.

The family income supplement is a pale shadow of the supplementary benefit scheme. Any attempt to extend the supplementary benefit scheme to the working population will be resisted, not undermine work incentives. For these reasons, poverty, even narrowly confined to income only, will continue to exist in Britain.

The inability of the government to solve the problem of poverty among the working poor means that any real improvement in the supplementary benefit scales is impossible. These scales were calculated at least thirty years ago and, though they have been increased several times since, they have not been basically re-thought. To solve the problem of low pay and poverty, as at present defined, means some reduction of inequality. To improve the scales of supplementary benefit (i.e. to raise the poverty line) means a further reduction of inequality. The prospects are, therefore. that Britain will go on trying to help its poor ; but until the question of inequality comes into the political arena, poverty will continue to exist.

1591. Geyelin, Philip. In Britain, symptoms of an identity crisis. *International Herald Tribune* 18 Jul. 1982 ; 4.

1592. Gilbert, B. *Evolution of national insurance in Great Britain*. Batsford, 1666.

1593. Gough, I. and T. Stara. Low incomes in the United Kingdom. *Manchester School* 36, 1968.

1594. Harrison, J.F.C. *Common people*. London, Barnes and Noble, 1984. p. 445.

1595. Hatcher, J. *Plague, population and the English economy, 1348-1530*. London, Macmillan, 1977.

1596. Hill, Reuben. *et. al. Family development in three generations* Cambridge, 1970.

1597. Holterman, S. Areas of urban deprivation in Great Britain. *Social Trends* (6) London, HMSO, 1975.

1598. Kaldor, N. *Causes of the slow rate of growth of the U.K. economy*. Cambridge University Press 1966.

1599. Land, H. *Large families in London*. London, Bell, 1970.

1600. Laybourn, Keith and Jack Reynolds. *Liberalism and the rise of labour, 1890-1918*. London, St. Martin's Press, 1984 p. 237.

1601. Lee, Ronald. Population in Pre-industrial England : An Econometric analysis. *Quarterly Journal of Economics* 87 (4) November 1973.

1602. Lydall, H. and D. Tipping. *Distribution of personal wealth in Britain.* Bulletin of Oxford Univ. Institute of Economics and Statistics, Feb. 1961.

1603. Nettl, J.P. and R. Robertson. Industrialization, development or modernization. *British Journal of Sociology* 17 (13) Sep. 1966.

1604. Nicholson, J.L. *Redistribution of income in the United Kingdom in 1959, 1957 and 1953.* London, Bowes and Bowes, 1965.

1605. Poverty and disability. London, the Disability Alliance, 1976.

1606. Routh, G. *Occupation and pay in Great Britain. 1906-1960.* Cambridge, 1965.

1607. Rowntree, B.S. *Poverty : A study of town life.* London, Macmillan, 1901.

1608. Sharpston, Michael. Britain as an underdeveloped country. *World Development* 2 (1) Jan. 1975 ; 49-54.

1609. Sinfield, A. *Poverty research in Britain and Europe.* Washington, Bureau of Social Science Research, Nov. 1967.

1610. Stanton, D. Take-up debate on the UK family income supplement. *Policy and Politics* 5 (4) Jun. 1977.

1611. Tawney, R.H. *Equality*, London, Allen & Unwin, 1931.

1612. Taylor, A.J. *ed. Standard of living in Britain in the industrial revolution.* London, Methowen, 1979.

1613. Townsend, Peter. *Poverty in the UK.* Penguin, 1979.

1614. Townsend, Peter. *Poverty, socialism and labour in power.* London, Fabian Society, 1967.

1615. Wedderburn, D. Poverty in Britain today—The evidence. *Sociological Review* 10 (3) Aug. 1962.

1616. Wilding, P. *Poverty : The facts in Wales.* London, Child Poverty-Action Group, 1977.

1617. Wolf, R.D. *Economics of colonialism. Brtian and Kenya, 1870-1930* London, Yak Univ. Press, 1974.

1618. Wrigley, E.A. Family limitation in pre-industrial England. *Economic History Review* Feb. 1966.

UNITED NATIONS

1619. Joshi, Nandini. *Powers vs poverty : A view of UNCTAD*. Ahmedabad, New Order Book Co., 1980. p. 84.

1620. Nye, Joseph. UNCTAD : Poor nations pressure group. In *Anatomy of influence* Ed. by Cox Jacobson. New York, Yale, 1977.

UNITED STATES OF AMERICAN

1621. Aaron, Herry. Rejunvenating. U.S. Social Security. *Economic Impact* (4) 1980 ; 59-62.

1622. Achenbaum, W. Andraw. America as an aging society : Myths and images. *Daedalum* Win. 1986 : 13-30.

1623. Ackerman, Frank and Andrew Zimbalist. Capitalism and inequality in the United States. In *Capitalist system*. Ed. by Reich Edwards and Weills Kopf. N.J., Prentice-Hall, 1978.

1624. Bagdikian, Ben H. *In the midst of plenty : A new report on the poor in America*. New York, Signet Books, 1961.

1625. Black, Eugene R. *Address to the Economic and social council of the United Nations, April 24, 1961*. New York, 1961, (Mimeograhed).

1626. Blan, P.M. and O.D. Duncan. *American occupational structure*. New York, John Wiley, 1967.

1627. Boom in trouble. *International Herald Tribune* 18 Jul. 1984 ; 4.

1628. Bremner, Robert H. *From the depths : the discovery of poverty in the United States*. New York Univ. Press, 1956.

1629. Broom, L. and N. Glenn. *Transformation of the Negro*. London, Harper, 1965.

1630. Cantwell, N. Exploitation of Children. *Ideas Forum* 7, 1981.

1631. Cheshyre, Robert. Americans on poverty line. *Amrita Bazar Patrika* 17 Aug. 1983 ; 6.

1632. Child poverty rising in in USA. *Statesman* 6 Oct. 1986 ; 6.

1633. Clendinen, Dudley. In U.S. South, heat and dust : People, animals and crops suffer in record drought. *International Herald Tribune* 18 Jul. 1986 ; 1.

1634. Cohen, Wilbur J. and E. Sullivan. Poverty in the United States. *Health, Education and Welfare Indicators*, Feb. 1964.

1635. Cox, K.R. *Location and public problems.* Chicago, Maaronfa, 1979.

1636. Cutright, P. National political development : Measurement and analysis. *American Sociological Review* 28, Apr. 1963.

1637. Dasgupta, Barun. US economy : Gloomy prospect. *Mainstream* 26 Jul. 1986 ; 31-32.

The American "dream" is fast turning into a long "nightmare." Late in 1984, the Bank of America warned that with debts rising and income slowing down, a decline in consumer spending was becoming inevitable. The US Department of Commerce also foresaw a decline in the growth of consumption expenditure in constant dollars from five per cent in 1984 to 3.1 per cent in 1985.

Today, the stark reality can no longer be hidden. Real wages are falling. Consumer credit with its higher interest rates is fast eating up the family savings. And more and more (62 per cent at the present reckoning) American wives with young children are being forced to take up jobs to supplement their household steadily fallling real wages.

The decline started in 1973 when the Arab oil embargo sent the first wave of shiver through the well-oiled American industry. Since then, successive increases in oil price have pushed up the price level faster than wage increase. Average weekly earning since 1973 have fallen by 14.3 per cent, after accounting for inflation. Medium household income had declined by six per cent to $ 26.433 in the period 1973-1984. Workers in the organised sector are being deprived of the cost of living advantage that they had wrested during the years when inflation was very high.

The persistent urge for cost reduction leads to retrenchment in which young workers—the latest to enter the workforce—are sacked first. Cost control has been responsible for real eduction of wages in a number of industries by five per cent in manufacturing industry and as much as 15 per cent in construction industry.

What has been the extent of erosion of real wages since 1973 ? To quote an American economist : one who was 30 in 1949 could see his real earning go up by 63 per cent by 1959 when he reached 40. But one who was 30 in 1973 found his real earnings fall by one per cent when he turned 40 in 1983.

The average American wage earner does not want to accept easily a fall in living standard. Faced with the steadily declining real wages, he resorts more and more to his credit cared. No wonder that the ratio of consumer debt to income has now reached an all-time high.

While at one end this is increasing the debt burden on the individual wage-earner, at the other end it is generating demand and keeping the wheels of industry moving. Economists agree that unless the workers pile up debt to "fuel" the economy, America's much-vaunted economic growth will slow down from an anticipated three per cent to less than two per cent in the second half of the current year. In the long run, they concede, if the growth rate does not grow, it will not only bring about a basic change in the American's living standard but change the nation's entire economy.

An increase in the real wages of workers, it is argued, can be effected only through a "steady and strong" growth in productivity. But the prospect for such a growth, it is grudgingly admited, is very bleak in the foreseeable future.

1638. Drogin, Bob. Poverty in USA. *Deccan Herald* (Bangalore) 3 Mar. 1985 ; 6.

At least 20 million Americans now suffer from varying degrees of hunger in a "public health epidemic" that is growing because of Reagan administration cuts in federal nutrition assistance programmes, according to a yearlong, privately funded national medical survey.

The report by the Physician Task Force on Hunger, a group of 22 prominent doctors and academicians, was the most comprehensive attempt to study the extent of hunger and malnutrition in the United States since a controversial White House task force said last year that it was unable to "substantiate allegations of rampant hunger" in the nation.

But the physicians' group declared that hunger be not difficult to find and blamed the alleged increase on "governmental failure" by the administration. Hunger could be radicated in six months, it predicted, if $ 5 billion to $ 7 billion were spent to restore or expand nutrition programmes.

"Hunger is a political problem, and out Government leaders must end their Laisse z-faire attitude towards this serious epidemic." I Larry Brown, task force Chairman and a faculty member at Harvard University School of Public Health, said at news conference last week. He said that hunger had reappeard after being "virtually eliminated" in in the 1970s.

Spokesman for the White House and the Department of Health and Human Services said that they had not seen the 147-page survey, titled "Hunger in America The Growing Epidemic," and would not comment on it.

But the report is quite likely to fuel the national debate over budget priorities as Congress considers the administration's proposal to cut $ 800 million in fiscal 1986 from federal nutrition in fiscal 1986 from federal nutrition programmes including school lunch and breakfast, the child care food programme and special supplemental feeding for pregnant women, infants and children.

Members of the physicians group will testify this month before the House education and labour committee, which opened hearings on Tuesday into the proposed 16 per cent cut in spending for subsidised meals for school children. Committee staff members estimate that about 7.3 million children and 17,900 schools could be forced out of the programme if the cuts are enacted.

"This, we believe, would be a national tragedy—a tragedy for this generation of young people and those who follow." Gene White, an official with the American School Food Service Association, told the committee.

Members of the physicians group acknowledged that their estimates were imprecise, but Brown said that up to two-thirds of the 20 million classified as hungry are children. Many Americans, he said. go hungry several days to a week each month when they run out of money or food stamps.

Most often, hunger in America is seen as moderate malnutrition or "silent undernutrition", causing undersized infants and children, lower resistance to infections and chronic diseases and cognitive impairment said Dr. Aaron Shirley, Head of the Mississippi Medical and Surgical Association.

1639. Duncan, Greg J. *et. al. Years of poverty, years of plenty.* Ann Arbor, University of Michigan, 1984. p. 198.

1640. Economic/Navigation. *International Herald Tribune*, 25 Jun. 1986 ; 4.

1641. *Economic report of the President of the United States for 1964.* Washington, US Govt. Printing Office, 164.

1642. *Examination of the War on poverty*, Washington, July. 10, 13 & 18 1967, Committee on Labour and Public Welfare. (Hearings before the Sub-committee on Employment Manpower and poverty. 90th Congress, IST Session on 5. p. 408.

1643. Felder, Herry E. *Changing patterns of black family income, 1945-1982.* (Joint Centre, New York, for political Studies, 1964. pp. 62.

1644. Fink, Leon. *Workingmen's democracy : the knights of labour and American politics.* London, University of Illinois Press, 1983. pp. 256.

1645. Fisher, A.G.B. *Clash of progress and security.* New York, Augustus. M. Kalley Publishers, 1935.

1646. Flynn, Charles L. *White land. black labor. Caste and class in late 19th century Georgia.* London, 1983. pp. 207.

1647. Foner, Philip S. *History of the labor movement in the United States,* New York, 1980.

1648. Gibson, Rose C. Blacks in an aging society. *Dacdalus* Win 1983 ; 349-72.

1649. Glazer, Nathan. Paradoxes of American poverty. *Public Interest* Fall 1965.

1650. Gordon, Margaret S. *Ed. Poverty in America* San Francisco, Chandkar Publishing, 1965.

1651. Green house, Steven. Fading American dream : Millions learning to cope with downword mobility. *International He ald Tribune* 19-20 Jul. 1986, 1,6, 48, 1980.

1652. Gutkind, Efraim. *Poverty matrix : Patterns of economic behaviour among the American Poor.* (Ph. D. thesis) Univ. of California.

1653. Hagestad, Gunhald O. Aging society as a context for family life. *Daedalus* Win. 1986 ; 119-40.

1654. Hareven, Tamena K. Family time and historical time. *Daedalus.* Spr. 1977. 57-70.

1655. Harrington, Michall. *Other America : Poverty in the United States,* New York, Macmillan, 1962.

1656. Haveman, Robert H. creating jobs. *Economic Impact* (Washington) (4) 1984 ; 63-70.

1657. Hill, R.B. and Regina Nixan. *Youth employment in American industry.* Transaction Books, 1984 ; p. 121.

1658. Hispanic poverty grows. *International Herald Tribune* 4 Sep. 1986 ; 4.

1659. Hoerder, Dirk *Ed. American labour and immigration history, 1877-1920s : Recent European Research.* London, University of Illinois Press. 1983 p. 284.

1660. Humphrey, Hubert H Investing in America's future. In *War on poverty.* New York, 1964 : 31-48.

1661. Jackson, E.F. Status consistency and symptoms of stress. *American Sociological Review* 27, 1962.

1662. Jackson, E.F. and P.J. Burke. Status and symptoms of stress : Additive and interaction effects. *American Sociological Reivew,* 30 Aug 1965.

1663. Kain John *ed. Roce and Poverty.* Prentice-Hall, 1969.

1664. Kaiser, Kobert. Help for America's poor has not been enough. *International Herald Tribune* 14 Nov. 1984 ; 4.

1665. Katz, Michael B. *Poverty and policy in American history.* New York, Academic Press, 1983. p. 303.

1666. Keyserling, Loon H. *Progress or poverty : The United States at the cross-roads.* Washington, conference on Economic Progress, Dec. 1964.

1667. Kolko, Gabriel. Causes of poverty. In *Wealth and power in America.* New York, Praeger, 1962 ; 70-95.

1668. Kolko, Gabriel. Extent of poverty. In *Wealth and Power in America.* New York, Praeger, 1962 : 96-110.

1669. Kolko, Gabriel. Income inequality and consumption. In *Wealth and power in America* New York, Praeger, 1962 ; 111-34.

1670. Kolko, Gabriel. *Wealth and power in America : An analysis of social class and income distribution.* New York, Praeger, 1962.

1671. Kurdyumov, N. Growing burden of unemployment on US working people. *Soviet Review* (New Delhi) 6 Sept. 1982 ; 31-32.

1672. Landecker, W.S. Class crystallization and class consciousness. *American Sociological Review* (New Delhi) 6 Sept. 1912 ; 31-32.

1673. Landecker, W.S Class crystallization and its urban pattern. *Social Research* 27, 1960.

1674. Lenski, G.E. Social participation and status cryststallization, *American Sociological Review* 21, 1956.

1675. Lenski, G.E. Status crystallization : A non-vertical dimension of social status. *American Sociological Review* 19 Aug. 1954.

1676. Lindert, Peter. H. *Fertility and scarcity in America.* Princeton. 1978.

1677. Lindsey, Robert. Urbanization quickness on Hawaii's island of Mawi. *International Herald Tribune* 14 May 1986 ; 4.

1678. Low-cost food plans—New regional estimates. *Research and Statistics No. 28.* Social Security Administration, Oct. 1959.

1679. Lydall, H. and J.B. Lansing. Comparison of the distribution of personal income and wealth in the United States and Great Britain. *American Economic Review* 49, Mar. 1959.

1680. Lynes, T. *National assistance and national prosperity.* Welwyn, Codicote Press, 1962.

1681. Malcom, Andrew H. Young and poor : A growing class in U.S. *International Herald Tribune* 29 Oct. 1985 ; 1,4.

1682. Mayer, Jean. Nutritional status of American Negroes, *Nutritional Reveiw* 23 (6) Jun. 1965.

1683. Mclanahan, Sara. Family Structure and the reproduction of poverty. *American Journal of Sociology* 9 (4) Jan. 1985 ; 873-82.

1684. Miller, Herman P. *Income of the American people*. New York, John Wiley & Sons, 1955.

1685. Miller, Herman P. *Rich man, poor man : A study of income distribution in America.* New York, Crowell, 1964.

1686. Miller, S.M. American lower class. *Social Research*, Spr. 1964.

1687. Miller, Herman P. Changes in the number and composition of the poor. In *Poverty in America* Ed. by M.S. Gordon. San Francisco, 1965 ; 81-101.

1688. Morgan, James N. *et al. Income and welfare in the United States.* New York, McGraw-Hill, 1962.

1689. *Negro family : the case for national action.* Washington, US Deptt. of Labour, 1964.

1690. Nehgarten, Bernice. L. and Dail A. Age in the aging society *Daedalus*, Win. 1986 ; 31-50.

1691. North, Donglass, C. *Economic growth of the United States, 1790-1860.* New York, Norton, 1960.

1692. Ornatim, O. *Poverty amid affluence* New York, Twentieth century Fund, 1966.

1693. Parsons, T. Tull citizenship for the Negro American, a sociological problem. *Daedalus* 94 (4) Fall 1965.

1694. Paying for aging society. *Japan Echo* 12 (1) 1985: 57-58.

1695. Poverty US style. *Nagpur Times* 27 Nov. 1984;6.

1696. Preston. Samuel. Children and the elderly : Divergent paths for America's dependents. *Demography* Nov. 1984; 435-57.

1697. Preston. S.H. Children and the elderly in the US. *Scientific American* Dec. 1984; 44-49.

1698. Raspberry. William, Underclass : Self-help may work. *International Herald Tribune* 20 Jun. 1986;6.

1699. Reason : Interview in the Charles Murray. *American Review* (2) 1986; 49-54.

1700. Reich, C.A. Mew property. *Yale Law Journal* 73 (5) Apr. 1964.

1701. Reston, James. Irony of poverty *Amrita Bazar Patrika* 29 Nov. 1984.

1702. Riley, M.W and John W. Longevity and social structure; the added years. *Daedalus* Win. 1986; 51-76.

1703. Schlesinger. A.M. *Colonial merchants and the American revolution 1763-76.* New York, 1918.

1704. Schware, Robert. U.S. : Poverty amidst plenty. *Patriot* 19 Nov. 1982;4.

Never so many millionaires, never so many unemployed. Government figures pegged the unemployment rate in the United States at 10 per cent this month, the worst unemployment level since the great depression of the 1930. Unemployment in Youngstown, Ohio, hit the 20.9 per cent mark, the highest in the nation. Various other cities throughout the country have office rates around 20 per cent.

The depression in America today is characterized by these two extremes : conspicuous living. It-up and spending lavishly on the one hand; pain, worry, and poverty on the other.

The number of US millionaires grew over 10 per cent last year, to 5, 74, 342. More millionaires defined as those persons with more than one million dollars in assets live in New York state than in any other state. California, Illinois, and Ohio run a close second; the farming state of Idaho has the most millionaires in proportion to population, with 26. 46 millionaires for every 1,000 residents.

Fascinating as it might be to examine this trend. in what follows I shall offer some thoughts on the significance of the employment predicament in this country.

The post-war peak of 11,260,000 unemployment persons is more than double the 5,156,000 of 1974. More than half that increase has taken place during the 20 months since President Reagan took office.

President Reagan always manages to find a whipping boy for (scapegoat) for the present trend and the accompanying despair and disillusionment of a growing number of Americans with the US economic system, namely the previous Democratic administration. But the employment situation has in fact been getting worse under both Democrats and Republicans. Of the nearly five million who have become unemployed since the cyclical rise in unemployment began in 1979, two million occurred under former President Carter, with the lion's share under Reagan. Too often, President Reagan is more concerned with identifying a single political target for the mounting crisis than with a concrete programme for recovery.

President Reagan said at a 28 October press conference : "There is some sunshine on the horizon" and "we are going to stay the course". He added that the country's biggest problem at present "may be fear-fear that we're adrift, that there is no plan, that no one is doing anything to make things better". In declaring there was nothing to fear but fear. Reagan minted no new platitude; President Roosevelt had said the same thing back in 1933, and Hoover said it repeatedly for three years before him.

But whereas Roosevelt instilled hope and courage in the people during the early 1930s and made clear that he had the people's interests at heart and would mobilize the power of the government to help them. Reagan has not been able to convince the nation that he cares deeply that people are suffering and that he shares with them their despair at the blighted prospects this depression had brought. To many, America no longer seems a land bright with hope and promise; a mood of apprehension persists that corresponds to the fear of a patient that he or she will never recover.

To let the President know that millions of Americans need jobs and homes, and that his policies and budget cuts are hurting large segments of the population, members of church, and other action groups, for example, have set up tent communities across the nation in a 1930s like protest against President Reagan's economic policies. The tent cities, called "Reagan Ranches" by the coalitions of labour and community groups that have set them up, are in Lansing, Michigan : St. Louis, Missouri : Columbus, Ohio : Atlanta, Georgia; Houston, Texas Boston, Massachusettes; Philadelphia Pennsylvania; and

New Orleans, Louisiana. Atleast 30 more cities are expected to have tent cities by mid-November.

In the 1930s there was scarcely a city in the country that did not harbour atleast one tent city, then known as "Hoovervilies". In empty lots in the big cities, homeless families, threw together makeshift shocks of boxes and available scrap metal. St. Louis had the largest Hooverville, which had over a thousand jobless souls. This and other encampments of squatters were where the dispossessed stood their last stand.

Whether this depression deepens or takes a turn for the better it will be interesting to see if questions are raised about capitalism itself or whether the unemployed will meekly accept their lot.

In earlier periods of depression, revolutionary spirits burgeoned when conditions began to improve slightly. They tended not to heighten at the bottom of the trough of the depression, as in 1932. Two years later, in 1934, for example, violent strikes shook the country. From the lettuce fields of California to the tomato fields of New Jersey, farmers went on strike. In Des Moines, Iowa, union electrical workers pulled a control switch that caused a massive power outage, plunging some 160,000 people into darkness and paralyzing the entire city, Copper mines in Butte, Minnesota closed the Anaconda pits for months; meanwhile striking cooks, waiters, and busboys from the famous Waldorf-Astoria hotel in New York City paraded down Park Avenue singing the "International". On Labour Day, 1934, Italian, French, Portuguese, and other textile workers began the largest single strike ever undertaken in this country that shut down the textile industry in twenty states.

Although many in this country are dispirited, the radical tempo has not yet quickened. We are in the doldrums at present, waiting for a wind of change.

1705. Shostak, A.B. and W. Gomberg *eds. Blue-Collar World : Studies of the American Workers.* N.J., Free Press, 1964.

1706. Silberman, Chaules E. *Crisis in Black and White.* New York, Random House, 1964.

1707. Still too much poverty, *International Herald Tribune* 29 Aug. 1986;4.

1708. Unemployment in U.S. held at 7 per cent in October. *International Herald Trbiune* 8-9 Nov. 1986; 15.

1709. US poverty rate unexpectedly high for 1983. *Amrita Bazar Patrika* 13 Aug. 1984; 7.

1710. Vinovskis, Maris A. Fertility decline in the West as a model for developing countries today : the case of 19th century America. In *FDLDC*; 229-53.

1711. Wines, Michael. Rich in U.S. get richer. *International Herald Tribune* 28 Jul. 1986; 3.

1712. Wriggius, W. Howard. Third World strategies for change : the political context of North-South interdependence. *In Reducing global inequities*. Ed. by W.H. Wriggins and Gunnar Adler-Karlssora. New York, 1978; 21-120.

The United States no longer holds the commanding position it had in the 1950s even should its domestic differences and post-Watergate political disenchantment be overcome. Soviet military power has, on balance, been increasing. But Moscow's capability remains constrained by a restless Eastern Europe, the capability and policies of neighbouring China, and an increasingly rigid institutional framework at home. Western Europe and Japan, despite their recent recession and the obvious susceptibility of both to raw-material power exerted by certain Third World states, will again be important centers of policy initiative and sources of technology, markets, and credits Third World states will seek. The oil-producing states will also become centers of financial support and policy initiative; some will even develop substantial military capabilities. Accordingly, there will be more centers of significant economic, political, technological, and military power to which Third World states may turn. And in general, where there are alternatives available, there usually is more potential room for maneuver than when a state has no alternative but to turn to either superpower.

There are now more voices that can speak a consequential "nay" to block constructive action. On the other hand, the United States is liable to remain so pre-eminent in the world economy and in the political context of the non-communist world that there will be few aspects of the world political economy that can be reliably reshaped without its constructive participation.

Despite the lessened preeminence of the superpowers, relations between them will continue to affect Third World capabilities. The existence of the two superpowers constrains each from using its available force against most Third World states, even when the latter act in ways that in earlier periods would have ensured retaliation. The nuclear standoff, therefore, strengthens Third World capability in both economic and politico-diplomatic domains. At the same time, such inhibitions of the superpowers provide greater scope for the stronger Third World states to move with impunity against the weaker ones should the former so desire, a possibility that will tend to work against the Third World solidarity we are exploring.

Competition for influence among Moscow, Peking, and Washington will persist even as they become more interdependent. This will mean that certain Third World states, particularly large and potentially consequential states or those located near the fault lines where the Soviet and American "spheres of influence" converge—such as in the Middle East, Central Europe, and Northeast Asia—can threaten to move from one to the other/or act in other ways designed to enhance their bargaining position *vis-a-vis* one of the three superpowers.

The homogeneity of the Third World will decline during the 1980s. Already in the last half of the 1970s there is perceptible increase in differentiation within the Third World. To be sure, there always were substantial differences, depending upon precolonial history and cultures, which were completely different in many part of Asia, Africa, and Latin America, the length of colonial control and whether the imperial power was Great Britain, France, Holland, Portugal, or the United States. These differences out of the past will diminish over time.

But new sources of differentiation are likely to become more marked in the future. For example, since 1973, the room for maneuver of the oil-producing states has increased many times while the nearly 40 most seriously affected (MSA) states have experienced sharply worsening economic conditions. In between the two, a number of industrializing states—Brazil, Mexico, Taiwan, India, to name four—are shaping their futures along lines many Third World states have always hoped for : toward growing industry, an increasingly diversified economy, an expanding and more varied export sector, and a growing domestic technological capability.

Even the problem of debt burdens sharpens differentiations. The goals of greater equality and assured autonomy are being put forward with increasing vigour. However, they are not necessarily mutually consistent. For while equality can be achieved by the Third World *vis-a-vis* the North mainly by closer collaboration among Third World states, greater autonomy implies a reduced readiness for mutual collaboration. To be sure, successful politics usually implies the effective parallel working of contradictory principles. The goals themselves are not inherently contradictory : only the mean for achieving them may call for moving in opposite directions.

A major preoccupation of leaders of all regimes is how to remain in power. A good deal of effort is devoted to pursuing this objective. Indeed, a major element in some Third World activism *vis-a-vis* the North reflects the fact that one way to strengthen one's position in the domestic arena is to make gains—real or symbolic—from the North, the area of former colonial exploitation or of contemporary "oppression." When David stands up to Goliath, public, bureaucratic, and often military support at home are quickly generated, even if such actions economic relations. Any regime subject to public pressures in the North, quite as much as in the Third World, will use foreign policy postures and policies to help sustainits domestic support.

To be sure, there are other ways of consolidating one's hold on power at home apart from standing up to the North. And there are reasons for attempting to change relationships with the North other than simply to retain domestic power. Nevertheless, a significant proportion of Third World activism *vis-a-vis* the North reflects the nearly universal goal of regimes seeking to remain in power.

Security or territorial preoccupations persist. Many Third World regimes feel themselves threatened by near neighbours, particularly where small states lie cheek by jowl with larger, more dynamic, and more powerful states. Other remain anxious that a near neighbour may become more powerful than at present, posing a real threat in the future even if there is none today. Then, too, there are unfulfilled territorial ambitions that gnaw at certain Third World leaders.

These familiar "security" goals have by no means been set aside with increased Third World activism, but persist as underlying concerns even if they may now be overlaid with increased emphasis on goals 1, 2 and 3 above. The resources Third World states devote to acquiring arms and the special bilateral relations many Third World states still retain—and even seek to encourage—with major powers of the North confirm the view that security is still an important goal relevant to North-South bargaining.

In addition, a number of Third World states that are neighbours of either superpower or of other major powers may feel threatened by their larger and better developed neighbour. The goal of security for them may call for developing close links with the other superpower or another major state to act as a balance to the neighbour's threatening power.

Arbitrary frontiers, scattered tribal brethren living in neighbouring states, recent military or political defeats that may have led to a loss of territory, recollections of a grander history—all these can evoke ambitions to gain or to regain territory.

Finally, a regime may feel itself threatened by internal movements that are receiving support from outside. Such regimes will seek military assistance and support that only outside major powers are in a position to provide.

1713. Young, O.R. *Resource regimes.* Berkely, Univ. of California Press, 1982.

1714. Zimenkov, Rudolf. *Unequal partnership—U.S. economic relations with developing countries.* New Delhi, Sterling, 1986. p. 102.

The gap between growth level and rates of the rich and economically weaker Third World countries, most of which are newly-free, continue to widen further despite concerted efforts by the latter to get equal and better terms in trade and economic cooperation with the free-market economy countries.

In spite of the fact that socialist countries' assistance has increased tremendously the bargaining power of the Third World countries, they continue to get a raw deal from the Western rich countries. According to a report of the Brandt Commission, the developing countries suffered a loss of more than one billion dollars in 1981 and 1982 in their export earnings as a result of the protectionist measure and unequal terms of trade. The volume of losses would be surely far bigger in the coming years as more restrictive barriers are put by the West.

Trade, is, of course, one of the spheres in which the developing countries suffer badly. Scientific and technical cooperation with such a country as the US causes a big drain of valuable resources from the developing countries. UNCTAD estimates show that in the early 80s, the losses of the developing countries in the purchase of technology from the US and its transnational corporations (TNCs) totalled 16,400 million dollars a year.

The author has thoroughly analysed the role of the US and its TNCs *vis-a-vis* the endeavours of the newly-free countries to overcome the aftermaths of colonial exploitation as the US happens to be the biggest exporter of capital (45 per cent of the direct total investment by developed Western countries) to the Third World. The aggregate flow of funds from the US into the developing states increased from 4,500 million dollars in 1961 to 30,200 million dollars in 1982. While this is an impressive record, the structure of the flow of capital has undergone significant changes which are also very instructive.

UPPER VOLTA

1715. McSweeney, B.G. Time to learn, time for a better life—The women's education project in Upper Volta. *Assignment Children* (49-50) 1980 ; 109-27.

URUGUAY

1716. Alisky, Marvin. *Uruguay : A contemporary survey.* New York, Prayer, 1969. p. 173.

1717. Brannon, R.H. *Agricultural development of Uruguay.* New York, Prayer, 1968.

1718. Daly, Herman F. Uruguayan economy : Its basic nature and current problems. *Journal of Inter-American Relations* Jul. 1965 ; 316-30.

1719. Economic crisis in Uruguay. *Amrtia Bazar Patrika.* 25 Jul. 1986 ; 8.

1720. *Economic, social and cultural problems. In Uruguay and the United Nations.* New York, Manhattan Publishing Co., 1958 ; 42-47.

1721. Fitzgibbon, Russell H. *Uruguay, portrait of a democracy.*

1722. Lindahi, Goran G. *Uruguay's new path : A study of politics during the first colegiado, 1919-33.* Stockholm, 1962.

1723. Pendle, George. *Uruguay.* New York, Oxford University Press, 1965.

1724. Redding, David C. Economic decline of Uruguay. *Inter-American Economic Affairs* Spr. 1967 ; 55-72.

1725. Tavlor, Philip B. *Government and politics of Uruguay.* New Orleans, Tulane University Studies in Political Science, 1960.

1726. Yaita, Engene. National economy of Uruguay. 1941-46. *Commercial Pan America* (179) May 1948.

VENEZUELA

1727. Bridges, Tyler. Venezuela's 'informal' economy. *International Herald Tribune* 25 Jul. 1986 ; 13.

1728. Gilmore, R. *Caudillison and militarism in Venezuela, 1810-1910.* Athens, Ohio University Press, 1964.

1729. Kuczynski, Pedro-Pablo. Economic development of Venezuela. In ; *Contemporary Venezuela and its role in international affairs.* Ed. by Robert D. Bond. New York Univ. Press, 1977 ; 45-90.

1730. Petras, J. and M. Morley. Venezuelan development model and U.S. policy. *Development and change* 7, 1976.

1731. State on spending spree for development plan. *International Herald Tribune* Jun. 1978.

1732. Survey of Venezuela. *Financial Times* (London) 17 Nov. 1975.

1733. Venezuela raises rate for debt repayments. *International Herald Tribune* 21 Jul. 1986 ; 7.

1734. Venezuela seeks putting off of debt repayment. *Financial Express* 9 Oct. 1982.

VIETNAM

1735. Chandola, Harish. How an economic zone works. *National Herald* 24 Dec. 1976 ; 5.

1736. Economic revolution a far cry for Vietnam. *Statesman* 16 Feb. 1982.

1737. Fifty-five years of the Communist Party of Vietnam. *Vietnam Courier* (2) 1985 ; 1-2.

1738. Ray, Baren. Vietnam's new thesis on economic development. *Mainstream* 21 Aug. 1982 ; 19-23.

The Fifth Congress of the Communist Party of Vietnam held last April was reported very briefly by the media in India and that too only in respect of some media in India and that too only in respect of some political and foreign policy questions. The main Political Report presented to and adopted by the Congress, however, contained an economic section which can be said to present a new thesis on the country's path of development, which will be of interest and relevance to many Third World countries. Not that an altogether new line was presented for the first time at the Congress ; as we shall see, the line had been in practice at least since 1978, but the Congress presented it in a coherent analytical frame which took off from the policy already put into action.

Vietnam, which has been a full CMEA member since 1978, is the most populous (after the USSR) and the poorest member of the Community. The population of the unified country reached 60 million in 1980 whereas its 1975 GNP was estimated to be 85 billion dollars, thus leaving a per capita annual income of about 140 dollars. After the liberation of the South in 1975, the resources of the South (which was and, it seems, still is, richer than the North) were tapped while there was faster development in the North.

The value of exports in 1976 increased by 70 per cent over 1975, while the 1977 increase over 1976 was 42 per cent. Concerning foreign trade Vice-Premier Le Thanh Nghi made an important policy pronouncement in April 1978 : that Vietnam would, focus on the export of products such as coffee, rubber, timber, shrimp, ink frozen pineapple, objects d'art and clothes, whilst international aid and credits would be used to import equipment and machinery, raw materials, fuel and fertiliser.

Further, to the extent that a commodity was highly priced on the world market and domestic requirements were limited, that commodity should be exported regardless of its sector of origin (emphasis added). The Vice-Premier stressed the importance of state monopoly of foreign trade and remarked upon the generous assistance provided by the Socialist countries. He argued that the failure of exports to keep up with imports was an organisational rather than an economic problem. Increased levels of exports would be forthcoming if markets were created and their existence was made known to all products. In line with this generally open outlook, Vietnam had joined the IMF and the World Bank in 1977 (the only CMEA) member in the latter, signed contracts on oil exploration with West European companies and even introduced quite liberal foreign investment laws.

1739. Vietnam on way to economic progress. *Patriot* 31 Aug. 1985 ; 4.

1740. Vietnam economy. *Vietnam Courier* (2) 1986 ; 6-8.

WEST INDIES

1741. Macmillan, W.M. *Warning from the West Indies.* London, Penguin, 1938.

YUGOSLAVIA

1742. Anil, R.N. Yugoslavia : Worker-run-economy. *Hindustan Times* 11 Dec. 1984 ; 9.

An Indian diplomat who is just back after a four year stint in Yugoslavia describes self-management as "a fascinating system", What began as a "Yugoslav Experiment," he says, "has become the envey of the outside world."

Under this system a centrally controlled economy has been replaced by a decentralised worker-run economy. The workers are the owners of the national resources. They enjoy the status of producers and managers of their own factory or enterprise and also play a dominant role in deciding the production targets, working conditions, salaries and bonuses, new recruitment and dismissals etc. Minimum salary is guaranteed to each worker according to his input.

Self-management is based on the belief that man's work is the basis for acquiring the fruits of social labour and managing social resources. According to Josip Broz Tito : "True freedom lies, first of all, in the right and possibilities of any man to autonomously decide on all essential questions of his own life." Man thus becomes the basic factor and creator in the society. He fixes his own targets taking into consideration all his resources and socio-economic interests and tries to achieve them. He thus becomes the centre of all development activity.

Before the introduction of the self-management system in Yugoslavia, the enterprises and establishments were organised and owned by the state and the directors, appointed by the state, were responsible for the overall working and performance of the enterprise. They had to report back to the 'administrative-operational leadership' in the state apparatus, who further reported to their respective ministries. In this set-up the bureaucracy had the upper hand, especially in the absence of mass social participation and control. The system led to the suppression of initiative and to the entrepreneurial capacities of the staff. Workers were not motivated enough within the existing remuneration system which was regulated by state decrees and acts. This led to the strategic decision to let the workers manage their own enterprises, thus eliminating the state's regulatory, supervisory and other functions.

The year 1950 marks the actual introduction of self-management in Yugoslavia. Gradually it was expanded to most of the enterprises, co-operatives, non-banking institutions, public services and even to governmental bodies and state management.

The whole process developed steadily but effectively throughout the fifties. By 1955 the self-management system became an integral part of the local communities and county districts. The 1968 constitutional amendment abrogated state ownership and gave self-managing autonomy to all enterprises and establishments. Another constitutional amendment in 1974 declared that self-management was a basic and invoilable human right of the workers. The results were encouraging. The country witnessed immense socio-economic and political transformation.

With this system Yugoslavia has managed to evolve a flexible, open and efficient socialist economy. Even in terms of international competition the system has proved effective. It has accelerated the production capacity of the whole society.

Even after 35 years a group of beaurocrats and intellectuals are not yet reconciled to the system. Foreign elements have been encouraging them. They blame the system for the country's economic crisis-growing rate of inflation, a whopping foreign debt of 20 billion dollars, high level of unemployment and unbalanced trade exchange.

1743. Rusinow, Dennison. Half full or half empty ? The mood in Belgrade *International Herald Tribune* 19-20 Jul. 1986;4.

1744. Yugoslavia and her economy. *Young Indian* (New Delhi) 29 Nov. 1973; 21-22.

Yugoslavia will celebrate her national day on November, 29. The country has attained many spectacular achievements during 30 years of the Socialist Federation Republic. Her endeavours to solve internationality conflicts, and her march towards economic development through devolution of power to worker collectives and self-management are evidences of her dynamism.

In Yugoslavia, there are six nationalists; they include the Slovens, Croats, Serbs, Moutenegrins, Macdenians and Moslems; each nationality constitutes a republic having its own national state. But each of them is a democratic community of all other nationalists or national minorities living there. There are two other minorities; the Albanians and the Hungarians. They are predominantly found in Kisovo and Vejuodina and enjoy the status of autonomous province; they are not only constituent parts of Serbia but also of the Federation.

The internationality conflict has posed a serious problem today in every country; it was responsible for break-up of several countries. The concept of a national-state, has served as a machination of imperialism to divide a country in the past; it was responsible for wars and it has still been the cause of the present conflict and tensions in the world; the latest being the Arab-Israel conflict.

The two-nation theory has proved illusory to peace; it has not brought any permanent solution to internationality conflicts.

The experience of India and also of other countries bear testimony of this fact. The problem stemming from internationality tension needs to be solved within the framework of a secular society; for, we are faced with new realities in the contemporary world. There is the problem of population explosion; there is a technological revolution; there is a spectacular growth of science; the expectation of the individual has gone up. All this has changed the pattern of social relation; the secular base of society has in fact become a reality. Any attempt to perpetuate the old social order is to put a brake to the whole historical process of human development and progress; it is bound to create serious tensions and convicts.

If Yugoslavia has solved the problem of internationality conflicts and tensions through devolution of power, "self-management," power to "work collectives", it is indeed a remarkable milestone in human development.

Economic development in this country deserves our particular attention. Yugoslavia had inherited a legacy of the colonial system. Her economy was a morass of backwardness. The per capita national income in the Kingdom of Yugoslavia before the Second War broke out had been hardly 150 dollars. The share of primary activities-agriculture and forestry in the national income was 52.6 per cent with industry and mining accounting for a mere 18.9 per cent. The pattern of the living of the people was largely agricultural with those who made their living from the land making up 76 per cent of the total.

1745. Yugoslavian economy looking up. *Patriot* 19 Jan. 1985;2.

ZAIRE

1746. Gambino, Anthony W. Zaire: Rights abuses must be curbed. *International Herald Tribune* 1 Sep. 1986; 4.

1747. Islam, Shada. Political outlook fails to match Zaire's economic upturn. *Pioneer* 21 Jan. 1985; 2.

Recent improvement in Zaire's economic performance might make Western bankers smile, but the country's volatile political situation continues to worry President Mobutu's friends and foes.

Reports of political unrest in Zaire are reaching the different groups of disenchanted Zairean politicians living in exile in Belgium with increasing frequency.

Nguza Karll Bond, Zaire's former Prime Minister who now heads a motley group of Belgian-based opposition groups known as the Congolese Front for the Restoration of Democracy, disclosed recently that discontented army officers had made an unsuccessful bid to topple Mobutu at the end of September.

The coup attempt was foiled, contends Nguza, because of information supplied by a foreign intelligence service to the President who was on an official visit to Rome.

More recent reports of an armed rebellion in the town of Moba in the country's mineral-rich Shaba province also worry Belgian politicians and businessmen.

Belgium has invested heavily in Zaire's copper and cobalt sector. There are about 110 Belgian officers in the Zairean army and thousands of "co-operants" sent to help Zaire implement its development plans. Belgian missionaries can be found in some of Zaire's most isolated regions.

Belgium's relations with its former colony have never been easy. The two countries have quarrelled frequently over political, diplomatic and economic issues.

Brussels has accused President Mobutu of mistreating political prisoners, violating human rights and economic mismanagement. The Zairean leader has denounced Belgian "meddling" in his country's internal affairs. He is particularly annoyed by Belgium's policy of harbouring Zairean political exiles.

Mobutu's much-publicised visit to Belgium last July, however, signalled a new Zairean interest in attracting Belgian aid and investments. The Belgian authorities stressed that they were impressed by the economic reforms undertaken by the new Zairean Prime Minister, Knego Wa Dondo.

ZAMBIA

1748. Nyerinda, V.G. *Zambia's response to human needs*. Lusaka, Zambia Council for Social Service, 1972.

1749. Outlook gloomy for beleaguered Zambian economy. *Baghdad Observer* 7 May. 1985; 5.

Zambia, once among the most prosperious countries in black Africa, has fallen on hard times, and businessmen and diplomats see little chance of the economy reviving in the next few years.

The country built its properity on a single commodity- - Copper— and Zambia has virtually no other source of foreign exchange now that world copper prices have plummetted.

Copper fetched an average on 1.58 dollars per pound between 1970 and 1974, but the price has since slumped to about 70 cents and industry sources say it seems unlikely to recover substantially in the near future.

President Kenneth Kaunda once said that Zambians were born with copper spoons in their mouths. But while this was a blessing until about 10 years ago, many now see it as a curse.

For not only is copper fetching low prices, but deposits now being mined are expected to be exhausted in 15 to 20 years and further reserves, if found, may be uneconomic to exploit.

Economists and businessmen here agree there is no short-term solution to Zambia's chronic problems, but say they would be alleviated by a devaluation of the kwacha, officially-worth 2.38 to the dollar but far less on the thriving black market.

A team from the International Monetary Fund (IMF) is in Zambia to negotiate a package of measures expected to inciude devaluation, although not necessarily by the usual means of an overnight cut in the value of the currency by a flat percentage.

Many economists believe Zambia may set the level of the Kwacha by auctioning foreign exchange, as does Uganda. Although Zambia is resisting IMF pressure for such a system, they say it may have little choice if it is to get loans it so badly needs.

The economists believe the government's reluctance to adopt this market-oriented approach stems partly from its strong commitment to state participation in the economy and partly from fears that Asians—who dominate the country's private sector—would corner the market in foreign exchange.

A devaluation, through auctioning of hard currency or other means, would make imported goods even more expensive and create new hardships for millions of Zambians who have already suffered considerably from their country's economic plight.

1750. Chela, Fred. Zambia's economic crusade. *Pioneer* 25 Jan. 1985 ; 6.

Zambia's President Kenneth Kaunda has launched an "economic crusade 1985" to revive the country's moribund economy. He has announced a series of austerity measures which are part of a package deal negotiated with the International Monetary Fund (IMF). In return, Zambia received an IMF loan to help it through the next difficult 18 months.

The crusade, he said; "will be a special onslaught on the elemental forces of recession, inflation and unemployment which continue to haunt us with increasing ferocity as our export advantage erodes."

The heart of the programme is an attempt to boost agriculture by making it more efficient and increasing exports to generate much—needed foreign exchange.

The task will be difficult : Kaunda has rightly said that Zambia was born with a copper spoon in its mouth, and mineral exports account for 97 per cent of exports account for 97 per cent of export earnings. All agricultural exports combined barely add up to three per cent.

In May Kaunda announced that the external debt totalled $ 4.5 billion; a financial report prepared by the National Commission for Development Planning has warned that the figure may rise to over $ 5.5 billion within three years. Certainly, the situation is going to get worse before it gets better.

Zambia is among the many nations to discover that a debt moratorium covers only repayment of principal not of interest, and that bankers fees for the dozen rescheduling agreements which have been signed are very costly.

Symbolic of the new tough approach, which was outlined by Kaunda in an address to businessmen and farmers in Lusaka recently, is the ban on new development projects unless they are considered essential and likely to generate foreign exchange.

1751. Harden, Blaine. Breakdown in Zambia : Debt backlog brings Chronic decay. *International Herald Tribune* 26 Sep. 1985 ; 1-2.

This country's tallest office building has only one elevator that works. Its ups and downs symbolize a chronic economic decay in Zambia and across much of sub-Saharan Africa.

Office workers stand in long lines all day outside the elevator, which serves 23 floors. When their turn comes, they pack themselves in, without bothering to press any buttons, and begging shouting out floor numbers. As if by magic, the elevator stops at their floors.

What they are shouting at, in country filled with machines that do not work for lack of money to buy spare parts, is not the elevator, but the elevator operator. They shout because he is standing on top of the elevator car, manipulating a jerry-rigged control device that, with frequest breakdowns, keeps the elevator moving and prevents Zambia's most prestitious building from losing its tenants.

The elevator car with the operator on its roof is among the oddest manifestation of Zambia's disintegrating economy.

What is less odd, but far more important, is that the country has almost no foreign exchange to import wheat for bread; to buy diesel fuel; to fix farm tractors, 62 per cent of which do not work; to upgrade factories, which operate at less than 32 per cent of capacity; or to pay off a growing foreign debt.

"What is happening is that Zambia is strangled, and not so slowly anymore," said an International Monetary Fund official who is a specialist on Zambia.

The economies of many countries in sub-Saharan Africa have been contracting for more than a decade, with declining per capital income and with population growth outstripping food output.

But what is happening to Zambia, as well as to countries such as Tanzania and Sudan, is a crisis of another, more disturbing order. International lending agencies, major donors and local bankers say Zambia is incapable of borrowing or producting its way out of debt.

"Rescheduling our debts and borrowing more money will give us some breathing space, but it will merely put off the evil day," said Francis

Nkhoma, general manager of Barclays Bank PLC in Zambia, "Frankly, we cannot generate enough money to pay the debts and buy the imports that keep the country going."

Interest payments on Zambia's debt would eat up 40 per cent of the country's export earnings, if Zambia met these payments, which it does not. Debt service drains away 82 per cent of new loans coming into the country.

1752. Simons, H.J. Zambia's urban situation. In *Development in Zambia*. Ed. by B. Turok. London, Zed Press, 1979.

1753. Zambia's economic crisis. Worsens. *Patriot* 28 Aug. 1984 ; 6.

ZIMBABWE

1754. Frankel, Glenn. Zimbabwe silos full, but dying goes on, *International Herald Tribune* 15 Jul. 1986 ; 1-2.

1755. Loewenson, R. Hunger in Zimbabwe. *International Herald Tribune* 7 Oct. 1986 ; 5.

Handicapped

1756. Bhawan Singh. Help for the handicapped. *India Today* 15 May 1984 ; 150.

1757. Bodhankar, V.G., Towards rehabilitation of the disabled. *Deccan Chromicle* 18 Mar. 1984.

1758. Habibulla, M.I., Avenues for employment and concessions for disabled. *Social Welfare* Mar. 1984 ; 30.

1759. Hurkat, P.C. Disability *versus* Employability. *Social Welfare* (New Delhi) Mar. 1984 ; 4-6.

At the end of the queue : The disabled population is, however, at the end of the labour queue in all lands and at all times including that of India. In the circumstances competitive employment is a distant unattainable goal. Most severe mentally and physically handicapped, therefore, need special arrangements for preparing them for entry into labour market. Advanced countries have solved the problem by establishing a network of sheltered workshops. They are truly the last resort for giving employment to physically handicapped with serious loss of functions. They focus on unskilled, labour-intensive work after proper training such as packaging, bench assembly, collecting, mail sorting, stuffing, mechanical assembly, wood working, metalworking, inspection, custodial work, manufacturing jobs, reclaimation, salvage operation etc. India has not yet experimented in this field. Sheltered workshops are indeed indispensable and will go a long way in ameliorating the difficulties of handicapped for these are the final major component of the rehabilitation system and provide employment for those who have few options in the competitive labour market. Sheltered workshops are thus not only the employers of last resort but also a source of service for those most in need—welfare for workfare in its true sense. The magnitude of services rendered by sheltered workshops will be obvious by the fact that they employed nearly 1 million separate clients during the last decade in U.S.A. While the manpower and veteran's programme together reached about 500,000 handicapped in the same duration.

The government must, however, the cautious from the very beginning to see that the employment programme designed for the disabled may not become employment programme for the ablebodied workers. It is suggested that the ratio of the staff in sheltered workshops must be 50:50 between disabled and ablebodied workers, and that, they must work on the principle of industry and commercial establishments. The products and services created by these workshops be subsidised by Government of India to make them competitive and be sold on the pattern of Khadi Gramodhyog. These workshops must also provide nonvocational services to the clients like developing skills of independent living—such as personal hygine, speech therapy, homemaker training, training in mobility, adult education, psychotherapy, transportation, housing and homebound employment. Such services by sheltered workshops will go a long way in inculcating a sense of workfare and will wean them away from public relief and charity. The private sector employers can do a wonderful job by providing suitable placements to the physically handicapped in their industrial and business establishments.

1760. Patel, Jagdish K. Education and training not enough, *Social Welfare* Mar. 1984 ; 10.

The existing programmes for the economic independence of the blind are woefully inadequate, and need revolutionising. A blind person is always regarded by the public as an expert at weaving, caning or on music. Can the blind do only mechanical, repetitive jobs ? Most organisations still stick to the traditional programmes for the blind.

Though there are several new professions such as physiotherapy, stenotyping, bank jobs, telephone operators jobs, motor engineering, carpentry etc., where the blind could be employed after training, such jobs are not within the reach of many blind. Similarly such occupations as poultry, dairy, fishing. piggery can be thrown open to the rural blind to ensure them economic independence.

The absence of adequate training programmes leads the blind nowhere. At the same time many blind are unable to get employment although they possess the necessary qualifications. This leads to frustration, withdrawal from society and manifestation of this dissatisfaction in various ways. The blind have reached a juncture where they do not know where to go and what to do. This sense of insecurity about the future is one of the greatest problems the blind face today.

The second problem of the visually handicapped is their own attitude. It has been found that though they often talk of their efficiency, ability and demand equal rights they also ask for special concessions and privileges. They ask for equal rights in respect of education and employment but in reality they exploit their blindness and whenever opportunity is available, they falsely play on the sentiments of the community and the Government.

Blindness is a physical muisance and, no doubt, causes trauma and maladjustment with society but it should be accepted by the blind person. This acceptance will lead him to conquer his handicap, making the best of his present situation. Blindness does not hamper the growth of personality or abilities. The blind have abilities which are at par with those of any sighted individual; it is just that they have to be carefully nurtured and developed.

If the blind develop a sense of self respect and can prove their talents, all their problems will be solved. I feel it is the attitude of expecting sympathy and special concessions that should be avoided. To overcome their problems the blind should have associations of their own where they can voice their opinions and prove their talents and skills from time to time. There should be solidarity among various organisations of and for the blind. These organisations should work together for the creation of facilities for training the blind in employment-oriented occupations. These organisations should also have programmes for the socio-psychological adjustment and integration of the blind by appropriate programmes.

These should be cooperation between organisations for the blind, voluntary organisations and the community. Each should understand more about the other by a two way system of exchange. This way, the problems and limitations of each group could be solved the easier way. More realistic and low-cost programmes should be developed whereby a greater number of blind can be economically rehabilitated.

1761. Ravindran Nair, G. Disabled : Give them a chance. *Social Welfare* Mar. 1984 ; 3-4, 38.

There are about 500 millions disabled people in the world making up more than 10 per cent of today's population. All of them need our help to stand on their own, live and work alongside the rest of humanity enjoying all the rights to which every human being is entitled. That this has been denied to them over the centuries was being realised by the world community culminating in the declaration of the year 1981 as the International Year of the Disabled Persons followed by the Declaration of the Decade 1983-92 as the International Decade of Disabled Persons.

Through a long span of time, mankind has been subjected to a myth of sorts that the disabled are useless, incapable of doing anything on their own, a species to be pited on and looked after so long as they are alive. The myth has already been broken long before and even now; that every country and every community is realising that the blind, the hearing handicapped or the crippled or paraplegic can stand on their own if society cares to give them a chance. All the same the prejudices persist in both developed and developing countries, although spurred by larger resources and greater awareness, some of the advanced societies might have forged ahead in providing both short-term and long-term measures aimed at the education, training and employment, sheltered or open, of the disabled communited. What the disabled ask for today is for something more basic : the restoration of the basic human rights which they cease to enjoy because of mere physical or mental disability. Here too the position is far brighter than even before.

In India we have come a long way from the position obtaining before Independence : the Employment Exchanges set up exclusively for the Physically Handicapped have sought to place the disabled in a variety of trades and vocations while the Vocational Rehabilitation Centres have trained them in different trades according to their aptitude and qualification. A fixed percentage of certain categories of jobs in both Government and Public Sector Undertaking is reserved for the disabled of different categories. The initiative taken by the Nationalised Banks, the Indian Railways, the P and T Department and several other organisations in providing financial assistance and other avenues for the employment of the disabled merits kudos. Today the Central Government as well as the

State Governments, the public and private sectors are seized of the problem as never before. We realise today that it is better to open up opportunities of employment to them than bear extravagant expenditure on their care that perpetuates their dependency. Self-reliance remains the motto of our National Plan of Action for the Disabled formulated during the IYDP.

The 1983 International Labour Conference held at Geneva took a positive step further : it adopted an international convention and recommendation on vocational rehabilitation and employment of disabled persons. By adopting a convention, which becomes binding on those Governments which ratify it, the ILO underlined the importance it attached to the formulation and implementation of coherent national policies in this field. Countries ratifying the convention are obliged, within their possibilities, to ensure that the appropriate vocational rehabilitation measures are made available to all disabled persons and promote opportunities for their employment in the open labour market.

What is envisaged is assistance and incentives to employers, establishment of various types of sheltered employment, encouragement of the production workshops and cooperatives by and for disabled persons, elimination of architectural barriers and provision of adequate means of transport, exemption from taxes or other charges on material and equipment for rehabilitation programmes and provision of partime employment and research.

A massive publicity drive needs to be mounted to focus on the tremendous potential that lies latent in the vast human resources lebelled as disabled. Together with the mass media, the community at large, the voluntary sector, the workers, the employers and, on top of all, the opinion leaders from the disabled themselves should join together to formulate a blueprint for action that would ensure the sustained training and employment of the disabled in vocations where they could function as effectively as anyone else. This should be the objective to be secured during the remaining nine years of the International Decade of Disabled Persons.

1762. Rehabilitating the handicapped. *Yojana* 1 May 1986 ; 29.

1763. *Towards a fuller life : Education and rehabilitation of handicapped.* Delhi, Dept. of Social Security 1967. p. 203.

Housing and Human Settlements

1764. Abraham, Amrita. Slum dwellers and the law. *Tribune* 31 Jul. 1985;4.

The Supreme Court judgement on the pavement dwellers in Bombay, delivered by a five–Judge Constitution Bench earlier this month, has been received, inevitably, with mixed feelings. The Municipal Commissioner, the Mayor and the Police Commissioner have welcomed it because stalled civic projects can now be carried out, because Bombay can be cleaned up and because there will be fewer impediments to traffic.

The civil rights groups which took up the cause of the pavement dwellers and petitioned the Supreme Court four years ago are deeply disappointed with the judgement.

The payment dwellers themselves, who number between 2.5 million to three million, are very anxious and troubled. Some of them are very angry.

The judgement held that no one had the right to encroach on public spaces like pavements. Even though the Judges recognised that it was dire poverty that brought hundreds of people everyday to Bombay in search of a living and that most of them found legitimate means of livelihood, and also that removing them from where they now lived would deprive them of their livelihood, they ruled that putting up dwellings on pavement was an act of trespass. The judgement, therfore, found that the Bombay Municipal Corporation Act (section 314) which empowered civic officials to remove objects or structures in such public places was not unfair or unreasonable.

The court directed the civic authorities not to demolish the hutments of the pavement dwellers before Oct. 31 this year one month after the monsoon is normally over. On the related question of slum dwellers, the Court ruled that such slum dwellers as had been "censused" by the State Government in 1976 and issued identity cards could not be evicted until they had been given alternative accommodation.

Pavement dwellers who happened to be "censused" (and a small number were so by accident) must also be given alternative sites but not necessarily before their hutments were demolished.

The Supreme Court had been petitioned in late 1981 by the People's Union for Civil Liberties and others after Mr. A.R. Antulay's Government set about demolishing hundreds of hutments in two large settlements in the city in pouring rain. The operation was carried out without notice; house-hold goods were destroyed and the people themselves were forced into buses and sent outside the city. The P.U.C.L. obtained a swift and temporary stay of the demolitions and deportations from the Bombay High Court. The matter was taken to the Supreme Court and an interim stay against the demolition of the hutments that came up before Oct. 1981, was granted.

The Court was then petitioned to direct the civic authorities not to carry out demolitions of hutments. essentially on the ground that no one ought to be deprived of his right to livelihood, and by removing the pavement dwellers "who had no other recourse" the Corporation would be so depriving them.

1765. Abrams, C. *Man's struggle for shelter.* Cambridge, M.I.T. Press, 1964.

1766. Abrams, Charles. Public housing mythds. *New Leader* 38 Jul. 1955, 3-6.

1767. Bapat, Meera. Slum areas legislation : Its relevance for slum improvement and upgradation. *Task forces on housing and urban development.* Planning Commission, Govt. of India. New Delhi, 1983.

1768. Bhargava, Gopal. Need for housing planning in urban India. *Young Indian* 19 Aug. 1971; 7-9.

1769. Bhargava, Gopal. Slums for urban India *Young Indian.* 28 Oct. 1971; 15-17.

1770. Blanchand, Paul. *Democracy and empire in the Caribbean.* New York, Macmillan, 1947.

1771. Chandra, Ramesh. Human settlements in developing countries *Indian and Foreign Review* 15 Oct. 1985; 4-5, 23.

The growth of urban human settlements in the world which had taken place during the last decade and which is projected to take place till the turn of the century, i.e., the year A.D. 2000 is phenomenal.

While the world population is estimated to increase by 1500 million, more than three quarters of the increase i.e., 1200 million people will be added to urban human settlements in more than 15 years. It has been estimated that in the developing countries, the percentage of the population living in urban settlements will rise from 28 per cent (1975) to 44 per cent.

In number this signifies a growth from 830 million to 2150 million.

In Africa, the urban settlements are expected to double their size from 160 million to 350 million.

In 1950 only two cities in the developing countries had over five million inhabitants. In 1980 there were 26 cities with a population of five million or more in the world of which 19 were in developing countries. By A.D. 2000 if the present trend continues, 58 cities of the world will have a population of five million or more, 44 of which will be in developing countries. It has been estimated that the population of slum and squatter settlements in urban settlement areas is increasing at twice the rates of growth of population of the cities. This is four times faster than the world population growth.

1772. Cobba, Hussain. More pressure on housing as the young set up own homes. *Baghdad Observer* 27 Aug. 1983; 2.

In several developing countries, Iraq no exception, the concept of the family is more extensive than the nuclear families of western societies. The institution has a wider connotation, frequently grouping cousins, uncles and distant relatives in a fairly extended kinship system. Among its most recurrent characteristics, the joint or extended family, especially the rural one, is organised in such a way that property and income are pooled together and likewise expenditure is not accounted for individually. This structure and its evolution has a definite impact on the whole national economic system.

As it is generally believed, an evolution from the social and economic system of the extended family to a nuclear family, is the direct result of an accumulation of economic factors. The extended family being in the main coined with subsistence and agricultural societies. The nuclear family emerges from the split and disintegration of the former as urbanisation gathers momentum and living standards are uplifted.

The disintegration of the system of the joint family and its split into smaller families may be taken as one measure of economic and social development. Such inferences however the normally qualified by the reservation that the structural change in the system of the family must accord with the rate of growth and development of the whole economy including industry, agriculture and services.

The rapid disintegration in the last ten years of the extended Iraqi family, (consisting 7 to 15 members), in favour of a much smaller family unit (3 to 7 members) is a phenomenon easily fitting conventional analysis.

The onset of fast development in the 1970s and especially after the oil price adjustment in 1974, has markedly accelerated the process of breaking up the standard size of the Iraqi family. Such factors as urbanisation, high living standards, stupendous expansion in public amenities and government financial help encouraging early marriages, lay behind the erosion of the sociological foundations of the joint family.

Government policy in this respect appears to have been in favour rather than in opposition of this trend. President Saddam Hussein expounding on the issue told an economists meeting in 1974 that the "wide scale state provision of housing (to citizens) is an effective way to accelerate the natural process of breaking up the (joint) family. State mortgages or the provision of building lots of land at nominal prices or free of charge will have similar consequences."

Before the 1970s, the only practical form of insurance and social security available to the disabled and weaker persons revolved around the extended family. The introduction of the all embracing state social security system has reduced dependence on the support of the joint resources of the big family. Pension and social security laws, the social welfare law seeing to the needs of the aged, disabled and those unable to work for one reason or another, must have left their imprints on the structure of the family.

Education has been another area where by virtue of being provided free by the state, has replaced reliance on the collective pool of financial resources of the joint family to send one's children to school.

1773. Daker, L.W., Roofs for roofless millions. *Indian Express* (New Delhi) 1 Feb. 1984;6.

1774. Dasgupta, Shibani. Stemming the urban slum epidemic (in India) *Link* 14 Sep. 1986; 12-13.

1775. Dogra, Bharat. Urban ghettos. *Hindustan Times* Weekly 24 Mar. 1985.

1776. Drakakis-Smith, D. *Urbanization, housing and the development*. London, Croom-Helm, 1981.

1777. Dwyer, D.J. *People and housing in Third World cities* London, Longman, 1975.

1978. Ferguson, T. and M.G. Pettigrew. *Study of 718 slum families rehousing and morbidity and mental health.* Baltimore, 1962.

1779. Ganguly, A.K. Housing problem : Wanted a national policy, *Amrita Bazar Patrika* 20 May 1986: 6.

1780. *Global review of human settlements.* United Nation, Habitat, 1976.

1781. Gujral, I.K. Housing explosion needed. *Socialist India* 29 May 1971 ; 35-37.

1782. Hai, Le Thach. Slum Clearance in Ho Chi Minh City. *Vietnam Courier* (2) 1985 : 24.

Slums are a common phenomenon in the growth of big cities under the capitalist system. The situation is even worse in the underdeveloped countries, which have suffered from old and new colonialism. In the case of Saigon under US occupation, a third element came to make the situation truly-desperate : during the war years, the brutal "rural pacification" policy of the United States and its stooges caused hundreds of thousands of rural people to leave their native villages and their fields for the "capital" where they lived in tens of thousands of hovels, in fact anything that could shelter them from rain and sun. A family for instance crowded into the body of a discarded taxi and made it their home for years. Small wonder that in 1971 an investigating team of United Nations specialists made this remark : "Something till worse than the existence of so many hovels in this city is the relative scarcity of even those hovels."

According to statistics from the General Housing Department of the Saigon regime, before liberation Saigon had as many as 3,200 hectares of its area occupied by slums. Recent investigations have provided more details : 28,000 hovels, 194,967 houses without running water, 122,877 houses without electricity and 124,011 houses without electricity and 124,011 houses without toilets. In 25,995 of those hovels, there is only 1-2 square metres of floor space for each person. But the most burning question is to rehouse the nearly 100,000 persons living in 16,821 shanties along the drainage canals. These hovels are not only dreadful dwellings but also pose a serious threat of pollution due to the garbage and human waste dumped into the canals.

Against such a background, the housing problem for this city of more than 3.5 millions with a very high population growth rate is a most urgent once.

The Resolution of the 3rd Congress of the Party Organsation of Ho Chi Minh City and the Resolution of the City Party Committee dated April 10, 1984, gave top priority to the housing problem.

After on-the-spot investigations and careful discussions with the district and wart authorities, the city administration has worked out a bold programme to build 10,000 apartments for families of government employees and workers, disabled soliders and revolutionary martyrs and members of the armed forces. This is to be carried out along with the removal of most of the shanties now standing along the canals. The programme is expected to be completed before April 39, 1985, the 10th anniversary of the liberation or Saigon. The cost inolved is estimated at 1.2 billion dong. Of this, the city budget will bear 30-40%, a major financial effort in the present economic situation. The remaining 60% will be covered by the welfare funds of factories and enterprises and also by the population's own contributions.

Immediately after the programme was endorsed by the city, many districts set out to built houses in the framework of this plan.

In Tan Binth district, even before they were allocated money from the city budget, the authorities of the 9th ward decided to built four of the ten planned apartments with a view to rapidly rehousing people now living in the most precarious and unhygienic conditions. Other wards followed suit in a concerted effort to get 100 apartments ready for their occupants on National Day (2 September 1984).

The movement spread quickly to the entire city. Binh Thanh district along in 1984 completed more than 200 apartments, 20 of them with bricks contributed by the local organization of the Ho Chi Minh Young Pioneers. In the 10th district, after the completion of 80 apartments, the local authorities began the construction of 100 multi-storeyed houses in Aug. 1984, and another 300 in Nov. Constraction is also going apace in the 1st, 2nd, 5th, 6th, 8th, 11th, Phu Nhuan an Go Vap inner-city districts and the Duyen Hai and Cu Chi outlying districts. In Cu Chi in particular, with the number of disabled soldiers and revolutionary martyrs occupying a sizable proportion of the population, the local authorities have allocated 200 apartments to their families.

On the occassion of National Day 1984, 750 apartment houses were allocated. The plan to allocate 3,500 apartments on the occasion of the 40th anniversary of the Vietnam People's Army (22-12-1984) was also fulfilled. If account is taken of the nearly 1,000 families of working people, who were accommodated in houses not fully occupied by decision of the Prime Minister, in 1984 alonge more than 5,000 families of working people were rehoused. This represents a significant step in the long-term programme for slum clearance.

The housing programme in Ho Chi Minh City has received effective assistance from many localities in the North, especially Hanoi, Haiphong and Thanh Hoa province, through the exchange of commodities from Ho Chi Minh City for building materials, especially cement. The Ministry of Building, for its part, has also helped speed up the building tempo in in order to quickly do away with one of the ugliest vestiges of US neo-colonialism and the US War of aggression in the South.

1783. Hardoy, J.E. and D. Satterthwaite. *Shelter : Need and response.* New York, John Wiley, 1981.

1784. Hole, V. Social effects of planned rehousing. *Town Planning Review* 25 (2) Jul. 1959 ; 161-73.

1785. Home for the homeless. *International Herald Tribund* 5 Nov. 1986 ; 4.

1786. Houses for the homeless. *Deccan Herald* (Bangalore) 23 Jan. 1985 ; 8.

1787. Housing for poor—A challenging field for town planners. *Pioneer* 22 May 1986.

1788. Housing problem *Searchlight* (Patna) 21 Oct. 1985 ; 4.

1789. Housing the poor. *Statesman* (New Delhi) 4 Sep. 1986 ; 6.

1790. Iyer, S.S. and K.K. Verma. *Roof over their heads. A study of night-shelters in Delhi.* Delhi School of Social Work, 1964. p. 59.

1791. Jagmohan. Human settlements *Hindustan Times* Sunday Magazine 18 Dec. 1983 : 1-3.

The problem of human settlements is one of the most complex one of our times. Its dimension can be seen from the fact that at present two-fifth of the world population live in homes without the barest of necessities. About 800 million people are living in poorly built dwellings. About 1.3 people do no have access to clean water, and about 1.8 billion are without facility of sewage disposal. And requirements are daily mounting. It has been estimated that to meet the human settlements' needs of the projected population by the turn of the century, about 900 million new houses, 1,500 million new work places and 20 million miles of new transportation lines will have to be constructed.

Like other developing countries, India faces serious challenges in the realm of human settlements. What sets India apart is the severity of its problem. Its population of 658 million is spared over 329 million hectares and is concerntrated in 575, 916 rural settlements and 3,245 urban settlements. It is one of the most densely populated countries in the world. It accounts for about 15 per cent of world's population in a land area constituting only 2.4 per cent of the world total. As such, the per cent capita availability of land in the country comes to 0.43 hectare in 1981, as compared to 4.14 hectares in USA, 8.43 hectares in USSR, 1.91 hectares in Burma and 0.98 hectare in China and Pakistan. Under the impact of growing population, per capita availability of land in India has progressively declined over the past decades ; in 1981, it was nearly half of the per capita figure for 1951.

Growing urbanisation of the world population has further complicated the problems of human settlements. The 20th century has been called the Age of Urbanisation. In 1900, about 8 per cent of the world population lived in urban areas. By 2000, this percentage will rise to 50, and about 3 billion people will be living in the cities. Out of these 3 billion people, 66 per cent will be in the cities of the developing countries.

India is no exception to this process of urbanisation. Though our rate of urbanisation is comparatively low, the size of our urban population is very large. According to 1981 Census, it is 156 million—fourth largest urban population amongst the countries of the world. In number, only three countries have more urban population than India. These are USA, USSR and China. By 1985, India will outpace both USSR and USA, and will have the second largest urban population in the world, next only to China.

By 2000. India will have 350 to 400 million people living in its urban areas. There will be 20 cities, rather super-cities, lation each, and 600 cities with population ranging from 50,000 to 500,000.

1792. Jamaal, Majeed. Low cost housing. *Mainstream* Jul. 1986 : 21-22.

1793. Jha, L.K. Housing for millions. *Financial Express* 18 Oct. 1983; 5.

Shelter is a basic economic need, ranking next in importance only to food and clothing. Unfortunately while food and clothing do receive the attention and priority they deserve in programmes of economic development, housing is usually looked upon as a part of social welfare measures. Along with education and health care, it is treated as an adjunct to the development process—as a resource-absorbing rather than a resource generating activity. This misconstrued approach has resulted in some neglect of housing in our development plans as well as some faulty policies. In consequence housing shortage has been getting worse and more acute from plan to plan, even year to year.

So long as people satisfy and particular need through their own efforts and resources, it does not have much significance as on economic activity. It is when people have to depend on the resources and efforts of others for satisfying a need, that a new industry comes into existence. In places where people cook their own foods, there are no restaurants. The catering industry comes into existence when there is a demand for cooked food. Likewise, in regard to housing in most cities, particularly the larger ones, people can no longer look after their own housing needs, undertaking their own construction out of their own resources. They have to hire or purchase the accommodation they need, while there are builders engaged in construction work to satisfy the needs of others and not their own.

Apart from satisfying a basic need, housing has a major contribution to make to the development process. It has a tremendous potential for generating employment and will help alleviate the unemployment problem. The National Buildings Organisation estimated in 1980 that investment of Rs. 1 crore in housing would provide direct employment to 923 men for a year and indirect employment to 1477 men, both skilled and unskilled. The tradition of saving in order to invest in a house is firmly rooted in Indian society. People who do not think of investing in shares and securities do invest in housing. A step up in housing activities will generate more savings in the community.

The material inputs for housing are also easily provided. Bricks create no problem. Their supply can be augmented at will. With abundant deposits of limestone in the country as well as the capacity to fabricate cement plants, the expansion of cement production does not face any foreign exchange constraint.

In nevertheless there is a growing shortage of housing, it is largely because of weaknesses in the policy framework. In the absence of a clear blueprint for the development of housing, a series of divergent decisions, *ad hoc* in character, affecting housing are taken from different angles by different agencies of the Central Government, the state governments as well as local authorities. In the event. house-building has become a difficult operation with so many hurdles to clear that only those who are highly resourceful in more senses than one, can really go ahead.

There are, of course, institutions which stand ready to help intending house-builders with finance, but the availability of finance cannot help if building sites are not available, cement is in short supply and the clearances necessary for construction to start difficult to obtain. To start with I propose therefore, to concentrate on the impediments and obstacles which slow down progress in this vital sector.

1794. Karkal, G.L. Problems of urban housing and slums. *Indian Journal of Social Works* Apr. 1970 : 35-42.

1795. Krack, Erhard. Tackling a major social problem. *Problems of Peace and Socialism* Oct. 1986 ; 100-06.

1796. Kulkerni, G.B. Housing : A serious problem. *Economic Times* 1 Aug. 1981.

1797. Kumar, Tej B. Housing the millions. *Indian & Foreign Review* 15 Jul. 1980 ; 15-18.

1798. Lall, Vinay D. Low income housing. *Economic Times* 67 Aug. 1986 ; 5.

1799. Lawson Roger and Cindy Sterens. Housing allowances in West Germany and France. *Journal of Social Policy* 3 (3) 1974.

1800. Mabogunjie, A.L. *et al. Sheter provision in developing countries.* New York, John Wiley, 1978.

1801. Menon, A.G. Large scale construction on rural housing as an anti-poverty strategy. In *EAPS* ; 127-31.

If poverty is defined as the lack of basic human needs-foods, clothing and shelter-provision of any of them would be an anti-poverty measure. The purpose of this paper, accordingly, is to suggest the organized construction of a large number of dwelling units for the rural poor-the landless-agricultural labourers and members of the less privileged classes of society, who are also for the most part, agricultural workers and also landless—as an anti-poverty strategy.

It has been estimated that to wipe off the existing deficit in housing, to replace units that will go out of use and to allow for the needs of the increase in population, a minimum of 10,000 dwelling units per 1 million inhabitants will be required to be constructed per annum in the next few decades.

In a copy of a draft proposal for an "Asian Housing Programme : 6 million Rural Houses in 1976" under which it has been suggested that, largely through community action and self-help, and after adequate preparation, 6 million houses can be got constructed, in the rural areas in 16 Asian countries (with an estimated total population of 600 million) by 1976, using, for the most part, local material and skills. The economic implications of such a programme, the relationship of the value added to the GNP, has been brought out in Annex. 1.

As the proposal has been drawn up for consideration by countries having a variety of economic and geographic conditions, it is necessarily couched in the most general terms. The methodology advocated is stated merely as being "self-help". The implications for employment creation and for integrated community development would be clearer if a specific example is discussed. This is done in the following paragraphs.

In India, it had long been recognized that land reform, by itself, sometimes worked to the disadvantage of the very section of the community that it is designed to benefit, viz., the landless poor. This is because not all the landless can hope to get land to cultivate, and landlords, with reduced areas for self-cultivation, no longer feel obliged to provide housing-sites to the landless. This has been sought to be corrected by the Government, by acquiring land and distributing it as housing-sites to the landless poor and other under-privileged, classes.

1802. Mitra, Arup. Government policy for slum improvement. *Mainstream* 19 Jul. 1986; 27-29.

It is not that the growing significance of the slums has been overlooked by the planning authorities before laying down the social objectives in the plan documents: rather it has always been recognised that housing is a burning problem for the millions of shelterless people. It has been emphasised, "in India housing sector has always been given due importance in the development programme under the Five Year Plans", and that the provision of shelter is crucial to the development and improvement of the quality of life of the people.

In this wider perspective therefore, it is of relevance to evaluate the programmes and measures undertaken so far to tackle the problematic issues arising in the context of slums. Moreover, the angle from which the slum problem has been visualised in Indian context has to be emphasised to judge its appropriateness and effectiveness in reducing the intensity of the slum problem.

The earliest attempt made in the context of public housing was the social housing scheme introduced in the First Plan. Thereafter, the integrated subsidised housing sector for industrial workers and Economically Weaker Sections (EWS) was introduced in 1952. Low income group housing scheme (1954) and middle income housing scheme (1959) were also undertaken to deal with the housing problem. In the context of the growth of slums, the first attack was make in 1956, that is, slums, the first attack was made in 1956, that is, slum clearance scheme or slum area Act, 1956. But as a result of the recognition of the fact that the policy of clearance of the slums cannot be successful in the fact of growing problems, the policy measures had to take a different turn from clearance to improvement following the recommendations of the Sixth Housing Ministers' Conference in 1962.

It was then realised that improvement of slums at site would be preferable to a policy of relocation of slum dwellers and construction of tenements and, therefore, the scheme for environmental improvement of slums was formulated in 1972 and the amenities to be provided under the scheme were water supply, swerage, community baths and latrines, street lights, widening and paving of lanes. During the Fifth Five Year Plan in 1974, the scheme was transferred to the State sector as a part of the Minimum Needs Programme and was intended to cover all cities with a population of above three lakhs. The scope of the scheme was further widened in 1978 to cover all urban areas irrespective of the size of their population.

In the Fifth Five Year Plan, the Integrated Urban Development Programme (IUDP) along with the Integrated Development of Small and Medium Towns (IDSMT), was introduced initially in the four metropolitan cities of Bombay, Calcutta, Delhi and Madras and later extended to cover all towns with a view to providing assistance to the State Governments to implements the land acquisition, development and disposal programmes, urban renewal and redevelopment projects and provision of urban infrastructure. But when it was realised that the bulk of the resources were sanctioned simply for land acquisition, revised guidelines were given in 1978 for providing water supply, sewerage, transportation facilities and health facilities. But so far, as Task Forces on Housing and Urban Development (1983) writes, IUIP has never been evaluated.

The Sixth Five Year Plan also recognised the poor environmental condition and insanitation in the slums and attached considerable importance to the programmes concerning the provision of basic amenities and purification of slum areas :

> "A particular area becomes a slum not because of its structure but because of its environment and insanitation. Of the urban population nearly a fifth is estimated to constitute slum population. The slum population in 1985 needing attention is estimated to be about 33.1 million. Of this only 6.8 million have been covered by March 1980. It is proposed to cover about 40 per cent of the remaining slum population that is 10 million slum population by 1985. Assuming per capita investment of Rs. 15.0 the total cost of this programme during the plan would be Rs. 15.1 crores. Depending on the strategy to be adopted in the area, facilities to be provided under the programme are water supply, storm water drains, paving of streets, street lighting and community latrines. Areas inhabited by scheduled castes are to be given to priority." (Sixth Five Year Plan : Para 14. 26, page-225.)

The Sixth Five Year Plan and the Twenty Point Programme of the Government are also said to have accepted all the objectives of the International Year of Shelter for the Homeless (IYSH).

1803. Mukherjee, D. Housing for the homeless. *Patriot* (New Delhi) 7 May 1986; 4.

1804. Murison, H.S. and J.P. Lea. *Housing in Third World Countries.* London, Macmillan, 1979.

1805. Nair, K.K. Radical face-lift for Dharavi slum. (Bombay). *Blitz* 6 Dec. 1986; 23.

1806. Parekh, H.T. Finance for housing. *Economic Times* 1 Aug. 1981; 4.

1807. Parmar, Suresh K Housing neglect continues. *Hindustan Times* 17 Jul. 1971; 9.

1808. Payre, G. Urban housing in the Third World. London, 1977.

1809. Pyne, Biren. Housing for the people. *Amrita Bazar Patrika* 28 May 1984; 6.

1810. Ramamurty, P.R. Housing for the poor. *Free Press Journal* 24 Mar. 1986; 6.

During the last two decades there has been a tremendous increase in the world population : in a quarter of century, 1950 to 1975, the world population has been doubled from around 2500 million to nearly 4000 million. It is the developing countries which have borne the brunt of the rise, and hence, of the consequences. Statistical analysis indicates that the annual growth rate of the poor in the developing countries has been almost three times in contrast to the developed ones. Among the three basic requirements of man, namely, food, clothing and shelter, shelter has been the most neglected aspect as far as availability, standard and affordability are concerned.

The choice is clear. The choice is a home : however humbler it is, and an abode at his village or native place faced with repeated famine and shrinking employment opportunities, or occupation with some nomial earnings coupled with risk or no shelter to the workers and family. The priority on bread wins. The housing need is relegated to second place. Meanwhile, the problem has intensified in magnitude and complexity and the earlier benevolent approach to construct housing for the poor has been replaced by a more urgent and realistic search for a solution of their shelter needs.

Before a housing scheme is considered one has to look into it from the viewpoint of the would be occupants. Broadly speaking, the problems of the rural poor and the so called urban poor have to be considered in different contexts. In the rural areas where housing shortage is estimated to be around 18.8 million (1985), it is not so much a question of shelter as that of land.

Since the beginning of the industrial age, the demographic trend has been more towards urbanisation. In India today the urban population constitutes 23.7% of the total population as against 11% in 1901. In fact, the rate of migration amounts to a mass shift of a population of 4 million annually—a growing and colossal trend. Migration is not the only problem. There is a natural increase in the population of urban area All this has resulted in a high demand for low-cost housing units as also an everwidening gap between supply and demand, the demand outstripping the supply. For example, in Bombay, the demand works out to about 60,000 units per year while the supply from the public and private sectors is 20,000 units per year. The costs are so forbidding that only about 20% of the population can afford to take advantage of such housing units. As a consequence the pavement dwelling and slum formation are the only possible (though illegal) modes of shelter. It is predicted that by the year 2001, out of 15 million people, 60% will be slum-dwellders.

Earlier, the major policy thrust had been to provide houses to low and middle income groups or special categories of economically weaker sections. The slums, where the urban poor have taken refuge, were then considered as undesirable and as blots on the metropolitan areas, and hence were sought to be cleared. The various slum clearance schemes introduced since then only added to the imbroglio, since in view of the formidable costs of rehabilitation. Scarce resources and the rapid growth of slums as also problems of social and economical dislocation, such schemes are highly impractical.

1811. Rew, A.W. *Access and implementation in low-income housing in metro Manila*. Bangkok, 1977. (Mimeo).

1812. Risbud, Neelima. Sheltering the urban poor. *Link* 21 Sep. 1986 ; 9-12.

1813. Ribens, Monique. Rare move to help the homeless, *Tribune* (Chandigarh) 22 Apr. 1986 ; 4.

As Ambassadors from all over the world arrive at the United Nations each day, they are confronted by homeless men and women, dressed in rags and blankets and huddled over steam gratings in front of the U.N. Secretariat building – poignant reminders of a growing tragedy in the U.S.A., and throughout the world.

Recent reports show that despite the vaunted U.S. economic recovery, poverty at the local level has not abated. More and more Americans are hungry and homeless.

In May, 1984, the US Department of Housing and Urban Development estimated that 250,000 to 350,000 people are homeless in America. Advocates of these "street people" put the figure at up to two million.

New York and Washington, home of many foreign diplomats, alone have 50,000 without homes and between 5,000 and 10,000 living on the streets.

The US situation, mirrored in every major city around the world, is of growing international concern,

At its 37th Session, the U.N. General Assembly proclaimed 1987 the International Year of Shelter for the Homeless.

Its principal objective is to secure a political commitment by the international community to improve the shelter and neighbourhoods of the poor and disadvantaged, particularly in developing countries. Top priority is being given to the task of providing shelter for the homeless in those countries.

The call to action has its roots in the world's burgeoning population. As U.N. Secretary-General Javier Perez de Cuellar reminded delegations in a recent report, world population will increase to six billion from the present four billion within the next 14 years "and it is not expected to stabilise until the middle of the next century."

He pointed out that the pressure on resources—including shelter—already has put many countries under heavy stress, particularly in the "gigantic urban agglomerations" that are a spreading phenomenon.

As Rafael M. Sales, Executive Director of the U.N. Fund for Population Activies (UNFPA), pointed out, the number of cities of four million people or more has increased within a decade from 28 to 41. He added : "The number of such cities in the world is projected to rise to 66 by the year 2000."

How are Governments and the private sector to provide shelter for such a concentrated mass of humanity ? The challenge already is almost too great, even in industrialised nations.

In the U.S.A., two elements of the problem are clear : the ranks of the homeless are swelling and there is not enough shelter to meet the increasing demand. The solutions being offered—temporary housing or soup-kitchen meals—arem many aruge, merely band-aids for a gaping would that is growing and festering.

1814. Rup Narain. Those shelterless unfortunates. *Janata* (Bombay) 30 Sep. 1956.

1815. Sahai, B.M. Housing the millions. *National Herald* (New Delhi) 26 Oct. 1983 ; 5.

1816. Saini, N.S. Human settlements : New Scenario. *Link* 21 Sep. 1986; 5-8.

1817. Schorr, Alvin L. Housing policy and poverty. *COP* ; 113-23.

1818. Schorr, A.L. *Slums and Social insecurity.* London, Nelson, 1964.

1819. Schumacher, E.F. Paterns of human settlement. *Gandhi Marg* Jul. 1976 ; 162-74.

1820. Sehgal, K.C. Politics of slums. *Hindustan Times* 12 May 1982.

1821. Sen, Amiya. Providing shelter to millions. *Amrita Bazar Patrika* 29 Oct. 1984 ; 6.

1822. Sen, N.N. Houses for rural poor. *Amrita Bazar Patrika* 12 Dec. 1983 ; 6.

1823. Sewalia, G.P. Housing needs more money. *Hindustan Times* 18 Jul. 1986 ; 23.

1824. Stokes, Bruce. Roof over one's head. In *Helping Ourselves.* London, W.W. Norton, 1981 ; 61-75.

1825. Swami, N.V.R. Housing the millions. *Free Press Journal* 9 May. 1986 ; 6.

1826. Swami, N.V.R. Moving forward to the year of shelter. *Tribune* 13 May 1986 ; 4.

1827. Turner, J. Barriers and channels for housing development in modernizing countries. *Journal of the American Institute of Planners* 33(3) 1967.

1828. Turner, J.F.C. What to do about housing—as part in another development. *Habitat International* 5(1-2) 1980 ; 203-11.

1829. Whither housing *Hindustan Times* 22 Jul. 1986 ; 9.

1830. Wilner, D.M. *et al. Housing environment and family life.* Baltimore, Johns Hopkins Press, 1962.

1831. Liyn, Guo. Housing headachestrik cities. *China Daily* 11 Jun. 1986 ; 4.

Human and Civil Rights

1832. Humphrey, Hubert H. Civil rights and poverty. In *War on poverty.* London, 1964 ; 95-106.

1833. Johnston, R.J. Individual freedom and the world economy. In *WIC* ; 173-95.

1834. Seymour, James D. *China rights annals.* New York, M.E. Sharpe, 1985. p. 195.

Imperialism

1835. Amin, Samir. *Imperialism and unequal development.* Sussex, Harvester Press, 1977. p. 267.

1836. Clark, Grover. *Balance sheet of imperialism : Facts and figures, on colonies* London, 1936.

1837. Rhodes, R *ed. Imperialism and underdevelopment.* New York, Monthly Review Press, 1970.

Income Distribution

1838. Aaron, H and M. Meamire. Public goods and income distribution. *Econometric* 38 (6) Nov. 1970.

1839. Adelman, Irma and Sherman Robinson. *Income distribution policies in developing countries.* Stanford University Press, 1977.

1840. Ahmed, Mahfooz. Mass poverty, income distribution and the role of fiscal, monetary and pricing policies. In *EAPS* ; 178-82.

Mass poverty has emerged as the major problem facing several developing countries in the ECAFE region, despite impressive economic growth in some countries and great potential for rapid development opened by the 'Green Revolution'. The phenomenon raises many conceptual problems, and often it is difficult to clearly identify its scope. Some identify poverty with subsistence living, while others distinguish between "absolute" and "relative" poverty. Poverty, in some instances, is related to the capacity to work, human dignity, state of unemployment, etc.

In the ultimate analysis, however, mass poverty and income distribution are one and same problem, and distinction such as "absolute" and "relative" poverty are illusory. Indeed "poor" are located on the lower end of the income distribution and distinguished from the "non-poor" by certain "acceptable minimum living standards" relevant to a particular country at a particular time. It follows that the "acceptable minimum" differs from country to country and will rise as the economy progresses.

The variety of concepts and definitions create confusion which is compounded by the complex problem of measuring mass poverty. Indeed, it is impossible to objectively determine the magnitude of poverty with available information,

While there is an urgent need for improving the data base for measuring the poverty situation in detail, the available imformation and techn iques of measurements at hand, provide a meaningful basis for arriving at a broad profile of poverty in certain countries of the region.

On a liberal assumption about the minimum acceptable living standard, it appears that 35-50 per cent of the total population is living below the "poverty line" in India, Pakistan, Bangladesh, Sri Lanka, Indonesia, Thailand and the Philippines.

This represents a staggering magnitude and presents a challenge for policy makers in these countries, a challenge which is varied in scope and content. Indeed, efforts are also needed for those who are at the lowest end of the distribution below the poverty line and those who are "just above" it.

There is close interdependence between mass poverty on the one hand and level and rate of development, structure of production and the state of the distribution of income, wealth, and access to opportunities on the other. Unemployment, undermployment and extent of existing income inequality are different manifestations of the phenomenon of poverty and thus form its integral parts.

The relations and interaction between these different variables provided a broad framework and determines the scope of policies. The relevant sets of policies in this context are :

(i) Policies leading to high capital formation and mobilization of saving and hence to rapid economic growth ;

(ii) deliberate technological choices favouring labour intensive techniquies ;

(iii) policies designed to re-distribute "resources" which are at the root of the problem of income distribution and mass proverty ;

(iv) price, monetary and other policies with a view to changing relative factor, input and output prices which lead to greater labour intensity and desirable changes in the production structure ;

(v) fiscal policies for reducing income inequality and also inequality of wealth distribution.

1841. Aigner, Dennis and A.J. Heirs. Social Welfare view of the measurement of income equality. *Review of Income and Wealth* Mar. 1967.

1842. Bandhan, P.K. and T.N. Srinivasan. *Poverty and income distribution in India.* Calcutta, 1974.

1843. Bressler, Barry. Income distribution, relative poverty and family size. *Quarterly Review of Business and Economics* 14, Spr. 1974.

1844. Burkus, John. Some aspects of income redistribution through social security in four Western European countries. *International Labour Review* 97(2) Feb. 1968.

1845. Carnoy, Martin *et al. Can educational policy equalise income distributional in Latin America.* Saxon Farnborough, House, 1979.

1846. Champernowne, D.G. Comparison of measures of inequality of income distribution. *Economic Journal* 84(336) Dec. 1974.

1847. Dowling, J. Malcolm *et al.* Income distribution, poverty and economic growth in developing Asian countries. *Singapore Economic Review* 30(1) Apr. 1985 : 1-13.

1848. Dharma Kumar. Changes in income distribution and poverty in India. *World Development* Jan. 1974 : 31-42.

1849. Fleg, A.T. Role of inequality of income in the determination of birth rates. *Population Studies* 33(3) Nov. 1979.

1850. Flegg, A.T. Inequality of income, illiteracy and medical care as determinants of infant mortality in underdeveloped countries. *Population studies* 36(3) Nov. 1982.

1851. Frank, Charles R and R.C. Webb *eds. Income distribution and growth in the less-developed countries.* Washington, 1977.

1852. Kakwani, Nanak. *Income inequality and poverty.* Washington, World Bank, 1978.

1853. Lamale, H. Changes in concepts of income adequacy in the last century. *American Economic Review* 47, May 1958 ; 291-99.

1854. *Low income groups and methods of dealing with their problems.* Paris, OECD 1966.

1855. Ojha; P.D. and V.V. Bhatt. Pattern of income distribution in an underdeveloped economy : A case study of India. *American Economic Review* 54(5) Sep. 1964.

1856. Oshima, H.T. Income inequality and economic growth : *Malayan Economic Review* 15(12) Oct. 1970.

1857. Pabkert, Felix. Social security and income redistribution : A comparative study. *International Labour Review* 98(5) Nov. 1968.

1858. *Public expenditure on income maintenance programmes.* Paris, OECD, 1976.

1859. Reason, I Economics of the distribution of non-agricultural incomes and incidence of certain taxes. *Journal of the Statistical and social Inquiry society of Freland* 20(4) 1959-61.

1860. Repetto, Robert. Effects of income distribution on fertility in developing countries. In *FDLDC* ; 254-73.

1861. Sawyer, Malcolm. *Income distribution in OECD countries.* Paris, OECD, 1976.

1862. Sundrum, R.M. Income distribution, 1970-76. *Bulletin of Indonesian Economic Studies* 15(1) 1979 ; 137-41.

1863. Titmuss, R.M. *Income distribution and social change.* London, Allen & Unwin, 1962.

1864. Under, D. *Rich and poor countries : A study in problems of comparisons of real income.* London, Institute of Economic Affairs, 1966.

1865. World incomes rise but the poor gets the least. *Amrita Bazar Patrika* 16 Apr. 1984 ; 86.

Inequality

1866. Ackerman, Frank. and Andrew Zimbalist. Capitalism and inequality in the United States. In *Capitalist System.* Ed. by Reich Edwards and Weisskopf. Prentice-Hall, 1978.

1867. Aggarwal, Partap C. *Half-way to equality.* New Delhi, 1980.

1868. Aggarwal, Pratap C and M.S. Ashraf. *Equality through privilege.* New Delhi, 1976.

1869. Ahluwalia, Montek S. Inequality, poverty and development. *Journal of Development Economics* 3(4) 1976 Dec ; 807-42.

1870. Ahmed, Karuna. Towards equality : Consequences of protective discrimination. *Economic and Political Weekly* 13, 1978 : 69-72.

1871. Anandan, P.I. Coronation and the depressed classes. *Hindustan Review* (Calcutta) 24, 1911, 529-32.

1872. Aryamane, R.V. Backward classes in the Indian Constitution. *Political Scientist* (Ranchi, Bihar) 1-2, 1964-66, 27-36.

1873. Atkinson, A.B. *Economics of inequality Oxford*, 1975.

1874. Atkinson, A.B. On the measurement of inequality. *Journal of Economic Theory* 2(3) Sep. 1970.

1875. Baner, P.T. *Equality ; the Third World and Economic Delusion.* London, Weidenfeld & Nicolson, 1981.

1876. Berthond, R. *Disadvantage of inequality.* PEP, Macdonald Janes, 1976.

1877. Bose, Nemai Sadhan. *Racism, struggle for equality and Indian nationalism.* Calcutta, Firma Klm, 1981. p. 249.

1878. Bowles, G. Schooling and inequality from generation to generation. *Journal of Political economy* 80, 1972.

1879. Carter, Gwendolen. *Politics of inequality, South Africa since 1948.* New York, 1958.

1880. Chaudidas, R. How close to equality and scheduled caste ? *Economic and Political Weekly* 4, 14 Jun. 1969 ; 975-79.

1881. Chauhan, Brij Raj. Scheduled castes and scheduled tribes. *Economic and Political Weekly* 4, 25 Jan. 1969 ; 253-63.

1882. Chowdhury, G. Equality before the law in India. *Cambridge Law Journal* 19, 1961 ; 223-38.

1883. Chowdhury, S.R. Equality before the law in India. *Cambridge Law Journal* 19, 1961 ; 223-38.

1884. Coates, B.E. *et al. Geography and inequality.* Oxford, 1977.

1885. Cowell, F.A. *Measuring inequality* Deddington, Oxford, Philip Alan, 1977.

1886. Cowell, F.A. and F. Mehta. *Estimation and interpolation of inequality, measures.* London, School of Economic, 1981. (Mimeograph).

1887. Fernandes, Walter. *ed. Inequality—Its bases and search for solutions.* Indian Social Institute, 1986.

1888. Fields, G.S. *Poverty, inequality and development.* Cornell University, 1979.

1889. Galanter, Marc. *Competing equalities : law and the backward classes in India.* Delhi, Oxford University Press, 1984. p. 625.

1890. Gans, Herbert J. *More equality.* Random House, 1973.

1891. George, V. Explnations of poverty and inequality. In *PICMC* ; 1—23.

Inequality is used to refer to the unequal distribution of income and wealth as well as of status and power. It is a feature of all contemporary societies irrespective of economic development, political system or anything else. There may be legitimate debate about the extent of inequality in different societies but not about its existence. While acknowledging the importance of status and power in society, this chapter is concerned with inequalities of income and wealth only. An attempt to explain these inequalities, however, will throw some light on the former, for the two are related.

Poverty is not so easily defined; or rather there is not the same consensus of opinion as to its meaning as there is with regard to inequality. If it is confined to income and wealth, two main types of definitions have been used so far. The first definition is an 'absolute' standard which does not change much over time or across countries. Rowntree's work in Britain at the end of the last century was the first serious attempt to define poverty in absolute terms. His work has been extremely influential on subsequent studies and on social policy both in Britain and in other countries. According to Rowntree, a family is in poverty if its 'total earnings are insufficient to obtain the minimum necessaries' for the maintenance of merely physical efficienty. The 'minimum necessaries' were food, clothing, housing, heating, lighting and utensils for cooking and washing—all purchased at the lowest prices and in quantities necessary for physical subsistence only. Once the standard has been 'scientifically' decided, all that is needed is to update it to take into account the rise in prices of the basic necessities.

Experience since Rowntree has shown that an absolute definition of poverty is impossible to sustain over a long period of time during which the general standard of living has risen substantially. Rowntree himself partly acknowledge this in his second study in 1936 when his poverty line was 40 per cent higher than his former one, after taking into account the rise in prices. The improvement, however was much less substantial when the two poverty lines were compared with the prevailing level of wages.

The main reason is, of course, the very obvious fact that what are considered basic necessities as the acceptable amount and quality of basic necessities change over time. It is possible, however, to maintain an absolute definition of poverty over a short period of time. The official poverty line in the USA, for example, is adjusted annually according to changes in prices but not in wages. Thus the poverty line for a family of four constituted 55 per cent of the median income in 1959 and 38 per cent in 1972. As a recent OECD report observed, it is not surprising that the extenty of poverty declined during these thirteen years because 'economic growth is likely to eliminate much of it without any special income maintenance programmes'.

The second definition views poverty in relative terms. It is based on the notion that needs are not physiologically based but culturally determined. It has a long theoretical tradition with such diverse exponents as Hegel, Adam Smith and Marx. 'By necessities I understand,' wrote Adam Smith, 'not only the commodities which are indispensably necessary for the support of life, but whatever the custom of the country renders it indecent for creditable people, even of the lowest order, to be without.' This view of poverty remained dormant and had little influence on social science thinking and on social policy until the 1960s when poverty was 'rediscovered' in the USA and in Britain. Its influence, however, has been greater on academic thinking than on actual government policy. Nevertheless, several industrially advanced countries began in the late 1960s to raise their poverty line annually to keep pace with the rise in wages. This enabled the poor, or rather those who relied on social security benefits, to gain from rising national economic prosperity. Thus a relative concept of poverty was grafted on an absolute standard—producing an absolute muddle, as we shall see in the next chapter. No serious work has been done to determine the exact criteria to be used in estimating the level of the relative poverty line. With all its imperfections, the subsistence poverty line of Rowntree was based on some survey work within a conceptual framework. Townsend's recent work in rigorously defining relative poverty is a welcome advance but it needs to be put to the test of applied research.

A general acceptance of the relative view of poverty and a general rejection of the absolute standard, however, can lead to incongruous conclusions in comparative studies. It can, for example, lead to the conclusion that the extent of poverty in India is not too different from that in West Germany, that in underdeveloped countries the extent of poverty, using a relative standard, is lower than using an absolute yardstick; and *vice versa* the extent of poverty in affluent societies is higher if based on a relative rather than an absolute definition. It is thus important to keep the absolute definition of poverty in mind when one is discussing conditions in underdeveloped countries. It is only in industrially advanced and affluent societies that the absolute definition of poverty has lost most of its usefulness. Even in such societies it is useful to keep the notion in mind and perhaps use the term destitution to refer to it to avoid confusion with poverty used in relative terms.

Relative poverty is not the same as inequality. It is only the tail end of inequality that prevails at any one time. Where relative poverty begins on the ladder of inequality is a political issue decided in the political arena of a country. The higher up it is, however, the greater its effect on the income distribution of the country. An acceptance of a relative definition of poverty does not necessarily mean that poverty will always exist, because it is quite possible for governments to ensure that no one has an income below whatever the relative poverty line happens to be at any one time. Clearly, too, abolition of relative poverty does not mean abolition of inequality though it does mean a reduction of it. Indeed, governments of many industrially advanced countries have proclaimed their intention of abolishing relative poverty but certainly not inequality. In spite of the fact that relative poverty is the tail-end of inequality, it is viewed differently both morally and politically. In Marshall's words, 'Poverty is a tumour which should be cut out and theoretically could be; inequality is a vital organ which is functioning badly.' A less emotive and a more correct way of expressing this is to say that moderate inequality is acceptable but excessive inequality is not.

For purposes of explanation, poverty is best seen as part of inequality. To explain inequality is to explain both wealth and poverty, for the two are the extreme positions of income distribution in society.

1892. Griffin, Keith. *International inequality and national poverty* New York, Holms & Meier, 1978.

1893. Guhan, S. *Growth inequalities and poverty in Tamil Nadu.* Madras. Gren-Am, 1984. p. 38.

1894. Hughes, G.A. and I. Islam. Inequality in Indonesia. *Bulletin of Indonesian Fconomic Studies* 17 (2) 1981; 42-71.

1895. Inequality and economic growth. In *Profiles of rural poverty.* Geneva, ILO, 1979; pp. 10-18.

1896. Islam, I. *Issues in inequality and poverty during economic development. The case of Indonesia.* Cambridge University, 1983. Unpublished Ph. D. Dissertation.

1897. Jencks, Ch. *et al. Inequality.* Penguin, 1975.

1898. Khullar, M.M. Consequences of unequal society. *Patriot* 11 Jan. 1980; 4.

Inequality in a climate of high incidence of poverty insures prosperity for the privileged minority in the higher strata of society.

It provides physical comforts and conveniences of life such as big houses, private vehicles, coolers and air-conditioners, fabutious furnishings, rich variety of food, expensive clothing and a retinue of servants to the elite. In the existing socio-economic conditions and the political system of the country, wealth generates tremendous capacity for the rich to influence economic policies and political decisions through bribe, participation or patronage. Strategic control extends much beyond the time horizon of a single generation and thereby it becomes dynastic.

Glaring inequalities give rise to a parastic class which is arrogant, exploitative and immoral. Vast sections of society, victims of deprivation and destirution, are subjected to inferiority complex with the tragic consequence of loss of hope, initiative and dynamism. Unequal access to opportunities caused by class distinctions breeds conflict and social tension. To maintain this inegalitarian structure vested interests continue to reinforce concentration of wealth. In the ultimate analysis, the nation adopts a growth path which preserves and promotes economic oligarchy and leads to impoverisement of human qualities, wasteful utislisation of resources alongwith the certain of a fiscal system, which creates the illusion of reducing inequalities so as to create a semblance of social justice and thereby keep the credibility of the government.

It is unfortunate that after more than two decades of democratic planning, nearly 22 per cent of the population is in a state of severe destitution. In 1977-78 47.85 per cent of rural population, 40.71 per cent of urban population and 46.3 per cent of the total population was estimated to be below the poverty line. The literacy rate, according to the latest figures, ranged between 13.92 for Orissa, 8.46 Rajasthan and 8.72 in Bihar as compared to 29.3 for the country and 54.31 per cent for Kerala. In terms of per capita monthly consumer expenditure of the weaker sections in rural areas, it was as low as Rs. 26.91 in 1971-72. Regarding assets of rural households, 66.3 per cent is accounted for by land, 17.9 per cent by buildings and 4.6 per cent by durable household goods.

1899. Kundu, Amitabh. Absoluteness and relativity in the measurement of inequality and poverty. *Asian Economic and Political Review* 4 (34) 1979.

1900. Miller, S.M. *et al.* Proverty, inequality and conflict. *Annals* Sep. 1967.

1901. Parking, F. *Class, inequality and political order.* London, MacGibbon & Kee, 1971.

1902. Reich, Michael. *Racial inequality : A polilical-economic analysis.* Princeton. 1981. p. 345.

1903. Roberts, P. Income inequality in some Western countries : Patterns and trends. *International Journal of Social Economics* 5 (1978).

1904. Rodgers, Gerry. B. Demographic factors in poverty and inequality the macro level. In *Proverty and population.* Geneva, ILG, 1984, 69-126.

1905. Russett, Bruce *et al.* Health and population patterns as indicators of income inequality. *Economic Development and Cultural Change* 29 (4) Jul. 1981.

1906. Selden, Mark. Income inequality and the State. In *CRD*; 193-218.

1907. Sen, Amartya. *On economic inequality.* New Delhi Oxford Univ. Press, 1973.

1908. Steiner, G.Y. *Constitutional inequality : The Political fortunes of the equal rights amendment.* Brookings Institution, 1985. p. 113.

1909. Weeds, Erich. Income inequality, average income and domestic violence. *Journal of Conflict Resolution* 25 (4) Dec. 1981 ; 639-54.

1910. Wriggins, W. *et al. Reducing global inequalities.* New York. McGraw Hill, 1978.

Labour Force

1911. Davis, A. Motivation of the underprivileged worker. In *Industry and society.* Ed. by W.F. Whyte. New York, 1946.

1912. Dharmarajan, S. Labour scene in 1985. *Yojana* (New Delhi) 1 May 1986; 4-6.

1913. Ezekiel, Hannan, Population and labour force. In *Second India Overview*, New Delhi, Macmillan, 1978; 26-40.

1914. Galbraith, John Kenneth. Industrial escape. In *Nature of mass poverty*. Cambridge, 1979; 108-19.

1915. Gallie, Duncan. In *Search of the new working class*. Cambridge, 1978.

1916. Hasan, Amir. Bonded labour is a social problem, *Pioneer* 28 Sep. 1986; 4.

1917. Hirashima, S. ed. *Hired labour in rural Asia.* Tokyo, Institute of Developing Economies 1977.

1918. Kriesberg, L. Relationship between socio-economic rank and behaviour, *Social Problems* 10, 1963; 334-53.

1919. Lewis. W. Arthur. Economic development with unlimited supplies of labour. *Manchester School* 22 (2) May 1954.

1920. Lipton, Michael. *Labour and poverty.* Washington, World Bank, 1983. p. 148.

1921. Lockwood, D. *Blackcoated worker.* Lonodon, Allen & Unwin, 1958.

1922. Lockwood, D. New Working Class. *European Journal of Sociology* 1 (2) 1960.

1923. *Poverty and minimum living standards—The role of the ILO.* Report of the Director General to the 54th Session of the International Labour Conference. Geneva, 1970, p. 51.

1924. Saunders, Kay ed. *Indentured labour in the British Empire*, 1834-1920. London, Croom Helm, 1983. p. 350.

1925. Shiva Rao, B. *Industrial worker in India.* London, 1939.

1926. Streefkerk, Hein. *Industrial transition in rural India.* Bombay, popular prakashans, 1985.

1927. Thorner. Daniel and Alice. *Land and labour in India.* Bomabay, Asia, 1962.

1928. Young, M. and P. Willmott. Social gruding by manual workers. *British Journal of Sociology* 1956.

Land Reforms

1929. Albert, Paul. *Partnership or confrontation? Poor lands and* rich. New York. Free Press, 1973. p. 269.

1930. Bowman, Isaiah. *Limits of land settlement : A report on present day possibilities.* New York, Council on Foreign Relations 1937.

1931. Crocombe, Ron. *Land tenure in the Pacific.* Melbourne, Oxford Univ. Press, 1971.

1932. Kajita, Masaru. *Land reform in Japan,* Tokyo, 1959. p. 30.

1933. Krishnan, Jairam. Degradation and poverty. *Economic Times.* 13 Apr. 1986; 6.

India has a land mass of about 329 million hectares at least half of which is degraded and whose productivity is far below its potential. In agriculture, out of 143 million ha. at least 40 million ha., are degraded. In the forestry sector, out of 75 million ha., 30 million ha. are without tree cover and 10 million ha., have only some shrubs. The pasture and grazing lands and other uncultivable lands are largely degraded.

In these categories of land approximately 175 million ha. consists of degraded lands and grazing lands, have been the most neglected and are perhaps, the most degraded areas.

There are wastelands due to water erosion (73.6 million ha.) which includes sheet erosion, ravines, riverines, water-logging and gully erosion. Wastelands due to wind erosion (12.9 million ha.) include shifting sand dunes, extra moisture stress and coastal dunes. Wastelands due to salinity and alkanity are about 7.5 million ha.

In terms of geographical distribution, Rajasthan has the highest area of wastelands with 18 million followed by Madhya Pradesh with 13 million ha. and Maharashtra with 12 million ha. Uttar Pradesh has 6.6 million ha. of wastelands. State-wise distribution is given in Annexure-I.

There is an alarming loss of good forests and good agriculture lands, anywhere from 1.5 to 2.5 million ha. per year. The loss in forest million ha. per year. If defoıestation continues at the present rate, there will be hardly any forests left at the turn of the century. Further, agriculture and food security would also be seriously affected.

1934. Krishnan, Jairam. Wastelands development : Requirement of funds. *Economic Times* 13 Apr. 1986;6.

1935. Krishnan, T.N. Demographic transition in Kerala : Facts and factors. *Economic and political weekly* (Special Number) 11(31-33) Aug. 1976.

1936. *Poverty and landlessness in rural Asia*. Geneva, ILO, 1977.

Living Standard

1937. Abel-Smith, Brian and Christopher Bagley. Problem of establishing equivalent standards of living for families of different composition. In *COP*; 86-99.

What criteria should be used to decide whether two households of different composition are at the same standard of living ? Given a poverty line for a household consisting of husband and wife, how much extra is needed for children of different ages to provide the same standard of living ? The question arises whatever method is used for establishing the original poverty line.

A solution to this problem is needed not only to make possible measures of poverty but also to operate programmes which attempt to combat poverty with cash grants. In both research and policy, much more attention has tended to be devoted to establishing the poverty level than to securing equity between different types of household. For example, the early crude calculations of the numbers of the poor in the USA virtually ignored the problem altogether. Though many countries do not have the elimination of poverty as the sole or necessarily the principal aim of their social security policy, the lack of equity in the treatment of households of different composition is a remarkable feature of most income maintenance programmes.

Bagley has demonstrated the anomalous provisions for children within existing British provisions for social security. There are three sets of provisions for children. The first-national assistance (now supplementary benefit)—is subject to a test of means. The second is benefit as of right which comes in two parts—family allowances for all second and subsequent children and national insurance benefits available only for children of the sick, unemployed etc. The third consists of allowances for children in the income-tax. The first and third but not the second provide allowances which differ according to the age of the child. The second (and in certain circumstances the third) vary the allowances according to the number of children in the family.

From 1948 onwards the National Assistance Board (now the

Supplementary Benefits Commission) has employed a uniform national scale for calculating the needs of household members. This scale represents the minimum level of living which is normally provided to those who apply for help and have no other resources. The subsistence scale has been revised periodically to take account of changes in prices and on occasions changes in the national income. The scale excludes rent for which separate provision is made.

The National Assistance Board increased the benefits for a married couple (excluding rent) by 18-19 per cent for a child under 5, 22-3 per cent for a child aged 5-10, 26-8 per cent for a child aged 11-15. The same percentages are used irrespective of the number of persons in the household. The variations between the highest and lowest percentages for each age group cannot be explained by price changes or by the desire to round each allowance figure to the nearest 6d. The Board has never explained precisely how it calculates its allowances.

1938. Bagley, C. *Cost of a child.* London, Institute of Psychiatry, 1969.

1939. Birla Institute of Scientific Research Economic Research Division Standard of living. In *World economic profile.* New Delhi, Macmillan, 1955; 117-31.

1940. Drewnowski, and W. Scott, *Level, of living index.* Geneva, U.N. Research Institute for Social Development Report No. 4, Sep. 1966.

1941. Franklin, N.N. Concept and measurement of minimum living standards. *International Labour Review* Apr. 1967.

1942. Wedderburn, Dorothy. Cross national study of standards of living of the aged in three countries. In *COP*; 193-204.

It is not the purpose of this paper to stray back to topics discussed earlier at this conference, in particular the conceptual problems involved in the definition of poverty. Nevertheless some references must be made to these matters because the interpretation of the preceding discussion of measures of poverty among the old depends very much upon such questions as whether income is a satisfactory measure of resources, and whether the 'income unit' or the 'family' is the appropriate grouping to use for the analysis of poverty.

The argument for using a wider concept of financial resources than income, at least when studying the standard of living of the old is a strong one. There is a widespread belief that, insofar as people are financially able to, they will save while they are working in order to have some assets to use in old age. There has also been widespread speculation about whether old people with assets do in fact use them when they retire, or whether they have not, by this time, acquired a habit of irrationally clinging to what savings they have. The information about the value of asset holdings obtained in the cross-national survey was rather scanty. Linking it with what we know from other studies, however, we can draw certain conclusions.

First, in all three countries, but more particularly in Britain, there remain considerable proportions of old people with no liquid assets, or with assets of such low value as to be insignificant. Between a quarter and 45 per cent, varying as between men, women and couples, in all countries, had no or very small amounts of liquid assets. There is also a high correlation between income level and asset ownership, particularly in Britain and the United States. Although there may be individuals with low incomes and large assets, it is mostly the people with incomes above the poverty levels discussed here, who are the owners of large assets. It can be argued that for a study of poverty it would be more satisfactory to devise some means of combining income and liquid assets into a single economic indicator. (Not owner-occupied houses or life insurance because these are so often non-relizable assets). It has been suggested that the assumption should be made that individuals will consume what assets they possess, evenly over the remaining years of life expectancy. Income levels would then be raised by an appropriate share of assets. But Morgan *et al.* who have made such a calculations report that "Adult heads over 65 with inadequate incomes receive on average only $135 or 0.7 of their average budget requirements from investment of their capital in annuities.

But a wider definition of assets than a purely financial one may also be of particular relevance to discussions of poverty among the old. On the one hand it is sometimes argued that the 'needs' of old people are less than the needs of younger age groups because they are entering their period of low incomes, with a home which is already equipped, and with stocks of clothing and household lines built up during their working life. On the other hand it can also be asserted that poverty and low incomes, where they occur among the old, are long-term features of the old people's existence. Indeed this is one of the special characteristics of the elderly's poverty, that there is little expectation of moving out of the condition for the rest of their life. Within the framework of the cross-national study it was impossible to investigate such matters as stocks of durable goods, clothing, etc. This would, however, be a very fruitful area for investigation, and specially on a comparative basis. Some work done on these lines in Britain suggests that at least in that country the low income groups are likely to have extremely low levels of stocks of many items of household equipment.

Finally, there is the question of help from the family to its older members. This involves not only the conceptual question of what is the most appropriate grouping for which resources should be measured—income unit, household or something wider still. It is also of relevance in assessing the role of the family in the 'culture' of poverty. First, however, it should be noted that our definition of income in the cross-national survey included all regular cash allowances received from any family members outside the dwelling. It did not include gifts in kind from such family members, because the questions were not asked in such a way as to enable us to put a money value upon them.

The cross-national survey established, however, that such help in kind was quite frequent, was probably not of great monetary value, and was sometimes two-way, that is from old to young as well as young to old. It makes very little difference to our estimate of poverty among the aged. Intra-household transfers are a different matter, however. For, of old people with surviving children, 42 per cent in Britain live with at least one child and 20 per cent in Denmark and the United States. Moreover it is among the poorest, particularly the poorest single and widowed women, that sharing house in this way is most common. In the United States and Britain for instance, more than 70 per cent of the women in the lowest quartiles of the income distribution are living with relatives; in the highest it is only 40 per cent. The estimate of the amount of poverty among the old might, therefore, be changed if the income receiving unit was defined more widely to include all members of the household. But without detailed evidence of the financial position of the rest of the household no superficial assumptions should be made. For we also know that, particularly in Britain and to some extent in the United States, significant proportions of the elderly women were living with unmarried daughters who themselves may well not have had a very high income.

Malnutrition

1943. Beenstook, M. Cost of nutrition in Indonesia and the poverty line. In *Health, migration and development*. Gower, 1980.

1944. Heller, P.S. and W.D. Drake. Malnutrition, child morbidity and the family decision process. *Journal oj Development* Economics 6(2) Jun. 1979.

1945. Luck, J. *War in malnutrition and poverty.* New York. 1946.

1946. Malnutrition : Silent death. *Blitz* (Bombay) 16 Aug. 1986; 3.

1947. Rao, Radhakrishna. Way to fight malnutrition. *Tribune* 2 May 1986; 4.

Among the important foodcrops of the world cassava occupies the sixth place and because of its tremendous commercial potential; about 80 countries round the world have taken to its cultivation. In 1983, the world cassava production stood at 188 million tonnes, corresponding to an average energy equivalent of 10.50 million tonnes of cereal grains.

In Asia, India and Thailand are the major producers of this highly favoured tuber. While in India cassava is grown in about 3.5 lakh hectares with an annual yield of 58 lakh tonnes, in Thailand about 1.23 million hectares are under cassava cultivation. In 1984 alone, Thailand exported cassava worth about $660 million.

Cassava, popularly known as tapioca, is easy to grow as it is tolerant to droughts and diseases and has no fixed harvest time. As a rained crop it is grown in the lower slopes of the hilly regions in South India. The average tapioca yield in India–90 per cent of it is grown in Kerala, Tamil Nadu and Assam—is about 20 tonnes per hectare. Field experiments conducted at the Agricultural Research Station at Mannuthy in Kerala have shown that 20 tonnes of cassava yield per hectare under sole crop stand can be increased by three to four tonnes by intercropping with groundnut.

As per the recent projection of the National Commission on Agriculture, the production figure of tapioca should be 40 million tonnes from an extended area of over one million hectares by the year 2000. Of the total cassava output in the country about 70 per cent is used as food, 20 per cent as animal feed and 10 per cent as industrial raw material. The starch extracted from cassava is used in leather and textile industries.

1948. *Report of the panel on composition and nutritive : value of flour.* London, HMSO, 1955.

Management

1949. Nair, K. Ramachandra. Poverty and its management in Third World. *Economic Times* 25 May 1984; 5.

When basic needs are not met individuals and families are said to be in poverty. Poverty is difficult to define. There are however, two broad concepts of poverty : relative poverty and absolute poverty. Relative poverty is often measured in terms of inequality in income distribution. Absolute poverty is measured in terms of some kind of notion of 'subsistence' considered appropriate in the circumstances of the particular family or society concerned.

In the Third World countries absolute poverty is malnourishment and undernourishment on a mass scale. Besides food intake, minimum subsistence needs of clothing, housing, education and health are also to be taken into account in ascertaining the level of poverty. Social functioning is adequate only if these needs are met. A minimum income is, therefore, necessary to fulfill the needs. This minimum income is generally referred to as the 'poverty' line. The number of persons or families below this line can then be counted as absolutely poor.

Poverty also means 'want' and 'deprivation'. These are closely interlined in the analysis of the dynamics of poverty. The dynamics of poverty are reflected in such factors as below average education, low quality education, hindrances to study, substandard housing, poor health values, illness, lack of hygiene, low life expectancy, high infant morality, unemployment, and underemployment, homelessness, family breakdowns and the consequent social and psychological stresses. Though many of these are not suspectable to accurate empirial measurement, they give an overall idea of mass poverty in a society. What is being witnessed in most parts of the Third World is grinding poverty of which the human society should be really ashamed of. What then should be done to alieviate mass poverty ?

It is reported that 48 per cent of the world's population is spread in 32 countries in Asia, Africa and Latin America which account for a mere 4.5 per cent of the world GNP and they enjoy less than US $330 per capita GNP. On the other extreme, 28 of the richest countries mostly in Europe and North America having only a population of 13.5 per cent account for 58 per cent of the World GNP and they enjoy a per capita GNP of more than US $7590 which is 23 times more than that of the poorest group. India ranks 12th from the bottom up, with a per capita GNP of just $210 which is lower than that of average of the poorest group. The world is thus divided into the poor and the rich and the bulk of the absolutely poor in the world are found in the poor countries of the Third World. It follows from the above that the eradication of mass poverty depends upon the nature of global environment and the pattern of world development,

Mass Media

1950. Bandyopadhyay, D. TV and anti-poverty programmes. *Mainstream* 18 Feb. 1984 ; 7-9.

With its expansion to cover 70 per cent of rural population of our country, TV can and should play an effective interventionist role in dissemenating the required information and knowledge about the anti-poverty programmes.

Though important, transmission of information is not the end of the process. The beneficiary groups having got the knowledge may not be able to do anything further unless their dependency and fear psyche could be substantially altered. Awakening of consciousness and raising of aspiration to seek a change from the present state of socio-economic stagnation is an essential pre-requisite for successful implementation of this package of programmes. Audio-visual media of TV could fulfil this purpose significantly provided innovative and imaginative software could be produced.

Requirement of the TV software can be assessed by looking into the contents of a few programmes.

The most important instrument designed for the alleviation of poverty is the Integrated Rural Development Programme. The basic philosophy of the programme is to provide income-generating assets to the assetless to take them above the poverty line. Since the entire assetless and poverty-stricken population cannot be covered all at once there has to be a choice. The principle accepted is "bottom-up": the poorest of the poor to be selected first to be followed by other layers of poverty groups. This basic principle is not well known not only to the beneficiary groups but to many in the operational agencies charged with the implementation of the programmes. That apart even where it is known it is hardly ever followed :

The process suggested is that after the family survey, that households should be selected by the meeting of the whole village to avoid any manipulation, favouritism, partiality and all that. This method also ensures a degree of democratic participation in the process of selection. But it is hardly followed anywhere.

Rural TV programme can in the first place properly inform the procedure continuously so that the implementing machinery becomes apprehensive of the retribution that may follow any significant deviation, and the beneficiary groups also become aware of how the programme should be implemented. Regional TV centres should select some blocks at random, interview the officials and beneficiaries, ascertain how the process of selection was followed and telecast it with commentary whether the correct methodology was adhered to. It should also live telecast the whole village or gaon-sabha meetings in which the beneficiaries are selected. Telecast of live situations of correct and wrong processes in the local language with the local faces appearing on the TV screen will have a salutory effect on the local potential beneficiary goups and would perhaps prevent gross misuses of abuse of selection procedure in future. A two-way information flow system may be evolved not only for the selection process but also for other items of activity included in the package.

The most difficult part of the programme is the selection of income-generating scheme for the beneficiary households. Initial assetlessness significantly reduces the asset absorptive and retentive capacity. Ideally each household should have a custom-made investment pattern. In actual practice, only a few schemes are pushed irrespective of the capability or willingness of the beneficiaries to accept them. Since targets have to be achieved within a given time-frame, assets are often very thinly spread to achieve the number, sacrificing the content. Moreover, quite a few beneficiaries are incapable of managing and holding on to lumpy investments which are only considered bankable and viable by the bankers.

What most of these households require is the conglomeration of micro-investments on a variety of items which are within the management capabilities of these households which may make the households viable.

1951. Berelson, B and M. Janowitz *ed. Reader in public opinion and communication.* New York, Free Press, 1966.

Middle Classes

1952. Abercrombe, Micholas and John Urry. *Capital, Labour and the Middle Classes, London,* George Allen & Unwin, 1983. p. 175.

Migration and Immigration

1953. Carruthers, Nirman and Aidan R. Fukai. International Migration. *World Politics* Oct. 1982 ; 106-20.

1954. Galbraith, John Kenneth. On Migration. In *Nature of mass Poverty.* Cambridge, 1979 ; 120-39.

1955. Grigg, D.B. Migration and overpopulation. In *Geographical impact of migration.* Ed. by P.E. White and R.I. Woods. London, Longmans, 1980 ; 60-83.

1956. Harris, J and M.P. Todaro. Migration, unemployment and development : two sector analysis. *Aemrican Economic Review* Mar. 1970.

1957. How to move millions, and how not to. *Asiaweek* 4 May. 1986 ; 52.

1958. Jerome, H. *Migration and business Cycles.* New York, National Bureau of Economic Research, 1926.

1959. Jones, Catherine. *Immigration and social policy in Britain.* London, Taristock Publications. 1977.

1960. Land, Thomas. Growth industry in poverty and hope. *Amrita Bazar Patrika* 4 Nov. 1985 ; 7.

They man Greek Fishing boats, do domestic chores in patrician homes in Rome and labour in Catalanian fields. They are illegal aliens, mainly from North Africa but increasingly also from Asia, who hold no work permits, valid visas or passports. They are insecure and unwelcome in their host communities and they are ruthlessly exploited.

Their number is in the region of 600,000 in Italy, 300,000 in Spain and 40,000 in Greece. But this may be a very conservative estimate. For illegal aliens are a growth sector of international migration, encouraged by poverty and hope. They number several million in North America and hundreds of thousands in West Germany, France, Belgium and Sweden.

A global study published by the UN International Labour Organisation concludes that controlling the twilight world of clandestine migration is beyond the scope of any government acting alone. Tough immigration laws and barriers erected in one country merely divert the flow to another with a more easy going approacch to illegal immigration.

Coercive deportation procedures are applied very seldom in Southern Europe. In 1982, Spain expelled some 2,800 foreigners, a third of whom had committed offences more serious than illegal residence. In the same year, Italy expelled 5,000 in addition to 15,000 illegal aliens who agreed to their departure. But at least 10 times as many aliens entered these countries during the same year as "tourists" and "students", in order to seek employment.

The foreigners do the lowest paid, dirty and dangerous jobs which the natives reject despite their record unemployment levels. In Italy, the study found that the desire of many middle class women to take up emploment has led to a "tremendous demand for domestic staff which the national workforce is unable to meet a kind of irresistible invitation to which young girls from the Third World are now responding."

The ILO study offers little hope for an early control of the illegal traffic in labour because it springs from the widening income gap between the rich and the poor continents. But the wealthy nations could collectively confront the issue if they were prepared to spend more on development assistance and insisted on linking aid with job creation in the poor countries.

1961. MacDonald, J.S. and L.D. *Invisible immigrants.* Runnymede Industrial Unit, 1972.

1962. Martine, George. Adaptation of migrants or survival of the fittest.—A Brazilian case. *Journal of Developing Areas* 14, Oct. 1979.

1963. Oberai, Amarjit S. and H.K. Manmohan Singh. Migration, remittances rural development : Findings from a case study in the Indian Punjab. *International Labour Review* Mar—Apr. 1980.

1964. *Role of immigrants in the labour market.* (Project export by the unit for manpower studies) London, Dept. of Employment, 1977.

1965. Salt, J. Geographical pattern of demand. In *Migration in post-war Europe by* J. Salt and H. Clout. Oxford, 1976.

1966. White, P.E. and R.I. Woods. *eds. Geographical impact of migration.* London, Longmans, 1980.

1967. Zachariah, K and J Coude. *Migration in West Africa.* Washington, World Bank, 1981.

Multinational Corporations

1968. Ade-Lawal, N. MNCs impact on developing countries. *India Quarterly* Jul-Sep. 1983.

1969. Astapovich, A.Z. *Strategy of transnational corporations*. Moscow, Progress, 1983.

1970. Attar Chand. Developing Countries and multinational Corporations. *Industry and Economy* (Bombay) Feb. 1980.

1971. Bereznoy, A. Multinational Companies of Hongkong, Taiwan and South Korea. *For Easter Affairs*. (1) 1983 ; 180-89.

1972. Bergsten, G Fred *et al*. *American multinational and American interests*. Washington, 1978.

1973. Casson, Mark. *Alternatives to the multinational enterprise*. London, Macmillan, 1979.

1974. Chadha, Chetan. Drugs and baby foods: Suray on the Third World. *World Focus* (75) Mar. 1986 ; 7-9.

1975. Chandhoke, Neera. Some social, poiitical and economic implications of multinational involvement in post-colonial societies. In *GGTOS* ; 185-96.

1976. Chellappa, D. *Transnational corporations*. Madras, New century Book House, 1985.

1977. Christy, V. Compaign for the heartland. *Multinational Monitor* 10-11 Jun. 1983.

1978. Code for multinationals. *Amrita Bazar Patrika* 21 Jun. 1985.

1979. Das, Nabagopal. Multinationals in India. *Amrita Bazar Patrika* 9. Jan. 1985 ; 6.

1980. Datta, Pradip. Making NNCs acceptable in Third World. *Telegraph* (Calcutta) 9 Nov. 1982 ; 6.

1981. Deo, Som. *Multinational Corporations and the Third World*. New Delhi, Ashish Publishing House, 1986 ; p. 221.

1982. Durrning, John H. Multinational enterprises and trade flow of Less Developed, Countries. *World Development* Feb. 1974 ; 131-38.

1983. Dutt, R.C. Overview. In *GGTOS* ; 197-204.

1984. Franko, I.G. Multinationals : The end of U.S. dominance, *Harvard Business Review* 56(2) Nov-Dec. 1978.

1985. Freeman, D.L. Testimonial for multinations. *Mainstream* 20 Mar. 1979.

1986. Furtado, Celso. Dependence in a unified world. *Alternatives* (Delhi) 8(2) Jun. 1982 ; 245-70.

1987. Glynn, Leonard. *Multinationals in the world of nations*. New York, 1983.

1988. Hamilton, Geoffrey. International code of conduct for multinationals. *Multinational Business* (3) 1983.

1989. Harjinder Singh. TNCs exploit Nambia's resources. *Patriot* 27 May 1985 ; 4.

1990. Howard, Michael C. Transnational Corporations and the Island nations of the South Pacific. In *GGTOS* : 117-60.

1991. Iranov, I. Transnationals in developing countries : Social implications. *Soviet Review* (New Delhi) 28 Oct. 1982.

1992. Khan, Rasheeduddin Khan. New global Leviathans. *World Focus* (75) Mar. 1986 ; 3.

The global economy in the second half of the 20th century is dominated by the transnational corporations (TNCs). Investment, technology, trade and the decisive instruments of what is called 'market economy' are all controlled by the TNCs. This is a phenomenon both new and unique in the economic history of mankind.

In the 19th century, the logic and repercussion of production processes of emergent capitalism in Europe led to the formation of transcontinental and transoceanic imperialism, resulting in the subjugation of almost two-thirds of the diverse human race in Asia, Africa, Pacific and the Caribbean by just about eight major West European colonial powers, for more than a century and a half. While building of vast kingdoms and even empires over contiguous areas and regions was a phenomenon even of the feudal and pre-feudal stages of socio-political development in world history. global imperialism was a direct consequence of the dialectics of capitalist expansionism.

Similarly while cartels, monopolies and oligopolies were a phenomenon of developed capitalism, politically supported by direct colonialism and administrative imperialism, the TNCs as 'global companies' operating at the time of the liquidation of settler-bureaucratic empire system is a phenomenon which is new, different and distinct, whose economic, political and human implications have to be carefully and comprehensively analysed. Because in the mid 20th century, marked ironically at one level by the massive process of political decolonisation that has brought into being about 120 new states as sovereign entities, the rise and expansion of TNCs, and 'planetary enterprises' having a 'global reach', have simultaneously also brought into being what may be called 'autonomous economic dominions', more powerful than most sovereign states, indeed even a combination of states, with an arena of operation cutting across national frontiers and hemispheres.

It has now been established without doubt that the TNCs latent power overwhelms national sovereignties, their operations transgress terriotiral laws and regulations, their dominance vitiates and subordinates national economies and priorities, and their massive economic control negates the very structure of political independence and sovereign jurisdiction of states gained after more than a century of colonial domination. Due to these attributes and propensities the TNCs should be recognised as new global leviathans, which are sustained as functioning structures of neocolonialism by the inequitous provisions of the Bretton Woods-GATT regime, and the entailing world monetary and financial institutions, which are loaded in favour of the developed capitalist countries.

TNCs are the product of far-reaching inventions, discoveries and basic changes in many branches of science and technology—especially in electronics, energy, chemical and synthetic industries and communications-that has ushered in the epoch of the second industrial revolution. The computer revolution, with micro-processors and micro-chips, which has brought into being the Technetronic Age, has increased the gulf between the 'advanced' and the 'backward' economies, and generated production processes for which even the entire globe appears a limited arena of operation. We therefore witness a basic contradiction between global economic processes, and global political reality. Precisely when after a long struggle, for independence against colonialism, political territorial sovereignties have emerged, they appear obsolete and meaningless in a world dominated by giant TNCs, whose political links with the ex-colonial countries and the world's biggest power, the United States, make them new sovereigns without crowns, new masters casting a shadow on the fragile structures of political independence of two-thirds of mankind. And what is their profile ?

Most of the decolonised territories are mini and micro-states, small both in area and population, and of course low not only in their GNP and per capita income but also in practically all other recognised indicators of socio-economic development like per capita protein consumption, energy consumption, literacy, availability of physician, life expectancy, access to celan drinking water etc., covering the entire spectrum of what is called the quality of life.

1993. Kowalewski, David. Asian strike against transnationals : Characteristics and consequences. *Asian Profile* Jun. 1986 ; 287-99.

1994. Kumar, K. Third World multinationals : *International Studies Quartely* 26(2) 1982 ; 397-424.

1995. Mehta, Balraj. IMF-World Bank in league with MNCs. *World Focus* (75) Mar. 1986 ; 18.

1996. Mehta, Satish C. Multinational Corporations in a developing economy : the experience of Nigeria. In *GGTOS* ; 87-116.

1997. Mishra, Girish. Multinationals and developing countries. *New Wave* (New Delhi) 27 Jul. 1986 ; 9-14.

With the end of the Second World War the process of the break up and final collapse of colomalism began with the Indian sub-continent going out of its ambit. By the end of the 1960s this process was almost complete. Now, except for Namibia and South Africa, colonialism has been wiped out.

It did not, however, mean that imperialism or the erstwhile colonia powers quietly retired. No, a new strategy was formulated to continue the economic hold over the erstwhile colonies. This strategy came to be known as "Neo-colonialism."

Neo-colonialism brings about a reconciliation between political independence of a country and its economic dependence. Under the old-style colonialism an imperialist nation hunting for sources of valuable raw materials and minerals, markets, and avenues for the investment of surplus capital had to hoist its own flag over the country grabbed by it ; the colonial power had to establish its own rule with "suitable" institutions and governmental apparatus and the police and army to keep the native population under control.

With the passage of time and changing world situation, this kind of arrangement became outdated and very expensive and strenuous. The two

World Wars weakened the colony-holding big imperialist powers ; the pressures from American finance capital for dismantling the barriers for its operation in other parts of the world mounted ; the October Revolution and, later the emergence of a world socialist systems signified a shift in the world balance of forces in favour of the colonial peoples fighting for their independence : and, above all, the growing power of liberation struggles of the subjugated peoples made it impossible for imperialist countries to continue their rule.

They were forced to recognise that "their interests in the developing countries no longer required the protection of governors in ceremonial dress, and expensive colonial administrations." They had to withdraw and some did with a show of "dignity" while others did after a lot of bloodshed.

Judith Hart has rightly remarked that the withdrawal of colonial powers or the process of decolonisation was "not the result of any romantic vision of the quality of peoples. It was an overdue recognition that twentieth century capitalism no longer required colonialism to serve its purposes, and that political and military costs of maintaining it were both high and unnecessary.

The United States had demonstrated clearly during the period between the wars, and in the decade after the war, that there were other methods of maintaining economic dominance. The USA was dominating the countries of Latin America not by direct political presence but through American private capital.

1998. Mishra, Girish. Taming MNCs : Need for a code of conduct. *World Focus* (75) Mar. 1986 ; 10-14.

The term 'multinational corporation' (MNC) is not a very old one. It originated barely 26 years ago when David E. Lilenthal (who had occupied very important positions under various US presidents from Roosevelt onwards) delivered a paper at the Carnegie Institute of Technology in April 1960, which was entitled "The Multinational Corporation". Three years later, 'Business Week' came out with a special report, "Multinational Companies".

Thirteen years later in 1973, the UN Department of Economic and Social Affairs came out with a study Multinational Corporations in World Development, trying to impart a precise meaning to the term. To quote : "The term 'multinational' signifies that the activities of the corporation or enterprise involve more than one nation. Certain minimum qualifying criteria are often used in respect of the type of activity or the importance of the foreign component in the total activity. The activity in question may refer to assets, sales, production, employment, or profits of foreign branches and affiliates."

The Group of Eminent Persons Constituted by the UN to study the impact of MNCs came out with the statement that "Multinational Corporations are enterprises which own or control production or service facilities outside the country in which they are based. Such enterprises are not always incorporated or private ; they can also be cooperatives or state-owned entities." It went on to underline the fact that MNCs could not be ignored in any meaningful discussion of world economic problems as they "are important actors on the world state....The total value of international trade. Their spread and growth has been one of the outstanding phenomena of the last two decades, and in many countries, outside the centrally planned economics, they have significantly increased their share of national output."

At present there are about 200 large MNCs which operate simultaneously in 20 or more different nations and are joined together by common ownership and management strategy. According to one authoritative estimate, the value added annnually by each of the top ten MNCs is greater than the GNP of some 80 member-states of the UN and it is predicted that by the end of the century 300 giat corporations will account for the largest proportion of world industrial production. General Motors' sales are larger than the national income of the Netherlands and the profit of Standard Oil Company of New Jersey in any given year is larger than the GNP of Costa Rica.

Among the MNCs the most powerful are those originating in the USA. In fact, directly or indirectly US giants control almost all the MNCs operating in the world. This fact needs to be borne in mind to grasp the implications of the struggle of developing countries to tame or discipline the MNCs.

Multinationalisation of large US monopoly firms started around the beginning of this century when the export of capital was undertaken on a large scale. It received a fillip during the twenties. During the thirties the export of capital slowed down but was resumed with greater vigour after World War II. During the fifties and sixties foreign investment of American firms increased at 10 per cent per annum (compound) and at this rate it doubled in less than a decade. After

1970 the rate of growth has increased and USA's foreign private investment will reach enormous proportions by the turn of the next century.

Up to World War II, in spite of huge foreign investments, most of the large US firms were, ton quote 'Business Week', "domestically oriented enterprises with international operation" but an important change took place during the following 15 years. "In industry after industry, US companies found that their overseas earnings were soaring, and that their return on investment abroad was much higher than in the US. As earnings abroad began to rise, profit margins from domestic operations started to shrink....This is the combination that forced development of the multinational company."

American corporate business does not think that its expansion abroad has come to an end. Instead it is relying heavily on the continued penetration of other countries' economics for its future properity. The American business no longer thinks that its own country is now the "land of opportunity." It believes that foreign markets offer the biggest potential for future growth. There are solid reasons to think so. Foreign sales of US companies have been growing at a much faster rate, profitability abroad is fantastically higher and by setting up factories in foreign lands they can avoid tariff and other barriers and get various tax concessions given by local governments.

The MNCs want monopolistic control over the foreign sources of raw materials and other such products and over foreign markets so that they can buy and sell on advantageous terms, transfer orders from one subsidiary to another and transfer their investments from one country to another whenever they think that by doing so they can maximise their profits and put pressures on host countries to come to terms with them. As one American expert has remarked : "for this what they need is not trading partners but 'allies' and clients willing to adjust their laws and policies to the requirements of American Big Business."

1999. Puri, Rama. Common heritage of mankind *versus* multinational *versus* multinational mining consertia. In *GGTOS* ; 161-84.

2000. Rothschild, Matthew. *Multinational look at the transnational Corporation*.Sydney, 1982.

2001. Saini, Mahander Kumar, *ed*, *Global giants the other side*. Delhi, Indian Institute of Research on Transnational Corporations, 1986. p. 222.

In the contemporary are the effects of Multinational Corporations

(MNCs) on various facets of development have been a subject of critical analysis both by well known institutions of the world including the United Nations System and its various agencies as well as by the different faculties of the universities and by individual scholars. In this connection several appropriate questions have been asked. More important amongst them include : (1) Is the national state strong enough to resist the effects, (evil, of course) of MNCs on different aspects of national life ? (2) Are the MNCs sensitive enough to adjust their operations to suit the local needs ? (3) Do the MNCs help the host country to achieve self reliance ? (4) Up to what extent do they restrict the development of endogeneous culture in view of their cultural and economic power ?

The spectrum of answers to these questions is very wide. The supporters of MNCs (including their home governments) not only defend their action in host countries but extend all the necessary help in the achievment of their goals. They are also backed by World Bank and IMF whose endless efforts for privatisation of national economics of the Third World countries have already shown miracle results in Latin America which is in the total grip of "debt-trap". Other developing countries are also fast moving in that direction. Through enormous profits which MNCs earn in Third World countries and repatriate them both by overt and covert means by transfer pricing to their home countries. In fact they are the main vechicle of neocolonialism.

These global giants control finances, technology and management which are essential for industrialisation and development of the Third World countries. After the fall of colonialism in Third World (though some pockets still exist) and for meeting, the imperative need of development for fulfilling the basic needs of teeming millions the newly liberated countries had no alternative but to open their economies to the Multinationals both under the pressure of international loan giving agencies like the World Bank and IMF and their erstwhile masters backed by the States of America which had drawn a plan of dominating the world after the World War II.

The plan included a system of military alliances for the containment of communism ; in political terms, to defend the democratic systems and to manage the left over colonies without physical occupation and in economic terms, to preserve the world capitalist system through the domination of MNCs.

The phenomenal growth of MNCs after the World War II, like the development of science and technology, is unprecedented in human history. Today they exercise tremendous influence or more appropriately power over the lives of citizens and governments of their home countries. In the Third World countries their influence is no less At time they have not even hesitated to organise coup de etate against those Third World governments which wanted to say good bye to them lock stock and barrel.

Visualising the control of MNCs over their economies, the Third World countries had been demanding at various world forums a mechanism to control them.

2002. Saini, Mahander Kumar. India : Undulating policy postures. *World Focus* (75) Mar. 1986 ; 15-21.

Multinational corporations (MNCs) or transnational Corporation (TNCS) in India today are the East India Company and Dutch East India Company of yesterday with a similar ideology of profit—making through exploitation of domestic resources with an equally subtler mechanism backed by financial and technological advancement of high order and the newer rubric of management administration. These economic entities were known to us prior to India's becoming a British colony, during the colonial rule, after the independence under all the previous Prime Ministers and now under Rajiv Gandhi's regime. After 1950 they have been continuously drawing the attention of the international community due to their increasing role in world economic relations. It is worthwhile to recapitulate the different phases of their roles in Indian society. They have passed through at least three phases : (1) Control era : Nehru's time 1947-62, (2) Decontrol era : Indira Ghandhi's time 1966-77, and Janata regime 1977-79, and (3) Free multinational era : Mrs. Gandhi's second term 1980-84, and beginning of 1985 with Rajiv Gandhi's government. Each phase has its own characteristics.

Soon after independence the Nehru government came out with the first Industrial Policy Resolution in 1948 which emphasised the need of participation of foreign capital and industrial expertise for rapid industrialisation of the country. The majority interest in ownership and effective control should, as a rule, be always in the Indian hands. Elaborating the need to control the foreign capital (MNCs) which dominated the country due to its past association, Jawaharlal Nehru stated in Parliament that the object of regulation was utilisation of foreign capital in a manner most advantageous to the country. Foreign capital was to supplement Indian capital as in many cases scientific, technical and industrial knowledge and capital equipment can best be secured alongwith foreign capital. As a follow-up action similar principles were emphasised in the First Five Year Plan.

However, in the late fifties MNCS were permitted with minority equity participation to meet the foreign exchange components for import of machinery and equipment. With progress in the field of technology the government's approach towards foreign investments and collaboration with MNCs became increasingly selective. MNCs were extended a number of concessions. After the Second Industrtial Policy Resolution (1956), the government appointed the Mudaliar Committee to suggest general guidelines for cases in which foreign collaboration might be allowed. The committee in its report recommended a liberal approach to foreign collaboration in the case of substantially export-oriented industry. In 1969 the government issued an illustrative list of industries where :

(*a*) foreign investment might be permitted ;

(*b*) only foreign technical collaboration (but not foreign investment) might be permitted ; and

(*c*) no foreign collaboration (financial or technical) was considered necessary.

The policy was further liberalised through Industrial Licencing Policy (1970). The thrust was to technological gaps in the engineering and chemical industries. Majority foreign participation was to be considered if the development of a paticular industry was vital and essential in the national interest and in other cases where a huge amount of foreign exchange was involved. To boost up the export, collaboration with MNCS in trading was also allowed.

In this era many MNCs could get a foothold in Indian economy, while some of the sectors like drugs were almost totally under their control as was revealed by the Hathi Committee Report. But the emphasis on public undertakings and the public sector development for realising socialism (many of the important undertakings developed with socialist help) kept the MNCs, if not under total control, at least at a low key in the economic sector.

Soon after Nehru's death Pakistan attacked India and the old MNCs operating in India tried to pressurise the Indian government. These companies refused to market the petroleum products which India was getting from USSR on rupee payment basis. In the 1971 Indo-Pak conflict ESSO, Caltex and Burma Shell were not prepared to process additional crude, even though they were operating much below their capacity. Soon after the Indo-Pak War of 1965, Indira Gandhi became the Prime Minister ; she went to the polls in 1967 and returned with a majority in Parliament. For some years thereafter she remained busy in consolidating her position. During this time the emphasis was on the sector and strengthening the concept of self-reliance.

In 1973 the Government enacted the Foreign Exchange Regulation Act, 1973 through which all the foreign companies were asked to reduce their equity participation to 40 per cent. This was done with a view to increase government control over the operation of MNCs in India. However, FERA proved otherwise. It increased the hold of MNCs over the Indian economy. In name all foreign companies after reduction of their equity to 40 per cent became Indian companies and consequently they were permitted to enter into those areas of the economy which were not open to them prior to FERA. Concessions which were available to Indian companies were extended to them like incentives and concessions for establishing industries in backward regions of the country. Certainly this role of MNCs in India's industrial development was against the proclaimed policy of self-reliance.

One of the most subtle methods of operation of neocolonialism is the MNCs. The modus operandi is (a) use of MNCs as a vehicle of export of capital to the developing countries; (b) use of MNCs as vehicles of unequal terms of trade; (c) use of MNCs for access to the markets of the developed countries; (d) aid; and (e) transfer of technology. During the control era and decontrol era, multinationals have used all these methods of operations, of course not with as much intensity as they are doing now in the "Free Multinational Era" which started in the post-Janata period but achieved its peak during the first year of Rajiv Gandhi's government.

2003. Saini, Mahander Kumar. Multinationals and Third World. In *Aspects of nonalignment*. Ed. by M.K. Saini. New Delhi, Kalamkar, 1980 ; 110-16.

004. Saini, Mahander Kumar. Multinational corporations and mini-multinational corporations in Third World Industrialization. In *GGTOS* ; 25-48.

2005. Saini, Mahander Kumar. *Politics of Multinational's* Delhi, New Delhi, Gitanjali Prakashan, 1981. p. 342

The development of science and technology in the twentieth century in the West was contemporaneous both with the emergence of Multinational Corporations (MNCs) and the national liberation movements in many colonies in Asia, Africa and Latin America. Consequently, amongst the many links between the erstwhile colonialists and the former colonies, the one in the form of MNC became overwhelmingly important in due course of time and posed a formidable challenge to planned independent economic and political development of the Third World countries. It is very well known that for the maximization of profit and for making their position and interest secure, the MNCs invariably resort to all kinds of chicanery such as encouraging political corruption, creating lobbies to favour vested interests and instigating coups d' etat in host countries. Once allowed to enter a developing country they operate like an octopus by entrenching themselves in the society. As a result, the drainage of wealth from the developing countries to the developed world and the dependence of the former on the latter continues unabated—a phenomenon not very unlike the one existed under colonialism. The old relationship between the coloniser and the colonised is replaced by business relations between two sovereign nations where interests are represented by the MNCs.

The MNCs are systematically eroding national sovereignty of the developing countries. Amongst the various methods of neo-colonialism the MNCs have established a novel pattern of exploitation through the mechanism of maximum influence in return for minimum investment transfer pricing, unequal terms of trade, transfer of obsolets technology and brain drain. It is imperative for the Third World to be on its guard against them.

2006. Singh, Harjinder. TNCs emploit Namibia's resources. *Patriot* 27 May 1985 ; 4.

2007. Stamp, Maxwell. Multinational corporations and private overseas investment. *World Development* 2(2) Feb. 1974; 123-29.

2008. Sweezy, P.M. On the new global disorder. *Monthly Review* Apr. 1979.

2009. Tomilnson, B.R. continuities and discontinuities in Indo-British economic relations : British multinational corporations in India. In *Imperialism and after*. Ed. by W.J. Monmseu and J. Osterhammel. London, 1986 : 154-66.

2010. Utrecht, Ernest. Economic development through export processing Zones (EPZs) : A brief survey. In *GGTOS* ; 49-76.

2011. Utrecht, Erust. *Social and cultural impact of the activities of TNCs in Southeast Asia*. Sydney, 1982.

2012. Wells, Louis T. *Third World Multinationals*. Cambridge, MIT Press, 1983.

2013. Wells, Lous T. Third World multinationals may benefit the West. *Asian Wall street Journal* 13 Dec. 1983.

2014. Whichard O, U.S. direct investments abroad in 1980. *Survey of Current Business* 61, 1981 ; 20-39.

National Integration

2015. Chatterji, Bhola. Poverty hinders national integration. *Amrita Bazar Patrika* 30 Jan. 1985 ; 6.

The twentieth century's greatest man of peace-Mohandas Karamchand Gandhi—was done to death because his theme song was universal brotherhood of man. About three and a half decades later one of the most celebrated statespersons of our time—Indira Gandhi—was gunned down because she refused to give way to the forces—social, religious and political—of anti-reason and irrationality. Both of theme lost their lives to diabolical forces which were the sworn enemies of secularism and democracy.

Secularism and democracy are the prop and stay of the Indian policy. Only on the basis of secularism and democracy can 700 million Indians of different religions, languages, cultures and ethnic origins be integrated into a nation. The assassination of Mahatma Gandhi was a stern reminder that the nation could take nothing for granted. The murder of Indira Gandhi rudely brought home to every sensible Indian the fact that something is rotten in the state of India, that Indians are not an integrated nation and that they are still prisoners of the vile passion and prejudice which politics of religion breed.

Justice, it is said, must not only be done, it must be seen to be done. Likewise, it is not enough to say that India has a secular Constitution, but secularism must be seen to be practised and that too at every level of the polity.

Can it be honestly claimed that the state unfailingly lives up to the magnificent promises of the Constitution ? Could it be disputed that the word and deed of the men who rule often reflect the wishes and aspirations of the dominant majority, which is but one among the many communities that constitute the nation ? These are facts that cannot be wished away. The nation will have to face its moment of truth if it is determined to make sure that Mahatma Gandhi and Indira Gandhi did not die in vain.

The country is passing through a crisis. Crisis of confidence, of ethics and morality in politics, of values in public life. A climate of violence and anti-reason pervades society; and forces of disunity and destabilisation are at work to wreck it from within and outside. Indeed, the country has miles to go before it can claim to have fulfilled the task. And what is that task ? "Millions of minds have to be convinced and millions of hearts have to be converted," in Arnold Toynbee's memorable expression, into accepting the basic truth that none will survive if the nation disintegrates, if the country falls apart. To talk about secularism in the given context, is not a futile academic exercise, certainly not to the people whose existence depends on the correct practice of it.

A brief digression : Independence came to a truncated ancient land that hardly had the time to rejoice at its liberation from colonial bondage. The country was overhelmed by uprooted humanity and an unprecedented communal carnage. But it did not disintegrate. Nothing daunted, Jawaharlal Nehru exhorted his countrymen to battle against whatever sought to destory India even before it could doff its swaddling clothese. He reminded his countrymen that they had made "a tryst with destiny" which could be redeemed only by lighting a lamp in the millions of homes where darkness reigned.

2016. Rajeshwara Rao, C. CPI proposals at National Integration Council. *New Age* 13 Apr. 1986 ; 4.

Poverty alleviation pragrams should be implemented properly under the supervision of committees of beneficiaries and corruption eliminated.

Drought-prone and flood-prone areas must be provided with immediate relief and permanent schemes to prevent floods and drought drawn up.

Public sector to be strengthened and expanded with the help of workers' unions and their leaders. Statutory minimum wage should be provided for workers in the unorganised sector.

Full neutralisation for the rise in the cost of living for all workers and employees, including government employees.

Cheap inputs and their easy availability, as also regular marketing mechanism, for handloom weavers and handicraftsmen.

Special measures to improve the status of tribal people, including return of their alienated lands and facilities to utilise forest produce freely: assistance to develop their cultures and languages.

Special development programmes for the least developed areas like the states of the north-eastern region.

Old Age Care, Pension and Insurance

2017. Bhim Sain. In the winter of our lives. *Newstime* (Hyderabad). 17 Aug. 1986 ; 4.

2018. Chandra, Suresh. Looking after older citizens. *Decean Chrrmide* 27 Jul. 1986 ; 6.

2019. Cole, D and J. Utting. *Economic circumstances of old people.* Codicote, 1962.

2020. Communities for the old people. *Japan Times Weekly* 23 Aug. 1986 ; 12.

2021. Esptein, L.A. Retirement income and measures of need. *Research and statistics Note* (2) Washington, 1964.

2022. Lin, Xin. Nationwide concern for elderly. *Beijing Review* 3 Sep. 1984 ; 4.

2023. Misra, Jayshree. Give them a helping hand. *Times of India* 26 Jul. 1986.

2024. Old contemptibles. *Pioneer* 27 Jul. 1986 ; 4.

"Grow old along with me, the best is yet to be". These off-repeated brave lines now mock the old in the face, especially in this country. The old and the very old now constitute a big section of the population, thanks to the slight improvement in modern medicine and health services. But by prolonging life beyond the Psalmst',s three score and ten, no service has been rendered to the helpless and lonely aged. With the disintegration of the joint family system the old people in the majority of homes are leading a life of unberable hardships and humillation. Social security is virtually non-existent in this country. The token relief prescribed by the state for the old and destitute does not touch even the fringe of the problem.

In other countries. especially in the West, where conditions are much better for the old people, there is now an increasing realisation that not enough is being done for the so called senior citizens of the state. Britain's old are getting older and there are many more of them. A survey shows that in 1951 there were an estimated 271 people in England and Wales aged over 100; by 1981 that figure had risen nine-fold to 2,410. The numbers aged over 65 have been rising steadily for 30 years so that the proportion of the population past near-retirement age reached 15 per cent in 1981 against just 11 per cent in 1951. By the early 1990s, a 'London Times' survey shows, the numbers aged over 65-age of retirement in U.K. will have risen by something over a further 500,000.

The age of retirement in most cases, is fixed at 58, even though the person, concerned is physically fit and mentally alert and capable of rendering useful service for at least ten years to come. It is not suggested that the old people should be retained when they reach the age of retirement, especially in a country where unemployment among the young is assuming menacing proportions. But when there are no social security provisions and very few-state-run homes for the aged, it is only fair that some provisions should be made to provide alternative employment even on a bare living age for the physically fit and mentally alert "old people" arbitrarily retired at the age of 58 or so, not only on humanitarian grounds but also for increased production and productivity.

It is noteworthy that the crises that have occurred in the U.K., Australia and the United States both in the cost of caring for the elderly through large-scale provision of Old People' Homes and the difficulties of monitoring and maintaining standards in them, have led to rethinking over the vexed problems of the aged. To put it bluntly: the old and the very old be disowned or drawned. The sensible and humanitarian thing to do is to cannot use all the usable in some capacity or other for the benefit of the community and not to create an explosive situation with millions of old people taking to the street agitating for humanitarian treatment by a state pledged to egalitarianism and claiming to be a crusader for human rights.

2025. Orshansky, Mollie. Budget for an elderly couple. *Social Security Bulletin* 23(12) Dec. 1960.

2026. Paillat, Paul, Old people. *In Low income groups and methods of dealing with their problems.* Paris, OECD, 1969.

2027. Problems of an aging Japan. *China Daily* 4 Oct. 1986:4.

2028. *Report of the enquiry into the financial and other circumstances of retirement pensioners.* London, HMSO, 1966.

2029. Seiritsu, Ogura. Proposal for phasing out public pensions. *Japan Echo* 12(1) 1985: 59r64.

With US President Ronald Reagan's landslide reelection late last year, people have begun to speak of the collapse of the "New Deal coalition" that has guided American economic and welfare thinking ever since the 1930s. The traditional policies of the Democratic Party's liberals, who advocate welfare and fairness for all, were unable to turn back the enthusiasm for a strong and economically reinvigorated America as promised by Reaganomics.

Japan, too, has seen the rise of a conservative philosophy extolling the virtues of small government, a shift reflected in efforts to build a more dynamic society by means of an administrative reform compaign and deregulatory programs in several fields.

Looking forward to Japan in the twenty-first century, we see that the largest and darkest cloud on the horizon is a demographic structure top-heavy in the old-age brackets. It is now virtually certain that the graying of Japanese society will take place with a swiftness surpassing that in any Western country. Can Japan overcome the attendant problems and maintain its dynamism and prosperity ? Or will the economy enter a period of protracted stagnation due to the side effects of the aging process. If the economy falters, it will become extremely difficult to provide the pensions and other services of an ample welfare system, and the productive population may have to shoulder the world's heaviest burden of tax and social security payments. In that event, Japan will be a far cry from the Japan of the high-growth days, when saving and investment levels were high, technological progress was rapid, and workers were diligent.

In his article Ogura Seiritsu argues that now is the time to embark on reform of Japaness welfare policies to avert an economic downturn over the long-run. In 1951, he reports, tax and social security payments combined were 33% of gross national product, a level well below that in Britain, France, and West Germany and somewhat below that in the United States. But the aging of the population will inevitably entail a considerable expansion of outlays for social security programs, the majority of which supply medical care and pensions.

According to a projection he has made on the premise that the existing set-up will remain in force, in the year 2025 Japan will have to spend 2.5 times more than it does today on social security benefits. Perhaps 45% of the monthly salaries of workers will have to be deducted from paychecks to cover social security premiums.

Ogura also analyzes saving behaviour. Traditionally the Japanese have been prudent savers. laying aside a large portion of their income for old age, and the economy has had a very high saving rate. The financial assets of the average person have risen over that person's lifetime, and the money put away by each age group has exceeded the amount saved by the same age group in earlier years. So far, Ogura reports, the expansion of pension benefits has not a large negative impact on the accumulation of saving deposits. As society ages and each productive worker carries a heavier tax and social security burden, however, the high saving rate will be bound to decline if people can look forward to living on pensions in old age.

2030. Shandas, E *et al. Old in three industrial societies.* London, Rontledge and Kegan Paul, 1968.

2031. Sharma, O.P. Aged population: Do they need more attention. *Economic Times* 1 May 1986:5.

2032. Steiner, Peter O and Robert Dorfman. *Economic status of the aged.* Besheley, 1957.

2033. Varsha Rani. Helpage : Infusing a new life. *Times of India* 26 Jul. 1986.

2034. Wedderburn, D. Financial resources of older people : A general review. In *Old people in three industrial societies.* Ed. by E. Shanas, *et al.* New York, 1967.

2035. Wilson, T *ed. Pensions, inflation and growth.* London. Heiremann, 1974.

Policy Framework

2036. Namboodiripad, E.M.S. Not by planning alone. *Seminar* (328) Dec. 1986; 25-27.

2037. Galbraith, John Kenneth Framework of policy. In *Nature of mass poverty Cambridge*, 1979; 92-107.

2038. Galbraith, John Kenneth. Political origins of error. In *Nature of mass poverty.* Cambridge, 1979; 23-43.

2039. Gumaste, Vasant. Anti-poverty programmes. *Economic and political Weekly* (Bombay) 18 Jan. 1986; 140.

2040. Haber, A. Poverty budgets : How much is enough. *Poverty and Human Resources Abstracts* (Ann Arbor). 1 (3) 1966.

2041. Horowitz. David. Strategy of the war against poverty. In *Abolition of poverty.* New York, Prayer, 1969; 110-56.

2042. Keynes, J.M. Economic possibilities for our grandchildren. In *Essays in persuasion.* London, 1952.

2043. Miller, S.M. and M. Kein. Poverty and policy. In *Social problems* Ed. by H.S. Becker. New York, John Willy, 1966.

2044. Moolgaokar, S. Moving to twenty-first century. *Mainstream* 24(45) 12 Jul. 1986;9, 31.

2045. Panigrahi, Chintamani. Anti-poverty measures and employment promotion in India. In *EAPS*; 153-62.

Removal of poverty has now been accepted as the foremoset national task. The problem has become so acute and challenging that many noted economists and social scientists in our country have applied their minds seriously to define the dimensions of poverty in figurative terms. Some have defined the poverty line in terms of a minimum calory requirement (of about 2,250 units), or alternatively as minimum per capital expenditure of twenty Indian rupees per month at 60-61 prices.

According to some in 1960-61, 57.8 per cent of the rural and 7.6 per cent of the urban population were below poverty line, In 1967-68, the percentage of poor in the rural population increased to 70 per cent compared with 57.8 per cent in 1960-61. Some other economists are of the view that the extent of rural poverty is on the decline. Accordingly to their studies, the percentage of rural population below the poverty line declined from 62.4 per cent in 1956-67 to 37.1 per cent in 1967-68.

But whatever may be the findings of different studies in this respect, the Planning Commission of India's estimate is that 57 to 60 per cent of the agricultural labourers live below the poverty line. In addition, the non-agricultural rural workers, like artisans, constitute another small section of the poor in the countryside. The Approach Paper to the Fifth Plan prepared by the Planning Commision states that 220 million out of 558 million persons in the country are estimated to live below the poverty line.

The major causes of poverty in India are underdevelopment

inequality, under-employment. She had all these things in her mind, when Prime Minister Indira Gandhi gave the clarion call to our countrymen in 1970, for straining every nerve to remove this blot of poverty from the face of India.

We must now try to comprehend, in brief, the extend and magnitude of the problem of unemployment in India as it stands today.

India is now soon going to launch its giagantic Fifth Plan. In the First Five Year Plan, non-agricultural employment to the extent of 5.5 million was provided.

In the Second Plan, the backlog of unemployment was estimated at 5.3 million, of which 2.8 million was in rural areas and 2.5 million in urban areas. Thus 17 million persons were in need of employment by the end of the Second Plan, while the actual employment that could be created during the Second Plan was not more than 8 million.

So, at the beginning of the Third Plan the backlog of unemployment were 9 million. In the Third Plan, the additional labour force potential was estimated at 17 million.

Thus 26 million new jobs were required to be provided in the Third Plan for wiping out unemployment. As against this 14.5 million new employment opportunities could be created between 1962-67, still leaving a formidable backlog of over 11 million persons needing employment by the end of the period.

The estimated employment in 1969 was 16.63 millions and in March 1972 the estimated employment was 17.98 million. With the launching of various employment programmes during the last three years of the Fourth Plan, the total employment provided can go up to 19 million. Even then the Fifth Plan will have a backlog of about 15 million unemployed persons. This no doubt registers improvement over the previous plans.

However, the estimates of unemployment in India are not precise. Information which is available relates to the number of job-seekers on the live Registers of employment Exchanges. But it has it limitations. Becuase all of the registrants are not necessarily unemployed and all those who are without jobs do not necessarily register their names.

2046. Policies of development. In *Profiles of rural poverty*. Geneva, ILO, 1979; 19-24.

2047. Policy options for poverty alleviation. *Kurukshetra* Nov. 1985; 4-6.

2048. Rangachari, K. Policy for poverty : Where there is a will. *Statesman* 19 Dec. 1980; 6.

2049. Reddy. K. Mahipal Anti-poverty plans. *Newstime* 26 Mar. 1986 ; 7.

The emphasis on anti-poverty programmes in the 1986-87 budget with a 65 per cent increase in the outlay, apparently justifies the Union Finance Minister's claim that the budget pulsates with the aspirations of the poor. The substantial increase in the allocations for anti-poverty programmes translates the government's rhetoric into reality which is a welcome step provided it siphons off the benefits to the deserving poor. The country seems to be poised for making deeper inroads into the citadels of poverty. The primary objective of these anti-poverty programmes must be to create and transfer resources in favour of the underprivileged. But the past experience has shown that the plethora of anti-poverty programmes have not been able to make a meaningful dent on rural poverty owing to enormous leakages in their implementation.

The benefits did not properly percolate to the targeted groups due to wrong choice of beneficiaries. Middle men and the bureaucracy have, to a large extent, gained rich dividends as it is evident from the serious lapses in the implementation. The lapses are due to lack of political will, conceptual flaws in the institutional framework and apathy of the bureaucracy towards the alleviation of poverty. First of all, the institutional structure and local elected bodies through which these schemes are implemented, must be rejuvenated, and revitalised and made aware of their responsibility.

The working of the IRDP and other related programmes have to be revised. The important facet of rural transformation strategy for banishing poverty is skill formation which should be performed through TRYSEM.

The quantum jump in allocations for anti-poverty programmes will provide only a temporary relief. The permanent solution for poverty eradication is revival of rural economy through intensifying agriculture.

2050. Rein, Martin and S.M. Miller. Poverty, policy and purpose : the dilemmas of choice. In *Economic progress and social welfare*, Ed. by L.H. New York, 1966.

2051. Rein, Martin and S.M. Miller. Poverty programme and policy priorities. *Transaction* 4(9) Sep. 1967.

2052. Sanwal, Mukul. In defence of anti-poverty programmes. *Yojana* (New Delhi) 1 Oct. 1985; 22-24.

2053. Sawhny, Karan. Anti-poverty schemes : Programmed to failure. *Statesman* 18 Oct. 1984; 6.

2054. Sen, Amartya. *Levels of poverty : Policy and change.* Washington, World Bank, 1980. p. 91.

2055. Sen, Amartya. Positive anti-poverty action is the real issue, not just the sanctity of controls. *Telegraph* (Magazine) 5 Jan. 1986; 4-9.

2056. Shakeel Chandra. Stress on anti-poverty schemes. *Industrial Times* 3 Mar. 1986; 3-4.

The impact of the deadly left book unleashed by the government of India when it hiked suddenly and steeply, the prices of administered commodities, particularly petrol and petroleum products, had somewhat been softened by the Union budget which mercifully has spared the common man of more tax burden. This is not to say that the tidal wave of public resentment and anger has subsided. What is percepitable is a definite decrease in its intensity as a result of Vishwanath Pratap Singh's careful balancing of political considerations and hard economic necessities. He has very ably corrected, to a great extent, the pro-rich tilt which was discernible in the last budget.

Perhaps the most welcome proposal of Budget' 86 is a provision of a large sum of money for anti-poverty schemes like the integrated Rural Development Programme and the National Rural Employment Programme which will greatly benefit the poor, especially in the rural areas. Any anti-poverty programme in under-nourished, over-worked, famished India is welcome. Another good feature of the budget is its equitious nature. It has indeed raised the stakes of the poor in the economy—perhaps for the first time since Independence.

The simplification of the tax structure (MODVAT) is bound to yield rich dividends. Already there is a demand to enlarge it and bring more industries under it.

In short, the budget has seen the beginning of the implementation of the long-term fiscal policy on a sure note. This would go a long way in achieving the targets of the Seventh Plan. The budget is but a small step in the right direction. It may well turn out to be a big leap for India which is preparing in right earnest to enter the 21st century as a leader in the comity of nations—strong, sovereign and self-reliant.

2057. Singh, Tarlok. Policy for poverty concentration areas. *Mainstream* 22 Oct. 1983; 33-36.

The approach to the problem of poverty has to be necessarily multi-dimensional. The policy framework within which any specific thrust can be pursued effectively has at least five major components.

These are :

1. Reorientation of social, economic and industrial priorities to subserve the basic needs of the mass of the population, with emphasis on development of human resources and social services and the requirements of the weaker socio-economic groups.

2. Structural and institutional changes, with emphasis on distributional policies, agrarian reform, reorganisation and strengthening of the unorganised segments of the economy.

3. Developing for each region in the country a composite rural-industrial structure appropriate to local conditions and resource endowments in which agriculture and industry are planned together as a system along with the necessary economic and social overheads.

4. Following up concrete strategies for bringing about a fundamental transformation in the specific conditions that govern in each area the life and livelihood of each of the socio-economic groups most affected by the condition of poverty. These include a large proportion of small farmers, the vast majority of marginal farmers, tenant-cultivators, landless labourers, rural artisans and those engaged in traditionally poor occupations. There is certainly a place in the scheme of development for picking out the poorest among these groups for special support. But more broadly conceived programmes are essential for achieving any significant progress.

5. There are large areas in the country which are relatively easy to identify which can be correctly described as Poverty Concentration Areas. Besides areas under extreme pressure of population, Poverty Concentration Areas clearly include tribal areas, hill areas, drought-prone and desert areas, chronically

flood-affected areas, coastal areas affected by salinity, and much of the north-east region of the country. (These latter areas have been recently studied in some depth under the appeal-lation of 'Backward Areas' by a National Committee appointed by the Planning Commission with B. Sivaraman as Chairman).

Together the Poverty Concentration Areas of the country hold a very large proportion of the poor. Aided by wide strategies encompassed under the first-four policy directions mentioned above, a national focus on Poverty Concentration Areas would now constitute a major contribution to the attack on poverty.

For several years attempts have been made to identify backward regions, districts and areas. Every State has its own view about areas which require additional support by way of development because of their backwardness. Often the focus has been on attracting increased investment or assistance from the Centre and on expansion of credit by banks and other financial insititutions which work under guidelines set by the Centre.

There are many obvious overlaps between the approach of identifying Backward Areas and Poverty Concentration Areas. When an area is described as backward, we have an view specially the state of the infrastructure, its weak base in natural resources and endowments and, consequently, its low levels of productivity. Weakness in these respects is invariabily accompanied by weakness in education, health, and other social indicators. In focussing attention on poverty concentration in an area, the primary emphasis is on people, their conditions, occupations, skills, productivity, etc. Concern with Poverty Concentration Areas should lead us, within each area, to identification of the socio-economic groups whose poverty has to be diminished as speedily as possible. There is an intimate relation between strengthening the economy of an area and dealing through direct measures with the poverty of specified socio-economic groups. Neither approach is sufficient by itself. Making out an area on pertinent grounds as a Poverty Concentration Area implies action both in terms of the economy and resource base and in terms of the population and the socio-economic groups of which it is composed.

2058. Sukhatme, P.V. Wasteful programmes will not do. *Economic Times* 26 Jun. 1986.

Poverty is a relative concept. It varies with the general level of living in a society, which in turn varies overspace and time. The connotation of poverty in richer societies, like the U.S.A., is sure to be different from that in poor societies, like India or Bangladesh. Similarly, the connotation of poverty in India of ancient times was presumably somewhat different from what we understand as poverty today. But this also means that it is possible and meaninfgul to define or measure poverty in an absolute sense for a particular society at any point in time . . . . Absolute poverty is best defined in terms of an income level demarcating the poor from the rest.

The question is how to arrive at this income. In poverty in India (Dandekar and Rath) this level of income is arrived at for the different States of India, by ascertaining with the help of actual household expenditure data for different categories of rural households, classified on the basis of their average per capita consumption expenditure on all items, collected by the N.S.S.O. in 1961-62, that level of total per capita expenditure at which the average household in the group was able to provide to its members food giving 2250 calories per person per day. No such norm(s) was specified about the non-food part of the household expenditure : whatever such households spent on non-food items was considered adequate for defining the poverty line. This was one way of arriving at the level of total income (or expenditure) by which a normal household in rural India (state-wise could be considered to be poor or otherwise.

It may be pointed out that it is quite possible that there were households who, though below this level of total income (or expenditure), were in fact able to ensure the specified calories to their members by either a "judicious" choice of the items of food and their quantities or by spending more on food and less on non-food than the general run of the poor. Similarly, there may be many non-poor households whose members did not actually consume food that ensured the specified calories. Obviously the proportion of such households in the expenditure categories higher or lower than the poverty line was not high; otherwise the average calorie figures for such categories would have been the reverse of what was actually observed.

2059. War on poverty. *Madhya Pradesh Chronicle* 9 Aug. 1983; 4.

2060. War on poverty. *Decean Chronicle* 12 Mar. 1986; 6.

Population

2061. Adegobola, O. New estimates of fertility and child mortality in Africa, South of the Sahara. *Population Studies* Nov. 1977.

2062. Agarwal, S.N. *Population* New Delhi, NBT, 1978.

2063. Aird, Fertility decline in China. In *FDLDC* : 119-228.

2064. Aird, J.S. Population growth in the People's Republic of China. *In Chiness economy post Mao.* Washington, JEC, Govt. Printing Office, 1978, 439-75.

2065. Allman, James. *Natural fertility and associated intermediate variables in some Arab Countries.* Battelle FDP Working Paper No. 7, Feb. 1979.

2066. Andorka, Rudolf. *Determinants of fertility in advanced societies.* London, Methuen, 1978.

2067. Andorka, Rudolf. *Population and socio-economic change in peasant societies : the historical record of Hungary : 1700* to the present. Rome, FAO, 1978.

2068. Anker, Richard *et al. Fertility determinants in developing countries. A case study of Kenya.* Liege, Ordina, 1982.

2069. Anker, Richard and J.C. Knowles. Emrpirical analysis of mortality differentials in Kenya at the macro and micro levels. *Economic Development and cultural change* 29 (1) Oct. 1980.

2070. Antonovsky, Aaron and Judith Bernstein. Social class and infant mortality. *Social science and Medicine.* 11, 1977; 453-70.

2071. Arthur, Brian W and G. Mc Nicoll. Analytical survey of population and development in Bangladesh. *Population and Development Review* 4(1) 1978.

2072. Arthur, Brian W. and G. Mc Nicoll. Optimal time paths with age dependence : A theory of population policy. *Review of Economic Studies.* 44(1) Feb. 1977.

2073. Bad Population policy. *International Herald Tribune* 30-31 Aug. 1986; 4.

2074. Banister, J and S.H. Preston, Mortality in China. *Population and Develapment Review* 7, 1981; 98-110.

2075. Basu, A.B. Need for population control in India economy. *Economic studies* 22 (2) 1981; 143-46.

2076. Becker, G. *Human Capital* Columbia Univ. Press, 1964.

2077. Berelson, B. *Ed. Population policies in developed countries.* New York, 1974.

2078. Blaikie, Piers, M. *Family planning in India.* London, Edward Arnold, 1975.

2079. Blandy, Richard J. Welfare analysis of fertility reduction. *Economic Journal* 24, 1974.

2080. Bondestam, L and S. Bergstrom. *Poverty and population control.* London, Academic Press, 1980.

2081. Bose, S.K. Challenge of numbers of, not of poverty. *Northern India Patrika.* 8 Nov. 1985; 4.

2082. Brody, J.A. Prospects for an aging population. *Nature* 6 Jun. 1985; 463-66.

2083. Brown, Lester R. *Population growth, food needs and production problems world population and food supplies, 1980.* Madison, Wis. American society of Agronomy, 1965. (Special Pub. no. 6).

2084. Caldwell, John C and Chukuka Okonjo *eds. Population of tropical Africa.* New York, 1975. Columbia University.

2085. Caldwell, John C. Fertility in Africa. In *FDLDC*; 79-118.

2086. Carr-Saunders, A.M. Fallacies about over-population. *Foreign Affairs* 9(4) Jul. 1931.

2087. Carr-Saunders, A.M. *et al. Population problem : the experts and the public.* London, George Allen & Unwin, 1938.

2088. Carr-Saunders, A.M. *World population : Past growth and present trends.* Oxford, 1936.

2089. Cassen, R.H. *India : Population, economy and society.* London, Macmillan, 1978.

2090. Cassen, R.H. Population and development : A survey *World with Development* 4, 1976; 785-830.

2091. Charles, R.J. Third World's struggle to use people power. *Futurist* 8, Dec. 1974; 285-86.

2092. Cleland, Wendell. *Population problem on Egypt.* Ephrata, Pa, Science Press, 1936.

2093. Crole, A.J, *et al. Human fertility in Russia since the 19th Century.* Princeton, 1979.

2094. Crocker, W.R. *Japanese population problem. The Coming crisis.* London, George Allen & Unwin, 1931.

2095. Davis, Kingsley. *Population of India and Pakistan.* Princeton, 1951.

2096. Davis, Kingsley. Population policies : Will the current programme succeed ? *Science* 10 Nov. 1967.

2097. Demeny, Paul. On the end of the population explosion. *Population and Development Review* Spr. 1979.

2098. Eberstadt, Nick. Recent in declines fertility in less Developed Countries, and what population planning may learn from them. In *FDLDC*; 29-71.

2099. Eggebeen. David and Peter Uhlenberg. Changes in the organization of men's lives, 1960-80. *Family Relations* Apr. 1985; 251-57.

2100. Ehrlich, Paul. *Population bomb* New York, Ballantine, 1968.

2101. Enke, S. Reducing fertility to accelerate development. *Economic Journal* 84 (334) Jun. 1974.

2102. Fawcett, C.B. Some factors in population density. *Problems of Population*, 1931. London, International Union for the Scientific Investigations of Population Problems.

2103. Ferenczi, Imre. *Synthetic optimum of population.* Pan's, League of Nations, 1938.

2104. Firebangh, Glenn. Population density and fertility in 22 Indian Villages *Demography* 19 (4) Nov. 1982.

2105. Flinn, M.W. *European demagrophic system, 1500-1820.* Brighton, Harvester Press, 1981.

2106. Frank, Odile. Infertility in Sub-Saharah Africa. *Population and Development Review* 9 (1) Mar. 1983.

2107. Frederiksen, P.C. Further evidence on the relationship between population density and infrastrcutre. *Economic Development and Cultural Change* 29 (4) Jul. 1981.

2108. Frisch, Rose E. Population, nutrition and fecundity. In *FDLDC*; 319-36.

2109. Fuchs, R.J. and G.J. Demko. Population distribution policies in developed socialist and western countries. *Population and Development Review* Sep. 1979.

2110. Geisert, Harold L. *World population pressures.* Washington, 1958 p. 46.

2111. Ginzberg, Eli. *Human resources : The wealth of a nation.* New York, 1958. p. 183.

2112. Glass, D.V. *Population policies and movements in Europe.* Oxford, 1940.

2113. Goodstadt, L.F. China's one-child family : Policy and public response. *Population and Development Review* 8, 1982; 37-58.

2114. Gottfried, R.S. *Epidemic disease in 15th century England : The medical response and the demographic consequences.* Leicester Univ. Press, 1978.

2115. Gwatkin, D.R. Political will and family planning : The implications of India's emergency experience. *Population and Development Review* 5, 1979; 29-59.

2116. Harvey D.W. Population, resources and the ideology of science. *Economic Geography* 50, 1974; 256-77.

2117. Hashmi, Sultan S. Population aspects. In *EAPS*; 163-77.

Today, the population base in the less developed countries is as large as 2800 millions. The rate of population growth is 2.5 per cent per annum, implying doubling of the population in 28 years. As economic development has been handicapped by the lead taken by the growth of population, no significant progress in raising the living standard of the people is being made. Under such demographic conditions, it is difficult to expect that a viable socio-economic development which will generate modernisation necessary to faciliate demographic transition from high to low level of fertility will be achieved. This is the dilemma which most of the developing countries of the world, and of the ECAFE region in particular, are faced with today.

Between 1900 and 1950 the rate of population growth in the ECAFE region averaged around 0.7 per cent per annum. As of 1940, the total population of the region number around 1,216 million. It was a period of high fertility and high mortality. The expectation of life at birth ranged between 30 to 40 years, implying that most people were dying before completing their productive and reproductive periods. Until 1940 a modest rate of economic growth of 2 to 3 per cent per annum was sufficient to off-set the effect of population growth and to show some progress. In addition, the communications media in those days were much less improved and the aspirations of the people were moderate.

The sudden rise in the annual rate of growth in the ECAFE region from 0.8 per cent in the 1940s to 1.9 per cent in the 1950s swelled the population size to 1460 million by 1955 and to 1600 million by 1950. This upsurge alarmed many planners in the ECAFE region as the targets set in the development plans were not achieved. In many countries the 1960/1961 round of censuses indicated a larger population size than was projected for planning purposes. This major set-back to development brought awareness among the planners of the effect of population on economic development. This concern was reflected in the First Asian population Conference organized by ECAFE in New Delhi in 1963. The Conference was attended by representatives of ECAFE member governments and experts in population and development planning. After reviewing the demographic situation and examining the implications of population growth for economic and social development planning, the Conference made a number of recommendations including positive action by governments to moderate the rate of population growth. Recognising the interrelationship between population and economic and social development, the Conference also rccommended that "A national population policy should be integrated with policies and programmes in related economic and social spheres."

It was a significant step in the history of development planning that the definite role of population was identified. By the early 1960s several countries had established family planning programmes. But these programmes were established in the Ministry of Health, and were not made an integral part of the development strategy and planning as was recommended by the first Asian Population Conference (APC). In actual practice only the symptoms and consequences of population growth heve been considered since the first APC. The unindirectional focus on the effect of population on economic and social development and the neglect of the feed back effect of changes in economic and social development have resulted in imbalanced development.

The review and appraisal of the United Nations First Development Decade (1960-1970) has shown that the performance of developing countries on the average fell short of the target of 5 per cent per annum or growth in gross national product. They were able to achieve an annual rate of increase of about 2 per cent in their per capita gross domestic product during the period 1960-67. The review also showed that the performance of many countries "with low per capita income and large population has been totally inadequate". The review prepared by ECAFE for countries of the region also drew the same conclusions. A more recent report prepared by the UNCTAD on trade and development policies in the 1970s maintained that about three-quarters of the total population of the Third World lived in countries where the economic growth rates were significantly below the contemplated target.

The relationship between population change and development has already been covered to some extent in the previous sections. So far, poverty, which is a negative phase of economic and social development has been indirectly dealt with. In this section, an attempt is made to show the interrelationship between determinants of population change and of poverty. Each of the determinants of population change, i.e., fertility, mortality and migration, has a close interaction with both the positive and the negative phases of development. The rate of population growth, which is a by-product of fertility, mortality and migration, has a positive association with the negative phase of development of poverty.

The concept of poverty has so far not been defined precisely for generic reasons. Poverty is a relative term. Who is poor cannot be determined without a reference to who is rich within a given context. What are the determinants of poverty ? This is a somewhat difficult question which should be examined by researchers, planners and policy makers for improving implementation of anti-poverty strategies and plans.

The magic figure of "40 per cent" population below the poverty line for the less developed countries is commonly being used. The statistical bases of this figure are not yet known. As poverty is a relative term, the same proportion of the poor in each country will have different meanings depending upon the level of development. For example, 40 per cent in a country with a per capita income of less than 100 US dollars will have a different meaning than a country with a per capita income of 150 to 2,000 dollars as regards to subsistance, although not, perhaps with an impoverished individuals perception of his plight.

2118. Hanser, P. *ed. World population and development : Challenges and prospects.* New York, Syracuse University Press. 1979.

2119. Hell, Broner and L. Robert. Growth and Survival. *American Review* Sum. 1973.

2120. Henry, Alice and P. Piotrow. Age at marriage and fertility. *Population Reports* Nov. 1979.

2121. Hofferth, Sandra I Updating children's lifecourse. *Journal of Marriage and the Family* Feb. 1985; 93-115.

2122. Horowitz, David. Population. In *Abolition of Poverty*. New York, Prayer, 1969; 49-71.

2123. *Kenya Population Census*. Nairobi, Govt. Printer, 1962.

2124. Kirby, E. Stuart. Population pressure. In *Economic development in East Asia*. London, 1967; 32-41.

2125. Krishanaji, N. Poverty and fertility : A review of theory and evidence. *Economic and Political weekly* 18 (19-21) May. 1983.

2126. Lee, Ronald Denos *ed*. *Population patterns in the past*. New York, Academic Press, 1977.

2127. Masrick, G. and M.J. Bane. *Nation's families*; 1960-1990. Cambridge. 1980.

2128. Mauldin, W. Barker *et al*. Conditions of fertility decline in developing countries, 1950-1975 : *Studies in Family Planning* See also *FDLDC*; 72-96.

2129. McFalls, Joseph A. Frustrated fertility : A population Paradox. *Population Bulletin* May 1979.

2130. McGurk, H. *Growing and changing*. Methuen, 1975.

2131. McKeown Thomas. *Modern rise of population*. New York, Academic Press, 1976.

2132. Mitra, Asok. *India's population : Aspects of quality and control*. New Delhi, Abhinav Publication, 1978.

2133. Morawetz, David, Basic needs policies and population growth. *World Development* 6 (11-12) 1978.

2134. Morris, M. David *Measuring the condition of the world's poor : the physical quality of life index*. New York, Pergomon Press 1979.

2135. Morrison, Malcolm H. Work and retirement in the aging society. *Daedalus* Win. 1986; 269-94.

2136. Morrison, Thomas K. Effects of population size and population density on the manufactured exports of developing countries. *Southern Economic Journal* 43 (3) Jan. 1977.

2137. Myrdal, Gunnar, Economic effects of population development. In *Economic development*. Bombay, Vora, 1966; 33-52.

2138. Nevett, A. *Population explosion or control.* London, Chapman, 1964.

2139. Ohlin, Goran. *Population control and economic development.* Paris, OECD, 1967.

2140. Padmanabha, P. Population : Decisive decades ahead. *Economic Studies* 22 (1) 1981; 97-107.

2141. Page, H.J and R.J. Lesthaeghe *eds, Child-spacing in Tropical Africa.* London, Academic Press; 1981.

2142. Peterson, W. *Politics of population.* London, Gollanez, 1964.

2143. Petersen, William. American efforts; to reduce the fertility of Less Developed countries. In *FDLDG*; 337-62.

2144. Petersen, William. Some prstnlates of population in policy. *Population Review* Jan-Dec, 1971.

2145. Pifer, Alan. Public response to population aging. *Daedalus* Win. 1986; 373-96.

2146. Pitchford, J.D. *Population in economic growth.* Amsterdam, North Holland, 1974.

2147. Pitt-Rivers. G.H.L.F. *Problems of population.* London, George Allen & Unwin, 1932.

2148. Repetto, Robert. Population, resource pressure and poverty. In *Global possible.* Ed. by Robert Repetto. New Delhi, Segment Book Distributors. 1986; 131-70.

2149. Revelle, Roger *ed. Rapid population growth* 2 Vols. Baltimore; 1971.

2150. Ridker, Ronald G *ed. Population and development : The search for selective interventions.* Baltimore, 1976.

2151. Rodgers, Gerry. B. *Poverty and population ; Approaches and evidence.* Geneva, ILO, 1984. p. 213.

2152. Rossi, Alice S. Gender and parenthood. *American Sociological Review* Feb. 1984; 1-19.

2153. Rossi, Alice S. *Gender and the life course* New York, Aldine, 1985.

2154. Rossi, Alice S. Sex and gender in an aging society. *Daedalus* Win. 1986; 141-70.

2155. Schofiled, R.S. 'Crisis' morality. *Local Population Studies.* 9, 1972; 10-21.

2156. Schultz, T.P. *Economics of population* Reading, Mass, Addison Weekly, 1981.

2157. Scrimshaw, Susan C.M. Infant mortality and behaviour in the regulation of family size. In *FDLDC*; 295-318.

2158. Siegel, Jacob S and C.M. Taluber. Demographic prospectives on the long-lived society, *Daedaulus* Win. 1986; 77-118.

2159. Srivastawa, S.K. Challenge of growing population. *Economic Studies* 22 (1) 1981; 113-16.

2160. Stycos, J.M. Recent trends in Latin American fertility. *Population Studies* 32, 1978; 407-25.

2161. Sundara Rajan, K.S. India's population problem. *Finance and Development* 2 (3) Sep. 1965.

2162. Teachman, Jay *et al. Impact of family planning programme on fertility. Ed.* by C. Chandrasekaraw and A Hermalin. Dolhain, IUSSP. 1976.

2163. Thompson, Warren S. *Danger spots in world population.* New York, 1939.

2164. Thompson, Warren S. *Population problems* New York, McGraw-Hill, 1935.

2165. Titmuss, R.N. *Poverty and population* London. Macmillan, 1938.

2166. Torres-Gil, Fernando Latinization of a multigenerational population. *Daedalus* Win 1986; 325-48.

2167. United Nations. *Determinants and consequences of population trends.* New York 1973.

2168. Westoff, C. Fertility decline in the West : Causes and prospects. *Population and Development Review*, Mar. 1983; 99-105.

2169. Woods, Robert. Malthus, Marx and population crises. In *WIC*; 127-49.

2170. Wright, Harold. *Population* Cambridge, 1923.

2171. Xinzhong, Qian. China's population policy? Theory and methods. *Studies in family Planning* 14 (12) 1983; 295-301.

Psychological Factors

2172. Allen, Vernon L *ed. Psychological factors in poverty.* Univ. of Wisconsin, 1970.

Public Health

2173. Abel-Smith, B and A. Leiserson. *Poverty, development and health policy.* Geneva, WHO, 1978.

2174. Ali, C. Relief. Nutrition and health problems in the Nigerian/ Biafran War. *Journal of Tropica Pediat.* 16(2) Jun. 1970.

2175. Allbrook, D.B. Medical care, health and national development in Australia's neighbourhood. *Medical Journal of Australia* 2, 1972 ; 1045-50.

2176. Avom, Jerome L. Medicine, health and the geriatric transformation. *Daedalus* Win. 1986 ; 211-26.

2177. Bell, C.O. Basis of national health planning in Papura New Guinea, *Papua New Guinea Medical Journal* 15(4) 1972 ; 246-48.

2178. Bell, C.O. *Diseases and health services of Papua New Guinea.* Papua New Guinea, Dept of Public Health, 1973.

2179. Bennett, F.J. Primary health care and developing countries. *Social Science and Medicine* 13A, 1979 ; 505-14.

2180. Benyoussef, A. Health Service delivery in developing countries. *International Social Science Journal* 29(3) 1977 ; 397-418.

2181. Benyoussef, A and B. Christian. Healthcare in developing countries. *Social Science and Medicine* 11(6-7) 1977, 399-408.

2182. Brody, J.A. Length of life and the health of older people. *National Forum* Fall 1982.

2183. Brown, E.R. Public health to imperialism. *American Journal of Public Health* 66(9) 1976 ; 897-903.

2184. Bryant J. *Health and the developing world.* Ithaca, Cornell Univ. Press, 1969.

2185. Callahan, Daniel. Adequate health care and an aging society. *Daedalus* Win. 1986 ; 247-68.

2186. Cleaver, H. Malaria, the politics of public health and the international crisis. *Review of Radical Political Economics* 9(10) 1977 ; 61-80.

2187. Davis, Karen. Aging and the health care system : Economic and structural issues. *Daedalus* Win. 1986 ; 227-46.

2188. Dignan, J. *Social security—outline of a scheme of national health insurance.* Sligo Champion Publication, 1945.

2189. Djukanoric, V and E.P. Mach. *Alternative approaches to meeting basic health needs in developing countries.* Geneva, WHO, 1975.

2190. Dutt, G. Pada. Wanted a health programme. *Frontier* 31 May. 1969 ; 8-9.

2191. Fatal diseases : the big killers. *Blitz* 16 Aug. 1986 ; 7.

2192. Feudall, N.R. *Auxiliaries in health care : Programmes in developing countries.* Baltimore, Johns Hopkins Press, 1972.

2193. Frankel, Glenn. Even the diseases are segregated : Apartheid affects how young people live-and die. *International Herald Tribune* 17 Jul. 1986 ; 1-6.

2194. Frankenberg, R. Functionalism and after ? Theory and developments in social science applied to the health field. *International Journal of Health Services* 4(3) 1974 ; 411-27.

2195. Frenden heim, Milt. Rise in U.S. health costs is double the inflation rate. *International Herald Tribune* 28 Jul. 1986 ; 3.

2196. Gish, O. Resource allocation, equality of access and health. *International Journal of Health Services.* 3(3) 1973 ; 399-412.

2197. Golladay, F. *Health problems and policies in the developing countries. Washingtion,* 1980.

2198. Hall, T.L and A. Mejia. *Health manpower Planning.* Geneva, WHO, 1978.

2199. Harichandran. Health for all by 2000 A.D. a dream *Yojana* 1 Jun. 1986 ; 23-26, 33.

The trained manpower is one of the indicators of health development. In the International scene USSR has impressive availability of one physician for every 280 persons, Czechoslovakia one for 40 persons, West Germany one for 450 persons and so on. Among the low per capita income countries India stands in a better place but the availability is less than in Pakistan, China and Egypt. There is phenomenal increase in the case of allopathy medical practitioners. The number of registered medical practitioners increased from 59,338 in 1950 to 1,97,650 in 1975 and 2,68,712 in 1981. The number of practitioners per lakh of population increased from 16.5 in 1950 to 393 in 1981. All the system of medicines namely, allopathy, Indian systems of medicine and homoeopathy taken together had a total of 6.51 lakh medical practitioners in 1981. Of this allopathy accounted for 41.3 per cent (2.69 lakhs), Indian systems of medicine 41.9 per cent (2.73 lakhs) and homoeopathy 16.2 per cent (1.09 lakhs). In 1981, India had a total number of 3.78 lakh registered nurses, mid wives and health visitors. Of this, nurses accounted for 39.8 per cent (1.5 lakh,) midwives 38.3 per cent (1.45 lakh), ANMS 19.4 per cent (0.73 lakh) and health visitors 2.5 per cent (0.10 lakh).

An analysis of the data relating to different States would indicate that there is wide disparity in the availability of health manpower. Punjab tops the list with 128 doctors per lakh of population and Tamil Nadu stands second. Madhya Pradesh has the lowest availability of doctors namely 8 per lakh of population. Though all-India average of doctors per lakh of population was 39 in 1981, Rajasthan, Assam, Orissa, UP, Bihar and MP had a level much below this average. Thus it can be seen that there is a wide disparity in the availability of doctors in states. In the case of nurse-population ratio also there is a wide disparity. Maharashtra is per 1981 statistics had 54 nurses for a lakh of population whereas Tamil Nadu 52, Kerala 37, Punjab 35 and so on. Uttar Pradesh has the lowest in this regard and the ratio is 7 nurses for one lakh population.

The attainment of the objective of health for all 2000 A.D. will remain as a distant hope unless the packages are given due attention. The problem of under nutrition and malnutrition widely afflict a considerable section of the society. The prevailing high mortality rates among infants and the morbidity patterns have a link with malnutrition. The worst victims of this problem are children in the age group 0.6 years, pregnant women and nursing mothers. Surveys on nutrition reveal that nearly 50 per cent of the households in different states of the country consume food which is quite inadequate to meet their requirements either in calories or proteins or even both.

2200. Hellberg, J.H. Health planning in developing countries. In *Priorities in Malanesian development*. Ed. by R.J. May Canberra, Australian National University, 1973.

2201. Jain, Minu. Low funding of primary health centres : Health takes a back seat. *Times of India* 20 Jun. 1986.

2202. Jazairi, N. *Approaches to the development of health indicators.* Paris, OECD, 1976.

2203. Jha, L.K. Economics of health programme. *Mainstream* 26 Apr. 1986 ; 11-12, 27.

The contribution which Indians have made to the advancement of medical science and as practitioner of the art of healing through medicine and surgery is second to none in the world. Time and again, people who have gone for treatement to the best hospitals in America have found that the top man looking after them is an Indian. While I certainly feel proud of the contribution which they are making to the health of the mankind, I am even more concerned with thinking of ways in which their talent and services could help the well-being of the people of this country, particularly the poorest and those living far away from metropolitan cities like Bombay or Delhi.

It is not that the health of the Indian people has not recorded a substantial improvement in the years after Independence. The very fact that the average expectancy of life at birth has gone up from less than 30 years before Independence to above 50 years today is an eloquent tribute to the progress that has undoubtedly been made. Even so, the fact remains that far too many people in the country are victims of diseases which can be somewhat easily prevented or cured. The rate of infant morality is still too high. Although we have succeeded in the eradicating smallpox and plague, our efforts to eradicate malaria have not been quite so successful and there are signs of a setback. Further, many of the ailments which still afflict the poor in India but are not known in richer countries are the result of poverty and malnutrition as well as unhygienic conditions which do not come within the domain of the medical scientist as such. Yet, in the evolution of policies to remove these weaknesses and shortcomings, the involvement of medical science is essential.

2204. King, M. *Medical care in developing countries.* Nairobi, 1966.

2205. Kraut, H. and D. Cremer. *Health and nutrition in East Africa.* Munich, 1971.

2206. Lone, Salim. Crisis in health needs. *Congress Varnika International* (New Delhi) Sep. 1985 ; 32-34.

Critical health and essential survival needs amounting to hundreds of millions of dollers remain unment and pose a growing threat to the populations at risk in the drought-affected African countries, officials of the Office for Emergency Operations in Africa have warned. Vaccines, antibiotics, water pumps, tents, blankets and even clothes are amongst the items urgently needed, especially in areas where rain has brought chillier weather and added to the incidence of respiratory illnesses such as pneumonia. The fear of epidemics, such as the one that swept through the camps in Somalia and claimed at least 1,000 lives in April, is also growing.

The Office for Emergency Operations in Africa is spearheading a system-wide drive to help meet these emergency non-food needs. The recent Geneva Conference organized by the Office helped identify the resources to meet the most pressing necessity : food, valued at over a billion dollars. But non-food needs remained grossly underfunded.

"The world response in the billion dollars of foodgrains pledged for Africa must now be matched by support, for health, relief items and water," OEOA head Bradford Morse wrote in the New York Times. "Without these, many of the weakest victims, children and the old, many not live to see the food arrive."

The U.N. system has held a number of consultations with donor governments since the March Geneva Conference to alert them to the pressing dimension of the famine. The OEOA itself arranged specific country consultations for each of the 18 most affected nations with donor governments at which detailed lists of needs were presented. The Food and Agricultural Organization held a special session in Rome March 29 to discuss not only food aid but the need for basic agricultural/pastoral inputs—without which there would be no meaningful harvests in the drought-ridden communities even if the rains came.

UNICEF has launched a new appeal for $ 120 million for Africa's emergency health and survival needs, within their context of the overall OEOA assessment. And at its Executive Board deliberations late in April, UNICEF urged the represented governments to consider additional funding for those areas for which UNICEF holds responsibility within the U.N. system. In addition, UNICEF organized a special working-level meeting for donors on April 20 to focus on the financial needs in these sectors, and detailed presentations were made on the six most affected countries.

"Our calculations suggest that, at the moment, less than $5 million of UNICEF's estimated requirements for emergency support of $ 120 million can be identified," Mr. James Grant, the organization's Executive Director, told the donor' meeting, which was also addressed by OEOA Executive Co-ordinator Maurice Strong. As at the other U.N. meetings, observors reported, there was a lot of sympathy and support but actual commitments continued to be critically short of requirements.

"There is no question that we are very concerned about the adequacy of the response in non-food areas," Mr. Strong acknowledged at a press conference at U.N. headquarters. "These needs add up to about $ 600 million, and unless they are met quickly, we could revert to the kind of situation prevailing in late 1984 with massive numbers of deaths. We must explain to the richer countries that the absence of drugs and other medicines, tents and blankets, essential water supplies, etc. can all take a terrible toll. Food alone, especially for severely malnourished children, is not enough."

2207. Manchanda Madan Lal Health for all. *Hindustan Times* 6 Aug. 1986 ; 9.

Health is a state of complete physical, mental or social well-being and not merely absence of disease or infirmity. This guiding principle, according to WHO, is basic to human happiness and achievement of any State in this regard is of value to all-India, a member state of WHO, is signatory to Alma Ata Declaration of 1978 and a party to universal commitment to secure Health for All by 2000 A.D. The global strategy as adopted in 1981 is to achieve the goal through primary health care.

The task is by no means easy for a country of India's size inhabited by one-seventh of the total world population. If the present growth rate of 2.2 per cent per annum is allowed to remain uncontrolled, the population of 683 million, according to 1981 census, is likely to touch the staggering figure of 950 million by the turn of the century. In view of the magnitude of the problem, doubts have been often expressed that HFA is a utopia. A moderate view, however, is that the objectives are not beyond reach provided there is a sustained political will and support both at the Centre and in the States.

Health programme has been an integral part of our General National Development from Oct. 2, 1952. A vast infrastructure has been built during the past 34 years to provide primary health care to people in the rural areas, hilly and tribal belts. Under the HFA programme, not only we have cater for the rapidly growing population, but the urban poor and slum dwellers too have to be covered. The existing health care system is mainly curative. It has to be restructured to integrate promotive, preventive aspects at level of primary health care and new training and re-orientation programme for various health functionaries have to be launched. According to existing norms, huge number of Primary Health Centres and Sub-Centres have to be established and a large man-power, to man them and place in the field, is required.

2208. Marks, J. *Vitamins in health and disease*. London, Churchills, 1967.

2209. McNeill, W.H. *Plagues and peoples*. Oxford, Blackwell, 1977.

2210. Navarro, V. Underdevelopment of health or the health of underdevelopment. *International Journal of Health Services* 4(1) 1974 ; 5-27.

2211. Nowell, K.W. *Health by the people—Geneva, WHO*, 1975.

2212. Pathik, B and E Goon. Fiji School of medicine. *Public Health Papers* 70, 1978 ; 79-96.

2213. Riessman, C.K. Use of health services by the poor. *Social Policy* 5(1) May-Jun 1974.

2214. Rodgers, J. *Health and rural development*. Geneva, IUHEI, 1984 (Mimeo).

2215. Sapru, R.P. Public health care. *Tribune* 7 & 8 May 1986 ; 4.

2216. Schram, R. *History of the Nigerian health services*. Ibadan, 1971.

2217. Shagari, Shehu. Healthy children offer sure hope for the nation. In *Challenge of Change*. Lagos, 1980 ; 81-83.

2218. Sharma, A.D. Health for all by 2000 A.D. *Economic Times* 14 Sep. 1986 ; 5.

2219. Sharpston, M.J. Health and development. *Journal of Development Studies* 9(3) 1974 ; 455-60.

2220. Sick Society : Outdated approach to health—Poverty the biggest ailment. *Blitz* 16 Aug. 1986 ; 41-43.

2221. Sorkin, A. *Health economics in developing countries.* Lexington, D.C. Health, 1976.

2222. State health policy. *Economic Times* (New Delhi) 23 Aug. 1980; 7.

2223. Taylor, C.E. and M.F. Hall. Health, population and economic development. *Science* 157, 1967 ; 651-57.

2224. Tourse, M.P. Health rovolution. *World Health* Nov. 1979 ; 11-13.

2225. Winslow, C. *Cost of Sickness and the price of health.* Geneva, WHO, 1951.

2226. Yeborahafari, Ajoa. Crushing answer to malnutrition. *Mid-Day* (New Delhi) 16 Jul. 1986 ; 13.

In a picturesque village not far from the Ghanaian capital of Accra, people have learned a process which extracts the protein from green leaves and turns it into a powder which fights malnutrition.

The Red Cross worker who helped introduce the process believes it can help the estimated 42 per cent of children under five in her country with protein deficiencies. Already she says it has cut the incidence of malnutrition in the locality by more than half.

If not for a chance meeting on a Ghana-bound aircraft five years ago it might not have come about. Dede-Oforiwa Tetteh, a nurse who is deputy secretary-general of health with the Ghana Red Cross, was returning from Brirain when she got chatting with Dr. Peter Fellows, a food technologist at Oxford Polytechnic in England.

The talk turned to nutrition, and Tetteh told Fellows about the malnourished children in her home village, Kpone Bawaleshie. Seven out of ten were malnourished; she was wondering how she could help on her return.

Fellows, part of a small aid organisation called Find Your Feet (FYF), told her about the protein extraction process. The operation is simple : fresh green leaves are washed and mashed, pounded or crushed; the resulting green liquid is strained through a fine, clean cloth, and the juice is heated to boiling point, then strained a second time. The solidified protein remains in the cloth and is air dried into a powdery substance, which is added to food in quantities of one teaspoonful daily.

According to another method, the final product can be a moist green cake, or even a juice. Although the potential of leaf protein has long been recognised, it has not been widely taken advantage of.

Refugee Problem

2227. Buxton, D.F. *Economics of the refugee problem.* London, Focus, 1938.

RURAL AREAS

2228. Advance of rural poverty. In *Profiles of rural poverty.* Geneva ILO, 1979 ; 4-9.

2229. Ahluwalia, Montek S. Rural poverty and agricultural performance in India. *Journal of Development Studies,* 4, 1977 ; 298-323.

2230. Aubert, Vilhem. Rural poverty and community isolation. In *COP* ; 236-50.

The income statistics of Norway suggest that poverty is to a large extent a rural phenomenon. Of the 50,000 who in 1962 were employees in agriculture, forestry and fishery, 32 per cent earned less than 4,000 kroner ($ 570) per year, and 27 per cent earned between 4,000 and 8,000 kroner. Exactly one half of a total of 7,800 providers who earned less than 4,000 and whose total household income was between 4,000 and 8,000 belonged to the agricultural occupations. The great majority of these providers were independent farmers and/or fishermen. Of those households whose incomes were less than 4,000, and where the poverty cannot be explained by youth, old age or disability, a large share were independent farmers or fishermen.

The evidence on rural poverty is too fragmentary and insufficiently analyzed to permit safe conclusions. It must also be borne in mind that the same cash income lasts longer in a rural district than it does in a city. The production of milk, meat and fish for home consumption, as well as the greatly reduced building costs in the countryside, should be taken into account when rural and urban income levels are being compared. Nevertheless, it may be claimed that a large share of those whose major problem is poverty, are to be found in the isolated rural regions of Norway. There is reason to believe that for those who live in poverty in the cities, poverty is more frequently accompanied by other major problems, Mental illness, alcoholism or some other disability is very often a concomitant, or even a cause, of their underprivileged position.

The preceding does not imply that the Norwegian countryside is characterized by poverty. Rural poverty is not characteristic of any large region, but is found in relatively small pockets in the remote mountain districts, on the west coast, and in the north. To some extent the poverty may be gleaned from the income statistics. Since these are organized on the basis of the municipality as the smallest unit, however, the smallest pockets of poverty are not easily located.

A special analysis of the income levels in the inland districts of the two northernmost countries, Troms and Finnmark, has been undertaken by the Directorate of Labour. The analysis reveals incomes which are only half of the national average for taxpayers, and in some municipalities considerably less. In the whole area the per capita income is one-third of the income per taxpayer, and in the one municipality down to one-fourth, while the per capita income for the nation is one-half of the taxpayer income. It means that substantially larger households must subsist on an income of less than half the national average,

Scarcity of natural resources is the basis cause of this poverty. The areas under scrutiny are hardly industrialized; farms are small and agricultural conditions generally unfavourable; communications are poor and distances very great. Although these factors are particularly powerful in Northern Norway, they are also present in many Southern Norwegian areas, where they sometimes lead to poverty, but often not. In addition to the poor resources, the inland municipalities of North Troms and Finnmark are characterized by a net increase of the population in recent years. More and more people have to subsist on the same meagre resources. Emigration has not in this region served as a safety valve as has been the case in many other non-industrialized rural regions. The Directorate of Labour's report explains this partly by the prevalence of Lappish-speakers in these areas, the Lapps being reluctant to leave their traditional habitat and community to seek employment under different and unfamiliar conditions. The language barrier is a crucial hindrance to emigration, but there are probably other obstacles to be overcome. We shall later return to this ethnic problem.

2231. *Australian economic policies.* Sydney, A.I.I.A., 1938.

2232. Bardhan, P.K. On the minimum level of living and the rural poor. *Indian Economic Reivew* 5 (1) Apr. 1970.

2233. Byerlee, D and C.K. Eicher. *Rural employment and economic development.* Michigan State University, 1972.

2234. Castro, Alronso *et al.* Indicators of rural inequality. *World Development* 2 (5) 1981.

2235. Challenge to the Third World. In *Profiles of rural poverty.* Geneva, ILO, 1979 : 47-49.

2236. Coombs, P.H. *ed. Meeting the basic needs of the rural poor.* New York, Pergammon, 1981.

2237. Coombs, P.H. and M. Ahmed, *Attacking rural poverty.* Baltimore, Johns Hopkins Univ. Press 1974.

2238. Fighting rural poverty. *Amrita Bazar Patrika* 7 Apr. 1986 ; 9.

2239. Fighting rural poverty. *Amrita Bazar Patrika* 18 Jul. 1985 ; 6.

It is evident from Prime Minister Rajiv Gandhi's observations at the parliamentary consultative committee attached to the Planning Ministry that he is not satisfied with the pace at which the anti-poverty programmes are being implemented. He expressed doubts, which are also shared by the Planning Commission whether the benefits are really reaching those for whom these programmes are meant. It had been realised at the beginning of the sixth plan, that in spite of the phenomenal progress achieved during the last twenty-five years in both agricultural and industrial sectors, the economic condition of the rural poor did not substantially improve. It is the big farmers and their proteges who reaped the fruits of rural development. For this reason, it was necessary to formulate specific programmes to benefit the weaker sections of the rural community. This goal was sought to be attained through the national rural employment programme and the integrated rural development programme. The former can only provide temporary relief to small farmers and landless labourers for a short period during the slack season by creating additional job opportunities with the ultimate aim of strengthening the rural economy as a whole. The integrated rural development programme is more important because it seeks to reduce the number of people below the poverty line on a permanent basis. It is obviously because of this that the Prime Minister laid more emphasis at the consultative committee on the need for implementing the programme with the sense of urgency the situation calls for. But it is the State Governments which are entrusted with task of executing the programme with the help of loans from the commercial banks as also Central assistance.

The Prime Minister's directive that the anti-poverty programmes should be aimed at helping the poorest among the poorer sections is apparently meant for the State Governments. This reorientation is essential according to him, if the number of those living below the poverty line is to be brought down to 10 per cent by 1994-95. If some aberrations have been noticed in the identification of beneficiaries it is mainly because of lack of vigilance on the part of the State Governments. His contention that there should be some selectivity in favour of those families "at the lowest ranges of incomes even among the mass of the poor" is beyond dispute as this is the real aim of the antipoverty programmes. But there may be difference of opinion on whether the result would be better if locally elected representatives are associated with the selection of beneficiaries. As the local panchayats are controlled by different political parties, the selection may not be impartial. His proposal for monitoring the progress at regular intervals by the Centre might prove a more effective remedy as this would make the State Governments, with which the responsibility for overall supervision rests, more alert. The commercial banks also came under severe criticism for their delay in sanctioning loans and insistence on adequate security which the rural poor cannot furnish. A change in this policy is reasonable to expect because of the Prime Minister's exhortation to banks not to make a fetish of banking principles while extending loans to the rural poor and Dr. Manmohan Singh's observation that the banking system has been coverted from "class banking to mass banking after nationalisation". A close cooperation among the State Governments, local panchayats, and the commercial banks is essential to attain the goal Mr. Gandhi has placed before the country.

2240. Gadam, Sudhakar. IRDP failure blamed on bad planning. *Economic Times* 11 Sep. 1986.

2241. Ganguli, B.N. Rural communitarianism. An alternative. path to development. In *Indian Economic Thought* New Delhi, 1977 ; 86-102.

2242. Ghate, Prabhu, *Direct attack on rural poverty*. New Delhi, concept, 1985.

2243. Guhan, S. Rural poverty : Policy and play acting. In *India : Degradation and development*, Ed. by A.B. Shah. Vol. 2. Hyderabad, 1982.

2244. Humphrey, Hubert H. Rural poverty. In *War on poverty*. New York, 1964 ; 65-82.

2245. Inayatullah. C. Political context of programmes of rural development and rural poverty. In *EAPS* ; 114-26.

Eradication of rural poverty seems to be the declared policy objectives of almost all countries in Asia. To a varying degree, they stress the need of creating a society free of poverty and exploitation. To achieve this purpose various types of programmes of rural development have been introduced. However, rural poverty, both absolute and relative, tends to persist in spite of these programmes. In fact it is possible that ranks of the rural poor, which include the agricultural labourers, the village artisans, the landless tenants and the small landowners may be swelling as more and more small landowners are pushed over the wall of self-subsistence.

Not only the rural developement programme introduced by most Asian countries, have marginal effect on absolute poverty, but they also have made no significant impact on reduction of economic, social and political inequalities. Under certain circumstances, they, in fact, have increased these inequalities, thus reinforcing and strengthening the pre-existing inegalitarian rural social structures and making them less amendable to rapid and peaceful transformation.

A possible explanation of the ineffectiveness of these programmes seems to be that, in general, they are intended to be instruments of achieving goals other than eradication of poverty and inequality such as raising agricultural productivity, controlling political discontent and winning political support for national elites. Within the constraints in which such elites operate, these goals are much more important to them and have greater political pay off than the goals of eradication of poverty.

Major programmes of rural development in Asia could be placed in three main categories :

(1) The programmes intended to alter property relations in favour of the less privileged such as land reforms which may be called *equality-oriented programmes* ;

(2) the programmes oriented to spread new technology-oriented programmes ;

(3) the programmes oriented to raise community solidarity by introducing new groups and institution such as cooperatives, local government and community development. These programmes may be called solidarity-oriented programmes.

Impact of these programmes on rural poverty is determined by :

(1) Strategy they follow to affect poverty ;

(2) their instrumental adequacy ; and

(3) sequences of their introduction.

Impact of a programme is enhanced if it incorporates a strategy of manipulating the direct rather than indirect causes of poverty. An indirect strategy lacks control over unanticipated consequences which could defeat the original purpose. In general the rural development programmes in Asia have followed an indirect strategy. It was expected that diffusion of improved technology and stronger community institutions would raise production and strengthen sentiments of self-help in the community which would eradicate poverty. This strategy was obviously not effective in assisting the poor strata.

The second determinant of the impact of a programme is its size and magnitude. A programme may diagnose the causes of povery correctly and may follow a direct strategy. But if its magnitude is not adequate to effect poverty its impact would be considerably limited. This, for instance, is true for several land reform measures carried out in various countries of Asia where due to high ceiling placed on land to carried out in various countries of Asia where due to high ceiling placed on land to be resumed, not enough land could be available for redistribution among the poor.

Thirdly, the effect of rural development programmes would be determined by the sequence in which they are introduced in a country. If, for instance, introduction of adequate land reform measures are followed by technology-oriented and solidarity-oriented programmes, their impact on poverty would be much more significant than when such programmes are diffused in inegalitarian communities. In the first case, their fruits would be shared by the most and in the second case only by a few. Similarly, new institutions introduced, after extreme social inequalities have been eradicated, would be much more effective than they are introduced in an inegalitarian social structure where they would become instruments of the powerful.

2246. Joshi, Navin Chandra. Removing rural poverty. *Mainstream* 2 Apr. 1983; 32-33.

The recent studies have brought out the wide gap that exists between intention and reality in relation to schemes to help the rural poor. A study published by the Indian Institute of Management. Ahmedabad, has concluded that these programmes have, by and large, failed to benefit the poorest of the poor. Indeed, the sample surveys have revealed that on an average only about one-fourth of the intended population has been covered by the implementing agencies. The picture emerging from another report, submitted by an expert group appointed by the Planning Commission to assess the overall impact of rural anti-poverty schemes, is equally distressing.

The rural poor in India can fairly be identified as being composed of small and marginal farmers, landless agricultural labourers, rural artisans and persons engaged in traditional occupations. Actually all the unemployed, under-employed and even some employed persons are poor because of their low producitivity and low wages. Some Backward and all the Scheduled Castes and Scheduled Tribes people are below the poverty line.

An important principle of state policy laid down in our Constituion is that social economic and political justice shall be secured for all people. It is mentioned that the state is to direct its policy in such a manner as to secure the distribution of ownership and control of material resources of the community to subserve the common good and to ensure that the operation of the economic system does not result in the concentration of wealth and means of production to the common detriment. One policy instrument for fulfilling the aforesaid principle of state policy is the nature and pattern of income distribution amongst the different sections of our society. The recent studies on income distribution, however, make disturbing reading and it seems the Directive Principles of State Policy will never be achieved unless some radical methods are now adopted.

The Reserve Bank of India figures reveal that in rural areas the bottom 20 per cent of the population has only nine per cent of the aggregate income while the top five per cent has 17 per cent of the income. The National Council of Applied Economic Research has found in a study on the basis of 1975-76 data that three per cent households possess 50 per cent of agricultural land while 75 per cent possess only 10 per cent. Evidently, the major factor accounting for wide inequalities in income distribution in India is the highly inequitable distribution of privately owned means of production.

Of the seventy-five million households engaged in agriculture, more than 50 per cent are marginal holders with less then one hectare of land. Another 20 per cent have between one and two hectares. When Indian agriculture was operated traditionally, the small farmer was not in such a disadvantageous position as he is today when agricultural operations have been modernised. Earlier, his productivity per acre was more on small farms but with the introduction of new capital—intensive technology, the advantage of higher productivity has shifted to big farms, making matters worse as far as inequality in earning capacity is concerned.

Privately-owned land constitutes the bulk of private wealth in India. Various land reform legislations starting from Zamidari abolition in 1959 to ceiling on ownership of land of 1970s are concerned with this asset.

Although land ceiling laws were enacted in almost all States, the results achieved so far have not been significant due to the high ceiling level, large number of exemptions from the law, *mala fide* transfers, partitions and poor implementation of the law. A very negligible portion of agricultural land has been declared surplus for distribution to agricultural workers and small holders. This failure to achieve significant redistribution of land compels us to look elsewhere for eradication of rural poverty.

2247. Juyal, B.N. and Vikashbai. Gandhian approach to rural development. *Ideas in Action* 129, 1979 ; 17-24.

2248. Karkal, Malini. Misleading results of IRDP. *Economic Times* 26 Jun. 1986.

It is generally commented that though the Integrated Rural Development Programme (IRDP) has its major objective of poverty alleviation, the implementation of the programme had emphasis on quantity rather than quality. In deciding the eligibility for assistance under the IRDP programme annual income of the family is taken as a criteria and in many instances landholding alone is used as a criteria for beneficiary choice. For the landless a certificate stating the applicants income per annum is adequate. In neither of the cases actual varification of the documents is required.

Information about land holdings is available with the Block Development Officer. This information is relied upon for all official work. However these documents are not updated for long periods of time to assure their reliability. This was confirmed by comparing the detailed information available at the BDO's office and that obtained from visits to individual households and looking through the documents on land ownership. An enquiry of this nature was made in one village in Thane district. The figures from the BDO's office showed that in the village there were 47 farmers with land holding between 2.5 to 5 acres. Whereas those with holdings of less than 2.5 acres were 79. The house to house enquiry showed that the figures were 72 and 276 respectively.

In the recent years for several government programmes it is found that the quantitative targets and official pressures to meet them, have led to several malpractices. One therefore suspects that the above mentioned under reporting of small and marginal farmers is also one of the ways of showing that the poverty needs in the area are fewer.

The Concurrent Evaluation of IRDP : The Main Findings of the Survey for October-November 1985, published by the Department of

Rural Development of the Ministry of Agriculture shows that selection of beneficiaries varied from State to State. Further, the report also mentions that there was time lag in providing assistance to the selected beneficiaries varied from 3 to 4 months, to 2 years. Surprisingly, though the basic objective of the IRDP programme is to lift the beneficiary from his income level, the questionnaire itself did not have provision for enumerating family incomes. Information that some of the sources have indicated that to begin with, many of the beneficiaries—sometimes to the extent of 50 per cent, were ineligible for the benefits of the programme.

IRDP programmes were introduced in the Sixth Plan on realisation that in spite of the growth in the aggregate national income the distribution of the gains was uneven. Those who benefited from the growth were those who owned land and other productive assets, or were skilled in different types of work. Whereas those who were resourceless and unskilled wage earners were left outside of these newly generated incomes. IRDP programmes were specifically designed to meet this shortcoming, and help the poor to overcome their poverty. In the light of the earlier experience that the benefits do not reach the deprived and the poor. It was most essential that the IRDP programmes and then their monitoring through the evaluation surveys, laid emphasis on qualitative aspects of the programme. Experience however shows that the emphasis is on quantitative dimension and the results which are presented in overall statistical terms, continue misleading the actual gains in terms of narrowing the differences.

IRDP therefore is another government programme that has expanded the number in government service and the expenses on paper work and other activities without showing results that the programme was initiated for.

2249. Krishna Mohan Rao, G. New 20-Point Programme : Thrust on rural poverty. *Mainstream* 13 Sep. 1986 ; 12-13.

The Centre has come out with a new revised 20-point programme with alleviation of rural poverty as its main thrust. On August 20 the new revised 20-point programme was tabled in Parliament by ABA Ghani Khan Choudhury, Minister for Programme Implementation suggesting that this programme will henceforth be monitered at the Centre by his ministry and not by the Planning Commission.

Its objectives were spelt out by the Government as : "eradicating poverty, raising productivity, reducing income inequalities, removing social and economic disparities, and improving the quality of life."

This revised new programme raises the immediate question—how is it different from the previous 20-point programme announced in 1975 and 1982 ?

The new 20-point programme marks a dramatic shift from the old one. Certainly, this new revised programme is the most coherent of all the three with the emphasis wholly on rural development, and poverty alleviation. "The war on poverty is our first priority" says the introductory note. Ghani Khan Choudhury viewed that the 20-points must be "restructured" from time to time in the light of "achievements and experience". By and large its basic elements are the same as the organic constituents of the anti-poverty thrust of the 7th Plan.

In the present revision poverty alleviation has been accorded top priority with emphasis on eradication of rural poverty. The innovative feature of this restructured programme is "responsive administration" which means, says the documents : "Simplify procedures; delegate authority; enforce accountability; evolve monitoring system from block to national level—and attend promptly and sympathetically to public grievances."

2250. Lipton, Michael Rural development and the retention of the rural population. *Canadian Journal of Development Issues* 1982.

2251. Makkar. S.L. Eradication of poverty from rural India : Some steps. *Kurukshetra* Feb. 1986 ; 19-21.

Appropriate Technology is stressed as being a dynamic and flexible concept which must be responsive to varying conditions and the existing situation in different regions of the country and different sub-regions within a region. The appropriate technology can prove an instrument for improving the economic levels of the poorest people. The development of appropriate technology relatively low cost, employment oriented, based on local needs and conditions of the country is considered highly fruitful. The natural resources should be exploited in such a way that they give maximum returns. Appropriate technology is that which is biophysically viable, economically feasible and socially acceptable. Appropriate technologies will be suitable for adoption on farms, which tend to enhance the use of available local resources. The appropriate technology is determined by the conditions of the country itself. The selection and application of appropriate technology implies the use of both large scale and low cost small scale technologies dependent on objectives in a given set of circumstances. It can be helpful to narrow down the inequalities of wealth and income by taking technology to rural areas from urban areas and laboratories through young hands and fresh minds keeping in view the environments. It can play a significant role in removing poverty by reducing the number and percentage of population below the poverty line. It is the young man who can take technology to village level from urban centres for structural changes in the life of the poor villagers. The youth of our country can play an important role in improving the socio-economic conditions of the poor villagers by increasing the productivity all round including the reasonable distribution of production.

2252. Manjeet Kaur. Rural poverty : A threat to stability. *Real India* (New Delhi) 1 Mar. 1980 ; 15.

2253. Massive effort to alleviate rural poverty. *Employment News* 3 May 1986 ; 2.

2254. Mathew, T.I. Rural social security. In *EAPS* ; 106-13.

In spite of different viewpoints on the concept of social security, there is a general concensus that social programmes are aimed to guarantee to the widest possible sections of the population, benefits in the event of :

(i) loss of income due to sickness, maternity, injury, disability, old age, death of the breadwinneer and unemployment;

(ii) a morbid condition requiring medical care of a preventive or curative nature; or

(iii) responsibility for the maintenance of children. The significance of social security programmes for anti-poverty strategies is easily perceived.

Minimum wages as well as the policy measures for maintenance of real incomes from employment are relevant to those who posses jobs. But can the possession of jobs alone ensure protection against the loss of income, on account of the various contingencies just enumerated, and keep the people above the poverty line ? In many developed countries, the benefits provided under social security schemes help to keep large numbers of the people above the poverty line.

If income redistribution is accepted as a necessary weapon in the anti-poverty strategy, social security becomes at once relevant. Social security programmes generally bring about a redistribution of income from the healthy to the sick, from the employed to the unemployed, from the childless to those with children, and from the currently employed to those who have retired from wage-earning employment.

While the potentialities of effective-social security programmes, which bring about this type of "horizontal" redistribution of income, are well known is the fact that appropriately designed and efficiently administered social security programmes could also be counted upon a useful instruments of "vertical" redistribution of income between population groups at different levels of income, i.e., the transfer of incomes from the higher income-groups to lower income-groups. This redistributive role of social security programmes has long been recognised in many developed countries in Western Europe and, emperically proved by recent studies. In the Asian region, Japan has also, to some extent, succeeded in combining social security schemes with fiscal instruments to effect redistribution of income so as to improve the position of needy persons in the lower income groups.

2255. Mathew, T.I. Social security for rural population in India *International Labour Review* 108(4) Oct. 1973.

2256. Mehmet, Ozay. Rural poverty and policy interventions under trusteeship. In *Development in Malaysia* London, 1986 ; 46-74.

2257. Nellor, John W. *et al. Developing rural India : Plan and practice.* Ithaca, Cornell Univ. Press.

2258. Minhas, B.S. Rural poverty, land redistribution and development *Indian Economic Review.* 5, Apr. 1970.

2259. Nadkarni, M.V. Overpopulation and the rural poor. *Economic and Political Weekly* 13 Mar. 1976.

2260. Pande, S.K. Bonds of rural poverty. *Business standard* (Calcutta) 17 Aug. 1980 ; 4.

2261. Prasad, Pradhan H. and G.B. Rodgers. *Caste, class and landholding in the analysis of the rural economy.* Geneva, ILO, 1983 (Mimeo).

2262. *Profiles of rural poverty.* Geneva, ILO, 1979. p. 50.

2263. Rajaraman, Indira. Growth and poverty in the rural areas of the Indian state of Punjab, 1960-61 to 1970-71. In *Poverty and landlessness in rural Asia.* Geneva, ILO, 1977 ; 61-74.

2264. Rao, V.K.R.V. How to increase rural employment. *Socialist India* (New Delhi) 24 Jul. 1971 : 11-12.

2265. Reddy, J. Ramadas. Why poverty continues ? *Yojana* 1 Dec. 1986 ; 20-22.

2266. Reddy, L. Udaya Bhaskara. Socio-economic conditions of rural poor : A study. *Kurukshetra* (New Delhi) Mar. 1986 ; 18-20.

The study of the rural poor has assumed a significant importance in the context of the massive welfare programmes initiated by Government of India to achieve a better standard of rural life. If these programmes make an impact and enable the rural poor to raise their living standards, it would be a long way in ushering in the desired changes in socio-economic life of rural poor in India. The Government recognised that something needs to be done for uplifting the rural poor. As a response to the situation and to bring about necessary changes, the Government introduced development planning, the mobilization of resources, the upgrading of manpower and skills, the fostering of orientation and attitude conducive to development and the implementation of a large number of programmes and projects.

The development programmes introduced by Government have made very little impact on rural poor. They have been suffering under a misguided form of development not designed with the primary purpose of uplifting their welfare in mind. One of the most depressing features of our planning is the persistence of poverty withont an end. Many of our poorest have accepted poverty without demur as being their perennial fate. According to recent estimates more than 50 per cent of rural population is living below the poverty line. Thus a study of rural poor in Indian context assumes a significant importance.

2267. Rempel, H and R.A. Lobdell, Role of urban-to-rural remittances in rural development. *Journal of Development Studies* 14, 1978 ; 324-41.

2268. Rodgers, Gerry B. Conceptuialisation of poverty in rural India. *World Development* 4(4) Apr. 1976.

2269. Roy, Bunker, Rural poverty, Urban ignorance. *Hindustan Times* 19 Oct. 1980.

2270. Roy, Durgadas, Rural development challenge. *Tribune* 1 Oct. 1986 ; 4.

2271. Sahai, B.M. Rural development for removal of poverty. *National Herald* 9 Mar. 1984 ; 5.

2272. Sinha, Jagdish. Planning and Rural poor *Maintstream* 26 Jul. 1986 ; 28-30.

Planning has been considered the best path of economic development growth and common welfare all over the world. Planning in India was started after Independence and by now we have passed through more than three and half decades of the planning era, and have entered the Seventh Five Year Plan (1985-90).

Right from the very start of planning (The First Five Year Plan 1950-51 to 1955-56) till today economic development and growth with social justice has been an important consideration in our planning process. The attempt of Indian Planners has closely been associated with social justice in the economic growth policy of India. The Third Plan document had said : "Ever since Independence, two main aims have guided India's planned development to build up by democratic means a rapidly expanding and technologically progressive economy and a social order based on justice and offering equal opportunity to every citizen". The slogan of *Garibi Hatao* in 1971 was, in fact, intended to increase the welfare of poorer sections in society, particularly in the villages of India.

The planners in India have been considering rural development, the rural poor in particular, as an important tool for national progress and prosperity. They will seem to be very serious and positive about the upliftment of millions of the rural poor through various rural-oriented schemes and programmes like the Integrated Rural Development Programme, (IRDP), National Rural Employment Programme, (NREP), Integrated Tribal Development Programme (ITDP), Rural Labour Employment Guarantee Programme, (RLEGP) and Minimum Needs Programme, (MNP) which are supposed to be implemented under the Five Year Plans, intended to pay attention to the socio-economic problems of economically and socially backward communities living in the villages of India. All the economic, social, political and ethical logic also goes in favour of distributing the gains of national development more in favour of the havenots. The Rawlsian conception of Justice has also strongly influenced the Indian socio-economic policies and programmes which are to improve the conditions of millions of poor people. Rawls has said : "The social objective is to maximise the welfare level of the least advantaged numbers in society." (John Rawls, A Theorty of Justice, Cambridge, Massachusetts, 1972, pp. 286-87).

In the objectives of the approved Seventh Plan (1986-80) all the rural development programmes and schemes basically are very much intended to improve the poor socio-economic conditions, health, education and nutrition of the distressed and depressed sections of the rural population, with the target of reducing the poverty ratio from 37 per cent in 1984-85 to 25.8 per cent in 1989-90 (about 11 per cent decline in five years). (see "Seventh Plan Approved" : Editorial, Southern Economist, Vol 24, Nov 15, 1985). This means planners do recognise the real needs and expectations of millions of people who live below the poverty line in villages, and, therefore they express their strong desire for development based on growth with social justice in the distribution of national gains, giving top priority to poverty alleviation programmes in the list of Seventh Plan objectives. Dr. V.K.R.V. Rao the noted economist, has also accepted that "growth, employment, social justice and quality of life are integrated and linked together—through plans, programmes and policies in the process of economic development." (Mainstream, June 21, 1980).

2273. Siwal, Beg Raj. Rural poverty and rural development. *Economic Studies* 22(5) 1981 ; 273-78.

2274. Thippaiah, P and M. Devendra Babu. Tackling rural poverty. *Yojana* 30(22) 1 Dec. 1986 ; 12-15.

2275. Wedekin, K.E. Soviet rural society. *Soviet Studies*, 1970.

2276. War on rural poverty. *Pioneer* 10 May 1986 ; 4.

Slavery

2277. Andrade, F. *Freedom chooses slavery.* New York, 1959. p. 139.

2278. Banaji, D.A. *Slavery in British India.* Bombay, 1933.

2279. Davis, David Brion. *Problem of Slavery in Western Culture.* Ithaca, 1966.

Social Problems & Security

2280. Becker, H.S. *ed. Social problems.* New York, John Willey, 1966.

2281. Bose, Nirmal Kumar. Who are the backward classes. *Man in India* 34, 1954 ; 89-98.

2282. Bott, E. *Family and Social Network.* London, Tavistock, 1957.

2283. Central Social Welfare Board. *Report of the Advisory Committee of the Aftercare programme.* New Delhi ; 1955.

2284. *Circumstances of families.* London, HMSO, 1967.

2285. *Current issues in social security planning : Concepts and techniques.* Geneva, ISSA, 1972.

2286. Deutsch, Joseph. Philantropic motives and contribution policy. A note. *Public Choice* 44 (3) 1984; 501-8.

2287. Dentsch, K.W. Social mobilization and political development *American Political Science Review* 55, Sep. 1961.

2288. Dodd, Strart Center. *Social relations in the Near East. Beirut,* 1940.

2289. Ferraguti, S. New approach to social action in a traditional setting. *International Review of Community Development* (31-32) 1973.

2290. Forsyth, F.G. Relationship between family size and family expendi ture. *Journal of the Royal Statistical Society* (Series—A) 123, 1960, 367-93.

2291. Friedlander, W.A. *Introduction to social welfare.* Prentice—Hall, 1955.

2292. Galtung, J. Rank and social integration : A multidimensional approach. In *Sociological Theories in Progress. Vol. 1.* Ed. by J. Berger *et al.* Boston, 1966.

2293. George, V. *Social Security and society.* London, Rontledge and Kegan Paul, 1973.

2294. Hunt, A *et al. Families and their needs.* London. HMSO, 1973.

2295. Miller S.M. Comparative social mobility. *Current Sociology* 9, 1960.

2296. *Report on the world social stiuation.* New York, United Nations, 1961.

2297. Runciman, W.G. *Relative deprisation and social justice.* London, 1966.

2298. Somnels, A *ed. Social security and family law.* London, Oceana Publications, 1980.

2299. Sarkar, S.C. Social Security in India. *Khadigramodyog* Mar. 1971; 425-77.

2300. Schnalberg, A and D. Reed. Risk, uncertainty and family formation : The social context of poverty groups. *Population Studies* Jul. 1978.

2301. Singh, Joseph R. War On poverty : Need for social action. *National Herald* 26 Jan. 1980; 5.

2302. Wedgwood, J. *Economics of inheritance*. London, Rontledge and Kegan Paul, 1929.

2303. Whyte, W.F. *Street Corner Society*. University of Chicago Press, 1943.

Socialism

2304. Poverty has nothing to do with Socialism—Deng. *Ta Kung Pao* 5 Jul. 1984; 3.

2305. Sweezy, Paul M. Socialism in poor countries. *Monthly Review* Oct. 1976.

2306. Weber, M. Class, status, party. In *From Max Weber*. Ed. by Gerth H and C.W. Mills. London, 1958.

Suicide

2307. Gibbs, J.P. and W.J. Martin. Theory of status integration and its relationship to suicide. *American Sociological Review* 23, Apr. 1958.

Technology

2308. Amin, Samir. Transfer of technology. In *Imperialism and unequal development*. Sussex, Harvester Press, 1977; 169-80.

Technology was probably still largely autonomous with respect to the progress of fundamental science because the techniques in these new branches of activity—the industries—were mainly bssed on mechanics, which could be grasped by empirical experience without any thorough direct knowledge of its mathematical foundations. Again, in agriculture, observation and experience, without knowledge of the scientific secrets of biology, have made possible immense progress for thousands of years.

Pure science thus was separate from production practice and developed autonomously. This does not mean that science was independent of society, of course, but it was related to the ideological superstructure rather than serving the production base. The dominant branch of science was mathematics, the most advanced formalization of logic, whereas the natural sciences remained at best descriptive. Mathematics went hand in hand with philosophy and attempted to answer the questions raised by it (the infinitely small, for example). Of course, astronomy, which inspired mathematical research, was useful both to agriculture and to navigation, but it was even more necessaıy to the ideological constructs of cosmogony and religion.

These two sets of relationships have been upset in our century. Technology, having become an object of labour specialization, has been separated from production. On the other hand, pure science has passed into the direct service of technology. This is not only because progress in the (physical and biological) sciences has made prodigious strides since these sciences were launched in the nineteenth century; nor even because mathematics has been systematically made to serve science. It is also because technology is now derived explicity from science. The second scientific and technical revolution shifted the center of gravity from mechanical engineering to electronics (this basis of automation supplanting mechanization) and applied biology. Mere empiricism is no longer sufficient to ensure the progress of production techniques.

Does this means that the growing complexity of technology is the reasons for its divorce from production ? To all appearances it is, and it is this appearance which suggests that the progress of the productive forces, derived from that of technology, is neutral with respect to the social relations of production. But in fact, this separation stems primarily from the division of labour within trades, the fragmentation of jobs, and the consequent massive degradation of work. While fifty years ago it was still confined to certain jobs in the mechanized manufacturing industry, this degraded labour has now invaded the tertiary sector. Hence the worker has lost even partial control of the production process. Moreover, the fragmentation of jobs not only involves the performance of the job: it has spread to the giving of orders and even to design and policy-making, and to technological research itself. Control of invention is increasingly slipping from the grasp of the scientists themselves.

This evolution is the result of capital's domination of society. We need to rid ourselves of a whole set of myths about the organization of work, efficiency, etc. It has been demonstrated over and over again, with specific examples, that the main purpose of the organization of work as it is now—featuring the separation between the work of design and execution—is to reproduce the relations of domination which determine the relations of exploitation. Efficiency is always in relation to a system : here, the extortion of surplus value.

Thus, while the division of labour by trade or craft necessarily accompanies the commodity form of the product, the fragmentation of jobs within the trade determines the latter's capitalist commodity form. Since technology itself has recently become a commodity—a capitalist commodity—this has been followed by the separation of technological research from production, and by a certain form of division of labour within technological research itself. Technology is an object of buying and selling, in keeping with the buying and selling of the specialized capital equipment which is its material underprinning and in which it is incorporated. Today the monopolies control this technology; they can refuse to sell it, or insist on certain conditions and, in this way, appropriate some of the surplus value generated by the output obtained by means of this equipment.

If, then, the direct appropriation of the means of production was until recently the necessary medium of control by capital, this is no longer the case, at least not at all levels of the production process. It is sufficient to control its strategic focal points to get hold of the surplus value generated in the process as a whole.

It is in this context that the problems of the transfer of technology must be placed. Transfer of what? Transfer to whom ? If it is a question of modern technologies, we will have to bear in mind that these are capitalist technologies, and that they are, moreover, controlled by the monopolies. Hence we will be transferring, at the same time as the technology, the underlying capitalist relations of production. Moreover, by this transfer we will not be escaping the domination of imperialist capitalism. On the contrary, we will be extending its scope by integrating the periphery more firmly into the imperialist system. The work done in the last few years on the cost of this transfer is evidence of this—the cost turned out to be exorbitant. For example, the Andean Group of states has been paying prices for this kind of equipment, and for the relevant patents, which are many times their real cost of production. By this means, the surplus value generated at the periphery by "modernization" is largely transferred to the monopolies. Hence the countries of the periphery cannot hope to be able to take over and ensure for themselves their own ultimate autonomous dynamism. This could still be done in the nineteenth century—Germany, Japan, and others began by importing the technologies incorporated in this equipment. But, in this field as in others, imperialism involves a qualitative break. So we cannot really speak of "transfer" but only of the geographical shift of the place where the technology operates.

It is not a question of reducing the cost of this transfer, even if the cost were zero, the technologies of the imperialist centers would not be able to solve the problems of underdevelopment at the periphery. This technology is excessively costly, not only because of its capital-intensive nature, but because of the wasteful consumption patterns it brings with it, the exploitation of natural resources that it implies, etc. In other words, this technology presupposes imperialism, i.e., the excessive exploitation of natural resources that it implies, etc. In other words, this technology presupposes imperialism, i.e. the excessive exploitation of labor in the periphery. Thus it can only reproduce the relations of unequal development within the imperialist system.

If this transfer is not desirable, can we envisage another type, that of less advanced technologies ? The debate about "intermediate technologies" suggests such a course. But since history is not a linear advance, the present situation of the underdeveloped countries, shaped by imperialist domination, is not the same as that experienced by the now developed centers at a previous stage of their evolution. It is therefore no solution to borrow the technologies of nineteenth-century Europe, apart from the fact that they too brought with them capitalist relations of production.

There is no choice : we have to invent a new technology that can both establish socialist relations of production and develop the productive forces even beyond the level reached by capitalism.

This problem is not specific to the underdeveloped societies; it is a problem of the world system as a whole. We have mentioned the mass degradation of labour involved in the fragmentation of jobs. Automation does not involve a higher average level of skill than mechanization; on the contrary. As automation eliminates the simplest manual jobs in some sectors, the capitalist system develops new parasitic sectors of activity—usually in connection with the "selling costs" of monopolistic competition—which are in their turn affected by gradual degradation because of the fragmentation of tasks. Overall, the whole of social labor is devalued. Thus concrete and complex labor, creator of use-values, gradually gives way to abstract and simple labor, a uniform expending of energy, which makes still more realistic the analysis of value in Capital.

2309. Baranson, Jack. *Technology for underdeveloped area—An annotated bibliography* Oxford, Foreign Press, 1967. p. 81.

2310. Dubashi, Jay. Mixing technology with poverty. *Newstime* (Hyderabad) 14 Apr. 1986; 9.

A poor man cannot be employed in an atomic power station, except perhaps as a sweeper. He has to be employed in low-wage industries.

Otherwise, there will not be enough jobs to go around. The present economic crisis in Britain and elsewhere stems from the inability of new technology to create jobs, for that is not its main function. An atomic power station employs probably a tenth of the manpower required in coal-burning thermal stations of the conventional type and there are steel plants in Japan which need no more than 5,000 people to produce 3 to 4 million tonnes of steel a year. Technology is almost by definition a system in which machines takeover from men. In countries like India, we need a technology where machines as well as men will be required unitil such time as all manpower is absorbed.

The question of poverty is, therefore, only indirectly linked with the question of technology. China has been able to virtually do away with poverty—the grinding type of poverty which is still seen in India—without much technology. It is only in Japan that full employment and hi-tech go together for it is one of the very few countries where machines have not displaced men. By mixing poverty with technology, the Prime Minister is unnecessarily complicating the whole question of what technology should do in a country like India. We certainly could do with more and better technology, but that by itself will not help us do away with poverty.

2311. Parthasarathy, G. Social impact of hi-tech and public policy. *Link* 15 Aug. 1986; 6-8.

2312. Ramachandran, V. Development of appropriate technology and unemployment. *Khadigramodyog* 18 (1) Oct. 1971; 23-29.

2313. Roberge, Roger A. Peripheral industrialization and the technology transfer process. In *IDPR*; 1-15.

2314. Vepa, Ram K. Technology and rural uplift. *Indian Express* 8 Aug. 1986; 6.

It was fashionable at one time to talk of the need for Appropriate Technology for rural development. It was implied (and sometime explicitly stated) that such technology needs to be simple, even primitive, to match the limited skills available in the country side. There was also the larger assumption that the attitudes and motivations of these living in the villages were somehow different from those of the city dwellers.

Today there is some doubt whether these assumptions are valid. The rural-urban dichotomy may well be more in the minds of sociologists than in the field. It is doubtful whether in basic aspirations people, rural or urban, are (or ever were) different. Some years ago, when all-India Radio, under a culture-conscious minister, used to broadcast only "bhajans" for the villagers, it was noted during a survey that there was hardly any listening audience for such programmes. When a sarpanch was asked what type of music the village would like to hear, he answered : "The same as you people in towns do."

The same may well be true of Technology. It is now being recognised that Rural Technology is no different from its urban counterpart and if the problems of rural development are urgent and complex, as indeed they are, they need to attract the best, not the worst, technology. This is, perhaps, the weakness of the well-intentioned efforts of the Intermediate Technology Development Group (based on the concepts propounded by Schumacher) that second class technology is adequate to solve the problems of the Third World, at least as a transitional measure—till those countries can catch up with the more advanced ones.

2315. Xavier, Michall J. Japanese technology today. *Patriot* 29 Jul. 1386;4.

In the last 40 years since the end of World War II, Japan has risen from the ashes to become the third-ranking technological superpower in the world, behind the United States and the Soviet Union. Japanese automobiles, cameras, and all types of electronic products have advanced into world market dominance due to their superior performance.

Until recently, Japanese scientific developments came as a result of the post-war unified drive of government and private industry for accomplishment, with the Japanese population as beneficiaries but somewhat remote from the process. In recent years, however, popular interest in science and technology in the country has boomed. There are many new science magazines, articles on science appear frequently in newspapers, and television programmes on science have gained much popularity.

The average level of scientific understanding among the Japanese population in general has reached the level of Western Europe and the United States. This is an important factor in a dramatic turn of events in Japanese science ; a widely-supported national call for emphasis on basic research, now heard from every corner of Japanese society.

A check in text-books-even in the natural sciences-will show that there have been very few basic concepts or important methods developed in the past by Japanese scientists. In the flashier technological fields, the criticism is often heard that Japan simply uses its ingenuity upon fundamental breakthroughs discovered or invented in the West, Japanese science and technology up to now have largely-although not completely-developed from a base provided by importing, or to put it negatively, imitating. Although Japan has developed into a technological superpower, her original contributions to date to world science and technology have been minimal.

The call for basic research in Japan has been greeted with some skepticism abroad. The weak points of the Japanese scientific community are said to be the lack of scientific tradition and an environment that discourages originality. If Japan is to truly contribute original scientific research and original technological break-throughs, she must begin with the creation of an environment that will nurture pathfinding researchers.

Tribalism

2316. Cole, D. *Nomads and nomads.* Chicago, Aldine Press, 1975.

2317. Dalton, George. *ed. Tribal and peasant economics,* New York, Natural History Press, 1967.

2318. Kulkarni, M.G. *Problems of tribal developments : A case study.* Aurangabad, Parimal Prakashan. 1974.

2319. Middleton, J and D. Tait *eds. Tribes without rulers.* London, Routledge, 1958.

2320. Schapera, Iaac *ed. Migrant labour and tribal life.* London, Oxford Univ. Press, 1947.

2321. Tribal development (in India). *Madhya Pradesh Chromide* 15 Jul. 1985;4.

The fruits of the developmental programme have not reached those for whom they were meant. This which is common knowledge, was seen by the Prime Minister personally during the course of his four-day tour which has just concluded, of 27 sites in eighty predominantly tribal districts of Madhya Pradesh. That the Prime Minister took four-days off his busy schedule to go to the Adivasi areas and talk to them on a personal basis instead of addressing public meetings which are more spectacular than substantial is evidence of his deep concern for the lowliest and the lost. The impact of seeing things for himself led to the announcement that "a new programme would be formulated for extending the benefits of the Integrated Rural Development Projects to those economically weaker sections not yet covered by it. Mr. Gandhi also underlined the need for setting up small scale industries along side IRDP so that the beneficiaries could make most of the produce. It is to be hoped that these benefits would begin to flow sooner than later.

Progress is inadequate, not for want of projects. Most of the projects fail at the implementation level. They fail mostly because of the choice of wrong people to man them. Most of them are square pegs in round holes. Many consider their posting to remote areas as punishment. Mr. Gandhi said that Government "would see to it that the officers posted in the tribal areas changed their outlook and did not consider their posting there as punishment. Officers and men with a proper bent of mind should be given adequate training before being posted in tribal areas. Unless they are able to build rapport with the children of the jungles they would not be able to look after them, not in a spirit of condescension but in a spirit of real service. When Community Development Blocks were first introduced, Pyarelal, Gandhiji's secretary advised Prime Minister Lal Bahadur Shastri to withdraw the jeeps from the officers going to these Blocks. Unless the officers go to them as one among them if will not be possible to enlist their enthusiasm for developmental or any other kind of work.

The State's Seventh Plan of Rs. 7014 crores makes a provision of Rs. 1295 crores for the tribal sub-plan. Adding to this, the sum of Rs. 228 crores of special grant from the Central Government and other allocations, there is a total of Rs. 1902 crores for the development of tribal areas. This special allocation comes to about 18.50 per cent of the total allocation for the State's Seventh Plan for about 22 per cent of the population. And this is apart from expenditure on general development in which these areas also included. Selection of proper people with the right outlook and attitude to implement these programmes will make these vast resources go to where they are intended to go and not leave us wondering where they all went.

Underdevelopment

2322. Abalo, Carlos. Cancun ; "The magic of the market" and the reality of underdevelopment. *Comercio Exterior De Mexico* 27, Dec. 1981; 521-27.

2323. Abraham, M. Francis. *Perspectives on modernization Toward a general theory of Third World Development*. Washington, 1980.

2324. Acharya, Dhanraj. Problem of unemployment and underdevelopment. *Mainstream* (New Delhi) 9 (36) 8 May 1971; 17-18, 38.

2325. Agarwala, A.N. and S.P. Singh *eds. Economics of underdevelopment.* Oxford, 1958.

2326. Agarwala, A.N. *Some aspects of economic advancement of underdeveloped economics.* Allahabad, Kitab Mahal, 1958. p. 128.

2327. Albrecht, U. *et al.* Armaments and underdevelopment. *Bulletin of Peace Proposals* 5, 1974, 173-85.

2328. Alexander, Robert, J. *New development strategy.* New York, Orbis Boohs, 1976.

2329. Almond, G.A. and J.S. Goleman. *Politics of developing areas.* Princeton, 1960.

2330. Amin, S. *Accumulation on a world scale : A critique of the theory of underdevelopment.* New York, 1974.

2331. Amin, S. *Unequal development* Brighton, Harvester Press, 1976.

2332. Aseniero, George. Reflection on developmentalism From development to transformation. In *Development as social transformation.* London, 1985 ; 48-85.

2333. Bagchi, A.K. *Political economy of underdevelopment.* Cambridge, 1982.

2334. Bairoch, Paul. Historical roots of economic underdevelopment. In *Imperialism and after* Ed. by Wolfgang J. Mommsen and Jungen Osterhammel. London, Allen & Unwin, 1986 ; 191-216.

2335. Bauer, P.T. *Dissent on development* London, Weiden feld and Nicholson, 1976.

2336. Bernstein H *ed. Underdevelopment and development : The Third World today.* Penguin Books, 1973.

2337. Bhatt, V.V. *Development perspectives : Problem, strategy and policies.* Oxford, Pergamon Press, 1980.

2338. Bodenheimer, Suzanne. Dependency and imperialism : The roots of Latin Americans underdevelopment. *Politics and Society* May 1971.

2339. Brett, E.A. *Colonialism and underdevelopment in Kenya.* London, 1975.

2340. Brookfield, H.C. *Interdependent development.* London, Methura, 1975.

2341. Chenery, Hollis and Moises /syrquin. *Patterns of developments. 1950-70 New York*, 1975.

2342. Choudhry, Sand A. Food policy, inequality and underdevelopment (in Bangladesh). *Journal of contemporary Asia* 16 (2) 1986 : 131-43.

2343. Dasgupta, Sygata. Towards a no poverty society. In *EAPS* ; 21-38.

'Development' is also not a desirable ideal. For 'development' can work only when inequity, as a value, is enshrined in the society. If all people have cars in Varanasi, for example, nobody will be able to use a car in the city. Development is then functional only when a few people have access to it. In a modern society, where one pleads for equality, where the resources are limited and their indiscriminate, unsparing exploitation leads only to untimely exhaustion—liberation lies not in limited' growth but in the limitation of wants, in the lowering down of the standards of living of the few rich and powerful as also in the achievement of a no 'poverty', no 'development' society. The alternative plan for social change, the anti-thesis of development, will lead us to the latter in the shortest possible time, it will help liberation of all.

'Development' has been the undoing of the new nations. It has been responsible for much of the peacelessness, inequity and violence that stalks their world. Not only that; development has also seen the collapse of many a political regime. Led by the accredited leaders of these nations, the regimes, otherwise stable, could not fulfil the illusory goals provided by the thesis of development. Many tragedies took place thereafter ; mainly because the politics in the new nations, following the practice in the West, had become the politics of promise ! The latter held high hopes before the people and maintained that those who voted a leader to power had every right to expect a price for their choice. A rise in the standard of living, followed by a great deal of affluence in future, was obviously the price they expected. Yet no development did actually take place for the vast masses of people in these countries ; and as the bitter and the hungry were driven to the wall, they pulled down the established leaders.

The fashion in the developing nations has thus been to blame their administrators, the people and the leaders for the failures of development and to organise great whitch hunts from time to time. It is necessary to emphasise, in this context, that the administrators, politicians, and bureaucrats of the Third World, however inefficient they be, do not compare too unfavourably with their counter parts of the affluent nations. Neither are our people any less rational or change prone nor our religion any more monolithic or change resistant. Yet no development, worth the name, has taken place in these countries even though idle slogans continue to mislead the decision makers. All that they do is to create pockets of affluence and increase the areas of deprivation. As the promises given by the leaders of one group, after the other, fall on ground and blacken the fact of their heroes, people turn their backs to the latter and start questioning the credibility of this very institution of leadership itself! There is no other way out of this impasse but to persue the path laid down by the two of the great leaders of our time, Mao and Gandhi. Both these leaders stood firm against the politics of promise and refused to offer any bait to their followers save hardships and suffering, Gandhi had indeed come to the definitive conclusion that the model of development followed by the west was not, repeat not, a practicable phenomenon. He had accordingly called upon the people of India to look for their own models suited to their culture and genius as also to appreciate that there was no other way open to them but to build an altogether different type of society which will neither have affluence nor poverty.

But can 'development' and the 'affluence' of a few, made possible in the west, coexist with the vast area of 'poverty' of the Third World? Could a 'no affluence' society, deliberately created by social engineering, live together with the developed? It is possible, in other words, for the two worlds, one with a zero rate of growth and the other with an ever increasing one, to live in harmony? Will not one influence, contaminate or overpower the other? The answer to the question is three fold.

One, development and affluence are self destrictive. After the peaks are reached the steps are bound to be retraced. For over saturation creates inner contradictions in the affluent society and what Marx thought would happen to capitalism is already happening to the systems that produce affluence. They are collapsing under their own weight. Indiscriminate use of world's wealth depletes the total stock of resources and transforms the profile of the time honoured civilization. Even if the area of development is thus limited and only 6% of people use 70% of the resources of the world, the stock would one day be exhausted. The ecological disassters are pointer to that direction. But apart from it, there is a steady decline in the world food production as also in the nutritional standards of food consumption. If this process goes unbridled, man will soon lose the basic wherewithal of life. The reasons for this impending crisis even in the North World is often ascribed to the rate of population growth of the developing nations but are surely due as much to the man's total devotion to industrialization as to the process of 'megalopolis' building. Both these militate against the original values of life and will one day bring to a halt all further paces of development, whether the elite would want it or not. The process of return from the modern, affluent civilization to a saner, poorer standard of living will then begin.

Secondly, unbridled affluence destroys most of the social institutions which the human species have built with care over the last ten million years. Family, for example, is one such casuality. For the new culture of affluence seeks to erode the functions of family—four of which have from the time immemorial been its main tasks. These include, sex and procreation, inheritance, education and economic (and social) security of its members. If these were the purposes that the family served, the culture of the affluent society has made it unnecessary to look to the family any longer for meeting any of these basic needs. For socialisation of poverty makes inheritance and obsolete institution, the permissive society enables free use of sex ; and no member of the family not even the child or the women depend any longer on it either for their education or for security. Will there still be a need for this insititution ?

What is true of family is also true of the individual : The great advance of the mass society, a product of the affluent economy, has not only increased the loneliness of man but has also led to a new type of frustration which is created not by poverty but by affluence. The drug culture that keeps most of the people, who take the drugs, submerged in a coma during the period of its spell, may be considered as an aberration today ; but as affluence leads to over saturation, as the mass society smothers into smithereens the communities of the old and raises insular, isolating walls around individuals, the aberration of today will become the rule of tomorrow. If the disease spreads as it must, if the mass society gets increasingly atomised as it logically should, quite a few people may then remain submerged in the coma. Individuals will not need, under the circumstances, either family or sex ; and they could, during the period of the slumber, not even require much food. Cutting short the span of life, such a society will create an altogether different typology of human species than the one for whom the earth was made.

The 'Konarak' temple, which offers a three dimension treatment on sex education, was created, it seems at a time when most of the people of that part of the globe, saturated with a quest for spiritual liberation, were thinking of total renunciation. Today, when a great many people, saturated with affluence, are similarly planning to withdraw from the games of the living we need a new educative process to return from the high waters of affluence to a saner, poorer, standard of life. The lessons of affluence have, however, proved that it is not only the family and the individual but most of the other established institutions too are similarly changing beyond recognition. All the 'monoliths' built by the 'development' oriented society are today truly on the verge of a collapse.

2344. De, Nilish Chandra. *Overcoming underdevelopment*, Shillong, North-Eastern Hill University, 1986.

2345. De Silva, S.B.D. *Political economy of underdevelopment.* London, Routledge, 1982.

2346. Declerck, Roger P Management of development : the next decade. *Long Range Planning* 10 Jun 1977 ; 59-63.

2347. *Development as social transformation : Reflections on the global problematique.* London, Hodder and Stonghton, 1985. p. 281.

2348. Ezekiel, M. Impact and implications of foreign surplus disposal on underdeveloped economies : The international perspective. *Journal of Farm Economics* 42, 1980, 1063-77.

2349. Foster-Center, A. Neo-Marseist approaches to development and underdevelopment. In *Sociology and development Ed.* by E. De Kadt and G. Williams. London, Tavistock, 1974.

2350. Frank, A.G. *Dependent accumulation and under development* London, Monthly Review Press, 1979. p. 226.

2351. Frank, A.G. *Latin America : Underdevelopment or revolution.* New York. Monthly Review Press. 1969.

2352. Fank, A.G. Sociology of development and underdevelopment of Sociology. *Catalyst* (State University of New York in Buffalo) (3) Sum 1967.

2353. Furtado, C. Elements of a theory of underdevelopment—the underdevelopment structures. In *Underdevelopment and development.* Ed. by H. Bernstein. Penguin Books, 1973 ; 33-43.

2354. Gaulet, Denis. *Cruel choice : A new concept in the theory of development.* Cambridge, 1971.

2355. Ghosh, Pradip K. *ed. Development cooperation and Third World* Westport, Greenwood Press, 1984 p. 497.

2356. Griffin, Keith *Underdevelopment in Spanish America.* London, Allen & Unwin, 1968.

2357. Gupta, H.C. *Problems and processes of economic planning in underdeveloped economies.* Allahabad, Kitab Mahal, 1958. p. 260.

2358. Hagen, Everett E. *Economics of development.* Homewood, illinois, Irwin, 1975.

2359. Holsti, K.J. Underdevelopment and the gap theory of international conflict. *American Political Science Review* 69. 1975 ; 827-39.

2360. Hyden, G. *Beyond Ujamaa in Tanzania : Underdevelopment and an uncaptured peasantry.* London, Heinemann, 1980.

2361. Hyden, G. *No shortents to progress : African development management in perspective.* London, Heinemann, 1983.

2362. *Interdependence and development.* Paris, OECD, 1979. p. 109.

2363. Jain, Hem Chand. Main Causes of unemployment and underdevelopment. *Khadi Gramodyog* (New Delhi) May 1976 ; 554-68.

2364. Kadt, E and G. Williams *eds. Sociology and development.* London, Tavistock, 1973.

2365. Kasdan, Alan R. *Third Word : A new focus for development* Cambridge, 1973.

2366. Kay, G. *Development and underdevelopment : A Marxist analysis* London, Macmillan, 1975.

2367. Keenan, K.S. Social work approaches to balanced development. *Cultural Studies,* 12 (3) Jan. 1970.

2368. Khan, Mahmood Hasan. *Underdevelopment and agrarian structure in Pakistan.* Boulder Westview Press, 1981. p. 308.

2369. Kitching, G. *Development and underdevelopment in perspective : Populism, nationalism and industrialism.* London, Methuen, 1982.

2370. Kohr, Leopold. *Development without aid.* Llandybie, 1973 p. 227.

2371. Leipziger, Danny M *ed. Basic needs : The development.* Cambridge, 1981.

2372. Leys, C. *Underdevelopment in Kenya : The political economy of Neo-colonialism.* London, Heinemann Educational Books, 1975.

2373. Luckham, Robin. Armaments, underdevelopment and demilitarization in Africa. *Alternatives* 6 (2) Jun. 1980 ; 179-246.

2374. Macpherson, S. *Social policy in the Third World : The social dilemmas of underdevelopment.* Sussex, Wheatsheaf Books, 1985. p. 220.

2375. Mukherji, Shekhar. *Mechanism, of underdevelopment, labour migration and planning strategies in India.* Calcutta, Prajna, 1981. p. 190.

2376. Myrdal, Gunar. *Development and underdevelopment : A not on the mechanism of national and international economic inequality.* Caiso, Cairo, 1955.

2377. Myrdal, Gunnar. *Economic theory and underdeveloped regions.* London, Methuen University Paperbacks, 1963.

2378. O, Keefe, P. *et al*., *eds Kenyan underdevelopment : A case study of proletariamigration.* London, International African Institute, 1977.

2379. Orridge, A.W. Uneven development and nationalism. *Political Studies* 29, 1981; 1-15. 181-90.

2380. Rodgers, Gerry B. *Child work, poverty and underdevelopment* Geneva, ILO, 1981.

2381. Roxborough, I. *Theories of underdevelopment.* London, Macmillan, 1979.

2382. Rubinson, Richard *ed. Dynamics of world development.* London, Sage, 1981.

2383. Seers, Dudley. Meaning of development. *International Development Review* 11(4) 1969.

2384. Smith, Tony. Underdevelopment of development literature. *World Politics* 31(2) Jan. 1979 ; 247-88.

2385. Stewart, F. *Technology and underdevelopment*. London, Macmillan, 1977.

2386. Uri, Pierre. *Development without dependence*. New York, Prayer, 1976.

2387. Van Der Kraan, Alfons. *Lombok : Conquest, colonization and underdevelopment*. Singapore, Heinemann, 1980. p. 290.

2388. Vogeler, Ingolf and Anthony R. De Souza *eds. Dialectics of Third World development*. Montclair, 1980.

2389. Wallman, Sandra *ed. Perceptions of development*. New York, Cambridge University Press, 1977.

2390. Walton, John. *Reluctant rebels : comparative studies of revolution and underdevelopment*. New York, Columbia University Press, 1984, p. 243.

2391. Wilber, Charles K. *ed. Political economy of development and underdevelopment*. New York, Random House, 1972.

2392. Williams, G. Rural Underdevelopment. In *Social development in Nigeria*. Ed. by E.O. Akeredolu. Ibadan, 1979.

Unemployment

2393. Abdullah, Farooq. Educated unemployed. *Seminar* (328) Dec. 1986 ; 23-24.

2394. Acharya, Dhanraj. Problem of unemployment and underdevelopment. *Mainstream* 9 (36) 8 May 1971 ; 17-18, 38.

9395. Action plan to tackle unemployment. *Business Standard* (Calcutta). 20 Jan. 1983 ; 5.

2396. Bardhan, P.K. Wages and unemployment in a poor agrarian economy. *Journal of Political Economy* (3) 1979.

2397. Bhattacharya. Vivek. Unemployment in rural India. *Khadigramodyog* Nov. 1971 ; 123-32.

2398. Blanchard, Francis. New cures for old ills of poverty, unemployment. *International Herald Tribune* 6 Feb. 1985 ; 6.

2399. Blanchard, Francis. Steady growth in world unemployment *Statesman* (New Delhi) 6 Feb. 1985 ; 7.

2400. Blaug, Mark *et al. Causes of graduate unemployment in India*. London, Penguin, 1969. p. 312.

2401. Bose, Arun. Commitment to give employment or allowance to all ? *Young India* (New Delhi) 29 Apr. 1971 ; 7-8, 21.

2402. Bose, Arun. Problem of the unemployed. *Indian Left Review* 10(2) Mar-Apr. 1971 ; 19-22.

2403. Bose, Arun. Problem of the unemployed—a rejoinder *Indian Left Review* (3) May-Jun. 1671 ; 89-93.

2404. Chakravarty, Sukhamoy. Problem of unemployment. *Indian Left Review* 1(2) Mar-Apr. 1971 ; 28-30.

2405. Dantwala, N. Rural unemployment : Facts and Issues. *Economic and Political Weekly* 14(25) 23 Jun. 1979.

2406. Das, Nabagopal. Unemployment in India : Need for a different planning strategy. *Amrita Bazar Patrika* 13 Aug. 1985 ; 6.

2407. Das, Nabagopal. Unemployment in India. *Amrita Bazar Patrika* 25 Aug. 1986 ; 6.

2408. Deshpande, V.D. Unemployment in rural areas. *Economic Times* 21 May 1986.

2409. Dubashi, Jay. Jobless will remain jobless. *Sunday Mail* 20 Jul. 1986 ; 10.

2410. Dubashi, Jay. Unemployment : Jobs for the jobless. *India Today* 30 Sep. 1983 ; 82-83.

2411. Economics of unemployment. *Sentinel* (Assam) 26 Sep. 1983 ; 4.

2412. Educated. Unemployed. *Statesman* 18 Aug. 1986 ; 6.

2413. Educated unemployed—a symposium *Seminar* (New Delhi) (120) Aug. 1969 ; 10-38.

2414. Forester, T. Who exactly, are unemployed ? *New Society* 13 Jan. 1977.

2415. Forum of Education. *Educatea unemployment in India : Challenges and responses.* Delhi, Hindustan Publishing Corporation, 1982.

2416. Ganguly, A.K. Tackling unemployment. *Hindustan Times* 18 Apr. 1983, 9.

2417. Gheevala, C.L. Challenge of unemployment. *Swarajya* (Madras) Annual Number 1972 ; 113-18.

2418. Ghodke, Manju. Number of jobless continues to swell. *Economic Times* 11 Sep. 1986.

2419. Ghosh, B.N. Underemployment, show motion and ex-efficiency : A critique of Folke Dovzing. *Asian proflle* Dec. 1985 ; 577-80.

2420. Ghosh, D. Unemployment—Some policy issues. *Economic and Political Weekly* 6 Feb. 1971 ; 425-28.

2421. Gupta, Anand P. Poverty and unemployment *Economic Times* 21 Oct. 1981 ; 5, 22 Oct. 1981 ; 5.

2422. Hill, M. *Men Out of Work* Cambridge, 1973.

2423. Hossain, Alamgir. Unemployment in Bangladesh. *Pioneer* 12 Dec. 1986 ; 5.

2424. How to live with high unemployment. *Telegraph* (Calcutta) 21 Aug. 1985 ; 6.

Rajiv Gandhi is perhaps the First Prime Minister of the country to have expresscd himself as forthrightly as he did before trade unionists on Monday on the issue of surplus staff with the public sector. Few would disagree with the proposition that ideally money should be saved by getting rid of surplus staff and used in setting up new industries with modern technologies. This would lead to a cut in unit costs and also the creation of some new employed in lieu of the jobs lost. But there are some new employments in lieu of the jobs lost. But there are some negative aspects to this scenario. First, far fewer new jobs will be created than will be lost. Second, the new jobs will almost always require greater technical skills than the old jobs. Thus the net effect will be to improve the employment prospects of skilled new entrants into the job market, but finding suitable jobs for the older and less skilled people thrown out of employment will be very difficult. Also, with the present high interest rate structure in the country, the capital cost of new technology in India will be higher than in the advanced countries from where it is brought and this will get reflected prices for the Indian consumer than his western counterpart.

But despite this, technological upgradation cannot be avoided and if Indian costs are ever to approximate to international levels then the public sector, which provides many crucial inputs for the economy, will have to slowly cut its excssively high wage bill. Modern computerised large scale techology is notoriously low in its job potential and the sooner everyone acknowledges this the better. Even now, a steel plant is an emotive issue with a state and attracting one is equated with seeking to promote economic uplift of a region. But the direct job potential aside, even the development of ancillaries cannot be guaranteed. Thus, the draft of the Seventh Five Year Plan that we have been publishing, indentifies the central element in the development strategy of the Plan as creating 'productvie employment' but does not mention large scale industry at all in the context. Instead, its emphasis is on the additional job potential of agriculture through better irrigation and improved technology for low productive areas.

The secenario of the future is a shift away from urban centres, a regeneration of the countryside which will provide both employment and the buying power that will create the demand for mass consumption goods. Enthusiastic young entrants into politics with a burning zeal for promoting social uplift should now look to the villages for the right arena instead of seeking to improve the lot of industrial workers or government office clerks. The predominant social conflict in the near future will be the painful task of redeploying the highly vocal and politically powerful surplus manpower in the public sector. Since the oil price rise the west has been able to bear very high levels of unemployment without total social disruption because of elaborate systems of social security. It is in that direction that the Prime Minister's thoughts should now turn.

2425. Humphrey, Hubert H. Jobs for people : the employment crisis. *In war on proverty*. New York, 1964; 143-70.

2426. James, Ralph C. Labor mobility, unemployment and economic change : An Indian case. *Journal of Political Economy* 67 (6) Dec. 1959; 545-59.

2427. Jha, Gunanand. Unemployment : Its causes and cure. *Indian Nation* (Patna) 10 Nov. 1985; 4.

2428. Jha, L.K. Problem of unemployment among the educated. *Financial Express* New Delhi 14 Sep. 1984; 12.

The problem of unemployment among the educated is one of the gravest that we are facing today. Not only does it represent in economic waste in the sense that the tremendous investments in educational system turn out to be largely infructuous, but even more serious are the social and political consequences of frustration among the youth. The attempt to get preferential treatment in the matter of recruitment leads to corruption, nepotism, casteism and other evils. Educated, jobless young men often embark on illegal activities in the economic field, and sometimes indulge in violent crimes. Therefore. We cannot afford to shut our eyes to this problem in the vain hope that somehow or other it will go away. We have to attack it frontally.

There are two sets of cases-and remedies-which need to be analysed in an attempt to deal with the issue. On the one hand we must ask whether the academic institutions are providing the kind of education for which there is need in the society. Secondly, we should also ask whether in the economic system as a whole. there are any deficiencies or shortcomings which come in the way of making full use of the talent which comes out, or can come out, of the educational system. I believe, on both sides-the supply of trained manpower and the demand for it-there are weaknesses which need to be remedied.

According to figures published by the Directorate-General of Employment and Training, over 33,000 vacancies in 1980 and 35,000 and in 1981 had to be cancelled because suitably qualified candidates were not available. In 1981-82, according to the Union Public Service Commission, it was difficult to find suitable candidates for over 350 posts. These figures suggest that while there is a surplus of people with general education, there is a shortage of those with more specialised education, for which there is a growing need. But there are other figures which suggest that there are too many specialists in certain fields. According to the National Sample Survey Organisation, there were over 1,200 agricultural graduates looking around for jobs some time back.

Clearly, there are imbalances between the pattern of demand for qualified candidates and the pattern of supply of educated personnel. A drastic reform of the educational system to gear it to meet the manpower needs of the country is clearly needed.

This is not a new thought. It has been voiced by educationists and others time and again. Yet, surprisingly little is being done to bring about a change. This not just because governments, with their deep commitment to remaining where they are, have an inbuilt bias against change. The malady is deeper. The pressure from the public is for more degree colleges, much less for vocational institutions. And governments, with their instinct for self-preservation, succumb to such pressures. So, we must ask what can be done to eradicate this bias.

The Prime reason why there is a public clamour for more degree colleges and all parents who can afford to do so want to send their children to institutions where they can get a degree, is that governments, insist on a degree as a prerequiste for being considered for most government jobs. And since the Government is the largest employer, parents feel that they owe it to their children to qualify them for entry into government service.

During the days I was Governor of Jammu & Kashmir, I had occasion to enquire into the problems of unemployment among the educated. One of the conclusions which I had reached on that occasion was that the !ink between a degree and recuitment to government services should be a snapped. Recruitment to all the non-specialist services should be a just after the plus two stage in education. Thereafter, depending on the services to which a successful candidate is assigned, he should have further education, even of the degree standard, but in subjects which would be relevant to the service for which he has been selected. Thus, someone who is chosen for IAS could study subjects like sociology, economics, politics and law, apart from English language which continues to be as important as in the past for a variety of reasons. Those selected for the Indian Foreign Service could be asked to take up history, foreign languages, international law and other similar subjects: Those recruited for the Indian Audit and Accounts Service could have papers in accountancy, commerce, economics. And so on.

Such a change would bring about a major transformation in the educational system. It would eliminate the waste which takes place when someone with a degree in engineering or industrial chemistry or even a mathematician or a Sanskrit scholar gets into one of the generalist services.

2429. Joshi, Navin Chandra Spectre of unemployment. *National Herald* 19 Apr. 1983; 5.

2430. Joshi, Navin Chandra. Unemployment-back to square one. *Hindustan Times* 21 Nov. 1985; 26.

At the beginning of the Sixth Plan (March, 1980) about 12 million persons were unemployed in the country, of whom 3.37 million were educated (matriculation or above). The Plan estimated that there would be about 34 million fresh entrants in the labour force during 1980-85. Taking the backlog of the unemployment and freshers together, about 46 million people were looking for jobs during the Sixth Plan period.

Although the growth of employment during the Sixth Plan is said to have touched 5.2 per cent, yet roughly 3.3 per cent had been added to the unemployed force. With the total labour force in the 15-59 age-group estimated at 27 crore now, the unemployment figure runs pretty high.

The programmes included in the Plan were expected to generated equivalent to 34 millions standard people. If all new employment were to be on full time basis, the total jobs created in the Plan period could accommodate about 34 millions poople. Which is why, now at the beginning of the Seventh Plan, we are back to square one as far as the unemployment situation in the country is concerned. This is a matter of serious concern on the part of planners and economic administrators. We will not be able to make any dent on the existing problem of uneployment by the end of the Seventh Plan period

In fact, unemployment has been increasing ever since we launched the planning process. Both its size and the rate of growth have been on increase. While the percentage of unemployment to the total labour force at the end of the First Plan period was 2.9, it went up to 3.7 at the end of the Second Plan and jumped to 4.5 at the end of the Third Plan. After the three year period of Annual Plans it was 9.6 per cent. Subsequently, the average percentage of unemployment to total labour force was estimated at 10.4 per cent.

The Planning Commission reckons the country's labour force at 268.05 millions in 1985, implying an addition by about 34.23 millions during the Sixth Plan period. This gives us an averge growth rate of 2.54 per annum. At the beginning of the Seventh Plan (April, 1985) the backlog of unemployment is estimated to be around 44 million persons. The existing population of the country, as per the Approach Paper of the Seventh Plan, is 803 millions.

Assuming growth rate of population and labour force at 2.48 & 2.54 per cent respectively, the estimated labour force in 1990, the terminal year of the Seventh Plan, will be 340.74 million, implying an addition to the labour force of 38,53 millions. Obviously, the Indian economy will have to generate additional employment opportunities for a labour force the size of which may be around 55 to 65 millions people.

It may be noted that rural unemployment is much more serious than that in urban areas. While the rural sector poses the problem of landless workers and marginal farmers, the urban sector faces the challenge of providing white collared jobs. The organised sector of the economy absorbs about 11 per cent of the annual increase in the labour force while the remaining 91 per cent is engaged in the unorganised sector.

2431. Kalra, B.R. Unemployment : Dimensions and policy perspectives. *Financial Express* 17 Aug. 1985 ; 5.

2432. Kelkar, D.Y. Employment generation. *Economic Times* 21 May. 1986.

2433. Krishna, Daya. Planning for poverty : Five crore Indians are unemployed. *Organiser* (New Delhi) 6 Jul. 1986; 9.

2434. Krishna, R. *Rural unemployment : Concepts and estimates for India.* Washington, 1976.

2435. Krishnamurthy, J. *Employment situation in India.* (Mimeo). Washington, World Bank, 1978.

2436. Labor : Employment and Unemployment. In *Nippon*; *1985-86.* Tokyo, Kokusli-Sha corporations, 1985; 40-41.

2437. Lawson, Roger, Social security, employment and the single-parent family. In *Social Security and Family Law*. Ed. by A. Samuel London, Ocean Publications, 1980.

2438. Mahajan, V.S. Rural industrialization and unemployment. *Economic Studies* 22 (1) 1981; 81-86.

2439. Mahajan, V.S. Unemployment Problem in India. *Economic Studies* 22 (6) 1981; 289-92.

2440. Measuring unemployment ; NSS concepts. *Economic Times* 11 Sep. 1986.

2441. Meher, M.R. Unemployment *Capital* (Calcutta) 20 Apr. 1972 ; 644-45.

2442. Melman, Seymour. Inflation and unemployment as products of our economy. *Bulletin of Peace Proprosals* 9 (4) 1979; 359-74.

2443. Mounting unemployment. *Link* 20 Feb. 1953.

2444. Nabagopal, Das. Creating new job opportunities to reduce unemployment *Capital* (Calcutta) 30 Dec. 1971; 71-72.

2445. Oberai, Amarjit S. Migration, unemployment and the urban labour market. *International Labour Review* Mar-Apr. 1977.

2446. Panda, Rajaram. Global unemployment. *Newstime* 4 Mar. 1984; 8.

The post-War world is plagued by several crises. The superpower conflict, the mounting poverty in several Third World countries and their failure in combating it, the escalating nuclear arms race, the maddening diversion of valuable resources towards unproductive purposes, the mounting debt burden of many Latin American and South Asian countries are some of the major problems that mankind is facing in the 1980s. The widening gulf between the rich and the poor has taken the North-South dialogue to a stalemate. The call for South-South cooperation has not brought any meaningful result for the creation of a new world economic order. All such issues have divided the world into two conflicting blocs : the developed and the developing ones. However, one problem, namely unemployment, has not spared either of the two blocs. Both the Third World and the Western industrialised countries are facing the acute problem of increasing unemployment.

In the 1970s, more than 200 million people flooded the labour market of the Third World. It is expected that by the turn of the century, an additional 500 million world would swell the labour force. This means that more than 30 million new jobs will have to be created in each of the remaining years of this century to keep pace with the expansion of the world labour force. The International Labour Office in its first comprehensive study of the global scene entitled "World Labour Report" comes out with these grim findings.

The need to tackle the ever-increasing problem of unemployment calls for systematic planning at the global, regional and national levels. However, any attempt to tackle the problems ahead must precede our understanding about the complexities of the world labour scene.

The post-War world scene is not gloomy on all fronts. The world after the War in general has experienced an era of unprecedented prosperity. The sixties and the seventies alonge accounted for a record 65 per cent increase in per capital income. This rosy picture is, however, unlikely to be repeated in the coming decades. There are clouding doubts on the possible revival of the world economy as the gulf between the developed and the developing ones is constantly widening. While demands have increased, the size of the resource cake has decreased. The already visible sign of a general economic decline further blurs the prospect of providing full productive employment for the world's labour force for the coming few years.

On the other hand, as the disparities between the prosperious countries of the North and the developing economies of the South widen, it would sharpen tensions and contribute to social instability. This would also put increasing premium on South-South cooperation of which the regional cooperation movements in Asia and Africa would form a part. It is projected that between 1980 and 2000, the world population will increase from 4.4 billion to about 6 billion. Most of this increase will take place in the Third World. Thus any international action to combat poverty and unemployment needs to be focussed in this direction. The urgency for such an action is more if the economic performance of the countries of the Third World *vis-a-vis* the developed ones is assessed. It may be noted that even during the last two decades of sustained world economic growth, the Third World lagged behind the developed North.

The widening income disparity between the North and the South has resulted in a steady and increasing flow of migrants across frontiers in search of work. Their intrusion into the territory of others has often resulted in a backlash. Their social unacceptability by the native population of the country where they have chosen to live and work has resulted in their perpetual sense of insecurity. As a result, the Indian labour in the Gulf region is no longer welcome. Nor are they liked in the African countries. The image of Indian labour in Hongkong and other Southeast Asian countries is not good either.

2447. Poverty, unemployment and inequality. *Facts For You* (New Delhi) Dec. 1984; 9-11.

2448. Poverty and employment, *National Herald* 20 Dec. 1985; 5.

2449. *Poverty and employment in the rural areas of developing countries. Report-II.* Geneva, ILO, 1979.

2450. Poverty can't be removed only by more employment. *Pioneer* 6 Sep. 1983: 4.

2451. Radhakrishnan, E.P. Unemployment : A global perspective. *National Herald* 12 Sep. 1983; 7.

2452. Rao, V.R. Educated unemployment. *Indian Lobour Jorunal* Apr. 1972; 537-50.

2453. Reddy, Jaipal. Non-combustible. *Seminar* (328) Dec. 1986 ; 33-38.

2454. Seaberry, Jane. U.S. jobless rate jumps to 7.3 per cent in biggest rise since May 1980. *International Herald Tribune* 8-9 Mar. 1986 ; 1, 11.

2455. Sen, Lalit K. Growth centers and rural unemployment in India. *Economic Affairs* Aug. 1970 ; 329-39.

2456. Sengupta, Arjun. Problem of unemployment. *Indian Left Review* 1 (2) Mar.-Apr. 1971 ; 30-36.

2457. Shanta Kumar, G. Asean employment perspectives : Singapore and Malaysia. *Asian Thought and Society* 10 (29) Jul. 1985; 96-114.

2458. Shishkov, Y. Recession and unemployment in the capitalist countries. *International Affairs* (Moscow) Jan. 1984; 37-65.

The 1980-83 world cyclic crisis which hit all the capitalist countries has turned out to be the longest and most severe in the past 50 years in its economic and social aftermath. A most ugly feature of the present level. In 1932 the fully unemployed averaged 24 million, with another 6 million partially employed. In 1982, according to official statistics, the unemployed in the OECD countries comprised 30.3 million; in 1983 the number was expected to hit the 33-34 million mark. Obviously, these figures are understated. In reality unemployment is 40-50 per cent higher.

Mass joblessness has exacerbated the class tensions in the capitalist countries, intensified the internal political instability and advanced to the forefront the imperative need for drastic social reforms in the bankrupt "welfare society" which made the ruling circles of many Western countries announce, at least officialy, the fight against unemployment a priority task. But the army of "redundant people" continues to grow instead of diminishing. Western economists estimate that it will keep on increasing through the mid-1980 or, probably, the late 1980s.

What is the cause of the growing unemployment ? The main cause, of course is curtailed production as the result of continuing recession. Over 3 million workers were laid off in 1979-82 in the US manufacturing industries. A total of 3,140,000 industrial and 767,000 agricultural workers lost their jobs over the same period in the ten Common Market countries. The recession has been accompanied by massive bankruptices of small and medium-size enterprises and farms. In 1979 over 58,000 farms went out of business in the six largest Western countries; in 1982 the number of bankrupt farmers almost doubled to 102.000. Many of the ruined small businessmen and farmers add up to the army of unemployed.

Can this mass, skyrocketing unemployment be explained by cyclic causes alone? If plummeting business activity is the sole cause, why then wasn't the 1974-75 slump accompanied by such a huge growth in redundancy ? In 1974-75 the unemployment level (i.e., the share of the unemployed in the total number of able-bodied population) increased 0.3 per cent per one per cent decrease in the rate growth of Western countries' aggregate gross national product. In 1979-82 the ratio was 1 : 0, 7. Moreover, in between the two crises, when business activity somewhat revived, the level of unemployment in most Western countries (except the USA) practically remained the same. In the Common Market countries it even rose to 5.5 per cent in 1979 as against 4.3 per cent in 1975.

Such "behaviour" of unemployment is somewhat strange for "normal" capitalist development. In the past century and a half, since capitalist economy has been following a cyclic pattern of development, slowdowns sent unemployment up and the periods of revival and upswing sent it down. Of course, a minimal contingent of unemployed (which Marx called an industrial reserve army) has been always there as an industrial reserve.

For a decade now the absolute and relative unemployment parameters have been practically independent of the changes in the economic cycle, which can be easily seen from the diagram where aggregate data are cited for seven leading countries of state-monopoly capitalism (the USA, Japan, West Germany, Britain, France, Italy and Canada) accounting for almost 80 per cent of the OECD countries' total number of employment and 83 per cent of their GNP. In the late 1950s and in the 1960s fluctuations in the unemployment and its level could be rather clearly associated with the ups and downs of business activities; from 1973 the trend changed : unemployment dynamics have been almost autonomous ever since reacting only on recessions, not recoveries.

One of the reasons for this anomaly is the demorgraphic peculiarities of manpower reproduction. In the 1950s and early 1960s there was a temporary rise in the birth rate in several Western countries, and in the 1970s the young generation born in those years flooded the labour market. The peak years in individual countries are different : Britain and Italy, 1979-80; West Germany, 1980-82; Australia, 1987-88; Japan, 1988-89; and Ireland, the mid-1990s.

2459. Shukla, Tara. Agricultural unemployment : Problems and prospects. *Economic Times* 11 Sep. 1986.

2460. Sinfield, Adrian. Poor and out of work in shields. In *COP* 220-35.

Some of the disabled said they had refused to go on the Disabled Persons' Register as they believed this hampered them in competing in the open market and encouraged employers to consider them only for lower paid jobs. It also appeared to provide confirmation to assistance officers that such men, applying for aid for themselves and their families, should be wage-stopped (see below) without attention to previously high earnings. Most of the disabled and some of the older workers were registered at the exchange as 'light labourers'. In an area where men with a skill or training were having to take jobs as labourers and the number registered for this occupation far exceeded vacancies, this classification seemed tantamount to 'reject'.

The extent to which the employment exchange helped those with the handicaps of no skill, inexperience, old age and poor health or disability seemed severely limited by three factors—the economic situation in the area, the exchange's emphasis on its dependence upon the good will of employers and Ministry of Labour policy to submit those most industrially qualified for a job. It was the decision of the employer to notify, and to continue notifying, the exchange of any vacancies and many employers seemed to expect the exchange to save them some of the invidious problems of selection and rejection. If a firm felt the exchange was being too persistent in sending old, disabled or otherwise 'unsuitable' applicants for jobs, then it could discontinue notification of jobs and reduce the exchange's opportunity to place even its most suitable registrants. Obviously there was need for a delicate balance in relationships, but the existing balance seemed to be weighted heavily against the unemployed man.

Although a few employers believed that the exchange was trying to make them accept 'the dregs', this seemed unlikely. Employment exchange policy was to submit 'those most industrially suited' for a job and this is what it set out to do. The criteria for suitability became difficult when a clerk had to choose among many unskilled labourers with little knowledge of their employment experience to help differentiate them. It seemed likely that for want of other criteria those last out often became the first submitted, or some judgement of suitability in terms of personal appearance was made. Alternatively, if the clerk recognized the arbitrariness of such a decision, he might send them all for the job and both men and employers objected.

In the existing economic situation and without any change in policy, it seemed that little could be done to help those disadvantaged in the search for work. There was often a likelihood that such disadvantages might become more formally disqualifying factors for submission to work.

The effect of unemployment on the life of a man and his family was hard to measure in one or two brief interviews. It was clear that men played down the impact while they were still unemployed. Once the crisis was over some of the more central issues were discussed more openly, an indication of how deeply unemployment could strike at a family's security. The laconic way in which men referred to their misfortunes seemed to be often due to the fact that unemployment was now part of their way of life and they had come to regard it fatalistically as 'just one of those things.'

Those who seemed to make the most adjustment in their days because of unemployment were of two kinds—the very recently unemployed who said they were confident of a swift return to work and those out of work over a year with little expectation of further employment. The first tended to regard the unemployment at least at first as a break or a chance to relax, or as one said,. "It gives you a chance to spend your money'. The second, all older or considerably handicapped, appeared to be gradually withdrawing from the outer community, some becoming highly suspicious of all with whom they had contact. When asked if he saw any friends, one man aged 60 and living alone said that he had his radio : it was better than bringing in people and kept him company.

The rest of the unemployed appeared reluctant to make even minor adjustments in their lives because they seemed to regard these as acknowledging that they might be out of work for many more months. The three effects of unemployment most commonly mentioned were depression, irritability and the problem of passing the time and these were often linked together. Married men rarely referred to the loss of income directly as their wives did, but they did complain about the loss of freedom this brought.

2461. Singh, Chander Uday. Protection of unemployment. *Free Press Journal* 14 Oct. 1985 ; 7.

Finance Minister V.P. Singh's widely—appreciated address at the joint annual meet of the World Bank and IMF in Seoul last week included some stinging reference to the increasingly protectionist trading environment faced by Less Developed Countries (LDC's) attempting to boost exports to the developed West. He buttressed his appeal for a more open trade policy with facts gleaned from recent reports by the World Bank itself, UNCTAD, and the International Labour Organisation. And what he made explicit was that in seeking to restrict Third World entry to their markets, the developed countries were only harming themselves.

The proposition is by now almost beyond debate. Numerous studies by reputed economists and international organisations have established that Third World countries faced with declining exports inevitably out back on imports, reducing thereby the markets for Western product and technology. One result is that there is a demonstrable increase in redundancy and unemployment in export-based industries in the West each time Western nations curb imports from the developing world.

An ILO study some years ago pointed out that whereas some 850,000 jobs in sunset industries were lost as a result of imports from the Third World, more than 2.4 million jobs in OECD countries were directly attributable to exports to the nations of the South. A more recent ILO survey explained that one in 10 American workers in manufacturing owed their jobs to exports, and 40 per cent of the export growth in the U.S. was contributed by Third World countries.

Recent empirical data bears out these studies. Protectionist policies adopted by Western nations this decade have been directly responsible for a contraction in LDC exports from $ 616 billion in 1980 to $ 523 billion in 1984. But this decline forced the Third World as a whole to reduce its own import bill, and that in turn has eaten into Western export industries. Despite a 6.5 per cent export growth in 1984 over 1983, OEDC exports growth in 1984 over 1983, OEDC exports in 1984 were down two per cent compared to the 1980 level.

The link with unemployment can also be established. Arjun Sengupta, a member of the executive board of the IMF, stated last month that the rate of unemployment in industrial countries, which remained stable at around 3.5 per cent from 1967 to 1976, has been steadily rising since then. An OECD study released last week predicted that unemployment in Europe would touch a post-war peak of 11 per cent this year. Significantly, the two nations which have managed to stabilise unemployment after an increase in 1980-83 are the United States, at 7.5 per cent of the labour force, and Japan, at 2.5 per cent. Both have witnessed booming exports in the last two year.

Nor is protectionism beneficial to consumers in the West. An analysis by the American Federal Reserve Bank published on August 28 estimated that consumers in the country had ended up paying $ 14 billion to $ 19.5 billion extra last year only on account of tariffs and other protectionist measures imposed on imports of automobiles, sugar and clothing. The analysis also pointed out that new restraints on steel imports would cost consumers another $ 2 billion a year.

Yet trade curbs continue inexorably to increase, with domestic pressure groups in industrial countries continously seeking further protection. And indications are that the vicious cycle of protection and relation will grow worse in the immediate future, jeopardising in the process any hope of pulling out of the current recessionary phase. The 1985 UNCTAD report pointed out that exports from OECD countries now account for 30 per cent of their aggregate gross domestic products, making it clear that import curbs and retaliation can only be counter-productive in the long-run.

2462. Singh, YR. Training for Self-employment. I-VIII. *Employment News* (New Delhi) 16 April-31 May 1986.

2463. Sinha, Arati. "Developed" World with more unemployed ? *Patriot* 11 Jun. 1985 ; 4.

The just-released *OECD Economic Outlook, No 37 of June 1985*, makes for instructive reading, bringing as it does to the fore the major economic issues in the closing decades of the twentieth century, which had begun with high expectations from a changeover to socialism from capitalism but which seems to be ending with a lot of questions regarding the economic future of the world.

The socialist sector is under attack not only in Mrs Thatcher's Britain but also in post-revolutionary China. The people's Republic of China had emerged upon the world scene with the philosophy of two worlds—the world of the exploiters and the world of the poor—but now seems to have found hitherto unpearceived virture in the capitalist West, especially in the US, the country which after the revolution in had derided the most and which in turn had exhibited unremitting enmity toward the PRC for over two decades in the fifties and the sixities.

Several countries in Eastern Europe have also gone in for reforms providing for larger scope for the market forces, underlining the doubts about the workability of socialism, except that the Soviet Union still has not found it necessary to make any comparable institutional change to call into question the viability of the non-capitalist, socialist enterprises in that country.

The point to which I am trying to draw attention is the distinctly different outlook that marks the closing years of the twentieth century, apart from the opening years. An optimism about the future was the distinctive characteristic of the early decades, while in the closing years of the twentieth century an overwhelming pessimism seems to have settled upon all, and most of all on the leaders on the Left, many of whom seem to have resigned to the continued domination of the capitalists for many years to come.

And the evidence for this is not only the agreement that the CPI-M-led Left Front Ministry has entered into with the leading capitalist, Mr. R.P. Goenka (the agreement is between Mr Goenka and the West Bengal Government). The initiative clearly has been handed over to the capitalists. And it is here that the utter relevance of the OECD Economic outlook lies.

Formally, the OECD consists of just twenty-four countries; but these are among the richest and include all the major economic nations with the exception of the Soviet Union. What these 24 countries do determine, the economic future of the non-socialist (and now also part of the socialist) world.

The OECD nations are also the leading capitalist nations and they illustrate the possibilities and limitations of the capitalist mode of development at the end of the twenteith century. The report enables the readers to see what can be expected from taking the capitalist path.

The first fact that has to be noted is the extraordinary domination of just one country over the capitalist world. The growth in the world trade during the second half of 1984 slackened, according to the OECD Economic outlook, "as the United States import growth slowed and the fall in the OPEC, imports accelerated." There is no mention of the industrialised countries of Europe or of Japan as a major factor in determining the growth in world trade, except that the countries constituting the OPEC have been mentioned. But the predominance of the US is wide-spread and continuing.

Thus, the appreciation of the US national currency determined the terms of trade of the different countries. "The slowdown in the increase in the export prices of manufactured goods (read, the products of the capitalist West) came to an end in 1984. The principal reason for this was the appreciation of the dollar, which tended to raise local currency prices. United States exporters tended not to lower their prices in line with the appreciation of the dollar, while other exporters raised their prices as a result of reduced competition from the United States", the OECD report says.

2464. Sule, Surekha. Female unemployment : Nature and dimensions. *Economic Times* 11 Sep. 1986.

2465. Suri, Kamla. Unemployment at peak in Kerala, Tamil Nadu. *Economic Times* 11 Sep. 1986.

2466. Thakur, Dalip S. *Poverty, inequality and unemployment in rural India.* Delhi, B.P. Publishing Corporation, 1985.

2467. Unemployment in India. *Times of India* 4 Dec. 1985 ; 8.

2468. Unemployment problem of rich. *Economic Times* (New Delhi) 11 Jun. 1986 ; 8.

2469. Unemployment Scales a peak. *Financial Press* 29 Dec. 1984 ; 8.

2470. Unemployment time bomb. *Pioneer* 14 Mar. 1986 ; 4.

An engineer is at times hoist on his own petard. This is tragic, but the engineers can console themselves with the thought that accidents will happen even in the best regulated families. What is, however, worse than dying for qualified engineers is trying to make a living by begging due to prolonged unemployment. It's a matter of regret—many will call it shame—that unemployment among engineers has reached such a stage in Bihar that out of sheer desperation 50 unemployed engineers resorted to begging in the streets of Patna to focus public attention on their plight. A Patna message states that the Bihar State Unemployed Civil Engineers' Association said in a statement that they resorted to begging after about 2000 unemployed engineers were denied jobs by the Government. The Association claims that no engineer has been recruited by the State Government for the past six years.

While unemployed engineers are cooling their heels in their homeland and are holding "begging protests" in sheer frustration and anger, the powers-that-be keep complaining about the "costly brain drain" and exhorting the talented expatriates to spurn the siren song of "filthy lucre" abroad and return to "Mother India" to save the poor in the homeland. The day the news item of the engineer' begging protest in Patna was published in the newspapers, another arresting item about the brain drain found aprominentplace in the Indian Press. Dr. Vijay Kumar Sharma, an Assistant Professor of the Institute of Engineering and Technology in Lucknow, went on record with the statement that an estimated 14,000 Indians are currently attending U.S. universities and the total number of Indians residing there has risen from 1 lakh in 1971 to 5 lakhs in 1985.

It is intriguing to note that the Indians residing in the USA are in the category of the top 7 per cent of income earners there in various professional categories. The situation indeed is Gilbertian Engineers are being churned out in reckless profusion in this country without any proper planning for their intake. The problem has not cropped up overnight. There was sharp fall in the demand for engineers from 19,000 in 1965 to 11,400 in 1968, which works out to a 40 per cent reduction. The supply of engineers, on the other hand, steadily increased from 21,200 in 1964 to 34,000 in 1969, registering a 43 per cent rise. The figures are admittedly outdated. In recent years there has been a further steep increase in the number of engineers desperately looking for non-existent jobs.

It is all very well for the Government to say that they should take advantage of the liberal loans from banks and other Government sources for exploring avenues of self-employment. It is nobody's secret that while skilled and semi-skilled technicians in the intermediate reaches can eke out a living in their "self-employed" capacity, our engineers holding a bit of parchment have neither the training, nor the experience nor the skill to set themselves up either as engineering consultants or as owners of small engineering units with very inadequate resources.

It is this disquieting uncertainty about the future and lack of opportunities for the better skilled professionals that triggered off the brain drain which enabled the Western countries to exploit the skill of our talented men on whose education the country keeps spending millions of rupees. Without a stepped up economic growth and proper planning which alone can create more job opportunities, white collar unemployment will keep swelling in this country to the bursting point. It is a safe bet that angry and frustrated engineers and other professionals who take to the street for begging to register their protest will not agree to die quietly in the street. Massive unemployment snowballing dangerously year after year is high explosive which may burst suddenly and rock the country like a seismic upheaval.

2471. Urban employment. *Financial Express* (New Delhi) 28 Jul. 1986 ; 5.

2472. Visaria, Pravin. *Poverty and unemployment in India.* Washington, World Bank, Jul. 1978.

2473. Vyas, H.K. unemployment mounts in capitalist world. *New Age* 7 Nov. 1982 ; 11.

In the post-Second World War Years Western publicists used to write volumes trying to belittle the economic development in the socialist countries and singing pontific praises for the showpieces of capitalist economy, particularly West Germany and Japan as the outstanding examples of "free" economy.

Gone are those days. At present the socialist countries are showing constant and steady economic growth, there is no inflation and price rises, there is no unemployment and the wages of the workers and earnings of the cooperative farmers are rising.

Except for some difficulties in Poland, caused by mistakes of the former regime and a determined counter revolutionary onslaught financed by the West, the overall picture of the situation in the socialist countries show a completely opposite picture of what one sees in the Western capitalist countries and the United States of America.

Inflation high prices, reduced social benefits, and staggering and rising unemployment are plaguing the economies of these countries. Now even the News week columnist. Anthony Samson has to write in his journal of "the spectre (of unemployment) haunting the west".

In a way admitting the superiority of socialism, he says : "As a new generation in western Europe is confronted by the prospect of long-term unemployment, the politicians will face a second challenge—a challenge from Eastern Europe".

He goes on to say about the Eastern European regimes that "they can honestly say that they offer one benefit that Western Europe does not : guarantee of a job".

Further on he says" . . . . this promise from the east will inevitably begin to look more attractive to the young people".

What has prompted such comments from even a columnist of the Newsweek ? We shall deal with it presently, analysing the situation in the western capitalist countries.

In the socalled leader of the capitalist world, United States of America, the unemployment figure as per the last month's record went up to 10.1 per cent—first double digit rate since the dark days before World War II.

2474. West Europe unemployment high. *China* Daily 3 Jul. 1986 ; 4.

2475. World lacks jobs. *International Herald Tribune* 16 Jun. 1986 ; 6.

For most people in the industrial world, the time continue to be prosperious. But unemployment remains high and even appears to be rising, although the world is in the fourth year of recovery from the last recession. As in the United States, the unemployment rate in Britain rose a little last month—in Britain, to 13.3 per cent of the labour force compared with 7.3 per cent in the United States. For the 12 countries of the Common Market, the rate is nearly 12 per cent. Even in Japan, where it is still under 3 per cent, the trend is slowly upward.

Sometimes in the 1970s there was a silent and profound change in the politics of economics. The unemployment rate was no longer the single crucial number that could swing elections. Memories of the bad years in the 1930s and, for the Europeans, the post-war 1940s, had faded. A substantial structure of social security and unemployment benefits had been written into law, and the fear of losing a job no longer went so deep. As the privotal number in election campaigns, unemployment was replaced by inflation. To push inflation down, governments throughout the world have resorted to policies that have left the numbers of people without jobs far above the levels that, until the mid-1970s, were traditional.

In the United States, the massive loss of industrial jobs is chiefly attributed—correctly—to the excessively high exchange rate of the dollar. But over a longer period there is a pattern of decline in manufacturing employment that is common to all the advanced industrial countries, even Japan. Productivity has typically risen much faster in manufacturing than in most other sectors of these economics. The consequence has been a slow shift of labour from manufacturing and farming into the service industries and public employment. But the service industries have not been growing fast enough to accommodate this redistribution.

A high general level of unemployment is not the only measure of the social damage that results. Another is the length of time that each person remains unemployed, and it has generally been increasing. Still another is the age distribution of unemployment. Americans worry, with good reason, about unemployed youth. But the Europeans have far more to worry about. In the United States, one out of every seven working people under the age of 25 is out of a job. In France it is one out of four, and in Spain nearly half are not working.

Of all the industrial countries, only Japan has cut inflation without letting unemployment rise to levels that, at any time before the last dozen years, would have been considered intolerable. In Europe and North America there have been endless attempts to bring down both together, and none has worked. It is correct to celebrate the return to (comparatively) low inflation. But it would be quite wrong to ignore the costs at which it has been accomplished.

Untouchability

2476. Bonarji, N.B. Untouchability and the law. *Times of India* 8 Jul. 1956 ; 8.

Urbanization and Urban Poverty

2477. Abu-Lughod, J and R. Hay *eds. Third World Urbanisation.* London, Methuen, 1979.

2478. Aiyar, Swaminathan S. Neglect of urban poverty. *Indian Express* 3 Sep.1985 : 6.

2479. Attar Chand Employment potential in rural and urban centres. *Careers Digest* (New Delhi) Jun. 1979 ; 452-53.

2480. Bhargava, Gopal and R.K. Arora. Urban explosion 2,000 A.D. *Patriot* 23 Dec. 1986 ; 4.

2481. Bhatti, S.S. Ruralise cities, don't urbanise villages. *Link* 15 Aug. 1986 ; 21-27.

2482. Blume, Otto. Poverty of old people in urban and rural areas. In *COP* ; 184-92.

When I write about poverty, my understanding is that there is no generally valid definition of the concept of poverty which would be appropriate at all times and in all regions. In order to define the concept in operational terms, one must proceed from conventional assumptions. A person is described as poor if his total life situation lies below a subsistence level which is acknowledged as the minimum by the dominant public consensus. As in the case of the West German Federal Social Assistance and Youth Welfare Laws the terms 'poverty' is defined as a condition below a subsistence minimum. The term is applied when somebody is unable to achieve subsistence, that is, his requirements for food, clothing and shelter. This term is also used if he is unable to satisfy his cultural and social requirements e.g., if his ability to maintain contact with his environment is seriously impaired, on account of his inability to obtain essential material goods by his own strength and effort. It is not a necessary condition, however, for such an individual to regard himself as being poor. The term has to be defined independently of the subjective judgements of those concerned.

By old people I mean men and women who have completed their sixty-fifth year of life. As physiological and chronological age do not coincide, it is entirely a pragmatic problem at what age one speaks about people as being old. The pensionable age of manual workers and of white collar workers in the Federal Republic of Germany is 65. This has become the conventional strat of 'old age' on account of the fact that those who are employed have to leave their place of employment in almost all cases when they reach this age. This policy is the result of collective and other agreements governing the conditions of employment. This applies also to civil servants. They, too, are pensioned off at the age of 65, though at 62 in the case of poor health.

All the statements in this paper with regard to the situation of old people derive from the findings of empirical social research. Probability sampling methods have been used in these investigations. Between 1961 and 1966 sample surveys were undertaken in six large cities, in one highly industrialized rural area, in one less highly industrialized rural area, and in six predominantly agricultural rural areas. Interviews were conducted on the basis of standardized questionnaires. Certain groups of questions were not subject to any modification, especially those which concerned data about income and contacts with the social environment. Data was compiled on 11,000 punchcards, which form the basis of our analysis. The results are only representative for those urban and rural areas in which these investigations were carried out but may be regarded as valid for these areas. Almost 100 per cent correspondence was obtained in the results for the six large cities. Regional differences do not seem to have had an effect to any significant extent. (Tests were carried out in Bremen in the North, and Stuttgart in the South of the Federal Republic.) But as we shall show, there are greater differences between rural and urban conditions.

Why did we not conduct an investigation representative for the whole of the Federal Republic? In accordance with the Federal Social Assistance Law, responsibility for measures to support old people is vested in local government bodies, i.e., in urban and rural councils. This law has been in force since 1962. In the early 1960s neither rural nor urban authorities were in possession of adequate information (apart from routine statistics) concerning the situation of old people. Hence, it was not known how many old people were in need, nor the actual nature of their needs.

2483. Bromley, R and C. Gerry *eds. Casual work and poverty in Third World cities.* Chichester, Wiley, 1979.

2484. Castells, M. *Urban question.* London, Edward Arnold, 1977.

2485. Chandrachud, M.G. Employment for urban poor : Planning and problems. *Economic Times.* 8 Oct. 1986 ; 5.

2486. Cohen, A. *Custom and politics in Urban Africa.* London, 1969.

2487. Ezekiel, Hannan. Urbanisation. In *Second India Studies Overview.* New Delhi, Macmillan, 1978 ; 41-53.

2488. Fox, R.G. *ed. Urban India : Society, space and image,* Providence, Brown Univ. 1967.

2489. Fried, R. *Planning the eternal city.* Yale University Press, 1973.

2490. Gans, Herbert J. *Urban villagers.* New York, Free Press, 1962.

2491. Goldstein, Sidney. *Measurement of urbanization and projection of urban population.* Liege, 1975.

2492. Goyal, Radhika. Hope for the urban poor. *Sunday Observer* (New Delhi) 14 Dec. 1986 ; 20.

2493. Growing cities. *Indian Express* 21 May 1986 ; 6.

2494. Gugler, J. Overurbanization reconsidered. *Economic Development and Cultural Change* 31, 1982 ; 173-89.

2495. Gulati, L. Rationing in a peri-urban community. *Economic and Political Weekly* 19 Mar. 1977.

2496. Gupta, K.N. Employment schemes for urban poor. *National Herald* 17 Oct. 1984 ; 7.

2497. Humphrey, Hubert H. Urban poverty. In *War on poverty*. New York, 1964 ; 49-64.

2498. Isaac, B. Peasants in cities : Ingenious paradox or conceptual muddle. *Human Organization* 33(3) 1974.

2499. Jha, S.S. *Structure of urban poverty*. Bombay Popular Prakashan 1986 p. 184.

2500. Kalpagam, U. Coping with Urban poverty in India. *Bulletin of Concerned Asian Scholars* 17(1) Jan-Mar. 1985 ; 2-19.

2501. Khakhar, K.K. *Urbanisation and role of industrial estates : the USA, the UK and the Indian experience. New Delhi, Ashish*, 1985. p. 113.

2502. King, A.D. Colonial *Urban development* London, 1976.

2503. Kundn, Amitabh. *Measurement of urban processes*. Bombay, Popular Prakashan, 1980. p. 260.

2504. Lewis, Oscar. Urbanization without breakdown : A case study. *Scientific Monthly* 75, 1952 ; 31-41.

2505. Little, Menneth. *West African Urbaniz ation*. Cambridge, 1965.

2506. Ma, Laurence J.C. and E.W. Hanten. *ed. Urban development in modern China*. Boulder, Colo, Westview Press, 1981. p. 264.

2507. Mac Sweeney, A.M. Study of poverty in Cork City. *Studies* (Dublin) 4, 1915.

2508. Mangin, William, *ed. Peasants in cities*. Boston, 1970.

2509. Mazumdar, Dipak. Urban informal sector. *World Development* 4, 1976 ; 655-79.

2510. Mohamed, Ahmad Hussain. *Urban Politics in India.* New Delhi, Deep & Deep, Publications 1986. p. 250.

2511. Naik, R.D. *Some structural aspects of urban family.* Bombay, Somaiya, 1981. p. 120.

2512. New Loan Scheme for Urban poor. *Indian Express* 29 Aug. 1986 ; 1.

2513. Norwood, H *ed. Urbanisation and Housing in Papua New Guinea.* Univ. of Papua, New Guinea.

2514. Parkin, D. *ed. Town and Country in Central and Eastern Africa,* London, 1975.

2515. Pirenne, H. *Medieval Cities.* Princeton, 1939.

2516. Radhakrishan, V. Bane of urbanisation. *Free Press Journal* 28 Nov. 1983 ; 4.

2517. Rose, R *ed. Management of urban change in Britain and Germany.* London, Sage Publications, 1974.

2518. Santos, M. *Shared space : the two circuits of the urban economy in underdeveloped countries.* London, Methnen, 1979.

2519. *Social aspects of the industrialization and urbanization of Africa to the South of Sahara.* Paris, Unesco. 1956.

2520. Taper, B. Lover of cities. *New Yorker* 4 Feb. 1967 ; 39.

2521. Teja (Dr. Jayanti Dharma) feels urbanites must fight rural poverty. *Deccan Herald* 6 Mar. 1983 ; 6.

2522. Urban poor (in India). *Financial Express* (New Delhi) 30 Aug. 1986 ; 5.

The recognition that poverty is not a wholly rural phenomenon is reflected in the self-employment programme for the urban poor (SEPUP), announced to Thursday by the Finance Ministry. In its broad thrust, it is an analogue of the old Antyodaya programme for the rural poor, who were sought to be provided with an income-yielding asset by bank loans with an element of capital subsidy (to be provided by the Union Government) and concessional interest rates. Thirty three kinds of urban self-employed have been identified and these are to be given loans up to a maximum of Rs. 5,000 at an interest of 10 per cent, provided the family income is less than Rs. 600 per month. Seventy-five per cent of the amount borrowed is to be returned, in three years in monthly instalments with a three month initial grace period. (The other 25 per cent will be provided by the Union Government to the bank which will keep it in fixed deposits to be adjusted after the rest of the loan has been repaid). There is to be no security other than the assets created out of the loans.

There can be no quarrel with the principle of the scheme. Providing some initial support for the highly vulnerable members of the informal urban service sector is a long overdue component of a strategy of poverty alleviation. Strange as it may sound to some ears, these self-employed persons are entrepreneurs in every sense of the term. If entrepreneurship in the more formalised sectors of the economy is worthy of assistance for economic reasons, there is no reason why these persons should be denied it. Looked at from this angle, the new programme is not so much a case of social concern as an economic catalyst. Not that social concern would not be justified in the case of these vulnerable people. They are not the beneficiaries of the formal social security system that employees in organised industry, commercial establishments and the Government enjoy. Unlike the latter, they are the victims of *bandhs* and *hartals*, since their livelihood for the day is lost. Even so, it is necessary to emphasise the economic dimension of the programme and its growth rather than welfare implications.

As a banking proposition for entrepreneurial support. the programme may give rise to some misgivings. But these could be exaggerated. The risk of "bad debts" are there, no doubt, but at a venture, one could say that this is no greater than in the higher levels of economic activity. Indeed, whatever else may happen, it is unlikely that these assisted activities will become "sick industries" to the point of posing an independent problem in itself, as is happening with better organised sectors. This is so, if only because one has to have a certain level of health before one becomes "sick". By definition, these people are far from being at that level of health. Bad debts from them are less likely to break the banks than industrial and agricultural bad debts.

Wages

2523. Flinn, M.W. Trends in real wages, 1750-1850. *Economic History Review* 27, 1974.

2524. Poverty of wages. *Financial Express* 23 Jan. 1983 ; 4.

Water Conservation

2525. Abbas, K.A. Water ! Water ! everywhere. *Blitz* 17 May. 1986 ; 24.

2526. Dighe, Sunil Islands of prosperity. *Economic Times* 21 May. 1986 ; II.

2527. Drinking water for all by 1911. *Yojana* 1 May 1986 ; 19-20.

India's Commitment to the UN Drinking Water Supply and Sanitation Decade is definite and unhesitating as is clear from the fact that the Plan allocation (Rs. 49 crore in 1951-56) for water and sanitation rose to Rs. 3908 crore which later was further raised to 4177.51 crore in the Sixth Plan.

At the beginning of the decade (1981) only 77.7 per cent of the towns and cities and 31 per cent rural people had adequate supply of drinking water. Only about 0.5 per cent of rural people had some sanitary facility for disposal of human waste. Almost the entire rural population, some 52 crore of them, defacated in the open.

In arandom survey in urban areas it was found that 27 per cent had flush latrines, about 67 per cent had dry latrines and some 33 per cent had no latrines at all. Such statistics may be cold and nauseating, but, without them the country cannot work out solutions to this problem. After various studies and their evaluation the Government of India is determined to go ahead with the programmes to make available drinking water to all citizens by March 1991. For waste disposal the target is to cover 80 per cent for urban areas and 25 per cent for rural areas. The estimated expenditure is Rs. 14,700 crore, which will cover 95 per cent of the people. Five per cent, who cannot be covered, will be covered in Eighth Plan.

In the Code of Basic Requirements of Water Supply, Drainage and Sanitation, as well as the National Building Code, a minimum of 135 litre per consumer day (Iped) has been provided with all residences, which are provided with full flushing system for excreta removal. The earlier manual had recommended certain requirements for domestic, non-domestic, fire demand and industrial needs. The present committee has reviewed these figures and the following recommendations have been made.

2528. Linh, Dinh Cac. Water Conservation. *Vietnam Courier* (Hanvi) (2) 1986 ; 17-18.

2529. Mathur, Jag Mohan Drinking water for rural masses. *Yojana* 1 May 1986 ; 17-18.

Water is A Basic Necessity for every one, but unfortunately many of our 5.76 lakh villages have been facing scarcity conditions for years. In places like Rajasthan, people have to wait for hours to collect one pitcher of water tanker brought by the train. In hilly areas also the plight is the same. In many tribal and backward areas unhygienic water collected during the rainy season is the only source of drinking water. Thus, the provision of drinking water is one of the basic needs of our vllages. But during the initial period of our national planning, this aspect did not receive enough priority. A national water supply programme was taken up as early as 1954, but allocations made for this were too meagre. Until the ned of the Fourth Five Year Plan, i.e., 1974, total investment made by the Central and State Governments for providing water supply and sanitation facilities was only Rs. 855 crore. Of this, 65 per cent went to the Urban areas.

During the Fifth Five Year Plan it was realised that no improvement in the living standard of the people could be brought about without providing safe drinking water and sanitation. From this Plan Rural Water Supply became the part of minimum needs programme. During the Plan period more than Rs. 381 crore were spent on rural water supply.

Luckily when Sixth Five Year Plan was launched there was increasing awareness, both nationally and internationally, of the importance of safe drinking water supply. The drought of 1979-80 which was accompanied by an acute shortage of drinking water in many parts of the country added urgency to the search for a lasting solution. At international level, the United Nations Water Conference called for a ten year campaign to provide access to safe drinking water and sanitation to all people and the decade beginning from 1981 was designated as the International Drinking Water Supply and Sanitation Decade.

2530. Nimbkar, B.V. Water conservation in drought prone areas. *Economic Times* 21 May 1986.

2531. Om Narain, Water resources : Need for policy. *Deccan Chromide* 24 Jul. 1986 ; 6.

2532. Parvaiz, M. Aslam, Why a national policy for water management? *Yojana* 1 May 1986 ; 10-11.

2533. Rath, N and A.K. Mitra. Utilisation of Canal Water. *Economic Times* 21 Mar. 1986.

2534. Shinde, Annasaheb P. Some issues relating to national water policy. *Economic Times* 21 May 1986 : III.

2535. Sitapati, P. New strategy for integrated water management. *Yojana* 1 May 1986 ; 12-13, 18.

2536. Srivastava, Sudhir K. Water management, a formidable challenge. *Yojana* 1 May 1986 ; 7-9.

2537. Suraj Bhan. Soil Conservation in watershed management. *Yojana* 1 May 1986 ; 14-16, 23.

2538. Water crisis in Israel *Deccan Chromide* 24 Jul. 1986 ; 6.

Women

2539. Abbas, K.A. Work culture for women (in India) *Blitz* 6 Dec. 1986 ; 24.

2540. Abbott, Joan. Employment of women and the reduction of fertility. *World Development* 2 (2) Feb. 1974 : 23-26.

2541. Anker, Richard *et. al. Interactions between women's roles and population trends in the Third World.* London, Crown Helm, 1982.

2542. Anker, Richard. *Research on women's roles and demographic* Geneva, ILO, 1980.

2543 Banerjee, Nirmala. Women and poverty : Report on a Workshop. *Economic and Political Weekly* 18 (40) Oct. 1983.

2544. Barry, Kathleen. *Female Sexual Slavery.* New York, Prentice-Hall, 1979.

2545. Bernstein, Hilda. *For their triumph and their tears* : Women in *Apartheid South Africa.* London. 1975.

2546. Bhatt, Ela. Law is anti-poor *Telegraph* (Calcutta) (Sunday) 25 May 1986 ; 11.

2547. Bhattacharjee, Abhijit. Poverty amidst plentry. *Hindustan Times Sunday Magazine* 26 Jan. 1986 ; 5.

2548. Birks, J.S. and S.E. Letts. Women in rural Arab Society : Old roles and new in the Sultanate of Oman. *Journal of Gulf and Arabian Peninsula Studies* 3, 1977.

2549. Buvinic, M. *et al. Women's issues in Third World Poverty.* John Hopkins, 1982.

2550. Caplan, P. and J.N. Bujra *ed. Women united, women divided.* London, Tavistock, 1979.

2551. Driving away poverty (Women in China) *Women of China* (12) Dec. 1986 ; 1-5.

2552. Everett, Jana and Mira Savara. Bank loans to the poor in Bombay : Do women benefit ? *Journal of Women in Culture and Society* 10 (2) Win 1984, 279-90.

2553. Gupta, A.K. *Women and Society—The development perspective.* New Delhi, Deep & Deep, Publications 1986. p. 350.

2554. Heinen, Jacqueline. Women's double workshift ; Changing patterns in women's employment. *International Viewpoint* 10 Mar. 1986 : 11-15.

2555. Hoskins, D and L. Boxby. *Women and social security.* New York, US Social Security Administration, 1973.

2556. In rural Africa, development is women's work. *International Herald Tribune* 17-18 May 1986 ; 4.

2557. Joshi, H. Prospects and case for employment of women in Indian cities. *Economic and Political Weekly* Annual Number, Aug. 1976.

2558. Kamermav, Sheila B. Women, Children and poverty. *Journal of Women in Culture and Society* 10 (2) Win 1984 ; 249-71.

2559. Khaing, Mi Mi. *World of Burmese Women.* London, Zed Book, 1984.

2560. Marris, P. *Widows and their families.* London, Rontledge & Kegan Paul, 1958.

2561. Masden, D. Ennis. *Mothers above, alone.* London, 1969.

2562. Menon, Geeta. SEWA (Self-Employed Women's Association). before self. *Telegraph* (Calcutta) (Sunday) 25 May 1985 ; 16-18.

2563. Mies, Maria. Indian Women and leadership. *Bulletin of concemed of Asian Scholars* 9, 1977.

2564. Nelson, Barbara J. Women's poverty and women's citizenship. *Journal of Women in Culture and Society* 10 (2) Win 1984 ; 209-31.

2565. Omvedt, Gail Rural origins of women's liberation in India. *Social Scientist* 4 (4-5) 1975. (Special Number on Women).

2566. Omvedt, Gail. Women and rural revolt in *India. Social Scientist* Part I (61) 1977 Part 2 (62) 1977.

2567. Palmer, I. Women in rural development. *International Development Review* 22 (2-3) 1980 ; 39-45.

2568. Rowbotham, Sheila. *Women, resistance and revolution.* Harmondsworth, Penguin Books, 1974.

2569. Shen, Man-Ching. Role of women in society in Mainland China. *Issues & Studies* Nov. 1986 ; 97-109.

2570. Singleton, Kate. Men watch, women work in Yunan. *International Herald Tribune* 18 Jul. 1986 ; 8.

2571. Smith, J. *ed. Female labour supply.* Princeton, 1980.

2572. Smith, Joan. Paradox of women's poverty. Wage-earning women and economic transformation. *Journal of Women in Culture and Society* 10 (2) Win 1984 ; 291-310.

2573. Thitsa, Khin, *Providence and prostitution-Image and reality for women in Buddhist Thailand.* London, 1980.

2574. Treiman, D.V. and H.I. Hartman *eds.* Women, work and wages : *Equal pay for jobs of equal value.* Washington, 1981.

2575. United Nations. *Activities for the advancement of Women : Equality, development and pace.* New York, 1985. p. 69.

2576. Urdang, Stemphamie. *Revolution within a Resolution : Women in Guinea-Bissau.* Somerville, Mass., New England Free Press, 1974.

2577. Von Henting, Hanse. Sociological function of grandmother. *Social Force* May 1946.

2578. Women in rural development *FAO Review on Agricultural Development* 75, May-Jun. 1980 : 15-42.

2579. World Council of Churches. *Women in a Changing World. Prostitution and Tourism.* 11, Dec. 1981.

2580. Zeidenstein, S, *ed. Learning about rural women : Studies in family Planning.* London 1979.

2581. Zimmermann, Horst. Figures show that criminals are overwhelming, men. *Mid-Day* (New Delhi) 1 Jan. 1987 ; 11.

Youth

2582. Bhattacharya, Pranab. Youth and unemployment. *Deccan Chronicle* (Secundrabad) 9 Mar. 1986 ; 6.

Wanted seven young, energetic and dynamic Science/Commerce Arts graduates preferably between 20-25 years of age and having minimum of 6 to 7 years experience in the field of Marketing of Consumers Products for our new venture being coming out shortly. Salary commensurate with qualifications and experience.

This is but one of those several common adds regularly being noticed in the popular dailies. Many thousands of prospective aspirants try their luck knocking hard at the employer's door.

Strangely, every year, several million of fresh incumbents coming out of schools, colleges and universities add themselves under utter tragedy of unemployment thereby enhancing their experience as rich as only unemployed.

Though in every interview, the employer invariably asks about the job experience of the incumbents, there would hardly be any one available to give them a chance to acquire.

Youth unemployment is one of the most alarming aspects of the high jobless rate even in Western industrialised countries where according to a recent census as many as 8 million young people are out of work, many of whom cannot land a mere apprentice job. They are caught in a particularly frustrating jaws of Catch-22 trap—to get a job you to have an experience, to get experience you have to have a job.

Born during the prosperious 1960s, the grew up during the recession decade of the 1970s and now, half way through the 1980s, there are billions of young people of the "body-boon" generations who are unemployed and are well on the road to becoming a generation of unemployable misfits—seesawed between career and livelihood. The magnitude of the employment problem specially in the Third World is still worse and is almost beyond numerical calculation. An ILO forecast, further more views that the number of active young people in developing countries is expected to increase by an estimate, 25% by the year 2000.

The developing countries like India are therefore faced with the Herculean task of creating well over 100 million jobs in the next 15 years in order to absorb the projected 70 million increase in the Youth labour force and the 35 million shortfall of employment opportunities for the present day jobless youth.

2583. Dinesh Singh. Political will, national purpose *Seminar* (328) Dec. 1986 ; 14-19.

2584. Randhawa, M.S. Unemployment and rural youth. *Tribune* (Chandigarh) 23 Oct. 1985 ; 4.

The most urgent problem before the Punjab Government and the Union Government today is unemployment among the rural educated young men. According to a report of the Union Ministry of Education, whereas 18 per cent graduates with general education from the rural areas in the country were recorded as unemployed in 1972-73, their percentage increased to more than 19 in 1977-78. The position is much worse now and is a cause of violence, particularly in Punjab.

Connected with this problem is unrest among the Punjabi farmers who are by and large Sikhs. During 1966-1972 the hey-day of the Green Revolution-Sikh farmers prospered as they were getting remunerative prices, for their produce. Thanks to their enhanced incomes, they purchased tractors, dug tubewells and improved their farming systems. Since 1972, when the price of inputs rose sharply, the farmer has been a loser.

It is the manufacturers and seller of inputs who are now the beneficiaries of the agricultural revolution, while the farmers, who have become dependent on banks, are the sufferers. This is the situation in Punjab. The farmers are by and large followers of the Akali Dal, which believes in rural betterment. That is why the farmers voted en masse for this party in the recent elections.

Apart from unremunerative agariculture, the farmers have suffered from iniquitious taxation policies. The imposition of wealth tax and estate duty on agricultural land vitually broke the camel's back. Reservation of jobs for certain castes further added to the farmer's distress.

A large number of educated sons of farmers who were surplus to the requirements of farming used to go in for minor Government jobs in the old days. They suddenly found that so far as they were concerned, the doors of empolyment were shut. College education is no longer confined to urban areas in Punjab. The number of graduates from the rural areas is also substantial. These are the people who, due to unemployment and frustration, drifted to the ranks of the terrorists.